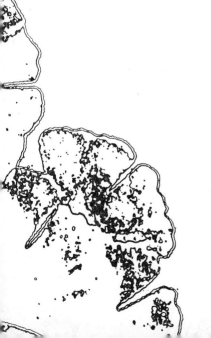

Peter Tompkins and Christopher Bird

The secret life of plants

Allen Lane

Portions of this work appeared in the November 1972 issue of *Harper's Magazine*

Copyright © Peter Tompkins and Christopher Bird 1973

First published in the U.S.A. by Harper & Row, Inc. in 1973

This revised edition first published in 1974

Allen Lane
A Division of Penguin Books Ltd
17 Grosvenor Gardens, London SW1

ISBN 0 7139 0594 8

Printed in Great Britain by
Ebenezer Baylis and Son Limited
The Trinity Press, Worcester, and London

Set in Monotype Garamond

Contents

Introduction   7

PART I MODERN RESEARCH

1 Plants and extrasensory perception   17
2 Mechanical uses of plants   27
3 Plants can read your mind   37
4 Visitors from outer space   52
5 Latest Soviet discoveries   65

PART 2 PIONEERS OF PLANT MYSTERIES

6 Plant life magnified a hundred million times   81
7 The metamorphosis of plants   97
8 Plants will grow to please   111

PART 3 TUNED TO THE MUSIC OF THE SPHERES

9 The harmonic life of plants   135
10 Plants and electromagnetism   146
11 Force fields, humans and plants   160
12 The mystery of plant and human auras   180

PART 4 CHILDREN OF THE SOIL

13 Soil: the staff of life   197
14 Chemicals, plants and man   217
15 Live plants or dead planets   230
16 Alchemists in the garden   243

Contents

PART 5 THE RADIANCE OF LIFE

17 Dowsing plants for health   263
18 Radionic pesticides   278
19 Mind over matter   296
20 Findhorn and the Garden of Eden   310

   Bibliography   321

Introduction

Short of Aphrodite, there is nothing lovelier on this planet than a flower, nor more essential than a plant. The true matrix of human life is the green sward covering mother earth. Without green plants we would neither breathe nor eat. On the under-surface of every leaf a million movable lips are engaged in devouring carbon dioxide and expelling oxygen. All together, twenty-five million square miles of leaf surface are daily engaged in this miracle of photosynthesis, producing oxygen and food for man and beast.

Of the 375 billion tons of food we consume each year the bulk comes from plants, which synthesize it out of air and soil with the help of sunlight. The remainder comes from animal products, which in turn are derived from plants. All the food, drink, intoxicants, drugs and medicines that keep man alive and, if properly used, radiantly healthy are ours through the sweetness of photosynthesis. Sugar produces all our starches, fats, oils, waxes, cellulose. From crib to coffin, man relies on cellulose as the basis for his shelter, clothing, fuel, fibres, basketry, cordage, musical instruments, and the paper on which he scribbles his philosophy. The abundance of plants profitably used by man is indicated by nearly six hundred pages in Uphof's *Dictionary of Economic Plants.* Agriculture – as the economists agree – is the basis for a nation's wealth.

Instinctively aware of the aesthetic vibrations of plants, which are spiritually satisfying, human beings are happiest and most comfortable when living with flora. At birth, marriage, death, blossoms are prerequisites, as they are at mealtime or festivities. We give plants and flowers as tokens of love, of friendship, or homage, and of thanks for hospitality. Our houses are adorned with gardens, our cities with parks, our nations with national preserves. The first thing a woman does to make a room liveable is to place a plant in it or a vase of fresh cut flowers. Most men, if pressed, might describe paradise, whether in heaven or on earth, as a garden filled with luxuriant orchids, uncut, frequented by a nymph or two.

Aristotle's dogma that plants have souls but no sensation lasted through the Middle Ages and into the eighteenth century, when Carl von Linné, grandfather of modern botany, declared that plants differ from animals and humans only in their lack of movement, a conceit which was shot down by the great nineteenth-century botanist Charles Darwin, who proved that every tendril has its power of independent movement. As Darwin put it, plants 'acquire and display this power only when it is of some advantage to them'.

At the beginning of the twentieth century a gifted Viennese biologist with the Gallic name of Raoul Francé put forth the idea, shocking to contemporary natural philosophers, that plants move their bodies as freely, and gracefully, as the most skilled animal or human, and that the only reason we don't appreciate the fact is that plants do so at a much slower pace than humans.

The roots of plants, said Francé, burrow inquiringly into the earth, the buds and twigs swing in definite circles, the leaves and blossoms bend and shiver with change, the tendrils circle questingly and reach out with ghostly arms to feel their surroundings. Man, said Francé, merely thinks plants motionless and feelingless because he will not take the time to watch them.

Poets and philosophers such as Johann Wolfgang von Goethe and Rudolf Steiner, who took the trouble to watch plants, discovered that they grow in opposite directions, partly burrowing into the ground as if attracted by gravity, partly shooting up into the air as if pulled by some form of antigravity, or levity.

Wormlike rootlets, which Darwin likened to a brain, burrow constantly downward with thin white threads, crowding themselves firmly into the soil, tasting it as they go. Small hollow chambers in which a ball of starch can rattle indicate to the root tips the direction of the pull of gravity.

When the earth is dry, the roots turn towards moister ground, finding their way into buried pipes, stretching, as in the case of the lowly alfalfa plant, as far as forty feet, developing an energy that can bore through concrete. No one has yet counted the roots of a tree, but a study of a single rye plant indicates a total of over thirteen million rootlets with a combined length of 380 miles. On these rootlets of a rye plant are fine root hairs estimated to number some fourteen billion with a total length of 6,600 miles, almost the distance from pole to pole.

As the special burrowing cells are worn out by contact with stones, pebbles, and large grains of sand, they are rapidly replaced, but when they reach a source of nourishment they die and are replaced by cells designed to dissolve mineral salts and collect the resulting elements. This basic nourishment is passed from cell to cell up through the plant, which constitutes a single unit of protoplasm, a watery or gelatinous substance considered the basis of physical life.

The root is thus a waterpump, with water acting as a universal solvent, raising elements from root to leaf, evaporating and falling back to earth to act once more as the medium for this chain of life. The leaves of an ordinary sunflower will transpire in a day as much water as a man perspires. On a hot day a single birch can absorb as much as four hundred quarts, exuding cooling moisture through its leaves.

No plant, says Francé, is without movement, all growth is a series of movements; plants are constantly preoccupied with bending, turning and quivering. He describes a summer day with thousands of polyplike arms reaching from a peaceful arbor, trembling, quivering in their eagerness for new support for the heavy stalk that grows behind them. When the tendril, which sweeps a full circle in sixty-seven minutes, finds a perch, within twenty seconds it starts to curve around the object, and within the hour has wound itself so firmly it is hard to tear away. The tendril then curls itself like a corkscrew and in so doing raises the vine to itself.

A climbing plant which needs a prop will creep towards the nearest support. Should this be shifted, the vine, within a few hours, will change its course into the new direction. Can the plant see the pole? Does it sense it in some unfathomed way? If a plant is growing between obstructions and cannot see a potential support it will unerringly grow towards a hidden support, avoiding the area where none exists.

Plants, says Francé, are capable of *intent*: they can stretch towards, or seek out, what they want in ways as mysterious as the most fantastic creations of romance.

Far from existing inertly, the inhabitants of the pasture – or what the ancient Hellenes called *botane* – appear to be able to perceive and to react to what is happening in their environment at a level of sophistication far surpassing that of humans.

The sundew plant will grasp at a fly with infallible accuracy, moving in just the right direction towards where the prey is to be found. Some parasitical plants can recognize the slightest trace of the odour of their victim, and will overcome all obstacles to crawl in its direction.

Plants seem to know which ants will steal their nectar, closing when these ants are about, opening only when there is enough dew on their stems to keep the ants from climbing. The more sophisticated acacia actually enlists the protective services of certain ants which it rewards with nectar in return for the ants' protection against other insects and herbivorous mammals.

Is it chance that plants grow into special shapes to adapt to the idiosyncrasies of insects which will pollinate them, luring these insects with special colour and fragrance, rewarding them with their favourite nectar, devising extraordinary canals and floral machinery with which to ensnare a bee so as to release it through a trap door only when the pollination process is completed?

Is it really nothing but a reflex or coincidence that a plant such as the orchid *Trichoceros parviflorus* will grow its petals to imitate the female of a species of fly so exactly that the male attempts to mate with it and in so doing pollinates the orchid? Is it pure chance that night-blossoming flowers grow white the better to attract night moths and night-flying butterflies, emitting a stronger fragrance at dusk, or that the carrion lily develops the smell of rotting meat in areas where only flies abound, whereas flowers which rely on the wind to cross-pollinate the species do not waste energy on making themselves beautiful, fragrant or appealing to insects, but remain relatively unattractive?

To protect themselves plants develop thorns, a bitter taste, or gummy secretions that catch and kill unfriendly insects. The timorous *Mimosa pudica* has a mechanism which reacts whenever a beetle or an ant or a worm crawls up its stem towards its delicate leaves: as the intruder touches a spur the stem raises, the leaves fold up, and the assailant is either rolled off the branch by the unexpected movement or is obliged to draw back in fright.

Some plants, unable to find nitrogen in swampy land, obtain it by devouring living creatures. There are more than five hundred varieties of carnivorous plants, eating any kind of meat from insect to beef, using endlessly cunning methods to capture their prey, from tentacles to sticky hairs to funnel-like traps. The tentacles of carnivorous plants are not only mouths but stomachs raised on poles with which to seize and eat their prey, to digest both meat and blood, and leave nothing but a skeleton.

Insect-devouring sundews pay no attention to pebbles, bits of metal, or other foreign substances placed on their leaves, but are quick to sense the nourishment to be derived from a piece of meat. Darwin found that the sundew can be excited when a piece of thread is laid on it weighing no more than 1/78,000 of a grain. A tendril, which next to the rootlets constitutes the most sensitive portion of a plant, will bend if a piece of silk thread is laid across it weighing but .00025 of a gramme.

The ingenuity of plants in devising forms of construction far exceeds that of human engineers. Man-made structures cannot match the supple strength of the long hollow tubes that support fantastic weights against terrific storms. A plant's use of fibres wrapped in spirals is a mechanism of great resistance against tearing not yet developed by human ingenuity. Cells elongate into sausages or flat ribbons locked one to the other to form almost unbreakable cords. As a tree grows upward it scientifically thickens to support the greater weight.

The Australian eucalyptus can raise its head on a slim trunk above the ground 480 feet, or as high as the Great Pyramid of Cheops, and certain walnuts can hold a harvest of

100,000 nuts. The Virginia knotweed can tie a sailor's knot which is put to such a strain when it dries that it snaps, hurling the seeds to germinate as far as possible from mother.

Plants are even sentient to orientation and to the future. Frontiersmen and hunters in the prairies of the Mississippi Valley discovered a sunflower plant, *Silphium laciniatum*, whose leaves accurately indicate the points of the compass. Indian liquorice, or *Arbrus precatorius*, is so keenly sensitive to all forms of electrical and magnetic influences it is used as a weather plant. Botanists who first experimented with it in London's Kew Gardens found in it a means for predicting cyclones, hurricanes, tornadoes, earthquakes and volcanic eruptions.

So accurate are alpine flowers about the seasons, they know when spring is coming and bore their way up through lingering snowbanks, developing their own heat with which to melt the snow.

Plants which react so certainly, so variously, and so promptly to the outer world, must, says Francé, have some means of communicating with the outer world, something comparable or superior to our senses. Francé insists that plants are constantly observing and recording events and phenomena of which man – trapped in his anthropocentric view of the world, subjectively revealed to him through his five senses – knows nothing.

Whereas plants have been almost universally looked upon as senseless automata, they have now been found to be able to distinguish between sounds inaudible to the human ear and colour wavelengths such as infra-red and ultra-violet invisible to the human eye; they are specially sensitive to X-rays and to the high frequency of television.

The whole vegetal world, says Francé, lives responsive to the movement of the earth and its satellite moon, to the movement of the other planets of our solar system, and one day will be shown to be affected by the stars and other cosmic bodies in the universe.

As the external form of a plant is kept a unit and restored whenever part of it is destroyed, Francé assumes there must be some conscious entity supervising the entire form, some intelligence directing the plant, either from within, or from without.

Over half a century ago Francé, who believed plants to be possessed of all the attributes of living creatures including 'the most violent reaction against abuse and the most ardent gratitude for favours', could have written a *Secret Life of Plants*, but what he had already put into print was either ignored by the establishment or considered heretically shocking. What shocked them most was his suggestion that the awareness of plants might originate in a supramaterial world of cosmic beings to which, long before the birth of Christ, the Hindu sages referred as 'devas', and which, as fairies, elves, gnomes, sylphs and a host of other creatures, were a matter of direct vision and experience to clairvoyants among the Celts and other sensitives. The idea was considered by vegetal scientists to be as charmingly jejune as it was hopelessly romantic.

It has taken the startling discoveries of several scientific minds in the 1960s to bring the plant world sharply back to the attention of mankind. Even so there are sceptics who find it hard to believe that plants may at last be the bridesmaids at a marriage of physics and metaphysics.

Evidence now supports the vision of the poet and the philosopher that plants are living, breathing, communicating creatures, endowed with personality and the attributes of soul. It is only we, in our blindness, who have insisted on considering them automata. Most extraordinary, it now appears that plants may be ready, willing, and able to cooperate with humanity in the Herculean job of turning this planet back into a garden from the squalor and corruption of what England's pioneer ecologist William Cobbett would have called a 'wen'.

I

Modern research

Plants and extrasensory perception

The dust-grimed window of the office building facing New York's Times Square reflected, as through a looking-glass, an extraordinary corner of wonderland. There was no White Rabbit with waistcoat and watch chain, only an elfin-eared fellow called Backster with a galvanometer and a house-plant called *Dracaena massangeana*. This particular adventure in wonderland started in 1966. Clee Backster, America's foremost lie-detector examiner, had been up all night in his school for polygraph examiners, teaching the art of lie-detection to policemen and security agents from all over the world. On an impulse he decided to attach the electrodes of one of his lie-detectors to the leaf on his dracaena – a tropical plant with large leaves and a dense cluster of small flowers, known as the dragon-tree because of the popular myth that its resin yields dragon's blood. He was curious to see if the leaf would be affected by water poured on its roots, and if so, how, and how soon.

As the plant thirstily sucked water up its stem, the galvanometer, to Backster's surprise, did not indicate less resistance as might have been expected by the greater electrical conductivity of the moister plant. The pen on the graph paper, instead of trending upwards, was trending downwards, with a lot of saw-tooth motion on the tracing. It was in fact showing a reaction similar to that of a human being experiencing a brief emotional stimulus.

A galvanometer is that part of a polygraph lie-detector which, when a weak current of electricity is run through a live human being, will cause a needle to move, or a pen to make a tracing on a moving graph of paper, in response to mental images, or the slightest surges of emotion, as they occur to the human guinea pig. It was invented at the end of the eighteenth century by a Viennese priest, Father Maximilian Hell, S.J., who was court astrologer to the Empress Maria Theresa; but was named after Luigi Galvani, the Italian physicist and physiologist belatedly credited with discovering animal electricity. The galvanometer is now used in conjunction with an electric circuit called a Wheatstone Bridge, in honour of the English physicist and inventor of the automatic telegraph, Sir Charles Wheatstone.

In simple terms, the bridge balances resistance, so that the human body's electrical potential can be measured as it fluctuates under the stimulus of thought and emotion. The standard police procedure is to feed carefully structured questions to a suspect and watch for those which cause the needle to jump. Veteran examiners, such as Backster, claim they can identify deception from the patterns they produce on the graph. The most effective way to trigger a reaction in a human being strong enough to make the galvanometer jump, is to threaten his well-being. Backster decided to do exactly that to the plant. He dipped a leaf of the dracaena in his cup of hot coffee; there was no reaction to speak of on the meter.

He studied the problem several minutes, then conceived a worse threat: he would burn the actual leaf to which the electrodes were attached. The very instant he got the picture of flame in his mind, and before he could move for a match, there was a dramatic change in the tracing pattern on the graph in the form of a prolonged upward sweep of the recording pen. Backster had not moved, either towards the plant or towards the recording machine. Could the plant have been reading his mind?

He left the room to fetch some matches and returned to find another sudden surge had registered on the chart. Reluctantly he set about burning the leaf. This time there was a lower peak of reaction on the graph. Later, as he went through the motions of pretending he would burn the leaf, there was no reaction whatsoever. Mysteriously the plant appeared to be able to differentiate between real and pretended intent. In order to establish what was happening and how, he now began on a meticulous investigation of the phenomenon he had just witnessed. His first move was to make sure he had not over-looked any logical explanation for the occurrence. Was there something extraordinary about the plant? About him? About the particular polygraph instrument? Enlisting collaborators, he went on to use other plants and other instruments in other locations all over the country. More than twenty-five different varieties of plants and fruits were tested, including lettuces, onions, oranges and bananas. The observations, all bearing a resemblance, seemed to demand a new view of life.

At first he considered that his plants' capacity for picking up his intention must be some form of extrasensory perception; then he quarrelled with the term. ESP is held to mean perception above and beyond varieties of the established five sensory perceptions of touch, sight, sound, smell and taste. As plants give no evidence of eyes, ears, nose, or mouth, and as botanists since Darwin's time have never credited them with a nervous system, Backster concluded that the perceiving sense must be more basic. This led him to hypothesize that the five senses in humans might be limiting factors overlaying some kind of primary perception, possibly common to all nature. 'Maybe plants see better *without* eyes,' Backster surmised: 'Better than humans do with them.' With the five basic senses, humans have the choice of perceiving, poorly perceiving, or not perceiving, at will. 'If you don't like the look of something,' said Backster, 'you can look the other way, or not look at all. If everyone were to be in everyone else's mind all the time it would be chaos.'

To discover what his plants could sense or feel, Backster enlarged his office, and set about creating a proper scientific laboratory. During the next few months, chart after chart was obtained from all sorts of plants. The phenomenon appeared to persist even if the plant leaf was detached from the plant, or if it was trimmed to the size of the electrodes; amazingly, even if a leaf was shredded and redistributed between the electrode surface there was still a reaction on the chart. The plants reacted not only to threats from human beings, but also to unformulated threats such as the sudden appearance of a dog in the room, or of a person who did not wish them well. Backster was able to demonstrate that the movements of a spider in the same room with a plant wired to his equipment could cause dramatic changes in the recorded pattern generated by the plant just *before* the spider started to scuttle away from a human attempting to restrict its movement.

'It seems,' said Backster, 'as if each of the spider's decisions to escape was being picked up by the plant, causing a reaction in the leaf.'

If a plant is threatened with overwhelming danger or damage, Backster observed that in self-defence it 'passes out', rather in the way that a human does. This was dramatically demonstrated one day when a lady physiologist from Canada came to Backster's laboratory to watch his experiments. The first plant gave no response whatsoever. Nor did the second; nor the third. Backster checked his polygraph instruments, and tried a fourth and a fifth plant; still no success. Finally on the sixth, there was enough reaction to demonstrate the phenomenon.

Curious to discover what could have influenced the other plants, Backster asked: 'Does any part of your work involve harming plants?'

'Yes,' the lady physiologist replied. 'I terminate the plants I work with. I put them in an oven and roast them to obtain their dry weight for my analysis.'

Forty-five minutes after the visitor was safely on her way to the airport, each of Backster's plants once more responded fluidly on the graph. This experience made Backster realize that plants could intentionally be put into a faint, or mesmerized, by humans, that something similar could be involved in the ritual of the Rabbi before an animal is killed in the Kosher manner, tranquillizing it into a quiet death, possibly preventing its flesh from retaining a residue of 'chemical fear', disagreeable to the palate and perhaps noxious to the consumer. 'It might be,' says Backster 'that a plant could appreciate becoming part of a "higher" form of life, rather than rotting on the ground.'

On one occasion, to show that plants and single cells were picking up signals through some unexplained medium of communication, Backster provided a demonstration for the author of an article appearing in the *Baltimore Sun*, subsequently condensed in the *Reader's Digest*. He hooked a galvanometer to his philodendron, then addressed the writer as if it were *he* who was on the meter, and interrogated him about his year of birth. Backster named each of seven years between 1925 and 1931 to which the reporter was instructed to answer with a uniform 'No.' He then selected from the chart the correct date which had been indicated by the plant with an extra high flourish.

To see if a plant could display memory, a scheme was devised whereby Backster would try to identify the secret killer of one of two plants. Six of Backster's polygraph students, some of them veteran policemen volunteered for the experiment. Blindfolded, they drew from a hat folded slips of paper on one of which were instructions to root up, stamp on and thoroughly destroy one of two plants in a room. The criminal was to commit the crime in secret; neither Backster nor any of the other students was to know his identity; only the second plant would be a witness. By attaching the surviving plant to a polygraph and parading the students one by one before it, Backster hoped to establish the culprit. Sure enough, the plant gave no reaction to five of the students, but whenever the actual culprit approached it caused the meter to go wild.

Backster was careful to point out that the plant could have picked up and reflected the guilt feelings of the culprit; but as the villain had acted in the interests of science, and was not particularly guilty, it left the possibility that a plant could remember and recognize the source of severe harm to its fellow.

Another interesting observation was even better suited to the mysterious world of Sax Rohmer and Bulwer Lytton. When a girl was murdered in a large New Jersey factory, Backster was retained by the police to give conventional lie-detector tests to prime suspects. As a large maintenance crew had been on hand at the factory on the evening of the murder, the interrogation of so many possible suspects might be a lengthy procedure. He therefore suggested that a polygraph be attached to each of the two house plants that were in the office where the body was found. One by one the maintenance crew would be asked to enter an adjoining office. If both the plants reacted to one particular individual, then conventional polygraph tests would be administered and the murder might be rapidly solved.

The workers began to parade through the adjoining office and the plants gave no unusual response. The greatest reaction came from the seasoned law enforcement officers when Backster requested them to place the plants in safe custody for the night as 'the sole witnesses to the homicide'. The next day the plants still gave no reaction; but neither they nor Backster could be faulted. The criminal turned out not to have been a worker at the factory.

In another series of observations, Backster noted that a special bond of affinity appeared to be created between a plant and its keeper, even though they were not in close proximity. With the use of synchronized stop-watches, he was able to note that his plants continued to react to his thoughts and attention from the next room, from down the hall, even from several buildings away.

He was even able to establish that his plants had shown positive signs of response at the very moment he had decided to return to New York from a fifteen mile trip to New Jersey. Whether it was relief, or welcome, Backster could not tell. In his office the original dracaena, the plant from which all his observations stemmed, showed a corresponding reaction on the chart at the very time that he was projecting a slide of it when he was away on a lecture tour.

Once attuned to a particular person, plants appeared to be able to maintain a link with that person, wherever he might be, even among thousands of people. This was shown one New Year's Eve in New York City when Backster went out into the bedlam of Times Square armed with a notebook and stop-watch. Mingling with the crowd, he noted his various actions such as walking, running, going underground by way of subway stairs, nearly getting run over, or having a mild fracas with a newspaper seller. Back at the laboratory, he found that each of three plants, monitored independently, showed similar reactions to his slight emotional adventures.

Backster has no idea what kind of energy wave may carry man's thoughts or internal feelings to a plant. He has tried to screen a plant by placing it in a Faraday cage as well as in a lead container. Neither shield appeared in any way to block or jam the communication channel linking the plant to the human being. The carrier wave equivalent, whatever it might be, Backster concluded, must somehow operate beyond the electromagnetic spectrum, and from the macrocosm down to the microcosm.

One day when Backster happened to cut his finger and dabbed it with iodine, the plant that was being monitored on the polygraph immediately reacted, apparently to the death of some cells in Backster's finger. Though it might have been reacting to his emotional state at the sight of his own blood, or to the stinging of the iodine, Backster was beginning to find a recognizable pattern in the graph when a plant was witnessing the death of some living tissue. Could the plant, he wondered, be sensitive on a cellular level all the way down to the death of individual cells in its environment?

On another occasion the typical graph appeared as Backster was preparing to eat a bowl of yogurt. This puzzled him till he realized there was a chemical preservative in the jam he was mixing into the yogurt that was terminating some of the live yogurt bacilli. Another puzzling pattern on the chart was finally explained when it was realized the plants were reacting to boiling water which was killing bacteria as it ran down the waste-pipe of the sink.

In order to explore the idea that some sort of cellular consciousness must be common to all life, Backster found a way of attaching electrodes to infusions of all sorts of single-celled creatures such as amoebae, paramecium yeast, mould cultures, scrapings from the human mouth, bloodcells, and even spermatozoa. All were subject to being monitored on the polygraph with charts just as interesting as those produced by the plants. Sperm cells turned out to be surprisingly canny in that they seemed to be capable of identifying and reacting to the presence of their own donor, ignoring the presence of other males. Such observations seem to imply that some sort of total memory may go down to the single cell, and by inference, that the brain may be just a switching mechanism, not necessarily a memory storage organ.

[23]

'Sentience,' says Backster, 'does not seem to stop at the cellular level. It may go down to the molecular and beyond. All sorts of things which have been conventionally considered to be inanimate may have to be re-evaluated.'

Convinced he was on the track of a phenomenon of major importance to science, Backster was anxious to publish his findings in a scientific journal so that other scientists could check his results. But personal involvement in his experiments and even prior knowledge of the timing of an experiment was often enough to tip off a plant into non-cooperation. He realized that he would have to devise an experiment in which all human involvement was removed. The entire process would have to be automated. The test he finally chose, after two and a half years of trial and error, was to kill live cells by an automatic mechanism at a random time when no humans were in or near the office, and see if the plants reacted.

Using the brine shrimp that are sold as food for tropical fish, he rigged up a device which would automatically tip them from their bowl into a pot of boiling water. A mechanical programmer actuated the device at random so that it was impossible for Backster or his assistants to know when the event would occur. As a control, other dishes were programmed at other times to dump plain water containing no brine shrimp. Three plants would be attached to three separate galvanometers in three separate rooms. A fourth galvanometer was to be attached to a fixed value resistor to indicate possible variations caused by fluctuations in the power supply, or by electromagnetic disturbances occurring near or within the experiment's environment. Light temperature would be kept uniform on all plants which, as an extra precaution, would be brought from an outside source, passed through staging areas, and hardly be handled before the experiment.

Plants selected for the experiment were of the *Philodendron cordatum* species because of its large leaves, firm enough to withstand comfortably the pressure of electrodes. Different plants of the same species would be used on successive test runs. In scientific terms, Backster wished to prove that,

there exists an as yet undefined primary perception in plant life, that animal life termination can serve as a remotely located stimulus to demonstrate this perception capability, and that this perception facility in plants can be shown to function independently of human involvement.

The results of these experiments showed that the plants did react strongly and synchronously to the death of the shrimp in boiling water; and the automated monitoring system, checked by visiting scientists, showed that plants reacted consistently to the death of the shrimp in a ratio that was five to one against the possibility of chance. The experiment and its results were written up in a scientific paper published in the winter of 1968 in Volume X of *The International Journal of Parapsychology* under the title 'Evidence of Primary Perception in Plant Life'.

More than seven thousand scientists asked for reprints of the report on Backster's original research. Students and scientists at some two dozen American universities indicated they intended to attempt to 'replicate' Backster's experiments as soon as they could obtain the necessary equipment.* Foundations expressed interest in providing funds for further experiments. The news media, which at first ignored Backster's paper, went into a flurry of excitement over the story when in February 1969 *National Wildlife* published a feature article which attracted such world-wide attention that secretaries and housewives began talking to their plants, and *dracaena Massangeana* became a household word.

Whereas the readers seemed to be most intrigued by the thought that an oak tree could actually quake at the approach of a woodchopper, or that a carrot could shiver at the sight of rabbits, the editors of *National Wildlife* were more concerned about the application of Backster's phenomenon to medical diagnosis, criminal investigation and espionage. Some aspects of this were so fantastic that they dared not as yet repeat them in print. *Medical World News* of 21 March 1969 commented that at last ESP research was 'on the verge of achieving the scientific respectability that investigators of psychic phenomena

* Backster has been loath to give out the names of these establishments so as not to have them importuned by outsiders until they have accomplished their tests and can make considered announcements of their results at a time of their own choosing.

have sought in vain since 1882 when the British Society for Psychical Research was founded in Cambridge'.

Now that funds were forthcoming, Backster was able to invest in more expensive equipment, including electrocardiographs and electro-encephalographs. These instruments, normally used for measuring electrical emissions from heart and brain, recorded the difference in the potential discharge of plants without putting current through them. The cardiograph gave readings more sensitive than the polygraph; the encephalograph gave readings ten times more sensitive than the cardiograph.

A fortuitous occurrence led Backster into another realm of research. One evening, as he was about to feed a raw egg to his dog, he noticed that as he cracked the egg, one of his plants attached to a polygraph reacted strenuously. The next evening he watched again as the same thing happened. Curious to see what the egg might be feeling, he attached it to a galvanometer, and was once more up to his ears in research.

For nine hours Backster got an active chart recording from the egg which corresponded to the rhythm of the heartbeats of the chicken embryo. But the egg had been bought at the local delicatessen and was unfertilized. Later, breaking the egg and dissecting it, he was astonished to find that it contained no physical circulatory structure of any sort to account for the pulsation. He appeared to have tapped some sort of force field not conventionally understood within the present body of scientific knowledge.

He concluded by putting one egg on the cardiograph and, at the other end of the office, dumped another egg in scalding water. The first egg showed a sharp reaction to the death of its partner. Such was the importance of this discovery that Backster temporarily abandoned his experiments with plants. Indeed, it gave rise to profound implications about the origin of life and could form the subject of another whole book.

2

Mechanical uses of plants

The next man to probe the mysteries of plant communication was Pierre Paul Sauvin, an electronics specialist from West Patterson, New Jersey, who happened to hear Backster interviewed on a radio programme, hosted by Long John Nebel.

An assiduous investigator of ESP and of the phenomenon of remote hypnotism, Pierre Paul Sauvin was equally at home in the 'state of the art' and 'feasibility considerations' of the engineer, mostly because of his training and employment for several large corporations, including Aerospace and International Telephone and Telegraph.

When Long John – a professional sceptic – roped Backster into a corner to get him to describe some practical uses for his discovery of primary perception in plants, Backster suggested that in jungle warfare soldiers in dangerous territory could wire up the local plants to act as 'stress alarm indicators' and avoid being ambushed. 'But if you really want to make a psychologist sit up and take notice,' he said, 'you could instrument a plant to activate a small electric train, getting it to move back and forth on no other command than that of human emotion.' This notion, though singularly impractical, could be spelled out in Sauvin's electronics jargon as an 'anxiety response device', and it fired him to make experiments of his own.

Sauvin claims that many of his insights and ideas for inventions come to him in psychic flashes, as if he were merely acting as a medium. He says he sometimes gets the factual data necessary for an invention without fully understanding the principle, or how it relates to the whole, and must get further details by questions addressed to 'levels beyond'. Using high voltage generators Sauvin can put 27,000 volts through his

[27]

body and remotely activate a large bulb filled with helium to serve as an electronic ouija board, its dark rings flowing in one direction or the other in answer to his questions. He also developed a system guaranteed to hypnotize even the most recalcitrant person by means of an unstable platform in a pitch black room and the swaying of a rainbow pattern of light that causes the subject to lose his balance.

With such expertise it was not long before Sauvin had a toy electric train running round a track, reversing its direction in response to Sauvin's thought and emotion, relayed to a plant. Later he was able not only successfully to demonstrate the performance before an audience in Madison, New Jersey, but to make the train start and stop at will under the klieg lights of a television studio. As the engine moved around the track it would activate a switch leading to Sauvin's body in such a way as to give him a sharp electric shock. Just ahead on the track, another switch was wired to a galvanometer attached to an ordinary philodendron. As the philodendron picked up Sauvin's emotional reaction at being shocked, the galvanometer needle would jump and throw the switch, reversing the train. The next step was for Sauvin to simply remember the sensation of being shocked and project it in order for the plant to activate the switch.

Though Sauvin had long been interested in parapsychology and was fascinated with the psychological implications of a plant responding to human thought and emotion, his main preoccupation was the development of a foolproof plant device that could be activated by any human being. Whether plants were 'conscious' or not, Sauvin was convinced they had an energy field similar to the energy field generated by a human being, and that somehow an interaction of these fields could be put to use. The problem was to develop equipment sensitive enough to take advantage of the phenomenon in an absolutely reliable way. Perusing the endless stream of trade journals that passed across his desk as a technical writer for I.T.T., Sauvin was struck by a series of articles in *Popular Electronics*, on unusual electronic circuits and exotic weaponry, by a mysterious writer named L. George Lawrence. The author, intrigued by the Russian development of animal guidance systems for training cats to pilot nonjammable air-to-air missiles right on to target, speculated in his articles on training plants to respond to the presence of selected objects and images, evidently for a similar purpose. After much work Sauvin eventually produced an instrument through which he hoped to be able to distinguish very fine changes in the field of plants. The sensitivity achieved was one hundred times greater than could be obtained with Backster's galvanometer, and enormous amounts of electronic 'noise' were eliminated.

What Sauvin was now measuring was no longer voltage amplitude but phase shift, or the fine lag between two running voltages. The result gave Sauvin an instrument roughly comparable to an ordinary light dimmer switch in which a plant leaf acted as the switch. Variations of apparent resistance in the leaf would cause a light to get brighter or dimmer depending on the response of the plant to outside effects.

As soon as his device was functioning, Sauvin set about monitoring plants around the clock. To catch the tiniest nuances of phase shift Sauvin hooked his plants to an oscilloscope, a big electronic green eye with a figure eight of light whose loops changed shape as the current from a plant varied, making patterns much like the fluttering of the wings of a butterfly.

Simultaneously, a varying tone was produced by current run through an amplified tone oscillator which enabled Sauvin to hear minute changes in vibrations, and know how his plants were reacting. A bank of tape recorders kept a permanent record of this oscillating tone, along with a monotonous beep every second from an international time signal broadcast. With a stop-watch he could check the effect he was having on his plants from a distance, wherever he happened to be.

Some of Sauvin's strange electronic equipment now came into its own, especially a complex system of automatic phone-answering and recording devices. For some years he had been writing for various specialized magazines, under various pseudonyms, while retaining his regular job. He had devised an ingenious system whereby when he was at work he was yet able to consult with his editors and answer their queries. By means of a small radio transmitter strapped to his leg and a battery of automated and preprogrammed tape recorders at home, he could communicate via his home telephone, receiving messages and giving answers, all from his work desk. A simple trick such as running the finger along a pocket comb close to the telephone would identify the caller by the particular soundwave which had been generated. As a cover for his own low-toned conversations from his desk, Sauvin developed the habit of humming to himself most of the time he was at work.

This Heath Robinson equipment served Sauvin admirably for remote controlled communication with his plants. He could call his own number and speak to his plants directly; he could monitor the tones of their responses via the amplified audio-oscillator, and from wherever he might be, he could control the light, colour, temperature or recording equipment in his quarters. To make his switching device more sensitively sophisticated, he hoped to devise a means of getting the plants to trigger a light source which in turn would cause a culture of micro-organisms to move through a glass phial and thus trigger another switch.

When electroding his plants Sauvin gradually realized that he obtained the best results from plants with which he could establish a special rapport. This he would accomplish by putting himself into a light trance, wishing the plant well, tenderly touching or washing its leaves till he could feel his own energy emanations entering and interplaying with those of the plant. Like Backster, he found that his plants reacted most strongly to the death of living cells in their environment, and most consistently to the death of human cells.

He also found in the course of his various experiments that the simplest signal he could transmit to his plants, extra-sensorily, to which they would respond with a sharp enough reaction, was a light electric shock administered to himself. This he did by swivelling his desk chair and then grounding the accumulated static charge by touching his finger on his metal desk. His plants several miles away would react with an instant surge. Just as with the train experiment, Sauvin eventually found that he merely needed to remember or re-feel a shock for his plants to pick up the signal, even from his holiday cottage eighty miles away.

Mechanical uses of plants

One of Sauvin's problems when he was away for several days was to keep his plants sharply attuned to himself, rather than to their immediate environment. Thus he had to devise some more effective means of attracting their attention than addressing them over the long distance telephone. Since they reacted most strongly to any damage done to himself or to any part of his own energy field, he experimented with *remotely* killing a few cells of his body in the presence of the plants. The system worked admirably. The difficulty lay in obtaining cells that would remain alive for protracted periods. Blood worked well enough, hair was difficult to kill, but sperm worked best of all, because, as Sauvin explained, it was easier to obtain than bleeding, and much less painful.

These experiments led Sauvin to wonder if plants might not just as well react to emotions of pleasure and joy as to pain and shock. Besides, he was tired of shocking himself. He soon found that his plants did react to joy and pleasure, but with wave patterns that were not sharp enough to trigger a switch reliably. Undaunted, he decided on a more daring experiment. On holiday with a girl-friend at his cottage he established that his plants, eighty miles away, would react with very high peaks on the tone oscillator to the acute pleasure of sexual climax, going right off the top at the moment of orgasm.

All of which was very interesting and could be turned into a commercially marketable device for jealous wives to monitor their philandering husbands, by means of a potted begonia; but it was not yet conducive to a simple, foolproof system of getting a plant to trigger a switch reliably. It did not rule out the possibility that his plant might at any time react to some stimulus in its own environment, such as the sudden appearance of a cat, or of a bird outside the window snapping up an insect. He therefore wired three plants, each set in a different room, in a different environment, to a single circuit which could only be activated if all three plants reacted synchronously. By keeping the plants in separate environments Sauvin hoped the required stimulus would be synchronous only when it came from him, wherever he might be. This was still not positively foolproof, because at times one plant or the other might not fully react to the stimulus. However, it was unlikely that any random stimulus would affect all three plants at once, and thus it was a step forward.

Sauvin was now anxious to release his data confirming Backster's findings and to make public his own contribution to a science which he felt had a potential for the world no less great than Marconi's use of radio waves. Unable to interest the mass media, or such conservative journals as *Science* or *Scientific American*, he decided to angle his material to the engineering and mechanical journals to which he was already a regular contributor. To incite the interest of the editor of a car magazine he concocted a story about a device that would enable him to start his car by remote control by means of thought waves to a plant. With the help of a small radio transmitter this proved to be a simple enough operation, the only technical difficulty being the designing of a gadget that would give just the right pressure to the ignition key, repeat the pressure if the engine failed to catch, and release pressure the moment it did. The device was designed to appeal to a citizen with the prospect of being able to wake up on a frosty morning and get his car and heater started while still comfortably enjoying his breakfast. But for Sauvin there was one defect; a plant was not really needed. The device could be operated directly by radio.

To include his beloved plants in a worthwhile gadget, attractive to car and home owners, Sauvin worked out a system whereby a man returning on a snowy night could approach his garage and signal his pet philodendron to open the doors. Here the plant's function of responding only to its master would make it admirably burglar-proof.

To arouse the interest of serious scientists and to attract the necessary funds for a proper laboratory, Sauvin hit upon the idea of showing that an aeroplane could be flown by thought control with the aid of his plants attached to his sensitive devices. For years Sauvin, already a licensed pilot, had enjoyed the hobby of flying model planes, some with a wing-spread as large as six feet, controlling them entirely from the ground by radio signals, getting them to bank, loop, speed up, slow down and even land. By a slight adaptation to his transmitter equipment, Sauvin was able to start, stop or affect the speed of a model plane in flight by transmitting a thought to a plant.

In the sensitivity of plants Sauvin also saw a means of detecting a potential hijacker at an airport before he could board a plane. He suggested 'Operation Skyjack', a system whereby plants could be used in conjunction with galvanometers, gyrating magnets and other sensitive devices to pick up the turbulent emotions of a hijacker while he was being screened by security officials.

Already the U.S. Army has taken an interest in devising ways of measuring the emotional responses of people via plants, without having to sensitize the plants to a special person beforehand. And at Fort Belvoir, Virginia, funds have been provided for research on plant experimentation. The U.S. Navy is also showing interest. Eldon Byrd, an operations analyst with the Advanced Planning and Analysis Staff of the Naval Ordnance Laboratory in Silver Spring, Maryland, has been repeating Backster's experiments with some success. Like Backster, Byrd found that by merely thinking of harming a plant's leaf, it was possible to make the polygraph needle jump. His experiments involved monitoring a plant's reaction to stimuli from water, infra-red and ultra-violet light, fire, physical stress, and dismemberment.

Byrd believes the galvanometrical effect produced by a plant is not caused by electrical resistance in the leaf, but by a change of biopotential in the cells from outside to the inside membrane, as defined by the Swedish Dr L. Karlson who has shown that a cluster of cells can change polarity, though the energy which causes cells to become polarized is not known. Byrd believes that a voltage change in the cells is what is being measured, and that it is the mechanism of consciousness which causes the change in potential.

Byrd's research supports Backster's observations that plants exhibit a quality of awareness and an empathy to other organisms that are stimulated in their presence. Like Backster, he also found that plants tended to 'faint' under excess stress, suddenly ceasing to respond even to the most basic stimuli, such as light and heat. Like Backster and Sauvin, Byrd was able to demonstrate on television a plant's reaction to various stimuli, including his *intent* to burn it. On camera Byrd showed that a plant would respond to his shaking a spider in a pill box with only about a second's delay, and that the response continued for as long as a minute. There was also a strong reaction when he cut the leaf from another plant.

A revolutionary new lie-detector device known as a Psychological Stress Evaluator, has now been made available to Byrd. The theory behind it is that the human voice normally operates in both audible frequencies and inaudible frequency modulations. The inaudible vibrations disappear from the voice when a person is under stress; and although the ear does not note the difference, the machine, according to the inventor, can trace the fluctuations on a chart. Byrd is working on a means of adapting this device to use in conjunction with plants.

In Japan a soft-spoken doctor of philosophy and successful electronics engineer from Kamakura, a charmingly gardened retreat not far from Yokohama harbour, has developed a similar lie detector into a device with the most fabulous results yet achieved in the plant kingdom. A regular consultant on lie detection for the Japanese police, Dr Ken Hashimoto read about Backster's laboratory experiments and decided to wire one of the family cacti to an ordinary polygraph by means of acupuncture needles.

His intent was more revolutionary than Backster's, Sauvin's or Byrd's. He hoped to enter into actual conversation with a plant; to do so he counted on an improvement he had made in the Japanese procedure for lie detection. To simplify and make less expensive the process of police interrogation, Dr Hashimoto developed a system, similar to Dektor's, whereby nothing more than a cassette tape is needed to record the reactions of a suspect. Electronically transposing the modulations of the suspect's voice, Hashimoto was able to produce on paper a running graph reliable enough to pass muster in a Japanese law court.

It now dawned on Hashimoto that by reversing the system he might be able to transform the tracings from a graph into modulated sounds, giving voice to a plant. His first experiments with a cactus similar to the giant saguaro of California and the Arizona desert, but much smaller, were a failure. Loath to conclude that either Backster's reports or his own equipment was defective, Hashimoto decided that it might be he who was having trouble communicating with the plant, despite the fact that he is one of Japan's leading researchers into psychic phenomena.

His wife, on the other hand, who loves plants and is renowned for her 'green thumb', soon got sensational results. As Mrs Hashimoto assured the plant that she loved it, there was an instant response from the cactus. Transformed and amplified by Dr Hashimoto's electronic equipment, the sound produced by the plant was like the high-pitched hum of very-high-voltage wires heard from a distance, except that it was more like a song, the rhythm and tone being varied and pleasant, at times even warm and almost jolly.

John Francis Dougherty, a young American from Marina Del Rey, California, who witnessed one of these conversations, says it sounded as if Mrs Hashimoto, speaking in modulated Japanese, was being answered by the plant in modulated 'cactese'. Dougherty further reports that the Hashimotos became so intimate with their plant that they were soon able to teach it to count and add up to twenty. In answer to a query as to how much two and two make, the plant would respond with sounds which, when transcribed back into inked tracings, produced four distinct and conjoined peaks.

Dr Hashimoto, who got his doctorate from Tokyo University, and is chief of the Hashimoto Electronics Research Centre, as well as managing director and chief of research for the Fuji Electric Industries – which produce the huge animated electrical signs that illumine Tokyo – has since demonstrated the adding capacities of his cactus to audiences all over Japan.

Asked to explain the phenomenon of his talking and adding cactus, Dr Hashimoto, who is also, surprisingly, one of Japan's best-selling authors – his *Introduction to ESP* is in its sixtieth printing and his *Mystery of the Fourth Dimensional World* is in its eightieth – answered that there are many phenomena that cannot be explained by the theories of present-day physics. He believes there is a world beyond the present three-dimensional world defined by physics, that this three-dimensional world is merely a shadow of a fourth-dimensional, nonmaterial world.

He further believes that this fourth-dimensional world controls the three-dimensional material world through what he calls 'mind concentration' or what others call psychokinesis, or mind-over-matter.

3

Plants can read your mind

While Backster and Sauvin were developing their experiments in the eastern part of the United States, in Los Gatos, California, a research chemist named Marcel Vogel began to probe into the realm of creativity. He had been challenged to give a course on the subject for the engineers and scientists of International Business Machines, the firm with which he worked. It was only after he had taken on the job that he realized the enormity of it. 'How does one define creativity?' he found himself asking. 'What is a creative person?' To answer these questions, Vogel, who had studied for years to become a Franciscan priest, began writing an outline for twelve two-hour seminars which he hoped would represent an ultimate challenge to his students.

As a boy, Vogel's curiosity about creativity had first been stirred when he wondered what caused the light in fire-flies and glow-worms. Finding nothing on luminescence in the great libraries he informed his mother that he would write a book on the subject. Ten years later his *Luminescence in Liquids and Solids and their Practical Application* was published in collaboration with Chicago University's Dr Peter Pringsheim. Two years after that, Vogel formed his own company called *Vogel Luminescence* in San Francisco and it soon became a leader in the field. Over a period of fifteen years Vogel's firm developed a variety of new products; the red colour seen on television screens, fluorescent crayons, tags for insecticides, a 'black light' inspection kit to determine, from their urine, the secret trackways of rodents in cellars, sewers and slums, and the psychedelic colours popular in new age posters.

By the mid 1950s, Vogel was bored with his day to day tasks of administering a company, and sold it to go to work for I.B.M. There he was able to devote his full time to research, delving into magnetics, optic-electrical devices, and liquid crystal systems, developing and patenting inventions of crucial significance to the storage of information in computers, and winning the awards which adorn the walls of his San Jose home.

During the Creativity course which Vogel was asked to give at I.B.M. one of his students gave him an *Argosy* magazine with an article on Backster's work entitled 'Do Plants Have Emotions?'. Vogel's first reaction was to throw the article into the waste-paper basket, convinced that Backster was just another charlatan unworthy of serious consideration. Yet something about the idea gnawed at his mind. A few days later, he retrieved the article and completely reversed his opinion.

The article, read aloud to his seminar students, aroused both derision and curiosity; but all agreed that it would be interesting to experiment with plants. That same evening, one of the students called Vogel's attention to the latest issue of *Popular Electronics* which referred to Backster's work, and included a wiring diagram for an instrument called a 'psychanalyser' which would pick up and amplify reactions from plants and could be built for less than twenty-five dollars.

Vogel divided his class into three groups and challenged them to repeat some of Backster's experiments. By the end of the seminar, not one of the three teams had achieved any success. Vogel, on the other hand, was able to report that he had replicated certain of Backster's results, and proceeded to demonstrate how plants anticipate the act of having their leaves torn and react with even greater alarm to the threat of being burnt, or uprooted – more so even than if they are actually torn, burnt or otherwise roughly treated. Naturally he wondered why he alone seemed to be successful.

Between the ages of eleven and fourteen, Vogel had read everything he could get his hands on which might explain the workings of the human mind. Dipping into books on magic, spiritualism and hypnotic techniques, he was soon giving stage demonstrations as a teenage hypnotist. With fascination he went on to study Mesmer's theory of a universal fluid whose equilibrium or disturbances explained health or disease, Coué's ideas of auto-suggestion as they related to painless child-birth and self-betterment, and the postulates of various writers on 'psychic energy'. This was a term popularized by Carl Jung who, though he differentiated it from physical energy, believed it to be incommensurable. Now Vogel reasoned that if there was a 'psychic energy' then, like other forms of energy, it must be storable. But in what? Staring at the many chemicals on the shelves of his I.B.M. laboratory, he wondered which of them could be used to store this energy.

In his dilemma, he consulted a spiritually gifted friend, Vivian Wiley, to see if she could help. When she came to his laboratory and went through the chemicals laid out for her, she said that, in her judgement, none offered any promise of a solution for Vogel's problem.

Vogel suggested she ignore his preconceived ideas about chemicals and use anything which might intuitively occur to her. Back in her garden, Vivian Wiley picked two leaves from a saxifrage, one of which she placed on her bedside table, the other in the living-room. 'Each day when I get up,' she told Vogel, 'I will look at the leaf by my bed and *will* that it continue to live; but I will pay no attention to the other. We will see what happens.'

A month later, she asked Vogel to come to her house and bring a camera to photograph the leaves. He could hardly believe what he saw. The leaf to which his friend had paid no attention was flaccid, turning brown and beginning to decay. The leaf on which she had focused daily attention was radiantly vital and green, just as if it had been freshly picked from the garden. Some power appeared to be defying natural law, keeping the leaf in a healthy state. Curious to see if he could get the same results as his friend, Vogel picked three leaves from an elm outside his I.B.M. laboratory, took them home and laid them on a plate of glass near his bed. Each day, before breakfast, Vogel stared concentratedly at the two outer leaves on the glass for about one minute, exhorting them lovingly to continue to live; the centre leaf he assiduously ignored. After a week, the centre leaf had turned brown and shrivelled, whereas the outer leaves were still green and healthy-looking. Even more interesting was the fact that the severed stems of the live leaves appeared to have healed the wounds caused by ripping from the tree.

Vogel was convinced that he was witnessing the power of 'psychic energy' in action. If the power of the mind could keep a leaf green, Vogel wondered what its effect might be on liquid crystals, an intensive study of which he was pursuing for I.B.M. Trained in microscopy, Vogel had taken hundreds of colour slides of liquid crystal behaviour magnified up to three hundred times. While making the slides, he realized that, by 'relaxing his mind', he could sense activity not visually revealed in the microscopic field.

I began to pick up things at the microscope which eluded others, not with ocular vision but with 'my mind's eye'. After becoming aware of them, I was led by some form of higher sensory awareness to adjust the lighting conditions to allow these phenomena to be optically recordable to the human eye or to a camera.

He reached the conclusion that crystals are brought into a solid, or physical, state of existence by *preforms*, or ghost-images of pure energy which *anticipate* the solids. Since plants could pick up a human intention to burn them, for example, there was no doubt in his mind that intent was one kind of energy field.

By the autumn of 1971, Vogel's microscopic work was taking up most of his time, and he was forced to abandon his research on plants. He was only stimulated to continue later when an article on such work appeared in the *San Jose Mercury*, as a result of which he was besieged on the telephone for information.

Vogel realized that, before he could observe with precision the effects on plants of human thoughts and emotion, he would have to improve his technique of affixing electrodes to the plant leaves in such a way as to eliminate what he considered to be the major source of spurious data – or engineer's 'noise' – which caused the pen-recorder to drift on the chart. Backster's system of clamping the electrodes to the leaves seemed to Vogel to cause the plant to respond to random electro-magnetic frequencies, such as 60-cycle hum, or any electro-static phenomenon such as a vacuum cleaner in the atmosphere around it, which in turn caused the pen-recorder to wander.

Vogel also found that some of the philodendrons he worked with responded faster, others more slowly, some very distinctly, others less distinctly, and that not only plants, but also their individual leaves, had their own unique personalities. Leaves with a large electrical resistance were especially difficult to work with; fleshy leaves with a high water content were the best. Plants appeared to go through phases of activity and inactivity, full of response at certain times of the day or days of the month, 'sluggish' or 'morose' at other times.

To make sure that none of these recording effects was the result of faulty electroding, Vogel developed a mucilaginous substance composed of a solution of agar, with a thickener of karri gum and salt. This paste was brushed on to the leaves before gently applying *carefully polished* 1 × 1-1/2 in. stainless-steel electrodes. When the agar jelly hardened around the edges of the electronic pick-ups, it sealed their faces into a moist interior, virtually eliminating all the variability in signal output caused by pressure on leaves when clamped between ordinary electrodes. This system produced for Vogel a base line on the chart that was perfectly straight, without oscillations.

Having eliminated these random influences, Vogel began a new round of experiments in the spring of 1971 to see if he could establish the exact moment when a philodendron entered into recordable communication with a human being. With a philodendron attached to a galvanometer which produced a straight base line, Vogel stood before the plant, completely relaxed, breathing deeply and almost touching it with outspread fingers. At the same time, he began to shower the plant with the same kind of affectionate emotion as would flow to a friend. Each time he did this, a series of ascending oscillations was described on the chart by the pen holder. At the same time Vogel could tangibly feel, on the palms of his hands, an outpouring from the plant of some sort of energy. After three to five minutes, further release of emotion on Vogel's part evoked no further action from the plant, which seemed to have discharged all its energy in response to his ministrations. To Vogel, the interreaction between himself and the philodendron appeared to be of the same order as that evoked when lovers or close friends meet, the intensity of mutual response evoking a surge of energy until it is finally expended and must be recharged. Like lovers, both Vogel and the plant appeared to remain suffused with joy and contentment.

In a botanical nursery, Vogel found that he could easily pick out a particularly sensitive plant by running his hands over a group until he felt a slight cooling sensation followed by what he describes as a series of electrical pulses, indicating a powerful field. If he increased the distance between himself and such a plant, he found, as Backster had, that he could get a similar reaction from it, first from outside the house, from down the block, and even from his laboratory in Los Gatos, eight miles away.

In another experiment, Vogel wired two plants to the same recording machine and snipped a leaf from the first plant. The second plant responded to the hurt being inflicted on its neighbour, but *only when Vogel was paying attention to it*. If he cut off a leaf while ignoring the second plant, the response was lacking.

From his own experience, Vogel knew that masters of the art of Yoga, and teachers of other forms of deep meditation such as Zen, are unaware of disturbing influences around them when in meditative states. An electro-encephalograph picks up from them quite a different set of brain waves from those when the same persons are alert to the everyday world around them. Thus it became clearer to him that a certain focused state of consciousness on his part seemed to become an integral and balancing part of the circuitry required to monitor his plants. A plant could be awakened from somnolence to sensitivity by his giving up his normally conscious state and focusing a seemingly extraconscious part of his mind on the exact notion that the plant be happy and feel loved, that it be blessed with healthy growth. In this way, man and plant seemed to interact, and, as a unit, pick up sensations from events, or third parties, which became recordable through the plant. The process of sensitizing both himself and the plant, Vogel found, would sometimes take only a few minutes, at other times nearly half an hour.

Asked to describe the process in detail, Vogel said that, first he quietens the sensory responses of his body organs, then he becomes aware of an energetic relationship between the plant and himself. When a state of balance between the bio-electrical potential of both the plant and himself was achieved, the plant was no longer sensitive to noise, temperature, the normal electrical fields surrounding it, nor to other plants. It responded only to Vogel, who had effectively tuned himself to it – or perhaps, simply hypnotized it.

Vogel now felt confident enough to accept invitations to lecture and to give demonstrations on television. At one lecture he said unequivocally:

'It is fact: man can and does communicate with plant life. Plants are living objects, sensitive, rooted in space. They may be blind, deaf and dumb in the human sense, but there is no doubt in my mind that they are extremely sensitive instruments for measuring man's emotions. They radiate energy, forces that are beneficial to man. One can feel these forces! They feed into one's own force-field which in turn feeds back energy to the plant.'

The American Indians, said Vogel, were keenly aware of these faculties. When in need, they would go into the woods. With their arms extended, they would place their backs to a pine tree in order to replenish themselves with its power.

Sometimes he encountered sceptics or hostile observers in his audience. By paying attention to the emanation of negative attitudes, Vogel found he could isolate the individuals emitting them and counter their effect with a deep breath, learned in Yoga instruction. He would then switch his mind to another mental image just as if he were turning a dial to a different setting.

Vogel reiterates that,

'The feeling of hostility, of negativity, in an audience, is well known to all public lecturers and is one of the main barriers to effective communication. To counteract this force is one of the most difficult tasks in public demonstration of these plant experiments. If one cannot do this, the plant and therefore the equipment will "go dead" and there is no response until a positive tie can be re-established.'

Vogel has also said:

'It seems that I act as a filtering system which limits the response of a plant to the outside environment. I can turn it off or on, so that people and plant become mutually responsive. By charging the plant with some energy within me, I can cause the plant to build up a sensitivity for this kind of work.

'It is extremely important that one understand that the plant's response is, to my mind, not that of an intelligence in plant form, but that the plant becomes an extension of oneself. One can then interact with the bio-electric field of the plant, or through it, with the thought processes and emotions in a third person.'

Vogel concluded that,

'a Life Force, or Cosmic Energy, surrounding all living things is shareable among plants, animals and humans. Through such sharing, a person and a plant become one! This oneness makes possible a mutual sensitivity allowing plant and man not only to intercommunicate, but to record these communications via the plant on a recording chart.'

Because his observations indicated there was an interchange, even a fusion of energies between plant and man, Vogel wondered whether an exceptionally sensitive individual could actually get *into* a plant, as was reported of the sixteenth-century German mystic Jacob Boehme, who, as a young man, became illumined and described being able to see in another dimension. Boehme said he could look at a growing plant and suddenly, by willing to do so, mingle with that plant, be part of the plant, feel its life 'struggling towards the light'. He said he was able to share the simple ambitions of the plant and 'rejoice with a joyously growing leaf'.

One day Vogel was visited in San Jose by Debbie Sapp, a quiet self-effacing girl who impressed Vogel with her initial ability to enter into instant rapport with his philodendron, as established by his instrumentation.

When the plant was entirely calm, he asked her, point blank: 'Can you now get into that plant?' Debbie nodded assent, and her face took on an attitude of quiet repose, of detachment, as if she were far away in another universe. Immediately the recording pen began to trace a pattern of undulations revealing to Vogel that the plant was receiving an unusual amount of energy.

Debbie later described what happened in writing:

Mr Vogel asked me to relax and project myself into the philodendron. Several things took place as I began to carry out his request.

First, I wondered exactly how I would get inside a plant. I made a conscious decision to let my imagination take over and found myself entering the main stem through a doorway at its base. Once inside, I saw the moving cells and water travelling upward through the stem, and let myself move with this upward flow.

Approaching the spreading leaves in my imagination, I could feel myself being drawn from an imaginary world into a realm over which I had no control. There were no mental pictures, but rather a feeling that I was becoming part of, and filling out, a broad expansive surface. This seemed to me to be describable only as pure consciousness.

I felt acceptance and positive protection by the plant. There was no sense of time, just a feeling of unity in existence and in space. I smiled spontaneously and let myself be one with the plant.

Then Mr Vogel asked me to relax. When he said this, I realized I was very tired but peaceful. All of my energy had been with the plant.

Vogel, who was observing the recording on the chart, noticed an abrupt stop when the girl 'came out' of the plant. On later occasions, when she 're-entered' it, she was able to describe the inner make-up of its cells and their structure in detail. She specifically noted that one of the leaves had been badly burned by an electrode. When Vogel detached the electrode, he found a hole almost all the way through the leaf.

Vogel has since tried the same experiment with dozens of other people, asking them to go into a single leaf and look at the individual cells within it. All gave consistent descriptions of various parts of the cellular body down to the detailed organization of the DNA molecules.

From the experiment, Vogel came to the conclusion that, 'We can move into individual cells in our own bodies and, depending on our state of mind, affect them in various ways. One day, this may explain the cause of disease.'

Knowing that children are more 'open-minded' than adults, Vogel has begun to teach children how to interact with plants.

First, he asks them to feel a leaf, describe its temperature, consistency and texture in detail. Next, he lets them bend leaves and become aware of their resiliency before going on to gently stroke their upper and under sides. If his pupils take pleasure in describing to him the sensations they feel, Vogel asks them to take their hands away from the leaves and try to feel a force or energy emanating from them. Many of the children instantly described a rippling or tingling sensation.

Vogel noticed that those children who felt the strongest sensations were wholly engrossed in what they were doing. Once they felt the tingling, he would say: 'Now completely relax and feel the give and take of the energy. When you feel it pulsing, gently move your hand up and down over the leaf.' Following his directions, the young experimenters could easily see that, when they brought their hands down, the leaves fell away. By continued repetition of this motion, the leaves would begin to oscillate. With the use of both hands they could actually get a plant to sway. As they gained confidence, Vogel urged them to move further and further away from the plant.

'This is basic training,' comments Vogel, 'to develop an expanded awareness of a force which is not visible. The awareness established, they see they can operate with this force!'

Adults, according to Vogel, are much less successful than children and this leads him to think that many scientists are not going to be able to repeat his or Backster's experiments in laboratories. 'If they approach the experimentation in a mechanistic way and don't enter into mutual communication with their plants and treat them as friends, they will fail!'

Indeed, Vogel has been told by one doctor working at the California Psychical Society that he has had not a single result, though he had worked for months. The same is true for one of Denver's most renowned psychoanalysts. Vogel comments that,

Hundreds of laboratory workers around the world are going to be just as frustrated and disappointed as these men until they appreciate that the empathy between plant and human is the *key*, and learn how to establish it. No amount of checking in laboratories

[46]

is going to prove a thing until the experiments are done by properly trained observers. Spiritual development is indispensable. But this runs counter to the philosophy of many scientists who do not realize that creative experimentation means that the *experimenters must become part of their experiments*.

This highlights the difference in approach between Vogel and Backster, indicating, perhaps, that Vogel is establishing a type of hypnotic control over his plants. Sceptics are achieving a reverse effect, yet Backster's plants, left strictly alone, will react to their environment quite normally.

Vogel says that even when a person *can* affect a plant, the result is not always a happy one. He asked one of his friends, a clinical psychologist, who had come to see for himself if there was any truth in the plant research, to project a strong emotion to a philodendron fifteen feet away. The plant surged into an instantaneous and intense reaction and then, suddenly, 'went dead'. When Vogel asked the psychologist what had gone through his mind, the man answered that he had mentally compared Vogel's plant with his own philodendron at home, and thought how inferior Vogel's was to his. The 'feelings' of Vogel's plant were evidently so badly hurt that it refused to respond for the rest of the day; in fact, it sulked for two weeks thereafter.

Vogel could not doubt that plants have a definite aversion to certain humans, or, more exactly, to what those humans are thinking. This being true, Vogel considers that it might be possible, one day, to read a person's thoughts through a plant. Something of the sort has already taken place. At Vogel's request, a friend who was a nuclear physicist began to work on a technical problem. As he was cogitating, Vogel's plant registered a series of tracings on the recorder for 118 seconds. When the tracing fell back to base line, Vogel informed his friend that he had stopped his train of thought. The friend corroborated. Had Vogel actually captured a thought process on a chart via a plant? When after a few minutes, the physicist at Vogel's request began to think of his wife the plant again recorded a tracing, this time for 105 seconds. It seemed to Vogel that, right in front of him in his living-room, a plant was picking up and passing on a man's mental impressions of his wife. If one could interpret such tracings, could one not know what the man was thinking?

After a break for a cup of coffee, Vogel almost casually asked his friend to think once more of his wife in the same way he had thought of her before. The plant registered another 105-second-long tracing very similar to the first. To Vogel this was the first time a plant seemed to have recorded a similar thought spectrogram and duplicated it! Perhaps, he thought, it is only a matter of time before chart patterns can be decoded into the message units which will be able to describe thought processes.

Having established that plants respond to individual humans and to other plants, Vogel next experimented with people in groups. While he was entertaining a group of sceptical psychologists, medical doctors and computer programmers at his house, he let them look over his equipment for hidden devices and gimmicks which they insisted must exist. Then he asked them to sit in a circle and talk in order to see what reactions the plant might pick up. For an hour, the group conversed with hardly a response from the plant. Just as they had all concluded that the whole thing was a fake, one of them said: 'How about sex?' To their surprise, the plant came to life, the pen-recorder oscillating wildly on the chart. This led to speculation that talking of sex could stir up in the atmosphere some sort of sexual energy such as the 'orgone' discovered and described by Dr Wilhelm Reich, and that the ancient fertility rites in which humans had sexual intercourse in freshly seeded fields might indeed have stimulated plants to grow.

On another occasion, the plant responded to an audience's reaction to a spooky story told in a darkened room lit only by a red-shaded candle. At certain points in the story, such as: 'The door of the mysterious cabin in the forest began slowly to open . . .', or, 'Suddenly, there appeared round the corner a strange man with a knife in his hand . . .', or 'Charles bent down and raised the lid of the coffin', the plant seemed to pay closer attention. To Vogel, this was evidence that a plant can measure 'figments of the imagination', as being converted to energy by the group as a whole.

Vogel stresses that experiments with plants can be extremely dangerous to those who do not have the ability properly to alter their states of consciousness. 'Focused thought,' he says, 'can exert a tremendous effect on the body of a person in a higher mental state, if he lets his emotions interfere.'

'No one,' says Vogel, 'who is not in sound bodily health should become involved with plants or any other kind of psychic research.' Though he has not been able to prove it, Vogel feels that a special diet of vegetables, fruits and nuts, rich in minerals and proteins, allows the body to build the kind of energy necessary for such work. 'One draws energy at high levels,' he says, 'and this requires good nutrition.'

Asked how the higher energies, such as thought, might operate on the physical bodies of living organisms, Vogel says he has now begun to speculate on the strange properties of water. As a crystallographer, he is interested in the fact that, unlike most salts, which have one crystalline form, core samples of glacier ice have more than thirty different forms. 'Uninitiated persons, when first looking at them,' says Vogel, 'could conclude that they were observing as many different substances. And they would be right in their own way because water is a real mystery.'

Vogel makes the prediction, which he stresses is as yet far from established fact, that since living things all have a high water content, the vitality of a person must be in some way related to the rate of respiration. As water moves around the body and through its pores, charges are built. Vogel's first clue about his postulate on water came from the fact that some 'psychics' have lost several pounds of body weight during sessions in which they expended vital, or psychic, energy. 'If we could weigh a person doing psychic research on a sensitive scale,' suggests Vogel, 'we would find that there is a loss of weight in each case. It is a water loss, as it is in persons who go on crash diets.'

Whatever the future brings, Vogel believes that his research with plants can help man to the recognition of long-ignored truths. By developing simple training kits, which he is presently designing, he thinks he can teach children to release their emotions and watch the effects in a measurable way.

'They can thus learn the art of *loving*,' says Vogel, 'and know truly that when they think a thought they release a tremendous power or force in space. By knowing that they *are* their thoughts, they will know how to use thinking to achieve spiritual, emotional, and intellectual growth.

'This is no machine to measure brain waves or any gimmick to help people to become seers or mystics,' Vogel insists, 'but one to help children to become *simple, honest human beings.*'

Asked to sum up the importance of his research with plants, Vogel replied:

'So much of the ills and suffering in life comes from our inability to release stresses and forces within us. When a person rejects us, we rebel inside and we *hold on to this rejection.* This builds a stress which, as Dr Wilhelm Reich showed so long ago, becomes locked in as muscular tension, and if not unlocked, depletes the body's energy field and alters its chemistry. My research with plants indicates one pathway to deliverance.'

For Marcel Vogel, plants have opened new horizons. The vegetal kingdom seems capable of picking up messages of intent, benign or malicious, that are inherently more truthful than when translated into words – a talent which all human beings may share but which they have momentarily occluded.

Two young Californian students of humanistic psychology and Hindu philosophy, Randall Fontes and Robert Swanson, have now pursued Vogel's quarry into unbeaten ground. Using sophisticated equipment lent them by the IBM researcher, they have made a series of discoveries so surprising that despite their youth they have been granted funds and equipment by established universities to further probe the mysteries of plant communication.

Fontes' and Swanson's first discovery came virtually by accident when one noticed that the other's yawning was being picked up by a plant in the form of energy surges. Instead of ignoring the phenomenon as improbable, the two students followed up the clue remembering that in ancient Hindu texts an exaggerated yawn was considered a means by which a tired person could be recharged with vivifying *shakhti*, a postulated energy filling the universe.

[50]

Plants can read your mind

With the help of Dr Norman Goldstein, a professor of biology at State University in Hayward, California, Fontes went on to discover an electrical potential travelling from cell to cell in the ivy philodendron which gives a strong indication of the presence of a hitherto unsuspected simple nervous system. He has most recently been working with *Nitella*, an aquatic plant whose individual cells can measure two inches or more. At the Stanford Research Institute in California Fontes is cooperating with Dr Hal Puthoff, a physicist, and Pat Price, a former test pilot and chief-of-police, who has remarkable psychic powers. Price can get the *Nitella* to respond to his various mental projections almost unfailingly. This being so, Puthoff and Fontes are hopeful that by removing Price a considerable distance from the *Nitella* – say more than 1,000 miles – and by using sophisticated timing equipment, they will be able to establish whether Price can affect the plant at such a distance and whether the energy from his 'mental projection' moves faster than the speed of light. Meanwhile, Swanson is cooperating in the setting up of a parapsychologically oriented counselling centre at the John F. Kennedy University in Martinez, California, where one of Swanson's goals is to determine just which people affect plants telepathically and which do not.

4

Visitors from outer space

One day late in October 1971, a blue Volkswagen carrying some unusual scientific equipment drove into Oak Grove Park near Temecula, a tiny southern California village not far from the famous Mount Palomar Observatory. Out of the driver's seat stepped L. George Lawrence, a forty-seven-year-old Silesian-born electronics engineer. Lawrence and a field assistant had come to this remote desert-like spot to record signals from wild-growing oak trees, cacti, and yuccas. He had chosen the park because, in his words, it is 'an electromagnetic "deep-fringe" area, with no man-made interferences and thus ideal for getting clean, uncontaminated plant reactions'. His apparatus, very different from that of Backster, Sauvin, and Vogel, incorporated, in a temperature-controlled bath, living vegetal tissue shielded behind a Faraday tube that screened out even the slightest electromagnetic interference. Lawrence had found that living vegetable tissue was able to perceive signals far more delicately than electronic sensors and it was his belief that *biological* radiations transmitted by living things were best received by a *biological* medium. Electrodes were not attached to Lawrence's desert plants because the plants were far enough away from their neighbours to rule out signal interference. Instead, he trained a lensless tube with a wide aperture at a target plant. At greater distances he substituted a telescope for the lensless tube, and made the plant more visible by hanging a white cloth on it. The living tissue was able to pick up a directional signal from as far away as a mile. Perturbations of the living tissue were detected, not visually through a pen-recorder, but aurally by means of a continuous, low even whistle, which changed into a series of distinct pulses whenever it was disturbed by signals from a plant.

On their first day at Oak Grove Park Lawrence and his

assistant took a break for a late afternoon snack, seating themselves about ten yards from their instrument which was left pointing randomly at the sky. As Lawrence bit into a 'Hebrew National' knockwurst, the steady whistling sound from his equipment was interrupted by a series of distinct pulsations. Lawrence, who had not yet digested the knockwurst, but had well digested the Backster effect, thought the signals might have been caused by his killing some of the cells in the sausage. Second thoughts reminded him that pickled sausage meat is biologically dead. As he checked his instrumentation, to his amazement the audio signal continued to produce a distinct chain of pulses for over half an hour before the even whistle returned, indicating that nothing more was being received. The signals must have been coming from somewhere, and since his device had been continuously pointed upward towards the heavens, Lawrence was faced with the fantastic thought that *something or someone was transmitting from outer space*. The possibility of life beyond earth was both disturbing and exciting to him and his colleague, but they were loath to jump to a premature conclusion that they had picked up an intelligent signal from trillions of miles away through a plant tissue. Lawrence therefore determined to spend several months improving his equipment, making it into what he termed a 'biodynamic field station designed for interstellar signal reception'. This he did, and by April 1972, his equipment was sufficiently refined for him to attempt to point it once more in the same direction which had brought the reaction on the earlier occasion. The alignment then had been celestial coordinates near *Ursa Major*, the Great Bear. This time he drove out to the Pisgah Crater, a volcanic butte, 2,300 feet above sea level, in the middle of the arid Mojave Desert, and surrounded by some thirty square miles of flat lava beds with not so much as a blade of grass. Aligning his telescope – coupled with the Faraday tube, a camera, an electromagnetic interference monitor and the tissue chamber – in the general direction of *Ursa Major*, Lawrence switched on his audio signal. After a ninety-minute interval, his equipment again picked up a recognizable, though briefer, pattern of signals. According to Lawrence, the periods between rapid series of pulse trains ranged from approximately three to ten minutes over a stretch of several hours as he monitored a single spot in the heavens.

It was a repetition of his 1971 observations and Lawrence began to wonder whether he had not accidentally stumbled over a scientific discovery of major proportions. He had no idea from where the signals might be coming or what or who was sending them, but it seemed to him highly possible that galactic drift played some role in their origin. 'The signals might be spilling over from the galactic equator which has a dense star population,' said Lawrence. 'We could be getting something from that area rather than from *Ursa Major*.'

He decided to continue the tests from his laboratory, pointing his machine at the same coordinates, leaving it on round the clock. Lawrence says that he had to wait weeks and sometimes months for the signals to come through, but when they did they were unmistakable. One signal produced a Brr-r-r-r-r beep-beep-beep type of audio pulse which Lawrence maintains no earthly entity has achieved.

Pressed to speculate on the nature of the strange signals, Lawrence stated:

'I don't believe they are directed at earthlings. I think we are dealing with transmissions between peer groups, and because we don't know anything about *biological communications* we are simply excluded from these "conversations". I also believe that the energy transmitted must be fantastically high since, at this basic level of its development, our instrumentation is not at all sophisticated and it would take a tremendous amount of power to create any response in it from such astronomical distances. The signals therefore, may be of an emergency nature. Something may be happening up there and someone may be desperately calling for help.'

Deciding that his findings may be of crucial significance and could herald a new and as yet unimagined system of communication, Lawrence sent a copy of his October 1971 tape, together with a seven-page report, to the Smithsonian Institution in Washington, D.C. where it is preserved as a potentially historical scientific document. The report concludes:

An apparent train of interstellar communication signals of unknown origin and destination has been observed. Since interception

was made by biological sensors, a biological-type signal transmission must be assumed. Test experiments were conducted in an
electromagnetic deep-fringe area, the equipment itself being
impervious to electromagnetic radiation. Follow-up tests revealed
no equipment defects. Because interstellar listening experiments
are not conducted on a routine basis, the suggestion is advanced
that verification tests should be conducted elsewhere, possibly
on a global scale. The phenomenon is too important to be
ignored.

Lawrence says the instrumentation tape, as a mere audio
presentation, is unpleasant to listen to, but reviewers of the
tape have conceded that 'a fascinating degree of enchantment'
tends to emerge after the tape has been played back three or
more times, typically over a period of weeks.

The tape contains a short, incremental series of deep
harmonious oscillations resembling nonsense chatter or background modulations. An intelligent character of the overall
pulse train is implied by discrete spacing patterns, apparent
repetitions of sequences, and highly attenuated electromagnetic
noise.

Lawrence's most important conclusion that biological type
sensors are needed in order to intercept biological signals
applies particularly to communications from outer space.
As he puts it: 'Standard electronics are next to worthless here,
since "bio-signals" apparently reside outside the known
electromagnetic spectrum.'

Lawrence points out that in the 1950s scientists who had
previously insisted that our small planet was unique in the
universe began, on the basis of careful celestial observations
and other inferences, to admit that we may not be alone in the
cosmic immensity, and to concede the possible existence of
extraterrestrials whose development might be far superior to
our own.

In the early nineteenth century Karl Friedrich Gauss, the
German mathematician and physicist, proposed that man
might make known to cosmic beings his presence on earth
by cutting huge swathes hundreds of miles long in the Siberian
taiga to form a right angle. This was followed by the suggestion
of the Austrian astronomer, J. J. von Littrow, that geometric

canals be dug in the Sahara, filled with kerosene and set aflame at night, and the recommendation of the French Scientist Charles Gros that a vast mirror be built to reflect sunlight directly at Mars.

These far-fetched ideas were updated when, in the summer of 1927, Jorgen Hals, a Norwegian radio engineer, was listening to short wave station P.C.J.J. transmitting from Eindhoven in the Netherlands and heard strange echoes. Only a quarter of a century later were these echoes finally considered to derive from the possible existence of a communications probe sent from afar to transmit and monitor the solar system for intelligent life and retransmit live radio-frequency emanations back to its distant 'home-world'.

In September 1953, C. W. Bradley of London picked up the call letters of the American station KLEE-TV in Houston, Texas, on his living-room television tube. Over the next several months the same letters were observed on TV screens in the offices of Atlantic Electronics Ltd in Lancaster. What was eerie about these receptions was not that the TV signal had been sent from so far away, since this happens often enough to cause no surprise, but that the signal had been sent about three years prior to the time of its reception, the call letters KLEE having been changed to KPRC in 1950. Explanations that the signals could have been stored in a 'plasma cloud' hovering above the earth which released the data in a broadcast for all to see gave no reasons as to how this could have been done or why, and suggestions that the whole thing was merely a meaningless – though extremely expensive – hoax seem far-fetched.

That scientists are still hotly pursuing the subject of communication with extraterrestrial intelligences, shortened into the acronym CETI, is evidenced by a top-level international conference held in September 1971 at the Byurakan Astrophysical Laboratory in Soviet Armenia. Sponsored by the science academies of the U.S.A. and the U.S.S.R., the conference was attended not only by astronomers but by biologists. anthropologists, historians and cryptographers.

Most of their projects, Lawrence complains, assume that signals must come by radio since that is the most efficient means of communication known to the scientists of this planet. If they became converted to his idea of receiving biological signals, Lawrence feels they would have a much better chance. The notion is echoed by Joseph F. Goodavage, author of *Astrology, The Space Age Science,* who, in an article for *Saga* magazine (January 1973), states that:

Rigid enforcement of established Scientific Method, as a kind of quasi-religion – with its burdensome ritual and tradition – may be the most serious obstacle in the path of direct communication between *Homo sapiens* and other civilizations that may be thriving throughout interstellar, intergalactic space.

Employed as an instrumentation engineer for a Los Angeles space-science corporation, Lawrence decided to design some more sophisticated transducers – or converters of one type of input energy into another type of output energy. Knowing that a mechanical device which could use heat, environmental pressure, electrostatic fields, and gravitational changes simultaneously was not up to the task, he theorized that a plant might be able to turn the trick because it had the necessary components built in by nature.

When he began to study the problem in 1963, Lawrence found he could get no help from plant specialists and biologists because none of them knew enough physics, and especially electronics, to visualize what he was driving at. In his search for a biological system for radiating and receiving signals, Lawrence began by going over the experiments made in the 1920s by the Russian histologist Alexander Gurwitsch and his wife, who proclaimed that all living cells produce an invisible radiation. Gurwitsch had noticed that the cells in the tips of onion roots seemed to be dividing at a definite rhythm. Believing this due to an extra unexplained source of physical energy, Gurwitsch wondered whether it might not come from nearby cells.

To test out his theory he mounted one root tip in a horizontally oriented thin glass tube to act as a ray gun. This he pointed at a similar onion root tip, also protected in a tube, but with a small area on one side exposed naked to serve as a target. After three hours of exposure, Gurwitsch examined sections from the target root under his microscope. When he compared the number of cell divisions, he found twenty-five per cent more in the exposed, irradiated area. The receiver root had seemingly picked up a vital energy from its sender neighbour.

To try to block the emission, Gurwitsch repeated the experiment with a thin shield of quartz between the roots, but obtained essentially the same results. However, when the quartz was coated with gelatine, or a simple sheet of glass was substituted, no enhanced cell division could be observed. Since glass and gelatine were known to block various ultra-violet frequencies on the electromagnetic spectrum, Gurwitsch concluded that the rays emitted by the cells of an onion root tip must be as short as or shorter than ultra-violet. Because they apparently increased cell division, or 'mitosis', he called them 'mitogenetic rays'.

Gurwitsch's findings had created a furore in the scientific world as laboratories hastened to check them. Since the wavelengths claimed for the new rays were more powerful than the ultra-violet frequencies which reach the earth from the sun, many biologists could not believe that living processes were capable of generating them. In Paris two researchers reported similar results; in Moscow one of Gurwitsch's own countrymen showed that he could increase the budding of yeast more than twenty-five per cent by exposing it to 'mitogenetic' rays from onion roots.

A pair of scientists at the Siemens and Halske Electric Company near Berlin came to the verdict that the radiation was a fact; and in Frankfurt, a researcher actually succeeded in measuring it, not through its effect on vegetal life, but with electrical instruments. On the other hand, equally reliable Anglo-Saxon investigators could detect no effects. In the United States, when the prestigious Academy of Sciences issued a report that Gurwitsch's discovery was not replicable, and therefore strongly suggested it might be the product of his imagination, Gurwitsch was sped into limbo.

Though Lawrence lacked an ultra-violet spectrometer to detect 'mitogenetic' radiation, he was fascinated by Gurwitsch's system of *directing* the energy. His observations also nudged Lawrence almost involuntarily to the position that there was a psychological, or 'mental', factor involved in Gurwitsch's

[58]

maverick work. Continuing to probe further with a sensitive high-impedance device of his own design, Lawrence sought to discover whether individual cells in a quarter-inch slice of onion, attached to a Wheatstone bridge and an electrometer, would react to various stimuli. He found that they seemed to respond to irritations such as a puff of smoke, or even to his mental image of their destruction, in about one hundred milliseconds, or one tenth of a second.

What seemed most odd to Lawrence was that the reaction of the onion tissue seemed to change depending on whether he, or someone else, was directing thought at it. People with 'psychic gifts' seemed to elicit much stronger responses than the practical-minded Lawrence. As he commented: 'If one can cause, or get something to cause, harm to a cell – assuming that the cell has a cellular consciousness – the reaction pattern in it will change from experimenter to experimenter.'

It was when Lawrence came across Backster's work that he decided to build a sophisticated psycho-galvanic analyser or plant response detector. With his new equipment, he got a series of 'wild' tracings from his plants; but because of what he retrospectively calls his 'ignorance and classical Prussian orthodoxy', he ascribed these effects to faults in his instrumentation. Nevertheless, his suspicion that plant tissues could pick up human thought and emotion slowly became more concrete in the light of Backster's achievements.

During his appointment as an assistant professor and Director of Audio-Visual Services at the California State College at San Bernadino, Lawrence attracted the attention of a sociologist colleague, Dr Mary Cisar. Because one of her best-loved house plants had mysteriously died, Lawrence purchased a philodendron for her and asked her to cooperate on some experiments with him after she had lived with it for a few weeks. When Dr Cisar made a flying trip to visit her father, Lawrence was able to note, with the help of synchronized watches, that her plant responded at certain times of day whenever she became excited or anxious. Though this seemed to confirm similar observations of Backster's, Lawrence's cautiousness still inclined him to believe that they might be due to 'bugs' in his instruments.

In October 1969, Lawrence began to publish a series of popular articles based on his reading and research, the first of which appeared as 'Electronics and the Living Plant' in *Electronics World*. Lawrence told his readers that, for the first time in the millennia since the first green leaves poked their heads out of Paleozoic swamps, plants were at last beginning to be studied for their 'electrodynamic properties'.

Four main questions, said Lawrence, were starting to attract serious attention: Could plants be integrated with electronic read-outs to form major data sensors and transducers? Could they be trained to respond to the presence of selected objects and images? Were their alleged supersensory perceptions verifiable? Of the 350,000 plants species known to science, which were the most promising from the electronic point of view?

Providing detailed instructions for investigating the behaviour of living plant cells with micro-electrodes, Lawrence also reported that in the 'Moon Garden' at Farmingdale, New York, scientists had been able in the 1960s to induce what appeared to be 'nervous breakdown' and 'complete frustration' in plants being tested as possible space foods. Even earlier, he said, L. Ron Hubbard, founder of Scientology, had noted in his East Grinstead laboratory that a tomato pricked on one side shuddered on the other.

Lawrence warned his readers that work with plants was not just a matter of electronic expertise and that working with the Backster Effect involved much more than the mere ability to construct top quality electronic equipment. 'There are certain qualities here,' he wrote, 'which do not enter into normal experimental situations. According to those experimenting in this area, it is necessary to have a "green thumb" and, most important, a genuine love for plants.'

Half a year later Lawrence followed up his revelations with an even more controversial article in the same magazine. Entitled 'Electronics and Parapsychology', Lawrence's article began by asking: 'Does man possess latent sensitivities that have been stifled by modern communications systems?' He then pointed out that although the fledgling science of parapsychology, long suspect because of an occult background, was having to fight for acceptance, the application of electronic instruments was not only permitting dramatic new experiments and bringing forth stunning discoveries but might in time rival the orthodox communications arts and sciences currently in use.

Stressing that the need for machine systems, capable of testing ESP in an unbiased, impartial manner had been recognized fifty years ago when an Italian scientist, Federico Cazzamalli, developed an ultra-high-frequency apparatus for testing human telepathy, Lawrence reported that the Italian's experiments had never been repeated because the Fascist dictator, Benito Mussolini, had declared the work secret.

In yet another article, this time in the June 1971 issue of *Popular Electronics*, Lawrence provided any researcher wishing to investigate communication with plants with detailed diagrams and a parts list for a 'response detector' allowing for extremely sensitive tests. Warning that constant repetition was an important factor in such testing, Lawrence stated that if a plant specimen is stimulated continuously, badly injured, or infrequently watered, it would tire quickly, or even lapse into shock and die. Researchers were therefore cautioned to be gentle with their plants and allow them to rest after experiments. The area in which plants live must be quiet, he added, 'so that the stimuli can be effectively applied with a minimum of power-line noise or disturbances from radio frequency transmission to cause faulty indications'.

Lawrence's ideas about plants were corroborated and elaborated upon by Jan Merta, a Czech publisher and student of physiological psychology, whose psychic gifts allow him to plunge an iron bar into a blacksmith's forge, heat it to incandescence, then calmly brush sparks off its white-hot end with his bare hand as easily as he would rub dust from a shelf. Freshly settled in Canada, Merta supported himself for two months by working as a troubleshooter for a large Montreal grower and importer of tropical plants. When clients in office and residential buildings complained that their plants were getting sick, Merta was sent to find out what was wrong. He often noticed the marked difference between the thousands of healthy plants in the firm's extensive greenhouses, and the languishing appearance of a single plant when it was taken away. Shock and loneliness were apparently cause enough for it to pine and in some cases to die. However, plants that were returned to the greenhouses would immediately regain their normal lush health.

As the result of hundreds of 'house-calls', Merta also noticed that plants thrived better when constantly communicated with by office workers and home owners than if left to themselves. Examples of the majestic *Ficus benjamini*, some nearly thirty feet tall, transported from Florida, though in excellent condition upon arrival, when placed around a fountain in a shopping centre's indoor circular solarium, started to wilt within two days in spite of careful watering and feeding. Yet those in heavily travelled passageways leading to the solarium retained their radiant vigour. To Merta this was a sure sign that the *Fici* enjoyed being admired by the passers-by.

In 1970, when Lawrence read that in the Ukraine radio frequencies and ultrasonic vibrations had been used to stimulate cereal grain seeds to produce higher yields as far back as the early 1930s and that the United States Department of Agriculture had successfully experimented in the same way, he gave up his college position and set about independently developing advanced equipment with which he hopes that seed grains can be provoked, on a commercial scale, to grow better and faster. 'If a plant seedling can be stimulated on a parapsychological basis, as the famous plant breeder Luther Burbank knew, then I don't see why,' says Lawrence, 'we can't transmit specific signals to whole fields of crops to stimulate their growth without all these damned soil-killing fertilizers.'

He began to work on special sound-type plant stimulation techniques which he combined with Backster Effect methods in order to stimulate his plants in a wireless fashion. Lawrence, torn between his interest in stimulating plant growth electrically and his projects to achieve interstellar communication, feels that the effort to contact extraterrestrial life is more important in the long run because 'if routine results can be achieved in CETI, many questions attached to riddles in the plant kingdom will be answered as a consequence'.

Visitors from outer space

On 5 June 1973, the research division of Anchor College of Truth in San Bernardino announced that it was inaugurating the world's first biological-type interstellar communications observatory under the direction of L. George Lawrence, now also a vice-president of Anchor. For the new research programme Lawrence has designed what he calls a Stellartron, which combines in one three-ton instrument the features of a radio telescope and the biological signal-receiving system of the biodynamic field station.

Anchor president, Ed Johnson, told the press that since radio astronomy had failed to detect intelligent signals from space, the college was backing Lawrence's idea that radio transmission was out of date and that biological communication should be given a trial.

Pointing out that in our own galaxy alone there are some 200 billion stars, Lawrence says that if one assumed each of them to have at least five companion planets, a total of one trillion might consequently be available for study. Even if only one planet in a thousand has intelligent life this would amount to one billion in our galaxy alone. Multiplied by the ten billion galaxies believed to comprise the observable universe, then there may be 10,000,000,000,000,000,000 planets capable of sending some kind of signal to Earth.

Anchor's founder, Reverend Alvin M. Harrell, thinks that contact with another race in the universe will trigger a tremendous explosion of knowledge. As Harrell says: 'Given the destructive brutality of humankind, we may expect any newly discovered civilization to be infinitely more loving and compassionate than we are.'

Lawrence observes that:

Perhaps plants are the true extraterrestrials for they converted an early mineral world into a habitat suitable for man by processes that border on near-perfect magic! What remains to be done now is to remove all traces of occultism and make plant response, including communications phenomena, a verifiable component of orthodox physics. Our instrumentation concepts reflect this effort.

If Lawrence is on the right track, the ardently desired prospect of producing hardware to move man into the vastness of interstellar space on Columbian voyages of discovery will be rendered as obsolete as Columbus's flagship, *Santa Maria*. Lawrence's research, suggesting as it does that intelligences are communicating instantly across distances requiring millions of light-years to reach, indicates that what is needed is not spaceships but the proper 'telephone numbers' to contact them. Though the work is still in an exploratory stage, his bio-dynamic field station may be a step towards plugging into the universal switchboard, with plants as the pretty, cheerful and efficient co-operators.

5

Latest Soviet discoveries

Recent interest and experiments in communication with plants have not been limited to the United States. Millions of newspaper readers in the U.S.S.R. were introduced to the ideas that plants communicate their feelings to man in October 1970 when *Pravda* published an article entitled, 'What Leaves Tell Us'. 'Plants talk . . . yes, they scream,' declared the official organ of the Communist Party. 'It only *seems* that they accept their misfortunes submissively and silently bear pain.' *Pravda*'s reporter, V. Chertkov, tells how he witnessed these extraordinary goings-on for himself when he visited the Laboratory for Artificial Climate at the renowned Timiryazev Academy of Agricultural Sciences in Moscow.

Before my eyes a barley sprout literally cried out when its roots were plunged into hot water. True, the plant's 'voice' was registered only by a special and extremely sensitive electronic instrument which revealed a 'bottomless vale of tears' on a broad paper band. As though it had gone crazy, the recording pen wriggled out on the white track the death agony of the barley sprout, although, to look at the little plant itself, one would never have guessed what it was going through. While its leaves, green as ever, stood upright, the plant's 'organism' was already dying. Some kind of 'brain' cells within it were telling us what was happening.

Pravda's reporter also interviewed Professor Ivan Isidorovich Gunar, head of the Academy's Department of Plant Physiology, who, with his staff, had performed hundreds of experiments, all of which confirm the presence of electrical impulses in plants similar to the well-known nerve impulses in man. The *Pravda* article noted that Gunar talked about plants as he would about people, distinguishing their individual habits, characteristics and proclivities. Chertkov wrote that,

c

He even appears to converse with them, and it seems to me that his plants pay attention to this good, greying man. Only persons invested with certain power are like this. I have even been told of a test pilot who talked to his misbehaving aeroplane, and I myself have met an old captain who talked with his ship.

When Gunar's chief assistant, Leonid A. Panishkin, a former engineer, was asked by the *Pravda* reporter why he gave up the technology in which he was trained in order to work in Gunar's laboratory, he replied: 'Well, there I used to be involved with metallurgy; here there is life.' He said he was particularly interested in searching out those conditions which might best suit the specific needs of plants and how they react to light and darkness. By using a special lamp which shone with the same intensity as the sun he had found that plants tired in an over extended day and needed rest at night. He hoped that it might one day be possible for plants to turn lights on or off in a greenhouse at will. According to *Pravda*, when the roots of Panishkin's beans were chilled, then warmed with hot water, the recording pen did not immediately indicate a reaction, as if the plant was 'remembering' the cold, and was somewhat loath to respond. This had convinced the researcher that there really were elements of memory in vegetal life.

The studies of the Gunar team may open up new vistas in plant breeding since in their laboratory it has been found that individual plants more resistant to heat, cold and other climatological factors can be selected within minutes by testing them with their instruments, although these qualities have heretofore taken geneticists years to establish.

In the summer of 1971, an American delegation from the Association for Research and Enlightenment (A.R.E.), founded by the seer and healer Edgar Cayce at Virginia Beach, Virginia, visited the U.S.S.R. The Americans – four medical doctors, two psychologists, one physicist and two educationists – were shown a film by Panishkin entitled *Are Plants Sentient?* The film demonstrated effects produced on plants by environmental factors such as sunlight, wind, clouds, the dark of night, the tactual stimulus from flies and bees, injuries produced by chemicals and burning, and even the very proximity of a vine to a structure to which it might cling. The film showed further that the immersion of a plant in chloroform vapour eliminates the characteristic biopotential pulse normally apparent when a leaf is given a sharp blow; it also indicated that the Russians are now studying the characteristics of these pulses to establish the relative degree of a plant's health. One of the doctors, William McGarey, stated in his report that the intriguing part of the film was the method used to record the data. Time-lapse photography made the plants seem to dance as they grew. Flowers opened and closed with the coming of darkness as if they were creatures living in a different time zone. All injury-induced changes were recorded by sensitive instruments from a polygraph attached to the plants.

In April 1972, *Weltwoche*, a Swiss newspaper published in Zurich, came out with an account of both Backster's and Gunar's work which it said had taken place simultaneously and independently. That same week the Swiss article was translated into Russian in a weekly review of the foreign press, *Za Rubezhom* (Abroad), published in Moscow by the U.S.S.R.'s Union of Journalists, under the caption: 'The Wonderful World of Plants'. These scientists, said the Russian version, are

proposing that plants receive signals and transmit them through special channels to a given centre where they process the information and prepare answering reactions. This nervous centre could be located in root tissues which expand and contract like heart muscle in man. The experiments showed that plants have a definite life-rhythm and die when they don't get regular periods of rest and quiet.

The *Weltwoche* article also caught the attention of the editors of the Moscow newspaper *Izvestia* who assigned their reporter M. Matveyev to write a story for the paper's weekly magazine supplement. Although the reporter referred to Backster's suggestion that plants might have memory, language and even rudiments of altruism, he strangely omitted Backster's most startling discovery that his philodendron had perceived his *intent* to harm it. Deciding that a 'sensation was being propagated in western newspapers', Matveyev travelled to Leningrad where he interviewed Vladimir Grigorievich

Karamanov, Director of the Laboratory of Biocybernetics of the Institute of Agrophysics, in order to get an authoritative opinion.

The Institute of Agrophysics was founded over forty years ago at the behest of the renowned solid-state physicist, Academician Abram Feodorovich Ioffe, who became particularly interested in the practical application of physics to the design of new products, first in industry, then in agriculture. After the institute opened its doors, Karamanov, then a young biologist, was inspired by Ioffe to familiarize himself with the world of semiconductors and cybernetics and, in due course, began building microthermisters, weight-tensometers and other instruments to register the temperature of plants, the flow-rate of fluid in their stems and leaves, the intensity of their transpiration, their growth rates and characteristics of their radiation. He was soon picking up detailed information on when and how much a plant wants to drink, whether it craves more nourishment or feels too hot or cold. In the first issue of *Reports of the U.S.S.R. Academy of Sciences* for 1959, Karamanov published 'The Application of Automation and Cybernetics to Plant Husbandry'.

According to the *Izvestia* reporter, Karamanov showed that an ordinary bean plant had acquired the equivalent of 'hands' to signal to an instrumental brain how much light it needed. When the brain sent the 'hands' signals, 'they had only to press a switch, and the plant was thus afforded the capability of independently establishing the optimal length of its "day" and "night".' Later, the same bean plant, having acquired the equivalent of 'legs' was able instrumentally to signal whenever it wanted water. 'Showing itself to be a fully rational being,' the account continued, 'it did not gulp down the water all at once but limited itself to a two-minute drink each hour, thus regulating its need for water with the help of an artificial mechanism.'

'This was a genuine scientific and technical sensation,' concluded the *Izvestia* reporter, 'a clear demonstration of twentieth-century man's technical abilities.'

Asked whether he thought Backster had discovered something new, Karamanov somewhat disparagingly replied:

'Nothing of the sort! That plants are able to perceive the surrounding world is a truth as old as the world itself. Without perception, adaptation does not and cannot exist. If plants had no sense
organs and didn't have a means of transmitting and processing
information with their own language and memory, they would
inevitably perish.'

Karamanov, who throughout the interview made no
comment on plants' ability to perceive human thought and
emotion – Backster's real and truly sensational discovery – and
seemingly oblivious to Backster's success in getting his
philodendron to recognize a 'plant assassin', rhetorically
asked the *Izvestia* reporter: 'Can plants discern shapes? Can
they, for instance, differentiate between a man who causes them
hurt and another who waters them?' Replying to his own
question, while at the same time putting Backster into what he
considered to be a proper perspective for Soviet readers,
Karamanov said:

'Today I cannot answer such a question. And not because I doubt
that Backster's experiments were immaculately set up and repeatedly
performed (though perhaps a door slammed, or a draught wafted
into the room, or something else). The fact is that neither he, nor
we, nor anyone else in the world is yet ready to decipher *all* plant
responses, hear and understand what they "say" to one another,
or what they "shout at us".'

Karamanov also predicted that in the long run it would be
possible cybernetically to direct all the physiological processes
of plants, not, as he put it, 'for the sake of sensation, but for the
advantage of plants themselves'. When, with the help of
electronic instruments, plants are able to auto-regulate their
environment and establish the best conditions for their own
growth, this should be also a long step towards larger harvest
of cereal grains, vegetables and fruits. Making clear that the
achievements were not just around the corner, he added, 'we
are not just learning to talk with plants and understand their
peculiar language. We are working out criteria which will
help us to control the life of plants. Along this difficult but
fascinating road, a multitude of surprises still await us.'

The *Izvestia* article was followed that summer by a story in

[69]

the monthly magazine *Nauka i Religiya* (Science and Religion), which has the dual aim of putting forward the latest findings in world science while at the same time playing down – in a section headed 'The Theory and Practice of Atheism' – the church-defended notion of a spiritual world hierarchically beyond that of man.

The author of the article, an engineer called A. Merkulov, went further than the *Izvestia* weekend supplement and recounted how the plant of the 'American criminologist' Backster had not only responded to the scalding death of brine shrimp but also to the killer of its vegetal neighbour. Such response to people's moods, he added, has also been detected at the State University in Alma Ata, capital of the remote Soviet Kazakh Republic at the foot of the Tien Shan mountains which separate the U.S.S.R. from China. There in a district of huge apple orchards scientists have found that plants repeatedly reacted to their owners' illnesses and to their emotional states. They also confirmed the long-held view that plants have short-term memories. Beans, potatoes, wheat and crowfoot (*Ranunculus*) after proper 'instruction', seemed to be able to remember the frequency of flashes from a xenon-hydrogen lamp. The plants repeated the pulsations with what Merkulov called 'exceptional accuracy' and since crowfoot was able to repeat a given frequency after a pause as long as eighteen hours, it was possible to speak of 'long-term' memory in plants.

After this response the Kazakhe scientists went on to condition a philodendron to recognize when a piece of mineralized rock was put beside it. Using the system developed by Pavlov with dogs, they simultaneously 'punished' a philodendron with an electrical shock each time a mineralized ore was placed next to it. The plant, anticipating the hurtful shock, would get 'emotionally upset' whenever the block of ore was put beside it, thereby showing a conditioned reflex. Furthermore, it could distinguish between mineralized ore and a similar piece of barren rock containing no minerals, a feat which might indicate that plants will one day be used in geological prospecting. Merkulov concluded by suggesting that the control of all processes in plant growth was the ultimate goal of all the new experimentation. In an institute of physics in the Siberian city of Krasnoyarsk, he wrote,

Physicists are even now regulating the growth of a monocellular seaweed, Chlorella. Experiments are continuing and becoming increasingly complex, and there is no doubt that in the not distant future scientists will be able to control the growth, not only of the simplest, but of higher plants.

Towards the end of 1972 Soviet readers were given more food for thought in an article 'Answer Me, Flower!' by Professor V. N. Pushkin, published in the popular colour magazine *Znaniya Sila* (Knowledge is Power) issued by the 'Knowledge' society, the leading organization for popular science in the U.S.S.R. Pushkin, a doctor of psychological science, began with a complete description of Backster's shrimp experiment. He told his readers that one of his young colleagues, V. M. Fetisov, was the first to make him aware of Backster's achievements and had persuaded him to embark on 'Backster Effect' experiments by bringing an ordinary potted geranium from his home and attaching it to an encephalograph in Pushkin's laboratory. Their experiments led them to believe that a hypnotized person should be able to send emotions to a plant more directly and spontaneously than a normal person. Of the expediency of using hypnosis, Pushkin wrote:

If a plant is generally able to react to a person's psychological states, surely it will respond to a strong emotional disturbance. But fear, happiness, grief? How can one evoke them on command? It is possible to eliminate the difficulty with hypnosis. A good hypnotist is able to awaken in his subject the most varied and at the same time sufficiently powerful experiences and, as it were, plug in to a person's emotional sphere. This is exactly what was needed for our experiments.

To this end Pushkin and Fetisov agreed to work with a young Bulgarian hypnotist, Georgi Angushev. From the many people whom he hypnotized Angushev selected those who most easily went into trance. Even with these specially chosen individuals, it was a long time before the researchers got their first encouraging results.

One day they began working with a young girl named

Tanya who was described by Pushkin as of 'lively temperament and spontaneous emotionality'. Seating her in a comfortable armchair about eighty centimetres from a flower to which the encephalograph had been attached, Angushev put her into hypnotic trance, then suggested to her that she was one of the most beautiful women in the world. Immediately Tanya beamed, her expression showing that the attention from people surrounding her was giving her great pleasure. At the climax of these pleasurable experiences the pen-recorder, which had been tracing a level line on the strip-chart, drew a series of nervous waves.

Angushev next told Tanya that a strong cold wind had come up, turning the weather harsh and raw. Tanya's reaction changed abruptly. She began to shiver like a person in light summer clothing put out in frosty weather and her face contorted with a mixture of sadness and pain. At the height of her torment, the plant registered another strong wavy line on the chart. After this Angushev arbitrarily suggested either positive or negative feelings to his subject and the flower always responded with the appropriate reaction. To prove that the response was not the result of chance events taking place in the room, the Muscovite psychologists switched on their encephalograph and let it run for long periods between their experiments. During these times there were no reactions of any kind.

Pushkin and Fetisov decided to see whether the plant could detect a lie, as Backster had claimed. It was suggested to Tanya that she think of a number from one to ten. At the same time she was told she would never reveal the number, even if pressed to do so. When the researchers counted slowly from one to ten, pausing after each digit to inquire whether it was the one she had thought of, each time Tanya responded with a decisive 'No!' Though the psychologists could not see any difference in her answers, the plant gave a specific and clear reaction to her internal state when the number five was counted. It was the number which Tanya had selected and promised not to reveal.

As a result of his many experiments in this field, Pushkin concluded that vegetal cells in the flower react to processes taking place in the nervous system of human subjects or in what is somewhat vaguely referred to as their 'emotional states'. Seeking a meaning for the flower's reaction he wrote: 'Perhaps between two informational systems, the plant cells and the nervous system, a specific link exists. The language of the plant cell may be related to that of the nerve cell. These wholly different living cells seemed to be able to "understand" one another.' Whatever the truth may eventually turn out to be, says Pushkin, one thing is sure: 'Research into the plant and man interrelationships can shed light on some of the most urgent problems in contemporary psychology.'

The magic and mystery of the world of plants lying behind these scientific doings has also recently become the subject of a new book entitled *Grass* by a popular writer, Vladimir Soloukhin, which appeared in four issues of the three million circulation magazine *Nauka i Zhizn'* (Science and Life) at the end of 1972. Soloukhin had read with fascination about Gunar's work and wondered why it had not evoked more excitement among his fellow Russians. 'Perhaps the elements of memory in plants are superficially treated,' he writes, 'but at least there they are in black and white! Yet no one calls his friends or neighbours, no one shouts in a drunken voice over the telephone: Have you heard the news? Plants can feel! They can feel pain! They cry out! Plants remember everything!' During his own inquiries, however, Soloukhin learned that a prominent member of the Soviet Academy of Sciences, working in the Siberian research centre of Akademgorodok, had stated:

Don't be amazed! We too are carrying out many experiments of this kind and they all point to one thing: plants have memory. They are able to gather impressions and retain them over long periods. We had a man molest, even torture a geranium for several days in a row. He pinched it, tore it, pricked its leaves with a needle, dripped acid on its living tissues, burned it with a lighted match, and cut its roots. Another man took tender care of the same geranium, watered it, worked its soil, sprayed it with fresh water, supported its heavy branches, and treated its burns and wounds. When we electroded our instruments to the plant, what do you think? No sooner did the torturer come near the plant than the recorder of the instrument began to go wild. The plant didn't just get 'nervous', it was afraid, it was horrified. If it could have, it would have either thrown itself out of the window or attacked its torturer. Hardly had this inquisitor left and the good man taken his place near the plant than the geranium was appeased, its impulses died down, the recorder traced out smooth – one might almost say tender – lines on the graph.

Unknown to Soloukhin was the fact that, in addition to plants' ability to recognize friend and foe, the Soviet scientists have also noticed that one plant supplied with water can somehow share it with a deprived neighbour. In one institute of research a corn stalk planted in a glass container was denied water for several weeks. Yet it did not die; it remained as healthy as other corn stalks planted in normal conditions near by. In some way, say Soviet botanists, water was transferred from healthy plants to the 'prisoner' in the jar. Yet they have no idea of how this was accomplished.

In his book, *Grass*, Soloukhin takes the Soviet people to task for their lack of sensitivity to the vegetal world around them. Targets of his criticism include agricultural bureaucrats, individual collective farmers, *kolkhozniks*, lumber executives, and even sales girls in Moscow flower shops. 'Human observation,' he writes, 'is so precise that we begin to notice the very air we breathe only when it is insufficient for our needs. More exactly, I should say "value" rather than "notice". We do not really value air, or even think about it, so long as we can breathe normally, without difficulty.' He adds that though man prides himself on his vast knowledge, he is like a radio technician who knows how to repair a receiver without understanding the theoretical essence of radio waves, or like our cave-men ancestors who put fire to use while unaware of the process of rapid oxidation. Even today, we squander heat and light yet have not the slightest clue to, or interest in, its original essence. Man is equally callous, he says, to the fact that the land around him is green.

We trample grasses into dirt, we strip the land with bulldozers and caterpillar treads, we cover it with concrete and hot asphalt. Disposing of wastes from our infernal industrial machines we dump upon it crude oil, rubbish, acids, alkalis, and other poisons. But is there that much grass? I, for one, can imagine man in a boundless, grassless wilderness, the product of a cosmic, or perhaps humanly non-cosmic, catastrophe.

Seeking to re-evoke wonder for nature in the hearts of an over-urbanized Soviet youth, Soloukhin tells the story of a prisoner who, incarcerated in a dank cell, finds among the pages of an old book, given to him by a kindly jailer, a tiny seed smaller than a pin-head. Overcome with emotion at the first visible sign of real life he has seen for years, the prisoner imagines that the microscopic seed is all that remains from the former luxuriant and festive plant kingdom in the great world outside the prison. Planting the seed in a bit of earth in the sole corner of the cell afforded a ray of sunlight, and watering it with his tears, the prisoner waits for a wonder to unfold.

Soloukhin accepts this wonder as a true miracle ignored by man only because it is repeated thousands of billions of times daily. Even if all the world's chemical and physical laboratories with their complex reagents, precise analyses, and electronic microscopes were placed at the prisoner's disposal, he continues, even if the prisoner studied the seed's every cell, atom and atomic nucleus, he still would not be able to read the mysterious programme lying within the seed, to lift the impenetrable veil which could cause it to transform itself into a juicy carrot, a sweet-scented herb or a radiantly coloured aster.

Soloukhin was fascinated with the statement by I. Zabelin, Doctor of Geographical Sciences and Moscow University professor, who in his article 'Dangerous Delusions' in one of the U.S.S.R.'s leading opinion forums, *Literaturnaya Gazeta* wrote: 'We are only beginning to comprehend the language of nature, its soul, its reason. The "inner world" of plants is hidden from our gaze behind seventy-seven seals.' Though these lines were in no way emphasized in the printed column, says Soloukhin, 'they appeared to me as bold-face type'.

Soloukhin recounts that when in 1922 Howard Carter discovered and opened Tutankhamen's tomb the heart-breaking wreath of field flowers, placed in the coffin by the pharaoh's young widow, moved and enthralled him even more than the opulence of the treasure he had discovered. 'All the royal pomp and splendour paled before this faded bunch of flowers, which still preserved traces of their once fresh colours and overwhelmingly reminded us that a thousand years is but the briefest of moments.'

Soloukhin has recently attacked the obtuse views of Soviet agricultural officials. Writing in the October 1972 issue of *Literaturnaya Gazeta*, he deplores the abandon with which generations-old natural Russian meadowlands have been allowed to deteriorate while fields needed for cereal crops are being ploughed and planted to grasses for animal fodder. 'We could cover Europe with hay and green grass from our meadows and build a haystack extending from the Mediterranean to Scandinavia,' he writes. 'Well, why don't we?' His rhetorical question only provoked an angry rebuttal from the U.S.S.R.'s Deputy Minister of Agriculture who insisted on upholding the *status quo*. Like writers in so many other countries, Soloukhin is unremittingly denouncing unecologically-minded industrialists in his country who are turning the rivers and lakes into cesspools, and despoiling its forests, all in the name of increased production. Seeking to reverse a half century of communist dicta, this passionate lover of nature exhorts his countrymen to cooperate with it, rather than subdue it.

That the Soviets are bent on introducing the idea of substituting the burning of coal, oil and natural gas – which in reality are merely three forms of preserved solar energy – for new, more direct and pollution-free ways to tap the sun, is revealed by an article in the first 1973 issue of *Khimiya i Zhizn'* (Chemistry and Life). The article pointed to the research of the American Nobel Prizewinner, Melvin Calvin, in photosynthesis wherein he discovered that plant chlorophyll under the influence of the sun's rays can give up electrons to a semiconductor such as zinc oxide. Calvin and his co-workers created a 'green photo-element' which produced a current of approximately 0.1 micro-amperes per square centimetre. After several minutes, the article went on, the plant chlorophyll becomes desensitized or 'exhausted' but its life could be extended by the addition of hydroquinone to the salt solution which acts as an electrolyte. The chlorophyll seems to act as a kind of electron pump passing them from the hydroquinone to the semi-conductor. Calvin has calculated that a chlorophyll photo-element with an area of ten square metres could yield a kilowatt of power. He thinks that such photo-elements could be manufactured on an industrial scale within the next quarter century and would be a hundred times cheaper than the silicone solar batteries now being experimented with. Even if the direct conversion of sunlight into energy via plant chlorophyll is not realized by the year 2000, says the *Chemistry and Life* article, it wouldn't put too much of a burden on man to wait a few decades longer considering the millions of years it took to convert plants into coal.

Meanwhile Professor Gunar, together with an increasing number of young Soviet scientists, was continuing to probe into the possibility that the reactions of plants might serve as an index of frost, cold and heat resistance in varieties of barley and cucumbers, and of disease potentials in potatoes. The original inspiration for his detailed study of plants may possibly be found in an article published in 1958 by his colleague A. M. Sinyukhin. This article refers to an outstanding Indian physiologist and biophysicist whose work was little known during his lifetime and rarely cited since his death. However, it was heralded as early as 1920 as introducing a new epoch in the development of world science by Kliment Arkadievich Timiryazev, in whose honour the Moscow Agricultural Academy is named. The Indian scientist, wrote Timiryazev, developed new apparatus startling in its simplicity and sensitivity to counter the entrenched idea of the German botanists that communication in plant tissue was simply hydrostatic. In so doing, he was able to measure in hundredths of a second the time needed for a signal to travel along the stems of various plants.

Sinyukhin made clear that the U.S.S.R.'s plant men were so impressed by the achievements of this Indian scientist that they were going to mount a research campaign based directly upon his long-ignored conclusions. In December 1958, a meeting was held in the main conference hall of the U.S.S.R. Academy of Sciences in celebration of the hundredth anniversary of the Indian sage's birth. Three leading academicians summed up for the huge crowd assembled the fantastic break-throughs which the Indian had made not only in plant physiology but in physics and in the vital and until then unheard of links between them.

'Many years, during the course of which whirlwind developments have taken place in biophysics,' said A. V. Lebedinskii, one of the leading Russian pioneers in radiobiology and space medicine, 'separate us from the time this Indian's work appeared. But, reading his works today, one still senses in them an unexpected and fruitful source of a whole chain of ideas in contemporary science.'

In this great work, said another speaker, 'The green world of plants, seeming to us so immobile and insensitive, came miraculously to life and appeared no less, and often even more, sensitive than animals and man.'

Six years later the Soviet Union honoured this neglected scientist by publishing in two handsomely illustrated volumes his selected works, together with copious commentaries including one entire book which had first made its appearance over half a century before, in 1902: *Response in the Living and Non-Living*. In these works Sir Jagadis Chandra Bose managed to accomplish the essential requirement of the twentieth century: an amalgamation of the wisdom of the ancient East with the precise scientific techniques and language of the modern West.

2

Pioneers of plant mysteries

6

Plant life magnified a hundred million times

In the old state of Bengal, there stands on four acres of ground off the Acharya Prafullachandra road, north of Calcutta University, a complex of buildings made of fine greyish and purple sandstone in the classical design of pre-Mohammedan India. The main building, known as the Indian Temple of Science, bears an inscription: 'This temple is dedicated to the feet of God for bringing honour to India and happiness to the world.'

Inside the entrance are glass cases containing a series of intriguing instruments devised more than fifty years ago to measure the growth and behaviour of plants, down to their minutest detail, by magnification of these processes up to 100,000,000 times. The instruments stand in their cases, in mute testimony to the genius of a great Bengali scientist whose work ranged over the fields of physics, physiology, and psychology; he was a man who found out more about plants than anyone before and perhaps since, but who remains almost unmentioned in classical histories of subjects in which he specialized.

The buildings and their gardens are the Institute of Research built by Sir Jagadis Chandra Bose of whom, nearly half a century after his death, the *Encyclopaedia Britannica* could only say of his work in the field of plant physiology that it was so much in advance of his time that it could not be precisely evaluated.

Bose's father, not wanting his son to go to an English school where he would be taught to imitate all things western, sent the boy to a simple village school, or *pathasala*. He went at the age of four and was carried to his classroom on the shoulders of a reformed gang-robber, or dacoit, who could find employment after a long prison sentence with no one but Bose's father. From this dacoit the boy absorbed stories of savage battles and adventurous escapades, but he also was exposed to the natural goodness of a man who had been befriended after being rejected by society as a criminal.

'No nurse,' Bose wrote in his later life, 'could have been kinder than this leader of lawless men. Though he scoffed at the juridical strictures of society, he had the deepest veneration for natural moral law.'

Bose's early contacts with the peasantry in the 1850s were crucial to his own appreciation of the world. Much later he told an academic gathering:

'It was from those who till the ground and make the land blossom with green verdure, from the sons of fisherfolk who told stories of the strange creatures that frequented the depths of mighty rivers and stagnant pools, that I first derived a lesson of that which constituted true manhood. From them, too, I drew my love of nature.'

Later when he graduated from St Xavier's College, his brilliant teacher, Father Lafont, was so impressed by the young man's aptitude in physics and mathematics, that he wanted him to go to England and read for the Civil Service examinations. However, Bose's father, who had personally experienced the deadening nature of that profession, advised his son against it. Instead, the young man went to Christ's College, Cambridge, where he was taught physics, chemistry and botanical sciences by such luminaries as Lord Rayleigh, discoverer of argon in the air, and Francis Darwin, son of the evolutionary theorist. Having taken his tripos there Bose went on to take his B.Sc. at London University in the following year. On his return to Calcutta he was appointed professor of physics at The Presidency College, reputedly the best in India. However, the principal of the college and the Director of Bengal's Public Instruction, who both maintained the view that no Indian was competent to teach science, protested violently against the appointment, which had been made over their heads. Not only did they refuse him any facilities for research, but his salary was to be half that of an English professor. Bose responded by refusing to touch his monthly salary cheque for three years, even though this meant that he had to live in poverty. Such was the brilliance of his teaching that his lectures were always packed. In the end the authorities had to bow to his obvious talents and pay him the proper salary.

Bose had no other financial resources and only a twenty foot square room to serve as a laboratory, and an illiterate tinsmith whom he trained as his mechanic. Nevertheless in 1894 he began work to see if he could improve the instruments recently devised by Heinrich Rudolph Hertz to transmit 'Hertzian' or radio waves through the air. Hertz, who had died that same year at the premature age of thirty-seven, had startled the world of physics by fulfilling in his laboratory the prediction of the Scottish physicist, James Clerk Maxwell, some twenty years before, that the waves of any 'electrical disturbance in the ether' – the variety and scope of which was far from known – would, like those of visible light, be reflective, refractible and polarizable.

While Marconi in Bologna was still trying to transmit electric signals through space without wires, a race he was to win officially against similar efforts by Lodge in England, Muirhead in the United States, and Popov in Russia, Bose had already succeeded. In 1895, the year before Marconi's patent was issued, a meeting was held in the Calcutta Town Hall, which was presided over by the Lieutenant-Governor of Bengal, Sir Alexander Mackenzie. At this meeting Bose transmitted electric waves from the lecture hall through three intervening walls to a room seventy-five feet away where they tripped a relay which threw a heavy iron ball, fired off a pistol, and blew up a small mine.

In England Bose's achievements now began to attract the attention of the Royal Society which, at Lord Rayleigh's behest, invited him to publish a paper in its proceedings on the 'Determination of the Wavelength of Electric Radiation', offering him a subsidy from its parliamentary grant for the advancement of science. This was followed by Bose being awarded a doctorate of science by London University. Invitations to address meetings came from the British Association for the Advancement of Science and from the Royal

Institution. Of his lecture on his apparatus for investigating electromagnetic waves *The Times* wrote: 'The originality of the achievement is enhanced by the fact that Dr Bose had to do the work in addition to his incessant duties and with apparatus and appliances which in this country would be deemed altogether inadequate.' The *Spectator*, echoing this accolade, announced: 'There is something of rare interest in the spectacle of a Bengali of the purest descent lecturing in London to an audience of appreciative European savants upon one of the most recondite branches of modern physical science.'

Back in India, Bose was encouraged to find that a memorial signed by Lord Lister, President of the Royal Society, and other eminent scientists, had been sent to the Secretary of State for India recommending that a centre for research and advanced teaching in physics 'worthy of that great Empire', be established under Bose's direction at Presidency College. Despite this recommendation, and an immediate grant by the Imperial Government of £40,000 to set up the centre forthwith, the Bengal Education Department succeeded in so tying up the project that it never came to fruition. Bose's disappointment was great and it was only softened by a visit from the poet and Nobel prizewinner Rabindranath Tagore, who, not finding Bose at home, left a huge magnolia blossom in token of his respect.

In 1898 Bose published four papers on the behaviour of electric waves in the *Proceedings of the Royal Society* and in Great Britain's foremost popular scientific journal, *Nature*. The following year he noticed the strange fact that his metallic coherer became less sensitive if continuously used but returned to normal after a period of rest. This led him to the conclusion that metals, however inconceivably, might exhibit a recovery from fatigue similar to that which took place in tired animals and people. Further work began to convince him that the boundary line between so-called 'non-living' metals and 'living' organisms was tenuous indeed. Moving from the domain of physics into that of physiology, Bose began a comparative study between the curves of molecular reaction in inorganic substance and those in living animal tissue. To his awe and surprise, the curves produced by slightly warmed magnetic oxide of iron showed striking resemblance to those of muscles. In both, response and recovery diminished with exertion, and the consequent fatigue could be removed by gentle massage or by exposure to a bath of warm water.

Other metal components reacted in animal-like ways. A metal surface etched with acid, when polished to remove all trace of the etching, exhibited reactions in its acid-treated sections which could not be elicited from those which remained untreated. Bose ascribed to the affected sections some kind of lingering memory of the treatment. In potassium he found that the power of recovery was almost totally lost if it were treated with various foreign substances which seemed to parallel the reactions of muscular tissue to poisons.

In a presentation to the International Congress of Physics held in 1900 at the Paris Exhibition entitled *De la Généralité des Phénomènes Moléculaires Produits par l'Électricité sur la Matière Inorganique et sur la Matière Vivante*, Bose stressed the 'fundamental unity among the apparent diversity of nature', concluding that 'it is difficult to draw a line and say that here the physical phenomenon ends and here the physiological begins'. The Congress was astonished by Bose's suggestion that the gulf between the animate and inanimate might not be as broad and unbridgeable as was generally believed.

Physiologists were less enthusiastic because Bose's research overlapped on to territory which they considered their private preserve. At a meeting of the physics section of the British Association at Bradford, they listened in hostile silence while Bose read a paper contending that Hertzian waves could be used as a stimulating agent on tissues, and that metal response was analogous to that of tissues. To meet the physiologists on their ground, Bose meticulously adapted his experiments to an accepted 'electromotive variation' to which they were accustomed, and again got similar curves of muscles and metals responding to the effects of fatigue or of stimulating, depressing and poisonous drugs.

Then it dawned on Bose that if the striking continuity between such extremes as metals and animal life were real, he should also be able to get similar effects in ordinary vegetable plants which, because they were held to have no nervous system, were universally reckoned as unresponsive. Experimenting first with horse-chestnut leaves and then with carrots and turnips, Bose found that they responded to various 'blows' in much the same way as had his metals and muscles, and that plants were clearly sensitive down to their roots. He also discovered that plants could be as successfully anaesthetized as animals and that when the narcotic vapour was blown away by fresh air, like animals, they revived. Using chloroform to tranquillize a large pine tree, Bose was able to uproot it and transplant it without the usually fatal shock of such operations.

Sir Michael Foster, Secretary of the Royal Society, came to Bose's laboratory to see for himself and Bose showed the Cambridge veteran some of his recordings. 'Come now, Bose,' the older man said jocularly, 'what is the novelty of this curve? We have known it for at least half a century!'

'But what do you think it is?' Bose persisted quietly.

'Why, a curve of muscle response, of course!' said Foster testily.

Looking at the professor from the depths of his haunting brown eyes, Bose said firmly: 'Pardon me, but it is the response of metallic tin!'

Foster was aghast. 'What?' he shouted, jumping from his chair, 'Tin? Did you say tin?'

When Bose showed him all his results, Foster was so impressed that he invited Bose to give an account of his discoveries at another Friday Evening Discourse at the Royal Institution and offered personally to communicate his paper to the Royal Society in order to secure his priority.

At the evening meeting of 10 May 1901, Bose marshalled all the results obtained over four years and demonstrated each one of them with a comprehensive series of experiments. He ended by saying:

'I have shown you this evening autographic records of the history of stress and strain in the living and non-living. How similar are the writings! So similar indeed that you cannot tell one apart from the other. Among such phenomena, how can we draw a line of demarcation and say, here the physical ends, and there the physiological begins? Such absolute barriers do not exist.

[86]

'It was when I came upon the mute witness of these self-made records, and perceived in them one phase of a pervading unity that bears within it all things – the mote that quivers in ripples of light, the teeming life upon our earth, and the radiant suns that shine above us – it was then that I understood for the first time a little of that message proclaimed by my ancestors on the banks of the Ganges thirty centuries ago: "They who see but one, in all the changing manifoldness of this universe, unto them belongs Eternal Truth – unto none else, unto none else!" '

Bose's lecture was warmly received, and to his surprise, his views went unchallenged, despite the metaphysical note at its end. Sir William Crookes even urged that the last quotation should not be omitted when the address was published. Sir Robert Austen, one of the world's authorities on metals, praised Bose for his faultless arguments, saying: 'I have all my life studied the properties of metals and am happy to think that they have life.' He confessed confidentially that he had formed a similar opinion but had been rebuffed when he had once hesitantly hinted at it before the Royal Institution.

A month later Bose repeated his lecture and demonstrations before the Royal Society. Afterwards, Sir John Burdon Sanderson, the principal authority on electro-physiology, began by complimenting Bose on his acknowledged work in physics but followed with the remark that it was a great pity that he had wandered from his own field of study into areas which belonged properly to the physiologist. Since Bose's paper was still under consideration for publication he suggested that its title be changed from 'Electrical Response in . . .' to 'Certain Physical Reactions in . . .' thus leaving to the physiologists the term 'response' with which physicists should not be concerned. As for the electrical response of ordinary plants, which Bose had described at the end of his address, Burdon Sanderson denied categorically that such things were possible since 'he himself had tried for many years past to obtain them and had never succeeded'.

In his reply Bose said candidly he understood that the facts experimentally demonstrated were not questioned by his critic. If, therefore, he was not being impugned on the basis of this evidence, but was being asked to make modifications which altered the whole purpose and meaning of his presentation, on the basis of authority alone, he would have to decline. It seemed incomprehensible, he said, that any doctrine could be advocated before the Royal Society which suggested that knowledge could not advance beyond known bounds. Unless he were shown on scientific grounds where his experiments were faulty or defective, he would insist his paper be published as he had written it. At the end of his rebuttal when no one rose to break the icy silence which hung over the hall, the meeting was adjourned. The outcome of this challenge to so eminent an expert as Sir John was that Bose's paper, like many other notable papers in the past, was buried in the Society's Archives.

However, the controversy had elicited the interest of Bose's former teacher, Professor Sidney Howard Vines, the well-known botanist and vegetable physiologist at Oxford, who asked if he could witness Bose's experiments. Vines brought with him Horace Brown, another expert in the peculiarities of plant-life, and T. K. Howes, who had succeeded T. H. Huxley at the Natural History Museum in South Kensington. 'Huxley would have given years of his life to see this experiment.' Howes exclaimed when he saw the plant respond to stimulus. He thereupon, as secretary of the Linnean Society,* invited Bose to repeat all his experiments before his society and offered to publish the paper rejected by the Royal Society. Bose accepted with delight, and the new presentation before the Linnean Society took place on 21 February 1902. Afterwards he wrote to his friend Tagore: 'Victory! I stood there alone, ready for hosts of opponents, but in fifteen minutes the hall was resounding with applause. After the paper, Professor Howes told me that as he saw each experiment, he tried to get out of it by thinking of a loophole of explanation, but my next experiment closed that hole.'

The President of the Linnean Society wrote to Bose a few days later:

* The Linnean Society, named after Carl von Linne or Linnaeus (1707–78) the great Swedish botanist whose *Genera Plantorum* is considered the starting point of modern systematic botany, was organized at the end of the eighteenth century when Sir J. E. Smith, its first president, acquired Linnaeus' botanical library from his widow.

It seems to me that your experiments make it clear beyond doubt that all parts of plants – not merely those which are known to be motile – are irritable, and manifest their irritability by an electrical response to stimulation. This is an important step in advance, and will, I hope, be the starting point for further researches to elucidate what is the nature of the molecular condition which constitutes irritability, and the nature of the molecular change induced by a stimulus. This would doubtless lead to some important generalities as to the properties of matter, not only living matter, but non-living matter as well.

In 1902 Bose published the results of his experiments, which were the substance of the lectures he had given in London, Paris and Berlin, in a book entitled *Response in the Living and Non-Living*. Then he began to concentrate on determining how mechanical movements in plants might be similar to those in animals and humans. Since he knew that in plants there was respiration without gills or lungs, digestion without a stomach, and movements without muscles, it seemed plausible that there could be the same kind of excitation as in higher animals but without a complicated nervous system.

He concluded that the only way to find out about the 'unseen changes which take place in plants' and tell if they were 'excited or depressed' would be to measure visually their responses to what he called 'definite testing blows' or shocks. He wrote that:

In order to succeed in this, we have to discover some compulsive force which will make the plant give an answering signal. Secondly, we have to supply the means for an automatic conversion of these signals into an intelligent script. And, last of all, we have ourselves to learn the nature of these hieroglyphics.

In this single statement Bose mapped out for himself a course for the next two decades.

He began by improving the optical lever which he had designed to magnify contractions in plants. It now became an optical pulse recorder, a device which made visible for the first time movements in plant organs hitherto hidden from the scientific world.

With the aid of this instrument, Bose was able to show the similarity in behaviour between skins of lizards, tortoises and frogs and those of grapes, tomatoes and other fruits and vegetables. He also showed that the vegetal digestive organs in insectivorous plants were very like animal stomachs; and that in response to light there were close parallels between leaves and the retinas of animal eyes. With his magnifier he proved that plants become as fatigued by continuous stimulation as animal muscles, whether they were hypersensitive mimosas or undemonstrative radishes. Indeed with the former he was able to demonstrate the characteristics of a nervous system. He experimented with heat and cold to ascertain the optimal conditions under which plant movement was best elicited. One day he found that when all motion stopped in his plant, it suddenly shuddered in a way reminiscent of the death spasm in animals. At death the plant threw off a huge electrical force. 'Five hundred green peas could develop five hundred volts,' said Bose, enough to fulminate a cook but for the fact that peas are seldom connected in series.

Though it had been thought that plants liked unlimited quantities of carbon dioxide, Bose found that too much of this gas could suffocate them, but that they could then be revived, just like animals, with oxygen. Like human beings, plants became intoxicated when given shots of whisky or gin, swayed like any bar-room drunkard, passed out, and eventually revived, with definite signs of a hangover.

These findings together with hundreds of other data were published in two massive volumes in 1906 and 1907. *Plant Response as a Means of Physiological Investigation*, ran to 781 pages and detailed 315 separate experiments. These went against an entrenched opinion which Bose thus explained:

From the plausible analogy of the firing-off of a gun by pulling a trigger, or the action of a combustion engine, it has been customary to suppose that all response to stimulus must be of the nature of an explosive chemical change, accompanied by an inevitable run-down of energy.

Bose's experiments, on the contrary, showed him that in plants, their movement, the ascent of their sap and their growth, were due to energy absorbed from their surroundings which they could hold latent or store for future use. These revolutionary ideas, and especially the findings that plants had nerves, were received with veiled hostility among botanists.

Bose's second volume, *Comparative Electro-Physiology*, set forth 321 additional experiments, and its findings also clashed with current teaching and doctrine. Instead of emphasizing the accepted wide range of specific differences between the reactions of various plant and animal tissues, Bose consistently pointed to a real continuity between them. Even more heretically, he held that the isolated vegetal nerve is indistinguishable from an animal nerve. He wrote that:

So complete, indeed, has that similarity between the responses of plant and animal, of which this is an instance, been found, that the discovery of a given responsive characteristic in one case has proved a sure guide to its observation in the other, and that the explanation of a phenomenon, under the simpler conditions of the plant, has been found fully sufficient for its elucidation under the more complex circumstances of the animal.

The authoritative scientific magazine, *Nature*, wrote of the first: 'In fact, the whole book abounds in interesting matter skilfully woven together and would be recommended as of great value if it did not continually arouse our incredulity.' It was equally ambivalent in its attitude to the second:

The student of plant physiology who has some acquaintance with the main classical ideas of his subject, will feel at first extreme bewilderment as he peruses this book. It proceeds so smoothly and logically, and yet it does not start from any place in the existing 'corpus' of knowledge, and never attaches itself with any firm adherence. This effect of detachment is heightened by the complete absence of precise reference to the work of other investigators.

There were none of course, and the reviewer, limited by the compartmentalized science of his day, had no way of knowing he was dealing with a genius half a century ahead of his time.

Bose summed up his philosophy:

This vast abode of nature is built in many wings, each with its own portal. The physicist, the chemist and the biologist come in by different doors, each one his own department of knowledge, and each comes to think that this is his special domain unconnected with that of any other. Hence has arisen our present division of phenomena into the worlds of inorganic, vegetal and sentient. This philosophical attitude of mind may be denied. We must remember that all inquiries have as their goal the attainment of knowledge in its entirety.

The opposition to Bose's revolutionary findings, in some measure due to plant physiologists' inability to construct the delicate instruments he had devised, convinced him that he should develop an even more refined set of instruments for automatic stimulation and recording of response. This he succeeded in doing and the results were so convincing that this time they were published in the Royal Society's *Philosophical Transactions*. In the same year Bose published his third massive volume of experimentation as *Researchers on Irritability of Plants*; 376 pages, 180 experiments.

A repentant animal physiologist who had cast the single vote preventing publication of plant research by the Royal Society, came up to Bose to confess his misdeed and said, 'I could not believe that such things were possible and thought your oriental imagination had led you astray. Now, I fully confess that you have been right all along.' Bose, letting bygones be bygones, never divulged his name.

Bose's research was for the first time vividly recorded for the public in the British publication, *Nation*:

In a room near Maida Vale there is an unfortunate carrot strapped to the table of an unlicensed vivisector. Wires pass through two glass tubes full of a white substance; they are like two legs, whose feet are buried in the flesh of the carrot. When the vegetable is pinched with a pair of forceps, it winces. It is so strapped that its electric shedder of pain pulls the long arm of a very delicate lever which actuates a tiny mirror. This casts a beam of light on the frieze at the other end of the room, and thus enormously exaggerates the tremor of the carrot. A pinch near the right-hand tube sends the beam seven or eight feet to the right, and a stab near the other wire sends it far to the left. Thus can science reveal the feelings of even so stolid a vegetable as the carrot.

The vegetarian and anti-vivisectionist George Bernard Shaw having witnessed through one of Bose's magnifiers in his laboratory, a cabbage leaf going through violent paroxysms as it was scalded to death, dedicated his own collected works to Bose, inscribing them: 'from the least to the greatest living biologist'.

The acclaim which came in the British Isles was repeated in Vienna where it was the consensus of eminent German and Austrian scientists that 'Calcutta was far ahead of us in these new lines of investigation'.

In 1917 a knighthood was bestowed on Bose in recognition of his work. Even more gratifying to him was the opening of his own Institute for Research in Calcutta on the 30 November, on the occasion of his fifty-ninth birthday. During his speech at the ceremony Bose stated that it was his particular desire that any discovery made at his new Institute would become public property and that no patents would ever be taken out on them. This was consistent with his past refusal to patent the device which could have made him, instead of Marconi, the inventor of wireless telegraphy, and to turn his ideas to profit.

A year after the foundation of the Institute, Bose was able to announce that he had been able to devise a new instrument, a crescograph, which could not only produce a 10,000-fold magnification of movement, far beyond the powers of the strongest microscope, but also could automatically record the rate of growth of plants and their changes in a period as short as a minute. With this instrument Bose showed the remarkable fact that growth proceeds in rhythmic pulses in countless plants, each pulse exhibiting a rapid uplift and then a slower partial recoil of about a fourth of the distance gained. The pulses in Calcutta averaged about three per minute.

By watching the progress on the chart of his new invention, Bose found that growth in some plants could be retarded and even halted by merely touching them, and that, in others, rough handling stimulated growth, especially if they were sluggish and morose.

To determine a method which would allow him *instantly* to show the acceleration or retardation of a plant's growth in response to a stimulant, Bose now devised what he called a 'balanced crescograph', which would allow the plant to be lowered *at the same rate* at which it was growing upward, thus reducing the marking of its growth on the chart to a horizontal line and allowing any changes in *the rate* to express themselves as curves. The method was so extremely sensitive that Bose was able to detect variation of the rate of growth as hyper-minimal as 1/1500 millionths of an inch per second.

In America, the *Scientific American*, referring to the significance of Bose's findings for agriculture, wrote: 'What is the tale of Aladdin and his wonderful lamp compared to the possibilities of Dr Bose's Crescograph? In less than a quarter of an hour the action of fertilizers, food, electric currents and various stimulants can be fully determined.'

During Bose's trip to Europe in 1919 and 1920 the usually reserved *Times* wrote 'While we in England were still steeped in the rude empiricism of barbaric life, the subtle Easterner had swept the universe into a synthesis and had seen the *one* in all its changing manifestations.'

But even those bold statements and the announcement that Bose was to be made a Fellow of the Royal Society, in May 1920, could not stem the all too familiar intimations of the doubters and pedants.

Professor Waller, an old adversary of Bose's, upsetting the general atmosphere of cordiality and recognition, wrote to *The Times* to question the reliability of Bose's magnetic crescograph and to ask for a demonstration of it in a physiological laboratory before experts. The demonstration, which took place at London University on 23 April 1920, was a complete success. Lord Rayleigh joined with several colleagues in a letter to *The Times* stating 'We are satisfied that the growth of plant tissues is correctly recorded by this instrument and at magnification of one million to more than ten million times.'

Bose also wrote to *The Times* on 5 May:

Criticism which transgresses the limit of fairness must inevitably hinder the progress of knowledge. My special investigations have by their nature presented extraordinary difficulties. I regret to say that during a period of twenty years, these difficulties have been greatly aggravated by misrepresentation and worse. The obstacles deliberately placed in my path I can now ignore and forget. If the result of my work, by upsetting any particular theory, has roused

[94]

the hostility here and there of an individual, I can take comfort in the warm welcome which has been extended to me by the great body of scientific men in this country.

During still another trip to Europe in 1923, the year that saw the publication of Bose's detailed 227 page work, *The Physiology of the Ascent of Sap*, the great French philosopher Henri Bergson said, after hearing Bose lecture at the Sorbonne: 'The dumb plants had by Bose's marvellous inventions been rendered the most eloquent witnesses of their hitherto un-expressed life-story. Nature has at last been forced to yield her most jealously guarded secrets.'

More Gallicly humorous, *Le Matin* stated: 'After this discovery we begin to have misgivings, when we strike a woman with a blossom, which of them suffers more, the woman or the flower?'

In 1924 and 1926 there appeared two more volumes of experiments totalling more than 500 pages: *The Physiology of Photosynthesis* and *The Nervous Mechanism of Plants*. In 1926 Bose was nominated a member of the League of Nations Committee on Intercultural Cooperation, other eminent members of which were Albert Einstein, N. A. Lorentz and Gilbert Murray.

However, the Indian Government had yet to be jolted into awareness of the importance of Bose's work, and in the same year Sir Charles Sherrington, President of the Royal Society, Lord Rayleigh, Sir Oliver Lodge and Julian Huxley, all signed a memorial to the Viceroy of India pleading for the expansion of the Institute.

All his life Bose had emphasized to a scientific community steeped in a mechanistic and materialistic outlook, the idea that all of nature pulsed with life and that each of the interrelated entities in the natural kingdom might reveal untold secrets could man but learn how to communicate with them.

In 1929 Bose, now in retirement, summed up his scientific philosophy in the lecture-hall of his own Institute. Standing under a bronze, silver and gold relief of the Hindu sun-god rising in his chariot for his daily cosmic fight against the powers of darkness, an image which he had first seen depicted in an ancient cave fresco at Ajanta. Bose said,

[95]

'In my investigations on the action of forces on matter, I was amazed to find boundary lines vanishing and to discover points of contact emerging between the Living and the non-Living. My first work in the region of invisible lights made me realize how in the midst of luminous ocean we stood almost blind. Just as in following light from visible to invisible our range of investigation transcends our physical sight, so also the problem of the great mystery of Life and Death is brought a little nearer solution, when, in the realm of the Living, we pass from the Voiced to the Unvoiced.

'Is there any possible relation between our own life and that of the plant world? The question is not one of speculation but of actual demonstration by some method that is unimpeachable. This means that we should abandon all our preconceptions most of which are afterwards found to be absolutely groundless and contrary to facts. The final appeal must be made to the plant itself and no evidence should be accepted unless it bears the plant's own signature.'

7

The metamorphosis of plants

Why botany, a potentially fascinating subject, dealing with plants, living and extinct, their uses, classification, anatomy, physiology, geographical distribution, should have been from the beginning reduced to a dull taxonomy, an endless Latin dirge, in which progress is measured more by the number of corpses catalogued than by the numbers of blossoms cherished, remains a mystery. Young botanists still struggle through the jungles of Central Africa and Amazonia in search of polysyllabic specimens to add to the 350,000 already on the books. But what makes plants live does not appear to be within the scope of the science. Nor has it been since the fourth century B.C. when Theophrastus, a disciple of Aristotle from the island of Lesbos, first catalogued a couple of hundred species in his nine books *On the History of Plants* and six *On the Causes of Plants*. This was increased to four hundred medicinal plants when Dioscorides, a Greek physician to the Roman army, published his *Materia Medica*. Throughout the Dark Ages, Theophrastus and Dioscorides remained the standard texts in botany. The Renaissance brought aesthetics into the field, with lovely woodcuts in large herbals such as those of Hieronymus Bock, but it could not rip botany from the rigorous grip of the taxonomist. By 1583 a Florentine, Andreas Caesalpinus, had classified 1,520 plants into fifteen classes, distinguished by seed and fruit. He was followed by the Frenchman, Joseph Pitton de Tournefort, who described some 8,000 species of plants in twenty-two classes, chiefly according to the form of corolla – the coloured petals of the flower.

This brought sex into the picture. Although Herodotus had reported almost half a millennium before Christ that the Babylonians distinguished two sorts of palms, and would sprinkle the pollen from one on to the flower of the other in order to secure the production of fruit, it was not till the end of the seventeenth century that it was realized that plants were sexual creatures with a flourishing sex life of their own.

A German named Rudolf Jakob Camerarius was the first botanist to demonstrate that pollen is necessary for the fertilization and seed formation of flowering plants. He was a professor of medicine and director of the local Botanical Gardens at Tübingen, and he published his *De Sexu Plantorum Epistula* in 1694. His theory that there could be a sexual difference in plants caused general astonishment. It was considered 'the wildest and most singular invention that ever evolved from a poet's mind'. There was a heated controversy which lasted for almost a generation before it was finally established that plants had sexual organs and could therefore be elevated to a higher sphere of creation.

Even so, that plants have distinct male and female organs was a fact that was quickly covered by the eighteenth-century establishment with an almost impenetrable veil of Latin nomenclature which stigmatized the labiate vulva, and mis-styled the vagina. The former they called stigma, the latter style; penis and glans were equally disfigured into filament and anther.

Whereas plants had been going through countless millennia of improvement to their sexual organs, often in the face of staggering climatic changes, and had invented the most ingenious methods for fecundating each other and for spreading their fertile seed, students of botany, who might have delighted in the sexuality of plants were frustrated by such terms as 'stamens' for the male and 'pistils' for the female organs. Schoolchildren might have been fascinated to learn that each corn kernel on a cob in summer is a separate ovule, that each strand on the pubic corn silk tufted around the cob is an individual vagina ready to suck up the pollen sperm brought to it on the wind, that it may wriggle the entire length of the stylized vagina to impregnate each kernel on the cob, that every single seed produced on a plant is the result of a separate independent impregnation. Instead of struggling with archaic nomenclature, teenagers might be interested to learn that each pollen grain impregnates but one womb, which contains but one seed, that a capsule of tobacco contains, on an average, 2,500 seeds, which require 2,500 impregnations, all of which must be effected within a period of twenty-four hours in a space less than one-sixteenth of an inch in diameter. Instead of using the wonders of nature to stimulate the budding minds of their pupils, Victorian teachers misused the birds and the bees to denature their own sexuality.

How many universities even now draw the parallel between the hermaphroditic nature of plants, which bear both penis and vagina in the same body, with the 'ancient wisdom' which relates that man is descended from an androgynous predecessor? The ingenuity of some plants in avoiding self-fertilization is uncanny. Some kinds of palm trees even bear staminate flowers one year and pistillate the next. Whereas in grasses and cereals cross-fertilization is insured by the action of the wind, most other plants are cross-fertilized by birds and insects. Like animals and women, flowers exude a powerful and seductive odour when ready for mating. This causes a multitude of bees, birds, and butterflies to join in a Saturnalian rite of fecundation. Flowers that remain unfertilized emit a strong fragrance for as many as eight days or until the flower withers and falls; yet once impregnated, the flower ceases to exude its fragrance, usually in less than half an hour. As in humans, sexual frustration can gradually turn fragrance into fetor. Similarly, when a plant is ready for impregnation, there is an evolution of heat in the female organ. This was first noted by the celebrated French botanist Adolphe Théodore Brongniart in examining a flower of the *Colocasia odorata*, a tropical plant grown in greenhouses for the beauty of its foliage. This plant, at the time of flowering, presents an increase of temperature that Brongniart compared to an attack of fever, repeating the phenomenon for six days, daily from three to six in the afternoon. At the proper time for impregnation Brongniart found that a small thermometer fastened to the female organ marked a temperature eleven degrees Centigrade higher than any other part of the plant.

The pollen of most plants has a highly inflammable character; when thrown on a red-hot surface it will ignite as quickly as gunpowder. Artificial lightning was formerly produced on the theatrical stage by throwing the pollen grains of the *Lycopodium* or club mosses on to a hot shovel. In many plants the pollen diffuses an odour bearing the most striking resemblance to the seminal emission of animals and man. Pollen, which performs the same function in almost precisely the same manner as does the semen of animals and men, enters the folds of the plant vulva and traverses the whole length of the vagina, until it enters the ovary and comes in contact with the ovule. Pollen tubes elongate themselves by a most remarkable process. As with animals and humans, the sexuality of certain plants is guided by taste. The spermatozoa of certain mosses carried in the morning dew in search of females, is guided by its taste for malic acid towards the delicate cups at the bottom of which lie moss eggs to be fertilized. The spermatozoa of ferns, on the other hand, liking sugar, find their femals in pools of sweetened water.

Camerarius's discovery of sex in plants set the stage for the generator of systematic botany, Carl von Linné, who dubbed the corolla petals 'curtains of the nuptial bed'. A Swede, who latinized his name to Linnaeus from a favourite linden tree while studying for the priesthood, he divided the plant world into species principally on the basis of variations in the male sexual organ or pollen-bearing stamens of each plant. With his penchant for looking, Linnaeus recognized some six thousand different species of plants. His system, referred to as the 'sexual system', was considered 'a great stimulus to students of botany'. But his monumental method of latinized classification turned out to be as sterile as that of any voyeur who only looks at bodies. Still in use today the unwieldy title of 'binomial nomenclature', the system grants to each plant a Latin name for species and genus, to which is added the name of the person responsible for first naming it; thus the garden pea you eat with chops is the *Pisum sativum Linnaeum*.

Raoul Francé, a true lover of plants, described Linnaeus's efforts in these words:

Wherever he went the laughing brook died, the glory of the flowers withered, the grace and joy of the meadows was transformed into withered corpses whose crushed and discoloured bodies were described in a thousand minute Latin terms. The blooming fields and the storied woods disappeared during a botanical hour into a dusty herbarium, into a dreary catalogue of Greek and Latin labels. It became the hour for the practice of tiresome dialectic, filled with discussions about the number of stamens, the shape of leaves, all of which we learnt only to forget. When the work was over we stood disenchanted and estranged from nature.

It needed a real poetic genius to break away from this mania for classification and to put life and love and sex back into the plant world. In September 1786, eight years after the death of Linnaeus, a tall, handsome man of thirty-seven, who had been spending his holidays at Karlsbad taking the waters and strolling with the ladies in the woods on long botanical expeditions, suddenly rebelled against the whole system. Incognito, with only his servant aware that they were heading south beyond the Alps for *das Land wo die Citronen blühen*, the traveller, in real life Privy Councillor and Director of Mines for the Duchy of Saxe-Weimar, was delighted at the beauty and variety of the southern vegetation beyond the Brenner Pass. This secret trip to Italy, the culmination of years of longing, was to constitute a climax in the life of Germany's greatest poet, Johann Wolfgang von Goethe.

On his way to Venice he stopped to visit the Botanical Gardens of the University of Padua. Strolling among the luxuriant plants, most of which grew only in hothouses in his native Germany, Goethe was overcome with a sudden poetic vision which was to give him insight into their very nature. It was also to give him a place in the history of science as the precursor of Darwin's theory of organic development, an achievement as little appreciated by his compeers as it was extolled by a later generation. The great biologist Ernst Haeckel considered Goethe to stand with Jean Lamarck 'at the head of all the great philosophers of nature who first established a theory of organic development, and who are the illustrious fellow-workers of Darwin'. For years Goethe had been distressed by the limitations involved in a merely analytical and intellectual approach to the plant world, typified by the cataloguing mind of the eighteenth century, and of a theory of physics, then triumphant, which submitted the world to blind laws of mechanics.

While still at Leipzig University Goethe had rebelled against an arbitrary division of knowledge into faculties which cut up science into rival disciplines. In Goethe's nostrils university science had the stench of a corpse whose limbs have rotted apart. The young poet, whose early verses glowed with a passionate delight in nature, was disgusted at the petty contradictions of university savants. He began to seek knowledge elsewhere, avidly studying galvanism and mesmerism and pursuing the electrical experiments of Winkler. Already as a child he had been fascinated by the phenomena of electricity and magnetism and struck by the extraordinary phenomenon of polarity. An urge to apprehend the tremendous secrets displayed all around him in constant creation and annihilation led him on to books on mysticism and alchemy. There he discovered Paracelsus, Jakob Boehme, Giordano Bruno, Spinoza and Gottfried Arnold. From Paracelsus, Goethe learnt that the occult, because it deals with living reality and not dead catalogues, might come closer to the truth than science. But above all, he learnt that the treasures of nature are not discovered by one who is not in sympathy with nature. He realized that the normal techniques of botany could not get near to the living being of a plant as an organism in a cycle of growth. Some other form of looking was needed which could unite itself with the life of the plant. To obtain a clearer picture of a plant, Goethe would tranquillize himself at night before going to sleep by visualizing the entire cycle of a plant's development through its various stages from seed to seed. In the splendid gardens at Weimar, in the *Gartenhaus* quarters given to him by the Duke, Goethe developed an acute interest for living plants, an interest which was sharpened by his friendship with the local apothecary, Wilhelm Heinrich Sebastian Buchholz, who kept a garden of medicinal herbs and plants of particular interest. Together they built up a special botanical garden.

In the grander Botanical Gardens of Padua, where Paracelsus had preceded him, Goethe was most impressed by a palm because he was able to discern in its fanlike quality a complete development from the simple lance-shaped leaves near the ground, through successive separations, up to a spatulate

sheaf where a branchlet of blossoms emerged, strangely unrelated to the preceding growth. From the observation of this
complex series of transitional forms Goethe obtained the
inspiration for what was to become his doctrine of the *metamorphosis of plants*. In a flash he realized what had been
accumulating in his mind through long years of association
with plants: the fan palm showed clear, living proof that *all* the
lateral outgrowths of the plant were simply variations of a
single structure: the leaf. *

At Goethe's request the Padua gardener cut from the fan
palm a sequence of modifications which Goethe carried away
with him in several pasteboard containers in which they
lasted for several years. The same palm tree still stands in the
Padua Botanical Gardens despite numerous intervening wars
and revolutions.

With his new way of looking at plants Goethe came to the
conclusion that nature, by bringing forth one part through
another, could achieve the most diversified forms through
modification of a single organ.

The variation of plant forms, whose unique course I had long
been following, now awakened in me more and more the idea that
the plant forms round about us are not predetermined, but are
happily mobile and flexible, enabling them to adapt to the many
conditions throughout the world, which influence them, and to be
formed and reformed with them.

Goethe also recognized that the process of development and
refinement of form in plants worked through a threefold cycle of
expansion and contraction. The expansion of foliage was
followed by a contraction into calyx and bracts; there followed
a splendid expansion into the petals of the corolla and a
contraction into the meeting point of stamen and stigma;
finally there came a swelling into fruit followed by a contraction
into seed. This six-step cycle completed, the essential plant
was ready to start all over again.

* Sir George Trevelyan in a chapter on Goethe's plant metamorphosis in his
forthcoming book on architecture, points out that by leaf Goethe did not mean
the stem-leaf, which is itself a manifestation of the basic organ. Some other
word, says Trevelyan, is needed such as 'phyllome' to imply the archetypal
ideal organ which underlies every organ of the plant and is able to transfer one
part into another.

Ernst Lehrs's thoughtful evaluation of Goethe in *Man or Matter*, says that another natural principle is implicit in this cycle for which Goethe did not coin a specific term 'although he shows through other utterances that he was well aware of it, and of its universal significance for all life'.

Lehrs calls this principle that of Renunciation.

In the life of the plant this principle shows itself most conspicuously where the green leaf is heightened into the flower. While progressing from leaf to flower the plant undergoes a decisive ebb in its vitality. Compared with the leaf, the flower is a dying organ. This dying, however, is of a kind we may aptly call a 'dying into being'. Life in its mere vegetative form is here seen withdrawing in order that a higher manifestation of the spirit may take place. The same principle can be seen at work in the insect kingdom, when the caterpillar's tremendous vitality passes over into the short-lived beauty of the butterfly.

Lehrs marvels at the powerful forces which must be at work in the plant organism at the point of transition from its green to its coloured parts. They enforce, he says, a complete halt upon the juices that rise up right into the calyx, so that these bring nothing of their life-bearing activity into the formation of the flower, but undergo a complete transmutation, not gradually, but with a sudden leap.

After achieving its masterpiece in the flower, the plant once more goes through a process of withdrawal, this time into the tiny organs of fertilization. After fertilization, the fruit begins to swell; once more the plant produces an organ with a more or less conspicuous spatial extension. This is followed by a final and extreme contraction in the forming of the seed inside the fruit. In the seed the plant gives up all outer appearance to such a degree that nothing seems to remain but a small, insignificant speck of organized matter. Yet this tiny, inconspicuous thing bears in it the power of bringing forth a whole new plant.

Lehrs points out that in its three successive rhythms of expansion and contraction the plant reveals the basic rule of its existence.

During each expansion, the active principle of the plant presses forth into visible *appearance*; during each contraction it withdraws from outer embodiment into what we may describe as a more formless pure state of *being*. We thus find the spiritual principle of the plant engaged in a kind of breathing rhythm, now appearing, now disappearing, now assuming power over matter, now withdrawing from it again.

Goethe saw in the changeableness of all the external characteristics of plants, nothing but appearance; he drew the conclusion that the nature of the plant was not to be found in these characteristics, but had to be sought at a deeper level. The thought became more and more alive in him that it might be possible to develop all plants from a single one.

This conceit was destined to transform the science of botany, indeed the whole concept of the world: with it came the idea of *evolution*. Metamorphosis was to become the key to the whole alphabet of nature. But whereas Darwin was to assume that external influences, like mechanical causes, work upon the nature of an organism and modify it accordingly, to Goethe the single alterations were various expressions of the archetypal organism (*Urorganismus*), which possesses within itself the capacity to take on manifold forms, and which at a particular time takes on that form which is best suited to the conditions of the external environing world. Goethe's *Urorganismus* is a sort of Platonic idea in the eye of the created mind.

Sir George Trevelyan explains the kernel of Goethe's philosophy as lying in a metaphysical concept of nature.

The godhead is at work in the living, not in the dead; it is present in everything in the process of development and transformation, not in what has already taken shape and rigidified. Thus, reason in its strivings towards the divine, is concerned with putting to use what has already developed and grown torpid.

Seeing that every part of the plant is a metamorphosis of the archetypal 'leaf' organ, Goethe came to the conception of an *archetypal* plant, or '*Ur-pflanze*', a supersensible force capable of developing into myriad different forms. This, says Trevelyan, is no single plant, but a force that holds the potentiality of every plant form within it.

All plants are thus seen as specific manifestations of the archetypal plant which controls the entire plant kingdom and gives the value to nature's artistry in creating forms. It is in ceaseless play within the world of plant form, capable of moving backwards and forwards, up and down, in and out, through the scale of forms.

Summing up his discovery Goethe asked: 'If all plants were not modelled on one pattern, how could I recognize that they are plants?' Filled with delight, he declared he could now invent plant forms, even if they had never been realized on earth before. Writing from Naples to his friend and fellow poet Johann Gottfried von Herder in Weimar, he said,

> I must tell you confidentially that I am very close to the secret of the creation of plants, and that it is the simplest thing one could imagine. The archetypal plant will be the strangest creature in the world, which nature herself ought to envy me. With this model and the key to it, one can invent plants endlessly which must be consistent – that is, if they did not exist, yet they could exist, and not some artistic or poetic shadows and appearances but possessing inner truth and inevitability. The same law can be applied to everything living.

Goethe now pursued the idea 'with joy and ecstasy, lovingly immersing myself in it in Naples and Sicily', applying the idea to every plant he saw, writing reports to Herder on what took place 'with as much enthusiasm as was manifested over the finding of the lost silver piece in the gospel parable'.

For two years Goethe observed, collected, studied phenomena in detail, made many sketches and accurate drawings. 'I pursued my botanical studies, into which I was guided, driven, forced – and then held captive by my interest.'

Goethe returned to Germany after two years in Italy, only to find that the new vision of life he had acquired was incomprehensible to his fellow countrymen.

> From Italy, rich in forms, I was plunged back into formless Germany, exchanging a sunny sky for a gloomy one. My friends, instead of comforting me and drawing me back to them, drove me to despair. My delight in things remote and almost unknown to them, my sorrow and grief over what I had lost, seemed to offend them. I received no sympathy, no one understood my language. I could not adjust myself to this distressing situation, so great was

the loss to which my exterior senses must become reconciled. But gradually my spirit returned and sought to preserve itself intact.

Goethe set his thoughts on paper in a first essay *On the Metamorphosis of Plants* in which he traced 'the manifold specific phenomena in the magnificent garden of the universe back to one simple general principle', and stressed nature's method of 'producing in accord with definite laws, a living structure that is a model of everything artistic'.

The essay, which was to generate the science of morphology in plants, was written in an unusual cryptic style, different from contemporary scientific writings. He did not pursue each idea to its full conclusion but left room for interpretation. Once more he found himself repulsed because his regular publisher refused the manuscript, telling him he was a literary man, not a scientist. When finally he managed to have it printed elsewhere, Goethe was further surprised to find it completely ignored by botanists and public alike. He commented that,

The public demand that every man remain in his own field. Nowhere would anyone grant that science and poetry can be united. People forgot that science had developed from poetry and they failed to take into consideration that a swing of the pendulum might beneficently reunite the two, at a higher level and to mutual advantage.

Goethe then made the mistake of giving away copies of the brochure to friends outside his immediate circle. These friends, said he, were by no means tactful in their comments.

No one dared to accommodate himself to my method of expressing myself. It is most tormenting not to be understood when one feels sure himself, after a great stress and strain, that one understands both one's self and one's subject. It drove one to insanity to hear repeated again and again a mistake from which one has himself just escaped by a hair's breadth, and nothing is more painful than to have the things that should unite us with informed and intelligent men give rise instead to unbridgeable separation.

To his newly acquired friend and fellow poet Johann Christian Friedrich von Schiller, Goethe gave a spirited explanation of his theory of the metamorphosis of plants with graphic pen sketches of a symbolic plant. 'Schiller listened and looked with great interest, with unerring comprehension, but when I had ended he shook his head, saying: "That is not an experience, that is an idea".'

Goethe was taken aback and a little irritated. Controlling himself he said: 'How splendid that I have ideas without knowing it, and can see them before my eyes.' From the argument Goethe was left with the philosophic concept that ideas must be clearly independent of space and time, whereas experience is restricted to space and time. 'The simultaneous and successive are therefore intimately bound together in an idea, whereas they are always separated in experience.'

It was eighteen years after the Congress of Vienna before references to the metamorphosis of plants began to appear in botanical texts and other writings, and thirty years before it was fully accepted by botanists. When the essay became known in Switzerland and France people were astonished to find that a poet 'normally occupied with moral phenomena associated with feeling and power and imagination, could have achieved such an important discovery'.

Late in life Goethe added another basic idea to the science of botany. A generation before Darwin, he realized that vegetation had a tendency to grow in two distinct ways: vertically and spirally. With his poet's intuition Goethe labelled the vertical tendency, with its sustaining principle, male; the spiral tendency, which conceals itself during the development of the plant but predominates during blossoming and fruiting, he labelled female. He explained that,

When we see that the vertical system is definitely male and the spiral definitely female, we will be able to conceive of all vegetation as androgynous from the root up. In the course of the transformation of growth the two systems are separated, and take opposite courses to be reunited on a higher level.

Goethe held a lofty and comprehensive view of the significance of the male and female principles as spiritual opposites in the cosmos. Also it seemed to him a truly magical phenomenon that the action of the root of a plant is directed earthward towards moisture and darkness, whereas the stem or trunk strives skywards in the opposite direction towards the light and the air. To explain it Goethe postulated a force opposite, or polar, to Newton's gravity, to which he gave the name *levity*.

'Newton,' says Lehrs, 'explained to you – or at least was once supposed to explain, why an apple fell; but he never thought of explaining the exact correlative but infinitely more difficult question, how the apple got up there.'

The concept led Goethe to a picture of the earth as being surrounded and penetrated by a field of force in every respect the opposite of the earth's gravitational field. Lehrs continues:

As the gravity field decreases in strength, with increasing distance from the centre of the field, that is, in the outward direction, so does the levity-field decrease in strength with increasing distance from its periphery, or in the inward direction ... This is why things 'fall' under the influence of gravity and 'rise' under the influence of levity.'

Lehrs adds that if there were no field working inwards from the cosmic periphery, the entire material content of the earthly realm would be reduced by gravitation to a spaceless point, just as under the sole influence of the peripheral field of levity it would dissipate into the universe. 'Just as in volcanic activity heavy matter is suddenly and swiftly driven heavenwards under the influence of levity, so in a storm does light matter stream earthwards under the influence of gravity.'

When Goethe died on 22 March 1832, twenty-seven years before Darwin was to proclaim his principle of organic evolution, he was considered Germany's greatest poet with a universal mind capable of compassing every domain of human activity and knowledge. But as a scientist he was considered a layman.

Though a genus of plants, the *Goethea*, was named after him, as was a mineral – goethite, it was more as a courtesy to a great man than to a scientist. In due course Goethe was credited with having coined the word 'morphology' and of having formulated the concept of botanical morphology which persists to this day. He was credited with the discovery of the volcanic origin of mountains, of establishing the first system of weather stations, of being interested in connecting the Gulf of Mexico with the Pacific Ocean, and of wanting to build steamships, and flying machines; but the scope of Goethe's formulation of the metamorphosis of plants had to await the advent of Darwin to be fully appreciated, and even then it was largely misunderstood.

As Rudolf Steiner was to write, almost a hundred years later:

It was from observations similar to those of Goethe that Darwin proceeded when he asserted his doubt as to the constancy of the external forms of genera and species. But the conclusions which the two thinkers reached were entirely unlike. Whereas Darwin considered that the whole nature of the organism was, in fact, comprised in these characteristics, and came to the conclusion, therefore, that there is nothing constant in the life of the plant, Goethe went deeper and drew the inference that, since those characteristics are not constant, what is constant must be sought in something else which lies beneath changeable externalities.

8

Plants will grow to please

Goethe's poetic notion that a spiritual essence lay behind the material form of plants was put on a firmer basis by a medical doctor and a professor of physics at the University of Leipzig. Credited with over forty papers on such subjects as the measurement of electrical currents and the perceptions of colours, Gustav Theodor Fechner came to his profound understanding of plants in a totally unexpected way. In 1839 he began to stare at the sun in the hope of discovering the nature of afterimages, those strange pictures which seem to persist on the retina of the eye even after the cessation of normal visual stimulus. A few days later, he was horrified to realize that he was going blind. Exhausted from over-work and unable in his new affliction to face his friends and colleagues, he retired to a darkened room with a mask over his face, to live in solitude praying for recovery.

One spring morning three years later, sensing that his sight had been restored, he emerged into the light of day; joyously walking along the Mulde river he instantly recognized that flowers and trees along its banks were what he called be-souled.

As I stood by the water and watched a flower, it was as though I saw its soul lift itself from the bloom and, drifting through the mist, become clearer until the spiritual form hung clearly above it. Perhaps it wanted to stand on the roof of its budding house in order better to enjoy the sun. Believing itself invisible, it was quite surprised when a little child appeared.

The result was *Nanna, or the Soul-Life of Plants*, which was published in Leipzig in 1848. Although scathingly rejected by his fellow academicians, it became so popular that it was still being printed in Germany three-quarters of a century later.

In his introduction, Fechner explained that he happened on

the title by accident. At first he thought of calling his new book *Flora*, after the Roman goddess of flowers, or *Hamadruas*, after the wood nymph which the Hellenes recognized as living only as long as the tree of which it was the spirit. But he rejected the first as too botanical, the second as too classically stiff and antiquarian.

One day while reading Teuton mythology, Fechner learned that Baldur, god of light, had like Actaeon peeping at Diana, secretly gazed upon the naked form of the flower-princess, Nanna, as she bathed in a stream. When her natural loveliness was enhanced by the energy over which Baldur ruled, his heart, said the legend, was pierced, and the marriage of Light and Flowers became a foregone conclusion.

Fechner's awakening to the soul life of plants turned him from professing physics to professing philosophy, a branch of knowledge of which he took a chair at Leipzig the same year that *Nanna* appeared; though even before his realization that plants had undreamt-of sensitivity, Fechner had concerned himself with cosmic problems in a *Little Book of Life After Death*, only posthumously published in Dresden in 1936, and in *Comparative Anatomy of the Angels*, a work which he considered so risqué that he wrote it under the pseudonym of Dr Mises.

In the *Little Book* Fechner put forward the idea that human life was lived in three stages: one of continuous sleep from conception to birth, one of half-wakefulness which humans called terrestrial life, and one of fuller alertness which began only after death.

In *Comparative Anatomy* he traced the path of evolution from monocellular organisms through man on to angelic higher beings spherical in form and capable of seeing universal gravitation as ordinary humans perceive light, of communicating not acoustically but through luminous symbols.

Fechner introduced *Nanna* with the concept that whether plants have a soul or not changes one's whole insight into nature. If man admits to an omnipresent, all-knowing and almighty God who bestows animation on all things, then nothing in the world can be excluded from this munificence, neither plant nor stone nor crystal nor wave. Why should universal spirit, he asked, sit less firmly in nature than human beings, and not be as much in command of nature's power as it is of human bodies?

Anticipating Bose's work, Fechner further reasoned that if plants have life and soul, they must have some sort of nervous system, hidden perhaps in their strange spiral fibres. Going beyond the limitation of today's mechanistic physiology, Fechner referred to 'spiritual nerves' in the universe, one expression of which was the interconnection of celestial bodies, not with 'long ropes' but with a unified web of light, gravity, and forces yet unknown.

The soul, said Fechner, received sensations, in a manner analogous to that of a spider which is alerted to outside influences by its web. It seemed reasonable to him to accept that plants had nerves, their purported absence being due to man's ignorance rather than to any innate vegetal deficiency.

But this nervous system was no more linked to a plant's psyche than is the body of a man to his soul. Both were diffused throughout, yet separated from all the organs which they directed. 'None of my limbs anticipates anything for itself,' wrote Fechner, 'only I, the spirit of my whole, sense everything that happens to me.' He held that the two entities were two different sides of one reality, the mind appearing subjectively, the body objectively, as a circle is either concave or convex depending on whether the observer stands inside it or outside. The confusion resulted because it was difficult to hold both points of view simultaneously. Basic to his animate philosophy was the axiom that all life is *one* and simply takes up different shapes in order to divert itself. The highest good and supreme end of all action is the maximum pleasure not of the individual but of all, said Fechner, and on this he based all his rules for morals.

Since spirit to Fechner was a deistic universal, it was useless to refer to souls as wholly individual, whether vegetal or human. Nonetheless they were the only criteria for forming a conception of other souls and making themselves known to them by outward physical signs. To the undoubted irritation of today's prevalent school of behaviourist psychology, Fechner also maintained that in its soul alone was the true freedom of any creature.

[113]

Because a plant is rooted, it necessarily has less freedom of movement than an animal, Fechner declared, though by moving its branches, leaves and tendrils as it sees fit, it behaves much like an animal which opens its claws upon capture or runs away when frightened.

More than a century before experiments in the Soviet Union apparently convinced the Russians that plants can auto-regulate their own needs with the help of man-designed instrumentation, Fechner asked,

'Why should we believe that a plant is not any less aware of hunger and thirst than an animal? The animal searches for food with its whole body, the plant with portions of it, guided not with a nose, eyes or ears but with other senses.'

It seemed to Fechner that 'plant people', calmly living their lives in the spots of their rooting, might well wonder why human bipeds keep rushing about. 'In addition to souls which run and shriek and devour, might there not be souls which bloom in stillness, exhale fragrance and satisfy their thirst with dew and their impulses by their burgeoning?' Could not flowers, Fechner asked, communicate with each other by the very perfumes they exude, becoming aware of each other's presence in a way more delightful than by means of the verbiage of humans which is seldom delicate or fragrant except, by coincidence, in lovers?

Fechner wrote:

From *inside* comes the voice and from inside comes the scent. Just as one can tell human beings in the dark from the tone of their voices, so in the dark, every flower can be recognized by its scent. Each carries the soul of its progenitor.

Flowers having no fragrance he likened to animals which live alone in the wilds, and those with perfume to gregarious beasts.

In the end, posited this German sage, was it not one of the ultimate purposes of human bodies to serve vegetal life surrounding them by emitting carbonic acid for the plants to breathe, and by manuring them with human bodies after death? Did not flowers and trees finally consume man and by combining his remains with raw earth, water, air and sunlight, transform and transmute human bodies into the most glorious forms and colours?

Fechner's 'animism' for which he was so wrathfully castigated by his contemporaries, led him to issue, two years after *Nanna*, a book on atomic theory in which, long before the birth of particle physics, he argued that atoms were centres of pure energy and the lowest elements in a spiritual hierarchy. The following year he brought out *Zendavesta*, its title inspired by the sacred writings of the ancient Zoroastrians who claimed that their great religious leader Zarathustra had taught his people how to breed the food plants that still today form our chief source of nourishment. The original *Zendavesta* might be considered the first book on agriculture. Fechner's work was characterized by the younger American philosopher William James as a 'wonderful book by a wonderful genius'. Its fascinating and complex philosophy contained such concepts as that of 'mental energy' which appealed strongly to Sigmund Freud and without which the edifice of psychoanalysis might never have been built.

Though Fechner heroically attempted to put forward what his contemporaries, and many present-day philosophers, would call 'an idealistic view of reality', he ceaselessly tried to reconcile it with the methodology of modern science in which he was trained.

Perhaps this was why this Leipzig physician and physicist, characterized as one of the most versatile thinkers of the nineteenth century, was so excellent an observer of the details of the vegetable world surrounding him.

In *Nanna* he described the sex organs of plants – which in humans St Paul considered so uncomely – as marvels of beauty, lyricising on the manner in which plants lure insects to wriggle into their genitalia to drink the hidden nectar and thus shake fertilizing pollen from the anthers on to the stigma of their petals.

Fechner marvelled at how plants could intentionally devise the most sophisticated systems to spread their species, how the puffball waits to be trodden upon in order to produce a cloud of minute spores carried a great distance by the wind, how the maple casts off propeller seeds that spin away with a passing breeze, how fruit trees seduce birds, beasts and man into distributing their seeds afar, neatly packaged in nourishing manure, how viviparous water lilies and ferns reproduce tiny but perfect plants on the surface of their leaves. He also delighted in the idea that the sensitive tips of a plant's roots enabled it to maintain a sense of direction; and that the climbing tendrils of plants repeated perfect circles in the air as they searched for purchase.

Although Fechner's work was not taken seriously, one Englishman whose life ran parallel to his, had the daring to recognize that some mysterious force in plants had the characteristics of sentience or intelligence. After publishing his *Origin of the Species* in 1859, Charles Robert Darwin devoted the greater part of his remaining twenty-three years not only to an elaboration of his theory of evolution but to a meticulous study of the behaviour of plants.

In *The Power of Movement in Plants* published just before his death, Darwin developed the idea that their habit of moving at certain times of the day was the common inheritance of both plants and animals. The most striking part of this similarity, he wrote, was 'the localization of their sensitiveness, and the transmission of an influence from the excited part to another which consequently moves'. But he stopped short of asserting that plants had nervous systems because he could find no such system. Nevertheless, he could not get out of his mind that plants must have sentient ability. In the very last sentence of his massive volume, referring to the properties of a plant's radicle – that part of its embryo which develops into the primary root – he stated boldly:

It is hardly an exaggeration to say that the tip of the radicle acts like the brain of one of the lower animals: the brain being seated within the anterior end of the body, receiving impressions from the sense organs, and directing the several movements.

In an earlier book *The Fertilization of Orchids*, published in 1862, one of the most masterful and complete studies of a single species of plant life ever to appear, Darwin set forth in highly technical language the way insects caused the fertilization of those unusual flowers which he had learned about by sitting on the grass for hours and patiently watching the process. In more than a dozen years of experiments conducted on fifty-seven species of plants Darwin found that products of cross-pollination resulted in more numerous, larger, heavier, more vigorous and more fertile offspring, even in species that are normally self-pollinating, and put his finger on the secret for the production of such copious amounts of pollen. The immobile plants were betting on the fact that, though the odds were millions to one against it, if their pollen could mix with a far-away relative, the children were likely to attain what came to be known as 'hybrid-vigour'. Of this Darwin wrote that:

the advantages of cross-fertilization do not follow from some mysterious virtue in the mere union of two distinct individuals, but from such individuals having been subjected during previous generations to different conditions, or to their having varied in a manner commonly called spontaneous, so that in either case their sexual elements have been in some degree differentiated.

The thrust of Darwin's theory of evolution and of the survival of the fittest indicated that something more than chance was in play. That this something might accommodate to the wish of man was the next extraordinary development.

In 1892, ten years after Darwin's death, a fifty-two page nurseryman's catalogue; *New Creations in Fruits and Flowers*, published in Santa Rosa, California, created a sensation in the United States. Unlike similar booklets which had thus far included not more than half a dozen novelties among the hundreds advertised, this catalogue contained not a single plant known to man.

Among its horticultural marvels were a hardwood giant Paradox walnut which, growing as fast as a spongy pulpwood, could form a hedge tall enough to screen a house within a few years; a giant daisy named after Mount Shasta with mammoth snow-white petals; an apple, sweet on one side and sour on the other, and a cross between a strawberry and a raspberry which, though it did not fruit, seemed as strange to followers of the theory of natural selection as would the mating of a chicken with an owl.

When the catalogue finally made its way six thousand miles to the Netherlands, it caught the eye of an Amsterdam professor, Hugo de Vries, a geneticist who was later to become celebrated for carrying forward Darwin's life work with his own theory of mutation. De Vries was astonished at the apparent ability of one man to bring into the world botanical specimens undreamt of by nature. To satisfy his curiosity, he set off across the world to California to visit the publisher of the catalogue. His name was Luther Burbank. In his front garden stood a fourteen-year-old Paradox walnut larger than the Persian variety four times its age, and a 'monkey puzzle tree' which could stun passers-by by dropping twenty-pound nuts on their heads. In the little cottage where Burbank worked there was neither library nor laboratory and his notes were kept on tearings from brown paper bags or on the backs of letters and envelopes. Throughout the evening the bewildered de Vries, who had expected files of carefully recorded data which might reveal Burbank's secrets, questioned the plant-breeder only to be told that his art was basically 'a matter of concentration and the rapid elimination of non-essentials'. As for his laboratory, Burbank told de Vries: 'I keep it in my head.'

The Dutch scientist was no more perplexed than were hundreds of his American confrères who, lacking any rational explanation for Burbank's methodology, often branded the wizard a charlatan. Burbank's own evaluation of the botanical fraternity did little to appease their collective ire. In 1901 he told the San Francisco Floral Congress:

'The chief work of the botanists of yesterday was the study and classification of dried, shrivelled plant mummies whose souls had fled. They thought their classified species were more fixed and unchangeable than anything in heaven or earth that we can now imagine. We have learned that they are as plastic in our hands, as clay in the hands of the potter or colour on the artist's canvas and can readily be moulded into more beautiful forms and colours than any painter or sculptor can ever hope to bring forth.'

Such statements infuriated the narrow-minded, but de Vries, who accepted Burbank as a born genius, wrote of his work that 'its value for the doctrine of evolution compels our highest admiration'.

As his biographers almost inadvertently make clear, Burbank

was and remains an enigma. Born in 1849 in the rural Massachusetts village of Lunenburg, the lasting impressions from his schooling came from his reading of Henry David Thoreau and of the other great naturalists, Alexander von Humboldt and Louis Agassiz. But these were overshadowed by Charles Darwin's massive two volume *The Variation of Animals and Plants Under Domestication,* which he read shortly after its publication in 1868. Burbank was deeply impressed by its theme that organisms vary when removed from their natural conditions.

While still in Massachusetts, Burbank one day happened upon a seed ball in his patch of potatoes – a vegetable which almost never sets seed and is therefore propagated from the buds, or 'eyes', of its tuber. Because he knew that potato seeds, if they could be found, would not grow tubers true to type, and instead would produce a curious batch of mongrels, he excitedly thought that one of them might develop into a potato miracle. One of the twenty-three seeds in the ball gave rise to an offspring that managed to double the average yield. It was smooth, plump, an excellent baker, and unlike its red-skinned progenitor, it was a cream-white colour. Today the new potato, which was christened the Burbank, dominates the U.S. potato market.

Shortly after Burbank's arrival in Santa Rosa, Darwin's *The Effects of Cross and Self Fertilization in the Vegetable Kingdom* came out, and Burbank was particularly struck by a challenging introductory statement: 'As plants are adapted by such diversified and effective means for cross-fertilization, it might have been inferred from this fact alone that they derived some great advantage from the process.'

To Burbank, this sentence seemed both a blue-print and a command. If Darwin had drawn plans, he would carry them out. His first chance came in March 1882 when a variety of plums known as prunes were coming into their own in hundreds of Californian orchards as a new money-making fruit. They were easily dried and thus easily shipped and hard to spoil. He was asked by a banker if he could deliver twenty thousand young prune trees for a two hundred acre planting by December. The banker was anxious not to miss the bonanza but everyone had told him it was impossible to produce a crop so quickly. Burbank knew that if the man had given him two years nothing would have been simpler than to sprout plum trees from seed, bud them with prunes in the late summer and after cutting off the original plum tops, watch them develop into prune seedlings the following year. How, he asked himself, could he turn the same trick in eight months? It suddenly struck him that almonds, a member of the genus *Prunus*, would sprout much faster than the hard stones of plums. After buying a sackful of the oval-shaped nuts, Burbank forced them to sprout in warm water, copying a method he had used with corn in Massachusetts, which had allowed him to beat other farmers to the market by more than a week. Even so, the little seedlings were not ready for budding until June, and time was running short. With a cash advance from the banker, Burbank hired all available nursery help in the region. They worked round the clock; when the job was finished, Burbank prayed that his tiny seedlings would grow into five-foot trees in the four months remaining before the contract called for delivery. His luck held: before Christmas he was able to deliver 19,500 trees to the overjoyed banker. Other nurserymen were left gasping at a feat which produced a $6,000 windfall for Burbank. For him the lesson was that mass production was one of the keys in revealing the as yet undisclosed secrets of nature.

Thus began Burbank's pomological revolution which led to the development of new prunes and plums – including one, the 'Climax', which tasted like a pineapple, and another which tasted like a pear – that today still account for over half of California's giant crop. There followed the ever popular Burbank 'July Elberta' peach, a luscious Burbank 'Flaming Gold' nectarine, a bush-type chestnut which bore a crop six months after its seed was put in the ground, a white blackberry the colour of an icicle, and two quinces that were so good that most nurseries still stock no other. In developing new fruit, Burbank was so adept and fast that he could race through thousands of cross-pollinations while orthodox plant specialists in laboratories were pedantically pouring over sheaves of notes involving only a few dozen. He was accused of trickery and of buying his new creations abroad, which of course he did, for

Burbank was convinced that plants, like people, would behave differently when away from home. He would therefore order experimental varieties to cross with home-grown stand-bys from as far away as Japan and New Zealand. In all, he introduced over a thousand new plants, which if evenly spaced over his working career, amounted to a never before seen specimen every three weeks. Despite the backbiting of envious and narrow-minded scientists, this miracle making was heralded by professional experts big enough to recognize genius when they saw it, even if it passed their understanding.

Liberty Hyde Bailey, the universally recognized dean of American botany, who had earlier told a world horticultural congress that 'man could not do much to produce variations in plants', came from Cornell University to see what Burbank was doing to create such a furore. After his visit to Santa Rosa he wrote in an issue of *World's Work* magazine:

Luther Burbank is a breeder of plants by profession, and in this business he stands almost alone in this country. So many and so striking have been the new plants that he has given to the world that he has been called the Wizard of Horticulture. This sobriquet has prejudiced a good many people against his work. Luther Burbank is not a wizard. He is an honest, straightforward, careful, inquisitive and persistent man. He believes that causes produce results. He has no other magic than that of patient inquiry, abiding enthusiasm, an unprejudiced mind, and a remarkably acute judgement of the merits and capabilities of plants.

This was a delight to Burbank, who smarted from the ugly rumours circulated about his work by the orthodox. He told a packed lecture-hall at Stanford University that 'Orthodoxy is ankylosis – nobody at home: ring up the undertaker for further information!'

Professor H. J. Webber, a geneticist in charge of plant breeding at the U.S. Department of Agriculture, maintained that single-handed Burbank had saved the world nearly a quarter of century in plant-breeding time. David Fairchild, who spent years exploring the world for new plants which might prove commercially useful in the United States, though baffled by Burbank's methods, summed up his impressions of his visit to Santa Rosa in a letter to a friend: 'There are those

who say Burbank is not scientific. It is true only in the sense
that he has tried to do so much, and has been so fascinated by
the desire to create that he has not always noted and labelled
the footsteps which he has taken.'

At his experimental farm where forty thousand Japanese
plums or a quarter of a million flowering bulbs could be seen
growing at the same time, Burbank would walk down a row of
thousands of plants – whether tiny seedlings just breaking
ground or chest-high flowers nearing maturity – and without
breaking his stride pick out those likely to succeed.

One wide-eyed county farm adviser described this in his
own words:

He'd go along a row of gladioli, yanking out the ones he didn't
want as fast as he could pull them up. He seemed to have an instinct
that told him if a tiny plant would grow up to bear the kind of fruit
or flowers he wanted. I couldn't see any difference between them,
even if I stooped and looked closely, but Burbank did no more than
glance at them.

Burbank's catalogues gave the impression that he employed
thousands of workers. 'Six new gladioli, the best of a million
seedlings.' 'The growing of ten thousand hybrid clematis
plants for several years to get a final six good ones.' 'Discard-
ing eighteen thousand calla lilies in order to get one plant.' 'For
twenty-five cents, as gorgeous an effect is readily produced
with this new zinnia as an outlay of twenty-five dollars would
purchase if expended on dahlias.' 'My Royal Walnut can out-
grow ordinary walnuts eight to one and promises to revolu-
tionize the furniture business and also perhaps the cord-wood
industry.'

The earthquake of 18 April 1906, which all but devastated
San Francisco, reduced Santa Rosa to a mass of flaming
splinters and rubble. However, the remarkable thing was that
not a pane of glass in Burbank's huge greenhouse not far from
the centre of town was even cracked. Burbank was less amazed
than his fellow townsmen, though he was careful not to broach
the subject directly in public. He had an idea that his communing with the forces of nature and the cosmos had a great deal to
do with his brilliant, and seemingly unique, success with plants
and this might well have protected his greenhouse.

His indirect allusions to the personalization of his plants are illustrated by an article he wrote in 1906 for *Century Magazine*. He asserted that:

The most stubborn living thing in this world, the most difficult to swerve is a plant once fixed in certain habits. Remember that this plant has preserved its individuality all through the ages; perhaps it is one which can be traced backward through eons of time in the very rocks themselves. Do you suppose, after all these ages of repetition, the plant does not become possessed of a will, if you so choose to call it, of unparalleled tenacity?

To Manly P. Hall, founder and president of the Philosophical Research Society of Los Angeles and a student of comparative religion, mythology and esoterica, Burbank revealed that when he wanted his plants to develop in some particular and peculiar way not common to their kind, he would get down on his knees and talk to them. He wrote that:

Mr Burbank also mentioned that plants have over twenty sensory perceptions but, because they are different from ours, we cannot recognize them. He was not sure that the shrubs and flowers understood his words, but he was convinced that by some telepathy, they could comprehend his meaning.

Hall later confirmed what Burbank told the famous Yogi, Paramahansa Yogananda, about his development of the spineless cactus, a years-long procedure during which Burbank pulled thousands of cactus thorns from his hands with pliers. Burbank said:

'While I was conducting my experiments with cacti, I often talked to the plants to create a vibration of love. "You have nothing to fear." [I would tell them.] "You don't need your defensive thorns. I will protect you".'

Burbank's power of love, reported Hall,

greater than any other, was a subtle kind of nourishment that made everything grow better and bear fruit more abundantly. Burbank explained to me that in all his experimentation he took plants into his confidence, asked them to help, and assured them that he held their small lives in deepest regard and affection.

Helen Keller, deaf and blind from infancy, after a visit to Burbank, wrote in *Outlook for the Blind*:

He has the rarest of gifts, the receptive spirit of a child. When plants talk to him, he listens. Only a wise child can understand the language of flowers and trees.

Her observation was particularly apt since all his life Burbank loved children. In his essay, 'Training of the Human Plant', later published as a book, he anticipated the more humane attitudes which came after him and shocked authoritarian parents with the words:

It is more important for a child to have a good nervous system than to try to 'force' it along the line of book knowledge at the expense of its spontaneity, its play. A child should learn through a medium of pleasure, not of pain. Most of the things that are really useful in after life come to the children through play and through association with nature.

Burbank, like other geniuses, realized that his successes came from his having conserved the wonder and exuberance of a small boy for everything around him. He told one of his biographers:

'I'm almost seventy-seven, and I can still go over a gate or run a foot race or kick the chandelier. That's because my body is no older than my mind – and my mind is adolescent. It has never grown up and I hope it never will.'

It was this quality which so puzzled the scientists who looked askance at his power of creation and bewildered audiences who expected him to be explicit as to how he produced so many horticultural wonders. Most of them were as disappointed as the members of the American Pomological Society who, gathered to hear Burbank's lecture entitled 'How to Produce New Fruits and Flowers', gaped as they heard him say:

'In pursuing the study of any of the universal and everlasting laws of nature, whether relating to the life, growth, structure and movements of a giant planet, the tiniest plant or of the psychological movements of the human brain, some conditions are necessary before we can become one of nature's interpreters or the creator of any valuable work for the world. Preconceived notions, dogmas and all personal prejudice and bias must be laid aside. Listen patiently, quietly and reverently to the lessons, one by one, which Mother Nature has to teach, shedding light on that which was before a mystery, so that all who will, may see and know. She conveys her truths only to those who are passive and receptive. Accepting these truths as suggested, wherever they may lead, then we have the whole universe in harmony with us. At last man has found a solid foundation for science, having discovered that he is part of a universe which is eternally unstable in form, eternally immutable in substance.'

Though he did not know of him, Burbank would have agreed with Fechner, 'that it is a dark and cold world we sit in if we will not open the inward eyes of the spirit to the inward flame of nature'.

That plants were able to reveal their secrets was accepted as natural by a remarkable agricultural chemist named George Washington Carver. Born just before the American Civil War, he overcame the handicap of his slave descent and went on to receive public recognition for his many scientific discoveries.

From the time he was able to get about for himself in the surrounding countryside young Carver began to display an uncanny knowledge of all growing things. Local farmers in Diamond Grove, a tiny community in south-western Missouri, remembered the weak-looking boy roving for hours through their holdings examining plants and bringing back certain varieties with which he could miraculously heal sick animals. On his own, the child planted a private garden in a remote and unused bit of ground. With the remnants of cold frames and other stray material he built a secret greenhouse in the woods. When asked what he did by himself so far from the farmyard, Carver replied firmly, if enigmatically. 'I go to my garden hospital and take care of hundreds of sick plants.' Farmers' wives from all over the countryside began to bring him their ailing house plants. Gently caring for them in his own way, Carver often sang to them in the same squeaky voice which characterized him in manhood, put them in tin cans with special soil of his own concoction and tenderly covered them at night. When the owners saw their plants again they would ask how he could work such miracles. Carver only said softly: 'All flowers talk to me and so do hundreds of little living things in the woods. I learn what I know by watching and loving everything.'

After working his way through high school in Kansas and Simpson College in Iowa, Carver enrolled at the Iowa State College of Agriculture. He studied under Henry Cantwell Wallace, editor of the popular *Wallace's Farmer*, a man whom he much admired. One of Wallace's sayings that 'nations endure only as long as their top-soil', left a lasting impression on him. Often he found time to take Wallace's six-year-old grandson on long walks into the woods to talk with plants, little suspecting that the hand he was holding would be that of a Secretary of Agriculture, and later, two years before Carver's own death, Vice-President of the United States.

By 1896 Carver had his master's degree and was invited to join the faculty. At the same time the founder and president of the Normal and Industrial Institute, Booker T. Washington, who had heard of Carver's brilliance, asked him to come to Tuskeegee, Alabama and run the Institute's Agricultural Department. Like Bose, he decided that he could not let the prospect of a comfortable and well-paid post on the Iowa State faculty dissuade him from serving his own people. So he immediately accepted the second offer.

Carver had not been in the south more than a few weeks when he discerned that the main problem facing the flat land spreading out in hundreds of square miles around him was slow poisoning. Monotonous planting of a single crop, cotton, year in, year out, had been sucking the fertility out of the soil for generations. To counteract the slow despoliation by thousands of sharecroppers, he decided to set up an experimental station. There he included a branch for teaching Blacks, and a private laboratory in which he would sit for hours communing with plants and into which he never allowed a single book to penetrate. He made his lectures as simple as possible. When the Chancellor of the University of Georgia, W. B. Hill, came to Tuskeegee to see for himself if it was really true that a Negro professor was as brilliant as rumour had reported, he declared that Carver's presentation of the problem of southern agriculture was 'the best lecture that it has ever been my privilege to attend'.

Each morning Carver would rise at four o'clock to walk in the woods before the start of the working day and bring back countless plants, many of them unknown to the average botanist, with which to illustrate his lectures. Explaining this habit to friends, he said, 'Nature is the greatest teacher and I learn from her best when others are asleep. In the still dark hours before sunrise God tells me of the plans I am to fulfil.'

For more than a decade Carver worked daily on experimental plots of soil trying to discover how to change Alabama's enthralment to 'ol' debbil cotton'. He treated one nineteen acre plot with rotted leaves from the forest, rich muck from the swamps, and barnyard manure instead of commercial fertilizer. This resulted in such rich harvests of rotated crops that Carver came to the conclusion that 'in Alabama the very fertilizers which existed in almost unlimited supply were allowed to go to waste in favour of commercial sold products'.

As a horticulturalist, Carver had noticed that the peanut was incredibly self-sufficient and could grow well in poor soil. As a chemist, he discovered that it equalled sirloin steaks in protein and potatoes in carbohydrates. Surely, he thought to himself, this remarkable ground fruit must hide hundreds of reasons for its creation. He locked himself in his laboratory and began breaking down the peanut into its chemical components and exposing each of his many nuts to different conditions of temperature and pressure. To his satisfaction he found that one third of the nut was made up of seven different varieties of oil. Working round the clock, he analysed and synthesized, took apart and recombined, broke down and built up the chemically differentiable parts of the peanut until at last he had two dozen bottles, each containing a brand new product.

At a meeting of farmers and agricultural specialists he demonstrated what he had been able to do in seven days and seven nights: a peanut-sized replica of the biblical account of creation. He begged his audience to plough up the soil-destroying cotton and plant peanuts in its stead, assuring them that it would produce a cash crop far more valuable than its sole existing use as food for pigs might indicate.

The audience was doubtful, the more so when Carver, asked to explain his methods, replied that he never groped for them but they came to him while walking in the woods in flashes of inspiration. To allay their doubts he began to issue bulletins, one of which stated incredibly that rich, nutritious and highly palatable butter could be made from the peanut. Whereas it took one hundred pounds of dairy milk to make ten pounds of butter, one hundred pounds of peanuts could produce thirty-five pounds of peanut butter. Other bulletins showed that a cornucopia of products could also be extracted from the sweet potato, a tropical vine of which most Americans had never heard, that throve in the South's cotton-debased soil. When the First World War broke out, Carver turned his mind to the shortage of dyestuffs. From the leaves, roots, stems, and fruits of twenty-eight different plants he created 536 separate dyes which could be used to colour wool, cotton, linen, silk and even leather.

At last his labours attracted national attention. When it was rumoured that at the Tuskeegee Institute they were saving two hundred pounds of wheat per day mixing two parts of ordinary flour with a new flour derived from sweet potatoes, a flock of dieticians and journalists came to investigate. Delicious breads made from the mixed flours were served with a sumptuous lunch of five courses, each made from peanuts or sweet potatoes, or, like Carver's 'mock chicken', from the two combined. The only other vegetables on the table were sheep sorrel, pepper grass, wild chicory and dandelions, served as a salad. The menu was designed to illustrate Carver's assertion that plants growing in nature were far better than those from which the natural vitality had been removed in cultivation. The food experts, who realized that Carver's contributions might go a long way towards helping the war effort, rushed to telephone their papers. Carver had become known to scientists the year before when he was elected a fellow of the Royal Society. Now he was in the national headlines.

By 1930, the peanut's one-time worthlessness had been converted, through Carver's clairvoyance and industry, into an income of a quarter of a billion dollars for southern farmers. Its oil alone was valued at $60,000,000 a year and peanut butter established itself as one of the favourite foods of even the poorest American child. He also discovered that peanut oil could help the atrophied muscles of polio victims. Results were so astonishing that he had to set aside one day each month to treat patients at his laboratory, but his feat remained un-recognized by the medical profession. Not satisfied with his achievements with peanuts, Carver went on to make paper from a local southern pine tree which ultimately encouraged foresters to cover millions of southern acres with productive forests where only scrub woods had existed.

In the midst of the depression Carver was invited to Wash-ington to testify before the powerful Ways and Means Com-mittee of the U.S. Senate which was considering a Bill designed to protect struggling American manufacturers. Dressed in his usual, seemingly eternally durable, two-dollar black suit with an ever-present flower in its button-hole and a home-made necktie, Carver arrived at Union Station. He called a porter to help him with his bags and direct him to Congress, but was rebuffed with the reply, 'Sorry, Pop, I ain't got time for you now, I'm expecting an important coloured scientist coming from Alabama.' Patiently Carver lugged his own bags to a taxi which took him to Capitol Hill.

The committee had accorded him ten minutes in which to testify. However when he began his presentations and took from his bag face-powders, petroleum substitutes, shampoos, creo-sote, vinegar, woodstains, and other samples of the countless creations concocted in his laboratories, the Vice-President overruled protocol and told Carver he could have as much time as he liked because his demonstration was the best that he had ever seen presented to a Senate Committee.

In half a lifetime of research Carver, though he created fortunes for thousands, rarely took out a patent on any of his ideas. When practically-minded industrialists and politicians reminded him of the money he might have made had he only afforded himself this protection, he replied simply: 'God did not charge me or you for making peanuts. Why should I profit from their products?' Like Bose, Carver believed that the fantasies of his mind, however valuable, should be granted free of charge to mankind.

This self-effacing quality was an enigma to two inventive geniuses and contemporaries who, unlike Carver, were cannily practical men even to the point of trying to buy Carver's services. Thomas A. Edison told his associates that 'Carver is worth a fortune' and backed up his statement by offering to employ the Black chemist at an astronomically high salary. Carver turned down the offer. Henry Ford, who thought Carver 'the greatest scientist living', tried to get him to come to his River Rouge establishment with an equal lack of success.

Because of the strangely unaccountable source from which his magic with plant products sprang, his methods, like those of Burbank, continued to be inscrutable both to scientists and to the general public. Visitors finding Carver pottering at his work bench amid a confusing clutter of moulds, soils, plants and insects were baffled by the utter, and, to many of them, meaningless, simplicity of his replies to their persistent pleas for him to reveal his secrets. 'The secrets are in the plants. To elicit them you have to love them enough.'

'But why do so few people have your power?' his questioner persisted. 'Who besides you can do these things?'

'Everyone can if only they believe it.' Tapping a large Bible on a table, he added, 'The secrets are all here. In God's promises. These promises are real, as real as, and more infinitely solid and substantial than, this table which the materialist so thoroughly believes in.'

In a celebrated public lecture, Carver related how he had been able to call forth from the low mountains of Alabama hundreds of natural colours from clays and other earths, including a rare pigment of deep blue. Egyptologists saw rediscovered in it the fabulous blue of the treasures of Tutankhamen's tomb.

Not long before his death a visitor to Carver's laboratory saw him reach out his long sensitive fingers to a little flower on his workbench.

He paused and after a moment of reflection smiled at his visitor, saying,

'When I touch that flower I am touching infinity. It existed long before there were human beings on this earth and will continue to exist for millions of years to come. Through the flower, I talk to the Infinite which is only a silent force. This is not a physical contact. It is not in the earthquake, wind or fire. It is in the invisible world.

'Many people know this instinctively, and none better than Tennyson when he wrote:

> Flower in the crannied wall,
> I pluck you out of the crannies,
> I hold you here, root and all, in my hand,
> Little flower – but if I could understand
> What you are, root and all, and all in all,
> I should know what God and man is.

What Carver did not know was that Tennyson's lines were spun directly from a Goethe couplet.

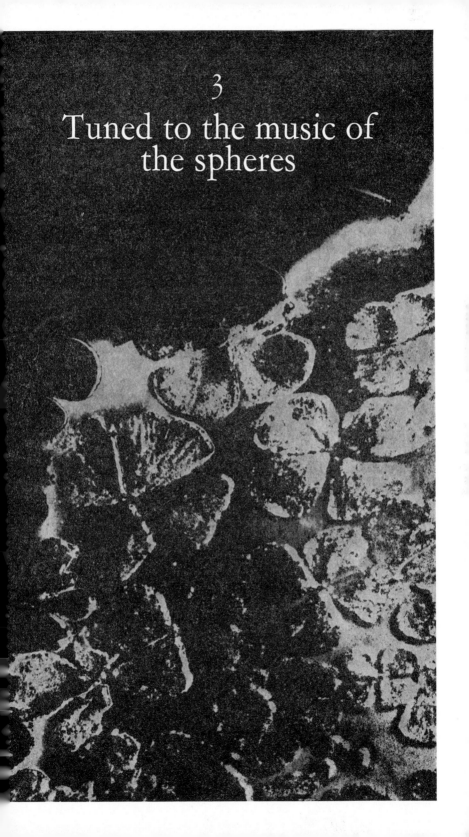

3
Tuned to the music of the spheres

9

The harmonic life of plants

It is said that Lord Krishna, the eighth and principle avatar and incarnation of Vishnu – a member, together with Siva and Brahma, of the Hindu deic trinity – used music to promote enthralling growth and bewitching verdure in the *Kunjavan* of Vrindavan, a city long famous for its saint-musicians. Much later Mian Tan Sen, one of the sages of the court of the famous Moghul emperor, Akbar, was reported to be able to perform such miracles with his songs as to bring on rain or light oil lamps and to vernalize plants and induce them to blossom simply by intoning devotional songs or *ragas* at them. This appealing idea is confirmed in Tamil literature which refers to the eyes, or buds, of sugar-cane growing vigorously in response to the mellifluous buzzing of speckled beetles and to the profuse oozing of sugary nectar from the golden flowers of *Cassia fistula* when serenaded with heart-melting melodies.

All this was familiar to a scholar of ancient Indian history and philosophy, Dr T. C. Singh, who was also head of the department of Botany at Annamalai University, south of Madras. He was interested enough in these old legends to want to make some experiments of his own. From studying the live streaming of protoplasm in the cells of an aquatic plant, *Hydrilla verticillata*, he went on to experiment with an electrically operated tuning fork placed six feet away from the plant. Through a microscope he observed that the fork's note, broadcast for half an hour just before six o'clock in the morning, caused the protoplasm to stream at a speed normally attained only much later, after sunrise. The same acceleration was achieved when a violin was played near the plants, and after a fortnight they were noticeably taller and stronger than the control plants.

Encouraged by this, Singh asked a musician friend of his, Gouri Kumari, to play a *raga* on his *veena*, a fretted lute-like instrument fitted with seven strings, to some balsam plants. Kumari played for twenty-five minutes at the same time every morning as the potted balsams, otherwise known as *Impatiens balsamina*, 'listened' in a normally lit and ventilated room. After a month-long excitatory period, the balsams were set outdoors on the first of November together with several control plants. Given equal amounts of water but no food, all the plants burst into bloom on 22 November and seemed to be growing at the same rate for a week thereafter. However, during the fifth week, the experimental balsams began to shoot ahead and, at the end of December, had produced an average of 72 per cent more leaves than the control plants and had grown 20 per cent higher.

Singh proceeded to adopt a system in which a large number of varieties of healthy potted plants of the same age and vigour were placed, one species at a time, in a semicircle within a radius-distance of ten feet from the place of musical excitation. A similar number of the same species were kept far away. For several weeks just before sunrise each species was subjected to more than half a dozen separate *ragas*, one per experiment, played on the flute, violin, harmonium, and *veena*; the music lasted for half an hour daily and was scaled at a high pitch with four to five principal frequencies between 100 and 600 cycles per second. From all this experimentation Singh was able to state, in the magazine of the Bihar Agricultural College at Sabour, that he had 'proven beyond any shadow of doubt that harmonic sound waves affect the growth, flowering, fruiting, and seed-yields of plants'.

As a result of his success, Singh began to wonder whether sound, properly administered, could spur field-crops to greater yields. From 1960 to 1963 he piped the *Charukesi raga* on a gramophone by means of a loud-speaker to six varieties of early, medium and late paddy rice growing in fields in the state of Madras and in Pondicherry. The resulting harvests ranged consistently from 25 per cent to 60 per cent higher than the regional average. He also was able musically to provoke peanuts and chewing tobacco into producing nearly 50 per cent more than normal. Singh further reported that when the musically unaccompanied *Bharata-Natyam*, India's most ancient dance style, was executed by girls without trinkets on their ankles, the growth of Michaelmas daisies, marigolds, and petunias was very much accelerated, presumably from the rhythm of the footwork transmitted through the earth; their flowering occurred about a fortnight earlier than in controls.

Though the Indians of the subcontinent, both ancient and modern, appear to have been the first to produce a significant effect on plants with music or sound they are by no means the only ones. In 1960 in the agricultural community of Normal, Illinois, a botanist and agricultural researcher, George E. Smith, learned with interest of Singh's experiments while chatting with the farming editor of his local newspaper. Though somewhat sceptical, he planted maize and soyabeans the following spring in two identical greenhouses, both kept precisely at the same level of temperature and humidity. In one of the greenhouses he installed a small record player, and played Gershwin's 'Rhapsody in Blue' twenty-four hours a day. In due course he was able to report that the seedlings in that greenhouse sprouted earlier than those given the silent treatment, and that their stems were thicker, tougher and greener. In many subsequent experiments he got similar results.

Pressed to explain his results, Smith speculated that sound energy might increase molecular activity in the maize, and added that thermometers placed in the plots indicated that soil temperature was inexplicably two degrees higher directly in front of the loud-speaker. He was perplexed that the edges of the leaves of those corn plants growing in the slightly heated earth appeared a little burned but thought this might be due to excessive exposure to musical vibrations. It might be explained, one of his Kansas friends told him, by the fact that high-frequency waves had been used successfully to control insects in stored wheat and that the same wheat planted later, germinated faster than untreated grain.

The publicity given to Smith's experiments resulted in a letter from Peter Belton of the research branch of Canada's Department of Agriculture. Belton told him that he had broadcast ultrasonic waves to control the European corn-borer moth whose larvae extensively damage growing corn:

At first we tested the hearing ability of this moth, and it was obvious that it could hear sounds at about 50,000 cycles. These high-pitched sounds are much like those made by bats, the moth's natural enemy. We planted two plots of corn, each ten feet by twenty, and divided them with sheets of plastic eight feet tall capable of stopping this sound frequency. Then we broadcast the bat-like sound across two of the half-plots from dusk till dawn throughout the period the moths lay their eggs.

He went on to say that nearly fifty per cent of his ripe corn ears were damaged by larvae in the silent plots but only five per cent suffered injury in the plots where the moths had supposedly suspected bats might be lurking. A careful count also revealed sixty per cent fewer larvae in the sound plots, and the corn was three inches taller.

In the mid-1960s the varied efforts of Singh and Smith aroused the curiosity of two researchers at Canada's University of Ottowa, Mary Measures and Pearl Weinberger. Like L. George Lawrence, they were conversant with discoveries by Russians, Canadians, and Americans that ultrasonic frequencies markedly affect the germination and growth of barley, sunflower, spruce, Jack pine, Siberian pea tree, and other seeds and seedlings. The experiments indicated, albeit inexplicably, that enzyme activity and respiration rates in plants and their seeds increased when they were stimulated by ultrasonic frequencies. However, the very frequencies which stimulated some plant species inhibited others. Measures and Weinberger wondered whether specific *audible* frequencies in the sonic range would be as effective as music in enhancing the growth of wheat.

In a series of experiments lasting more than four years, the two biologists exposed the grains and seedlings of spring Marquis and winter Rideau wheat to high-frequency vibrations. They found that, depending on how long the wheat seeds had been vernalized, the plants responded best to a frequency of 5000 cycles a second.

Baffled by their results, the two researchers could not explain why audible sound had resulted in accelerated growth so striking that it seemed to promise to double wheat harvests. The effect could not have been produced by breaking chemical bonds in the seeds, they wrote in the *Canadian Journal of Botany*, since, to do this, one billion times as much energy as was added by the sound frequencies would be required. Instead, they suggested that sound waves might produce a resonant effect in the plant cells, enabling the energy to accumulate and affect the plant's metabolism.

An interesting and eventually very controversial series of experiments on the effects of music on plants was begun in 1968 by Mrs Dorothy Rettallack of Denver. She had enrolled for a degree for which she was required to conduct a laboratory experiment of her own choosing in biology. She vaguely recalled reading an article about George Smith's playing disc jockey to his cornfields and decided to follow his lead. She teamed with a fellow student whose family provided an empty room at home and furnished two groups of plants made up of a philodendron, corn, radishes, geraniums and African violets. Together, they suspended Grolux lights over one group and played the taped musical notes B and D struck on the piano every second, alternating five minutes of those wearisomely repetitive sounds with five minutes of silence. The tape played continuously twelve hours a day. During the first week, the African violets, drooping at the start of the experiment, revived and began to flower. For ten days all the plants seemed to thrive, but at the end of two weeks, the geranium leaves began to yellow. By the end of the third week all the plants, some of which had been actually leaning away from the source of the sound as if blown by a strong wind, had died, with the unaccountable exception of the African violets which somehow remained outwardly unaffected. The control group, allowed to grow in peace, flourished.

When she reported these results to her biology professor, Francis F. Broman, and asked if she could do a more elaborately controlled experiment for credit in his course, he reluctantly consented. 'The idea made me groan a little,' said Broman afterwards, 'but it was novel and I decided to okay it, even though most of the other students laughed out loud.' Broman made available to Dorothy Rettallack three new Biotronic Mark III Environmental Chambers 56 inches long, 26 inches high and 18 inches deep, recently purchased by his department, similar to large box-like home fish aquariums, which allowed for precise control of light, temperature and humidity.

Allotting one chamber for a control group, Mrs Rettallack used the same plants, with the exception of the violets, as in the first experiment, setting them in identical soil and affording them equal amounts of water on schedule. Trying to pinpoint the musical note most conducive to survival, each day she tried an F-note, played unremittingly for eight hours in one chamber and three hours intermittently in another. In the first chamber her plants were stone dead within two weeks. In the second chamber, the plants were much healthier than control plants which had been left in silence in the third chamber.

Mrs Rettallack and Professor Broman were nonplussed by these results. They had no idea what could be causing the disparate reactions and could not help wondering whether the plants had succumbed to fatigue, boredom or simply been 'driven out of their minds'. The experiments aroused a spate of controversy in the biology department, with both students and professors either dismissing the whole effort as spurious, or intrigued by the inexplicable outcome. Two students, following Mrs Rettallack's lead, ran an eight-week experiment on summer squashes, broadcasting music from two Denver radio stations into their chambers, one specializing in heavily accented 'rock', the other in classical music. The squashes were hardly in-different to the two musical forms: those exposed to Haydn, Beethoven, Brahms, Schubert and other eighteenth- and ninteenth-century European music grew *towards* the transistor radio, one of them even twining itself lovingly around it. The other squashes grew away from the rock broadcasts and even tried to climb the slippery walls of their glass cage.

Impressed with her friends' success, Mrs Rettallack ran a series of similar trials early in 1969 with sweet corn, squash, petunias, zinnias, and marigolds; she noticed the same effect. The rock music caused some of the plants at first to grow either abnormally tall and put out excessively small leaves, or remain stunted. Within a fortnight all the marigolds had died, but only six feet away identical marigolds, enjoying the classical strains, were flowering. More interestingly, Mrs Rettallack found that, even during the first week, the rock-stimulated

plants were using much more water than the classically enter-
tained vegetation. Despite this an examination of the roots on
the eighteenth day revealed that soil growth was sparse in the
well watered group, averaging only about an inch, whereas in
the second, it was thick, tangled and about four times as long.

Further experiments in which Mrs Rettallack submitted her
plants to 'acid rock' music, a particularly raucous and percussive type of music that subordinates harmony to volume
and tempo, revealed that all the plants leaned away from this
cacophony. When she rotated all the pots 180 degrees, the
plants leaned decidedly in the opposite direction. This convinced the majority of her critics that the plants were definitely
reacting to the sounds of rock music. Mrs Rettallack guessed
that it might be the percussive component in the music that so
jarred her plants and she therefore started yet another experiment. Selecting the familiar Spanish tune, 'La Paloma', she
played one version of it performed on steel drums to one
chamber of plants and another version played on strings to a
second. The percussion caused a lean of ten degrees *away* from
the vertical, which was very little in comparison with the rock;
but the plants listening to the fiddles leaned fifteen degrees
towards the source of the music. An eighteen-day repeat of the
same experiment using twenty-five plants per chamber including squash from seed, and flowering and leaf type plants from
greenhouses, produced largely similar results

Now she wondered how the plants would be affected by
more sophisticated music of both east and west. She chose some
Bach organ preludes and some classical Indian music played on
the *sitar* by Ravi Shankar. The plants gave positive evidence of
liking Bach since they leaned an unprecedented thirty-five
degrees *towards* the preludes. But even this affirmation was far
exceeded by their reaction to Shankar: in their straining to
reach the source of the classical Indian music they bent more
than half way to the horizontal, at angles of more than sixty
degrees, the nearest one almost embracing the loud-speaker.
Mrs Rettallack's next experiment, the playing of folk and
'country western' music to the plants seemed to produce no
more reaction on them than those in the silent chamber. Perplexed, Mrs Rettallack could only ask: 'Were the plants in

complete harmony with this kind of earthy music or didn't they care one way or the other?' On the other hand various jazz records such as Ellington, Brubeck and Armstrong caused 55 per cent of the plants to lean 15 to 20 degrees towards the loud-speaker, and growth was more abundant than in the silent chamber. Mrs Rettallack also determined that these different musical styles markedly affected the evaporation rate of dis-tilled water inside the chambers. From full beakers, 14 to 17 millilitres evaporated over a given time period in the silent chambers, 20 to 25 millilitres vaporized under the influence of Bach, Shankar and jazz; but, with rock, the disappearance was 55 to 59 millilitres.

Further experiments with the largely twelve-tone music of the neo-classicists showed that its dissonances, unlike those of rock, did not cause the plants to cringe. Root examination showed that the specimens in the rock chamber were scrawny, whereas those subjected to the *avant-garde* music were compar-able to control plants.

The publicity given to Mrs Rettallack's experiments in newspapers and on television produced an avalanche of mail. There was also much hostile criticism and questioning of her conclusions. Professional biologists pooh-poohed this 'pseudo-science' and called it 'pure garbage'. They felt that they had been ridiculed.

Meanwhile, Mrs Rettallack had been thinking along another line. The alarming effect which acid rock music had been shown to have on plants made her wonder whether the nation-wide craze for it among the younger generation might not be extremely deleterious to their development. Her doubts increased when she read an article in the Napa, California, *Register* stating that two doctors had reported to the California Medical Association that of forty-three musicians playing amplified hard rock music, forty-one had suffered permanent hearing loss.

Some of Denver's rock buffs also seemed deeply impressed by Mrs Rettallack's experiments. One long-haired musician, peering into the rock-suffused biotronic chamber, said to her: 'Man, if rock is doing *that* to plants, I wonder what it's doing to me?' His reaction led her on to try to determine if rock music has a particular effect on marijuana, prized for its ability to produce hallucinations in smokers and consumers of its leaves.

While delving in libraries to find material with which to give a philosophical underpinning to her experimental work, she came across a declaration in the *Book of the Secrets of Enoch* that everything in the universe, from the herbs of the field to the stars of the heavens, had its individual spirit or angel. She also noted that Hermes Trismegistus was reputed to have stated that plants had lives, minds and souls, even as did animals, men, and higher beings. Hermes, named 'thrice greatest' by the Greeks, was regarded as the originator of Egyptian art, science, magic, alchemy and religion.

Her research into ancient Chinese sources revealed that 'music, being intimately connected with the essential relations of beings and the vital spirits of men, is tuned to the tone of heaven and earth, and thus expresses all the frequencies of heaven and earth, as several zithers tuned to one tonic.' The priests of pharaonic Egypt, she found, had dedicated seven sacred sounds to the seven major planets to allow for the transmission of their power by the planetary deities to earthly worshippers. These sounds the Christians later incorporated into the ritual chants of their church, one of which has descended to modern times as the well-known *Gloria Patri*, the words of which begin: 'Praise God From Whom All Blessings Flow.'

That musical sound lies within the very hearts of atoms is the contention of a professor of chemistry, now retired after a long career at Johns Hopkins University, Donald Hatch Andrews. In his book, *The Symphony of Life*, Andrews invites readers to join him on an imaginary journey inside a magnified calcium atom taken from the bony tip of his forefinger. Inside the atom, says Andrews, there are shrill tones dozens of octaves above the highest tones of a violin, the music of the atomic nucleus, the tiny particle at the centre of the atom. If one listens closely, he continues, one is aware that this music is far more complex than familiar church music. There are many *dissonant* chords like those found in the music of today's modern composers.

The whole purpose of dissonant music, according to Cyril

Meir Scott, the English composer and theosophist, was to break up established thought forms. Discord – used in its moral sense – can only be destroyed by discord, he says, the reason for this being that the vibrations of beautiful harmonics are too rarefied to touch the comparatively coarse vibrations of all that pertains to a much lower plane. In this book *Music, Its Secret Influence Throughout the Ages*, Scott discusses the important mystical qualities of Richard Wagner's music. A profound spiritual principle lies behind his Ring of the Nibelungen and his aim, says Scott, was to reveal the mystic truth that each individual soul is unified in an all-pervading consciousness. Scott writes that,

In order to form this great scheme, Wagner had to break down many pre-existent musical conventions. In vain did the pedagogues of music look for adherence to their cherished rules of harmony. In vain did they look for correct modulations and resolutions and all the other technical appurtenances of the nineteenth century. In place of them they found unresolved discords, *false relations*, and transitions into keys which had no perceptible connection with the key just abandoned – all was seeming lawlessness, deliberate disregard of rule and precedent – scandalous *Freedom*!

To attain unity by breaking down barriers to unity and so set music free was one of the aims of Stravinsky and Schönberg. The Russian composer Alexander Scriabin also knew that he had a spiritual message to convey musically to the world as a benefit to his fellow humans. Like César Franck before him, the Russian was an exponent of higher worlds and sought to build a musical bridge between the angels, or *devas*, and man. Cyril Scott considered that he was the first European composer to combine a theoretical knowledge of ancient occult mysteries with tonal art. During the last fifteen years of his life before he died at forty-three, two years before the outbreak of the Russian revolution, Scriabin was working on his *Mysterium*, a masterpiece which was to combine music with colours projected on a huge screen behind the orchestra and exotic fragrances wafted into the concert hall. By harmonizing aural, visual and olfactory vibrations Scriabin sought to make of his audience 'experimental initiates' bringing them ecstatic visions and loosening the bonds which held their true selves in their physical encasements, just as the adepts of Heliopolis and other occult temples were reported to have done thousands of years ago.

So far, no researcher, with the exception of Hans Kayser, the German author of *Harmonica Plantarum* and other mathematically learned books on the relation of sound intervals to the growth of plants, seems to have become interested in the octaval correspondences between the shapes of plants and musical notes. Kayser observed that if one projects all tones within the space of one octave, in the same manner that the astronomer and astrologer Johannes Kepler worked out in his *Harmonia Mundi* for the solar planetary system, and if one sketches their angles in a specific way, one obtains the prototype of leaf form. The interval of the octave, the basis for music-making and indeed all sensation, thus contains within itself the form of the leaf.

Not only does this observation lend new psychological support to Goethe's metamorphosis of plants, which derive their development from the leaf form, but it casts new light on the ingenious classificatory system developed by Linnaeus. When one considers, says Kayser, that a passion-flower contains two ratios, a *five*-part petal and stamen arrangement and a *three*-part pistil, even if one rejects a logically reasoning intelligence, one must admit that in the soul of plants are certain form-carrying prototypes – in the passion flower's case musical thirds and fifths – which work, as in music, to shape the blossom forms as intervals. It is from this point of view that Linnaeus's system acquires a 'psychic' rehabilitation, concludes Kayser, for, with his 'sexual' classification scheme, the famous Swedish botanist hit on the psychic nerve of plants.

What humans are able to perceive consciously with their limited senses is but a minute fraction of what vibrationally affects them. The so-called scentless daisy may be as sweet-smelling as the rose – had people the olfactory ability to detect the particles the daisy throws off. Efforts to prove that a given sonic vibration will affect plants, or man, may, far from resolving the interactions of music and life, be only unravelling a wondrously resonating tapestry of influences into its separate, unrelated threads.

10

Plants and electromagnetism

If the response of plants to musical and other sounds is not yet sufficiently understood, the same may be said of their reactions to wavelengths that have come to be called electromagnetic. Man is still in the dark as to which of his countless devices that produce waves of electromagnetic energy are beneficial and which deleterious to living things.

It was the eighteenth-century French writer and astronomer, Jean-Jacques Dertous de Mairan, who began a study of the idea that the setting sun appeared to be causing his sensitive *Mimosa pudica* to fold their leaves just as they did when touched by his hand. He did not instantly assume that they were going to sleep as darkness fell. Instead he waited for the sun to rise again and put two of the mimosas in a pitch-dark closet. At noon he noticed that their leaves remained wide open; but at sunset they shut just as promptly as the ones on the drawing-room table. The plants, concluded Mairan, must be able to 'sense' the sun without 'seeing' it. He was unable to account for this and in his report to the French Academy he lamely suggested that his plants must be under the influence of *an unknown factor in the universe*.

Some two and a half centuries later Dr John Ott, who runs the Environmental Health and Light Research Institute at Sarasota, Florida, was able to confirm Mairan's observations. He began to speculate on whether this 'unknown energy' could penetrate a massive amount of earth, the only shield known to be able to block so-called 'cosmic radiation'. In order to test this he took six mimosas down a mine-shaft at noon to a point 650 feet beneath the earth's surface. Unlike those in the dark closet, Ott's subterranean specimens immediately closed their leaves without waiting for sunset; they did so even when incandescent bulbs were lit all around them. Except for the fact that he related the phenomenon to electromagnetism, of which little was known in Mairan's time, Ott was as much 'in the dark' about the cause of it as had been his eighteenth-century French predecessor.

All that Mairan and his contemporaries knew about electricity was what the Greeks had passed on to them concerning the properties of amber, or *electron* as they called it, which when vigorously rubbed attracted a feather or a piece of straw. They knew, too, that lodestone, a black ferrous oxide, could exert an equally inexplicable attraction on iron filings. Since this material was found in a region of Asia Minor called Magnesia, it was dubbed *Magnes Lithos*, or Magnesian Stone, a term shortened to *magnes* in Latin and to magnet in English.

The first man to link electricity and magnetism was the sixteenth-century savant, William Gilbert, whose medical skill and philosophical erudition won him appointment as personal physician to Queen Elizabeth I. Announcing that the planet itself was a globular magnet, Gilbert attributed to the lodestone a 'soul', since it was 'part and choice offspring of its animate mother, the earth'. Gilbert also discovered that materials other than amber could be caused to attract light objects if friction was applied to them. He designated them 'electrics' and coined the term 'electric force'. For centuries the forces of attraction in amber and lodestone were thought to be 'penetrating etheric fluids' (whatever they might be), emitted by the substances. Even fifty years after Mairan's experiments, Joseph Priestley, known principally as the discoverer of oxygen, wrote in his popular textbook on electricity:

The earth and all the bodies we are acquainted with, without exception are supposed to contain a certain quantity of an exceedingly elastic and subtle fluid which philosophers have agreed to term electric. The moment any body becomes possessed of more or less than its natural quantity, very remarkable effects arise from it. The body is said to be electrified and is capable of exhibiting appearances which are ascribed to the power of electricity.

By the twentieth century real knowledge about magnetism had progressed very little. In a text published soon after the Second World War, by Chicago's Museum of Science and

Industry, it is stated that human beings still do not know why the earth is a magnet, how magnetic materials can be mechanically affected by other magnets at a distance from them, why electric currents have magnetic fields about them or even why tiny atoms of matter, small as they are, occupy such empty but prodigious volumes of field-packed space. Three and a half centuries have elapsed since Gilbert's famous *De Magnete* was published, and yet the eminent Dr Jeno Barnothy wrote in 1964 that 'many theories were proposed to explain the origin of geomagnetism but none of these theories are entirely satisfactory'.

The same can be said for contemporary physics which has substituted for the idea of an 'etheric fluid' a spectrum of undulating or electromagnetic radiations, ranging from enormous macropulsations lasting several hundred thousand years each with wavelengths millions of miles long to super-rapid energy pulses alternating 10,000,000,000,000,000,000,000 times a second with wavelengths measuring an infinitesimal 10 billionths of a centimetre. The first type is associated with such phenomena as the reversal of the earth's magnetic field, the second with the collision of atoms, usually those of helium and hydrogen, moving at incredibly high speeds and converted to radiant energy termed 'cosmic rays'. In between lie countless bands of energy waves including gamma rays, originating in the nuclei of atoms, X-rays, originating in their shells, a collection of frequencies which because they can be perceived with the eye are called light, and those used in radio, television, radar and a growing multitude of applications from space research to electronic cooking.

The electromagnetic waves differ from sound waves in that they can travel through a vacuum, although no one has yet explained how they do so. Many scientists have concentrated on the physical properties of electromagnetism and how these might be applied to mechanical devices, but few have paid any attention over the years to how and why electromagnetic waves might affect living things.

One of the first men to experiment along this line was an independent-minded Scot, Maimbray, for whom no Christian name is known. In 1746 he put two myrtle shrubs next to an electrical conductor in Edinburgh and was amazed to see the shrubs grow three-inch branches and buds at a time when most other plants were dormant.

In 1749, Jean Antoine Nollet, a French abbot and physics tutor to the dauphin, was informed by a German physicist in Wittenberg that water, which normally issued drop by drop from a capillary tube, would run out in a constant stream if the tube were electrified. After repeating the German's experiments and adding some of his own, Nollet, as he later put it, 'began to believe that this electrical virtue employed in a certain manner might have some remarkable effect on organized bodies which can be looked upon, in some way, as hydraulic machines prepared by nature itself'.

He discovered that plants placed in metallic pots next to a conductor increased their rate of transpiration, and that seeds grown in electrified containers grew more rapidly than normal. His conclusion that electricity could profoundly affect the growth functions of life forms was formulated a few years before the famous occasion when Benjamin Franklin flew a kite during stormy weather and collected a charge of electricity from lightning. The bolt struck a metal point on the kite's frame with the result that energy ran down the kite's wet string into a Leyden bottle. This bottle was a device developed in 1746 at the University of Leyden by two researchers who were under the impression that electricity was a fluid. They hoped to fill a glass jar with it by means of a wire and an electrostatic generator; but no matter what they did, they could never detect electricity in the jar when their electric machine stopped turning, even when the jar was filled with water. When one of them grabbed the water-filled jar connected to the electric machine in one hand and simultaneously reached to remove the wire connected to the machine with the other, he felt a tremendous blow on the chest as he touched the wire and dropped the jar which shattered. Thus it was discovered that the water in the jar actually did contain electricity which could be discharged in one violent burst of energy.

The next efforts to adapt atmospheric electricity to the fructification of plants came in Italy when in 1770 Professor Gardini stretched a number of wires above a productive monastery garden in Turin. Within a short time, many of the plants began to wither and die. When the monks dismantled the wire, the garden revived. Gardini hypothesized that either the plants had been deprived of a natural supply of electricity necessary to their growth or that they had received an overdose.

When Gardini heard from France that the brothers Joseph-Michel and Jacques-Etienne Montgolfier had sent aloft an enormous balloon filled with heated air to carry two passengers on a 10-kilometre 25-minute trip over Paris, he recommended that this new invention be applied practically to horticulture by attaching a long wire to it along which electricity could be conducted from great heights into fields and gardens below.

These French and Italian reports caused little stir among the scientific pundits of the day who, even then, were beginning to pay more attention to the effects of electricity on inert, rather than on living, bodies. Nor were they impressed when yet another clergyman, Abbé Bertholon, came out in 1783 with a full-scale treatise, *De l'Electricité des Végétaux*.

Bertholon, who was considered something of a sorcerer, asked his gardener to stand on a slab of insulating material and sprinkle vegetables from an electrified watering can. The result was that his lettuces grew to an extraordinary size. He also invented what he called an 'electrovegetometer' to collect atmospheric electricity by means of an antenna, and pass it through plants growing in a field. He wrote that,

This instrument is applicable to all kinds of vegetal production, everywhere, in all weather; and its utility and efficacity cannot be ignored or doubted except by timid souls who are not inspired by discoveries and who will never push back the barriers of the sciences but will remain eternally within the narrow confines of a cowardly pusillanimity which, to palliate it, is too often given the name of prudence.

In his conclusion, the abbot boldly suggested that one day the best fertilizer for plants will come in electrical form 'free from the sky'.

The exciting notion that living things interacted and indeed were imbued with electricity advanced a giant step when in

November 1780, the wife of a Bolognese anatomist, Luigi Galvani, accidentally discovered that a machine used to generate static electricity caused the severed leg of a frog to jump spasmodically. When his attention was called to it, Galvani instantly wondered whether electricity was not in fact a manifestation of life, and wrote in his work-book: 'The electrical fluid should be considered a means to excite nervo-muscular force.'

For the next six years Galvani worked on the effects on muscular motion of electricity until he happened accidentally to discover that his frogs' legs would twitch just as well without the application of an electric charge if the copper wires they hung from were blown by the wind against an iron railing. Realizing that the electricity in the three-part circuit had to be coming from the legs or the metals, Galvani, who believed it to be a living rather than a dead force, decided it was associated with the animal tissue and ascribed the reaction to a vital fluid or energy in the frogs' bodies which he termed 'animal electricity'.

Galvani's findings at first received warm support from his compatriot Alessandro Volta, a physicist at the University of Pavia in the Duchy of Milan. But when Volta repeated Galvani's experiments and found he could elicit the electrical effect only when two different metals were used, he wrote to Abbot Tommaselli that it was obvious that the electricity came, not from the frogs' legs, but from 'the simple application of two metals of different quality'. Concentrating on the electrical properties of metals, Volta was led in 1800 to the invention of a pile of alternating zinc and copper discs with a piece of wet paper sandwiched between each two layers. Instantly chargeable, it could be used to produce electric current at will, not only once, like the Leyden jar, but thousands of times, and thus for the first time researchers were freed from their dependence on static or natural electricity. This first ancestor of our electric storage cell disclosed an artificial dynamic or kinetic electricity, which all but obliterated Galvani's notion of a special vital energy in living tissues.

Though at first Volta had accepted Galvani's findings, he later wrote: 'If we deprive animal organs of any electrical activity of their own and abandon this attractive idea which Galvani's beautiful experiments suggested, these organs can be regarded simply as electrometers of a new kind and of a marvellous sensitivity'. Despite Galvani's prophetic assertion, just before his death, that one day the analysis of all the necessary physiological aspects of his experiments 'would provide better knowledge of the nature of the life forces, their different duration, according to variations in sex, age, temperament, illnesses, and even the very constitution of the atmosphere', scientists neglected his theories and denied them in practice.

A few years earlier, unknown to Galvani, the Hungarian Jesuit Maximilian Hell had revived Gilbert's idea of 'soul-like' characteristics in the lodestone being transmitted to ferrous metals; and with this idea had invented a singular arrangement of magnetized steel plates to cure his own persistent rheumatism. His friend the Viennese physician Franz Anton Mesmer, who picked up an interest in magnetism by reading Paracelsus, was impressed with Hell's subsequent cures of a variety of afflictions in others, and embarked on a long series of experiments to check them. In so doing Mesmer became convinced that living matter had a property susceptible to being acted upon by 'earthly and celestial magnetic forces', which in 1779 he called 'animal magnetism' and to which he devoted a doctoral thesis entitled 'The Influence of the Planets on the Human Body'. Learning that a Swiss priest, J. J. Gassner, was healing patients by touch, Mesmer successfully adopted Gassner's technique and proclaimed that some people, himself included, were better endowed with the 'magnetic' force than others.

Though it seemed that these startling discoveries of bioelectrical and biomagnetic energy might open the door to a new age of research which could unite physics with medicine and physiology, the door was again slammed shut for more than a century. Mesmer's success in treating cases, where others had failed, provoked his Viennese medical colleagues to jealousy. Attributing his cures to witchcraft and the devil, they organized a commission to investigate his claims. When the commission reported unfavourably, Mesmer was expelled from the medical faculty and told to give up his practice. He moved to Paris in 1778 where he found 'people more enlightened and less indifferent to new discoveries'. But it was not long before the French physicians grew as angry and jealous as had their Austrian counterparts. Their clamour forced the king to appoint a Royal Commission to investigate Mesmer's claims, despite the fact that the eminent physician D'Eslon had championed Mesmer's scientific contribution as 'one of the most important of our age'. The commission returned a verdict that 'animal magnetism is non-existent and can have no salubrious effect', Mesmer was held up to public ridicule, and his popularity began to wane. He retired to Switzerland where one year before his death in 1815, he completed his most important work: *Mesmerism or the System of Reciprocal Influences; or The Theory and Practice of Animal Magnetism*.

In 1820, Hans Christian Oersted, a Danish scientist, found that a compass needle placed near a current-carrying wire always turned so that the needle became perpendicular to the wire. When the current was reversed, the compass needle pointed in the opposite direction. The fact that a force could act on the compass needle indicated that a magnetic field existed in the space around the wire. This led to one of the most profitable discoveries in the history of science when Michael Faraday in England and Joseph Henry in the United States independently realized the opposite phenomenon was equally valid, that a magnetic field could induce an electric current if the wire were moved through it. Thus the 'generator' was invented, and with it a whole new world of electrical appliances.

Today, books on what man can *do* with electricity fill thousands of shelves in this world's libraries, but what electricity *is* and why it functions are as much a mystery as they were in Priestley's day. Modern scientists still have no idea of the composition of electromagnetic waves. They simply use them for radio, radar, television and toasters.

Because of such a lopsided concentration on the mechanical properties of electromagnetism, only a corporal's guard of individuals has paid attention over the years to how and why electromagnetism might affect living things. A notable exception was Baron Karl von Reichenbach, a German scientist from Tübingen who in 1845 had discovered wood-tar products, including creosote, used for the preservation of above-ground fencing and underwater pilings. He became aware that specially gifted persons whom he termed 'sensitives' could actually see a strange energy emanating from all living things and even from the ends of bar magnets; this energy he called *Odyle* or *Od*. But, though his works were translated into English by a distinguished medical doctor, William Gregory, appointed professor of chemistry at the University of Edinburgh in 1844, as *Researches into the Forces of Magnetism, Electricity, Heat and Light in Relation to the Force of Life*, his attempts to prove its existence to his physicist contemporaries in England and on the continent were rejected out of hand.

Reichenbach indicated the reason why his 'odic force' was spurned when he wrote: 'Whenever I began to touch on the subject, I felt at once that I was harping on a string of an unpleasant tone. They coupled Od and sensitivity in their minds with so-called "animal magnetism" and "Mesmerism" and with that all sympathy was at an end.' The coupling was entirely unjustified, in that Reichenbach had clearly stated that though the mysterious odic force might resemble animal magnetism and was associated with it, it also could exist quite independently.

Years later, Wilhelm Reich contended that

the energy with which the ancient Greeks and the moderns since Gilbert were dealing was a basically different energy from that with which the physicists are dealing since Volta and Faraday, one obtained by the movement of wires in magnetic fields; different not only with regard to the principle of its production, but *fundamentally* different.

Reich believed that the ancient Greeks, with the principle of friction, had discovered the mysterious energy to which he gave the name 'orgone', so similar to Reichenbach's Od and to the ether of the ancients. Reich claimed that orgone is the medium in which light moves, and the medium for electromagnetic and gravitational activity, that it fills all space, though in different degrees and concentration, and is even present in vacuums. He considered it the basic link between inorganic and organic matter. By the 1960s, shortly after Reich's death, the evidence for the electrical basis of organisms was becoming overwhelming. As D. S. Halacy, a writer on orthodox science, stated it simply: 'The flow of electrons is basic to practically all life processes.'

The difficulties encountered in the period between Reichenbach and Reich stemmed partly from the vogue in science for taking things apart, rather than studying them as functioning wholes. Simultaneously the gulf widened between workers in what came to be known as the 'life sciences' and physicists who believed only what they could see or instrumentally measure. Meanwhile, chemistry concentrated on increasingly varied and smaller separate entities which, in their artificial re-combination, offered a cornucopia of fascinating new products.

The first artificial synthesis in the laboratory of an organic substance, urea, seemed to destroy the idea that there was a special 'vital' aspect in living things. The discovery of cells, the purported biological counterparts of the atoms of classical Greek philosophy, suggested that plants, animals and man himself were merely different associations of those building blocks or chemical aggregates, a notion enhanced by the succeeding discoveries of subcellular chromosomes, genes, and the 'ultimate' component, DNA. In the new climate, few took the initiative to delve deeper into the effects of electromagnetism on life. Nevertheless, individualistic mavericks occasionally brought forward an idea on how plants might respond to external cosmic forces and thus kept the findings of Nollet and Bertholon from expiring.

Across the Atlantic, William Ross, testing claims by the Marquis of Anglesey that seeds sprouted faster when electrified, planted cucumbers in a mixture of black manganese oxide, table salt, and clean sand watered with dilute sulphuric acid. When he applied an electric current to the mixture, the seeds sprouted well ahead of those in a similar but non-electrified mixture. Ross also buried a copper plate measuring fourteen inches by five feet under the end of three 100-foot long rows of potatoes and a zinc plate of equal size under the opposite end.

Connecting a copper wire on the surface of the ground to both plates, he created a weak battery. When he harvested the stimulated tubers, they averaged two and a half inches in diameter, whereas those in a control plot were less than the thumb-nail size of a narrowfat pea.

Believing that he had an important commercial application, Ross applied for a patent and sent in a report published by the U.S. Patent Office as 'Galvanic Experiments on Vegetation' in 1844.

A year later, the first issue of the London *Journal of the Horticultural Society* published a long account of the 'Influence of Electricity on Vegetation' by an agronomist, Edward Solly who, like Gardini, suspended wires in the air over garden plots, and, like Ross, tried burying them under the soil. But of Solly's seventy experiments with various grains, vegetables, and flowers, only nineteen were of any benefit, and nearly as many were harmful.

The conflicting results of these researchers made it obvious that the amount, quality and duration of electrical stimulation was of crucial importance to each form of vegetal life. But since physicists lacked instrumentation to measure its specific effects, and still knew little about how electricity, artificial or atmospheric, actually operated on plants, the experimental field was left to persistently curious horticulturalists or out-and-out cranks. Still, various observations on how vegetation had an electric quality continued to be recorded.

In 1859 an issue of the London *Gardeners' Chronicle* published a report of light flashes passing from one scarlet verbena to another and noted that the phenomenon could best be seen during crepuscular periods when a thunderstorm approached after a long spell of dry weather. This validated Goethe's discovery that the flowers of oriental poppies could be seen flashing at dusk.

It was not until the latter part of the century that new vistas were opened in Germany on to the exact nature of the electricity in the air. Julius Elster and Hans Geitel were the inventors of the photo-electric cell and first metered ultra-violet light. They also specialized in the spontaneous emission of radiation from inorganic substances which was coming to be called radioactivity. They now began a vast study of atmospheric electricity, which disclosed that the soil of the earth continually emits electrically charged particles into the air. Called *ions* from the neuter present participle of the Greek verb, *ienai*, meaning 'to go', these particles were either atoms, groups of atoms, or molecules regarded as having a net positive or negative charge by gaining or losing electrons.

Because on a clear day in good weather the earth has a negative electrical charge while the atmosphere is positive, electrons stream skyward from the soil and plants. During storms the polarity is reversed, the earth becoming positive and the base of the cloud layer negative. Because there are at any time an estimated 3,000 to 4,000 'electrical' storms raging over the surface of the globe, the charges lost by the earth in those areas favoured by balmy weather are thus replaced and a seesawing balance of electrical gradients is maintained. As a result of the ever-present flow of electricity it has been found that the voltage, or electric pressure, increases at higher altitudes. The chief difficulty in harnessing this vast reservoir of energy and putting it to work is said to be lack of precise knowledge of how it functions and of the laws which govern its operations.

A new assault on applying atmospheric electricity to the growth of plants began when a Finnish scientist called Selim Lemström made four expeditions to the subpolar regions of Spitzbergen, northern Norway and Lapland from 1868 to 1884. Lemström was an expert on polar light and earth magnetism, and he had a theory that the luxuriant vegetation in those latitudes could be attributed to what he called 'that violent electrical manifestation, the *Aurora Borealis*,' and not to the long summer days as popularly supposed.

It had been known from the time of Benjamin Franklin that sharp points were especially attractive to atmospheric electricity, and this led to the invention of the lightning-conductor. Lemström reasoned therefore that 'the sharp points of plants acted like lightning-conductors to collect atmospheric electricity and facilitate the exchange of charges of the air and ground'.

His studies of the rings of fir trees confirmed that the

annual growth fully correlated with periods of high aurora and sun-spot activity, the effects being most pronounced as one travelled north.

When he came home to verify these observations by experimentation, Lemström connected a series of flowers in metal pots to a static generator by an overhead network of wires sixteen inches above them and a pole set into the soil as a ground. Other pots he 'left to nature'. After eight weeks, the electrified plants showed gains in weight of nearly fifty per cent over their electrically deprived neighbours. When he transferred his apparatus into a garden he not only more than doubled the yield of strawberries but found them to be much sweeter; his harvest from barley plants increased by one third.

In a long series of experiments conducted as far south as Burgundy, Lemström's results varied not only with specific vegetables, fruits and cereals but also with temperature, moisture and the natural fertility and manuring of the soil. He reported his success in 1902 in a book *Electrocultur*, published in Berlin, and the term was included in the forthcoming edition of L. H. Bailey's *Standard Encyclopedia of Horticulture*.

The English translation of his book, entitled *Electricity in Horticulture and Agriculture*, which appeared in London two years after the German original, aroused the interest of the great physicist and believer in psychical research, Sir Oliver Lodge. Lodge solved Lemström's time-consuming difficulties by moving his wire network upwards as his plants grew; to allow the movement of people, animals and farm equipment through his electrified fields, he suspended his grid on insulators attached to high poles and this created an electromagnetic field.

During one growing season Lodge was able to increase the per-acre yield of Canadian Red Fife wheat by forty per cent and was pleased that the bakers who ground it to flour said it produced bread of a far better quality than that made from the wheat they were normally furnished.

After working with Lodge, his collaborator, John Newman, adapted the system to achieve over twenty per cent increase in wheat yields in Evesham, England, and in potatoes dug at Dumfries, Scotland. Newman's strawberries were not only vastly more productive than non-electrified equivalents but, like Lemström's, were more succulent and sweet; his sugar beets tested out as having greater than normal sugar content. Of passing interest, Newman published his report, not in a botanical journal, but in the fifth edition of the *Standard Handbook for Electrical Engineers* brought out by McGraw-Hill in New York. Ever since it has been more the engineering fraternity than the plant men who have assiduously pursued electrocultural efforts.

Force fields, humans and plants

Because their profession calls upon them for practical solutions to problems no matter how difficult they appear at first glance, engineers, unlike researchers in pure science, are less concerned with *why* or *how* something works than with *whether* it will work. This attitude frees them from the shackles of theory, which in the history of science has often caused pedants to disregard the brilliant new findings of geniuses because there was no theoretical basis to support them.

When an ingenious Hungarian refugee, Joseph Molitorisz, who escaped to the United States from his Soviet-occupied homeland and took an engineering degree, came across Abbé Nollet's ideas about electro-osmosis, he started thinking about how the Frenchman's efforts could be applied to agricultural problems. He puzzled over the idea that a redwood can raise its sap more than three hundred feet whereas the best man-designed suction pump can pull water up less than a tenth of that distance. There was evidently something about trees and electricity that defied laws of hydrodynamics in standard engineering. At a Californian agricultural research station run by the U.S. Government, Molitorisz decided to adapt what he had learned from Nollet to citrus orchards. In an early experiment he ran an electric current through citrus seedlings. When the current flowed in one direction, the growth of the tiny trees was speeded up but when the direction was reversed, the seedlings shrivelled. Evidently, the electricity somehow abetted the natural flow of electric current present in the plants or, when reversed, blocked it. In another experiment, partly inspired by his reading of Abbé Bertholon, Molitorisz applied a 58-volt current to six branches of an orange tree but left another six branches untouched, with the result that within eighteen hours, sap was freely circulating in the 'powered' branches while in the untouched branches there was very little sap flow. The harvesting of oranges is laborious because all the fruit does not ripen simultaneously and must be hand-picked over many days if it is not to rot on the branches. Molitorisz worked on the idea that picking costs might be reduced if he could get a tree to drop its ripe fruit through electrical stimulation. And this indeed he did. By wiring an orange tree to a source of direct current, he got it to drop its ripe fruit while the green oranges remained on its branches. Unfortunately even with this success he could not get funds for additional experimentation. However, Molitorisz, who has also invented an 'electrical flower pot', which can keep flowers alive much longer than is normally possible, believes that one day it will be easy to harvest the fruit of an entire citrus orchard by electricity and it will no longer be necessary to raise the pickers into the trees.

In Pennsylvania, another engineer, Dr Larry E. Murr, artificially simulated in his laboratory the electrical conditions of short thunderstorms and long periods of rainy weather. After seven years of work in his man-made 'mini-climate' he was able to get significant increases in plant growth by carefully regulating the voltage field strength over plants in lucite pots set on an aluminium plate to serve as one electrode, the other supplied by an aluminium wire mesh hung from insulating poles. Other voltages, he found, severely damaged the leaves of plants. Murr reached the conclusion that:

Whether or not we can augment acreage yield by maintaining artificially devised electric fields over crop areas is still a matter for speculation. The cost of achieving such gains by large-scale outdoor installations might be much more than they are worth. Nevertheless, the possibility exists.

Dr George Starr White, who published a book entitled *Cosmo-electric Culture*, discovered that metals like iron and tin could facilitate plant growth if bright pieces were dangled from fruit trees. His evidence was corroborated by Randall Groves Hay, an industrial engineer from Jenkintown, New Jersey. Where Hay attached metallic Christmas tree balls to tomato plants, they would bear their fruits earlier than normal. In his own words: 'At first, my wife would not let me hang the balls on the plants because she said it would look just too ridiculous. But when fifteen potted tomatoes hung with balls started to ripen in cold, inclement weather long before those of any other grower, she allowed me to continue.'

James Lee Scribner, an electronic engineer from South Carolina, experimented with the electronic bathing of seeds. He wired an aluminium pot to an ordinary electric outlet, then he spread between the electrodes a wet metallic mix made up of millions of zinc and copper particles. When it dried, electricity was able to filter between the electrode strips. A butter-bean planted in the aluminium pot grew to the amazing height of twenty-two feet, though such beans normally never exceed two feet. At maturity it produced *two bushels* of delicious beans. Scribner believes that:

It is the electron that is responsible before the photosynthesis can take place, for it is the electron that magnetizes the chlorophyll in the plant cell that makes it possible for the photon to assert itself and become a part of the plant in the form of solar energy. It is also this magnetism that draws the molecules of oxygen into the ever expanding chlorophyll cells of the plant, and so we must assume that moisture is in no way integrated into the plant through any absorption process whatsoever, for the integration of moisture is purely an electronic one. The so-called root pressure (moisture droplets) appearing on plant surfaces is not root pressure at all, but an abundance of electrons working with the rather excessive water energy in the bed.

In the Soviet Union, a commercial processing plant to treat seeds with electrical energy with a two-ton per hour capacity was reported in 1963. Results indicated that yields for the green mass of corn jumped 15–20 per cent over the average, oats and barley 10–15 per cent, peas 13 per cent and buckwheat 8–10 per cent. What promise this pilot project might hold to relieve Russia's persistent grain shortages was not mentioned. To an agricultural industry which has been forced to rely almost wholly on artificially produced chemicals not only to fertilize its soil but also to rid its crops of marauding pests, the electrocultural horizons being opened up afresh by engineers seemed dubious and unnecessary. This may explain why almost no money has been made available for more investigation.

A former director of the United States Department of Agriculture's Division of Agricultural Engineering Research, E. G. McKibben, complained as far back as 1962 that this policy was extremely short-sighted. In an address to the American Society of Agricultural Engineers McKibben said:

'The importance and the possibilities of the application of electromagnetic energy in its many forms to agriculture are limited only by the creative imagination and physical resources available. Electromagnetic energy is probably the most basic form. It, or something closely related to it, appears to be the basic substance of all energy and all matter and the essential fabric of all plant and animal life.'

McKibbon stressed that as yet undreamed achievements might be reasonably attained if only much more support was put behind electrocultural efforts but his plea has thus far fallen on deaf ears.

Even before McKibben made his appeal, brand new discoveries about the influence of magnetism on vegetation were being made. In 1960 L. J. Audus, a professor of botany at London University's Bedford College, while trying to find out exactly how plants respond to gravity, stumbled on to the fact that their roots are sensitive to magnetic fields. His pioneering paper 'Magnetotropism, a New Plant Growth Response' appeared in *Nature*. Almost simultaneously, two Russians, A. V. Krylov and G. A. Tarakanova, showed that tomatoes ripen faster nearer the south than the north pole of a magnet, but they were unable to explain the reason for it in their report.

In Canada, Dr U. J. Pittman, of the Agricultural Research Station in Lethbridge, Alberta, observed that all across the North American continent the roots of various domestic and wild cereal grains, as well as those of a number of species of weeds, consistently aligned themselves in a north-south plane parallel to the horizontal force of the earth's magnetic field. He also found that germination of certain cereals could be speeded up if their long axes and embryo ends were orientated towards the north magnetic pole. 'When Granny insisted that her pumpkin seeds be planted pointing north,' wrote Pittman in *Crops and Soils Magazine*, 'she may have been dead right!'

Yet another engineer, Dr H. Len Cox of Denver, Colorado, became interested in the idea of electroculture. There were large deposits of a useless but magnetizable ferrous ore called magnetite in near-by Wyoming, and he was able to bring back a lorry load and grind it into powder. After charging it in a magnetic field of undisclosed strength and mixing it with trace minerals, he sifted it into the soil of a garden plot where it would come into contact with the roots of red and white radishes. Though the green tops of the maturing plants seemed no different from similar radishes allowed to grow normally in a neighbouring plot, the activated radishes, when pulled from the ground, were on an average twice as large as the controls. Also their tap-roots were three to four times as long, which indicated that root stimulation seemed to have produced the increased growth. The same remarkable effect was shown in turnips, carrots, beans, lettuces and broccoli. Such was his success that Cox formed his Electroculture Corporation in 1970 in order to sell his product. Users reported that they not only got much larger yields but that the vegetables produced had a far better flavour, thus corroborating Lemström's report on his strawberries and Sir Oliver Lodge's bakers' comments on their bread. Cox cannot explain how the activator works, nor why the magnetized powder produces no results when shaken into flowerpots or greenhouse seed-boxes. It seems that the ferrous oxide, which when magnetized is called lodestone, radiates its power only when in contact with what Gilbert, in his day, called 'its animate mother', the earth itself.

In the early 1920s Georges Lakhovsky, a Russian-born engineer living in Paris, began to write a series of books which suggested that the basis of life was not matter but immaterial vibrations associated with it. 'Every living thing emits radiations', stressed Lakhovsky who advanced the revolutionary new theory that cells, the essential organic units of all living things, were electromagnetic radiators capable, like wireless sets, of emitting and absorbing high frequency waves.

The essence of Lakhovsky's theory was that cells are microscopic oscillating circuits. In electrical parlance such an oscillating circuit requires two basic elements: a capacitor, or source of stored electric charge, and a coil of wire. As the current from the current flows back and forth between one end of the wire and the other, it creates a magnetic field which oscillates at a certain frequency, or so many times per second. If such a circuit is greatly reduced in size, very high frequencies are obtained; Lakhovsky believed this to be what occurs in the microscropically tiny nuclei of living cells. In the small twisted filaments within cellular nuclei Lakhovsky descried the analogues to electrical circuits.

In his *Le Secret de la Vie*, published in 1925, Lakhovsky set forth a number of startling experiments upholding the idea that disease was a matter of disequilibrium in cellular oscillation. The fight between healthy cells and pathogens such as bacteria or viruses was a 'war of radiations'. If the radiations of the microbes were stronger, cells began to oscillate aperiodically and became 'diseased'. When they ceased to oscillate, they died. If the cellular radiations gained ascendance, the microbes were killed. In order that a diseased cell be restored to health, Lakhovsky felt it should be treated by means of a radiation of appropriate frequency.

In 1923, Lakhovsky designed an electrical apparatus emitting very short waves (with lengths of two to ten metres) which he called a radio-cellulo-oscillator. In the surgical clinic of the famous Salpetrière hospital in Paris he inoculated geraniums with cancer-producing bacteria. When the plants had developed tumours the size of cherry stones, one of them was exposed to radiation from the oscillator. During the first days the tumour grew rapidly, but after two weeks it suddenly began to shrink and die; after a second two-week period it fell off the afflicted plant. Other geraniums treated over different time periods also shed their cancers under the effect of oscillator radiations.

Lakhovsky saw these cures as supporting his theory. The cancer had been overcome by the enhancement of the normal oscillations of healthy cells in the geraniums. This was quite opposite to the approach of the radium specialists who proposed that the cancer cells be destroyed by external radiation.

In the development of his theory Lakhovsky was faced with the problem of the origin of the energy necessary for the normal production and maintenance of cellular oscillations. It did not seem probable that the energy was produced within cells any more than the energy in an electric battery or a steam engine was internally produced. He therefore came to the conclusion that the energy was externally derived from cosmic radiation.

To try to establish the cosmic origin of the energy Lakhovsky decided to dispense with the device he had invented to produce artificial rays and tap natural energy from space. In January 1925 he picked one of a series of geraniums previously inoculated with cancer and surrounded it with a circular copper spiral thirty centimetres in diameter, its two unjoined ends fixed in an ebonite support. After several weeks he found that whereas all the cancer geraniums had died and dried up, the plant ringed with the copper spiral was not only radiantly healthy but had grown twice as high as uninoculated controls.

These spectacular results led Lakhovsky into a complex theory as to how the geranium had been able to pick up from the vast field of waves in the external atmosphere the exact frequencies which enabled its cells to oscillate normally and so powerfully that the cancer-afflicted cells were destroyed.

To the multitude of radiations of all frequencies emanating from space and unceasingly traversing the atmosphere Lakhovsky gave the generic name *Universion*. Filtered by the spiral he concluded that they were brought specifically into action to restore the degenerating cells of the diseased geranium to healthy activity. To Lakhovsky the purpose of *universion* was to maintain, by resonance and interference, the natural vibration of healthy cells, and to re-establish the vibrations of unhealthy cells by eliminating the radiations of pathogens which differed from healthy cells in amplitude and frequency.

The *universion*, or collectivity of universal radiation, was not, in Lakhovsky's mind, to be associated with the notion of a complete vacuum in space with which physicists had replaced the ether of the nineteenth century. To Lakhovsky the ether was not the negation of all matter but a synthesis of radiation forces, the universal plexus of all cosmic rays. It was a ubiquitous and all-pervading medium, in which disintegrated elements were consigned and transformed into electrical particles.

Lakhovsky believed that with the recognition of this new concept the bounds of science could be extended and a basis laid for an attack on the most absorbing problems of life, including telepathy, the transmission of thought and by inference, man's communication with plants.

In March of 1927 Lakhovsky wrote a communication, 'Influence of Astral Waves on Oscillations of Living Cells' which was presented to the French academy by his friend the eminent biophysicist and discoverer of diathermy, Professor Jacques Arsène d'Arsonval.

By March of 1928, the geranium with the spiral around it had attained the abnormal height of four and a half feet and was flourishing even in winter. Sure that by his work on plants he had stumbled on a new therapy of unimaginable importance to medicine, Lakhovsky went on to develop a sophisticated therapeutic device for human beings which he called a multi-wave oscillator. It was successfully used in French, Swedish and Italian clinics to cure cancerous growths and lesions brought about by radium burns, goitres and a variety of diseases regarded as incurable. Lakhovsky, who was a prominent anti-Nazi, had to leave Paris when the Germans occupied it, and went to New York in 1941. The physio-therapy department of a large New York hospital employed his multi-wave oscillator to treat successfully arthritis, chronic bronchitis, congenital hip dislocation and other ills; and a Brooklyn urologist and surgeon, though he would not reveal his name, stated that he had used it on hundreds of patients to arrest bodily disturbances unamenable to other treatment. When Lakhovsky died in 1943, he had laid the basis for radio-biology. However, the medical profession refused to pursue his findings, and today use of the multi-wave oscillator for medical treatment is officially banned by U.S. health authorities.

While Lakhovsky was working in Paris, at the Texas State University a team headed by Professor E. J. Lund devised a way to measure electrical potentials in plants. In a series of experiments lasting more than ten years, Lund showed that plant cells produce electric fields, currents or impulses which, as Bose had implied, could serve as 'nervous systems'. Lund further demonstrated that the growth of plants was triggered by these electrical nervous systems rather than by growth hormones, or auxins, as was previously believed, and that the auxins were summoned and even transported by the cell-generated electric fields to the place where growth was known to occur. In an important but little-known book, *Bioelectric Fields and Growth*, Lund put forward the revolutionary finding that the electric pattern in plant cells changes nearly half an hour before the diffusion of hormones in them can be effective and growth detected.

Because most physicists still had no better means of detecting radiation than they had at the time of Mesmer's 'animal magnetism' or Reichenbach's 'odic force', the idea that living tissue could emit or respond to vibrations of energy was greeted with scepticism. Such was the case with the research of George Washington Crile, a surgeon and founder of the Cleveland Clinic, who published *The Phenomena of Life: A Radio-Electrical Interpretation* in 1936. This book offered evidence that the living organism is specifically adapted to the formation, storage and use of electrical energy, the genesis of which came, according to Crile, from ultra-microscopic units or furnaces in protoplasm which Crile called radiogens. Three years before his book appeared, Crile had pointed out in an address to the Congress of the American College of Surgeons that it would be possible for future skilled radio-diagnosticians to detect the presence of disease before it becomes outwardly apparent. For his efforts Crile was ridiculed by both his medical colleagues and the cellular biologists who accused him of having no solid grasp of the literature.

The effects of electromagnetic energy on living cells, both healthy and diseased, which most doctors and medical researchers, including cancer specialists, have yet honestly to confront, were finally to be revealed by the magic of time-lapse photography. Because most plants grow very slowly they look as unchanging to the human eye as if petrified. Only by looking away from plants for several hours, or, better, for several days, can one notice that they are different from the plastic flowers and shrubs which are supplanting living plants in florist shops across the world.

In 1927, an Illinois teenager, staring at the buds on a large apple tree in his front yard, wondering when they would open into flowers, realized that if he could take pictures of them in regular sequence he would be able to watch the buds unfold before his eyes.

Thus began the career of John Nash Ott, whose pioneering interest in time-lapse photography led him to unveil new mysteries in the kingdom of plants.

To experiment with exotic varieties of plants Ott built a small greenhouse, where he found that each variety of plant presented to him as many problems as would a different tribe to an anthropologist. Many of his charges seemed to act like temperamental prima donnas with deep psychological disturbances. As he consulted with university botanists and research scientists on the staffs of large companies, little by little the basic biological causes for his plants' misbehaviour became clear: they were extremely sensitive not only to light and temperature but to ultra-violet, TV and X-rays.

Ott's discoveries about light and temperature may lead to the explanation of many botanical mysteries, not the least of which is the tremendous size of plants growing high in the mountains of central Africa.

Over thirty years ago the English author Patrick Synge in his book *Plants with Personality* suggested that though no one had been able to produce a satisfactory theory on the origin of giantism in plants, it perhaps might happen on account of a complement of peculiar environmental conditions, namely, a low but moderately constant temperature, a consistently high humidity, and a strong intensity of ultra-violet light due both to the altitude and to the equatorial location.

In the European Alps vegetation growing high up tends

towards dwarfism, but in the Mountains of the Moon, or Ruwenzori as the Africans call them, Synge encountered heathers 'as mighty as great trees' and found shell-pink impatiens with flowers two inches across.

On the extinct volcano Mount Elgon, rising fourteen thousand feet on the Kenya-Uganda border, Synge found lobelias, which in England are tiny blue-flowered plants, growing nearly thirty feet tall, 'like gigantic blue and green obelisks'. He photographed them half covered with snow and with icicles hanging from the tips of their leaves. But when the same plants were brought back to England, they could not survive outdoors even in the mild winters of Surrey.

Synge's idea accorded with the hypothesis of the French chemist Pierre Berthelot, that it is the continuous presence of electricity high in the Alpine ranges that accounts for the luscious growth of plants in very poor soil. If the conditions enumerated by Synge are some day simulated by researchers, perhaps these giant plants will be successfully grown at sea level.

Ott's experiments in time-lapse photography were to lead him to the discovery that different wave lengths of light have a fundamental effect on photosynthesis, the process by which green plants convert light to chemical energy and by means of it synthesize organic compounds from inorganic ones, turning carbon dioxide and water into carbohydrates, with a release of oxygen. To attack this problem, he spent months building equipment which would allow him to take microscopic pictures of the streaming of protoplasm in the cells of Elodea grass while it was stimulated by direct unfiltered natural sunlight. Exposed to the sun's rays, the chlorophyl-containing bodies, called chloroplasts, which are the principal agents of photosynthesis, streamed in an orderly fashion around the edges of the obloid cells. But when the ultra-violet light in the sunlight was filtered out, some of the chloroplasts would drop out of the streaming pattern and huddle, immobile, in the corners. Cutting out the colours from the blue end of the spectrum toward the red increasingly slowed the chloroplast action.

Particularly fascinating to Ott was the fact that, at the day's end, all the chloroplasts slowed down and stopped, no matter how intensely they were subjected to artificial light. Only when the sun rose the next day would they resume the normal streaming pattern.

Ott realized that if the basic principles of photochemistry, as they applied to plant photosynthesis, had analogues in the animal world then, as the proponents of colour-therapy have long maintained, various frequencies of light might affect the physical well-being of humans by acting on the body chemistry in a way similar to the action of certain drugs on nervous and mental disorders.

In 1964 an article in *Time* magazine spurred Ott to research the effect of TV radiation on plants and humans. The story suggested that symptoms of nervousness, continuous fatigue, headaches, loss of sleep, and vomiting in thirty children under study by two U.S. Air Force physicians were somehow related to the fact that all of these children were watching TV from three to six hours on weekdays and from twelve to twenty hours on weekends. Though the doctors had concluded that the children were afflicted by prolonged idleness in front of the set, Ott wondered if some sort of radiation might not be at issue, particularly that of X-rays, which lie beyond ultra-violet in the energy spectrum.

To test this idea, Ott covered half of the picture tube of a colour TV set with a sixteenth of an inch of lead shielding, normally used to block out X-rays. The other half he covered with heavy black photographic paper capable of stopping visible and ultra-violet light, but allowing other electromagnetic frequencies to penetrate.

Ott placed six pots of bean sprouts in front of each half of the TV tube, a pair at three different levels from top to bottom. As a control, six more pots, each with its three bean sprouts, were placed outdoors, fifty feet from the greenhouse where the TV set was located.

At the end of three weeks, both the lead-shielded beans and those growing outdoors had risen to a height of six inches and appeared healthy and normal. The beans shielded from the TV only by the photographic paper had been distorted by toxic radiations into a vine-type growth. In some cases the roots appeared to have grown incongruously upward out of the soil. If TV radiation could make monsters of bean plants what might it do to children?

Several years later, when Ott was discussing the distortion of the beans with space scientists, he was told that the root growth of his bean plants exposed to radiation resembled that of wheat seedlings in a bio-capsule in outer space, where it was thought to be due to the weightless condition from lack of gravity. Some of the scientists seemed intrigued by his idea that not weightlessness but a general background radiation of an unspecified energy might cause the eccentric root growth.

Since general background radiation coming from the zenith, or the point directly overhead, penetrates through less of the earth's atmosphere and is therefore more powerful than that coming in at any other angle, Ott thinks that roots of plants grow downward to get away from the radiation directly above them.

Because of increasing difficulty in maintaining discipline in schools, children who are hyperactive or have difficulty concentrating have over recent years been administered so-called behavioural modification drugs or 'peace pills'. This practice has aroused a storm of controversy among parents, doctors and government officials. Though it has not been publicly suggested, Ott wonders whether this hyperactivity – and increasingly reported forms of lethargy including prolonged sleep – may be a result of exposure to radiation from TV sets.

Ott knew that since the radiation from a TV tube is contained in an extremely narrow band on the electromagnetic spectrum, biological systems sensitive to this narrow spike of energy could be as overstimulated by it as they would be by light focused through a magnifying glass. The only difference is that, whereas the magnifier concentrates the light in one direction, the specific energy emitted from the TV can travel in any direction where it meets no obstruction.

Ott's belief that electromagnetic radiation affects plants and animals in many unsuspected ways increased when he was called by Paramount Pictures in Hollywood to make time-lapse photos of flowers for a new picture, starring Barbra Streisand, based on the Broadway musical hit *On a Clear Day You Can See Forever*. In the story the heroine numbers among her extra sensory abilities that of making flowers grow as she sings to them. The studio wanted Ott to begin work immediately on geraniums, roses, irises, hyacinths, tulips, and daffodils for inclusion in this part of the film.

To duplicate as nearly as possible natural rays of outdoor sunlight, Ott had developed a new full-spectrum flourescent tube, with added ultra-violet. Because he had a tight deadline, he knew that only if the flowers would grow under the new lights could he hope for sucess. To his relief, all the flowers grew well. But Ott noticed that the best results came when the flowers were placed under the centre, rather than the ends, of the fluorescent tubes. He knew that the tubes worked on the same principle as the cathode guns in TV sets or in X-ray machines, but at much lower voltages, so low in fact that textbooks stated they could not produce harmful radiation. Suspecting the textbooks might be wrong, Ott placed two sets of ten parallel tubes end to end so that there were twenty cathodes in close proximity. When he sprouted the same kind of potted beans used in the TV experiments, he was startled to see that the ones close to the cathodes were stunted whereas those both at the centre of the tubes and ten feet away from them appeared normal.

After many more experiments with beans, Ott became certain that they are far more sensitive to trace amounts of radiation than the standard radiation-measuring equipment presently available. This, he thinks, is because whereas the instruments pick up only a single reading of energy the biological systems are exposed to its cumulative effects.

Ott was next confronted with the possibility that light frequencies could affect the development and growth of cancer.

His initial clue that there was a connection between light frequencies and cancer came when a physician in charge of cancer research at one of New York's largest hospitals agreed to ask fifteen human cancer patients to spend as much time as possible outdoors in natural sunlight without their glasses and avoid artificial light sources, including television.

By the end of the summer the doctor told Ott that it was the consensus of all those assisting in the project that fourteen of the patients had shown no further advancement in tumour development.

In the meantime, Ott had aroused the interest of a leading Florida ophthalmologist, who explained to him that a layer of cells in the retina of the eye, with no function in vision, showed abnormal response to tranquillizing drugs and asked if he would run toxicity tests of the drugs by utilizing microscopic time-lapse photography. Ott used a phase-contrast microscope equipped with a complete set of coloured filters, which permit the outline and details of cell structure to be clearly seen without killing them with stain as was previously necessary. This technique revealed that exposure to the wavelengths of blue light elicited abnormal pseudopodical activity in the pigment of the retinal cells whereas red light caused the cell walls to rupture. Even more interesting was the fact that when the cells were fed, by adding fresh media to the slide chambers, cell division was not encouraged at constant temperature, but if the temperature was lowered during the feeding accelerated division would take place within sixteen hours.

During their work the researchers also noticed that just before sunset the activity of the pigment granules within the cells would slow down and would return to normal only the next morning. It seemed to Ott that they were behaving just like the chloroplasts in the cells of Elodea grass. Perhaps plants and animals had more similarities in their basic functioning than had hitherto been suspected.

Ott suggests that the responses of chloroplasts and the pigment granules in retinal epithelial cells may be 'tuned' to the natural light spectrum of sunlight, under which all life on this earth has evolved. 'It would thus appear,' he says, 'that the basic principles of photosynthesis in plants, where light energy is recognized as a principal growth-regulating factor, might carry over from plant life and be equally important as a growth-regulating factor in animal life through control of the chemical or hormonal activity.'

Other studies of cellular behaviour have led Ott to conclude that malillumination or malradiation may be as important as malnutrition in the initiation of disease.

At the 1970 meeting of the American Association for the Advancement of Science, Dr Lewis W. Mayron, in his discussion of Ott's research with bean plants and rats exposed to TV radiation, concluded that 'the radiation has a physiological effect both on plants and animals which appears to be chemically mediated'. Mayron also commented on Ott's experiments with the effects of fluorescent tubes on beans, stating: 'The implications for human health are enormous when one considers the magnitude of the use of fluorescent lighting in stores, offices, factories, schools and homes.'

By the late 1960s the U.S. Congress had passed a Radiation Control Act by a vote of 381 to o. Florida Representative Paul Ropes, co-author of the act, credited Ott with 'getting us all started on the road toward control of radiation from electronic products'. Ott credits his plants with showing him the way to the light.

Since Ott's work, along with that of Gurwitsch, Rahn, Crile, and the proponents of electroculture all supports the earlier contentions of Galvani and Mesmer that living things have electrical or magnetic properties, it would have been strange had no one suggested that they must also have about them the same electromagnetic fields as those accepted in the world of particle physics. This was exactly the theory boldly advanced by two Yale University professors, one a philosopher, F. S. C. Northrop, the other, like Galvani, a medical doctor and anatomist, Harold Saxton Burr.

By asserting that electrical fields are the very organizers of life systems, Northrop and Burr offered chemists a new basis on which to explain how the thousands of separate constituents they had uncovered might be put together. They suggested to the biologists that their long hunt might be over for the 'mechanism' which assures that all the cells of the human body, replaced every six months, are properly aligned.

To prove their theory, Burr and his laboratory colleagues constructed a voltmeter of a new design, which drew no current from life forms to be studied and thus could not disrupt the total fields around them. Twenty years of research with this device and its more sophisticated descendants revealed to Burr and several of his associates astonishing things about the vegetal and animal world. Dr Louis Langman, an obstetrician and gynaecologist who worked with Burr's technique, found for example that the precise moment of a woman's ovulation can be measured with great accuracy and that some women ovulate over the entire menstrual cycle, in some cases without menstruation. Though the detection procedure is extremely simple, and in no way counters the rhythm method of birth control of the Catholic Church, it has yet to filter down to millions of women who would like to learn better how, or how not, to have children.

Burr himself determined that malignancies could be detected in certain organs before any clinical signs could be observed, and that the rate of healing in wounds could be reliably measured. The future location of a chick's head could be found and pinpointed in the egg from which it would hatch, without breaking it, during the first day of its incubation.

Turning to the world of plants, Burr measured what he came to call 'life-fields' around seeds, and found that profound changes in the voltage patterns were caused by the alteration of a single gene in the parent stock. Even more potentially interesting to plant breeders was his discovery that it is possible to predict how strong and healthy a future plant will be from the electrical diagnosis of the seed which produces it.

Because, of all living things, they seemed the most enduring and the least motile, Burr charted the life fields of trees on the Yale campus and at his laboratory in Old Lyme, Connecticut, over nearly two decades. He found that recordings related not only to the lunar cycle and to sunspots, which flare up at intervals with many years between them, but revealed cycles recurring every three and six months that were beyond his explanation. His conclusions seemed to make less suspect the long-mocked practices of generations of gardeners who claimed that their crops should be planted according to the phases of the moon.

One of Burr's students, Leonard J. Ravitz, Jr., who was to become a psychiatrist, was able to measure depths of hypnosis with the Burr-discovered techniques as far back as 1948. He went on to the not surprising conclusion that all humans are in hypnotic states most of the time, even when wide awake.

The continuous charting of life fields in people indicates a cyclic rise and fall of voltage, the peaks and valleys of which correlate to the periods when they feel good or bad, 'up' or 'down'. By plotting the curves in advance it is possible to predict highs and lows weeks in advance, as the students of bio-rhythms have proposed, going back to the time when they were first theorized by Dr Wilhelm Fliess, whose letters were so encouraging to Sigmund Freud during the years of Freud's self-analysis.

Burr's life work, as further developed by Ravitz, indicates that the organizing field around the 'bodies' of living things *anticipates* the physical events within them and suggests that the mind itself, as Marcel Vogel maintains, can, by modulating the field, affect positively or deleteriously the matter with which it is held to be associated. But these signposts had yet to be read by the leaders of organized medicine, and Burr's work has only recently begun to be seriously considered.

Medical pundits are now in for a further shock due to a startling discovery in 1972 at the Institute of Clinical and Experimental Medicine in Novosibirsk, a burgeoning industrial city of over a million people on the banks of Siberia's river Ob, which strongly supports the findings of Gurwitsch, Rahn and Crile.

S. P. Shchurin and two colleagues from the Institute of Automation and Electrometry have been awarded a special diploma by the U.S.S.R. State Committee for Inventions and Discoveries for discovering that cells can 'converse' by coding their messages in the form of a special electromagnetic ray.

The experimenters placed identical tissue cultures in two hermetically sealed vessels separated by a wall of glass, then introduced a lethal virus in one of the chambers which killed the colony of cells inside it. The second colony remained wholly unaffected. However, when they replaced the glass divider with a sheet of quartz glass and again introduced killing viruses to one of the colonies, the Soviet scientists were astonished to see that the second colony also met the same fate as the first, even though the viruses could not possibly have penetrated the barrier. Other first and second colonies of cells, separated by the quartz glass, both perished when only the first colony was murdered with chemical poisons or lethal radiation and the second left unexposed. What killed the second colony in each case?

Since ordinary glass does not permit ultra-violet rays to pass but quartz glass does, it seemed to the Soviet scientists that here was a key to the mystery. They recalled that Gurwitsch had theorized that onion cells could emit ultra-violet rays, and they resurrected his ideas from the limbo to which they had been consigned in the 1930s. Working with an electronic eye amplified by a photomultiplier and registered by a self-recorder which traced a graph marking the energy levels on a moving tape, they found that when life processes in the tissue cultures remained *normal*, the ultra-violet glow, invisible to the human eye but detectable as oscillations on the tape, remained *stable*. As soon as the affected colony began to battle against its infection, the radiation intensified.

Reports on this work in Moscow newspapers disclosed that, however fantastic it might seem, the ultra-violet radiation from the afflicted cells *carried information* encoded in the fluctuation in intensity which was somehow received by the second colony, just as words are transmitted and received in dots and dashes in the Morse code.

Since the second colony seemed in each case to die in exactly the same way as the first, the Soviets realized that it was as dangerous for healthy cells to be exposed to the transmitted signal of dying cells as it was for them to be exposed to viruses, poisons, and lethal radiation. It appeared that the second colony upon receiving the alarm signal from the dying first colony began to mobilize for resistance and that its very 'restructuring for war' against a nonexistent enemy proved as fatal as if it had indeed been attacked.

Moscow newspapers suggested that the Novosibirsk work may help to pinpoint what inner reserves the human body possesses to resist disease and quoted Shchurin on how it may help to open new horizons in diagnosis:

We are convinced that the radiation is capable of giving the first warning about the beginning of malignant regeneration and of revealing the presence of particular viruses. At the present time the early identification of many ailments, for instance the numerous forms of hepatitis, presents major difficulties.

Thus, fifty years after his work, his countrymen have finally brought recognition to Gurwitsch's brilliant research. Coincidentally they have also validated the work of another obscure compatriot, Semyon Kirlian, who has managed to capture on film extraordinary pictures of the force fields around humans and plants so accurately described and measured by Burr and Ravitz.

12

The mystery of plant and human auras

The long train was on the last leg of its journey from Moscow to Krasnodar, a south Russian inland port on the Kuban River, two hundred miles northwest of the volcanic Elbrus, Europe's highest mountain peak in the Greater Caucasus range.

In one of its 'soft' cushioned cars reserved for Soviet officials, a plant specialist, bored with watching the flat countryside, still only partly recovered in 1950 from the Nazi ravages of the 'Great Patriotic War', reopened his briefcase to check the condition of two similar leaves which he had plucked in a greenhouse before leaving the Soviet capital. Relieved to see that the leaves were still sparkling fresh and green in their bedding of moist cotton wool, he sat back in his fauteuil to admire the approach of the Caucasian piedmont.

Late that evening in a small Krasnodar apartment, a corner of which was fitted out as a miniature laboratory, Semyon Davidovich Kirlian, an electrician and amateur photographer, and his wife, Valentina, were making some adjustments to equipment they had begun building two years before the Nazi attack on their country.

With their new invention they had discovered they could photographically reproduce, without lens or camera, a strange luminescence which seemed to issue from all living things but was unapprehensible by the human eye.

A knock on the door surprised them, as no visitor was likely to call at that time of evening; they were even more surprised when a total stranger announced he had come all the way from Moscow to see if they could make for him photographs of the strange energy which he had heard they alone could make visible on film. From his briefcase the stranger pulled the two identical leaves and handed them to the Kirlians.

Excited at the prospect that their discovery was to be put to an official test, the Kirlians stayed up till after midnight, but were disappointed to note that while they could make excellent pictures of energy flares from one of the leaves, they could get only a weak facsimile from the other. They worked on through the night, trying to get photos of the luminescence as similar as the leaves themselves, but were wholly unsuccessful.

In the morning, crestfallen, they showed their results to the scientist, who shouted in amazement: 'But you've found it! You've proven it photographically!' He explained that one leaf had been plucked from a healthy plant, the other from a diseased specimen. Although the two leaves appeared identical to the human eye, the pictures plainly differentiated between them. Illness was evidently manifest in a plant's energy field before becoming visible as a symptom in its physical body.

That plants, as well as animals and human beings, have fields of fine sheaths of subatomic or protoplasmic energy which permeate the solid physical bodies of molecules and atoms was a centuries-old allegation by seers and philosophers. This extra dimension or 'aura' depicted in ancient iconography around the bodies of saints, with golden haloes around the heads, has been referred to by persons gifted with extrasensory perception since the beginnings of recorded history. By laying film or plate in contact with an object to be photographed and passing through the object an electric current from a high-frequency spark generator which put out 75,000 to 200,000 electrical pulses per second, the Kirlians had come across a way of photographing this 'aura' – or something akin to it.

Leaves from plants, sandwiched with film between the electrodes of their device, revealed a phantasmagoria hitherto restricted to clairvoyants, a micro-universe of tiny starry points of light. White, blue, and even red and yellow flares were pictured surging out of what seemed to be channels in the leaves. These emanations, or force fields round a leaf, became distorted if the leaf was mutilated, gradually diminishing and disappearing as the leaf was allowed to die. The Kirlians were next able to magnify this luminescence by adapting their photographic processes to optical instruments and microscopes. Rays of energy and whirling fireballs of light appeared to shoot out of plants into space.

The Kirlians also examined all kinds of 'inanimate' substances, including metal coins. Each had a different luminating pattern. Most interesting was the fact that while a two-kopeck coin showed only a constant glow around its edges, human fingertips seemed to shoot forth flaming energy in bursts like miniature volcanoes.

After their photographic demonstration of pathology in the leaf from the sick plant for the Muscovite visitor, it was another ten years before the Kirlians began to emerge from obscurity in the U.S.S.R.

In the early 1960s Dr Lev Fedorov of the U.S.S.R.'s Ministry of Public Health, struck by the possibilities of the new photography for medical diagnosis, awarded the Kirlians a first research grant but when Fedorov died soon thereafter, official funding from Moscow began to dwindle and academic sceptics were once more in control.

It was only when a journalist took up the Kirlians' story that interest was again aroused. 'This situation,' wrote I. Belov, 'is as bad as before the revolution, when the evil hand of Tsarist bureaucrats determined there was too much uncertainty in novelty. *Twenty-five years have passed* since the Kirlians made their discovery, yet the Ministries in charge still haven't released the funds.'

Belov's effort had its effects. In 1966, a conference bringing together many scientists interested in all aspects of what was coming to be called 'biological energy' was held in Alma Ata, capital of the Kazakh Republic. In proceedings of the conference, entitled *Problems in Bioenergetics*, a Moscow biophysicist, Viktor Adamenko, joined with the Kirlians to author a seminal paper 'On Research of Biological Objects in High-Frequency Electrical Fields'. The paper stressed the enormous difficulties of studying the spectrum of 'electrobioluminescence' but added that when these are overcome, 'we will be able to obtain important information about bioenergetic processes in a living organism'.

For all the mounting Soviet interest, it was another three to four years before American science – which had branded as fake Wilhelm Reich's 1939 discovery of a life energy in plants and humans which he called orgone – paid attention to the new developments. What attracted this attention was not the Soviet scientific publications but a book, *Psychic Discoveries Behind the Iron Curtain*, by two North American journalists, Sheila Ostrander and Lynn Schroeder, which appeared in the summer of 1970.

Excited by what she had read in the Ostrander-Schroeder volume, a former Broadway actress, now professor at the Neuropsychiatric Institute of the University of California at Los Angeles, Thelma Moss, Ph.D., wrote to Russia and received an invitation to visit Professor Vladimir Inyushin at Alma Ata.

Working with several colleagues, Inyushin had written up his research into the Kirlians' work in 1968 in a book-long scientific paper: *The Biological Essence of the Kirlian Effect*. Though Kirlian himself had maintained that the strange energy in his pictures was caused by 'changing the nonelectrical properties of bodies into electrical properties which are transferred to film', Inyushin and his collaborators went several steps further. They declared that the bioluminescence visible in Kirlian pictures was caused not by the electrical state of the organism but by a 'biological plasma body' which seemed to be only a new word for the 'etheric' or 'astral' body of the ancients.

In physics plasma is defined today as an electrically neutral, highly ionized gas composed of ions, electrons, and neutral particles which has been called the 'Fourth State of Matter' (after solids, liquids, gases). As far back as 1944, as the Allied armies were storming 'Fortress Europe', a book by the Russian V. S. Grishchenko, *The Fourth State of Matter*, appeared in French in Paris. Credit for coining the term bioplasma may thus belong to Grishchenko. The same year the discoverer of 'mitogenetic radiation', A. G. Gurwitsch, published his book in Moscow entitled *The Theory of a Biological Field*, summing up twenty years of work.

Inside the 'bioplasmic' body, said Inyushin, processes have their own labyrinthine motion, different from the energy pattern in the physical body, yet the bioplasmic body is not a chaotic, but a whole unified organism which acts as a unit, is polarized, gives off its own electromagnetic fields, and is the basis for 'biological' fields.

When Thelma Moss arrived on an evening flight in Alma Ata, she was invited by Inyushin to visit his laboratory and lecture to his students. Elated, she went to sleep sure that she would be the first American scientist to visit a Soviet institution engaged in studying Kirlian photography. The following morning when Inyushin came to pick her up at her hotel, he regretfully told her that 'permission for the visit had not come from Moscow'.

Moss was nevertheless able to learn from Inyushin that during six years of research with Kirlian photography he had been able to note that specific areas of the human body revealed characteristic colours which might prove significant in medical diagnoses. The clearest photos, he told Moss, were those taken at four o'clock in the afternoon, the worst at midnight. When Moss asked Inyushin point-blank if his 'bioplasma' body was what occult Western literature refers to as the 'aura' or the 'astral' body, he said: 'Yes!'

In ancient philosophies and in Eastern and Theosophical teaching, the energy body which duplicates the human body is also called the etheric body, fluidic body, or prephysical body. It is believed to be the unifying agent for the material body, a magnetic area where immaterial or subatomic vortices of the cosmos are transformed into the individual, the channel through which life communicates with the physical body, the medium for telepathic and clairvoyant projection. For decades scientists have been trying to find a way to make this body visible.

While Moss was in Alma Ata, the eminent American psychiatrist Montague Ullman, director of the department of psychiatry at the Maimonides Medical Center in New York City, was simultaneously interviewing Viktor Adamenko in Moscow.

Ullman was informed, somewhat to his surprise, that Adamenko and other Soviet scientists had been able to determine that the 'bioplasma' not only undergoes a drastic shift when placed in a magnetic field but is concentrated at hundreds of points in the human body which seem to correspond to the ancient Chinese system of acupuncture points.

Thousands of years ago the Chinese mapped seven hundred

points on the human skin as paths along which they believed a life force or vital energy to circulate. The Chinese insert needles at these points to correct imbalances in the energy flow, and to cure disease. Spots where the Kirlian lights flashed most brilliantly on a human body appeared to match the acupuncture points mapped by the Chinese.

Adamenko is still unsure about Inyushin's attribution of the phenomena to a 'bioplasma body', because there is as yet no 'rigorous proof' of its existence, and therefore prefers to define the visible emanations as 'a cold emission of electrons from the live object into the atmosphere'.

In the United States this 'cold emission of electrons' is almost universally translated as a 'corona discharge', which is compared to the static electricity emitted by a person after walking across a carpet and touching a grounded metal. The name is derived from the faintly coloured and luminous ring which surrounds celestial bodies and is visible through a haze or thin cloud or the luminous irregular envelope of highly ionized gas outside the chromosphere of the sun. But giving it an academic name has explained neither its substance nor its function.

As president of the American Society for Psychical Research, Ullman found it extremely interesting that Dr Anatoli Podshibyakin, a Kiev electrophysiologist, had discovered that bioplasma, if that is what it is, *instantly* reacts to changes on the surface of the sun even though cosmic particles, ejected by the sun, take about two days to reach the earth.

Many parapsychologists view man as an enmeshed, integral part of life on earth and in the universe. They maintain he is linked to the cosmos via his bioplasmic body, and reacts to changes in the planets as well as to the moods and illnesses of others, to thought, emotion, sound, light, colour, magnetic fields, the seasons, cycles of the moon, tides, thunder-storms, strong winds and even levels of noise. If there is a change in the universe and environment, say the parapsychologists, a resonance is produced in the vital energy of the human body which in turn affects the physical body. It is through his bioplasmic body that parapsychologists believe a man can be in direct contact with a living plant.

Still another U.S. parapsychological researcher, Dr Stanley

Krippner, director of the extraordinary Dream Laboratory at the Maimonides Medical Center in New York – where pictures have been successfully directed at sleepers in order to produce in their minds desired dreams – trekked to Russia in the summer of 1971. While in Moscow, Krippner was the first American invited to give an address on parapsychology to the Institute of Psychology in the Academy of Pedagogical Sciences. The lecture was attended by some two hundred psychiatrists, physicists, engineers, space scientists, and cosmonauts in training.

Krippner found out that Genady Sergeyev, a neurophysiologist working at the Ukhtomskii Military Institute in Leningrad, had made Kirlian photographs of Nina Kulagina, a sensitive who can, by simply passing her hand over but not touching them, move paper clips, matches, cigarettes, and other objects on a table top.

Sergeyev's photographs revealed that while Kulagina performs these psychokinetic feats, the 'bioplasmic field' around her body expands and pulses rhythmically and *a ray of luminescence seems to shoot out of her eyes.*

In the autumn of 1971, William A. Tiller, chief of the Materials Science Department at Stanford University (Palo Alto, California) and one of the world's experts on crystals, was the first American physicist invited by Edward Naumov, chief coordinator for Technical Parapsychology in Moscow, to investigate Kirlian photography in the U.S.S.R.

Although, like Moss and Ullman, Tiller was not permitted to visit Soviet laboratories, he was able to spend several days with Adamenko. When he returned to the United States, Tiller recommended in a highly technical report that the Kirlian method and devices, among others, were 'so important to parapsychological and medical investigations that attention should be focused on immediate construction of such devices and the duplication of the Soviet results'.

Tiller, who like Adamenko does not see the need for postulating any new 'bioplasma', and substitutes for it the 'cold emission of electrons', has been building extremely sophisticated equipment for taking Kirlian photographs in his Palo Alto laboratory.

One of the first actually to make Kirlian-type pictures in the United States was Thelma Moss, who worked on the project with one of her students, Kendall Johnson. With their apparatus, Moss and Johnson were the first Americans to take colour photos of leaves and pick up almost every region of the visible spectrum. American coins, appropriately enough, come out in red-white-and-blue, as do photos of the energy from the fingertips of the human hand.

Henry C. Monteith, an electrical engineer in Albuquerque, New Mexico, working at home, put together an apparatus consisting of two 6-volt batteries, a vibrator used to power automobile radios, and an ignition coil sold at all auto-supply stores. Like the Russians, Monteith found that a live leaf gave beautiful and varied self-emissions that cannot be adequately explained by conventional theory. He was further mystified when he discovered that a dead leaf gave, at most, only a uniform glow. Exposed to only 30,000 volts, the dead leaf did not reveal anything at all on film, even when bathed in water, but the live leaf shimmered in a radiance of self-emissions.

As the potential implications of a photographic process in existence for more than thirty years – which seemingly gave substance to the notion of the existence of an *aura*, a subject considered by most Western scientists to be on the 'lunatic fringe' of investigatory effort – began to be realized in the United States, demand mounted for more hard information. Stanley Krippner enlisted the cooperation of several financial backers and organized the First Western Conference on Kirlian Photography and the Human Aura in the spring of 1972 at Manhattan's United Engineering Centre, where a crowd of doctors, psychiatrists, psychoanalysts, psychologists, parapsychologists, biologists, engineers and photographers packed the ground-floor auditorium to overflowing. At the conference startling pictures by Moss and Johnson were shown of a leaf before and after being pricked. Done with Kirlian techniques, the photo of the wounded leaf revealed an enormous blood-red pond of energy in its centre which took the place of the bright azure and pinkish hue which showed up before the pricking.

The mystery of the link between human emotional or psychic states and emanations radiating from the fingertips is deepened by Moss's further finding that pictures of both her own and Kendall Johnson's fingers differ from day to day and hour to hour.

Since the photos of leaves change with variations in parameters, Moss conjectures that 'at whatever frequency we take a picture, we are resonating, or vibrating at the same frequency, *with one particular aspect of the material*; thus, not a whole picture, but different pieces of information are picked up'.

Tiller speculated that the radiation or energy coming out of a leaf or a human fingertip actually might be coming from whatever is present *prior to the formation of solid matter*. This, says Tiller, 'may be another level of substance, producing a hologram, a coherent energy pattern of a leaf which is a force-field for organizing matter to building itself into this kind of physical network'.

Tiller thinks that even if part of the network were cut away, the forming hologram would still be there. Apparently this is just what the Russians have been able to prove with a plant leaf. A picture printed in the *Journal of Paraphysics* (published in Downton, Wiltshire) shows a Russian Kirlian photograph of a leaf with one part cut away. Yet, where nothing would show ordinarily, the outline of the missing part of the leaf remains.

That this was not just Russian subterfuge was strikingly confirmed when Douglas Dean made photos of the fingertip of a New Jersey healer, Ethel de Loach, whose files bulge with successful case histories. One picture, taken while the healer was at rest, showed only a dark blue radiation streaming out of the skin and revealing the tip of the long nail. A second picture, shot when she was asked to heal, revealed in addition to the blue radiation an enormous orange and red flare leaping out of a point below the actual fingerprint. Both pictures were subsequently published on the cover of the medical journal *Osteopathic Physician*. Kirlian photos of faith healers reveal a smaller glow after healing, while those healed have greater emanations, indicating some sort of energy flow from the hands of the healer into the body of the patient, giving substance to Galvani's and Mesmer's theory of 'animal magnetism'.

At the Human Dimensions Institute at Rosary Hill College in Buffalo, New York, one of the professors, Sister M. Justa

Smith, a Catholic nun and biochemist, began thinking that healing energy coming from or through a healer's hands would have to affect the enzyme system *before* diseased cells could change to a state of health. Sister Justa – who had finished a doctoral dissertation proving that magnetic fields increase, while ultra-violet light decreases, enzyme activity – after engaging the cooperation of a healer, found that when he was in an 'optimum psychological state', or good mood, the energy coming from his hands could activate the pancreatic enzyme trypsin in a way which compared to the effects of a magnetic field measuring from 8,000 to 13,000 gauss. (Human beings normally live in a magnetic field of 0.5 gauss.) Sister Justa is continuing experimentation to find out whether a healer can activate other enzymes in the body and whether this activation can be of help to the maintenance of health.

How magnetic fields affect life and how they might be related to the energy of the 'aura' is a mystery only beginning to be unveiled. In recent years scientists have found, for instance, that snails perceive extremely weak magnetic fields and, since they can also distinguish their direction, could be said to incorporate structures which behave like navigational compasses.

It would seem that some correlation exists between the activity of the 'bioplasmic' or 'auric' fields – if that is what they are – around living things and their subjection to various types of radiation. Certainly there is no doubt, in light of the pioneering Soviet work and its American confirmation, that the health, physical or emotional, of plants and animals can be objectified with the Kirlian technique.

The main strength of the Russian research, according to Professor Tiller, is that 'it has been able to provide us with detectors and devices with which we can begin to show cause-effect relationships between psycho-energetic phenomena and the kind of read-outs which our colleagues find acceptable and that our logical system has come to accept as proof. We're *at that stage of naïveté* that we need this proof.'

The first Kirlian conference was so successful that a second meeting was held in New York's Town Hall in February 1973. One of the most striking presentations was that of Dr John

Pierrakos, a Greek-born psychiatrist who showed detailed drawings of auras which he can visually perceive around plants, animals and human beings and which he is able to monitor in continual movement around neurotically and psychotically disturbed patients. In her book *Breakthrough to Creativity*, published in 1967, Shafica Karagulla, M.D., reported how many physicians use their observations of the human energy field in their diagnostic work. Because they were guarded about discussing their unusual abilities outside their own circle, Karagulla did not refer to any of them by name. Pierrakos is perhaps the first physician publicly to state that his perceptions of the human aura assist him in his diagnoses.

'Man is an eternal pendulum of movement and vibration,' Pierrakos told the Town Hall audience.

His spirit is captured in a body in which forces throb and pulsate like the beat of a heart. Often, they thunder and quake in his body with strong emotions that shake the very foundations of his physical being. Life goes on, rhythmically and quietly pulsating with the warm feeling of love or cascading with avalanches of violent emotion, for movement and pulsation is life. When movement diminishes, the person becomes ill, and when the movement stops, the person is dying.

Pierrakos likened human bodies to time capsules in which biological functions are performed 'for a century or so' after which the capsule changes the shape of its existence. 'During this time, like the flower that brings the blossom and the seed that brings the flower and the fruit, man's time capsule has to become aware of what is going on within and without.' To do so, asserted Pierrakos, we must describe and understand, fuse and integrate two attributes: *life energy* and *consciousness* – the former seen as the aura around the body with gradations similar to that of the atmosphere which thins as it proceeds outward from the earth. Though to his Hellenic ancestors energy was 'something producing movement', Pierrakos holds that this nebulous definition should be made more precise. 'Energy is a living force emanated by consciousness,' he suggests. 'By observing the energetic field emanating from the body – not unlike the steam over boiling water which, correctly observed, gives an idea of the water's nature – I get an idea of what is happening in the body,' Pierrakos said.

In his pictures, Pierrakos illustrated the three layers he sees around most of his patients. The first, a dark band no more than one-sixteenth to one-eighth of an inch thick, lies close to the skin and looks like a transparent crystalline structure. The second, a broader dark blue layer, reminiscent of a cluster of iron filings, forms an ovoid envelope around the body when seen from the front. The third is a lightish blue haze of radiant energy which, when the patient is in good health, extends several feet away from the body and accounts for why we describe happy zestful persons as 'radiant'.

The energy field of plants can also be severely affected by disturbed patients, says Pierrakos.

In some experiments with plants conducted in my office with Dr Wesley Thomas, we found that a chrysanthemum's field contracts markedly when a person shouts at it from a distance of five feet, and loses its blue-azure colour, while its pulsation diminishes to one third. In repeated trials, keeping live plants more than two hours daily near the heads of screaming patients (a distance of three feet away), the lower leaves started falling down and the plant withered within three days and died.

Pierrakos related that the number of pulsations the energy field emits per minute is also an indication of the internal state of a human being. The pulsations are much slower in older persons than in children, and in sleep than in wakefulness.

The same kind of energy field observable in humans is seen by Pierrakos macrocosmically over the ocean with miles-high fountains of radiation bursting forth from narrower bands of pulsation below. Since the amount of activity in this earthly aura plotted by Pierrakos against the time of day reveals the lowest ebb just after midnight and the highest shortly following noon, this directly correlates with Rudolph Steiner's account of how the chemical ether is exhaled and inhaled by our planet.

A research team of physicists and electronics specialists is currently seeking to objectify Pierrakos's 'sensitive' sight. Under the auspices of the Centre for Bio-Energetic Analysis they are developing a means of detecting the radiations of the human animal and plant auras with a sensitive photomultiplier tube, an instrument which measures photons or light energy from the 'etheric' field around a body. In a preliminary report they stated in Town Hall that, to date, their work indicates strongly that human beings radiate a strange field, detectable by the tube, the properties of which remain to be analysed and explained.

Pierrakos, who can also see the energy pumping forth from plants and trees, warns of the danger of comparing the phenomena revealed by Kirlian photography to known radiations such as X-rays. 'The study of the aura could become completely mechanized and objectified without reference to the great phenomena of life within the entity,' he says.

In this observation Pierrakos is not far from the philosopher-mathematician Arthur M. Young, inventor of the Bell helicopter, who stresses that in the back of the whole hierarchy of active energies, known or unknown, may lie *intent*. 'Content requires substance,' says Young, 'whether by reference to actual physical objects or to human feelings or emotion. Substance is indeed what the work connotes, that which stands under – *sub stance* – the interactions of the physical world. To the physicist this is *energy*. To the human being it is *motivation*.'

Though *motivation* or *intent*, or some other agency of will, is it possible for living forms to effect changes in their own physical systems? Is it possible for plants and men – which materialists assert are only renderable at death into so much compost, soap, or chemicals – to grow the way they want?

In the Soviet Union, a country which was originally founded on the most materialist of philosophies, the developments resulting from Kirlian photography have raised certain profound questions about the true nature of life – vegetal, animal and human – about mind and body, about form and substance. Thelma Moss believes that research in the field has actually become of such great scientific importance to both the Russian and U.S. governments that they are keeping their official efforts strictly secret. Nevertheless, a spirit of friendly rivalry and of cooperation has arisen between groups, thus far small, of Russian and American scientists.

As Semyon Kirlian put it in a letter to the First Western Conference to take up the implications of his work, 'the new research will have such enormous significance than an impartial assessment of the methods will be carried out only by minds in succeeding generations. The possibilities are immense; indeed, they are practically inexhaustible.'

4

Children of the soil

13

Soil: the staff of life

The promise of large and quick profits has led modern farmers all over the world to use artificial rather than natural fertilizers to force from their land every ounce of productivity. Instead of keeping their soils in natural balance by patient and tender efforts they have sought to subjugate nature rather than cooperate with her. One example among thousands is Decatur, Illinois, a farming community in the heart of the United States maize belt. As the summer of 1966 was drawing to a close, steamingly hot and sultry, the maize stood in the fields as high as an elephant's eye, promising a bumper crop in every direction, perhaps eighty to a hundred bushels to the acre. In twenty years the farmers had almost doubled the land's yield by the use of nitrate fertilizers, unaware of the deadly danger they were courting.

The following spring one of Decatur's 78,000 inhabitants – a man whose living indirectly depended on the success of the maize harvest – noticed that a glass of drinking water from his kitchen tap had a strange taste. As the water was supplied directly from Lake Decatur he took a sample to the Decatur Health Department for testing. The results showed concentrations of nitrate that were not only excessive but potentially lethal. Nitrate, in itself innocuous to the human physical constitution, can become deadly when converted by intestinal bacteria: these combine nitrate with the blood's haemoglobin into methaemoglobin which prevents the natural transport of oxygen in the blood stream. This can cause a disease known as methaemoglobinemia which kills by asphyxiation and to which infants are particularly susceptible.

A Decatur newspaper ran a feature story suggesting that the city's water supply had become polluted with excessive nitrate and that fertilizers being poured on the surrounding maize fields might be the source of the trouble. This exploded like a bombshell in maize-belt communities because farmers were using nitrogen fertilizers to the exclusion of all others as the cheapest and indeed the only means to produce over eighty bushels of maize to the acre, the amount needed to make a profit. Maize is a heavy consumer of nitrogen which, under *natural* conditions, is stored in the soil as a part of its humus. For countless ages before man began to till the earth, humus was accumulated by return to the soil of decayed vegetable matter. When man began to harvest crops he saw to it that humus, rich in nitrogen and other elements upon which plants depend, was replaced in the form of animal wastes, straw and other components of farmyard manure. In many countries of the Far East man's own excrement was applied to the land instead of allowing it to float away through sewage systems into rivers. To give only one example of the waste which occurs in urban societies nowadays, there is an almost inexhaustible supply of natural manure in Sioux City, Iowa, where millions of animals have been fed, slaughtered and shipped to the nation's retail markets for over half a century. There a pile of steer manure has accumulated longer than a football field. This mountain of organic waste, which poses an appalling disposal problem to the city fathers, could easily be processed into natural soil-enlivening products if there were a real interest in saving the soil. This is by no means an exceptional case according to Dr T. C. Byerly, leader of the U.S.D.A.'s waste disposal programmes, who states that wastes from livestock operations in the U.S. are currently equal to that produced by the entire U.S. population and that by 1980 they will double in size.

Instead of returning this natural humus-nitrogen to the soil the county chose to apply artificial nitrogen fertilizers. In Illinois alone the consumption rose from ten thousand tons in 1945 to well over half a million tons in 1966, and is rising constantly. Since the amount of nitrogen applied is more than the maize can naturally take up, the excess washes out of the soil into the local rivers: in the case of Decatur, all the way into the drinking glasses of its citizens. A survey carried out on farms throughout the Middle West disclosed that the maize crops were so heavily fertilized with synthetic nitrogen that the carotene was not being converted into vitamin A and as a result the cattle feed produced was also deficient in vitamins D and E. The cattle were not only losing weight but also they were failing to reproduce satisfactorily, which meant a loss to the farmers. When certain strains of maize were cut for silage the nitrate content was so high that the silos blew up. The juice that flowed out of them killed every cow, duck and chicken unfortunate enough to drink it. Even when silos did not explode, the nitrogen-laden maize in them became lethal in the form of nitrous oxide fumes sufficient to kill a man unsuspectingly breathing it.

The swirl of controversy which broke upon the Illinois maize belt when the truth became public, had already arisen in American scientific circles. At the 1970 annual meeting of the American Association for the Advancement of Science, Dr Barry Commoner, Director of the Centre for the Biology of Natural Systems at Washington University in Saint Louis, Missouri, presented a prophetic paper on the relation between nitrogen fertilizer and the nitrate level in mid-western rivers. Two weeks later, a vice-president of the National Plant Food Association, a lobby whose goal is to protect the interests of the two billion dollar American Fertilizer industry, sent copies of Commoner's paper for rebuttal to soil experts at nine major universities. These men had spent most of their careers advising farmers that the best way to ensure bountiful crops is to apply artificial fertilizers to the land. Therefore many of them were as irritated at Commoner's allegations as were the fertilizer lobby officials and they rushed to take up cudgels in the lobby's and their own defence.

Commoner's only supporter was his colleague, Dr Daniel H. Kohl, an expert in the electronic process of photosynthesis. Kohl thought that the problem was so serious that even the fate of the planet might be at stake. Therefore he tried to ascertain, by isotopic analysis, exactly what was happening to the excess nitrogen fertilizer in Illinois soils. His efforts were immediately and viciously attacked by his departmental colleagues on the grounds that such work was not a proper part of the department's goal of pure research. However,

Commoner was undaunted by the antagonism of the majority of his academic colleagues and in 1971 published his book *The Closing Circle*. In it he pointed out that the new technology, which allowed more maize to be produced on less acreage than before, might be a success economically but was ecologically a disaster. He characterized the nitrogen fertilizer industry in its hurtling dash for profits as one of the 'cleverest business operations of all time'. Evidence suggests that in the presence of artificial nitrogen, the natural fixation of nitrogen from the air by soil bacteria stops and, as a result, it is increasingly difficult for farmers to give up the use of the artificial product. Like addictive drugs, fertilizer nitrogen creates its own demand, the buyers having been 'hooked' on the product.

Dr William Albrecht, a professor of soil science at the University of Missouri, who, more than a quarter of a century ago was almost alone in stressing the importance of healthy soil to crops, animals and men, considers that when it comes to food cows are more intelligent than people. However tall and green the grass may look when grown with an excess of artificial nitrogen the cow will refuse it and eat the surrounding grass shorter and shorter. Though she cannot classify forage crops by variety name, nor by tonnage yield per acre, the cow is more expert than any biochemist at assessing their nutritional value.

Albrecht's years of research were admired by Dr André Voisin, the Director of Studies of France's National Veterinary School at Alfort, near Paris. In 1959 Dr Voisin produced a book, *Soil, Grass and Cancer*, the theme of which is that man, in his effort to produce food for an exploding world population, has forgotten that his body comes from the soil. 'Ashes to ashes, and dust to dust,' says Voisin, is not merely a religious and philosophical doctrine but a scientific truth of such profundity that it should be engraved over the entrance to every Faculty of Medicine throughout the world.

Voisin's realization that plants and animals are intimately associated with the soil whence they originate was strengthened when he visited the Ukraine and saw that, within a few generations, the giant dappled Percheron draught horses from France had dwindled to the size of Cossack horses, though their blood-lines had been kept pure by the Soviets and their conformation remained the same, though miniaturized. This should remind us, says Voisin, that all living things are bio-chemical photographs of their environment. Our ancestors, he says, were well aware of the fact that the dust of the soil itself is what finally determines vigour and health. Developing his theme that the soil makes the plant, the animal and man himself, Voisin exposed his readers to a fascinating panoply of data which illustrates that animals and plants on the land, not chemists in laboratories, are the supreme judges of agronomic methods. Voisin also provided copious examples to prove that, by itself, chemical analysis of food-stuffs, plants and soil is insufficient to evaluate their essence. As he says, farmers have long been given advice on animal feeding on the basis of certain tests for nitrogen content; he goes on to quote R. L. M. Synge, the 1952 Nobel Prizewinner in chemistry, who considers it presumptuous to conclude anything about the real nutritive qualities of grass, or human food, in this way.

The Dean of Agriculture at the University of Durham was so impressed with Voisin's lecture to the British Society of Animal Production in 1957 that he summed it up for the assembled audience by saying: 'As Monsieur Voisin has forcibly explained to us, a herbage which appears ideal to the chemist as judged by his analysis is not necessarily ideal for the cow.'

While Voisin was in England, he visited one farm on which the incidence of a disease known as grass tetany afflicting a 150-head herd of cattle was particularly high. Voisin learned from the farm owner that his livestock had been foraging, not on seasoned pastureland, but on new sowings of young grass to which enormous applications of industrial fertilizer, particularly potash, had been applied. Voisin told the farmer that when potash is applied to grass and other forage plants, the plants gorge themselves immediately and indulge in what Americans call 'luxury consumption'. This results in a large and rapid increase in the potash content of the plants and it diminishes the quantity of other elements absorbed. If there is a lack of magnesium, tetany is likely to occur.

When a local veterinary surgeon arrived at the farm to care

for some of the stricken animals, Voisin asked him whether he knew to what extent his client had employed potash to fertilize his grazing land. The animal doctor, who had no idea that he was talking to one of the most distinguished French representatives of veterinary science, curtly replied, 'This question concerns the farmer. My role is to care for sick animals and to cure them.' Voisin was shocked at this stock reply. 'I think,' he wrote, 'that it is not merely a question of healing the animal or man stricken by disease; it is necessary to heal the soil so as not to have to heal the animal or man.'

In his opinion the rise of the artificial fertilizer industry has caused man mechanically and unthinkingly to rely to such an extent on its products that he has forgotten his intimate relationship with the soil as nature made it, and that his adulteration of the dust from which he springs may be sealing his destiny on planet earth. Though the origin of this predicament is hardly a century old, its progression has been geometric in the proliferation of degenerative diseases consequent on the over-use of artificial fertilizers.

It all started with Baron Justus von Liebig, a famous German chemist who published an essay in 1840, interestingly entitled *Chemistry in its Application to Agriculture and Physiology* in which he appeared to indicate that *everything required by living plants was to be found in the mineral salts present in their ashes* once the plants have been incinerated to destroy all the organic matter they contained. Though this theory ran directly counter to centuries of agricultural practice, and indeed to common sense, the visual results of the application of artificial fertilizers composed of nitrogen, phosphates and potash, together with calcium oxide, or lime, seemed to prove Liebig's theory, and resulted in the rocketing climb of fertilizer production by the chemical industry. This sudden blind dependence upon nitrogen, phosphorus, and potassium, the main constituents of artificial fertilizers, or NPK – after the first letters of their Latin names – is termed by Dr Albrecht the 'ash mentality', since ashes suggest the idea of *death* rather than a *living* utilization theory which was going by the board. It is a theory that like a senile yet undeposable king, still rules the world's agricultural realms.

An interesting study of people's dietary practices in relation to their health was carried out in the early years of this century by Dr Robert McCarrison, who headed the nutrition research department for the government of India. He spent some considerable time working among the peoples of the remote Gilgit Agency, a rugged, mountainous area in northern Kashmir. One of these peoples, the Hunzas, who claim descent directly from the soldiers of Alexander the Great, could walk 120 miles at a stretch in the roughest mountain country in the world, or cut two holes in a frozen lake and swim from one to the other under the ice for the fun of it. McCarrison was struck by the fact that with the exception of an occasional eye-inflammation due to badly ventilated fires in their huts, they were wholly free from disease and lived to a great age. Their health was matched by their superior intelligence, wit and urbanity. Though they were numerically few and their neighbours warlike, they were rarely attacked – because they always won. However, neighbouring people who lived in the same climate and geographical conditions were afflicted with many diseases, and it was this which started McCarrison on his comparative study of the dietary practices of Gilgit Agency peoples. Later, he extended it to various races all over India.

By feeding diverse Indian diets to rats – which are foolish enough to eat whatever humans will eat – McCarrison found that his rats reflected the conditions of growth, physique and health of the people eating the same foods. Those rats which ate the diets of the peoples such as the Pathans and Sikhs increased their body weight much faster and were much healthier than those ingesting the daily fare of peoples like the Kanarese and Bengalis. When offered the food of the Hunzas, which was limited to grain, vegetables and fruits along with unpasteurized goat milk and the butter made from it, the rodents appeared to McCarrison the healthiest ever raised in his laboratory. They grew rapidly, were apparently never ill, mated with enthusiasm and had healthy offspring. Throughout their lifetime they were gentle, affectionate and playful. When they were killed at twenty-seven months, the equivalent of fifty-five years in humans, autopsies showed that nothing whatsoever was wrong with their organs. In contrast to these

'Hunza rats', others contracted precisely the diseases of the people whose diets they were being fed, and even seemed to adopt certain of their behavioural characteristics. Many of them, snarling and vicious, had to be kept apart if they were not to kill each other. Illnesses revealed at autopsy filled a whole page. All parts of their bodies, from womb and ovary to skin, hair and blood and respiratory, urinary, digestive, nervous and cardio-vascular systems were afflicted.

During a lecture to the British College of Surgeons McCarrison described how in the course of more than two years, his rats fed on the diets of the more vigorous and well-developed Indian races never fell ill. But the *British Medical Journal*, in a leading article on McCarrison's address, concentrated only on the diseases which diet would help to prevent and completely overlooked the deduction that people's health, like rats' health, was dependent on the quality of their diet. Doctors, used to textbook explanations that pneumonia was due to exhaustion, chills, a blow on the chest, the pneumoccus microbe itself, weakness in old age, or other illnesses, were unimpressed with McCarrison's finding that, in every case, his laboratory rats had fallen ill with pneumonia because of faulty food. The same was true for diseases of the middle ear, peptic ulcers and other afflictions.

American medical circles were no more alert to the basic truth which McCarrison was propounding than their British colleagues. At his Mellon lecture they listened impassively when he said of the Hunzas: 'Indeed their buoyant abdominal health has, since my return to the West, provided a remarkable contrast with the dyspeptic and colonic lamentations of our highly civilized communities.' Then as now, the weight of McCarrison's evidence that Hunzas enjoy a remarkably long disease-free life failed to mobilize any medical research expedition to Hunza-land. His important data was buried in the *Indian Journal of Medical Research*. It did not receive wide publicity until 1938 when a British doctor, J. T. Wrench, brought out a book, *The Wheel of Health*. In the introduction to his work he asked controversially why young medical students were always made to study sick or convalescent people, never the ultra-healthy? Medical schools, he objected, taught only disease. 'Moreover, the basis of our teaching upon disease is pathology, namely the appearance of that which is dead from disease.' Then as today, it seems the emphasis was on *pathology*, not *ecology*.

Neither Wrench's admonition nor the startling evidence of McCarrison seemed to have any effect on the health authorities of the major countries of the world. In 1949 Dr Elmer Nelson, in charge of nutrition at the U.S. Food and Drug Administration, was reported by the *Washington Post* to have declared in court that:

It is wholly unscientific to state that a well-fed body is more able to resist disease than a less well-fed body. My over-all opinion is that there has not been enough experimentation to prove that dietary deficiencies made one more susceptible to disease.

Some time before McCarrison arrived in the Gilgit Agency, Albert Howard, a young mycologist and agricultural lecturer to the Department of Agriculture at Barbados, came to the conclusion that the true cause for plant diseases would never be solved by researchers sequestered in small laboratories and greenhouses full of flowerpots. As he put it, 'In Barbados I was a laboratory hermit, a specialist of specialists, intent on learning more and more about less and less.' However, in a tour of the Windward and Leeward Islands when he was advising people on how to grow cacao, arrowroot, ground nuts, bananas, citrus fruits, nutmegs and a host of other plants, he found that he was learning a great deal from these men who were in actual contact with the land. And this made him realize one of the fundamental weaknesses in the organization of the research into plant pathology. He wrote that,

I was an investigator of plant diseases, but I had myself no crops on which I could try out the remedies I advocated. It was borne in on me that there was a wide chasm between science in the laboratory and practice in the field.

Howard's first big chance to combine theory and practice came in 1905 when he was appointed Imperial Botanist to the Government of India. At the Agricultural Research Station in Bengal he decided to see whether he could grow such healthy plants that they would not require poison sprays to resist disease. Taking the natives of the region as his teachers, he made a close study of Indian agricultural practices and, as he put it, 'speedily found his reward'.

The Indians used no pesticides or artificial fertilizers but returned to the land carefully accumulated animal and vegetal wastes. Howard was so successful in following this practice that by 1919 he had learnt, in his own words:

how to grow healthy crops, practically free from disease, without the slightest help from mycologists, entomologists, bacteriologists, agricultural chemists, statisticians, clearing-houses of information, artificial manures, spraying machines, insecticides, fungicides, germicides, and all the other expensive paraphernalia of the modern experimental station.

He also discovered that his herd of work-oxen, that were fed only from the produce from his fertile land, never went down with foot-and-mouth disease, rinderpest, septicaemia or any of the other cattle diseases which frequently devastated the countryside for miles around. He wrote that,

None of my animals were segregated, none were inoculated; they frequently came into contact with diseased stock. As my small farmyard at Pusa was only separated by a low hedge from one of the large cattle-sheds on the Pusa estate, in which outbreaks of foot-and-mouth disease often occurred, I have several times seen my oxen rubbing noses with foot-and-mouth cases. Nothing happened. The healthy, well-fed animals failed to react to this disease exactly as suitable varieties of crops, when properly grown, did to insect and fungous pests – no infection took place.

His experiences had shown him that the basis for eliminating disease in plants and animals was the fertility of the soil. In order to bring his experimental station to the highest state of fertility he determined to copy the age-old practices of China and build a large-scale system for turning farm waste into humus.

Unfortunately, while the idea was taking shape in his mind, the Pusa research station had become, in his opinion, firmly established as 'a series of watertight compartments – plant-breeding, mycology, entomology, bacteriology, agricultural chemistry and practical agriculture'. Vested interests seemed to regard the organization as more important than its purpose. To enable him to make a comprehensive study of soil fertility and its many implications Howard needed complete freedom of action. His proposals involved 'overlapping', and he realized that there was no room for his method of working within the existing framework of the organization. He therefore laboriously collected funds to found a new centre, the Institute of Plant Industry at Indore, eight hundred miles north-east of Bombay, where he could work in his own way. A higher yield of cotton, the principal commercial crop around Indore, could only be achieved by raising soil fertility and so Howard was in his element. He started to develop what came to be known as the *Indore process* of humus production. Within a short time, the yields of his cotton were not only three times those of the surrounding countryside but also the cotton was remarkably free from diseases. Howard later wrote that,

These results were progressive confirmation of the principle I was working out – the connection between land in good heart and disease-free crops; they were proof that as soon as land drops below par, disease may set in.

Howard was firmly convinced that the two most important goals were to keep the texture of his soils right and not to overwork his land beyond a volume of operations for which it had sufficient natural reserves.

Based on his findings, Howard wrote a book *The Waste Products of Agriculture: Their Utilization as Humus* which was greeted with favourable and even enthusiastic reviews around the world. But when the book was circulated to agricultural scientists working on cotton problems in research stations all over the British Empire, the reception was hostile and even obstructive. This was because Howard's successful methodology challenged the ingrained attitudes that *breeding methods alone* could improve cotton yields and the quality of plant fibres and disease was to be reduced by *direct assault with pesticides*.

Furthermore, the time factor was ridiculed. How could one possibly waste several years bringing the land back into what

Howard called 'good heart'? This would demand the abandonment of chemical fertilizers and the time-consuming organization of Indore compost, a mixture of decaying animal and plant matter at a ratio of 3:1. As Howard states:

> The production of compost on a large scale might, therefore, prove to be revolutionary and a positive danger to the structure and perhaps to the very existence of a research organization based on the piecemeal application of the separate sciences to a complex and many-sided biological problem like the production of cotton.

Research workers on many other crops throughout the Empire took the same dour view as that of the cotton specialists and they were strongly supported by the moguls of the burgeoning artificial fertilizer and pesticide industries.

When Howard came home to England at the end of 1935, he was invited by the students of the School of Agriculture at Cambridge University to address them on 'The Manufacture of Humus by the Indore Method'. Because he had distributed printed copies of his remarks beforehand in order to ensure that a lively discussion would follow his lecture, practically the whole staff of the school was present when he mounted the lecture platform. Since he had been so consistently attacked by plant specialists in England, India, and other parts of the world, it was no surprise to Howard that nearly all of the school's faculty from chemists and pathologists to plant breeders heatedly opposed his remarks. Only the student body seemed enthusiastic and, as Howard recalled,

> vastly amused at finding their teachers on the defensive and vainly endeavouring to bolster up the tottering pillars supporting their temple. Here again I was amazed by the limited knowledge and experience of the world's agriculturists disclosed by this debate. I felt I was dealing with beginners and that some of the arguments put forward could almost be described as the impertinences of ignorance. It was obvious from this meeting that little or no support for organic farming would be obtained from the agricultural colleges and research institutes of Great Britain.

Howard was correct. When later he read to the British Farmers' Club a paper on 'The Restoration and Maintenance of Fertility', representatives of experimental stations and of the

[208]

fertilizer industry in the audience poured ridicule on his ideas. To their protestations, Howard replied that he would shortly have his answer 'written on to the land itself'. Two years later Sir Bernard Greenwell, who had meticulously followed Howard's directions on his two estates, gave an account to the club which more than bore out Howard's lifetime findings. But the scientists and the fertilizer salesmen, knowing that success was the one unanswerable argument in favour of organic farming, failed to attend the lecture.

Despite the truculence of these vested interests, Howard, like McCarrison, was knighted for his achievements. Yet only a few sensitive individuals began to follow his lead. One of these was Lady Eve Balfour who had since childhood suffered bad bouts of rheumatism and continual head colds each winter from November to April. Learning of Howard's research just before the Second World War, she initiated an Indore-type operation on her own farm at Haughley in Suffolk. Instead of bakers' loaves she ate only bread ground from her own compost-benefited wheat. During the winter following the change in her diet, she was entirely free from colds for the first time in her life and was no longer bothered with rheumatic pains in prolonged periods of cold, wet weather.

During the war, Lady Eve's book *The Living Soil* appeared in heavily rationed England. The result of long detective work in libraries and interviews with health specialists who were convinced of the soundness of Howard's and McCarrison's views, it amassed a compendium of scattered data on the links between humus-grown plants and the health of animals and humans fed upon them. Lady Eve compared man's prideful 'conquest of nature' with the conquest of Europe taking place under the Nazis. 'As Europe is in revolt against the tyrant,' she wrote, 'so is nature in revolt against the exploitation of man.'

Lady Eve soon discovered that her piglets, attacked at the age of one month by a disease called white scour, which the textbooks explained was due to iron deficiency, and for which accordingly they recommended doses of chickweed or other plants rich in that element, could be cured equally effectively by being fed actual soil from fields rich in humus to which no chemical fertilizers had been applied, whereas soil from land 'exhausted' from the application of fertilizers had no effect upon the disease's progress.

Another of Howard's followers was Friend Sykes, a British farmer and breeder of thoroughbred horses, who bought a 750-acre derelict farm in Wiltshire and planned to farm it in accordance with Howard's ideas. Sykes's previous experience as an agricultural consultant had taught him that on specialized farms, where only certain crops or one variety of animals were raised, the inevitable result was a weakening of stock and plants by disease. He concluded that outbreaks of disease could be completely eradicated by an 'enlightened practice of good husbandry', and particularly by the introduction of mixed agriculture. Sykes had been a student of ecology long before the subject became a household word and an opponent of DDT more than ten years before Rachel Carson shocked the world with her book *Silent Spring*. In his *Food Farming and the Future*, published in 1950, he wrote,

The first thing that Nature does when she has been treated with poison is to battle against it and try to breed a resistant strain of the form of life that is being attacked. If the chemist persists in his poisonous methods, he often has to invent more and stronger poisons to deal with the resistance that Nature sets up against him. In this way, a vicious cycle is created. For, as a result of the conflict, pests of a harder nature and poisons still more powerful are evolved; and who is to say, in this protracted struggle, man himself may not ultimately be involved and overwhelmed?

Sykes's experience with his crops, based on his intuition that the soil had a *latent fertility* which could be brought out simply by tending the land, and without the application of any fertilizer whatsoever, was little short of fantastic. A laboratory analysis of the soil on one of his fields indicated severe deficiencies of lime, phosphate and potash, and artificial fertilizers were recommended to correct the condition. Ignoring this report, Sykes simply ploughed and harrowed his field and, *without adding any fertilizer*, sowed oats. To the amazement of his neighbours his crop yielded ninety-two bushels per acre which was followed by an equally successful crop of wheat. After tilling the soil throughout the summer, he again sent a sample of it to the laboratory and found that the lime and potash had been completely restored and only a deficiency of phosphorus remained. The unanimous view of experts was that cereal crops could not be successfully grown without a heavy dressing of phosphates; but Sykes merely subsoil ploughed the acreage and achieved a second harvest of wheat even larger than the first. Subsoil ploughing digs deeper into the ground and aerates this otherwise packed and useless earth. When Sykes ordered his subsoiler plough, the agent who took his order said: 'What on earth do you want a tool like that for in this God-forsaken country? My firm has been in business over a hundred years and has never supplied such an implement before.' The following year Sykes's wheat crop, which had been undersown with rye grasses and clover, produced two and a half tons of hay to the acre in one cut. Then he reploughed his land, planted it with oats, and was rewarded with a crop yielding over one hundred bushels to the acre. A third laboratory analysis of his soil showed no deficiencies whatsoever.

Sykes described this procedure in an essay 'Farming for Profit with Organic Manures as the Sole Medium of Refertilization' in which he concluded that not only had he made money, but also he had made his livestock healthy and his plants disease-free without the use of poison sprays. In addition he had been able to plant the same wheat, barley and oats from their seeds six consecutive years although other farmers had had to make changes. His yields he described as enormous.

The *Soil Association* was formed by Friend Sykes, Lady Balfour and others with the object of uniting people, of whatever country, to work for a fuller understanding of the *vital relationships* between the soil, plant, animal and man. Its philosophy centred on the idea that when *quality is sacrificed to quantity*, total food supply diminishes. The Association began a research project on land donated in Suffolk, the referees for which stated:

Humanity has been badly frightened by the invention of the atomic bomb. Yet the slower but more widespread devastation wrought by exhausting the soil upon which we depend for subsistence, is ignored by the majority of people, who think of calamity only in terms of disaster or war. Wasteful exploitation of the soil's fertility is due in part to the desire for quick cash returns, but in a greater degree to ignorance. Many scientists and agriculturalists now realize that their knowledge of the natural processes underlying soil fertility is incomplete. They recognize that these processes are only partly explicable in terms of agricultural chemistry and that the purely inorganic approach to the study of soil science is a line of thought as dead as the mechanical determination of nineteenth-century physics. 'Dead' is the appropriate word, for the missing factor is that of life itself.

Shortly before the formation of the Soil Association in Britain, J. I. Rodale, editor of a health magazine in Pennsylvania also came across the work of Sir Albert Howard. Afterwards, he wrote that,

> To say I was stunned would be a definite understatement. Surely the way food is grown has something to do with its nutritional quality. Yet this theory had not found its way into the articles of any of the health magazines I was reading. To physicians and nutrition specialists carrots were carrots were carrots.

In 1942 Rodale bought a farm of his own in Emmaus, Pennsylvania. He also set about publishing Sir Albert Howard's book, *An Agricultural Testament* and launched a journal, *Organic Gardening and Farming*, which today, after three decades of growth, has some 850,000 subscribers. A companion magazine to enlighten the public on the links between health and organically grown foods, called *Prevention*, was started by Rodale in 1950 and now circulates to over one million readers increasingly anxious about the quality of American food.

Rodale's campaign was designed to educate the American public and show them that the soil is alive and clean. Below its surface the earth teems with organisms. Some of the most valuable are earthworms, called *Annelida* after the Latin word for rings, because they are made of one hundred to two hundred ring-like segments, each an independent miniature body with identical organs. They burrow into the ground to depths of more than the height of a tall man, acting as nature's plough, eating the soil as they move and ejecting it again as castings to produce rich top-soil. Called by Aristotle the 'intestines of the soil' they could also be considered its vascular system since, without them, soils get hard-packed as if their arteries had hardened.

In 1881, a year before his death, Charles Darwin brought out a book, *Vegetable Mould and Earthworms*, in which he made the statement that without worms vegetation would degenerate to the vanishing point. He estimated that in a single year more than *ten tons* of dry earth per acre passed through the digestive system of an earthworm and that in a field well populated with them *one inch* of top-soil would be created *every five years*. Darwin's earthworm book mouldered on the shelf for fifty years before it was re-examined; even then his ideas did not penetrate into the curricula of the agricultural schools. As a result, it is hardly appreciated that with heavy application of chemical fertilizers and pesticides, a field can lose its entire earthworm population, so important for keeping it in a healthy condition.

Sir E. John Russell, in his book *Soil Conditions and Plant Growth*, says that in one tiny gramme of soil treated with farm-yard manure there are some 29,000,000 bacteria; however, where chemical fertilizers are used, the number is cut almost by half. In an acre of rich earth, bacteria are estimated to weigh more than a quarter of a ton; as they die, their bodies become converted to humus enriching the soil in a natural way. There are, besides, myriads of other microscopical organisms: actinomycetes, filamentous forms resembling both bacteria and fungi; tiny algae, related to seaweeds; protozoa, animals made up of a single cell; and the strange chlorophyll-less fungi themselves ranging from one-celled forms to branched bodies including yeasts, moulds and mushrooms. The vegetative part of one of these fungi associates with the roots of many green plants in a mysterious way that is beneficial to both. The threads of these fungi, called *mycorrhizae*, are consumed by tree roots with which they were associated. This discovery was borne out by Sir Albert Howard who found that the roots of the healthiest French vines were rich in *mycorrhizae*; no artificial fertilizers had ever been used on them and they were noted for the high quality of their wines.

Another great advantage of natural agriculture, well known

to yesterday's farmer, has been forgotten in the highly specialized mono-crop agriculture of today; the advantage of symbiosis in plants. As the Russian essayist Soloukhin has pointed out in *Grass*, modern Soviet agronomy has lost all feeling for the benefits of plant companionships. Though the specialists mock the idea that cornflowers growing in a field of waving rye can have a beneficial effect on the crop, and consider the blue-blossomed plants as only noxious weeds. Soloukhin asks: 'If the cornflower were an evil weed, would not the farmers of the world have grown to hate it before the appearance of the learned agronomists?'

How many botanists, asks Soloukhin, realize that the first sheaf of rye harvest was lovingly decorated with a cornflower wreath and placed in front of an icon, or that cornflowers were held by country folk to supply bees with abundant nectar for honey even in the driest weather? Suspecting that all this folk wisdom had a solid basis in fact, Soloukhin checked in scientific literature and found evidence supporting the accuracy of peasant intuition. He read that if a hundred wheat grains are mixed with twenty seeds from the ox-eye daisy the sprouting wheat will be overwhelmed, but that if only one daisy seed is added, the wheat will grow better than if no daisies come up in its field. The same is true for rye and cornflowers.

Soloukhin's view on plant symbiosis supports that of Dr Joseph Coccanouer, an American professor of botany and conservation. In his book, *Weeds: Guardians of the Soil,* published nearly a quarter of a century ago, Coccanouer sets forth the thesis that, far from being harmful, plants usually considered noxious and troublesome such as ragweed, pigweeds, purslane and nettles, bring up from the sub-soil minerals, especially those which have been depleted from the top soil, and are excellent indicators of soil conditions. As companion crops they help domesticated plants to get their roots down to food which would otherwise be beyond their reach. He struck a warning note when he wrote, 'In America, in our frenzied efforts to take advantage of high prices for agricultural products, we are mining our soils instead of farming them.' The same was beginning to be true of Europe where, since the Second World War, few farmers have been practising the *law of return*, and instead are giving in to stimulation of the soil with artificial fertilizers for quick and profitable returns. Today, Americans live in a country where farming is becoming more and more mechanized and where food production is supposed to be the world's most efficient. Yet food prices continue to rise. It is still said that whereas in 1900 one U.S. farmer could feed only five people besides himself, today he can feed thirty. But Georg Borgstrom, a Michigan University food scientist, says these mathematics are illusory. At the turn of the century farmers not only worked their land and raised livestock, but also they delivered their own milk, butchered their own animals, churned fresh farm butter, salted meat, baked bread and farmed with draught animals for which they produced feed. Now the draught animals have been superseded by expensive machinery using increasingly costly and depletable fossil fuels, and the husbandman's arts have been taken over by factories. In less than twenty-five years several million poultry raisers, whose chickens roamed the land ingesting all sorts of natural mineral products and insects, have disappeared to be replaced by some 6,000 semi-automated outlets where broilers, packed wing to wing in cages, are fed diets full of artificial supplements.

All these off-farm activities figure in the high cost and dubious quality of food. In fact, if one divides the some twenty-two million workers building farm machinery and farm-to-market roads, delivering and processing farm produce and engaged in other food production tasks, it becomes clear that it takes about the same number of people to feed Americans today as it did in 1900. However, there are signs that the agricultural worm may at last be starting to turn and that university scientists are beginning to wake up to the views propounded so long ago by McCarrison, Howard, and Rodale. As if they were discovering something new, Drs Robert F. Keefer and Rabindar N. Singh, agricultural researchers at the West Virginia University in Morgantown, issued a press release on 4 March 1973 to the effect that 'what man eats is determined partly by the fertilizer that farmers put on their crops'. In their experiments the two professors say that they have determined that the amounts of trace elements in sweet and fodder corn, so important in the diets of animals and humans, are dropping dramatically due to the kinds and amounts of fertilizers grown in some soils.

Their somewhat belated rediscovery of this basic truth has also reinforced a survey conducted in eleven mid-western states where it was found that the iron, copper, zinc and manganese content in corn grain has fallen off severely in the past four years. The application of huge doses of nitrogen fertilizer such as that which has alarmed the citizens of Illinois, may, says Singh, 'have far-reaching effects on the health of animals and men'. He adds that work of another of his colleagues shows that fertilization of pastures with high rates of nitrogen may produce changes in the milk of grazing animals as revealed by feeding it to rats. 'Our study on sweet corn,' Singh cautiously concludes, 'is offered as a model only because a single dietary ingredient in man's nutritional status isn't likely to be significant.'

More encouraging is the fact that practical farmers are no longer waiting for the academic scientists to confirm what they can observe with their eyes. Watching the effects of chemicals, both fertilizers and pesticides, on their land, independent and intelligent observers are going ahead to right things before it is too late. Even if the steps are time-consuming, they know that, unless they are taken, the land which for centuries produced maize, beans and squash for the Indians and protein-rich prairie grass for millions of buffalo not only may give forth mineral-deficient crops but may not be able to afford them any crops whatsoever.

14

Chemicals, plants and man

In the early nineteenth century an American of English descent named Nichols cleared hundreds of acres of rich virgin land in South Carolina on which he grew crops of cotton, tobacco and corn, so abundant that with the revenue he built a big house and educated a large family. Not once in his lifetime did he add anything to the soil. When it became depleted and his crops dwindled, he cleared more land and continued his exploitation. When there was no more land to be cleared the family fortunes declined.

Nichols's son, grown to manhood, looked at the poverty-stricken acreage, took the famous journalist Horace Greeley's advice and moved west to Tennessee where he cleared two thousand acres of virgin land; like his father he planted cotton, maize and tobacco. When his own son was grown to manhood, the land was once more so depleted from having living things taken from it and none returned that he moved on to Horse Creek in Maringo County, Alabama, there to purchase another two thousand acres of fertile soil and raise a family of twelve children on the proceeds; the town became Nicholsville; Nichols became the owner of a sawmill, a general store and a grist mill. This man's son also grew up to see devastation where his father had grown rich. He decided to move further west and settled in Parkdale, Arkansas, where he bought a thousand acres of good land on the bayou.

Four moves in four generations. Multiplied by thousands, this is the story of how Americans raised food on a continent which was there for the taking. The great-grandson of the original Nichols, like thousands of other farmers, inaugurated a new era. After the First World War he began to farm rather than to exploit his new acreage by adopting the new government-recommended artificial fertilizers. For a time his cotton crops prospered, but eventually he noticed that his pest population was much greater than it had been. When the bottom fell out of the cotton market Nichols's son Joe decided that medicine not farming was to be his career. He was a fully-fledged physician and surgeon in Atlanta, Texas when at the age of thirty-seven he suffered a bad heart attack which nearly killed him. He was forced to give up his practice, knowing that his expectation of life was extremely poor. As he was casually leafing through the advertisements in a farming magazine one day he came across a line 'People who eat natural food grown in fertile soil don't get heart disease'. Quackery of the worst sort, he thought to himself. After all, J. I. Rodale, the editor of the magazine, wasn't even a doctor. However, his eye was caught by the advertisements for two books, *Agricultural Testament* by Sir Albert Howard and *Nutritional and Natural Health* by Sir Robert McCarrison. He promptly ordered them both, hoping to find the answer to the questions that nagged him – What is natural food? What is fertile soil?

I had a medical degree, was fairly intelligent, had read a lot, owned a farm, but I didn't know what was natural food. Like many another American who hadn't really investigated the subject, I thought 'natural food' meant wheat germ and black molasses, and that all natural food addicts were faddists, quacks and nuts. I thought you made land fertile by dumping commercial fertilizer on it.

Now, more than thirty years later, Joe Nichols's thousand-acre farm in Texas is one of the show places of the state; nor has he ever again been afflicted with a heart attack. He ascribes both successes to the advice which he took from Rodale, Howard, and McCarrison. On his farm, not another ounce of chemical fertilizer went into the land, nothing but natural compost.

Nichols realized it was the 'junk food' he had been eating all his life, food produced from poisoned land, that had led straight to a massive heart attack. A third book, *Nutrition and the Soil* by Sir Lionel Picton, convinced him that the answer to metabolic disease, whether it was heart trouble, cancer, or diabetes, was indeed natural poison-free food grown on fertile soil.

The food we eat is digested and absorbed from the intestine into the blood stream. Essential nutrients are carried to the individual cells all over the body, where repair work is done by metabolism, the process by which stable non-living matter is built up into complex and unstable living material, or protoplasm. The cell has an amazing capacity to repair itself provided it gets proper ingredients through proper nutrition; otherwise it becomes stunted or goes out of control. The cell, or basic unit of life where metabolism occurs, needs essential amino acids, natural vitamins, organic minerals, essential fatty acids, unrefined carbohydrates, and several more as yet unknown factors.

Organic minerals, like vitamins, are found in balanced proportions in natural food. The vitamins themselves are not nutrients, but substances without which the body cannot make use of nutrients. They are parts of an extremely complex, intricately interrelated whole. In 'balance' means that all the nutrients utilized by the tissues must be available to the cell simultaneously. Furthermore the vitamins essential to proper nutrition and good health must be natural.

There is a great difference between natural and synthetic vitamins, not a chemical but a biological difference. There is something missing in the artificial that is of biological or life-enhancing value. Not yet widely accepted, this fact has been unequivocally established by the work of Dr Ehrenfried Pfeiffer, a biochemist and follower of the great natural scientist and clairvoyant Rudolf Steiner. Dr Nichols thinks the Pfeiffer techniques can reveal exactly why natural foods or those containing natural vitamins and minerals and enzymes – another chemical compound, of vegetable or animal origin, which causes chemical transformation – are superior to those grown and preserved with chemicals.

When Pfeiffer came to the United States at the outbreak of World War II, and settled at Three-Fold Farm in Spring Valley, New York, he worked out Steiner's 'Biodynamic' system for making composts and for treating the land, and set up a laboratory to investigate living things without breaking them into chemical constituents.

Before his arrival in the United States Pfeiffer had developed in his native Switzerland a 'sensitivity crystallization method' to test finer dynamic forces and qualities in plants, animals, and humans than had thus far been detectable in laboratories. Dr Steiner, who had given a series of esoteric lectures at the Silesian estate of Count Keyserling in the 1920s for agronomists concerned about the falling productivity of their crops, had asked Pfeiffer to find a reagent which would reveal what Steiner called 'etheric formative forces' in living matter. After months of tests with Glauber's salt, or sodium sulphate, and many other chemicals, Pfeiffer discovered that if a solution of copper chloride to which extracts of living matter had been added was allowed to evaporate slowly over fourteen to seventeen hours it would produce a crystallization pattern determined not only by the nature but by the quality of the plant from which the extract was taken. According to Pfeiffer, the same *formative forces* inherent in the plant and acting to bring about its form and shape would combine with living growth forces to form the pattern of crystal arrangement.

Dr Erica Sabarth, current director of the Pfeiffer-established laboratory in Spring Valley, showed the authors rows of beautiful crystallizations, looking like exotic undersea corals. She pointed out how a strong, vigorous plant produces a beautiful, harmonious, and clearly formed crystal arrangement radiating through to the outer edge. The same crystallization made from a weak or sick plant results in an uneven picture showing thickening or incrustation.

Pfeiffer's method, says Sabarth, can be applied to determine the inherent quality of all sorts of living organisms. When a forester sent Pfeiffer two seeds taken from different pine trees, and asked if he could detect any difference in the trees themselves, Pfeiffer submitted the seeds to his crystallization tests and found that, whereas one crystal picture was an example of harmonious perfection, the other was distorted and ugly. He wrote to the forester that one of the trees should be a fine specimen, the other must have a serious defect. By return mail the forester sent Pfeiffer enlarged photographs of two grown trees: the trunk of one was mast straight; the other was so crooked it was useless for lumber.

At Spring Valley Pfeiffer developed an even simpler and less time-consuming method to demonstrate how life veritably pulsates from living soils, plants, and foods, but not from inorganic minerals, chemicals, and synthetic vitamins, which are relatively dead. Requiring none of the complex equipment of the standard chemical laboratory, it uses circular filter-paper discs fifteen centimetres in diameter, provided with a small hole in the centre for insertion of a wick. The discs are laid in open petri dishes in which stand small crucibles containing a 0.05 silver-nitrate solution. This solution climbs up through the wick and spreads over the discs until it has expanded about four centimetres from the centre.

From the brilliant-coloured concentric patterns Pfeiffer has been able to disclose new secrets of life. Testing natural vitamin C taken from such products as rose hips, he established that the pattern of vitality was far stronger than from artificial vitamin C, or ascorbic acid. Rudolf Hauschka, a follower of Rudolf Steiner, suggests that vitamins are not chemical compounds that can be synthetically produced but 'primary cosmic formative forces'.

Before his death, Pfeiffer pointed out in his own booklet *Chromatography Applied to Quality Testing* that Goethe had stated a truth more than 150 years ago which is of the utmost importance with regard to the recognition of natural biological quality: *The whole is more than the sum of its parts.* 'This means,' wrote Pfeiffer,

that a natural organism or entity contains factors which cannot be recognized or demonstrated if one takes the original organism apart and determines its component parts by way of analysis. One can, for instance, take a seed, analyse it for protein, carbohydrates, fats, minerals, moisture and vitamins, but all this will not tell its genetic background or its biological value.

In an article, 'Plant Relationships as Made Visible by Chromatography', published in the winter 1968, issue of *Bio-Dynamics*, a periodical to further soil conservation and increase fertility in order to improve nutrition and health, Sabarth stressed that the chromatographic technique 'especially reveals the quality, even the living force of the organism'. She added that she plans to explore the possibilities of the method not only as it applies to seeds and fruits but with regard to the roots of plants and all the other plant parts.

In modern processed foods the vitamins, trace elements and enzymes are removed, mostly so as to render the food more durable. As Nichols put it: 'They remove the life, in effect killing it, so that it will not live and die later.' The most poisonous foods in his view are the bleached flour that goes into white bread, white sugar, refined table salt and hydrogenated fats. A grain of wheat consists basically of the germ, the endosperm and the husk. There are three layers of husk, inside which is the more or less solid, white, starchy endosperm. Down at the thick end of the endosperm is a hard nutty kernel called the germ. This is the actual seed of the grain of wheat. The husk protects it from the outside and the endosperm feeds it until it is able to draw its own nutrition from the soil. Other grains – barley, oats, rye, corn – have analogous constructions, and bread can be made from all of them. Wheat germ is unusual in that it contains the entire Vitamin B complex, hence bread was called 'the staff of life'.

In milling modern white flour, the wheat germ and the outside layers of the grain are removed. This means that enzymes, vitamins, and minerals are all stripped from the whole wheat grain, including iron, cobalt, copper manganese and molybdenum. Nichols says there must be a significant interrelationship between these minerals and the vitamins in a grain of wheat that keeps them in balance.

From the earliest times, as we know from bread which has been found in the excavations of ten thousand year old lake dwellings in Switzerland, wheat has been ground between two circular stones. Mills were worked by hand until the advent of steam power, the first steam mill being erected in London in 1784. In stone mills, the entire kernel, husk, germ and endosperm, was ground into meal flour. In that process some of the husk was reduced to powder, which gives colour to the wholemeal. In Deuteronomy 32:14 man is enjoined to eat 'the fat of the kidney of wheat', meaning the germ.

The development of iron rollers by a Frenchman in the early nineteenth century brought with it a separation of wheat germ, husk and endosperm. They were first used in place of stones in Hungary in 1840. By 1880 their use had become universal. From a commercial point of view the roller mill had three advantages over the grinding stones. By separating the husk and germ from the flour, the miller had two products for sale instead of one. The husk and germ were sold as 'offal', or animal fodder. Removal of the germ made it possible to keep the flour in good condition for a much longer time, which increased the miller's profit. When the roller mill was introduced it became possible to adulterate wheat with six per cent of added water. For this the germ had to be removed and sold separately or the flour would not keep.

In so-called 'enriched' white bread, with the vitamins and minerals removed, nothing is left but raw starch which has so little nutritive value that even bacteria won't eat it. Into this insipid starch synthetic chemicals are arbitrarily injected which form only part of the missing Vitamin B complex, and are not properly ingestible by human beings because they are not 'in balance'. The natural Vitamin E is destroyed by the chlorine dioxide used for bleaching the flour and its removal from bread reduces the intake of a working man from about a thousand units a day to between two and three hundred. To compound this trouble, at the same time that white flour was being introduced into England, margarine, the invention of another Frenchman, was brought in as a cheaper substitute for butter. It too was devoid of vitamins A and D. The general health of the country deteriorated. Men from northern England and southern Scotland, large and powerful during the Napoleonic wars, became short and frail and unfit for military service at the time of the Boer War. A commission set up to investigate the phenomenon concluded it was caused by men moving to the cities where they lived not on wholesome country bread but on white bread and white sugar.

Equally detrimental to health are white sugar and glucose, the heavy syrup in which fruits are packed and the sweetener for most soft drinks. In the seventeenth century, European manufacturers developed a lengthy but effective sugar refining process. The resulting whiteness, expensively produced, made both sugar and flour into attractive delicacies for which even the poor were willing to pay. According to Nichols, however, white sugar is one of the most dangerous foods on the market. All the good part, the molasses, the vitamins and minerals are removed. There is nothing left but carbohydrates and calories – of which we have too many already. Today, refining is done for purely commercial reasons: the sugar keeps better. White sugar can be stored in 100-pound cloth sacks for years in dirty warehouses and still be sold for a profit.

Most table syrup, says Nichols, is nothing but corn starch treated with sulphuric acid, artificially coloured and flavoured. It goes straight into the blood stream causing instant hyperglycaemia – or too much sugar in the blood. This drowns the human cells in sugar. The pancreas, heeding the alarm, puts out too much insulin and produces a state of hypoglycaemia, or *too little* sugar in the blood. One of the less suspected poisons on the dining-room table is common refined salt or sodium chloride which if taken in quantity and over a long period causes high blood pressure and heart disease. Hydrogenated fats are also contributing causes of heart disease. These include most of the fats and oils commonly found in shortening, and in practically all commercially baked cakes, biscuits and bread. Much ice-cream is made from mellorine, a cheap hydrogenated oil. The hydrogenating process prevents the fats and oils from going rancid, but it also destroys the essential fatty acids. Nichols points out that whereas natural rice is one of the richest sources of natural vitamin B complex, white processed rice is nothing but raw starch; and the average Westerner's diet is already overloaded with carbohydrates.

Protein is one of the most important items in human diet and meat is the most popular source of protein in the West. But the prime steak of today usually comes from beef that has been force-fed with low quality protein hybrid grains sprayed with poisonous insecticides. This goes straight into the fat of the meat, especially into the marbling, and this, says Nichols, leads straight to heart disease. To fatten cattle and thereby increase profits, animals are often fed with diethylsitbestrol which can be carcinogenic in both men and women. Their organ meat is edible only if the animal has been fed organically. The livers of prime animals are often confiscated because they contain abscesses and toxic substances. Commercially reared chickens may have arsenic and stilbestrol in their bodies, and these will end up in the liver because it is the detoxifying organ of the body.

Store-bought eggs are mostly infertile, do not taste as good as fertile eggs, and are nowhere near as good for you, says Nichols, because there is a subtle biological difference. Hens that lay commercial eggs are cooped up where they cannot move, have seldom if ever seen a rooster, let alone been caught by one. 'How,' asks Nichols, 'can an unhappy hen lay a good egg?'

In the pyramid of life, plants play an essential role. Man cannot ingest essential elements directly from the soil. They must be brought to him through the good graces of living plants, which likewise feed all animals, directly or indirectly. Whether it is through plant or animal our bodies grow out of the soil. Micro-organisms break up the chemicals and make them acceptable to plants. Plants can synthesize carbo-hydrates from the air, rainfall and sunshine. But before the life processes can convert these carbohydrates into amino acids and proteins, they must have help from a fertile soil. Neither man nor animal can synthesize the necessary proteins from the elements. Animals can only assemble them from the amino acids, providing the necessary kinds and amounts of each can be collected or produced by plants with the help of microbes.

Protein-producing plants demand a long list of elements from the soil: nitrogen, sulphur, and phosphorus are required to make part of the protein molecule; calcium and lime are also required; and magnesium, manganese, boron, copper, zinc, molybdenum, and other elements are needed in connection with protein construction, even if only in such small amounts as are called 'trace'. If the soil is not properly fertile, not teeming with micro-organisms, the whole process grinds to a halt. To keep the micro-organisms alive great quantities of decaying organic matter need to be added to the earth. On the forest floor dead plant matter and dead animal matter go back into the land. Leaf mould, through decay, continues to give life to the land, returning to the soil what the tree took as nutrient. Fertile soil is full of life and death; death and decay of organic matter; life in the form of bacteria, moulds and earthworms.

It should be obvious that soil is vital to health. Healthy soil, properly composted, with the right bacteria, fungi and earthworms, free from chemical fertilizers and pesticides, produces strong healthy plants which naturally repel pests. Healthy plants make strong healthy animals and strong healthy human beings. Poor land grows poor food, poor in vitamins, minerals, enzymes and proteins; this produces poor, sick people. Worn out land causes people to leave the farms and go to live in the slums.

It is a fact that plants grown on well balanced fertile soils have a natural immunity to insects and disease, just as a properly nourished body has an immunity to disease. Bugs and worms tend to gravitate towards plants which have grown on poor soil. One of the worst weakeners of plants turns out to be chemical fertilizer, or NKP, which came into general use on farms at the end of the Second World War.

The end result of such chemical farming, says Nichols, is always disease: first to the land, then to the plant, then to the animal, then to man. 'Everywhere in the world where chemical farming is practised the people are sick. The only ones to benefit are the companies that produce the chemicals.'

Simultaneous with the application of fertilizers, the chemical companies began to douse the land with chemical pesticides, abetted by the government and with the tacit support of university professors. Three hundred million pounds of different chemical poisons are now produced under twenty-two thousand different brand names, which result in the destruction of wild life and essential insect and microbe life. Of mass spraying, Dr George J. Wallace, Michigan University zoologist, went on the record to say that it 'poses the greatest threat that animal life in North America has ever faced – worse than deforestation, worse than illegal shooting, worse than drainage, drought, oil pollution, possibly worse than all these decimating factors combined'.

Not only wild life but fish in fresh water and even in the ocean are gradually being poisoned by a combination of insecticides and herbicides. Yet the DDT which wiped out fish and small game left its prime target, the boll weevil, flourishing. Despite the application of chemical pesticides the insects are gaining the upper hand, doing $4 billion worth of damage to crops each year. And no amount of argument appears to put over the fact that *healthy* crops are naturally pest resistant, keeping the insects at bay. In her book *Silent Spring*, Rachel Carson long ago made clear that the environment, which supports human life, is being strained to the point of collapse.

When Nichols realized what was happening to the country as a result of both chemical fertilization and chemical pesticides he found a number of like-minded doctors and scientists and together they formed Natural Food Associates, of which Nichols became the first president. The object of the organization was to start a nation-wide campaign to set out the facts and alert public opinion to the dangers of poor food grown on poor soil. 'We are facing metabolic disaster,' said Nichols. 'We are a nation of sick people. Heart disease is rampaging through America; it is our Public Enemy number one. It is the leading cause of death among Americans.' This provoked an angry response. A campaign was launched to discredit the N.F.A., calling them food faddists, quacks and charlatans and decrying their theories as unscientific. Newspaper and magazine articles, even entire books, were published in a huge effort to destroy the credibility of the organization. In 1973 the Commissioner for the Food and Drug Administration was still insisting that:

Scientifically it is inaccurate to state that the quality of soil in the United States causes abnormally low concentration of vitamins or minerals in the food supply produced in this country . . . There is no relationship between the vitamin content of foods and the chemical composition of the soil.

Nichols and his colleagues on the N.F.A. are faced by a formidable opposition. However, he says that in the long run the country must give up chemical fertilizers and gradually revive the soil organically. Organic fertilizer can now be bought in a sack or packaged just like ordinary commercial fertilizer, and at no greater cost. There are deposits of raw

[227]

rock phosphate and potash with marine trace minerals and other deposits which have the advantage of being no longer needed after a few years of application. On the other hand, the chemical farmer is obliged to put on more and more fertilizer each year. Eventually the organic farmer will make more money, as it will cost him less to operate. Organic farmers dispute their opponents' assertions that there can never be enough organic matter to supply big farms. It is said that the farmer must steal from one acre to get natural fertilizer for another acre. In fact, by following a few simple rules he can grow his own organic matter on every acre and apply the method to any kind of agriculture. All animal manures, garbage, perhaps even sewage sludge, can be, and should be, composted and returned to the land. If we could halve the waste of these materials, says Nichols, we could double the fertility of our soils and thus double the food supply.

The restoration of soil fertility, according to Nichols and his fellow organic farmers, would go a long way towards solving problems of floods and water shortages. When the soil is fertile the rain will soak into the ground; but on poor ground it will wash away the top-soil. Unless the rain soaks in, the underground water level will continue to fall and no amount of dam construction on rivers will solve the water problem. A third of the arable top-soil in the United States has already been washed into the sea over the years, and it is still being lost faster than it can be replaced. During floods, millions of tons of rich top-soil are washed downstream. Soil erosion costs half a million acres of land a year. We live from about eight inches of top-soil, containing earth-worms, bacteria, fungi and other microscopic forms of life that provide us with vegetation, trees, insects, and animals. It is the greatest natural resource of any nation; civilizations of the past have been destroyed when their fertile soils were lost.

Certain that there will be an age of famine, Nichols says that a fertile soil will be the first essential in combating it. And the present campaign to promote the use of commercial fertilizers in the so-called underdeveloped nations of the world must cease if they are not to suffer a massive increase in metabolic disease and even worse famines than they are subjected to at present. Yet the chemical companies keep pouring out propaganda and pressure for greater consumption of their product. Dr Raymond Ewele, vice-president for research at the State University of New York, who has been considered one of the world's leading chemical economists, says blithely, that if 'Asia, Africa and Latin America are not using quantities of fertilizer approaching thirty million tons by 1980, they are almost certain to be engulfed in widespread famine'. Nichols is convinced that exploitation of the soil will inevitably lead to war, and he cites the lesson of Japan who invaded Manchuria because of her need for soyabean protein to feed her growing population. Peace in this world, says Nichols, depends on conservation of natural resources, not their exploitation.

15

Live plants or dead planets

Hereford is not only the name of a popular breed of beef cattle developed in one of the English counties bordering on Wales, it is also a small town on the upper reaches of the Palo Duro River, which runs through the Texas Panhandle, a 170-mile-square area of the Lone Star State which, about a century ago, was a wild short-grass prairie roamed by thousands of American bison. For millennia the flat plains of Deaf Smith County, of which Hereford is the seat, produced a rich herbage and a variety of succulent weeds whose roots extended through two to four feet of clay-loam topsoil into the *calicahi*, a subsoil rich in calcium and magnesium, drawing up these elements and depositing them as they died on the surface to maintain a vital protein-rich graze for the wild bovines. The minerals in the soil were delicately balanced and the humus naturally provided by the dying vegetation along with the bovine droppings was sufficient to hold its own against the harsh climate, hot and dry in summer, bitterly cold in the snow-sparse winters. It was only half a century ago that farming began in the region; the first furrows were cut into the land by the metal mould-boards of ploughs; golden grain was sown as far as the eye could reach. Where the land was not planted, herds of cattle replaced the buffalo.

As the years went by, the farmers realized that deep ploughing was hurting rather than helping the soil. So they switched to breaking up the rich clay-loam to a depth of merely six to eight inches with chiselling tools pulled by low-horse-power tractors. At the same time they were delighted to discover that water from underground aquifers could be pumped up and applied to the soil to supplement the rainfall from thunder-storms which intermittently turned the prairie skies into a dark panoply of lightning-threaded cumulus and the creeks into 'rivers a mile wide and an inch deep'.

By the time the children of the first generation of farmers had grown into manhood, things had begun to go wrong in Deaf Smith County. Dissatisfied by smaller harvests obtained from depleted soil, farmers began adding artificial fertilizers to their land as recommended by agricultural research stations and academic advisers. In less than a decade disaster was in sight. The chemicals were burning up the organic material in the soil, upsetting the delicate natural balance of minerals. As a result, the soil began to dissipate. When mixed with irrigation water it coagulated into enormous clods weighing up to fifty pounds each. To break them up the farmers had to resort to huge 135-horsepower tractors capable of dragging enormous chiselling tools through the bricklike consistency of their land. Some of the farmers, appalled at the prospect of an end to irrigation farming in the Panhandle, owing to the unmindful application of the wrong kind of nutrients to the once rich land, were determined to react.

One of these, Frank Ford, after graduating from Texas Agricultural and Mechanical University, purchased an eighteen-hundred-acre farm in Hereford on which the land was badly eroded because of the prevailing agricultural practices. Of his own land he said: 'There were gullies so deep you could hide a tractor in them.' Today those gullies have been filled, the land has been terraced, levelled smooth and brought back to health. 'If you fight nature in farming,' he says, 'you're bound to lose; it might take twenty years to lose, but lose you will. Whereas if you work with it, then every year your soil is stronger, your plants are stronger, your finances are stronger.'

He used natural manures and banished all pesticides and herbicides. He introduced ladybirds in quantity to kill brown mites and other pests and he relied on chisel ploughing to get rid of Johnson grass. He refused to plant seeds that had been chemically treated against wire-worm and rust. In addition to farming, Ford put capital into Arrowhead Mills which specializes in the production of high-quality stone-ground flour and other natural foods. To assure himself a steady supply of organic products Ford was able to persuade some of his fellow farmers to adopt organic methods, and to form a group whose aim was to grow healthier food and to protect and improve the soil of West Texas.

Working with this group is Fletcher Sims Jr who had studied soil and ecological sciences under Dr William Albrecht, author of *Soil Fertility and Animal Health*, which the ecologically-minded regard as a foundation work published years ahead of its time. Sims began to refresh his memory and to consult the literature to see what might best be done to help the fast-deteriorating Panhandle land. One of the first things he noticed was that in the feedlots tons of cattle manure were piling up which no one knew how to dispose of. Within a few years the waste from one lot two miles from his home had collected into a pile over fifty feet high covering forty acres, or more than thirty football fields. A fleet of bulldozers and other equipment worth a quarter of a million dollars was needed to pack it. Sims further estimated that feedlots throughout the nation contain millions of cubic yards of manure which will eventually become worthless as fungi reduce them to minerals.

At the same time it seemed to Sims that the agricultural schools were going out of their way to ignore the value of cattle wastes on the land. At one college tons of manure were being ploughed three feet under the soil, which Sims knew could only do violence to both soil and manure. In the process top-soil is buried, subsoil exposed, and the manure prevented from becoming aerobically fermented. At another Texas college an organic slurry was being pumped on to fields at concentrations that killed the crops; and at an experimental station raw manure was being dumped as a waste product at the rate of three hundred tons per acre. Other scientists were suggesting that building materials be made from manure, and one group in the state of Washington was even working on how to make livestock feed with it.

In the face of what he considered to be these asinine approaches, Sims decided to study how manure could best be turned into valuable compost. Nichols introduced him to the compost work that had been done by Dr Ehrenfried Pfeiffer at a research laboratory in Spring Valley, New York. During several visits there he was introduced to Pfeiffer's research which demonstrates unequivocally how life veritably pulsates from living food, soil and vitamins and how inorganic minerals, chemicals and synthetic vitamins are dead. Without the aid of complex equipment of the standard chemical laboratory, Pfeiffer developed a simple system for reading patterns on filter paper which revealed to him not just the *chemical* components of soils, composts or plants but their *biological* quality.

Sims learned that compost-making goes through distinct phases; one in which original starches, sugars, and other components are broken down by bacteria, fungi and other organisms; a second in which the new materials are consumed by micro-organisms to build up their own bodies. It is of the utmost importance that the right kind of microfauna and microflora be present and that the second phase be timed correctly so that there will not be too much loss of organic matter. As the director of the Spring Valley laboratory said,

If compost is not worked properly, the original proteins and amino acids break down into simple chemical compounds. In other words, organic matter gets lost as carbon dioxide, and as nitrogen escaping as ammonia and nitrates. Many gardeners think of their composts as 100 per cent organic because all their original materials are organic. But nature isn't that simple. Living cells have 70 to 90 per cent water, only 15 to 20 per cent proteins, amino acids, carbohydrates and carbon compounds. Only 2 to 10 per cent is mineral: potash, calcium, magnesium and the trace elements that are inorganic. The organic compounds can be preserved in the bodies of the micro-organisms. They escape when they become free in some stage of the breakdown. The N, P and K concept comes into its own only when compost has been mineralized but by then the biological values have been lost. In compost-making you need to have a quick method for telling whether bacterial action is breaking down nitrogen-containing compounds too fast, which is indicated by the ammonia smell. If compost piles heat too fast they must be turned to interrupt the ammonia production so that bacteria rebuild more stable nitrogen compounds in bacterial protein.

Pfeiffer's coloured chromatogrammes – or coloured concentric patterns on filter paper – define so well the various stages of fermentation, whether decomposition, humus formation, or mineralization, that after years of work the laboratory was able to develop a biodynamic compost starter with a proper population of micro-organisms for general use. One of Pfeiffer's chromatographic pictures illustrated how, though it contained an incredible 18 per cent organic matter, the material from a cranberry bog was biologically inert. Standard chemical analysis would not have shown this. A picture of adobe soil from California revealed that although it contained minerals it had no well-developed microflora, and thus was infertile. Without organic matter in the soil plants are driven to drink water and more water to counteract the excess of mineral salts. Though they look lush to the eye, they are no longer in balance, and therefore no longer resistant to disease. Pfeiffer's chromatogrammes had been able to establish also that certain plants, such as beans and cucumbers, grow better if planted close together, whereas other combinations such as beans and fennel, do not flourish. Furthermore, the storage together of such crops as apples and potatoes mysteriously robs each of its most life-giving properties.

It is only our human egotistical point of view that labels a weed a weed, said Pfeiffer. If they were viewed as a functioning part of nature, they would have much to teach. He proved that a whole group of weeds, including sorrels, docks and horsetails, are sure indicators that the soil was becoming too acidic. Dandelions, which lawn-owners so feverishly dig up, actually heal the soil by transporting minerals, especially calcium, upwards from deep layers. They are thus warning the lawn-owner that something is wrong with the life of his soil.

To Sims the prospects of Pfeiffer's unique tests seemed endless. They could be used to discern the germination properties of seeds. For instance, two chromatogrammes of wheat, one grown with inert chemicals, the other biologically, showed a marked difference. Furthermore, his process has conclusively proved that synthetic vitamin C, or ascorbic acid, is completely different from the vitamin C naturally derived from rose hips. The something missing in the acid is of biological value: though as yet no one can exactly say why. Using Pfeiffer's biodynamic starter, Sims launched out on a commercial compost operation in which he treated raw manure in such a way that micro-organisms broke up compounds in the waste and assembled them into new and beneficial ones. At the same time, disease organisms and seeds from weeds or grains were automatically destroyed by temperatures reaching 140° F and harmful chemicals were biologically degraded. The compost was turned from time to time. Within one month it had become a fine, dark brown, friable, earthy material, wholly devoid of manure odour. The cow dung was transformed, miraculously as it were, by *biological* action.

As the farmers began to buy Sims's product and apply it to their land, startling results were not long in coming. One farmer treated his soil with half a ton of biodynamic compost per acre, rejected all other fertilizers and insecticides, and supplemented some three inches of rain with only two irrigations. After two years he was able to harvest a fantastic $172\frac{1}{2}$ bushels per acre of maize, or more than double the maximum crop achieved on the artificially nitrogenized lands of Illinois. and over twenty-five tons of sugar beets per acre. Other farmers had equally dramatic results. One reporter wrote that anyone who wanted to convince himself of the advantage of biodynamic compost had only to drive along a particular road in Panhandle where from the car he could see on one side a beautiful crop of healthy maize plants coming up on a composted field and on the other a few sickly plants starting out of hard-packed and cracked ground.

South-eastward across the enormous state of Texas, Warren Vincent has been encouraging farmers to grow rice organically in order to combat barnyard or water grass, on which herbicides, of the kind used so devastatingly to defoliate the jungles of Vietnam, have been extensively applied. Vincent encourages his neighbours to rotate rice with Bahaia grass which turns the land back to sod, controls weeds, and makes an excellent pasturage for animals. An increasing demand for the nutritionally superior brown rice has spurred them on to grow their crops organically.

In northern California were other pioneers, the four Lundberg brothers, who, unlike most farmers, returned their rice straw and stubble to the soil, instead of burning their fields each year and creating smoke pollution in the air for weeks over the whole region. Although the Lundbergs belonged to a rice association which offered them an automatic market for white rice, and though converting to organic methods involved additional costs, they remembered that their father had taught them that any farmer worth his salt has an obligation to improve the land he uses and, if possible, leave it to the next generation in a better condition than when he took it over, a philosophy which, applied world-wide, could make of this planet a Garden of Eden.

In changing over to organic farming, the Lundbergs knew that they were in for a hard struggle. So dependent had they been upon chemicals that the task of conversion was frightening. When the rice paddies are flooded millions of so-called tadpole shrimps emerge wriggling from the soil. They churn up the fine silt and thus block from the water the sunlight and warmth needed to germinate the seeds. They also feed on the tiny rice shoots. Although the 'shrimp' are worse in some years than others, it is the practice of the rice farmers to insure themselves against heavy infestation by spraying their paddies with parathion, or other pesticides, and by treating their seeds before planting with various chemical products to prevent disease. The chemification does not stop at this point. Barnyard grass is controlled by one herbicide, the rice water weevil by another poison. Copper sulphate is applied in the water to control algae. A chemical is sprayed on the growing crop to combat mosquitoes and destroy the eggs and larvae of the rice leafminer. Leaf-hoppers and army-worms, sedges and broad-leaved weeds are fought with other, and different, toxic products. Nitrogen is added to the soil in the form of ammonium sulphate together with superphosphate to supply phosphorus. Iron and zinc are added in the form of ferric sulphate.

Despite generalized warnings against giving up this extended family of chemical products, the Lundberg brothers decided to try. They located a source of manure and composted it before working it into an initial seventy-six acres. Their first crop averaged 3,700 pounds per acre, low when compared to chemically treated rice, but high enough to be economically feasible, given the premium prices paid for organic rice. Their initial experiment persuaded them to convert the whole of their acreage to organic farming. They controlled pests by careful water manipulation and timing. By seeding the rice on the dry ground instead of in the water and then flooding the paddies, the sprouting grains had an even chance against the tadpole shrimp. To prevent seedling diseases, the Lundbergs use only healthy seeds which had not been chemically treated. By meticulously cleaning away weeds around their banks, they found that rice water weevils could not breed. Leafminers were controlled by fertile soil and water manipulation, mosquitoes by an insect control fish called gambusia which feeds on mosquito larvae and other unwanted insects. Like the farmers in south-east Texas, the Lundbergs decided to control weeds by rotating rice crops with a crop of barley followed by purple vetch. They worked the rice husks into the soil instead of burning them, and filling the air with smoke and ashes. The rice stubble and stalks were disposed of by irrigating the paddy immediately after harvest; and thus the decaying process was begun and humus was being restored to the land.

Another pioneer in California is Jack Anderson who farms in the Sacramento valley and has the only commercial organic tomato operation in the state. Like the Lundbergs he had to rely on his farmer's intuition to solve extremely complex problems. Worms are tomato growers' main worry: and in the United States canneries cannot accept deliveries with more than a two per cent worm damage. Almost all growers believe that this can only be achieved with the use of chemicals. However, Anderson thought that timing might be a crucial factor because experience had taught him that tomatoes plucked before September were not attacked by worms. Working on this basis, his crop was so successful that in two years he was able to double his acreage. Anderson hopes to expand his production each year although, like the Lundbergs and other organic farmers, he faces a marketing problem.

Organic farming has spread to dairy farmers and to fruit growers. Among the latter is Ernest Halbleib, who refutes the almost universal assertion that apple growers cannot succeed without chemicals. His view is that insects arrive in orchards just to point out the very mistakes that man is making. They become resistant to pesticides and whereas ten years ago one spraying was enough in the growing season it now has to be repeated many times. More than twenty years ago Halbleib went to Washington to testify to the F.D.A. against poison sprays, poison fertilizers and poison seed treatment, and nothing he said then would he take back today. Since then his fellow fruit growers have used over five hundred new chemicals on their trees. Today, there is not one apple grower in his fruit belt who is not in distress with toxified soil.

Lee Fryer, an agricultural and nutritional consultant in Washington D.C., states that in 1968 the amount spent on commercial fertilizers in the United States exceeded two billion dollars. This sum would buy more than 100,000,000 tons of Fletcher Sims's biodynamic compost, which, if applied at the rate of one ton per acre, would cover the whole state of California with enough left over for the six New England states. For the cost of only a few days of the Vietnam war, the whole of the United States of America's soil could be given an annual treatment. He points to the successful use of seaweed as a natural fertilizer and soil improver. It has been developed in the British Isles by W. A. Stephenson, author of *Seaweed in Agriculture and Horticulture*, who has built up a profitable business distributing seaweed fertilizer in liquid form all over the world.

One of the first to use seaweed commercially in the United States was Glenn Graber of Hartville, Ohio, who grows vegetables on four hundred acres of the blackest richest peat soil in the country. About 1955 Graber noticed that a destructive species of nematode or 'roundworm' was appearing on his land and that 'bluebottom' was wilting a large percentage of his crops as well as those of his neighbours. Because the plague hit at a certain time of year, blame was universally put on the weather. But Graber, whose soil had been analysed and indicated a lack of trace minerals, began to think what he could do to improve matters. He learned that marvellous things had been accomplished with seaweed at the Clemson College of Agriculture in South Carolina, where researchers had used seaweed meal and a liquid seaweed extract manufactured in Norway to achieve gains in sweet peppers, tomatoes, soya and lima beans, and peas. Graber decided to follow the Clemson example and ever since he has been applying sea kelp imported from Norway in granulated form to his land at the annual rate of two hundred pounds to the acre. Towards the end of the first season he noticed that healthy green mould was forming in the tracks of his farm equipment, that his nematode infestation was dramatically reduced and the bluebottom eradicated. Since then he has never put a pound of artificial fertilizer on his land and has relied completely on seaweed, rock phosphate from Florida and ground granite from Georgia, and on bacterial action and cover crops to produce nitrogen. As his soil improved, he abandoned the use of pesticides and turned instead to a spray of liquified kelp applied at the rate of three gallons per acre over crops throughout the season. Graber is not sure how the liquid seaweed acts as a pesticide and says no research has yet been done to find out. He does not entirely escape infestations of pests from his neighbours' fields, but he feels sure that when he loses ten per cent of his onion crop through maggot flies, his neighbours are losing over half theirs despite all the insecticides they try. He firmly believes that healthy plants on healthy soil can resist pests naturally. To prove it he took one visitor through a field of magnificent parsley which was swarming with leaf-hoppers that brushed against their trouser legs; but the parsley remained untouched. He no longer has to use a heavy plough, hauled by two tractors, to break up his ground. By simply cover-cropping his land with barley and rye, he not only adds humus and nutrients to the soil but allows it to be aerated by the plants' strong roots and by earthworms and micro-organisms which flourish in it. His dried earth problem has disappeared as if by magic.

His plants also have a stronger resistance to frost. In one particularly unseasonable cold spell when the mercury dipped to a chilly 20° F, he lost none of his freshly transplanted tomatoes and peppers, though he remembered that under the same conditions they all expired when artificially fertilized. Graber declares,

Organics to me is basically a means of developing a full nutrition food. In general agriculture as practised today, farmers wait until they get a problem and then try to eradicate. But seaweed is a preventative in advance because it gives a complete nutrition of all needed minor or trace elements.

Other vegetable farmers in his area have not as yet followed Graber into what he calls the 'pure organic method', but many of them have begun to adopt the use of seaweed and rock phosphate. However, they still resort to artificial fertilizers and pesticides when they get a bad infestation. Graber says the learning process is slow because the amount of insecticide the farmers need depends on how well they feed their soil. He himself has had only three bad insect problems in thirteen years, two of them after an application of lime to fields, through which, as he sees it, the soil balance was upset.

At present the marketing of organically-grown vegetables is necessarily expensive because there are so few outlets. Graber thinks that the only way is to work through large food chains that will agree to isolate organically-grown produce on different shelves from the conventional supplies. Such an approach has recently been pioneered in West Germany by Latscha Filialbetriebe of Frankfurt, a fast-growing family-owned supermarket chain with a bent for innovation. They have introduced chickens, eggs, fruit juices, apples and frozen green vegetables which are guaranteed to have only minimal quantities of 'residuals' such as antibiotics, hormones, lead and the full spectrum of pesticides. All plant products come from farms cultivated along organic gardening lines as developed by the German State Institution for Plant Protection in Stuttgart which rules out the use of artificial insecticides and fertilizers.

Latscha says that none of its controlled products costs more than fifteen per cent more than ordinary equivalents and that its juices and deep-frozen items can be offered at prices under those charged for standard brands. Though the premium it pays to a cooperative dairy to produce milk without such additives as chlorinated hydrocarbons and DDT is passed on to the customer, the certified milk has climbed to ten per cent of Latscha's sales and its over-all revenues have increased despite a generally falling market demand.

For all their success, Glenn Graber and other farmers like him feel that many organic proponents tend to be too 'purist' and, as such, have alienated the chemical interests who might well change their closed thinking if met half-way. 'It's about time the two camps got together to determine what's right and what's wrong,' says Graber. This is also the opinion of Dr John Whittaker, a veterinary surgeon in Springfield, Missouri, who is animal health editor for the remarkable new monthly, *Acres, U.S.A.* He says that what is needed is to create common ground on which organic-minded farmers can meet with farmers who honestly have accepted the pronouncements of science. He states that,

> On the one hand, the organic people have got to stop viewing the natural movement as a group of little old ladies working in geranium beds. The truth is there can be no sudden death of the technology now extant. There has to be a phasing down, a buffering process, a marriage. We have to learn from each other.

Asked how technology might harmonize with nature, Whittaker points to the development of metal proteinates in which technology has taken minerals and hooked them to organic matter such as protein. One of the clearest statements about how proteinates work is that of Whittaker's colleague, Phillip M. Hinze, who looks upon the physical body not only as a compilation of chemicals but as an electric complex as well. Hinze says that,

> The animal body may be thought of as a very complex battery that not only receives, stores and uses electricity for chemical purposes, but also maintains itself by assimilating vitamins, minerals, amino acids and other products. The body recognizes these substances when they come along. Every organic substance has an electromotive property which determines whether it can be assimilated. When an animal needs nutrients, a signal is sent out to capture that nutrient from food that has been ingested. If there is no sickness, and the needed ingredients are present, they will be assimilated. Unfortunately the needed ingredients don't always correspond with substances considered suitable for food. For instance, the requirements of the animal body for metals are often met by feeding rations containing inorganic forms of these metals. But it happens that inorganic forms of nutritionally essential

metals have different electromotive properties than the same metals complexed with organic materials such as amino acids. A pig can't eat a nail. It needs organic iron.

So does the soil; over harvested, over irrigated and over grazed, it no longer contains the necessary organic minerals to produce good food in the form of plants.

This truth has been recognized by Dr Mason Rose, Director of the Pacific Institute for Advanced Studies, one of the first educational institutions in Los Angeles to break away from the standard university compartmentalization of knowledge and to teach the manufacture of soil humus and the breeding of bacteria.

Other groups, aware that man, having fouled his nest, must now clean it, have been experimenting with ecological farming techniques. A salient example is the New Alchemy Institute, which projects a host of activities, including backyard fish-farming, in climates as varied as those of the Canadian Maritime Provinces, New Mexico, California, and Costa Rica. The New Alchemists say their trio of goals are 'To Restore the Lands, Protect the Seas, and Inform the Earth's Stewards'. This is what the planet's vegetal covering on *terra firma* has been doing since long before the advent of man to his stewardship. In that sense, plants are the oldest alchemists.

16

Alchemists in the garden

The medieval alchemist, whose dream of transmuting one element into another was ridiculed for centuries, may now be vindicated, thanks to the efforts of living plants.

Early this century a young Breton schoolboy who was preparing himself for a scientific career, began to notice a strange fact about the hens in his father's poultry-yard. As they scratched the soil they constantly seemed to be pecking at specks of mica, a siliceous material dotting the ground. No one could explain to Louis Kervran why the chickens selected the mica, or why each time a bird was killed for the family cooking pot no trace of the mica could be found in its gizzard, or why each day the flock produced eggs with calcareous shells though they apparently had not ingested any calcium from land which was entirely lacking in limestone. It took Kervran many years to establish that the chickens were transmuting one element into another.

Reading a novel by Gustave Flaubert called *Bouvard et Pécuchet*, young Kervran came across a reference to Louis-Nicolas Vauquelin, a celebrated French chemist, who, 'having calculated all the lime in oats fed to a hen, found still more in the shells of its eggs. Therefore, there is a creation of matter. In what way, no one knows.'

It seemed to Kervran that, if the hen had somehow been able to manufacture calcium in its own body, everything he was taught in his chemistry class needed reviewing. Ever since the end of the eighteenth century, when Vauquelin's contemporary Antoine Laurent Lavoisier, known as the 'father of modern chemistry', had laid down the principle that in the universe 'nothing is lost, nothing is created, everything is transformed', it had been believed that elements could be shifted about in different combinations but could not be transmuted one to another; millions of experiments appeared to verify Lavoisier's contention.

The first crack in this seemingly unshatterable wall around the atom came at the start of the twentieth century with the discovery of radioactivity, which showed that some twenty elements could indeed change into something different, apparently no longer obeying the law of the conservation of matter. Radium, for instance, disintegrates into electricity, warmth, light, and various substances such as lead, helium and other elements. With the advent of nuclear physics, man was even able to create certain elements which had been missing on the famous chart drawn by the Russian peasant genius Dmitri Mendeleyev, because they were thought either to have vanished radioactively in former times or to have never existed in a natural state.

Ernest Rutherford, the British physicist who first theorized the existence of the atom's nucleus, showed in 1919 that one could transmute elements by bombarding them with alpha particles – identical to helium atoms less their electrons – a practice which has continued to the present time, with increasingly 'heavier artillery'. But even these breakthroughs did not shatter Lavoisier's dictum about the eighty or more non-radioactive elements. Chemists still hold that it is impossible to create another element by chemical reaction, and even maintain that all reactions occurring in living matter are solely chemical. In their view chemistry can and must explain life.

As a young graduate engineer and biologist, Kervran remembered Vauquelin's experiment and decided to repeat it. He fed a chicken on oats alone, the calcium content of which he had carefully measured. He then checked the calcium content in both the eggs and faeces issuing from the chicken and found the bird had produced four times as much calcium as it had ingested. When Kervran asked his biochemist colleagues how the extra calcium originated, they replied it had come from the chicken's skeleton. This, Kervran realized, might do in an emergency, but if a chicken were required to make shells very long its skeleton would soon be reduced to pulp. In fact, a chicken deprived of calcium lays soft-shelled eggs within four or five days. However, if fed potassium, the chicken's next egg has a hard shell composed of calcium. The chicken is evidently capable of transmuting the element potassium, which is found in high concentrations in oats, into the element calcium.

Kervran also learned that about the time of Vauquelin's retirement, an Englishman, William Prout, made a systematic study of the variations in calcium in incubating chicken eggs and found that when chicks hatched they contained four times more lime than was originally present in the egg and that, furthermore, the lime content of the shell had not changed. He concluded that there had to be an endogenous formation of lime from within the egg. This was long before scientists knew anything about the atom, says Kervran, so it was too early to talk about atomistic transmutation.

One of Kervran's friends pointed out to him that as far back as 1600 a Flemish chemist, Jan Baptista Helmont, had planted a willow sapling in a clay pot containing two hundred pounds of oven-dried soils and for five years had given the tree nothing but rain or distilled water. When Helmont removed the tree and weighed it he found it had gained 164 pounds whereas the weight of the soil remained approximately the same. Helmont wondered if the plant had not been able to turn water into wood, bark and roots.

Another vegetal anomaly which interested Kervran was that of *Tillandsia*, or Spanish moss, which can grow on copper wires without any contact with the soil. When burnt there was no copper residue in its ash, but iron oxides and other elements, all apparently supplied simply by the atmosphere.

Henri Spindler, another French scientist, became fascinated with how *Laminaria*, a variety of algae, seemed to be able to manufacture iodine. Searching for answers in half-forgotten literature on the dusty shelves of libraries, Spindler found that a German researcher by the name of Vogel had planted cress seeds in a container covered by a glass bell jar and fed them nothing but distilled water. A few months later when Vogel burned the adult plants, he found they contained twice the amount of sulphur which had been present in their seeds. Spindler also uncovered the fact that, soon after Vogel, two Britishers by the names of Lawes and Gilbert discovered at the famous Agricultural Research Institute at Rothamsted,

England, that plants seemed to extract from the soil more elements than it contained.

For seventeen years the Rothamsted researchers cropped a clover field, mowing it two or three times a year, and sowing it only every fourth year, without adding any fertilizer at all. This piece of land gave cuttings so abundant that it was estimated that if one had to add what had been removed in the period between the arrival of one swarm of seventeen-year locusts and another, it would be necessary to dump on the field over 5,700 pounds of lime, 2,700 pounds of magnesia, 4,700 pounds of potash, 2,700 pounds of phosphoric acid, and 5,700 pounds of nitrogen, or more than ten tons of the products combined. Where had all these minerals come from?

Delving deeper into the mystery, Spindler came across the work of a Hanoverian baron, Albrecht von Herzeele, who, in 1873, brought out a revolutionary new book, *The Origin of Inorganic Substances*, which offered proof that, far from simply absorbing matter from the soil and the air, living plants are continuously creating matter. During his lifetime von Herzeele made hundreds of analyses indicating that, in seeds sprouting in distilled water, the original content of potash, phosphorus, magnesium, calcium, and sulphur quite inexplicably increased. Though the law of the conservation of matter held that exactly the same mineral content in plants grown in distilled water would be found as in the seeds from which they spring, von Herzeele's analyses proved also that not only mineral ash but every one of the plants' components increased, such as the nitrogen which burned off during incineration of the seeds.

Von Herzeele also discovered that plants seemed to be able to *transmute*, in alchemical fashion, phosphorus into sulphur, calcium into phosphorus, magnesium into calcium, carbonic acid into magnesium, and nitrogen into potassium.

One of the many odd facts in scientific history is that von Herzeele's writings, published between 1876 and 1883, were given the silent treatment by official academia, which was supporting the fashion that biological phenomena could be explained atomistically according to chemical laws. Indeed, most of Herzeele's works never found their way on to library shelves.

Spindler drew the attention of some of his colleagues to von Herzeele's experimentation. One of them was Pierre Baranger, a professor and director of the laboratory of organic chemistry at the famous École Polytechnique in Paris, which, since its establishment in 1794, has trained the best scientific and engineering minds in France. To check von Herzeele's work, Baranger began a series of experiments which were to last the best part of a decade.

These experiments amply confirmed von Herzeele's work and indicated that atomic science might be faced with a veritable revolution.

When Baranger announced his discoveries to the scientific world in January 1958, before a distinguished audience of chemists, biologists, physicists, and mathematicians at Switzerland's Institut Genévois, he noted that if his investigations were further developed a certain number of theories which did not seem to have the benefit of a sufficiently experimental basis might have to be modified.

This cautious approach dictated by scientific mores was made more explicit by Baranger in an interview for *Science et Vie* in 1959. 'My results look impossible,' said Baranger,

but there they are. I have taken every precaution. I have repeated the experiments many times. I have made thousands of analyses for years. I have had the results verified by third parties who did not know what I was about. I have used several methods. I changed my experimenters. But there's no way out; we have to submit to the evidence: plants know the old secret of the alchemists. *Every day under our very gaze they are transmuting elements.*

By 1963 Baranger had incontestably proven that in the germinations of leguminous seeds in a manganese salt solution, manganese disappeared and iron appeared in its place. Trying to shed more light on the mechanisms involved, he discovered a whole web of complexities related to the transmutations of elements in seeds, including the time of their germination, the type of light involved, even the exact phase of the moon.

To understand the enormity of Baranger's work one has to realize that nuclear science asserts that in order to form the stability of elements such gigantic 'energies of fixation' are needed that the alchemists, unable to produce and direct such energy, could never have transmuted one element into another as they claimed. Yet plants are constantly transmuting elements in a manner completely unknown to science without having to resort to enormous modern atom smashers. The tiniest blade of grass and the frailest crocus or petunia is able to achieve what modern-day alchemists known as nuclear physicists have heretofore found impossible.

In speaking of his new research, the quiet, courteous Baranger said: I have been teaching chemistry at the École Polytechnique for twenty years, and believe me, the laboratory which I direct is no den of false science. But I have never confused respect for science with the taboos imposed by intellectual conformism. For me, any meticulously performed experiment is a homage to science even if it shocks our ingrained habits. Von Herzeele's experiments were too few to be absolutely convincing. But their results inspired me to control them with all the precaution possible in a modern lab and to repeat them enough times so that they would be statistically irrefutable. That's what I've done.

Baranger established that seeds of Cerdagne vetch growing in distilled water showed no change in phosphorus or potassium content. But seeds growing in a calcium salt solution varied their phosphorus and potassium content by the enormous factor of ten per cent, and that calcium increased in both groups. 'I understand perfectly well,' Baranger told the science writers, who grilled him with every possible objection during the course of their interview, 'that you are astonished by these results. For they are astonishing. I understand perfectly well that you are seeking the error which could make nonsense of these experiments. But so far no such error has been found. The phenomenon stands: plants can transmute elements.'

As upsetting and contradictory as Baranger's experiments seemed, it was pointed out by *Science et Vie* that nuclear physics itself has reached a stage wherein its practitioners use four separate and quick contradictory theories about the atomic nucleus. Moreover, they add, the very secret of life has not yet been found, perhaps because no one has yet looked for it in the atomic nucleus. So far, they went on, life has been considered to be mainly a chemical and molecular phenomenon, but perhaps its roots are to be located in the most remote sub-basements and cellars of atomic physics.

The practical consequences of Baranger's findings cannot be overestimated. One of these is that certain plants can bring to the soil elements useful for the growth of other plants, which could lead to many changes in received doctrines about fallows, rotations, mixed crops, fertilizers, or, as Friend Sykes found out through actual trials on his Wiltshire land, the manuring of infertile soils. Moreover, as Baranger opines, nothing prevents us from thinking that certain plants are capable of producing rare elements of industrial importance. They appear to supply us with an example of subatomic transformation which we are not capable of performing in the laboratory without bringing into action particles of high energy in exactly the same way we are not capable of bringing about at ordinary temperatures the synthesis of innumerable products, either alkaloids or others, which are extracted from plants.

Kervran, a man with continuing ties to the land despite his urban academic duties, began to be fascinated by another phenomenon of a global nature which has long been known to agricultural specialists. He read in Didier Bertrand's *Magnesium and Life*, published in French in 1960, that each time wheat, maize, potatoes, or any other crop is harvested, elements in the earth used by plants in their growth process are taken out. Since virgin arable soil contains from 30 to 120 kilograms of magnesium per hectare, Bertrand stressed that most of the earth's arable land should long since have been exhausted of this element. Not only is this not the case, but in various parts of the world, such as Egypt, China, and the Po Valley in Italy, soils continue to remain highly fertile in spite of the enormous quantities of magnesium taken from them through harvests of crops over thousands of years. Is it because plant life is able to upset the periodic table of the elements, to make magnesium from calcium or carbon from nitrogen, for instance, that lands have been able to replace the products they need, wondered Kervran.

With the Celtic directness of a Breton, Kervran published his *Biological Transmutations* in 1962, the first of a series of books which offered a whole new perspective on living creatures.

It made clear that those who believe in a system of farming which takes into account chemistry alone are in for a rude shock and that man and animals nourished on diets formulated by chemists will not long survive. Kervran freely accepted the notion that Lavoisier was right as far as chemical reactions were concerned. The mistake made by science, he said, is to contend that *all* reactions in living organisms are chemical in nature and that consequently, life should be interpreted in chemical terms. Kervran suggests that the biological properties of a substance are only inadequately determined by chemical analysis.

Kervran wrote that one of the main purposes of his book was

to show that matter has a property heretofore unseen, a property which is neither in chemistry nor in nuclear physics in its present state. In other words the laws of chemistry are not on trial here. The error of numerous chemists and biochemists lies in their desire to apply the laws of chemistry at any cost, with unverified assertions in a field where chemistry is not always applicable. In the final phase the results might be chemistry, but only as a consequence of the unperceived phenomenon of transmutation.

Rudolf Hauschka in his brilliant book *The Nature of Substance* carries Kervran and Heerzele's ideas even further, saying that life cannot possibly be interpreted in chemical terms because life is not the result of the combination of elements but something which precedes the elements. Matter, says Hauschka, is the precipitate of life. 'Is it not more reasonable,' he asks, 'to suppose that life existed long before matter and was the product of a pre-existent spiritual cosmos?'

Supporter of Rudolf Steiner's 'spiritual science', Hauschka is lapidary in his approach when he states that the elements as we know them are already corpses, the residue of life forms. Though chemists can derive oxygen, hydrogen and carbon from a plant, they cannot derive a plant from any combination of these or other elements. 'What lives,' says Hauschka, 'may die; but nothing is created dead.'

Hauschka, who also duplicated many of Heerzele's experiments, found that plants could not only generate matter out of a non-material sphere, but could 'etherealize' it once more, noting an emergence and disappearance of matter in rhythmic sequence, often in conjunction with phases of the moon.

In Paris, Kervran, a pleasant and forthrightly cooperative man of seventy with a prodigious memory for detail, told the authors that powerful energies are at work in the germination process of seeds which synthesize enzymes, probably by transmuting matter within them. His experiments have also convinced him that lunar forces are extremely important in germination, though botanists have long asserted that only warmth and water are required.

'We cannot deny the existence of something just because we don't know about it,' said Kervran.

The kind of energies to which the great Austrian natural scientist and clairvoyant Rudolf Steiner refers as cosmic etheric forces must exist if only from the fact that certain plants will only germinate in springtime no matter what amounts of heat and water are administered to them during other parts of the year. There are varieties of wheat said to germinate only as the days lengthen, but, when days are artificially lengthened, the wheat does not always germinate.

We do not know what *matter* really is, says Kervran. We do not know what a proton or an electron is *made of*, and the words serve only to cloak our ignorance. He suggests that inside atomic nuclei may lie forces and energies of a totally unexpected nature and that a physical theory to explain the low energy transmutations with which he deals must be sought, not in the hypotheses of classical nuclear physics based on powerful interactions, but in the field of hyperweak interactions in which there is no assurance of the operation of the established laws of conservation of energy or even the existence of a mass/energy equivalent.

Physicists, says Kervran, are mistaken in claiming that physical laws are the same for the living as for inanimate matter. Many physicists declare, for instance, that a negative entropy, a force which in biology would build up matter, is an impossibility, since the second principle of thermodynamics of Carnot-Clausius, regarding the breakdown of energy, states that there is only positive entropy, i.e., that the natural state of matter is chaos and that all things run down and become random, losing heat and not acquiring it.

In contradiction to the physicists, Wilhelm Reich held that the accumulators he built to collect an energy, which he named 'orgone', permanently raised the temperature inside the accumulator tops, thus making nonsense of the second law of thermodynamics. Despite the fact that he demonstrated the phenomenon to Albert Einstein in his house in Princeton, and that Einstein confirmed the phenomenon, though he could not account for it, Reich was considered mad.

Reich maintained that matter is created from orgone energy, that under appropriate conditions matter arises from mass-free orgone, and that these conditions are neither rare nor unusual. All of this further suggests that in living nature there exists, below the level of Lavoisier's classical molecular chemistry, a deeper level of nuclear chemistry which associates and dissociates nucleons, the components of atomic nuclei. In molecular combinations heat energy is produced. At the nuclear level a much more powerful energy, that of fisson or fusion as in A or H bombs, must be added. What remains unexplained is why these fantastic energies are not released in biological transmutations.

Science et Vie has postulated that if plasma-type nuclear reactions take place in bombs, in nuclear reactors and in stars, then there must be a wholly different type of reaction, specifically utilized by life, which brings about fusion in a strangely quiet way. The magazine suggests the analogy of a strongbox which can be opened by dynamite or by a combination lock. Like the lock, the atomic nucleus can prove stubborn when confronted with blind violence but pliable to skilful manipulation. The secret of life, so long suspected by vitalists, is as much a secret as the locksmiths' combination. The cleavage between the animate and the inanimate is to be found at the level of manipulation of the nuclear lock. It appears that, whereas man has to use dynamite, plants and other living organisms know the combination.

Kervran also wonders whether micro-organisms can even take sand and make it fecund. After all, he maintains, humus comes today from organic matter but at one time there was no organic matter on earth.

This raises the question of whether Dr Wilhelm Reich was

not on the track of the discovery of the century when he purported that he had observed at the microscope energetic vesicles or 'bions' which are not alive but 'carry biological energy'. Exposed to sufficiently high temperatures and made to swell, all matter, even sand, undergoes vesicular disintegration, wrote Reich, and the resulting vesicles can later develop into bacteria.

Kervran, who has now retired from his duties as one of France's more eminent professors in order to embark on the career of a determined alchemist, asks why chemically pure reactions such as the combination of one atom of nitrogen and one atom of oxygen can be realized in a test tube only at extremely high temperatures and pressures whereas living organisms can perform the same feat at room temperature. He feels that the biological catalysts known as enzymes are in some way responsible.

In a yearbook entitled *Alchemy: Dream or Reality?* published in 1973 in Rouen by the students of the prestigious Institut Nationale Superieur de Chimie Industrielle, Kervran writes that micro-organisms are a concentration of enzymes. Their ability to transmute elements is not a mere hooking of peripheral electrons to form bonds as in classical chemistry but involves a fundamental alteration of the nucleus of elements.

Most transmutations have been observed to take place within the first twenty elements of the periodic table. They further always seem to involve hydrogen or oxygen. Thus the transmutation of potassium to calcium is accomplished through the addition of a hydrogen proton.

Kervran expects the phenomena he describes, and the data he supplies, to irritate chemists because it involves, not the displacement of electrons in the peripheral atomic layers and the chemical bonding in molecules which lie at the heart of their discipline, but the alteration in structural arrangements of atoms induced by enzyme activities in living matter. Since this takes place within atomic nuclei, a new science distinct from chemistry is involved.

Since nature's atom smashing, according to Kervran, is performed by biotic life, micro-organisms are thus nature's prime mover in maintaining balance in soils.

[253]

In Kervran's view some transmutations are biologically beneficial, others dangerous. Since the harmful ones can be countered, the whole problem of deficiencies in the soil remains to be reassessed. Indiscriminate application of NPK fertilizers to the land can alter the content in plants of just those elements necessary to healthful nutrition. In this connection, Kervran cites the work of an American researcher, who, knowing nothing of Kervran's theory of biological transmutations, found that in hybrid corn too rich in potassium the content of molybdenum decreases. 'What *are* the optimal quantities of these two elements in plants?' asks Kervran, then continues: 'This does not appear to have been studied, and there is not only one answer, since values differ not only between species but between varieties of the same species.'

Even if potassium fertilizers were no longer available to agriculturalists, Kervran says, this would represent no catastrophe since micro-organisms could produce potassium from calcium. If yeasts and moulds for penicillin are already being produced on an industrial scale, why not factories for growing micro-organisms for the transmutation of elements? Already in the late 1960s Dr Howard Worne started Enzymes, Inc., at Cherry Hill, New Jersey, where micro-organisms bombarded with strontium 90 were being mutated so as to produce enzymes that would transmute waste carbon into usable carbon simply by having micro-organisms ingest one material and excrete a new one. Dr Worne is now in New Mexico using micro-organisms to transform solid waste from garbage and stockyards into humus for the compost-hungry Western states and methane gas for the energy-hungry Eastern states.

The understanding of the phenomena of biological transmutation, though as yet unrecognized by the majority of the world's agriculturalists, seems to have been anticipated by the advocates of biological cultivation, who, above all, realize that a price must be paid for *reliance on chemistry in a biological context*. Cultivation based on classical chemistry alone, stresses Kervran, fails wherever intensive and abusive methods are employed. The marked crop increases, such as those for the Illinois corn, can thus last only a certain time.

Though not applied as abusively as in America, where huge areas have been lost to cultivation because of a surfeit, even the more limited European use of artificial fertilizers has led, says Kervran, to a mounting lack of resistance in plants to pests. The increase of infestation is no more than a consequence of biological imbalance.

'Classical soil scientists and agronomists attached to the dogma that biology equals chemistry,' writes Kervran,

cannot conceive that all that is in plants has not been put into the soil. They are not the people to advise farmers; farmers should be guided by the enlightened and intelligent agriculturalists who have long recognized the division between a purely chemical and biological agriculture. They might then achieve their own conversion, and carry out some of the experiments described in this book for themselves. If they are men of good faith, they will admit their past errors, but one doesn't ask that much – only that they act.

Pointing out that the great English astronomical physicist Fred Hoyle gave up the theory of the steady state universe which he utilized for nearly a quarter of a century and which made him famous, Kervran notes that Hoyle himself has recognized that if future observations confirm that physics has taken a wrong direction then 'the properties of matter, the laws of chemistry, for example, would be completely changed'.

It is in bulletins such as that of the British Soil Association that Kervran sees articles confirming his ideas of biological transmutation in the soil. In the French analogue of this bulletin, *Nature et Progrès*, one researcher reports that, after analysing month by month for one year the phosphorus content of identical soils, one benefited by fermented compost containing no phosphorus and the other by phosphorus-rich farmyard manure, the first sample had 314 milligrams of phosphorus at the year's end as against only 205 milligrams for the second. The researcher concluded: 'Therefore the soil containing the greater amount of phosphorus was the one without any external supply of this mineral. A miracle of the living soil.'

If Dr Barry Commoner sees the buyers of artificial fertilizer becoming 'hooked' on their product, Kervran says the same thing for plants. Offering them chemicals, he writes, is simply drugging them to achieve higher yields – for a time. He compares this process to stimulating human appetites with an *apéritif* and then not following it up with a meal.

Louis-Victor de Broglie, winner of the Nobel Prize for his prediction of the wave properties of the electron, has said: 'It is premature to want to assess vital processes according to the very insufficient physio-chemical concepts of the nineteenth or even the twentieth centuries.' Kervran, who puts this quotation at the start of the British edition of his book, adds:

Who is to say in which present-day branch of physics 'mental energy', the strength of will or character, should be placed? One can associate memory with information and negative entropy with cybernetics (or should it be chemistry?) but nothing tells us if intelligence itself will not someday be expressed by a physical or chemical law.

Jean Lombard, a geologist, in a preface to Kervran's second book, *Natural Transmutations*, published in 1963, stated that Kervran had opened up a wide field, which in itself could lead to clarification of confusions in geological theory. Lombard also wrote:

The true workers of science, who are always ready to welcome new suggestions, sometimes ask themselves if the greatest obstacle to the progress of science is not bad memory on the part of scholars; they wish to remind the latter that some of their predecessors were burnt at the stake because of proposed 'interpretations' which have now become foremost truths. If pioneers of science were still being burnt, I would not give much for Louis Kervran's skin.

Reviewing Kervran's third book, *Low Energy Transmutations*, published in 1964, Professor René Furon, of the Faculty of Sciences at Paris University, wrote: 'This book completes the two previous ones. It can no longer be denied that nature makes magnesium out of calcium (in some cases the reverse takes place); that potassium can come from sodium; and that carbon monoxide poisoning can occur without inhalation of CO gas.'

It appears that outside France, not Western, but Japanese scientists have been the first to take Kervran's work seriously. When Hisatoki Komaki, a professor of science, read a Japanese

translation of Kervran's book *Biological Transmutations*, he tied
Kervran's findings into ancient Eastern cosmology and wrote
to Kervran to say that the transmutation of sodium, a *yang*
element, into potassium, a *yin* element, was of far-reaching
interest, more especially since Japan has a paucity of potash
deposits but ample supplies of sea salt.

Komaki abandoned his teaching to become head of a
biological research labatory at the Matsushita Electric Company
and informed Kervran that he would try to confirm the sodium-
to-potassium reaction and interest his collaborators in applying
it on an industrial scale. Komaki's research proved to him that
various micro-organisms, including certain bacteria and two
species each of moulds and yeasts, were capable of transmuting
sodium into potassium and that the yield of bacteria themselves
was enormously raised when only a small amount of potassium
was added to the cultures. Komaki has placed on the market a
product made of brewer's yeast which, applied to composts,
raises the potassium content in them. How this process relates
to the action of Biodynamic sprays as conceived by Rudolf
Steiner and developed by Ehrenfried Pfeiffer remains to be
determined.

Kervran's work is also attracting important notice in the
Soviet Union. Professor A. P. Dubrov of the Institute of Earth
Physics of the U.S.S.R. Academy of Sciences, who has been
working on the links between radiosensitivity in animals and
the geomagnetic field, wrote to Kervran at the end of 1971 to
suggest that the magnetic field of the earth itself might well play
an important role in biological transmutation, and that elements
might be affected depending on whether biological forms are
oriented north-south.

In 1971, a Russian book, *Problems of Transmutations in Nature*,
was published in a limited edition in Yerevan, capital of the
Armenian Republic. Its editor, V. B. Neiman, notes in a lead
article, 'Transmutations in Nature: The Present Status of the
Problem and Objects for Further Study', that the fundamental
problems of entropy and negentropy must be re-examined, and
maintains that the diversity of elements on earth is due to a
series of nuclear transmutations with analogous processes
applied to biological phenomena.

Neiman dug out the most extraordinary quotation from Lenin's *Materialism and Empirocriticism*, proving that the father of the Soviet Union tried to incorporate in his materialistic philosophy a notion more palatable to vitalists and mystics than to hard-core Communist pragmatists. 'However miraculous, from the viewpoint of common sense,' wrote Lenin, 'the conversion of imponderable ether to ponderable matter may seem, it is but a further confirmation of dialectic materialism.'

In the same collection, P. A. Korol'kov contributed an essay on the 'Spontaneous Metamorphism of Minerals and Rocks', in which he shows how silicon can be converted to aluminium. In his summary of a conference held in July 1972, devoted to chrome deposition in the Urals, Siberia, Kazakhstan, and the Soviet Far East, Korol'kov comes to the conclusion that the traditional geological views on the genesis of chromite and associated ores do not accord with new data presented at the conference.

'The fact is,' writes Korol'kov,

that we are witnesses and participants in a scientific-technological revolution, that is, we are living in a time in which we are being subjected to a radical revision, not of minutiae, but of the basic status of an inherited natural science. The time has come to recognize that any chemical element can turn into another, under natural conditions. And I am not alone in maintaining this. I know a dozen persons in the U.S.S.R. who hold the same views.

If Soviet scientists are coming around to a whole new view of matter, and even citing Lenin on the possibility of its manufacture by the ether itself, it would seem that the ecological revolution so necessary to safeguard the future of humanity, and pleaded for in the United States since Fairfield Osborn wrote *Our Plundered Planet* shortly after World War II, may have a chance of taking place despite the host of adversaries who see in it the demise of their personal fortunes.

In a review of the American edition of Kervran's book for the International College of Applied Nutrition, V. Michael Walczak, M.D., an internist practising in Studio City, California, said of Kervran's work:

It offers a totally different approach to our understanding of nutritional supplementation of the elements and how it functions in the physiologic and biochemical pathways of our bodies. It attempts to prove that our concepts of simple supplementation for deficiencies is not only questionable, but in serious error.

Though many nutritionists untrained even in simple chemistry are giving people huge and unnecessary doses of calcium because it is the mineral in largest quantity in the body, Walczak, who is now limiting his practice to internal metabolism and nutrition, states that his own research shows that eighty per cent of his patients – with diets supplemented or unsupplemented – have *too much* calcium and too few trace minerals with respect to calcium. The lack of trace elements in soils, and in foods, Walczak maintains, leads to an imbalance in enzyme function.

Walczak says he is preventing disease by administering the right amounts of enzymes, hormones, vitamins, and minerals, which together he calls 'the key to life', and also curing a host of degenerative diseases. He concludes that the 'gold' which the medieval alchemists tried for centuries to derive from lead may very well turn out to be the secret for obtaining good health and long life.

Walczak's views are supported by Richard Barmakian, a nutritionist in nearby Pasadena, who wrote to Kervran's American publishers that the U.S. version of *Biological Transmutations* should prove to be 'the most significant work of this century, scientifically and possibly otherwise'. It was only after he had read the book that Barmakian thought he might at last get to the core of the problem of calcium-metabolism abnormalities and deficiencies which he says are 'so tragically prevalent in pseudo-civilized countries of the world today and especially in the U.S.A.'.

This view was echoed by *Organic Gardening and Farming*, now published by J. I. Rodale's son, Robert, which stated that Kervran had showed that current chemical treatment of the soil is totally wrong and is rapidly destroying the quality of the soil worldwide: 'We're sure that as our understanding of the life processes involved in organic farming grows, the scientific community will be in for many surprises.' The economist

Charles Walters, Jr., publisher of *Acres USA,* also concurs:

Louis Kervran has opened a door. His works have received important recognition from Russians, Japanese, French and Chinese who don't have to ask the United States Department of Agriculture and the petro-chemical firms what to think, as is the case with too many extension agents, land grant colleges and farmers under the thumb of bank examiners.

If doctors, nutritionists, editors, and economists in the United States are now beginning to see in Kervran the herald of a new age, as are professional scientists abroad, it may be that a revolution is at hand. Perhaps the time is near when the dictators of nutritional and agricultural policies, who have forced upon all natural life, from the smallest micro-organisms to human beings, a drenching of chemicals to the point where the only recourse against adulterated food products is the growing of one's own private garden under natural conditions, will have to listen to the prophets who have warned against the chemification of the soil since the beginning of this century.

In an age in which science itself has become so specialized and the science of life, or biology, so molecular that our technological society seems to be producing a crowd of white-coated 'idiot savants' who plead lack of competency in all but their own narrow divisions of knowledge, the broad outlooks of Goethe, Pfeiffer, Howard, Commoner and Voisin and the new discoveries by Louis Kervran may be the one antidote to catastrophe.

5

The radiance of life

17

Dowsing plants for health

On the brighter side of life, a French engineer, André Simoneton, has found a straw which may keep the population of the planet from going under; his device, usable by man, woman, or child, is designed to make it possible to select healthy food from bad before ingesting it: it is a simple pendulum attached to a short piece of string used by diviners of water, lost objects, or the future.

For millennia the art or science of dowsing with forked stick or pendulum has been practised by Chinese, Hindus, Egyptians, Persians, Medes, Etruscans, Greeks, and Romans. In the Renaissance it was revived by such notables as Goethe's predecessor as Director of Mines in Saxony, Christopher von Schenberg, who had his portrait painted holding a dowsing rod, a custom emulated in modern times by Lloyd George, who had himself photographed in the same pose.

Though dowsing has not yet been accepted as a science in America, in France it is no longer relegated to the domain of the witch and warlock – despite the fact that over the centuries many a French dowser has paid with his life for practising 'sorcery'. Among the more celebrated victims were Jean du Chatelet, Baron de Beausoleil, and his dowser wife Marine de Bertereau, who, working under the protection of Maréchal d'Effiat, Louis XIV's superintendent of mines, discovered several hundred profitable mines in France only to be arrested for sorcery and succumb in prison, she in Vincennes, he in the Bastille. The persecution has continued in France mostly against doctors who find themselves dragged before tribunals for perpetrating dowsing cures on patients officially declared uncurable.

That dowsing is no longer considered anathema by the Church is thanks largely to the efforts of a long series of

French abbés and the recent intercession in Rome of such an eminent churchman as Cardinal Tisserant.

In the scientific community the art is now on the fringe of recognition thanks to professors such as Yves Rocard of the Collège de France, head of the physics department of the prestigious Ecole Normale Supérieure, who is recognized not only as a brilliant physicist but as an admirable dowser. His book on the science of dowsing, *Le Signal du Sourcier*, as yet unpublished in English, has been translated in the Soviet Union where geologists have recently been dowsing for minerals from aeroplanes and helicopters, and also locating underground archaeological artifacts.

The Mecca for dowsers in Europe is located in a small Parisian side street, now lost between the luxury of the Faubourg Saint Honoré and the tourist-ridden arcades of the rue de Rivoli, appropriately named for Saint Roch, canonized for protecting the populace against various pestilences. The actual Kaaba is an old curiosity shop called the Maison de Radiesthesie, *'radiesthesie'* being generic for dowsing and for the search for radiations beyond the electromagnetic spectrum, an appellative given to the art by the Abbé Bouly, who coined it from the Greek for 'sensitivity' and the Latin for 'radiance'.

On the shelves of this now venerable institution, run for the last half century by Alfred Lambert and his wife, are scores of books on dowsing – dowsing for water, for objects, and for health. In addition to those written by Catholic clergymen, there are others by aristocrats such as Count Henry de France and Count André de Belizal and by several distinguished French physicians.

There are also brass and mahogany showcases protecting various exotic machines, some simple, some sophisticated, designed to tune in, amplify or shield radiations, healthy or toxic. The machines are used mostly by doctors from all over the world for diagnostic and curative purposes, though the fundamental instrument in each case is the simple pendulum. These lie in stacked drawers on velvet cushions designed in many shapes and sizes from various materials, including ivory, jade, and octagonal quartz or crystal, though any weight on any string or chain is said to be effective.

In the United States, Dr Zaboj V. Harvalik, a professional physicist recently retired from his post as scientific adviser to the U.S. Army's Advanced Material Concepts Agency to devote himself to private research, has turned his attention to the dowsing phenomenon and to how physical theory might help to explain it. As chief of the research committee of the American Society of Dowsers, Harvalik is helping to break down fifty years of prejudice in official circles against dowsing as a 'quack art'.

At his home in Virginia, Harvalik has made meticulous tests to reveal for the first time that dowsers react with varying degrees of sensitivity to polarized electromagnetic radiation, artificial alternating magnetic fields in a frequency range from one to one million cycles per second and to DC magnetic fields. Harvalik is convinced that dowsers pick up magnetic field gradients whether they are trying to find water, underground pipes, wires, tunnels, or geological anomalies.

Dowsing, however, appears to extend far beyond the detection of flowing water or the magnetic field gradients thought to be associated with water currents. In its broadest definition it is simply *searching* – for anything. The former president of the American Society of Dowsers, John Shelley, before his premature death in 1972, amazed his fellow naval reserve officers when at the end of a training session at the Pensacola, Florida, Naval Air Station he was able, by using only a small dowsing rod, to locate his government salary cheque, which his colleagues had conspired with the help of the paymaster to hide somewhere in a huge two-storey naval building with dozens of rooms branching out of its corridors.

Gordon MacLean, a research chemist for Pine State By-Products in Portland, Maine, who still works full time despite his eighty-odd years, will take any visitor out to the Coast Guard lighthouse at Portland Head and with his 'divining' rod accurately predict when the next oil tanker on its way into Portland harbour will appear on the horizon and where.

Perhaps the most celebrated American dowser is Henry Gross, also of Maine, to whose feats Kenneth Roberts, the American historical novelist, devoted three books in the 1950s. Like the French abbots, Gross is an expert at dowsing from maps. Sitting at his kitchen table, he pinpointed on a map of the British-governed island of Bermuda, on which no source of water had been found, just those spots where he said drilling would produce it. To everyone's amazement, Gross was correct.

To physicists like Harvalik the forces at work in *map* dowsing, which do not appear to be related to the magnetic gradients operative in *field* dowsing, are totally inscrutable. Obviously a dowser is contacting some source of information which can provide accurate data on areas, or parts of space, far removed from his own physical location. Rexford Daniels, whose Interference Consultants Company of Concord, Massachusetts, has been pioneering the study for twenty-five years of how proliferating electromagnetic emissions interfere with one another and may work harmful environmental effects on man, states that he has become convinced that some overall force exists in the universe which is itself intelligent and provides answers. Daniels theorizes that this force operates through a whole spectrum of frequencies not necessarily linked to the electromagnetic spectrum and that human beings can mentally interact with it. To Daniels dowsing is simply an as yet imperfectly defined though exceedingly useful communications system. In his eyes an important task confronting man now is to check out the system in all of its aspects.

The specific technique of dowsing food for freshness and vitality was learned by engineer Simoneton, now also in his eighties – though he looks like a successful French businessman in his sixties – from another extraordinary Frenchman, André Bovis, a fragile tinker who died in his native Nice during the Second World War. Bovis is most widely known for his experiments with pyramids built to the dimensions of the Great Pyramid of Cheops, which he found would mysteriously dehydrate and mummify dead animals without decomposing them, especially if they were placed in a pyramid at the relative height of the King's Chamber, or one-third of the way from the base to the summit.

Basic to Bovis's theory is that the earth has positive magnetic currents running north to south, negative magnetic currents running east to west. He says that these currents are picked up by all bodies on the surface of the earth, and that *any* body placed in a north–south position will be more or less polarized, depending on its shape and consistency. In human bodies these telluric currents, both positive and negative, enter through one leg and go out through the opposite hand. At the same time cosmic currents from beyond the earth enter through the head and go out through the other hand and foot. The currents also go out through the open eyes.

All bodies containing water, says Bovis, accumulate these currents and can radiate them slowly. As the currents go out and act and react against other magnetic forces in objects, they affect the pendulum held by the dowser. Thus the human body, as a variable condenser, acts as a detector, selector and amplifier of short and ultra-short waves; it is a go-between for the animal electricity of Galvani and the inanimate electricity of Volta.

At the same time the pendulum, says Bovis, acts as a perfect lie detector in that if a person is frankly saying what he thinks about some subject, it will not affect the radiations and thus not affect the pendulum; but anyone saying something different from what he is thinking changes the wavelengths, making them shorter and negative.

Bovis developed a pendulum from a similar device which he says was used by the ancient Egyptians, made from crystal with a fixed metal point suspended on a double strand of red and violet silk. He called it 'paradiamagnétique' because it is sensitive to objects which are either attracted or repelled by a magnet. Bodies which are attracted, such as iron, cobalt, nickel, magnesium, chrome, or titanium, he called paramagnetic; those which are repelled, such as copper, zinc, tin, lead, sulphur and bismuth, he called diamagnetic. By placing a small magnetic field in the form of a solenoid between the dowser and the pendulum he claimed to be able to pick up very faint currents such as those emanating from a nonfecundated egg. He explained the use of red and violet strands as increasing the sensitivity of his pendulum on the grounds that red light vibrations are the same as the atomic vibrations of iron, which are paramagnetic, and those of violet are the same as copper, which are diamagnetic.

[267]

Bovis found that with his pendulum he could tell the intrinsic vitality and relative freshness of different foods within their protective skins because of the power of their radiations. To measure with his pendulum the varying radiant frequencies produced by foods Bovis developed a *biomètre*, or simple ruler arbitrarily graduated in centimetres to indicate microns, which are thousandths of a millimetre, and angstroms, which are a hundred times smaller, covering a band between zero and ten thousand angstroms.

By placing a piece of fruit or vegetable, or any kind of food, at one end of the ruler, Bovis could watch his swinging pendulum change directions at a certain distance along the ruler, which gave him an indication of the degree of the food's vitality. According to Bovis the limit of any object's radiance is overcome at some point by the general telluric field surrounding it, and can thus be measured. Dowsers maintain that any two objects of the same material and size placed a yard or so apart will create two fields which will repel each other at a halfway mark easily noted with a pendulum. Increasing the size of one of the objects will cause its field to move closer to the smaller object.

Simoneton found that food which radiates 8,000 to 10,000 angstroms on Bovis' biomètre would also cause a pendulum to turn at the remarkable speed of 400 to 500 revolutions per minute in a radius of 80 millimetres. Foods which radiate between 6,000 and 8,000 spun it at a rate of 300 to 400, with a radius of 60 millimetres. Meats, pasteurized milk, and over-cooked vegetables, which radiate less than 2,000 angstroms, have not sufficient energy to make the pendulum spin. Although, as Kervran says in a preface to Simoneton's book *Radiations des Aliments*, the wavelengths which are picked up by the pendulum are of a totally unknown nature, the fact that they are measurable remains of great practical value.

After studying Lakhovsky, Simoneton reasoned that human nerve cells not only can receive wavelengths but must also be transmitters. Any receiver must enter into resonant vibration with a sender in order to pick up its emissions. Lakhovsky likened the system to two well-tuned pianos: when a note is struck on one it will cause the same note to vibrate on the other.

Some dowsers say that the prime sensor in the human body may be located in the area of the solar plexus. This appears to be borne out by Harvalik's most recent research. To shield parts of the human body from the effects of the ocean of magnetic forces surrounding it, Harvalik took an eight-foot by ten-inch strip of highly effective magnetic shielding and rolled it into a two-layered cylinder which could be lowered around the body to shield head, shoulders, torso, or pelvic area.

With the shield covering his head, Harvalik walked blindfolded across a level area known to produce dowsing signals and obtained a strong reaction over each of three dowsing zones. The same reactions were obtained with his head exposed but his shoulders shielded. Gradually lowering the shield, Harvalik found that he could pick up dowsing signals until he reached an area between the seventh and twelfth rib, that is to say from sternum to navel.

'These measurements,' says Harvalik, 'suggest that dowsing sensors must be located in the region of the solar plexus and that perhaps there are additional sensors in the head or brain.'

According to Bovis, wavelengths broadcast by an object are picked up by the nerves in a human arm and then amplified by means of a pendulum swinging at the end of a string. Others say that the prime sensor in the human body is located in the area of the solar plexus. Tests in which the solar plexus was shielded with mu-metal which interrupts all known radiations showed that a dowser could no longer dowse. When mu-metal was placed around the head and brain no interference with dowsing occurred.

With this background Simoneton had enough electrical engineering and radio knowledge not to dismiss Bovis as a simple quack, and was able to establish empirically that with Bovis's system he could measure specific wavelengths from foods that indicated both vitality and freshness. Milk, which he measured at 6.5 thousand angstroms when fresh, lost forty per cent of its radiation by the end of twelve hours and ninety per cent by the end of twenty-four. As for pasteurization, Simoneton found that it killed the wavelengths dead. The same he found true of pasteurized fruit and vegetable juices. Garlic juice, when pasteurized, coagulated like dead human blood and its vibrations dropped from around eight thousand angstroms to zero.

Dehydrated fruit, on the other hand, was found by experiment to retain its vitality; if soaked in water for twenty-four hours it would radiate almost as strongly as when freshly picked. Canned fruits remained perfectly dead. Water turned out to be a very strange medium; normally unradiant, it was capable of being vitalized by association with minerals, human beings or plants. Some waters, such as those at Lourdes, Simoneton found to radiate as high as 14,000 angstroms. The Czech-born psychic Jan Merta holds that the rind from apples, pears and other fruits and vegetables, when left to soak in a glass of water overnight, releases healthful vibrations into the water which can then be drunk to provide better nourishment than the rind itself.

In his book *Radiations des Aliments*, Simoneton divided foods into four general classes. In the first were those whose radiant wavelength was over and above the basic human wavelength of 6·5 thousand angstroms, up to ten thousand or more. This category includes most fruits, which run between eight and ten thousand at the peak of their maturity, and most vegetables *if fresh from the garden*; but by the time they are on sale in towns they have usually lost one-third of their potency, and another third has gone by the time they are cooked.

Simoneton says fruits are filled with solar radiation between the bands of infra-red and ultra-violet, and that their radiance rises slowly to a peak while ripening, then gradually decreases to zero at putrefaction. The banana, which has a span of twenty-four days from the time it is picked until it rots, is only healthily edible for about eight days. It gives off optimum vibrations when it is yellow, less when green, and minimum when black. Vegetables are most radiant and therefore healthier when eaten raw. The potato, on the other hand, which has a radiance of only two thousand angstroms when raw rises to seven thousand when boiled and to nine thousand when baked. The same applies to other tubers. Legumes such as peas, beans, lentils, chickpeas, rate seven to eight thousand when fresh. But they lose most of their radiance when dried; they become heavy, indigestible and hard on the liver, says Simoneton. To benefit from them they too should be eaten raw and freshly picked. Wheat has a radiance of 8·5 thousand angstroms; when cooked this rises to 9·0. Olive oil has a superior radiance of 8·5 thousand and is extremely durable. Six years later it still gives off around 7·5 thousand. Butter, which radiates about 8·0, is good for about ten days before it starts to fall off, reaching its lowest level in about twenty days. Ocean fish and shellfish are good foods with a bright radiance from 8·5 to 9·0, especially if caught fresh and eaten raw. This includes crabs, oysters, clams and other shellfish. Freshwater fish is much less radiant.

In Simoneton's second category he places foods radiating from 6·5 down to 3·0 thousand angstroms. These include eggs, peanut oil, wine, boiled vegetables, cane sugar and cooked fish. He rates a good red wine between four and five thousand, and says it is a better drink than devitalized city water, and certainly better than coffee, chocolate, spirits or pasteurized fruit juices which have virtually no radiance. Echoing Nichols, Simoneton says that whereas the juice of a fresh sugar-beet gives 8·5 thousand angstroms, refined beet sugar can fall as low as 1·0, and the white lumps that get wrapped in papers are down to zero.

Of meats, the only one that Simoneton includes in his top list of edible foods is freshly smoked ham. Freshly killed pork radiates at 6·5 thousand; but once it has been soaked in salt and hung over a wood fire its radiance rises to 9·5 or 10 thousand angstroms. Other meats are almost valueless, except as a digestive exercise. Cooked meats, sausages, and offal are all in Simoneton's third category; so are coffee, tea, chocolate, jams, fermented cheeses and white bread. In his fourth category are margarines, conserves, spirits, refined white sugar, and bleached white flour.

Applying his technique for measuring wavelengths directly to human beings, Simoneton found that the normal healthy person gives off a radiance of about 6·5 or a little higher, whereas the radiations given off by tobacco smokers, alcohol imbibers and meat eaters are uniformly lower. People suffering from cancer will give off a low wavelength of 4,875, long before any overt symptoms of the disease are evident. Therefore it should be possible to diagnose and take remedial steps well before the cancer has made serious inroads into the body's cellular tissue.

It is Simoneton's hypothesis that to be healthy human beings should eat fruit, vegetables, nuts and fresh fish that give off radiations higher than their normal 6·5 thousand. He believes that low radiance foods, such as meat and white bread, sap the body of its existing vitality instead of replenishing its energy. Developing this idea it struck Simoneton that the therapeutic powers attributed since the dawn of history to herbs, flowers, roots and barks, might not be due to their chemical content, but to the healthy wavelengths they radiate.

Paracelsus acquired much of his immense knowledge of the healing powers of plants from the lore of old European herbalists and from wise men of the East, but his main source was nature itself. According to his 'doctrine of sympathetic resemblances' all growing things reveal through their structure, form, colour, and aroma, their peculiar usefulness to man. He recommended that a physician should sit quietly in a meadow and he would soon notice how 'the blossoms follow the motion of the planets, opening their petals according to the phases of the moon, by the cycle of the sun, or in response to distant stars'.

A modern follower of Paracelsus who turned out to be an extraordinary wizard with herbs and plants was a London doctor, Edward Bach, who gave up his Harley Street practice to seek more natural means of restoring health to his fellow human beings. He considered that most of the so-called remedies gave the patient unnecessary pain and often did him more harm than good. He was determined to find remedies that would be gentle, sure, and would result in healing of both mind and body.

Like Paracelsus and Goethe before him, Bach was convinced that true knowledge was to be gained not through man's intellect, but through his ability to see and accept the natural, simple truths of life. Paracelsus had asserted that the further you search the greater you will realize the simplicity of all creation, and advised physicians to search within themselves for the spiritual insight that would lead them to sense and recognize the energies of plants. In pursuit of this idea, Bach wandered the English countryside and the Welsh mountains in search of the wild flowers he was convinced contained the secret of healing man's spiritual and physical ailments. He felt sure that disease of the body is not due primarily to physical causes, but can stem from disturbing moods or states of mind.

Like Paracelsus, Bach believed that everything that lives radiates light, and like Simoneton, he realized that plants with their high vibrations were able to raise the lowered vibrations of human beings. As he put it, 'herbal remedies have the power to elevate our vibrations, and thus draw down spiritual power which cleanses mind and body, and heals'. Bach compared his remedies to that of beautiful music or arrangements of colour, or any gloriously uplifting medium that gives inspiration; his cure was not to attack the disease, but to flood the body with beautiful vibrations from wild herbs and flowers, in the presence of which 'disease would melt away as snow in the sunshine'.

Myrna I. Lewis, co-author with Robert N. Butler, M.D., of a new book *Aging and Mental Health*, was amazed when recently taken by the Soviets on a visit to several sanitaria in the Black Sea city of Sochi to find ageing Soviet citizens afflicted with a variety of ills, both physical and mental, being treated not with drugs but with vibrations from flowers in greenhouses where they were led to smell specific blooms so many minutes a day. They were also being treated with music played in their rooms and the sound of the sea recorded on tapes.

Fundamentally, Bach maintains that it is up to the sick person to change his mind about his own illness, but that healthy aesthetic vibrations help him recover his desire to be well. He felt that a long bout of fear or worry could deplete an individual's vitality to the point where his body lost its natural resistance to disease, and could thus became the prey of any infection or illness. 'It is not the disease which needs the treatment,' said Bach. 'There are no diseases; only sick people.' During his search for wild flowers with medicinal properties Bach felt his senses quickening. Through a finely developed sense of touch he was able to feel the vibrations and power emitted by any plant he wished to test. Like Paracelsus, if he held the petal or bloom of some plant in the palm of his hand or placed it on his tongue he could feel in his body the effects of the properties within that flower. Some had a strengthening, vitalizing effect on his mind and body, others would give him pain, vomitings, fevers or rashes. His instinct told him that the best plants would be found blooming late in the year, when the days are longest and the sun at the height of its power and strength. The plants he chose were the most perfect of their kind, their bloom beautiful in shape and hue, growing in profusion.

Bach may have read that Paracelsus on his estate at Hohenheim had captured dew on plates of glass, gathering the dew under various configurations of the heavenly bodies, believing the water to carry within it the energy of these planetary combinations. Or he may have had a flash of intuition, early one morning walking through a field upon which the dew still lay heavy, in which he saw that each dew-drop must contain some of the properties of the plant upon which it rested and that the heat of the sun, acting through the fluid, would serve to draw out these properties until each drop was magnetized with power. If he could obtain the medicinal properties of the plants he was seeking in this way, the resulting remedies would contain the full, perfect and uncontaminated power of the plants, and they might heal as no medical preparations had been known to heal before. He collected the dew from certain flowers and shook the drops into small bottles, filling some with the dew from flowers which had been in full sunlight, and some from those still in shade. Though many of the flowers did not contain the healing properties he sought, Bach found the dew from each plant held a definite power of some kind, and that this power was stronger in plants that had been in sunlight.

The collecting of dew was a laborious process and therefore he decided to place a few blooms from a chosen plant in a glass bowl filled with water from a clear stream. After the flowers had been standing in the sunlight for several hours, he found that the water had become strongly impregnated with the vibrations and power of the plant. From these first experiments Bach went on to produce thirty-eight remedies, and he wrote a philosophic booklet to go with them. Thousands of patients throughout England and the world were to vouch for their efficacy, and many thousands still depend on this elixir of flowers to cure them of innumerable ailments.

Alick McInnes, a ruddy-cheeked Scotsman, is another man who can feel the radiations from flowers. Blindfolded he can put his hand over a flower, and tell from the wavelength of its radiation just what plant it is and what its medical properties may be. He had spent thirty years in India and it was at the Bose Institute near Calcutta that he first became aware that plants not only give off radiations which can be sensed by man, but are themselves sensitive to the radiations given off by humans. By the entrance to the Institute stands a luxuriant *mimosa pudica*. Visitors are requested to pick a small frond and place it in one of Bose's complicated machines which provides a schematic pattern of the vibrations of the plant on a sheet of paper. The visitor then places his own wrist inside the machine and watches as a duplicate of the pattern is produced, demonstrating that mimosa is so sensitive it can pick up and faultlessly reflect individual human radiations.

As McInnes interprets the phenomenon of human and plant radiations, each individual member of either kingdom modifies or qualifies with his own wavelength the fundamental energy radiating through him. The same applies, says McInnes, down to the finest particle of matter: 'Everything radiates wavelengths which can be identified as sound, colour, form, movement, perfume, temperature and intelligence.' The radiations may vary, but the same flower species always gives off the same radiation.

McInnes says he has found it possible to transfer flower radiations to water where the radiations will stay more or less indefinitely. He has some bottles with radiations still effective after twenty years. Each flower species has a time when its radiations can best be transferred to water, usually, though not always, when the flowers are at the peak of their maturity, which is also usually around a full moon. When conditions are right, transfer of the radiations or potencies, as he calls them, is instantaneous, and McInnes says the water can actually be seen to change, 'an awe-inspiring experience never to be forgotten'. The resulting potentized water McInnes calls an Exultation of Flowers, which he says is not a specific for the treatment of any particular disease, but operates in a subtle way on the radiations coming through the human body, on animals or the soil, and in so doing raises the vitality of the person, animal or soil concerned. When vitality is raised to the necessary level, illness disappears. The radiations in Exultation of Flowers are not identifiable by ordinary methods of chemical analysis nor can the impulses be identified by any measuring instrument available in Britain. Therefore McInnes is obliged by law to label his bottles 'Guaranteed Chemical Composition – 100% water, without herbal or chemical ingredients'. He points out that magnetized steel and ordinary steel show the same chemical ingredients but are obviously quite different from each other, and he still hopes that some new method will be devised to identify the radiations.

McInnes says his Exultation is just as good for a cow with milk fever in Scotland as it is for a man with asthma in California or a woman stung by a wasp in New Zealand. It can be used on a baby with a stomach-ache, on a hive of bees with 'foul brood', on strawberry plants with 'June Yellows' or on hens which have eaten poisoned grain. Sprayed on to the soil he says it increases the activity and quality of soil bacteria. But he warns that gardens which have been treated with chemical fertilizers will take longer to respond 'because the whole polarity of the soil has been geared to decay'. He says the vibrations of his Exultation channel fresh energy into the soil which counteracts disease, blight and pests.

In more than sixteen years since Exultation of Flowers was offered to the public many thousands of letters have been received reporting success in the treatment of nearly every diagnosable disease. McInnes believes that all forms of life are created to live in harmony, but mankind has so misused this dominion over created things that there is now disharmony everywhere, which is expressed in physical disease in human, animal and plant life, the life forces from the Source of

Creation becoming more and more distorted. Believing that in the Golden Age the lion would lie down with the lamb, he describes how, when he lived in Uganda, he would watch hundreds of animals making tracks through the elephant grass towards salt licks. Carnivores such as leopards and panthers trotted alongside tiny timorous deer that in other circumstances would tremble and run away.

In South India McInnes witnessed the strange spectacle of Ramana Mohan Maharshi on his evening walk. Within seconds of his leaving his house, cattle tied up in stalls in the village half a mile away would struggle to get out of their ties. When released they careered along the road to accompany the old man on his walk, followed by all the dogs and children of the village. Before the procession had gone very far wild animals and even snakes joined it from the jungle. Thousands of birds appeared, almost blotting out the sky. There were tiny tits, huge kites, heavy-winged vultures and other birds of prey, all flying in harmony around the Maharshi on his walk. When he returned to his room, said McInnes, all the birds, animals and children would quietly disappear.

As everything created is interdependent, says McInnes, it follows that what affects one form of life must affect all other forms as well. 'If we deliberately cause suffering and disease in other lives, we increase our own suffering and disease.' All creation, he says, is affected by disease inflicted on laboratory animals in what he believes to be a futile and fore-doomed attempt to combat illness. All creation is tormented through the ghastly agonies which the vivisectionist inflicts on helpless creatures. Any relief of illness supposed to be removed by knowledge gained at the expense of such agonies will be paid for many times over in increased suffering in some other part of the whole. All creation suffers when plants in their millions are burnt by chemical weed-killers.

Just as every created thing takes a knock for every victim of war or every inmate tortured in a concentration camp, so every created thing takes a knock when a rabbit dies of human-induced myxamatosis, when animals are hunted and killed for sport, or when terrified cattle are slaughtered in abbatoirs. 'All of Life,' says McInnes, 'is one. There is no exception.'

[277]

18

Radionic pesticides

Simoneton's dream that doctors with earphones would one day diagnose patients by tuning in to the frequencies given off by their ailing organs and then cure them by broadcasting to the organs more healthful vibrations has turned out to be closer to fact than fiction.

At the end of the nineteenth century Dr Albert Abrams, the son of a successful San Francisco merchant from whom he had inherited a vast fortune, travelled to Heidelberg to study advanced medicine. In Naples young Abrams watched the famous Italian tenor Enrico Caruso flick a wine glass with his finger to produce a pure tone, then step back and by singing the same note shatter the glass. This impressive feat awoke in Abrams the idea that he might have stumbled on a fundamental principle which could be tied into medical diagnosis and healing.

At the University of Heidelberg's medical school, from which he was to receive top honours and the gold medal, Abrams met a Professor de Sauer, who was engaged, many years before Gurwitsch had happened on 'mitogenetic radiation', in a bizarre series of experiments with plants. De Sauer told Abrams that, while transplanting onion seedlings, he had inadvertently left some of the uprooted onions next to those still growing in one of several flats. Two days later he noticed that the seedlings growing on the side of the flat next to the dying plants were different in appearance from those on the opposite side. De Sauer could not explain the reason for the difference but Abrams was convinced that the onion roots were emitting some strange form of radiation and linked this in his mind with the resonance phenomenon behind Caruso's voice-shattered glass.

Abrams returned to the United States to teach pathology at

Stanford University's medical school, of which he was later to become director of medical studies. A superb diagnostician and master of the art of percussion, he would tap the body of a patient to produce resonating sounds, which became clues to whatever ills might be afflicting the patient. One day Abrams noticed that when a nearby X-ray apparatus was switched on without warning it dulled the resonant note he was getting from his tapping. Perplexed, Abrams rotated his patient and discovered that the strange dulling occurred only while the man faced east and west, but that when he was aligned north and south the percussion note was continuously resonant. There seemed to be a relationship between the geomagnetic field and as with the grains researched by Pittman in Alberta, the electromagnetic field of individuals. Abrams later discovered a similar effect was produced by a man with a cancerous ulcer of the lip, even when the X-ray machine was not operating.

After several months of experimentation with persons afflicted with various maladies, Abrams concluded that nerve fibres in the epigastric region not only react by contracting to the stimulus of X-rays generated from a machine several yards distant, but appear to be in a state of permanent contraction in the case of a patient suffering from cancer, except when the patient is oriented in a north–south direction. Because of this similarity, Abrams concluded that the contractions, due in the first case to radiant energy rippling from an X-ray instrument, were in the second case taking place in response to vibrating molecules which were collectively forming the cancerous growth.

Abrams asked his houseboy, Ivor, who had accompanied him to class, to step on to the lecture platform, strip to the waist, and face west. As he tapped the boy just above the navel, Abrams told his students to listen carefully to the hollow, resonant quality of the note he was obtaining. He then asked one young doctor to hold a specimen of cancerous tissue in light contact with Ivor's forehead, applying it for a few seconds, removing it, and applying it again. As Abrams continuously percussed the abdomen, the class was amazed to hear the note change from resonance to dullness each time the specimen was placed on Ivor's forehead, apparently because of a contraction of muscle fibres. When Abrams substituted a tuberculous specimen for the cancerous one, the resonance of the note did not change. But when he began tapping an area just below the navel, the same effect was produced. Abrams was forced to the conclusion that unknown waves from diseased specimens could be received and recorded by a healthy human body and that they somehow altered the character of its tissues.

After months of work, Abrams was able to show that a series of what he called 'electronic reactions', varying from cancerous and tubercular to malarial and streptococcal, could be pinpointed on different areas of the trunk of a healthy person like Ivor. This led him to proclaim that the time-honoured idea that disease was of cellular origin was out of date and must be discarded. Instead, he maintained it was because the molecular constituents of cells undergo a structural alteration, specifically a change in the number and arrangement of their electrons, that they develop characteristics which only later become visible at the microscope. Exactly what caused the alteration Abrams did not know, nor does anyone today. He nevertheless suspected that forces could be discovered for correcting what he considered to be intramolecular aberrations, and even for preventing their occurrence.

Abrams next found that the radiation from a pathological specimen could be transmitted, like electricity, over a six-foot wire. When a sceptical doctor challenged Abrams to find the exact location of a tuberculosis infection in his lung for which he had been receiving treatment in a sanitarium, Abrams had the man hold one disc against his forehead and got another student to pass the second disc over the subject's chest until the percussing note changed in tone. The baffled man admitted Abrams had located the infection within centimetres.

Since one spot on the trunk of a healthy subject reacted to not just one but several pathological specimens, Abrams next began to conceive of an instrument which might differentiate between the wavelengths of all specifically diseased tissues. After months of research, he worked out what he called a 'reflexophone', an instrument very much like the rheostat – a continuously variable electrical resistor used to regulate current – that could emit sounds varying in pitch and thus obviate the necessity of having to tap a specific point on a body.

Different diseases could now be read from the dial: fifty-five for a syphilitic specimen, fifty-eight for sarcomatous tissue, and so on. Abrams asked his assistant to mix up the specimens and found he could infallibly select or 'diagnose', by checking the readings on his indicator.

Abrams's developments to this point ran not only decades ahead of, but directly counter to, the prevailing medical philosophy of his day. His statement that 'as physicians we dare not stand aloof from the progress made in physical science and segregate the human entity from other entities of the physical universe' was as incomprehensible to most of his medical colleagues as were the later pronouncements of Lakhovsky and Crile.

An even more fantastic revelation came when Abrams found he could diagnose the ills of the human body with his instrument from a single drop of the body's blood. Furthermore, by apparently inducting the effect from one reflexophone to another which contained three rheostats calibrated in units of 10, 1 and 1/25, he was able to determine not only from what disease a person was suffering but *to what stage it had advanced*.

Even more fantastic, Abrams found that if a woman was afflicted with a breast cancer, he could determine from her blood spot alone in which breast the cancer was located, merely by having a healthy percussed subject point with his fingertips to his own breasts. In exactly the same way, Abrams could reveal the exact site of tubercular or any other diseased condition whether focused in the lungs, bowel, bladder, one of the vertebrae; in fact, wherever in the body.

One day while Abrams was demonstrating to a class the reaction induced by the blood of a malarial patient, he suddenly turned and said, 'Well, there are upwards of forty of you physicians present, and probably all of you would prescribe quinine to a patient suffering from this disease, but can any one of you offer any scientific reason for so doing?' There being no reply, Abrams took out a few grains of sulphate of quinine and put them where the blood drop had been in the device. It produced exactly the same percussion note as malaria. He then placed the malarial material in the container *together* with a grain or so of quinine wrapped in tissue paper. Now the percussion which had produced a dull sound indicating malaria gave a resonant sound. To his amazed class Abrams put forward the suggestion that radiations emitted by quinine molecules *exactly cancelled* those from malarial molecules, that the effect on malaria of quinine was due to an unsuspected electrical law which should become the subject of intensive research. Various other known antidotes behaved similarly – mercury against syphilis, to cite but one example.

Abrams knew that if he could devise a wave-emitting instrument, similar to a wireless broadcasting station, which could alter the character of the waves transmitted by malarial or syphilitic tissue, he might cancel them out as effectively as did quinine or mercury.

Though at first he believed 'this was beyond the wit of man', he eventually built an 'oscilloclast' with the help of a friend, Samuel O. Hoffman, a distinguished radio research engineer who had achieved fame in World War I by devising a unique method for detecting German zeppelins approaching the U.S. coast even at a great distance. This oscilloclast or 'wave breaker' could emit specific waves capable of curing human afflictions by apparently altering or cancelling out radiations emitted by various diseases. By 1919 Abrams began teaching its use to physicians, who, because neither they nor Abrams could exactly explain how it effected cures, regarded it as nothing short of miraculous.

In 1922, Abrams reported in the *Physico-Clinical Journal* that for the first time he had effected over telephone wires the diagnosis of a patient miles away from his office, using nothing more than a drop of blood from the patient and analysis of its vibratory rates by his instruments. This somewhat eerie claim finally aroused the ire of the A.M.A. which published a defamatory article impugning Abrams in its journal as a quack, an article which was parroted in England in the *British Medical Journal*. This caused Sir James Barr, past president of the British Medical Association, who had been successfully using Abrams's methods in his own practice, to write in reply:

Radionic pesticides

You very seldom quote from the *Journal of the American Medical Association* and one might have expected that when you did you would have chosen a more serious subject than an ignorant tirade against an eminent medical man, against, in my opinion, the greatest genius in the medical profession.

Barr concluded that one day 'medical editors and medical men will begin to perceive that there was more to Abrams's vibrations than was dreamt of in their philosophy'.

Abrams's greatest discoveries were that all matter is radioactive and that the generated waves can be picked up across space by using human reflexes as detectors; also, that in many conditions of disease dull patches are consistently found at specific spots on afflicted patients' bodies.

When Abrams died in 1924, the vilification against him continued in the United States in eighteen separate and consecutive issues of *Scientific American*. One of the worst insinuations was that the 'Abrams box' had been devised for no other purpose than to make a financial killing by selling it to naïve physicians and an unsuspecting public. No one noted that Abrams, a millionaire in his own right, had written to Upton Sinclair, one of his American defenders, that he would donate his devices to, and work unremunerated for, any institute which would develop the 'Abrams box' in the interests of humanity.

The sanctions against Abrams and his work scared off all but a small minority of American doctors, most of whom were independent-minded chiropractors or, as they like to be called, 'drugless physicians'.

But a generation after Abrams's death one of these, living in the San Francisco Bay area, was visited by Curtis P. Upton, a Princeton-trained civil engineer whose father was a partner of Thomas Alva Edison. Upton's engineering mind led him to wonder whether the strange device used to cure human affliction might not be applied to pest control for agriculture. In the summer of 1951 he and his Princeton classmate William J. Knuth, an electronics expert from Corpus Christi, Texas, drove into the cotton fields of the thirty-thousand-acre Cortaro-Marana tract near Tucson, Arizona. Together they unloaded from the back of their truck a mysterious boxlike instrument about the size of a portable radio, complete with dials and a stick antenna. Only this time they went one better than Simoneton and McInnes. They would attempt to affect the field not directly but through the medium of photographs.

An aerial photograph of the field was placed on a 'collector plate' attached to the base of the instrument, together with a reagent known to be poisonous to cotton pests. The dials were set in a specific manner. The object of the exercise was to clear the field of pests without recourse to chemical insecticides. The theory behind the system, as 'way out' as anything so far reported on the nature of plants, held that the molecular and atomic make-up of the emulsion on the photograph would be resonating at the identical frequencies of the objects they represented pictorially. Though the American engineers did not know it, the same discovery had been made by Bovis in the 1930s. By affecting the photograph with a reagent known to be poisonous to cotton pests the Americans believed the cotton plants in the field could be immunized against the pests. Because the amount of poisonous reagent used was infinitesimal compared to the number of acres photographed, the reagent was thought to act in the same way that trace dosages of dilution function in Homeopathic Medicine.

Homeopathy is a method of treatment founded by Christian Samuel Hahnemann, a physician of note born in Meissen in Saxony in 1755. Hahnemann, who was also a chemist, a linguist, a translator of medical works, and the author of a comprehensive apothecaries' lexicon, got himself into serious trouble with the then equivalent of the F.D.A. by his discovery that small doses of what can cause the symptoms of a disease in human beings can also cure them. The original discovery was made by chance when the Countess of Cinchon, wife of the Spanish Viceroy to Peru, was relieved of malaria with an infusion of bark from a local tree which produced symptoms in her identical with those of malaria. Thereafter known as 'cinchon bark', the remedy was sold by monks in Spain to the rich for its weight in gold and given to the poor for nothing.

Spurred by this novel approach to medicine, Hahnemann made a methodical search for plants, herbs, barks, or any substance, including snake venom, which could produce symptoms similar to those of a known disease, and by administering them in small doses produced some near miracle cures. He found belladonna to be a remedy against scarlet fever, pulsatilla against measles, and gelsemium against influenza. Quite as extraordinary as Hahnemann's cures was his next discovery, that the more he diluted a remedy the more potent and effective it became, even if diluted to an infinitesimal one million to one. Rudolf Hauschka explains the phenomenon by suggesting that if matter is a condensation or a crystallization of cosmic forces, these forces would naturally revert to being more powerful as they were liberated from their material casing like jinns from a bottle.

Hauschka explains part of Hahnemann's secret as being in the rhythmic, mathematical fashion in which he shook his dilutions, rhythm having the same effect it has on humans of freeing the spirit from the clutches of the body.

But the authorities made short shrift of Hahnemann. Already in bad odour with his fellow physicians because he considered bleeding and cupping his patients to be a crime, Hahnemann next incurred the wrath of his fellow apothecaries when they saw the threat to their profits from the sale of drugs in such minute quantities. The moment Hahnemann's discovery was given to the public in the journal of Goethe's personal physician, Dr Hufeland, the Guild of Apothecaries (forerunners of today's pharmacists and the 'detail men' who each year press hundreds of new pills on doctors) saw to it that Hahnemann was brought before a court, found guilty, forbidden to dispense medicine, and compelled to leave town.

In Tucson in 1951, it would have been hard to find a scientist who would bet the small change in his pocket that Upton and Knuth's protective process could offer them any safeguards against marauding pests. Yet the two engineers pursued their course, repeating the process with aerial photographs covering the entire four thousand acres owned by the Cortaro Management Company, one of Arizona's biggest cotton growers. The company executives were gambling that, if the twelve varieties of pests that normally attacked their million-dollar crop could be kept at bay with so simple a device, they could save up to

$30,000 a year in operating costs by eliminating the use of insecticide sprays.

In the fall, the Tucson *Weekend-Reporter* ran an illustrated two-page spread headlined: 'Million Dollar Gamble Pays Off for Cotton Man'. The article stated that a 'Buck Rogers type of electronic pest control' had allowed Cortaro to achieve an almost twenty-five per cent increase in per-acre yield of cotton over the state average. W. S. Nichols, president of the Cortaro Management Company, stated in an affidavit that the treated cotton also seemed to have approximately twenty per cent more seed: 'This may possibly be the result of not destroying the bees, upon which the radionic process seems to have no effect.' Nichols further remarked that his hoe hands had noted an almost complete absence of snakes in the areas subjected to the strange treatment.

On the East Coast of the United States, one of Upton's Princeton classmates, Howard Armstrong, who had become an industrial chemist with many inventions to his credit, decided to try his friend's method in Pennsylvania. After taking an aerial photograph of a cornfield under attack by Japanese beetles, he cut one corner off the photo with a pair of scissors and laid the remainder together with a small amount of rotenone, a beetle poison, extracted from the roots of a woody Asian vine which the Japanese call 'roten', on the collector plate of one of Upton's radionic devices.

After several five- to ten-minute treatments with the machine's dials set to specific readings, a meticulous count of beetles revealed that eighty or ninety per cent of them had died or disappeared from the corn plants treated through the photo. The untreated plants in the corner cut away from the photo remained a hundred per cent infested.

After witnessing this experiment, B. A. Rockwell, director of research for the Pennsylvania Farm Bureau Cooperative Association in Harrisburg, wrote:

To control insect pests at a distance of thirty miles with no danger to man, plants or animals would perhaps be an accomplishment heretofore unrivalled in the scientific control of insects injurious to vegetation. To an individual with 19 years' experience in the research field this feat appeared unreal, impossible, fantastic, and crazy. Yet careful counts by the writer of the treated corn plants and untreated corn plants indicated definitely that the kill ratio was 10 to 1 in favour of the treated plants.

Upton, Knuth, and Armstrong combined their talents and the first letters of their names to form U.K.A.C.O. Inc. The new company's goal was to relieve farmers of unwanted pests by the new method, as scientifically inexplicable as it was simple and inexpensive. The company received the backing of General Henry M. Gross, one of Harrisburg's most distinguished citizens, head of the Selective Service Board for the State of Pennsylvania.

In the West, Upton and Knuth contracted with forty-four artichoke growers to treat their crop against plume moths. The contracts were written on the basis of 'no control – no pay'. All the growers paid the service charge of one dollar an acre, a tiny fraction of the costs of conventional spraying. In Pennsylvania Rockwell stated: 'Since farmers usually do not pay for a service unless there is value received, this is the best testimonial for the U.K.A.C.O. process which has come to my attention.'

Convinced that a radical new development for controlling pests was in the offing, Rockwell arranged contracts with his fellow farmers to run a long series of experiments under his supervision.

At this point, the new insecticideless method of treating crops piqued the curiosity of the United States Department of Agriculture's research station at Beltsville, Maryland, one of whose officials, Dr Truman Hienton, called General Gross to say that he would like to find out exactly how U.K.A.C.O. was achieving its results. When Hienton and two of his Ph.D. colleagues arrived in Harrisburg, they were informed that the principle behind the machine seemed somehow to be related to that of radio broadcasting. But when U.K.A.C.O.'s Howard Armstrong was asked at what wavelength he was broadcasting his treatments, he could only say he did not know.

Nevertheless in the summer of 1951 Armstrong was so successful that when insecticide salesmen visited the farms under treatment they were informed their products were no longer needed. The farmers themselves operated many of the treating devices which were left by Armstrong on their farms. This evidently raised the hackles of the American insecticide industry, which responded that winter to U.K.A.C.O.'s new technology in the same way that the British fertilizer industry had to Sir Albert Howard's recommendations. *Agricultural Chemicals*, the industry's mouthpiece, printed an article in its January 1952, issue, panning the U.K.A.C.O. process as fraudulent.

Rockwell never denied that the radionic process was *not always* successful. He himself stated plainly that certain tests could fail because of interference from standing irrigation pipes, high-tension wires, leaky transformers, wire fences, radar, plant pots, and various soil conditions.

During the 1952 growing season field corn was treated on 1420 acres belonging to sixty-one farmers on eighty-one separate holdings in five counties: 78,360 individual corn stalks were examined. Officers of the new Homeotronic Foundation worked with several Pennsylvania Farm Bureau officials and one from the Farm Bureau Association of the State of Ohio.

Armstrong next learned from the West Coast that representatives of insecticide companies in concert with U.S.D.A. employees had been visiting farmers who used the U.K.A.C.O. process and telling them it was an outright fraud. The U.K.A.C.O. team came to the conclusion that Beltsville was directly and intentionally preventing them from proceeding with their work and that lobbyists of the insecticide industry in Washington were putting extreme pressure on the government to stamp out the new pest-control methods which were so dangerously threatening to put them out of business. So effective was the campaign against U.K.A.C.O. that the company had difficulty soliciting new clients among farmers, who were becoming convinced by an army of U.S.D.A. agents that there was nothing to the Upton-Knuth-Armstrong treatments.

Meanwhile Upton, whose patent application had been rejected for 'lack of convincing evidence in the record from qualified experts with scientific backgrounds', submitted a twenty-two-page addendum to support his claim. The adendum pleaded that 'it is difficult to precisely define the nature and mechanism of the novel methods' and postulated that the process

comprehends the study and use of certain fundamental energy sources capable of affecting molecules, atoms and electrons through their characteristic harmonic potency resonance frequencies in which every particle of matter exhibits its own characteristic frequency under a controlled polarity in a magnetic field of motion.

In support of their allegations, the inventors cited the work of Dr Edward Purcell, co-winner with Dr Felix Bloch of a 1952 Nobel Prize in physics, who published an article in the 15 November issue of *Science News Letter* on the characteristic resonant frequency of elements when resonated in selected magnetic fields, and a report on the work of Dr Bloch, wherein he succeeded, by a process he designated 'nuclear induction', in turning atomic particles into what, in effect, were infinitesimal radio transmitters, whose broadcasts, if highly amplified, could be detected in loudspeakers. There was little doubt in Upton's mind that his 'radiotonic treatment', as he called it, made use of the type of energy involved in the Bloch study, which, as Upton wrote, had 'not heretofore been recognized by science – particularly in its applications to molecular structures of the complex nature of plant and animal life'.

Holding that the work of electronic experts and the detection of potentials by means of delicate apparatus had long since proven the existence and the measurability of various amplitudes of electrical potentials in living creatures, Upton referred to the writings of Drs George Washington Crile and Harold Saxton Burr.

When all this failed to get the patent accepted, General Gross brought into play his contacts on the boards of some of the nation's largest industrial companies and was able to introduce the process to the consideration of important scientists in the U.S. Government, including Vannevar Bush, science adviser to President Eisenhower. When Gross explained to them U.K.A.C.O.'s accomplishments and said they were based on the idea that every particle has its own generic frequency, as Dr Crile had so stoutly maintained, the scientists responded heatedly that the U.K.A.C.O.-obtained results were impossible.

Though Gross politely suggested that the scientists come to Harrisburg and talk with Rockwell and the farmers whose crops had been 'radiotonically' protected and see the results for themselves, they declined his invitation. Gross had no more success with the director of the Carnegie Institution in Washington, who flatly told him that there was nothing in the science of electronics to suggest that the U.K.A.C.O. process could work.

Dr Willard F. Libby, who devised the carbon-14 dating technique, and who was soon to win the Nobel Prize in chemistry, after hearing Gross out, discouragingly yet perhaps accurately told him that it would take more than a million dollars to research the 'box'.

What also may have alarmed the government was the idea that if a host of insects could be affected, even killed, simply by radiating a poison at them via a picture of the plants which they were attacking, then the same technique could be militarily applied to concentrations of troops or even the populations of whole cities in wartime. All this discouragement, added to the studied and seemingly successful efforts of governmental and industrial moguls to wean farmers away from the new approach to insect control, finally forced U.K.A.C.O. to close its doors. But the story of what came to be called 'radionics' was only beginning.

Thirty years before the demise of the U.K.A.C.O. enterprise, a young engineer for the Kansas City Power and Light Company, T. Galen Hieronymus, who was one of the first to be granted an amateur radio operator's licence before World War I, was asked by one of his neighbours, a Dr Planck, to machine various parts for some instrumentation which required precise components, such as strips of silver plate, cut to exact proportions down to the millimetre, and carefully wound coils. Beyond referring to a mysterious medical genius in San Francisco with whom he had studied fantastic new techniques to treat disease, Planck did not enlighten his young machinist as to the purpose of the new instruments he was helping to build. It was only after Planck died and his wife asked Hieronymus to come to the house to look over a workroom full of strange equipment and, because she had no use for it, select whatever he wanted, that Hieronymus learned the real purpose of the equipment he had been machining, and that the name of the unknown surgeon was Albert Abrams.

Meanwhile a vivacious young Los Angeles chiropractor, Dr Ruth Drown, was also making refinements on Abrams's devices. Drown's most startling accomplishment was her development of a camera which could be used to take pictures of organs and tissues of patients using nothing but a drop of their blood, even when the patients were hundreds or thousands of miles from her office. Even more startling, she could take pictures in 'cross-section' which cannot be done with X-rays. Though she received a British patent for this twenty-first-century apparatus, Dr Drown's claim was relegated by F.D.A. authorities to the realm of science fiction and her equipment was confiscated in the early 1940s. To make sure that her plight was suitably publicized, the same authorities saw to it that reports from *Life* magazine were on the scene. After the *Life* story presented her as a charlatan, Dr Ruth Drown died of grief – an unrecognized genius.

While Drown was working in California, still another of Abrams's followers, a Chicago doctor, G. W. Wiggelsworth, with the help of his brother, an electronics engineer who at first looked upon the oscilloclast as an outright fraud but finally became convinced of its efficacy, went on to improve the 'Abrams box' by substituting for resistance coils variable condensers, a change which he found vastly improved the tuning. Wiggelsworth christened his new device a 'pathoclast' or disease breaker, the users of which banded together into a Pathometric Association.

Hieronymus had earlier made a detailed study of his own of strange energies emitted, not from healthy or diseased tissues, but from metals. Working on his theory, he took sterling-silver objects, such as broken spoons, pepper-and-salt shakers, and anything else he could steal from his wife, and buried them in the Kansas prairie.

Knowing the location of the hidden silver, Hieronymus then 'worked backward', as he says, trying to find the emanations from it. To his surprise, he discovered that every so often he could find *no energy* emanating from the silver, and wondered if someone might have dug up his hoard. A few hours later the energy would be radiating as strongly as ever.

Hieronymus's eclectic mind next wondered whether the energy was undetectable at given times because it was radiating not upward out of the earth but downward toward the earth's centre. To find out, he took an eight-foot copper-clad steel ground rod and sledge-hammered it at an angle into the ground so that it would extend below the silver hoard. When the rod was at the level of the silver or below it, his device, to which the rod was attached, indicated a surge of energy; when he pulled the rod some distance above the silver, no energy was registered.

By repeatedly taking measurements over weeks, Hieronymus found that the energy from the silver seemed to be diverted downward for a few hours every two and a half days. Checking in an almanac he discovered that the cycle of diversions in some ways correlated with phases of the moon. What Pfeiffer had discovered about lunar influence with respect to plants seemed also to be applicable to metals.

Further work with buried metal also convinced Hieronymus that these energies were, like those in Abrams's experiments, strongly influenced by magnetic attraction. Thus, at least two twentieth-century researchers, one a medical man, like Mesmer, the other a laboratory researcher, like Reichenbach, appeared to have rediscovered the link between mineral magnetism on the one hand and 'animal magnetism' on the other.

Hieronymus suspected that the unknown energy emitted from metals might be somehow linked to sunlight; since it could be transmitted over wires, it might have an effect on the growth of plants.

To find out, Hieronymus placed some aluminium-lined boxes in the pitch-dark cellar of his Kansas City house. Some boxes he grounded to a water pipe and connected by separate copper wires to metal plates on the outside of the house exposed to full sunlight. Other boxes were left unconnected. In all of them Hieronymus planted seed grain. In the connected boxes the seeds grew into sturdy green plants. The seeds in the unconnected boxes had no trace of green and were anaemic and drooping.

This brought Hieronymus to the revolutionary conclusion that whatever caused the development of chlorophyll in plants could not be sunlight itself but something associated with it, which, unlike light, was transmittable over wires. He had no idea at what frequency this energy might be located on the electromagnetic spectrum, or even if it was related to it.

As Hieronymus continued to build instruments for the doctors, and to experiment with them, he grew more and more convinced that the energy being modulated by the devices had little to do with electromagnetism. This notion became a certainty when he found the device itself was short-circuited if bathed in light rays from the sun just as electrical circuits in a radio are shorted by being plunged into a bath of water.

Hieronymus next designed a special analyser, first with lenses, finally with a prism, by means of which he could identify, from the radiations they emitted, many of the elements on Mendeleyev's periodic chart. He found that the energy, when refracted through a prism, behaved in the same manner as light, except that the angles of refraction were much more acute, and that the energy from various elements came through at angles of refraction in the same order as the contents of their nuclei. His ability to detect a substance from its radiation alone convinced Hieronymus that disease was destroyed by the Abrams device and its descendants 'through a radiative attack on the binding energy which holds molecular structures together'.

The frequency of emanation, or angle of refraction, is in exact proportion to the number of particles in the nucleus of an element, says Hieronymus. The range of frequencies or angles of refraction from complex substances can thus be used to disclose what they contain. The energy emitted does not, like electromagnetic energy, attenuate inversely as the square of the distance from its source. It radiates out only a certain distance depending on the object from which it is emitted, on the direction it takes, and even on the time of day of its measurement. Something varies the amount of radiation emitted in the same way that fog, smoke or other materials altering the density of the air in our atmosphere vary the intensity of light from whatever source.

[293]

Trying to describe this radiation Hieronymus first came up with the cumbersome explanation: 'Energy obeying some of the laws of *electricity* but not all of them, and some of the laws of *optics*, but not all of them.' To obviate the repetition he finally coined the term '*eloptic energy*'.

This energy, he concluded, though independent of, was somehow affiliated with, electromagnetic energy. Because of the difference, Hieronymus inferred that their spectra of frequencies were necessarily related. He decided to refer to eloptic energy in all its wavelengths as a *fine medium* which, as he wrote, 'might be the same as that which used to be described by electronic engineers and physicists as "the ether" put in action at higher harmonics than so far experienced'.

The bacteriologist Otto Rahn, whose book on radiation from living things had so puzzled his colleagues ten years before, after examining Hieronymus's process and experiments, wrote to the inventor:

Since those radiations hold the secret of life, they also hold the secret of death. At present, very few people know about the possibilities, and very few know *all* the facts. It seems imperative that those few keep their knowledge to themselves, and divulge only as much as is necessary to perform the immediate applications to cure disease. Your discoveries open up great possibilities, as tremendous as those of the atom bomb, and just like atomic energy, these radiations may be used for the bad as well as for the good of humanity.

In 1949 Hieronymus was awarded United States patent number 2,482,773 for the 'Detection of Emanations from Materials and Measurement of the Volumes Thereof'. Other patents were later issued in the United Kingdom and Canada.

At the Heisley farm, together with a U.K.A.C.O. representative Hieronymus selected three ears of corn on each of which a corn worm was munching.

Isolating the ears so that the worms could not escape, Hieronymus began to treat them with his radionic broadcaster. He states that, after three days of treatment for ten minutes per hour round the clock, two of the corn worms were reduced to mush but the third was still wobblily intact. Another twenty-four hours of the same treatment and the stubborn worm was also mush. All that remained of the others was just 'wet places' on the corn ears.

Hieronymus was so stunned by the lethal potential of the tuned radiation that he resolved never to reveal *everything* about the make-up of his devices or their operation until he could one day find serious researchers of impeccable character to help him elucidate the exact potentials of his discoveries.

19

Mind over matter

About two decades before U.K.A.C.O.'s efforts to help the farmers of Pennsylvania were put to rout by the chemical manufacturers and the U.S.D.A., a book called *The Chain of Life* appeared in the United Kingdom in 1934 by the British surgeon, Guyon Richards, who had built up wide experience in medical problems as physician in charge of an entire district for the Indian Medical Service.

He was stimulated by the theories of a colleague, Captain Sandes, who had introduced him to the little known benefits of ionization and its remarkable effects on the treatment of disease, a branch of science later developed in Germany and, more particularly in the U.S.S.R., but almost wholly neglected in other countries. Richards became, as he put it, 'electrically-minded', and proceeded to make detailed galvanometric studies of plants and people in health and disease. Of Abrams, Richards said it was a pity that the very invention of the oscilloclast had, because its curative properties could not be exactly explained, obscured from the medical profession the important issues which Abrams had raised.

Richards's book restimulated interest in radionics among a small coterie of imaginative doctors who wanted to experiment with the new healing process. Looking for an engineer who could help them to build the strange new equipment, they sought out an 'English Hieronymus' and found him in the person of George De La Warr, a psychically-gifted civil engineer.

Having built a series of instruments covered in black leather, which came to be known as 'black boxes', about a year following the demise of U.K.A.C.O., the work of which they had no inkling, De La Warr and his osteopath wife Marjorie, found that they could affect the growth of diseased, or undernourished plants by focusing 'radionic' energy straight at them through a lens system, thus substantiating the claim of Hieronymus, of whom they were also unaware, that it was optically refractable.

Like the U.K.A.C.O. partners, the De La Warrs obtained successful results not only by directly radiating a plant, but also by beaming energy to it through one of its leaves or through its photograph. Why this should be so remained a mystery. They could only state: 'It is still problematical whether it is the apparatus, the photographic emulsion or the presence of a specific operator that produces the effects – or a combination of all these factors.' In De La Warr's view the emulsion on the negative received from the plant radiations of light, as well as other radiations, the precise nature of which was unknown. There was also evidence that a relationship existed between a plant and a leaf detached from it, or the expressed juice of that plant, just as it existed between a patient and his blood spot. De La Warr wrote that,

It would appear that each molecule of matter is capable of producing a tiny electrical voltage that is specific to itself, and which 'transmits' rather like a tiny radio transmitter-receiver. A collection of molecules, therefore, is capable of transmitting a generic pattern. This means that the signal from a plant or human is quite individual, and that each plant or person will receive a transmission on their own generic pattern. It is here that the photograph plays its part, as it is thought that the emulsion on the negative retains the generic pattern of the object photographed and can be induced to re-radiate as a carrier. Thus, with a photograph of a plant in circuit it is possible to affect that plant at a distance.

The theory was in no way airtight, but the results obtained by radionics were fantastic. Realizing that the presence of living organisms in the soil is a prerequisite to good husbandry, the De La Warrs wondered if they could not treat the soil itself through the cells living within it by radiating energy patterns effectively equivalent to plant nutrients. To attempt this they determined to photograph the soil of garden plots, treat the photographs radionically, and then plant vegetables in the treated soil to see how they would fare.

They began with cabbages. They removed all the top-soil

from two selected sites eighty feet apart, in the ground attached to their laboratory. They thoroughly sieved and mixed the soil to eliminate any possibility of variation, then spread it back on the sites, allowing it to settle for a week. On 27 March 1954 they began a month-long treatment of one site by radiating its photograph daily in their dark room, leaving the other site untreated. At the end of that time they planted in each piece of ground four young cabbages selected for their similarity. For two weeks they waited anxiously but there was no apparent difference in the rate of growth. Then suddenly the cabbages in the treated soil began to grow noticeably larger and continued to do so until the end of June. Photographs taken some four weeks before maturity revealed that the plants in the treated site were *three times larger* than those left to grow normally.

Encouraged by this success, the De La Warrs decided to repeat the experiment on a larger scale. They noticed that in one strip of garden three rows of peas thirty-seven feet long were growing so uniformly as to leave little doubt that the soil was of equal consistency throughout. The peas were uprooted and the site prepared for fresh planting. The strip was divided into fifteen plots, six of which were photographed from a bird's eye view and treated radionically every day for one month. Two plots were left untreated; seven others were used as buffers. At the beginning of August ninety-six Early English Winter-Resisting broccoli plants, all seven inches high, were set out, six to a plot. The radionically treated plots were re-photographed with the plants in them and irradiated daily until the experiment was concluded in mid-January 1955 after snow and ice had apparently stopped all growth. Accurate weighing of the plants under the scrutiny of an expert from Oxford University's Department of Agriculture, Dr E. W. Russell, who observed the experiment from beginning to end, revealed that an average *eighty-one per cent increase* in total crop yield had been obtained for the treated plants compared to the non-treated controls.

The De La Warrs next decided to broadcast treatment from their laboratories to a garden at Old Boars Hill, two miles from Oxford. They divided an equilateral plot into four squares and planted broadleaf beans in each square. A single square was photographed and irradiated from the beginning of May to the beginning of August 1955. At the end of the test, the height of the bean plants grown in the treated square was nine and a half inches greater than in all three other squares, and the number of pods considerably greater. Further experiments, in which the distance between treated soil and the laboratory extended as far as Scotland, were equally successful.

During the next growing season in 1956 they decided to ascertain whether an inert substance, if irradiated and mixed with soil, could re-radiate the nutritive energy patterns to the seeds during germination and growth. The substance they selected was 'vermiculite', a micaceous silica which was both chemically inert and insoluble in water. It was treated by being blown into the air in front of a radionic apparatus normally used for therapeutic purposes on humans. Then it was added to a grass seed mixture containing rye, cocksfoot and other varieties in a proportion of two parts vermiculite to one part grass seed. Treated and untreated vermiculite mixtures were sown in similar soils and similar boxes. The fantastic results, as confirmed by a leading agricultural firm, showed that the treated vermiculite produced a crop 186 per cent heavier in moist weight with a protein content 270 per cent higher. As a result of this and other experiments a nationally known plant-breeding establishment asked if they could conduct their own tests with the treated vermiculite on various types of seed. Under the firm's rigid test conditions, the phenomenal increases in growth obtained by the De La Warrs were no longer apparent. Far from being discouraged by this, the De La Warrs began to speculate about the possibility that their plants had been responding not to the radiations from their machines but to the human beings involved in the experiments. To test this idea they ran the very same tests the firm had performed on exactly the same plots. To the amazement of the establishment's horticultural staff, the De La Warrs were again successful in increasing growth with treated vermiculite, but, try as they would, the professional plant growers could not repeat their success. It was clear that a human factor was the crux of the problem. To determine the extent of this factor they again mixed vermiculite into the soil of potted oats. Their assistants, who daily poured measured quantities of water on to the seeds, were told which pots contained treated vermiculite and which did not. But they were not told *that none of the vermiculite used had been irradiated* and was as inert as when brought from the supplier. The oat seeds had received only such nutrient energy as was provided by the soil itself; yet the seedlings in those pots which the assistants believed contained treated vermiculite were coming up faster than the others. Human belief in a plant's growth was apparently acting as a nutrient actually to produce faster growth.

De La Warr, who considered this experiment the most important he had ever run, found himself face to face with a shattering new reality with the most far reaching implications: *the mind of a human being could affect cell formation!*

When De La Warr described this important experiment to one of Great Britain's leading physicists and suggested that a universal energy could be evoked by the proper attunement of one's thoughts, he was told curtly: 'I do not believe you, Mr De La Warr. If you can affect the number of atoms in a growing plant by your thought process, we must revise our concept of what constitutes matter.'

'Indeed we must,' said De La Warr, 'even if such revision posed a whole overhaul of existing knowledge. How, for instance, could this energy be incorporated into mathematical equations? What would happen to the law for the conservation of energy?'

When De La Warr realized that the real key to getting plants to flourish was simply asking them to do so, he published an article in his journal, *Mind and Matter*, asking readers to produce evidence to support his own experimental results which were so at variance with accepted and current materialistic atomic theory.

One of the most crucial steps in a fifteen-step procedure outlined in the article was that in which the experimentor was to hold bean seeds in his hands and invoke a blessing varying according to his faith or denomination, in a reverent and purposeful manner. Though warmly received by readers, the article evoked a harsh reply from officials of the Roman

Catholic Church who took umbrage because, as they pointed out, it was inadmissible for anyone below the rank of deacon to perform any act of blessing. Laymen were supposed only to ask the Creator to perform a blessing. To still the waters of protest, the De La Warrs renamed their experiment 'Increasing the Rate of Plant Growth by the Mental Projection of an Undefined Energy'.

Many of their readers reported success similar to that attained in America by the Reverend Franklin Loehr, whose seven hundred experiments on the effect of prayer on plants, conducted by one hundred and fifty persons, using 27,000 seeds under the auspices of Loehr's Religious Research Foundation in Los Angeles, were reported in his book, *The Power of Prayer on Plants*.

Loehr showed that the growth rate of plants could be accelerated as much as twenty per cent when individuals singly or in concert visualized the plants as thriving under ideal conditions. Though their experiments seemed to be acceptable from the evidence and pictures presented, the results were ignored by scientists on the basis that Loehr and his assistants had no scientific training and used relatively crude methods to measure growth.

However, Dr Robert N. Miller, an industrial research scientist and former professor of chemical engineering at Georgia Tech, began a series of experiments in 1967 with Ambrose and Olga Worrall whose feats of healing have become celebrated in the United States. Using an extremely accurate method of measuring plant growth rates developed by Dr H. H. Kleuter of the United States Department of Agriculture, with accuracies up to one thousandth of an inch per hour, Miller, working in Atlanta, Georgia, asked the Worralls to direct their thoughts at rye seedlings from Baltimore, some six hundred miles away.

Whereas the growth rate of a new blade of rye grass had been observed by Miller to stabilize at 0·00625 inch per hour, after he asked the Worralls to think of the seedling at exactly 9.00 p.m. the trace on a graph indicating growth rate began immediately to deviate upward and by 8.00 a.m. the following morning the grass was growing eighty-four per cent faster.

Instead of growing the expected one sixteenth of an inch in the interval, the seedling had sprouted more than half an inch. Miller reported that the dramatic results of his experiment suggest that the sensitive experimental technique could be used to accurately measure the effect of mind over matter.

The mysteries of how the human mind may act through radionic devices such as those of U.K.A.C.O., Hieronymus, or De La Warr are yet to be explained. In an amazing development, John Campbell, editor of *Astounding Science Fiction* – since become *Analog Science Fiction/Science Fact* – determined in the 1950s that a circuit diagram of Hieronymus's machine drawn in Indian ink worked as well as the machine itself. 'Your electronic circuit,' he wrote to Hieronymus, 'represents a *pattern of relationships*. The electrical characteristics are unimportant and can be dropped out completely.'

After a prolonged study of radionic devices sponsored by the foundation set up by Arthur M. Young, inventor of the Bell Helicopter, Frances Farrelly, who ran her own college for medical laboratory technicians, also came to the conclusion that the devices were not necessary to achieve effects. While working in England with a Harley Street physician, she found she could walk towards a patient with her hands outstretched and feel within her own body where the patient had trouble. As she says: 'I was beginning to run the instrument in my head, or mentally only.' Since then, Farrelly has been able to make diagnoses of ills of individuals not only without a radionics device but without a bloodspot or a photograph or anything at all. The mental image of a patient held in her mind is sufficient.

In the summer of 1973 Farrelly's talents were put to test in Prague when one of the participants in the First International Conference on Psychotronics – a Czech logism for the effects of mental energy on matter – lost a wallet in the cavernous four-storey Railway Workers' Building, site of the conference. Within minutes, Farrelly tracked it down, pinpointing its exact location inside a box at the back of a dark closet where a cleaning woman had placed it for safekeeping.

The following day she was confronted by a professor from the Czechoslovak Academy of Sciences who gave her a chip of mineralized rock and asked her before a large audience if she could state its origin and age. Rubbing the table before her to get a radionic type 'stick', Farrelly, after putting a dozen questions to herself, stated that the mineral in question came from a meteor and was about 3,200,000 years old, answers which exactly matched the most considered conclusions of expert Czech minerologists.

During her stay in England, Farrelly was intrigued that the De La Warrs seemed to have radionically detected that every living plant has a critical rotational position (C.R.P.), which is apparently established by the earth's magnetic field as the seed sprouts out of the ground. If the seedling is transplanted in such a way that it continues to grow in its C.R.P., it will thrive better than plants which have been transplanted out of that orientation. This phenomenon was also independently discovered by Hieronymus, who found that a reading on the dials of his radionic device was maximum when the plant was rotated in a given position with respect to a compass rose.

The De La Warrs had also found that, because of this apparent relationship with the geomagnetic field, a plant has a pattern of radiation around it. Nodal points within this pattern or web which seem to concentrate the field of radiation can be located by a portable detector with a probe and a rubbing plate similar to that on their radionics device.

In England Frances Farrelly found that with a simple dowsing pendulum she could locate on a tree and in the domelike geometric pattern around it nodal points of energy which could expose X-ray film.

This field of energy may be related in some way to a magnetic field, since both can be detected with dowsing methods. In Lorton, Virginia, the authors witnessed the incredible sensitivity to a magnetic field as displayed by Wilhelm de Boer, a *Rutenmeister*, or master dowser, who lives in the Hanseatic city of Bremen, West Germany. When Dr Zaboj Harvalik asked de Boer to walk through a magnetic field which could be switched on or off, each time the field was on de Boer's tiny dowsing rod delicately held in his fingertips would revolve. When the field was off, the rod would not move.

With the same rod de Boer measures the auras of trees and

people. First backing off from a large oak, he then advanced towards it until he was about twenty feet away, at which point the rod flipped downwards. On a smaller tree de Boer had to approach more closely before there was any reaction from the rod.

'This energy coming out of a large oak can temporarily increase the strength of a human aura, or a person's vitality,' said de Boer, demonstrating that it extended some nine to ten feet outward from Harvalik's chest but was double that length after Harvalik hugged a big oak for two minutes. De Boer related how the 'Iron Chancellor' of Germany, Bismarck, at the advice of his personal physician, would put his arms around a tree for up to half an hour to recover from the fatigue of pressing duties.

Harvalik stated that the aura de Boer was measuring might not be the same as that seen around human beings by sensitives, to which the Britishers, Dr Walter Kilner and Oscar Bagnall, devoted much attention, since it seemed to extend further from the body. As Harvalik put it: 'We don't really know exactly what this extended aura is and we certainly have no way to analyse it in a physics laboratory, at least not yet.'

Whether the auric field as measured by de Boer is the same as the one which contains the 'nodal points' as revealed on film by Frances Farrelly is also as yet unanswerable. It appears that when the material substance with which the field is associated is broken up, the field goes with the individual parts which remain in contact even at a distance. This led the De La Warrs to wonder if a slip cut from a plant and rooted would benefit from the radiations emitted by its 'mother' or pine away in the absence of such radiation. Incinerating a mother plant, roots and all, they found that its motherless children did not thrive as well as similar shoots taken from a mother which was permitted to continue growing.

Most incredible to J. I. Rodale, who successfully repeated the De La Warrs' experiment, was the allegation that the mother plant did not necessarily have to be growing near her children for them to benefit from her 'protection'. The mother could apparently be in the next city, the next country, across the ocean, or anywhere on earth. If so, suggested Rodale, it would tend to indicate that all living things, including human babies, get protective radiations from their mothers, that radiations might underlie 'love at first sight' and that people with 'green thumbs' are emitting radiations beneficial to their plants.

That an energy comes from the hands of a healer – as was claimed of Jesus Christ – and that this energy can increase the growth of plants seems to have been proved in a scientific experiment on sprouting seeds by Dr Bernard Grad, a research biochemist at Allan Memorial Institute of Psychiatry of McGill University in Montreal. Taking the 'healing controversy' into his laboratory, he performed some careful experiments with the cooperation of a retired Hungarian Army colonel, Oskar Estebany, who became aware of his own extraordinary healing powers during the Hungarian revolt against the Soviet occupation of his country in 1956.

Grad's meticulous experiments, written up in the *Journal of the Society for Psychical Research* and the *International Journal of Parapsychology*, indicated that the sprouting of grains and the total amount of green plant issuing therefrom could be significantly increased when compared to controls, by watering them with a solution sealed in bottles and exposed only to the healing energy of Estebany's hands.

In his first rigidly controlled experiments Grad convinced himself that by holding the cages of wounded mice, but not actually touching the animals themselves, Estebany could heal their wounds faster than if the mice were exposed to heat or left untreated. Estebany also could retard the growth of goiters produced in the mice by iodine-deficient diets and goitrogens and hasten their disappearance when the mice were returned to a normal diet.

Grad next experimented to see if the strange energy emitted from Estebany's hands could affect the germination of seeds and growth of plants. When Estebany held in his hands for thirty minutes vessels containing solutions with which plants were later watered it was found that this simple expedient produced faster germination and greater growth than in seedlings untreated by the Hungarian.

The next question which arose in Grad's mind was what

results might be obtained from subjects other than Estebany. From the many patients available at the institute he chose a twenty-six-year-old woman with a depressive neurotic reaction and a thirty-seven-year-old man with a psychotic depression. He also selected a psychiatrically normal man of fifty-two.

What Grad sought to ascertain was whether a solution held for thirty minutes in the hands of a normal individual when poured on plants would cause them to grow at a faster rate than plants watered with solutions held for the same amount of time by neurotics and psychotics.

After the threesome had held sealed bottles of saline solution, their contents were poured on barley seeds embedded in soil.

Grad found that the little plants watered by the saline solution held by the normal human being grew significantly faster than those held by the psychiatric patients, or by a control group left untreated. The plants treated by the psychotic grew the slowest. Contrary to Grad's expectations, the plants treated by the neurotic grew at a slightly higher rate than the controls.

Grad noticed that when the psychotic was given the sealed bottle to hold he expressed not the slightest reaction or emotion, whereas the neurotic immediately inquired about the reason for the procedure and, when told, responded with an expression of interest and what Grad termed a 'brightening of mood'. Grad also observed that she lovingly cradled the bottle in her lap as a mother would a child. Grad reached the conclusion that 'the important fact for the purpose of the experiment was not the state of her general diagnosis but of her mood *at the time* she was holding the bottle'. In his detailed account of the experiment Grad reported to the American Society for Psychical Research that it would seem that a negative mood, such as depression, anxiety or hostility while treating the solutions would result in an inhibition of cell growth when plants were watered with that solution.

Grad saw the implications of his experiment to be far-reaching. If a person's mood could influence a saline solution held in the hands, it seemed natural to assume that a cook's or housewife's mood could influence the quality of food prepared for a meal. He recalled that in various countries menstruating milkmaids were not permitted in that part of the dairy where cheese was being prepared because of a presumed unfavourable effect on the bacterial cultures and that during their menstrual period women have been held to negatively influence the canning of perishables, the stiffening of egg-white, and the survival of cut flowers. If Grad's experiments were correct it was not the menstruation but the depression created by it in certain women that had the affect, a discovery which removes from the realm of prejudice to the realm of science the biblical injunction against 'unclean' women.

The whole subject of radionics and the part played by the action of the human mind, and whether it interacts with various radionics devices designed by De La Warr, Hieronymus, Drown, Abrams and others, stands on the very frontier of physics and metaphysics and the no-man's land which lies between them.

As Galen Hieronymus said to the authors:

Is the force and its manipulation basically in the realm of the psychic? We know that powerful psychics such as Frances Farrelly can produce results with no help whatsoever from a device. Yet others seem to be helped by a radionics instrument even when like the De La Warrs, they have well-developed psychic powers.

In his unique paper, 'Radionics, Radiesthesia and Physics', published by the Academy of Parapsychology and Medicine, Professor William A. Tiller, chairman of the Department of Material Science at Stanford University, who devoted part of a year-long stay in England to the study of radionics at the De La Warr laboratories, presents a model to explain how the process works:

The basic idea in radionics is that each individual, organism, or material radiates and absorbs energy via a unique wave field which exhibits certain geometrical, frequency and radiation-type characteristics. This is an extended force field that exists around all forms of matter whether animate or inanimate. A useful analogy here is the physical atom that is continually radiating electromagnetic energy in the form of waves because of its oscillating electrical dipole movement and its thermal vibrations. The more complex the material, the more complex the wave form. Living things, like humans, emit a very complex wave spectrum of which parts are associated with the various organs and systems of the body.

Tiller holds that if the millions of new cells born in our bodies each day come into being in the presence of fields polarized by the radionic process, they tend to grow in a healthier configuration, which weakens the original field of an abnormal or diseased structure. Continued treatment eventually moulds the healthy organ structure and the condition is healed.

Another researcher to accept the power of the mind is a neurologist and medical electronics expert, Dr Andrija Puharich, who has recently reported some of the most awe-inspiring feats of psychic, or mental, power yet to confront physicists, psychologists, and other academicians. Author of *The Sacred Mushroom*, which dealt with the effects of hallucinogenic plants, such as peyote, a decade before the world's younger generation became absorbed with mindbending drugs, from marijuana to LSD, and of *Beyond Telepathy*, a decade before studies of direct idea transference from one human mind to another were considered anything but crazy by the 'responsible' scientific community, Puharich has now discovered a truly remarkable psychic in the body of a young Israeli, Uri Geller, whose abilities have startled hundreds of audiences and left most open-minded scientists aghast at their implications.

As Puharich told Connie Best, author of an article on Geller, 'The Man Who Bends Science':

We're trying to develop a model to explain how all these atoms can be taken apart. There are theories of annihilation and so on in microphysics, but there is no theory in the world that can explain this on a macroscopic scale. How can you take all these atoms apart or infinitely compress them to the point where they are so tiny they are invisible, have the thing parked in some unknown space, and then get the atoms back reassembled?

Geller not only can miraculously affect the so-called inanimate world but the world of living things as well. Before reliable witnesses he has placed his hands over a rosebud for slightly longer than a quarter of a minute, then opened them to reveal the rose in full and radiant bloom. As Connie Best comments:

Mind over matter

Physics is precise, unbending. Yet Uri Geller is finding loopholes in science wide enough to pluck a rose out of. Uri Geller is bending physics, forcing it to take account of the so-called 'paranormal' powers of the mind. How much will physics have to change? If the readings of meters reflect the wishes of lab assistants, if the presence of an experimenters is enough to embarrass sub-atomic particles, how are we to know where we stand?

As the Serbian-born American inventor and genius, Nikola Tesla, stated before his death: 'The day science begins to study non-physical phenomena, it will make more progress in one decade than in all the previous centuries of its existence'.

Perhaps that decade is upon us.

Findhorn and the Garden of Eden

The most advanced experiment involving human communication with plants has developed in a remote corner of northern Scotland. On a barren, wind-blown patch of gorse and sand overlooking the Firth of Moray, near the heath where the three prophetic witches met Macbeth, an ex-R.A.F. Squadron Leader turned hotel-keeper decided to settle with his wife and three young sons in the derelict corner of a caravan park on Findhorn Bay – a rubbish heap of old tin cans, broken bottles, brambles and gorse bushes. He was tall and ruddy and his name was Peter Caddy. Once he had walked two thousand miles in the Himalayas, crossing Kashmir deep into Tibet, and since young manhood he had been a follower of a school of adepts whose object was to bring back beauty and wonder to this planet. With his wife, Eileen, and with Dorothy MacLean, both of whom he considered 'sensitives' Caddy pulled up his roots and moved to Findhorn one snowy November day in 1962.

For some time the Caddys had been intent upon radically changing their lives by turning away from materialist pursuits in order to enter upon what Caddy calls a long period of training and preparation during which they would surrender everything, including all personal volition to what they term 'limitless love and truth'. To be fair, the one place the Caddys least expected to settle was the unsightly, overcrowded encampment of mobile houses known as Findhorn Caravan Park. For years they had scornfully hurried past it on their way to and from Forres. Now some mysterious force was overriding their aversion and guiding them to their new home, less than half an acre in a hollow not far from the main cluster of caravans. It was a patch of land composed mainly of sand and gravel, constantly swept by gale-force winds, only partially protected by a belt of spiny fir trees and tufts of broom and marram grass which kept the soil from blowing away. With winter coming it was a dismal prospect. Following the concept of the monks who used to build their monasteries by hand, putting love and light into the fabric of the building with every stone they laid, the Caddys cleaned and painted their caravan from top to bottom and polished all the furniture. Devotedly cleansing and hand-painting the caravan was a first step towards the creation of their own centre of light. Partly to increase this protective shield of light around them and partly as a source of healthy nourishment, they dreamt of establishing a garden once the dark Scottish winter was over.

During the short days and long nights Caddy pored over gardening books which he found contradictory in their recommendations. Written for horticultural enthusiasts living mostly on the mild south English coast, they were irritatingly irrelevant. He had never sown a vegetable seed in his life and felt like Noah when guided to build an ark where there was no water; but he dutifully forged ahead. Guidance was to be followed to the letter, or they might as well return to the world of business. His Rosicrucian master had taught him one prime rule of life: 'To love where I was, love whom I was with, and love what I was doing.'

To receive the arcane guidance on which the infant community planned its every move, Eileen would rise regularly at midnight and meditate for several hours, bundling herself in an overcoat against the chill of the Scottish nights. She had read in a book that everyone receives his spiritual name at some point in life and that only then can he begin his spiritual work. In 1953 she had felt the word Elixir branded on her forehead; so she adopted the name, and from then on her guidance was constant.

In her inner vision Elixir now saw seven cedarwood bungalows clustered together, in the midst of a splendid garden, all trim and neat. How this vision was to materialize in the constricted squalor of the caravan site remained a mystery. Yet all were prepared to put their faith in her vision.

The prospect of creating a garden seemed a superhuman task. The ground was made of fine dusty sand and gravel in which nothing grew but tough pointed grass. But Caddy cheerfully began to dig a strip of quitch turf three feet wide by nine feet long and laid it to one side. He then dug down eighteen inches, accumulating a pile of sand and gravel. In the clean trench he placed the strip of quitch turf upside down and broke it up with his spade. This was to ensure that the turf would not sprout its way back up to the surface, but provide nourishment as it disintegrated. After many hours of patient digging, raking out of stones and finally spraying with water, the plot was ready for seeding.

According to the local agricultural experts, and the available textbooks on gardening, nothing could be grown in the Findhorn soil except perhaps a few lettuces and radishes. Scanty fare for a family which had become accustomed at their hotel to daily steak or duck washed down with good red wine. Nevertheless, Caddy conscientiously sowed his lettuce seeds. To fend off the ever-present winds blowing across the Moray Firth, the Findhorners needed a slatted fence. Almost miraculously, the necessary wood was forthcoming from a man who was dismantling his garage. As soon as the fence was up a neighbour ran over to say that some barely damaged bags of cement had fallen from a truck across the road. In a short while they had a fenced concrete patio from which to admire – not thriving young lettuce, but stunted apparitions, attacked by wire-worms. Then, a neighbour chanced to pass and informed Caddy of a pile of seasoned soot just outside the entrance to the caravan park, an admirable antidote to wire-worms.

By the end of May they were eating luscious lettuces and radishes. A compost heap was essential if they were to grow a greater variety of vegetables, without the use of chemical fertilizers. Once again, a neighbour gave them a pile of rotting grass and a near-by farmer, grateful for a rescued sheep, gave Caddy a large load of cow manure. A friend who owned a riding stable allowed them to follow his horses with a bucket and a shovel. A near-by distillery supplied them with free peat dross and cummings, a potent barley germ fertilizer. They gathered seaweed from the beach. A bale of hay dropped from a passing truck almost at the gate of the park served to cover the compost heaps. Relying on such 'supermundane assistance' the Findhorners acted as if they were endowed. As one of them wrote: 'We could have been negative and said the soil was useless – as it was. Instead we put hard work and positive thought into everything we did.'

Caddy worked from morning till night, putting sweat and radiations into the soil, his object being to grow enough vegetables to provide a large part of their diet in the months to come. The pure air, sunlight, sea bathing and plenty of cold, pure water, would, they hoped, purify their bodies and endow them with energy. The theory was that the more refined their bodies became the more they would be able to absorb cosmic energies and the less solid food they would need. They planted watercress, tomatoes, cucumbers, spinach, parsley, marrow and asparagus. They planted hedges of blackberries and raspberries round their garden which was now spreading beyond the caravan till it covered two acres of ground, every bit of soil of which had to be manufactured from old turfs and new compost, every square inch manhandled several times in the process.

The neighbours were incredulous, especially when only the Caddys' cabbages and sprouts survived a plague of cabbage root grubs, and only their black currants grew healthily when the crop had largely failed in the rest of the county.

Findhorn lunches consisted of salads with over twenty ingredients; surplus quantities of lettuce, radishes, spinach and parsley were disposed of round the neighbourhood which was suffering a shortage. Their evening meals included two or three vegetables from the garden, freshly picked and freshly cooked. Stews from garden vegetables consisted of onions, leeks, garlic, carrots, parsnips, swedes, turnips, artichokes, kohlrabi, celery, marrow, potatoes, flavoured with all kinds of herbs.

Elixir was told to let her mind dwell on each ingredient as she cooked, and that her thoughts and feelings were important in the continuing cycle of life. She was to appreciate whatever she was doing, whether peeling a carrot or podding a pea, and to consider each vegetable as a living thing in her hands. Of the peelings and garbage nothing was to be wasted. All was to go back into the compost and the soil, constantly increasing the live vibrations.

When autumn came they were ready to preserve quantities of raspberries, blackberries and strawberries, putting up altogether a hundred pounds of jam. They pickled fifteen pounds of red cabbage, and large quantities of cucumbers. In a newly built garage they stored potatoes, carrots, beetroot, and the shelves were laden with shallots, garlic and onions. During the winter they prepared the earth for the following season and planted more fruit trees and bushes, including apples, pears, plums, greengages, cherries, apricots, loganberries and boysenberries. By May 1964 the fruit trees and bushes were bursting into bud. When the red cabbages matured one weighed a massive thirty-eight pounds and another forty-two. A sprouting broccoli mistakenly planted as a cauliflower grew to such enormous proportions that it provided food for weeks; and was almost too heavy to be lifted from the ground. By this time they were growing sixty-five different kinds of vegetables, twenty-one types of fruit and forty varieties of herbs.

In June 1964 when the County Horticultural Adviser came to take a sample of the soil for analysis, his first comment was that the soil would require a dressing of at least two ounces of sulphate of potash per square yard. Caddy replied that he did not believe in artificial fertilizers, that he was happy using compost and wood ash. The adviser said that would be totally inadequate. Six weeks later when the results of the analysis arrived he was forced to acknowledge that there were no deficiencies in the soil sample. All necessary elements, including rare trace elements, were present. He was so astonished by the results that he asked Caddy to take part in a broadcast about the garden in which he, the adviser, would take the chair and an experienced gardener using conventional methods with chemical fertilizers would debate with Caddy. This Caddy did, attributing his success to organic manure and compost. He did not feel that the time was appropriate to expound on the spiritual side of their endeavour. By this time Caddy was convinced that there must be some greater underlying purpose in their pioneering venture at Findhorn. Perhaps it was the nucleus of some larger experiment in group living, a sort of training course in the realization that Life is a whole.

[314]

For some time Dorothy McLean, who had been receiving spiritual guidance of her own, and had adopted the spiritual name of Divina, had been studying the aromatic plants in the garden and found that their unique wavelengths could affect different parts of the human anatomy as well as the human psyche, some plants being good for wounds, others for eyesight, others for human emotions. She realized that by raising the quality of her own vibrations she might eventually open the doors to a whole new spiritual realm of plant life. It became clear to her that plants are most susceptible to human thoughts and emotions, and that their energy can be affected. Poisonous and bad-tempered moods have as depressing an effect on plants as happy uplifting frequencies have a beneficial effect. Not only that, but the bad effects could come back to humans as they ate the produce they had infected with bad vibrations. Thus the cycle could become either viciously descending, leading to more and more misery, pain and disease, or hopefully ascending, leading to greater joy and greater light. Thus the most important contribution that man can make to his garden – even more important than water or compost – is the radiation in the form of strength, love and happiness which he puts into the soil while cultivating it. But there are other radiations besides the human ones that affect the soil and plants; those from the earth itself and from the cosmos, each of which contribute to fertility, and without which they would be sterile.

In the spring of 1967 Elixir received guidance that the garden was to be extended even further and made into a place of beauty. The centre was to be expanded and new bungalows built. The vision she had first received on arriving at Findhorn was now beginning to materialize. Money for neat cedarstrip bungalows turned up as if by miracle, and the bungalows were soon surrounded by impeccable flower gardens.

In 1968 Findhorn was visited by a number of accomplished gardeners and agricultural experts who were amazed at its remarkable success despite the poverty of the soil and the rigorous northern climate. When Sir George Trevelyan, a leading member of the Soil Association, came at Easter the daffodils and narcissi were the largest and most brilliantly coloured that he had seen. The root vegetables were the best he had ever tasted. Many fruit trees were in blossom and a vigorous young chestnut stood eight feet high among broad-leaved trees and shrubs thriving on the landward slope of windswept dunes. Sir George said he had seen enough to know that compost and straw mulch alone, mixed with poor and sandy soil, was not enough to account for such a garden. He therefore wrote to Lady Eve Balfour, the Hon. Secretary of the Soil Association, that there must be some Factor X to be taken into consideration, adding that if so much could be accomplished at Findhorn in such a short time, the Sahara could be made to blossom.

Other visitors to Findhorn were equally impressed by the superb produce and felt that such results could not have been achieved on such barren soil by means of compost and good husbandry alone. There must be some other factor to account for it.

Lady Mary Balfour, sister of Lady Eve, who describes herself as an 'ordinary gardener of the organic school' spent twenty-four hours at Findhorn in September of 1968 and wrote:

The weather throughout was grey and at times wet. Yet in retrospect I can see that garden in brilliant sunshine without a cloud in the sky, which must be due to the extraordinary brilliance of the blooming flowers I saw there. The flower beds were all a compact mass of colour.

Professor R. Lindsay Robb, a United Nations agricultural expert and professor of agriculture at various universities, visiting Findhorn just before Christmas one year, went on record to say that:

The vigour, health and bloom of the plants in the garden at mid winter on land which is almost a barren powdery sand cannot be explained by the moderate dressings of compost, nor indeed by the application of any known cultural methods of organic husbandry. There are other factors and they are vital ones.

Eventually Peter Caddy confided to Sir George Trevelyan the secret of their success at Findhorn. Dorothy McLean had apparently managed to get into direct contact with the Devas or angelic creatures who control the nature spirits that are said by clairvoyants to be everywhere at work nurturing plant life. Sir George, an advanced student of the arcane, and of the hermetic sciences, admitted that he was aware that a number of sensitives claimed to be in touch with the devic world and to be working with it, and that Rudolf Steiner had founded his biodynamic methods on such knowledge. Far from scoffing at Caddy's explanation he was prepared to give it credence and to validate it by suggesting that conscious investigation of such worlds is of the utmost importance to our understanding of life, and especially our understanding of the life of plants.

After this Peter Caddy published a series of pamphlets describing the true nature of the experiments at Findhorn. Divina contributed with detailed descriptions of the messages she said she received directly from the Devas of which she described whole hierarchies responsible for every fruit and vegetable, for every flower and weed. Here was a Pandora's box more phenomenal than the one opened in New York by Backster.

Findhorn quickly developed into a community of over a hundred members. Young spiritual leaders turned up to preach the gospel of a New Age, and a college was founded to teach its tenets. What had started as a miraculous little garden appeared to be turning into a true centre of light for the Aquarian Age, visited annually from every continent of the globe.

Parting the veil into other worlds and other vibrations beyond the limits of the electromagnetic spectrum may well go a long way to explain the mysteries which are incomprehensible to physicists who limit their outlook to what they can see with their physical eyes and their instruments. In the world of the clairvoyant, who claims to have mastered the art of etheric and astral vision, a whole new series of vistas opens up around plants and their relation to man, to the earth and to the cosmos. The growth of seeds and plants, as Paracelsus intimated, may indeed be affected very strongly by the position of the moon, the position of the planets, their relation to the sun and to the other stars of the firmament.

Fechner's animistic vision of plants being ensouled becomes less of a wild conceit, as does Goethe's concept of a prototype plant. Burbank's knowledge that whatever man wishes he can produce with the aid of nature or Carver's insistence that nature spirits abound in the woods and take part in the growth of plants may have to be reviewed in the light of the discoveries of the Theosophists and especially of such extraordinary seers of nature spirits as Geoffrey Hodson. The ancient wisdom, as detailed by seers like Mesdames Helena P. Blavatsky and Alice A. Bailey, throws quite another light on the energy of bodies, both of humans and of plants, as well as the relation of individual cells to the entire cosmos.

The secret behind Pfeiffer's biodynamic compost, which has been proved so highly effective scientifically, turns out to be a homeopathic wonder based on a fairyland creation of Rudolf Steiner's organic brews made by burying cow horns filled with cow dung and deer bladders filled with nettles and camomile leaves. Steiner's anthroposophy, or Spiritual Science, throws such a light on plant life and agriculture as to make scientists root in their tracks.

Aesthetically, the world of the devas and the nature spirits turns out to be even more full of colour and sound and perfume than the creations of Scriabin and Wagner, their gnomes, nymphs, and undines, their fire, water, earth, and air spirits closer to reality than the Holy Grail and the eternal quest it engendered. As Dr Aubrey Westlake, author of *Pattern of Health*, describes our imprisoned state, we are locked in a

valley of materialistic concepts, refusing to believe there is anything other than the physical-material world of our five senses. For we, like the inhabitants of the country of the blind, reject those who claim to have 'seen' with their spiritual vision the greater supersensible world in which we are immersed, dismissing such claims as 'idle fancies' and advancing far 'saner' scientific explanations.

The attraction of the seer's supersensible world, or worlds within worlds, is too great to forgo, and the stakes too high, for they may include survival for the planet. Where the modern scientist is baffled by the secrets of the life of plants, the seer offers solutions which, however incredible, make more sense than the dusty mouthings of academicians; what is more, they give philosophic meaning to the totality of life. This supersensible world of plants and man, only touched on in this volume, will be explored in another, *The Cosmic Life of Plants*.

Bibliography

Abrams, Albert, *New Concepts in Diagnosis and Treatment*, Philipolis Press, San Francisco, 1916
Iconography: Electronic Reactions of Abrams, San Francisco, 1923
Acharya Jagadis Chandra Bose, (Transactions of the Bose Research Institute, Calcutta, vol. 22,) Bose Institute, Calcutta, 1958
Acres U.S.A., a Voice for Eco-Agriculture (monthly newspaper), Raytown, Mo.
Adam, Michel, *La Vie et les ondes; l'œuvre de Georges Lakhovsky*, E. Chiron, Paris, 1936
Adamenko, Viktor, 'Living Detectors (on the Experiments of K. Bakster', *Tekhnika Molodezhi*, no. 8, 1970, pp. 60–62 (in Russian)
Adams, George, and Olive Whicher, *The Living Plant and the Science of Physical and Ethereal Spaces*, Goethean Science Foundation, Clent, Worcs., 1949
Albrecht, William A., *Soil Fertility and Animal Health*, Webster City, Iowa, 1958
Soil Reaction (pH) and Balanced Plant Nutrition, Columbia, M., 1967
Albus, Harry, *The Peanut Man*, W. B. Eerdman Publishing Co., Grand Rapids, Mich., 1948
Alder, Vera Stanley, *The Secret of the Atomic Age*, Rider, 1958–72
Aldini, Giovanni, *Orazione di Luigi Galvani*, Monti, Bologna, 1888
Allen, Charles I., *The Sexual Relations of Plants*, New York, 1886
Andrews, Donald Hatch, *The Symphony of Life*, Unity Books, Lee's Summit, Mo., 1967
Applewhite, P. B., 'Behavioral Plasticity in the Sensitive Plant, Mimosa', *Behavioral Biology*, vol. 7, February 1972, pp. 47–53
Arditti, Joseph, and Arnold Dunn, *Experimental Plant Physiology: Experiments in Cellular and Plant Physiology*, Holt, Rinehart & Winston, New York, 1969
Audus, L. J., 'Magnetotropism: A New Plant Growth Response', *Nature*, 16 January 1960

Bach, Edward, *Heal Thyself*, C. W. Daniel Co. Ltd, Rochford

Bibliography

The Twelve Healers and Other Remedies, C. W. Daniel Co. Ltd, Rochford, 1933

Backster, Cleve, 'Evidence of a Primary Perception in Plant Life', *International Journal of Parapsychology*, vol. 10, no. 4, Winter 1968, pp. 329–48

'Evidence of a Primary Perception at Cellular Level in Plant and Animal Life', unpublished, Backster Research Foundation, Inc., 1973, 3 pp.

Bacon, Thorn, 'The Man who Reads Nature's Secret Signals', *National Wildlife*, vol. 7, no. 2, February–March 1969, pp. 4–8

Bagnall, Oscar, *The Origin and Properties of the Human Aura*, University Books, New York, 1970

Baitulin, I. O., V. M. Inyushin and U. V. Scheglov, 'On the Question of Electrobioluminescence in Embryo Roots', *Bioenergetic Questions – and Some Answers*, Alma Ata., U.S.S.R. 1968 (in Russian)

Balfour, Lady Eve B., *The Living Soil*, Faber & Faber, 1943

Balzer, Georg, *Goethe als Gartenfreund*, Bruckmann, Munich, 1966

Barnothy, Madeleine F. (ed.), *Biological Effects of Magnetic Fields*, Plenum Press, New York, 1964

Barr, James (ed.), *Abram's Methods of Diagnosis and Treatment*, Heinemann, 1925

Basu, S. N., *Jagadis Chandra Bose*, National Book Trust, New Delhi, 1970

Beaty, John Yocum, *Luther Burbank, Plant Magician*, J. Messner, Inc., New York, 1943

Bentley, Linna, *Plants That Eat Animals*, Bodley Head, 1967

Bertholon, M. L'Abbé, *De l'Electricité des Végétaux*, Alyon, 1783

Bertrand, Didier, *Recherches sur le vanadium dans les sols et dans les plantes*, Jouve et Cie, Paris, 1941

Best, Connie, 'The Man Who Bends Science' . . . *And It Is Divine*, Shri Hans Productions, Denver, Colorado, May 1973

Bhattacharya, Benoytash, *Magnet Dowsing or The Magnet Study of Life*, K. L. Mukhopadhyay, Calcutta, 1967

'Billions of Transmitters Inside Us? An Unknown Bio-information Channel has Been Discovered: Using this "Wireless Telegraph", the Cells of the Organism Transmit Danger Signals', *Sputnik*, May 1973, pp. 126–30

Bio-Dynamics (periodical), Bio-Dynamic Farming and Gardening Association, Inc., Stroudsburg, Pa.

Bird, Christopher, 'Dowsing in the U.S.S.R.', *The American Dowser*, August 1972

Bibliography

'Dowsing in the U.S.A.: History, Achievement, and Current Research', *The American Dowser*, August 1973

Boadella, David, *Wilhelm Reich: The Evolution of His Work*, Vision Press, 1972

Bock, Hieronymus, *Teütsche Speiszkammer*, W. Rihel, Strasbourg, 1550

Bontemps, Arna, *The Story of George Washington Carver*, Grosset & Dunlap, New York, 1954

Bose, D. M., 'J. C. Bose's Plant Physiological Investigation Relating to Modern Biological Knowledge', *Transactions of the Bose Research Institute*, vol. 37, Bose Research Institute, Calcutta, 1947–8

Bose, Jagadis Chandra, *Izbrannye Proizvedeniya po Razdrazhimosti Rastenii*, I. I. Gunar (ed.), Izdatel'stvo Nauka, Moscow, 1964

'Live Movements in Plants', *Transactions of the Bose Research Institute*, vols. 1–6, Longmans, Green & Co., New York, 1918–1931

Response in the Living and Non-Living, Longmans, Green & Co., New York, 1902

Plant Response as a Means of Physiological Investigation, Longmans, Green & Co., New York, 1906

Researches in Irritability of Plants, Longmans, Green & Co., New York, 1913

The Physiology of the Ascent of Sap, Longmans, Green & Co., New York, 1923

The Physiology of Photosynthesis, Longmans, Green & Co., New York, 1924

The Nervous Mechanism of Plant, Longmans, Green & Co., New York, 1926

Plant Autographs and Their Revelations, Longmans, Green & Co., New York, 1927

Motor Mechanisms of Plants, Longmans, Green & Co., New York, 1928

Growth and Tropic Movements of Plants, Longmans, Green & Co., New York, 1929

'Awareness in Plants', *Consciousness and Reality: The Human Pivot*, Charles Musès and Arthur M. Young (eds.), Outerbridge & Lazard, Inc., New York, 1972, pp. 142–50

Boulton, Brett, 'Do Plants Think?', *Ladies' Home Journal*, May 1971

Bovis, André, pamphlets on dowsing, privately printed in Nice, 1930–45

Bibliography

Bragdon, Lillian J., *Luther Burbank, Nature's Helper*, Abingdon Press, New York, 1959

Brier, Robert M., 'PK on a Bio-electrical System', *Journal of Parapsychology*, vol. 33, no. 3, September 1969, pp. 187–205

Brown, Beth, *E.S.P. with Plants and Animals: A Collection of True Stories that Glow with the Power of Extrasensory Perception*, Essandess Special Edition, New York, 1971

Brown, Jr., Frank A., 'The Rhythmic Nature of Animals and Plants', *American Scientist*, vol. 47, June 1959, p. 147

Brunor, Nicola, *La medicina e la teoria elettronica della materia*, Istituto Editoriale Scientifico, Milan, 1927

Budlong, Ware T., *Performing Plants*, Simon & Schuster, New York, 1969

Burbank, Luther, *The Training of the Human Plant*, Century Co., New York, 1907

My Beliefs, Avondale Press, New York, 1927

How Plants Are Trained to Work for Man, P. F. Collier & Son, New York, 1921

Burbank, Luther, with Wilbur Hall, *The Harvest of the Years*, Houghton Miffin, Boston and New York, 1927

Burr, Harold Saxton, *Blueprint for Immortality: The Electric Patterns of Life*, Neville Spearman Ltd, London, 1972

Camerarius, Rudolf Jakob, *Uber das Geschlecht der Pflanzen (De sexu plantorum epistula)*, W. Engelmann, Leipzig, 1899

Carson, Rachel, *Silent Spring*, Hamish Hamilton, 1963; Penguin Books, 1970

Chase, Thomas T., 'The Development and Use of Electronic Systems for Monitoring Living Trees', M.S. Thesis, Department of Electrical Engineering, University of New Hampshire, November 1972, 48 pp.

Clark, Laurence, *Coming to Terms with Rudolf Steiner*, Veracity Ventures Ltd, Rickmansworth, 1971

Cocannouer, Joseph A., *Weeds: Guardians of the Soil*, Devin-Adair Co., New York, 1964

Commoner, Barry, *The Closing Circle* Jonathan Cape, 1972

Conrad-Martius, Hedwig, *Die 'Seele' der Pflanze*, Frankes Verlag, Breslau, 1934

Cremore, John Davenport, *Mental Telepathy*, Fieldcrest Publications Co., 1956

Crile, George Washington, *The Bipolar Theory of Living Processes*, Macmillan, New York, 1926

Bibliography

The Phenomena of Life: A Radio-Electrical Interpretation, W. W.
Norton, New York, 1936

Crow, W. B., *The Occult Properties of Herbs*, Aquarian Press, London,
1969

Culpeper, Nicholas, *Culpeper's English Physician and Complete Herbal
Remedies*, Wilshire Book Co., North Hollywood, Cal., 1972

Darwin, Charles R., *The Power of Movement in Plants*, Da Capo Press,
New York, 1966

Insectivorous Plants, J. Murray, London, 1875

The Movements and Habits of Climbing Plants, D. Appleton & Co.,
New York, 1876

The Variation of Animals and Plants Under Domestication, D.
Appleton & Co., New York, 1896

Davis, Albert Roy, and A. K. Bhattacharya, *Magnet and Magnetic
Fields*, K. L. Mukhopadhyay, Calcutta, 1970

Day, G. W. Langston, and George De La Warr, *Matter in the
Making*, Stuart, London, 1966

New Worlds Beyond the Atom, Stuart, London, 1956

de Beer, Gavin, *Charles Darwin: Evolution by Natural Selection*,
British Academy, 1958

De La Warr, George, 'Do Plants Feel Emotion?', *Electrotechnology*,
April 1969

'Seeds Respond to Sound of Music', *News Letter*, Radionic
Centre Organization, Spring 1969, pp. 6–7

De La Warr, George, and Douglas Baker, *Biomagnetism*, De La
Warr Laboratories, Oxford, 1967

De La Warr, Marjorie, 'Thought Transference to Plants', *News
Letter*, Radionic Centre Organization, Autumn 1969, pp. 3–11

'Plant Experiments – Series 2', *News Letter*, Radionic Centre
Organization, Summer 1970, pp. 1–72

Dibner, Bern, *Alessandro Volta and the Electric Battery*, F. Watts,
New York, 1964

*Galvani-Volta; A Controversy That Led to the Discovery of Useful
Electricity*, Burndy Library, Norwalk, Conn., 1952

Dr William Gilbert, Burndy Library, New York, 1947

Dixon, Royal, *The Human Side of Plants*, Frederick A. Stokes Co.,
New York, 1914

Dixon, Royal, and Eddy Brayton, *Personality of Insects*, Charles W.
Clark Co., New York, 1924

Dixon, Royal, and Franklyn E. Fitch, *Personality of Plants*, Bouillon-
Biggs, New York, 1923

[325]

Bibliography

Dodge, Bertha Sanford, *Plants That Changed the World*, Dent, 1963.

Dombrovskii, B., and V. M. Inyushin, 'This Experiment Calls for Thought' (on the experiments of C. Backster), *Tekhnika Molodezhi*, no. 8, 1970, p. 62 (in Russian)

'Do Plants Feel Emotion?', in *Ahead of Time*, Harry Harrison and Theodore J. Gordon (eds.), Doubleday, Garden City, N.Y., 1972, pp. 106–16

'Do Plants Have Feelings? Researcher Is Communicating', *Carlisle County News*, Bardwell, Kentucky, 8 March 1973

Dowden, Anne Ophelia, *The Secret Life of the Flowers*, Odyssey Press, New York, 1964

Drown, Ruth Beymer, *The Theory and Technique of the Drown H.V.R. and Radiovision Instruments* (private printing), Artists' Press, Los Angeles, 1939
The Science and Philosophy of the Drown Radio Therapy, Los Angeles, 1939

du Hamel du Monceau, Henri Louis, *La Physique des Arbres*, 1758

du Plessis, Jean, *The Electronic Reactions of Abrams*, Blanche and Jeanne R. Abrams Memorial Foundation, Chicago, 1922

du Puy, William A., *Wonders of the Plant World*, D. C. Heath & Co., Boston, 1931

Electroculture in Plant Growth, compiled by staff of *Organic Gardening and Farming*, Rodale Press, Emmaus, Pa., 1968

Ellicott, John, *Several Essays Towards Discovering the Laws of Electricity*, London, 1748

Elliott, Lawrence, *George Washington Carver: The Man Who Overcame*, Prentice-Hall, Englewood Cliffs, N.J., 1966

Emrich, Hella, *Strahlende Gesundheit durch Bio-electrizitat*, Drei-Eicken Verlag, Munich, 1968

'E.R.A.: Electronic Reactions of Abrams', *Pearson's Magazine*, 1922

Esall, Katherine, *Plants, Viruses and Insects*, Harvard University Press, Cambridge, Mass., 1961

'E.S.P.: More Science, Less Mysticism', *Medical World News*, vol. 10, no. 12, 21 March 1969, pp. 20–21

Fairchild, David, *The World Was My Garden*, Charles Scribner's Sons, New York and London, 1938

Faivre, Ernest, *Oeuvres scientifiques de Goethe*, L. Hachette, Paris, 1862

Farb, Peter, *Living Earth*, Harper Colophon Books, New York, 1959

Farrington, Benjamin, *What Darwin Really Said*, Schocken Books, New York, 1966

Bibliography

Faulkner, Edward H., *Plowman's Folly*, University of Oklahoma Press, Norman, Oklahoma, 1943-63

Fechner, Gustav Theodor, *Nanna oder über das Seelenleben der Pflanzen*, Verlag von Leopold Voss, Leipzig, 1921 (1st ed., 1848)

Zend-Avesta, Pensieri sulle Cose del Cielo e dell'Al di la, Fratelli Bocca, Milan, 1944

Life After Death, Pentheon Books, New York, 1943

Elements of Psychophysics, Holt, Rinehart & Winston, New York, 1966

Fenson, D. S., 'The Bio-electric Potentials of Plants and Their Functional Significance, I: An Electrokinetic Theory of Transport', *Canadian Journal of Botany*, vol. 35, 1957, pp. 573-82

'The Bio-electric Potentials of Plants and Their Functional Significance, II: The Patterns of Bio-electric Potential and Exudation Rate in Excised Sunflower Roots and Stems', *Canadian Journal of Botany*, vol. 36, 1958, pp. 367-83

'The Bio-electric Potentials of Plants and Their Functional Significance, III: The Production of Continuous Potentials Across Membranes in Plant Tissue by the Circulation of the Hydrogen Ion', *Canadian Journal of Botany*, vol. 37, 1959, pp. 1003-26

'The Bio-electric Potentials of Plants and Their Functional Significance, IV: Some Daily and Seasonal Changes in the Electric Potential and Resistance of Living Trees', *Canadian Journal of Botany*, vol. 41, 1963, pp. 831-51

Findhorn News (periodical), Findhorn Foundation, Findhorn Bay, Forres, Moray, Scotland

Foster, Catherine Osgood, *The Organic Gardener*, Vintage Books, New York, 1972

Francé, Raoul Heinrich, *Pflanzenpsychologie als Arbeitshypothese der Pflanzenphysiologie*, Frankh, Stuttgart, 1909

Das Sinnesleben der Pflanzen, Kosmos Gesellschaft der Naturfreunde, Stuttgart, 1905

La Vita Prodigosa delle Piante, Genio, Milan, 1943

Plants as Inventors A. & C. Boni, New York, 1923

The Love Life of Plants, A. & C. Boni, New York, 1923

Germs of Mind in Plants, Charles H. Kerr & Co., Chicago, 1905

Freedland, Nat, *The Occult Explosion*, Michael Joseph, 1972

Friend, Rev. H. Ideric, *Flowers and Flower Lore* (vol. II), George Allen & Co. Ltd

Fryer, Lee, and Dick Simmons, *Earth Foods*, Follett, Chicago, 1972

Bibliography

Galaxies of Life: The Human Aura in Acupuncture and Kirlian Photography, Krippner Stanley and Daniel Rubin (eds.), Interface, New York, 1973

Gallert, Mark L., *New Light on Therapeutic Energies*, James Clarke & Co. Ltd, London, 1966

Galvani, Luigi, *Commentary on the Effect of Electricity on Muscular Motion – A Translation of Luigi Galvani's De Viribus Electricitatis in Motu Musculari Commentarius*, E. Licht, Cambridge, Mass., 1953

Opere Scelte, Unione Tipografico Editrice Torinese, Turin, 1967

Geddes, Patrick, *The Life and Work of Sir Jagadis C. Bose*, Longmans, Green & Co., 1920

Gilbert, William, *De Magnete*, Van Gendt, 1959

Goodavage, Joseph F., *Astrology, The Space-Age Science*, Parker Publishing Co., West Nyack, N.Y., 1966

Grad, Bernard, 'A Telekinetic Effect on Plant Growth', *International Journal of Parapsychology*, vol. 5, no. 2, 1963, pp. 117–33

'A Telekinetic Effect on Plant Growth, II: Experiments Involving Treatment of Saline in Stoppered Bottles', *International Journal of Parapsychology*, vol. 6, no. 4, 1964, pp. 473–98

'Some Biological Effects of the "Laying on of Hands": A Review of Experiments with Animals and Plants', *Journal of the American Society for Psychical Research*, vol. 59, no. 2, 1965, pp. 95–127

Graham, Shirley, and George Lipscomb, *Dr George Washington Carver, Scientist*, Julian Messner, Inc., New York, 1944

Grayson, Stuart H., and Sara Swift, 'Do Plants Have Feelings? Cleve Backster's Remarkable Experiments Suggest Heretofore Unknown Levels of Consciousness in Living Things', *Dynamis*, vol. 1, nos. 6–7, November–December 1971, pp. 1–8

Grohmann, Gerbert, *Die Pflanze als Lichtsinnesorgan der Erde und Andere Aufsatze*, Verlag Fries Geistesleban, Stuttgart, 1962

Guilcher, Jean Mickel, *La vie cachée des fleurs*, Flammarion, Paris, 1951

Gumpert, Martin, *Hahnemann: The Adventurous Career of a Medical Rebel*, L. B. Fischer, New York, 1945

Gunar, Ivan I., *et al.*, 'On the Transmission of Electrical Stimulation in Plants', *Izvestiya* (News), Timiryazev Academy of Agricultural Sciences, U.S.S.R., no. 5, 1970, pp. 3–9 (in Russian with summary in English)

'The Evaluation of Frost and Heat Resistance of Plants Through Their Bioelectric Reactions', *Izvestiya* (News), Timiryazev

Bibliography

Academy of Agricultural Sciences, U.S.S.R., no. 5, 1971, pp. 3–7 (in Russian with summary in English) 'Bioelectric Potentials of Potato Tubers in Varying Phytopathological States', *Izvestiya* (News), Timiryazev Academy of Agricultural Sciences, U.S.S.R., no. 6, 1971, pp. 212–13 (in Russian with summary in English) 'Electro-Physiological Characteristics of Reproduction and the Combined Values for Hybrids of Winter Wheat in Connection with Frost Resistance', *Doklady* (Reports), Lenin Academy of Agricultural Sciences, U.S.S.R., no. 9, September 1971 (in Russian) 'The Influence of Thermic Factors on the Dormancy Potentials of the Root Epidermal Cells of Winter Wheat', *Izvestiya* (News), Timiryazev Academy of Agricultural Sciences, U.S.S.R., no. 2, 1972, pp. 12–19 (in Russian with summary in English)

Gupta, Monoranjon, *Jagadis Chandra Bose, A Biography*, Bharatiya Vidya Bhavan, Chaupatty, Bombay, 1964.

Gurvich, Aleksandr G., *Mitogenetic Radiation: Physico-chemical Bases and Applications in Biology and Medicine*, Medgiz, Moscow, 1945 (in Russian)

The Theory of the Biological Field, Sovyetskaya Nauka, Moscow, 1944 (in Russian)

Mitogenetic Analysis of the Biology of the Cancer Cell, All-Union Institute for Experimental Medicine, Moscow, 1937 (in Russian)

Gurwitsch, A. and L., *L'Analyse mitogénétique spectrale*, Hermann, Paris, 1934

Gurwitsch, A. G., *Mitogenetic Analysis of the Excitation of the Nervous System*, N.V. Noord-Hollandsche Uitgeversmaatschappij, Amsterdam, 1937

Haase, Rudolf, *Hans Kayser. Ein Leben fur die Harmonik der Welt*, Schwabe, Basle, Stuttgart, 1968

Hahn, Fritz, *Luftekektrizitat Gegen Bakterien für Gesundes Raumklima und Wohlbefinden*, Albrecht Philler Verlag, Minden, 1964

Hahnemann, Samuel, *The Chronic Diseases, Their Specific Nature and Homoeopathic Treatment*, W. Radde, New York, 1845

Halacy, Jr, Daniel S., *Radiation, Magnetism and Living Things*, Holiday House, New York, 1966

Hall, Manly Palmer, *The Mystical and Medical Philosophy of Paracelsus*, Philosophical Research Society, Los Angeles, 1969

Hapgood, Charles H., *Reports from Acámbaro* (unpublished manuscript)

Bibliography

Harvalik, Z. V., 'A Biophysical Magnetometer-Gradiometer', *Virginia Journal of Science*, vol. 21, no. 2, 1970, pp. 59–60

Hashimoto, Ven., *Chobutsurigaku Nyumon* (work in Japanese on fourth dimension), Tokyo, 1971

Choshinrigaku Nyumon (work in Japanese on psychical research), Tokyo, 1964

Hauschka, Rudolf, *The Nature of Substance*, Vincent Stuart Ltd, London, 1966

Henslow, George, *The Origin of Floral Structure Through Insects and Other Agencies*, D. Appleton & Co., New York, 1888

Hieronymus, Louise and Galen, *Tracking the Astronauts in Apollo '11' with Data from Apollo '8' Included*. A Quantitative Evaluation of the Well-being of the Three Men Through the Period from Two Days Before Liftoff Until the Quarantine Ended – A Consolidated Report, self-published, 4 September 1969

Hieronymus, T. Galen, *Tracking the Astronauts in Apollo '8'*. A Quantitative Evaluation of the Well-being of the Three Men Through the Period from Two Days Before Liftoff Until Two Days After Splashdown – A Preliminary Report, self-published, 30 December 1968

The Truth about Radionics and Some of the Criticism Made about It by Its Enemies, International Radionic Association, Springfield, Mo., May 1947

Hill, Harvey Jay, *He Heard God's Whisper*, Jorgenson Press, Minneapolis, 1943

Howard, Albert, *The Soil and Health*, Schocken Books, New York, 1972

The War in the Soil, Organic Gardening, Emmaus, Pa., 1946

Howard, Albert, and D. Wad Yeshwant, *The Waste Products of Agriculture: Their Utilization as Humus*, Oxford University Press, London and New York, 1931

Howard, Walter L., *Luther Burbank: A Victim of Hero Worship*, Chronica Botanica Co., Waltham, 1945

Luther Burbank's Plant Contributions, University of California, Berkeley, Cal., 1945

Hudgings, William F., *Dr Abrams and the Electron Theory*, Century Co., New York, 1923

Human Dimensions (periodical), Human Dimensions Institute, Rosary Hill College, Buffalo, N.Y.

Hunt, Inez, and Wanetta W. Draper, *Lightning in His Hand – The Life Story of Nikola Tesla*, Sage Books, Denver, 1964

[330]

Bibliography

Hutchins, Ross E., *Strange Plants and Their Ways*, Rand McNally & Co., New York, 1958

Hyde, Margaret O., *Plants Today and Tomorrow*, Whittlesey House, New York, 1960

Inglis, Brian, *The Case for Unorthodox Medicine*, Berkley Medallion Books, New York, 1969

Innes, G. Lake, *I Knew Carver*, self-published, 1943

Inyushin, Vladimir M., and N. N. Fedorova, 'On the Question of the Biological Plasma of Green Plants', Thesis (in Russian), Alma Ata, U.S.S.R., 1969

Jenness, Mary, *The Man Who Asked God Questions*, Friendship Press, New York, 1946

Jimarajadasa, Curuppmullagé, *Flowers and Gardens (A Dream Structure)*, Theosophical Publishing House, Adyar, Madras, 1913

Joachim, Leland, 'Plants – The Key to Mental Telepathy', *Probe, the Unknown*, no. 47329, December 1972, pp. 48–52

Journal for the Study of Consciousness, Santa Barbara, Cal.

Journal of Paraphysics, Paraphysical Laboratory, Downton, Wilts.

Journal of the Drown Radio Therapy, Hollywood, Cal.

Karlsson, L., 'Instrumentation for Measuring Bioelectrical Signals in Plants', *Review of Scientific Instruments*, vol. 43, no. 3, March 1972, pp. 458–64

Kayser, Hans, *Die Harmonie der Welt*, Akademie für Musik und Darstellende Kunst, Vienna, 1968

Akroasis: The Theory of World Harmonics, Plowshare Press, Boston, 1970

Harmonia Plantarum, B. Schwabe & Co., Basle, 1943

Vom Klang der Welt, M. Niehans, Zurich, Leipzig, 1937

Kervran, C. Louis, *Biological Transmutations*, Crosby Lockwood, London, 1972

A la Découverte des transmutations biologiques, une explication des phénomènes biologiques aberrants, Le Courrier du Livre, Paris, 1966

Preuves Relatives à l'éxistence de transmutations biologiques, échecs en biologie à la loi de Lavoisier d'invariance de la matière, Maloine, Paris, 1968

Transmutations Biologiques: métabolismes aberrants de l'azote, le potassium et le magnésium, Maloine, Paris, 1962

Bibliography

Les Transmutations biologiques en agronomie, Maloine, Paris, 1970

Biological Transmutations, Swan House Publishing Co., Binghamton, N.Y., 1972

'Alchimie d'hier et d'aujourd'hui', *L'Alchimie, Rêve ou Réalité*, Revue des Ingénieurs de l'Institut National Supérieur de Rouen, 1972–3

Kilner, Walter J., *The Human Atmosphere; or the Aura made Visible by the Aid of Chemical Screens*, Rebman Co., New York, 1911

King, Francis, *The Rites of Modern Occult Magic*, Macmillan, New York, 1970

Kirlian, Semyon D. and Valentina H., 'Investigation of Biological Objects in High-Frequency Electrical Fields', *Bioenergetic Questions – and Some Answers*, Alma Ata, U.S.S.R., 1968

'The Significance of Electricity in the Gaseous Nourishment Mechanism of Plants', *Bioenergetic Questions – and Some Answers*, Alma Ata, U.S.S.R., 1968

Kraft, Ken and Pat, *Luther Burbank: The Wizard and the Man*, Meredith Press, New York, 1967

Kreitler, Hans and Shulamith, 'Does Extrasensory Perception Affect Psychological Experiments?', *Journal of Parapsychology*, vol. 36, no. 1, March 1972, pp. 1–45

Kunz, F. L., 'Feeling in Plants', *Main Currents of Modern Thought*, May–June 1969

Lakhovsky, Georges, *La Cabale; Histoire d'une découverte (l'oscillation cellulaire)*, G. Doin, Paris, 1934

La Formation Néoplastique et le déséquilibre oscillatoire cellulaire, G. Doin, Paris, 1932

La Matière, G. Doin, Paris, 1934

La Nature et ses merveilles, Hachette, Paris, 1936

L'Origine de la vie, Editions Nilsson, Paris, 1925

L'oscillateur à longeurs d'ondes multiples, G. Doin, Paris, 1934

L'Oscillation cellulaire; Ensemble des recherches experimentales, G. Doin, Paris, 1931

La Science et le Bonheur, Gautier-Villars, Paris, 1930

La Terre et nous, Fasquelle, Paris, 1933

L'Alchimie, Rèveou Réalité, Revue des Ingénieurs de l'Institut National Supérieur de Rouen, 1972–3

Lawrence, L. George, 'Biophysical AV Data Transfer', *AV Communication Review*, vol. 15, no. 2, Summer 1967, pp. 143–52

'Interstellar Communications Signals', *Information Bulletin*, no. 72–6, Ecola Institute, San Bernardino, Cal.

Bibliography

'Interstellar Communications: What are the Prospects?', *Electronics World*, October 1971, pp. 34 ff.

'Electronics and the Living Plant', *Electronics World*, October 1969, pp. 25–8

'Electronics and Parapsychology', *Electronics World*, April 1970, pp. 27–9

'More Experiments in Electroculture', *Popular Electronics*, June 1971, pp. 63–8, 93

'Experimental Electro-Culture', *Popular Electronics*, February 1971

Leadbeater, C. W., *The Monad*, Theosophical Publishing House, Adyar, Madras, 1947

Lehrs, Ernst, *Man or Matter*, Harper, New York, 1958

Lemström, Selim, *Electricity in Agriculture and Horticulture*, Electrician Publishing Co., London, 1904

Lepinte, Christian, *Goethe et l'occultisme* (Publications de la Faculté des Lettres de l'Université de Strasbourg), Société d'Edition des Belles Lettres, Paris, 1957

Lewis, Joseph, *Burbank the Infidel*, Freethought Press Association, New York, 1930

Linné, Carl von, *Flower Calendar*, Fabel, Stockholm, 1963

Reflections on the Study of Nature, L. White, Dublin, 1784

Loehr, Rev. Franklin, *The Powers of Prayer on Plant*, Signet Books, New York, 1969

Luce, G. G., *Biological Rhythms in Psychiatry and Medicine*, U.S. Public Health Service, Publication No. 2088, 1970

Lund, E. J., *Bioelectric Fields and Growth*, University of Texas Press, Austin, 1947

Lyalin, O., and A. P. Pasiehngi, 'Comparative Study of Bioelectric Response of a Plant Leaf to Action of CO and Light', Agrophysics Research Institute, V.I. Lenin All-Union Academy of Agricultural Sciences, Leningrad. Bulletin issued by Institute of Plant Physiology, Academy of Sciences of Ukrainian S.S.R. Kiev, 6 March 1969

McCarrison, Robert, *Nutrition and National Health*, Faber & Faber, 1944

McGraw, Walter, 'Plants Are Only Human', *Argosy*, June 1969 pp. 24–7

Mackay, R. S. *Bio-Medical Telemetry*, Interscience, 1970

Magnus, Rudolf, *Goethe as a Scientist*, H. Schuman, New York, 1949

Manber, David, *Wizard of Tuskegee*, Crowell-Collier, New York, 1967

Mann, W. Edward, *Orgone, Reich and Eros*, Simon & Schuster, New York, 1973

Marha, Karel, Jan Musil, and Hana Tohà, *Electromagnetic Fields and the Life Environment*, San Francisco Press, San Francisco, 1971

Marine, Gene, and Judith Van Allen, *Food Pollution: The Violation of our Inner Ecology*, Holt, Rinehart & Winston, New York, 1972

Markson, Ralph, 'Tree Potentials and External Factors', in Burr, H. S., *Blueprint for Immortality: The Electric Patterns of Life*, Neville Spearman, London, 1972, pp. 166–84

Martin, Richard, 'Be Kind to Plants – Or You Could Cause a Violet to Shrink', *Wall Street Journal*, 28 January 1972, pp. 1, 10

Matveyev, M., 'Conservation with Plants', *Nedelya*, (weekend supplement of *Izvestia*), no. 17, 17 April 1972 (in Russian)

Merkulov, A., 'Sensory Organs in the Plant Kingdom', *Nauka i Religiya* (Science and Religion), no. 7, 1972, pp. 36–7 (in Russian)

Mermet, Abbé, *Principles and Practice of Radiesthesia*, Stuart & Watkins, 1959

Mesmer, Franz Anton, *Le Magnétisme Animal*, Payot, Paris, 1971
Memoir of F. A. Mesmer, Doctor of Medicine, on His Discoveries, Eden Press, Mt Vernon, N.Y., 1957

Mességué, Maurice, *C'est la nature qui a raison*, R. Laffont, Paris, 1972
Cherches et tu trouveras, La Passerelle, Paris, 1953
Des Hommes et des Plantes, R. Laffont, Paris, 1970

Meyer, Warren, 'Man-and-Plant Communication: Interview with Marcel Vogel', *Unity*, vol. 153, no. 1, January 1973, pp. 9–12

Miller, Robert N., 'The Positive Effect of Prayer on Plants', *Psychic*, vol. 3, no. 5, March–April 1972, pp. 24–5

Milne, Lorus and Margery, *The Nature of Plants*, B. Lippincott, Philadelphia, 1971

Mind and Matter (quarterly periodical), De La Warr Laboratories, Oxford

Mitchell, Henry, 'Spread a Little Sunshine and Love and Reap Sanity from Plants that really Care', *Washington Post*, 1 July 1973, pp. G1, G4

Morgan, Alfred P., *The Pageant of Electricity*, D. Appleton Century Co., New York, 1939

Mother Earth, Journal of Soil Association, London

Murr, L. E., 'Physiological Stimulation of Plants Using Delayed and Regulated Electric Field Environments', *International Journal of Biometeorology*, vol. 10, no. 2, pp. 147–53

Bibliography

'Mechanism of Plant-Cell Damage in an Electrostatic Field', *Nature*, vol. 201, no. 4926, 28 March 1964

Naumov, E. K., and L. V. Vilenskaya, *Soviet Bibliography on Parapsychology (Psychoenergetics) and Related Subjects*, Moscow, 1971. Translated from Russian by Joint Publications Research Service, J.P.R.S. No. 55557, Washington, D.C., 28 May 1972, 101 pp.

Natural Food and Farming (monthly journal), Natural Food Associates, Atlanta, Texas

Neiman, V. B. (ed.), *Problems of Transmutations in Nature: Concentration and Dissipation* (collection of papers, in Russian), Aiastan Publishing House, Erevan, Armenia, U.S.S.R., 1971

Nichols, J. D., *Please Doctor, Do Something*, Natural Food Associates, Atlanta, Texas, 1972

Nicholson, Shirley J., 'ESP in Plants', *American Theosophist*, pp. 155–8

Nollet, M. L'Abbé, *Recherches sur les causes particulieres des phénomènes électriques*, Paris, 1754
Lettres sur l'électricité, 1753

Norman, A. G., 'The Uniqueness of Plants', *American Scientist*, vol. 50, no. 3, Autumn 1962, p. 436

Northern, Henry and Rebecca, *Ingenious Kingdom*, Prentice-Hall, Englewood Cliffs, N.J., 1970

Obolensky, George, 'Stimulation of Plant Growth by Ultrasonic Waves', *Radio-Electronics*, July 1953

O'Donnell, John P., 'Thought as Energy', *Science of Mind*, July 1973, pp. 18–24

Old and New Plant Lore, Smithsonian Scientific Series, Smithsonian Institution Series, Inc., New York, 1931

Organic Gardening and Farming (monthly journal), Rodale Press, Emmaus, Pa.

Osborn, Fairfield, *Our Plundered Planet*, Little, Brown, Boston, 1948

The Osteopathic Physician, October 1972 (special issue devoted to Kirlian photography and bioenergetics)

Ostrander, Sheila, and Lynn Schroeder, *Psychic Discoveries Behind the Iron Curtain*, Bantam Books, New York 1970

Ott, John N., *My Ivory Cellar – The Story of Time-Lapse Photography*, self-published, 1958
Health and Light – The Effects of Natural and Artificial Light on

Bibliography

Man and Other Living Things, Devin-Adair, Old Greenwich, Conn., 1973

Paracelsus, *Sämtliche Werke von Theophrast von Hohenheim* gen. *Paracelsus,* 20 vols. R., Oldenbourg, Munich, 1922–65
Parasnis, D. S., *Magnetism,* Hutchison, 1961
Parker, Dana C., and Michael F. Wolff, 'Remote Sensing', *International Science and Technology,* July 1965
Payne, Alan 'Secret Life of Plants' Revealed by Biologist', *Performance,* vol. 1, no. 41, 29 March 1973
Pekin, L. B., *Darwin,* Stackpole Sons, New York: 1938
Pelt, Jean-Marie, *Evolution et sexualité des plantes,* Horizons de France, Paris, 1970
Perkins, Eric, *The Original Concepts of the Late Dr Albert Abrams.* A lecture delivered to Radionic Association, 17 March 1956, Radionic Association, Burford
Pfeffer, Wilhelm, *Pflanzenphysiologie,* W. Engelmann, Leipzig, 1881
Pfeiffer, Ehrenfried, *The Compost Manufacturer's Manual,* Pfeiffer Foundation, Philadelphia, 1956
Sensitive Crystallization Processes: A Demonstration of Formative Forces in the Blood, E. Weisesbuchhandlung, Dresden, 1936
The Earth's Face and Human Destiny, Rodale Press, Emmaus, Pa., 1947
Formative Forces in Crystallization, Anthroposophic Press, New York, 1936
Practical Guide to the Use of the Bio-Dynamic Preparations, R. Steiner Publishing Co., London, 1945
Weeds and What They Tell, Bio-Dynamic Farming and Gardening Association, Inc., Stroudsburg, Pa.
Philbrick, Helen, and Richard Gregg, *Companion Plants and How to Use Them,* Stuart & Watkins, 1967
Philbrick, John and Helen, *The Bug Book: Harmless Insect Controls,* self-published, 1963
Picton, Lionel James, *Nutrition and the Soil: Thoughts on Feeding,* Devin-Adair, New York, 1949
Pierrakos, John C., *The Energy Field in Man and Nature,* Institute of Bioenergetic Analysis, New York, 1971
Pressman, A. S., *Electromagnetic Fields and Life,* Plenum Press, New York and London, 1970
Preuss, Wilhelm H., 'Aus "Geist und Stoff", die Arbeiten von Herzeeles', in Rudolf Hauschka, *Substanzlehre,* V. Klosterman, Frankfurt am Main, 1942

Bibliography

Prevention: The Magazine for Better Health (monthly journal), Rodale Press, Emmaus, Pa.

Priestley, Joseph, *The History and Present State of Electricity with Original Experiments* London, 1767

Pringsheim, Peter, and Marcel Vogel, *Luminescence of Liquids and Solids and Its Practical Application*, Interscience Publications, New York, 1943

Puharich, Andrija, *The Sacred Mushroom: Key to the Door of Eternity*, Doubleday, Garden City, N.Y., 1959

Beyond Telepathy, Darton, Longman & Todd, London, 1962

Pullen, Alice Muriel, *Despite the Colour Bar*, S.C.M. Press Ltd., 1946

Pushkin, V. N., 'Flower Recall', *Znaniya Sila*, November 1972 (in Russian)

Rahn, Otto, *Invisible Radiations of Organisms*, Gebrüder Borntraeger, Berlin, 1936

Ravitz, L. J., 'Periodic Changes in Electromagnetic Fields', *Annals*, New York Academy of Sciences, vol. 46, 1972, pp. 22–30

Regnault, Jules Emile J., *Les Méthodes d'Abrams*, N. Maloine, Paris, 1927

Reich, Wilhelm, *The Discovery of the Orgone: Vol. I, The Function of the Orgasm, Sex-Economic Problems of Biological Energy*, Orgone Institute Press, New York, 1942

The Discovery of the Orgone: Vol. II, The Cancer Biopathy, Orgone Institute Press, New York, 1948

Reichenbach, Karl L. F. von, *The Odic Force; Letters on Od and Magnetism*, University Books, New Hyde Park, N.Y., 1968

Physico-Physiological Researches on the Dynamics of Magnetism, Heat, Light, Electricity and Chemism, in Their Relations to Vital Force, J. S. Redfield, New York, 1851

Retallack, Dorothy, *The Sound of Music and Plants*, De Vorss & Co., Santa Monica, Cal., 1973

Richards, Guyon, *The Chain of Life*, John Bale Sons & Danielsson Ltd, London, 1934

Robbins, Janice and Charles, 'Startling New Research from the Man Who "Talks" to Plants', *National Wildlife*, vol. 9, no. 6, October–November 1971, pp. 21–4

Rocard, Y., *Le Signal du sourcier*, Dunod, Paris, 1963

Rodale, J. I., *The Healthy Hunzas*, Rodale Press, Emmaus, Pa., 1949

Russell, Edward John, 'The Soil as a Habitat for Life', in Smithsonian Institution Annual Report, 1962

[337]

Bibliography

Russell, Walter B., *The Russell Genero-Radiative Concept*, L. Middleditch, New York, 1930
The Universal One, Briefer Press, New York, 1926
The Secret of Light, self-published, New York, 1947

Sanderson, Ivan T., 'The Backster Effect: Commentary', *Argosy*, June 1969, p. 26
Scott, Bruce I. H., 'Electricity in Plants', *Scientific American*, October 1962, pp. 107–15
Scott, Cyril Meir, *Music, Its Secret Influence Throughout the Ages*, Aquarian Publishing Co., 1969
Scott, G. Laughton, 'The Abrams Treatment', in *Practice; an Investigation* G. Bles, 1925
Selsam, Millicent, *Plants That Move*, Morrow, New York, 1962
Plants That Heal, Chatto & Windus, 1960
Semenenko, A. D., 'Short-Term Memory of Plants' (in Russian), Institute of Photosynthesis, Academy of Sciences of U.S.S.R. and Timiryazev Academy, Institute of Plant Physiology, Academy of Science of U.S.S.R., November 1968
Sergeyev, G. A., 'Principles of Mathematical Modulation of Bioplasmic Radiations of a Living Organism' (in Russian) in anthology *Voprosy Bioenergetiki*, Kazakh State University, Alma Ata, U.S.S.R., 1969
Shaffer, Ron, 'Your Plants May Be Perceptive', *Washington Post*, 18 April 1972
Sherrington, Charles Scott, *Goethe on Nature and Science*, Cambridge University Press, Cambridge, 1942
Simonéton, André, *Radiations des aliments, ondes humaines, et santé*, Le Courrier du Livre, Paris, 1971
Singh, T. C. N., 'On the Effect of Music and Dance on Plants', *Bihar Agricultural College Magazine*, vol. 13, no. 1, 1962–3, Sabour, Bhagalpur, India
Sinyukhin, A. M., and V. V. Gorchakov, 'Role of the Vascular Bundles of the Stem in Long-Distance Transmission of Stimulation by Means of Bioelectric Impulses', *Soviet Plant Physiology*, vol. 15, no. 3, May–June 1968, pp. 477–87 (in Russian)
Skutt, H. R., A. L. Shigo, and R. A. Lessard, 'Detection of Discolored and Decayed Wood in Living Trees Using a Pulsed Electric Current', *Canadian Journal of Forest Research*, vol. 2, 1972
Soloukhin, Vladimir, *Trava*. Grass (in Russian), serialized in *Nauka i Zhizn*, nos. 9–12, 1972

Bibliography

'Some Plants are "Wired" for Growth: Electricity in the Garden', *Washington Post*, 13 February 1968, p. 34

Spangler, David, *Revelation, The Birth of a New Age*, Findhorn Publications, Findhorn Bay, Forres, Moray, Scotland, 1971

Spraggett, Allen, *Probing the Unexplained*, World Publishing Co., New York, 1971

Steiner, Rudolf, *Agriculture*, Biodynamic Agricultural Association, London, 1924–72

Stephenson, W. A., *Seaweed in Agriculture and Horticulture*, Faber & Faber, 1968

Sutherland, Halliday, *Control of Life*, Burns Oates, 1951

Swanholm, A. L., *The Brunler-Bovis Biometer and Its Uses*, De Vorss, Los Angeles, 1963

Sykes, Friend, *Food, Farming and the Future*, Rodale Press, Emmaus, Pa., 1951

Humus and the Farmer, Faber & Faber, 1946

Synge, Patrick, *Plants with Personality*, Lindsay Drummond Ltd, London, 1939

Taylor, J. E., *The Sagacity and Morality of Plants*, Chatto & Windus, 1884

Thomas, Henry, *George Washington Carver*, Putnam, New York, 1958

Thompson, Sylvanus, *Magnetism in Growth* (8th Robert Boyle Lecture), Henry Frowde, London, 1902

Tiller, William A., 'On Devices for Monitoring Non-Physical Energies' (unpublished article, 41 pp.)

'Radionics, Radiesthesia and Physics', *Proceedings of the Academy of Parapsychology and Medicine, Symposium on the Varieties of Healing Experience*, 1971

Tompkins, Peter, and Christopher Bird, 'Love Among the Cabbages: Sense and Sensibility in the Realm of Plants', *Harper's Magazine*, November 1972, pp. 90–96

Turner, Gordon, 'I Treated Plants not Patients', *Two Worlds*, vol. 92, no. 3907, August 1969, pp. 232–4

Voisin, André, *Soil, Grass and Cancer*, Philosophical Library, Inc., New York, 1959

Volta, Alessandro, *Opere Scelte di Alessandro Volta*, Unione Tipografico editrice Torinese, Turin, 1967

Voprosy Bioenergetiki (Problems of Bioenergetics) (in Russian), Kazakh State University, Alma Ata, U.S.S.R., 1969

Bibliography

Watson, Lyall, *Supernature*, Anchor Press, Garden City, N.Y., 1973

Weeks, Nora, *The Medical Discoveries of Edward Bach, Physician*, C. W. Daniel Co. Ltd, Ashingdon, Rochford

Weinberger, Pearl, and Mary Measures, 'The Effect of Two Sound Frequencies on the Germination and Growth of a Spring and Winter Wheat', *Canadian Journal of Botany*

Westlake, Aubrey T., *The Pattern of Health; A Search for a Greater Understanding of the Life Force in Health and Disease*, V. Stuart, London, 1961

'What Noise Does to Plants', *Science Digest*, December 1970, p. 61

Wheaton, Frederick Warner, 'Effects of Various Electrical Fields on Seed Germination', Ph.D. dissertation, Iowa State University, Ames, Iowa, 1968

Wheeler, F. J., *The Bach Remedies Repertory*, C. W. Daniel Co. Ltd, Ashingdon, Rochford

Whicher, Olive, and George Adams, *Plant, Sun and Earth*, Verlag Freies Geistesleben, Stuttgart

White, John W., 'Plants, Polygraphs and Paraphysics', *Psychic*, vol. IV, no. 2, November–December, pp. 12–17, 24

Wickson, Edward J., *Luther Burbank, Man, Methods and Achievements*, Southern Pacific Co., San Francisco

'The Wonderful World of Plants', *Za Rubezhom*, no. 15, 7–13 April 1972, pp. 28–9 (in Russian)

Wrench, G. T., *The Wheel of Health*, Schocken Books, New York, 1972

Yogananda, Paramahansa, *Autobiography of a Yogi*, Rider, New York, 1950

Past Forgetting

Past
Forgetting

My Memory Lost and Found

Jill Robinson

Cliff Street Books
An Imprint of HarperCollins*Publishers*

HarperCollins books may be purchased for educational, business, or sales promotional use. For information please write: Special Markets Department, HarperCollins Publishers, Inc., 10 East 53rd Street, New York, NY 10022.

FIRST EDITION

Designed by Liane F. Fuji

Library of Congress Cataloging-in-Publication Data
Robinson, Jill.
    Past forgetting: my memory lost and found/Jill
Robinson—1st ed.
      p. cm.
    ISBN 0-06-019430-8
    1. Robinson, Jill—Health 2. Women novelists, American—20th
century Biography. 3. Epilepsy—Patients—England—London
Biography. 4. Amnesia—Patients—England—London Biography.
5. Memory. I. Title.
PS3568.028915Z472 1999
813'.54—dc21   99-34975

99 00 01 02 03 ❖/HC 10 9 8 7 6 5 4 3 2 1

FOR
STUART SHAW

I'll see you again.
Whenever Spring breaks through again;
Time may lie heavy between,
But what has been
Is past forgetting

—Noel Coward, *I'll See You Again*

Live as if you were living already for the second time. . . . There is
nothing which will stimulate a man's sense of responsibleness more
than this maxim, which invites him to imagine first, that the present
is past, and second that the past may yet be changed and amended.
Such a precept confronts him with life's finiteness, as well as the
finality of what he makes out of both his life and himself.

—Viktor F. Frankl, *Man's Search for Meaning*

Writers look for order and pattern in memory, fitting things together,
giving inner coherence to our lives.

—Doris Lessing

Acknowledgments

*I*wish to thank the following authors and publishers for granting their kind permission:

Alan Baddeley, *Your Memory, a User's Guide* (Penguin Books, 1983)

Victor E. Frankl, *Man's Search for Meaning* (Simon & Schuster, 1959)

Barry Gordon, *Memory, Remembering and Forgetting in Everyday Life* (Mastermedia Limited, 1995)

Donlyn Lyndon and Charles W. Moore, *Chambers for a Memory Palace* (MIT Press, 1994)

Steven Rose, *The Making of Memory* (Bantam Press, 1992)

Daniel Schacter, *Searching for Memory* (Basic Books, 1996)

Dore Schary, *Heyday, An Autobiography* (Little, Brown and Company, 1979)

M.R. Trimble, *Women and Epilepsy* (1991)

D. Upton, P. Thompson and R. Corcorau, *Cognitive Differences between Males and Females with Epilepsy*

Peter Wolson, *The Vital Role of Adaptive Grandiosity in Artistic Creativity* (Psychoanalytic Review, 82[4], August 1995)

Frances A. Yates, *The Art of Memory* (ARK Paperbacks, 1984; orig. 1966)
   And, Dr. K. J. Zilka MD, FRCP.
And with gratitude for their continuing interest and encouragement to
                     Ted and Vada Stanley
                              &
                     Bruce and Lueza Gelb.
   And also to Leon and Karen Allen, Martha Greene, Tony and
Chrissie Hoffman, Eddie and Rosetta Ishag, Rob and Sherry Johnson,
Mike and Suzie Little, Tom and Bridget McCabe.
   And, of course, to
                     Lynn Nesbit
                          &
                     Diane Reverand.
   And my thanks to Mary Carwile.
   And to Matthew Guma.
   My affection to Laurie Lipton, Corinne Lavrie, Angie Montagu,
Deborah Susman, Geraldine McEwan, Susan Granger, and Joanne and
Gil Segel.
   And always to Joy Schary and Jeb Schary.
And my love to Stuart Shaw, Jr., Susan Shaw, and Philip Shaw.
   Above all, my love and appreciation to Jeremy Zimmer and Johanna
Simmel for the example of initiative, resolution, and spirit they've shown
in the creation of their lives.

C • H • A • P • T • E • R

1

*I*t begins like this. I am awake. Sunlight comes through the window. A warm body sits next to me on the bed. A firm torso or arm, pressing close, male or female. Not sure. The sun frames the blond hair. Solid presence–stability.

Crisp, heavy sheets. This is a hospital somewhere. And I'm in it.

Looking hard against the sun, I can see the face. "So, you're captivating," I say, "and who are you?"

"I'm your husband," he says. "I'm Stuart."

"That's a beginning," I laugh, "and who am I?" I'd like to ask, "And where are we," but that's too much to know just now.

"You're Jill. You're a writer."

He's scared, I can hear that. But at the same time he's able to be reassuring. "You're going to be just fine."

I can tell he's lying. "I didn't ask."

He takes my hand. "But you will. Do you remember climbing out of the pool?"

"Yes," I say. Can he tell when I'm lying?

I remember swimming. I am stretching every muscle to match the drive of the woman leading aerobics before this—collar blade outlined in sweat, thigh bones shadowed like the ridge under Ava Gardner's brows. Am I in Palm Springs? Twenty laps. I've got nineteen. "You're there," I urge myself on, "just one more."

Now I'm here in this hospital. "So, did I hit my head?" I don't wait for an answer. "How long have I been out?"

"A while," he says.

I lean against his arm.

It is night. Someone brawny is sitting beside me. "Hello . . ."—male voice—"now have some soup." He tries to feed me. I can't taste the name of it. "You could have drowned," he's telling me, "but you got out of the pool somehow."

I touch his forearm lightly. "This is very patient, nice of you to sit here with me."

"I'm your husband."

"I know—but I don't know." Tears. "If you know what I mean."

Here's the next banner of time I catch hold of. A man in white comes in. He puts up the shade. Behind him the world is flat, plain, and soft green, like a land in an old-fashioned children's book. I've never been out of America. Our family doesn't fly. Not since Carole Lombard was killed in the plane crash.

"It's sweet outside," I say.

"Are you asking where you are?"

"Probably."

He's great looking. Blond, built like Spencer Tracy, he'll charm my father. "Are you my doctor?" I look him up and down.

He sits down next to me on the bed and puts his hand over mine. "I'm your husband, Jill. You're at the Stoke Mandeville Hospital near Tring."

Mandeville. *That's familiar,* I think.

"In England," he says.

"You know, I thought England looked like this." I don't want to ask how I got here. Not yet. My head's splitting. "The kids—is there a phone

I can use? I have to call my kids." I look him over. I can't make any connection here between him and my kids, Jeremy and Johanna. "Who's with them?"

"Jill." He's trying to get me to pay attention, to see how long I can hold onto what he tells me. "You've been in a coma and you've forgotten things. It's only temporary." He hopes. "Jeremy and Johanna are grown."

"I've been out so long?" I try to sit up.

"It will all come back." He's trying to reassure both of us. He sounds English. My life is over and I've come back in an old war movie.

"There's a piece missing," I explain. I touch his hand and I'm gone again.

I'm leaning against a man's chest. I'm seriously unhappy. "You'll remember soon."

Anger is the last thing I remembered before the seizure, which put me into the coma, shattered my ability to remember and erased years of recollection.

My husband and I had come to a spa outside London, where we live. We made a pact to get fit, he reminds me now.

"You didn't want to rush dressing to go in for breakfast. You were trying on outfits. So I went back to bed to read until you decided you were ready. Then you discovered I'd brought chocolate with me to the spa. You put on your bathing suit, said, 'Forget breakfast, I'm going swimming.'"

"So I was the one who was angry."

"Yes."

Is his voice appealing because it's familiar, or because the tone, the rhythm, appeals to my taste? Do I remember my taste? What if I've forgotten how I dress? It's okay. He won't mind. Maybe.

We're searching each other's faces. He's trying to see if I don't remember. I'm trying to show I do. "So we'd been away a while."

"Only a couple of days," he says.

"It just feels like forever," I say.

"You're playing it well." He strokes my hand.

I rub my eyes to blank out tears.

"After you went off to swim," he says, "I got up and went in for my circuit training. I was on my way when they called me."

"Have you told me what happened each time you've visited?"

"Yes," he says, "more or less."

"What about telling me more."

"A maid discovered you in a seizure at ten. You'd made it to our room," he's stroking my hand with his forefinger and leaning towards me with his head down, "at five minutes after ten, that is, you were still convulsing, half on the bed, half on the floor, when the housekeeper came in. They called me." He looks at his watch now. "I came in at ten-ten and you were still in the condition they call stasis."

"What happened next?" Do I really want to hear it?

"The ambulance came at ten-thirty. You were convulsing through around twelve. We rushed you in an ambulance over here. They decided it was best to sedate you. You were unconscious for a couple of days."

"Did I almost die?"

"Almost."

"That's interesting."

"Not to me," he says. If he isn't strong, he wouldn't be here. He could have taken off and I would never have known.

I think about all this for a minute, which is probably as long as I can hold onto it. "Did I pass out? Is that what happened?"

"Not exactly."

"Good. I'm sleepy."

Now I am awake. The world outside is light green. A visitor is here. "I'm confused about what's happened, but it seems best not to know." Tears come.

"It's all right." The man is very protective. I tell him I do know him. Just can't place him exactly. He sounds like Richard Burton; that's how I know the voice.

He hands me white roses. "Those are nice," I say.

"The flower of Yorkshire." He's testing me. This is supposed to mean something. Can I make this connection? "I'm your husband," he tells me. He lightly kisses me on the forehead, sits beside me and holds my hand.

"Did we go through this before?"

"Yes," he says, "we were at this spa—for our tenth wedding anniversary." He takes off his glasses and leans down to hold me. "I love you."

"Are the children scared? Did you tell them I'll be home soon?"

Now it's another morning. I am up early. I'm walking with a soft-armed woman in the garden. "It's wonderful to be outdoors."

"We walked by the rose garden yesterday."

"Oh, good, I'll have the surprise of seeing it all over again for the first time." And if we do something and I don't remember, then I can't miss it. It's the stretching, half a shadow, something I almost remember, that's a problem. Worse will be when it's a memory of a time I shared with someone and I don't have it, so in a way, they'll miss it, too. Solitary memories aren't as troubling. If you don't have them, you don't know.

My mind is still. I reach up to touch the branch of a tree. "This looks like a tree I love at home, a perfect tree, a jacaranda tree. Our family is known for being able to memorize easily—but I can't tell you your name. Today. Or his." I nod over in the direction of the visitor in white who's standing by the door to the garden. "And he's my favorite doctor."

She laughs, "That's your husband."

"Oh, really?" I laugh. "There's a surprise for you. Does he know I don't remember him?"

He kisses me on the forehead. He's immaculate in white jeans and shirt. He points out that he is my husband. He's brought me five peaches.

We sit in the hospital cafeteria, looking out at the garden.

He brings over plates, a knife for cutting the peaches, and some tea. "We were at Champney's, a health spa. You'd been swimming. You got out of the pool and someone found you in a seizure."

Do I hear impatience?

"What kind of seizure? A heart attack? I'm too young for a heart attack."

"No," he holds my hand gently and firmly, "it seems to be epilepsy, but they'll want to do more tests later."

Epilepsy. Julius Caesar had it. Where did I get that? Why do I think I know that?

"Did you see it?" I know it's not attractive. When I was a kid, I had a friend, Carol Steinman, who had epilepsy. She was never allowed on overnights and went to very few birthday parties. Everyone said you wouldn't want to see her have a fit, see her foam at the mouth, her eyes roll back, she'd wet her pants. At Will Rogers's stables by the polo field at home in L.A., they shot horses who had fits. "I didn't know I had epilepsy."

I'm slicing a peach, carefully. It works better with my left hand. It's as if this hand and I greet each other like old war buddies.

He's watching my hands. "It might be something no one wanted to tell you."

"Maybe I forgot." Maybe the "friend" who had epilepsy was me.

He takes the knife from me.

"Don't worry," I say, "I won't kill myself over this."

He hands me a slice of one of the peaches. It's pale. "This is a wonderful taste."

I look at him. "You're seeing if I remember the flavor. I don't. But right now it's bright and soft, sweet and sharp, all at once, maybe more a fragrance than a taste."

"I'm not testing you," he says.

"Not really," I say.

"You're going home today." A woman rolls up the shade with a snap.

I try to picture what home might be, but that doesn't stop the scene from unfolding. I walk up the dark driveway to my house. I open the door. The house is dark and still and empty. I walk through each room and not only is nothing here, I know I don't even remember what was here. The kids are really gone. I can't ask—even if I do find someone to ask—because you can't say you don't know where your kids are.

"I don't think I'm going," I say. I don't want to go back. I live in this empty room with a book I've got to finish writing and a couple of snaps of my family. I can't remember the book. But I take it for granted I do this—like I'm not surprised I walk or eat or have had these kids. But they are gone. I mustn't let on that this bothers me. I pull on a long blue denim skirt. But I don't want to go back, so I take off the skirt. I can dress later.

"Don't you remember home?" She hands me the skirt. "You'll be wanting to put this on, luv. You'll remember when you see it." She looks out the window. Is she trying to remember a home for me? Or for herself?

"I don't remember. But it's been a while, hasn't it?" I'm not sure how long. A few weeks, I guess. My mind has become a pool. I put a fact in, an idea; like an image, it dives under and may come up as something else, transformed. Or not come up at all.

A man walks in. He's wearing a tight suit. Of course this is a doctor. Easy to see. They all look orderly. Except my father's heart doctor, who had asthma from smoking but couldn't stop. What do I need this for? Pieces of memory I do not need come through like dive-bombers dropping old flyers. I wave my arms at them, "off, off." The doctor's unsettled. "It's okay," I tell him, "I remembered something I don't need."

"Yes." He clears his throat. That's dealt with. "How are you doing today," he says to the chart at the foot of the bed, "still confused?"

"I'm kind of drowsy."

"Well, you will be," he looks at my chart, "you're on phenytoin. You were in status epilepticus when you were brought in to Mandeville. You're lucky to be alive." He has on a striped shirt and matching tie. He's the kind of doctor who regards illness as a disciplinary problem and likes prescribing things you hate.

"I spoke to my wife's sister," the Englishman says to the doctor. I've forgotten the Englishman is in the room. He's standing by the window. "She doesn't remember any mention of epilepsy and there aren't any records in medical offices in L.A. Jill had two convulsions during her sleep that I told our London doctor about last year. And she was given phenobarbital every night as a child, which Dr. Earl thought indicated epilepsy."

"L.A. doctors are largely interested in drugs," I explain to the Englishman. "Mandeville . . . but I live in Mandeville Canyon." I can see Jane Fonda riding her horse down the road dappled by the trees. What kind of trees?

"Mandeville is the name of the hospital, Jill."

"Of course it is," I say. So when did they put a hospital on the polo field? This is too confusing to argue about, so I just say that I used to use speed, but haven't had a drug or a drink for a long time.

"Really?" The doctor doesn't sound convinced.

The Englishman presses my hand and says, "She hasn't, not since 1969. When I noticed she had the seizures at night, our doctor sent her to a neurologist, who recommended that she go on an anticonvulsant. But," he looks at me, "she wouldn't."

"If that's the stuff I'm on now," I'm sharp about this, "I don't want it! I can't write on this—can't hold onto what I'm thinking, which means no writing, can't catch what I see." I feel drugged, handcuffed, struggling in an empty room, trying to fit a big jigsaw puzzle together.

"I shouldn't worry about the writing for now, my dear. You've been seriously ill," the doctor tells my husband, as if I've said nothing, "but you might want to confirm the situation with a new EEG when you return to London."

"But I want to go home."

The Englishman takes my hand. "London," he says, "is home."

I catch "is home." I hear his resignation. Not frustration, exactly. He seems to accept difficulty. That may be useful. It's not easy with a wife who doesn't have a grasp of your name. I look him over. I catch his character. I don't need to know where we are. Or where we're going today. He'll keep me safe.

2

*T*he dark red Jaguar has a steering wheel on the wrong side and a chauffeur, a notion that doesn't startle me.

"So, you have a Jaguar?" The Englishman is pleased that I recognize the car. But I'm from L.A. We may forget the name and the face, but never the car. The car suits him. I might not have named it so quickly if it had been a midlist car.

Mark, the driver, a tall man with the awkward charm of a shy six-year-old, is uneasy. Should he say he notices I don't know him or keep it to himself? He's English. He keeps it to himself.

"I'm sorry, I can't remember you. But I know you," I say to him. I hug him lightly, he blushes, and we are all reasonably more comfortable. I take my husband's hand (his name's on the tip of my tongue) as we sit together in the back seat.

"Mark's a writer," my husband says, "and he works as a chauffeur and gives us free rides."

"Until I write the best-seller, Madam," Mark says, "then we'll all have drivers."

"Then I'll drive," I say. Not while I'm on this stuff. I can't take that risk with the kids. Mark will help.

"I can't wait to see Johanna. And Jeremy. Yes. Are they scared?" I'm standing on a cliff suddenly with a flooding river of fears stretching out below. "You didn't tell them I have—this?"

"This is epilepsy, Jill—not another word you don't want to say. Johanna said she's seen you in what she called 'space-outs' when you've been overtired, so she wasn't surprised. And Jeremy wanted to get on a plane and rush over, but I told him that wasn't necessary."

I hear the midnight phones hollow in the dark. I'd rush to New York (from where?) to see my mother, to be with my father. I see my father, his coat flying behind him like the nun in *Madeleine,* rushing to my grandmother.

Of course it is necessary. Jeremy shouldn't take a plane by himself. How far away are we?

I can tell by the way the Englishman talks about the children that these aren't his. This is another subject I'll drop. I also do not remember his. At least I'll see mine soon. I don't want anyone to know the scope of this thing until I've worked it out.

I have frustration enough for both of us. What do we grasp by instinct in a given moment, and what do we understand by memory? And what's the difference? He keeps his hand laid flat over mine as we're driven. I look at his profile, the dark blue eyes, long blond lashes. I don't remember how he became my husband, don't know anything about him or much about myself.

This is not my freeway. I've got an instinct for freeways. We're driving on another side. I'm not certain what other side, but it isn't what I'm used to. I have a feeling I'm off target here and it will be best to keep quiet. The man I'm riding with has enough on his mind. And the driver seems to know where we're going.

I feel a gathering chill, some nausea. I grab onto the door handle. The car swerves. It's not the car—it's me. I look at him. Maybe he can't see it. It must not show. I'm falling off the world.

"Are you all right?" He's scared.

No, I'm not. But I can't talk. I'm gripped. I don't like it. Want to get up out of it. I have a hunch, as my dad always said—about something—it's going to clutch me deeper if I fight it. I settle in, see where it goes; my God, like a sixties thing. A spinout. No, I mean the other word where I'm across the other room of my head, like a dance floor on its side. If it's an open tuna can and you're small and in it while it's spinning—and I'm off again the second I fall out, fall out, yes, that's the word, it's like fallout, say my mind blows up like a jigsaw, Dennis Hopper's paintings, ammies like lemon tusks, Billy Al's targets, atoms of images raining down. Out please, out–it's the bomb that becomes a fighter plane, hitting, then eases off, rocking away, like a shaky real old plane. It's weird, a kind of dizzy thing, but not exactly. Will the kids think I'm stoned? They have to know I wouldn't.

We are not on the freeway now. We are in the city. "I feel like I've been away for ages." What I really feel is, I've never been here.

"You may feel like you've never been here." The Englishman reads my mind. Easy read right now. A primer. No. A burnt-out library, all bare, charred shelves.

"No. It's just a little strange. How many weeks was I in the hospital?"

"Only a few days, it just seems long," he says. Seems even longer to him.

"This is Marylebone," he says. It's like Greenwich Village might have looked a hundred years ago. Small restaurants, useful little shops, images from Dickens and Rex Harrison movies. "It's below Regent's Park," he says. "You love to walk over there by the water and watch the swans."

But I hate to walk. Never mind. He doesn't need to know right now.

"We take friends to Shakespeare's plays here in the summer," he adds.

"We also do that at the Hollywood Bowl," I say.

"Probably," he says. Was that a scene from my life he was not in?—so, therefore, of little interest to him. This will be very depressing if everything I find to remember is before the Englishman came into my life. Nothing, and never forget this, existed before England got there and pulled it together.

There's really no scenery here. It's more like New York. I'm missing the mountains always on the edge of your eyes at home; to the left going up Sunset, to the right going down. Now we turn off and we're in the Upper East Side—hospitals, medical offices.

"This is Wimpole Street," he says.

"I can see the sign," I say, "and I've heard the name." I'm edgy and don't know why. "I know—Barrett and Browning." Tears. "I've lost my memory, not my brains." But how much of what we call brains is really memory? Can I be smart without it? How long will it stay away? Is it all erased, or is it in there somewhere under a dense new filing system?

The chauffeur turns off Wimpole Street and parks the car. I know I can't wait to see the kids, but my husband can. If he were really crazy about them, he'd have brought them to the airport. He picked me up from somewhere today. New York, probably. Or L.A. Does anyone go anywhere else?

"We're here." He's watching me. Do I know the house? It's large, red brick, two curved front bays with stone garlands, like a large-bosomed Victorian woman in a fancy bodice.

"But it's beautiful!" I exclaim. Clustered on the steps under the arc of a eucalyptus tree are pots of bright flowers, like storybook flowers, and juniper bushes like we have by my grandmother's grave at home. My father and I go there on her birthday and on Passover and Yom Kippur. After he says the prayers, he tells her what's been happening lately, how the movie reviews have been, what pictures he loves, and he tells her a joke or two in Yiddish. Then he breaks off a sprig of juniper between his forefinger and thumb and smells it as if he's catching her spirit. He puts the sprig in his pocket.

Before the Englishman has the key in the lock, a woman with thick, curly black hair and several earrings in her right ear springs out of the door and hugs me. She is plump, but very fast. When she greets me she has an easy Spanish accent, like L.A. Spanish. Maybe she came from California with me. "I'm okay," I tell her. I'm not. I don't want to go inside. She takes my suitcase from the driver. The Englishman's looking at the mail on a table in an entrance hall with a marble floor.

"This is our house," he explains. "The basement flats and the waiting room and two offices on the ground floor are rented; one to Fickling, the dentist, and the other to a sex therapist."

A young woman with silver eagle hair, maybe thirty, is standing in the foyer; she's not going to rush me. She's cool, elfin—sharp blue eyes—tiny perfect hands. She kisses me. She searches my face. "You don't know me? Is that bad? Or is that good?" she laughs, shrugs.

"All I remember is I'm crazy about you—you're not . . ." This could be my sister, but the age doesn't work, and she just isn't. "I'm really sorry."

She's holding my hands. "It's fine. I can tell you all my stories over again. I'm Laurie Lipton and I live in one of the apartments downstairs. I'm the artist. Gavin, the architect, rents the other flat."

"I wish the kids weren't at school today." Tears are starting.

The Englishman stops at the foot of the red carpeted stairs. "Jill," he puts one arm around me and one on the heavy, dark oak banister, "your children aren't here. Jeremy is thirty-four. I told you yesterday—and this morning. He's married and has a new baby, Phoebe. Johanna is married and lives in Connecticut and has a son, Justin. You can call them tonight."

"Why not now?"

"Jill," he says, "it's a different time zone."

Maybe I'll wait until I'm better, so they won't be uneasy. I hate when my mother isn't clear.

As he opens the door, I expect only the tasteful simplicity of the entry—never, never the wild wonder of this busy old library of color, of books and things.

I'm standing in the dining room of this house and I am amazed: paper masks and pictures all over the walls, plates with movie stars' pictures, antique toys perched on every surface, hedges of paper flowers tumbling down from the tops of bookcases, and swags of dark Liberty prints sweeping down over white lace curtains. It's not empty at all. When Johanna was born Jeremy went in and painted the walls of her room red, like his room. She belonged to his world and that was his color. My father's antique banks are everywhere—when did he give them to me? And the silver candlesticks. "These are my parents'," I say softly—and these big brass candelabra—Cary Grant bought them from my Aunt Lillian's shop. And the tall old art books, The Heritage Collection, children's classics. My brother is just beginning to read. He's the youngest. I reach up, "and these are my father's books, *Case History of a Movie* is terrific." I look at my hand; this is my mother's hand. This means my sister, Joy, and brother, Jeb, will be grown, too. This isn't memory. This is reason, which works slower than memory, like an old train. I think for a moment. Now I wonder if that process, my thinking, is to be trusted at all. There on the wall is a painting my mother did of me holding Jeremy when he was a baby. I look at my hand again. I don't want to look in a mirror. When I think too hard, I get dizzy. It's not a simple feeling. It spins off through visions I instantly forget.

"I've made some lunch," the Spanish woman with the curly black hair says.

"Don't you miss California?" I ask her. "It's all I remember."

"I've never been there," she says. She reminds me she is from Brazil. "I am Lilia, you see. You will be wonderful, you will see. I have ripe papayas. Oh, these are so perfect for the memory. You will tell me things about myself I have never dreamed. That is how good it will be."

The cool, young, silver eagle woman stands beside me and touches my arm lightly. "Do you know her?" She's looking at the large drawing of a serious, sharp-eyed woman. "She looks like Alan Rickman," I say.

"You haven't forgotten movie star names," my friend says.

"It's only my life I seem to be missing."

Sketched around the edge of a portrait is a strip of film with images of a child, writing. "I'm guessing the picture's me," I say, "which means I don't know her."

The Englishman is watching me. "This is Laurie," he puts his arm around her, "she's the artist. You may know her better."

"What I think I know about you may be what I know about my mother," I tell Laurie as we sit down at one of the tables. They're draped in my grandmother's shawls of wonderful old prints. "I'm confusing you, and being aware of the confusion doesn't fix it, although it's clear he's my husband," I say. I stroke the purple paisley and smooth out the toasty fringe that looks like peacock tails on one. "I've saved these for so long. My grandmother used to spread them out over her couch with the satin quilt my father gave her." I imagine the land in Russia looked just like this.

The Englishman goes into another room to make a call and I tell the artist, "I am blank one minute—then, the next instant, I'm here with you."

"Whoever I am." The artist looks at me with this sly glance she has.

"So," I ask her, "what does he do? How terrible I don't remember."

"He says he's a spy," Laurie smiles.

I think about it. "Could be." Could be I'm so caught up with my own work, I've never fixed on his enough for it to stay in my mind.

"He fixes businesses in trouble," Laurie says. "That's what he really does, but he works at home."

She's reading what's left of my mind. I'm confused again. I hate this about the kids being gone. I thought we were driving back and would be in L.A. any minute, winding up Mandeville Canyon, and there would be the kids, and the jacaranda trees. "I may be tired now," I say, and Laurie takes my hand in her own tiny hand. No wonder each line she draws is so precise, so smooth.

I listen to her carefully "So, we met in New York—of course, you sound like home."

"Yes, but we met here in London. You ran into me at a gallery and decided I was in trouble." Laurie explains. "I wanted to leave my Dutch husband. You weren't surprised I was leaving him. You said he wasn't difficult enough to wrestle through the time marriage takes to work. I would, I told you, but I have to live somewhere. I asked if I could rent the little studio flat in your basement and Stuart said, 'You can't rent it, but you can have it—you'll be here to keep Jill company when I'm on a business trip.'"

So he is like my father in this way, always generous. I wonder if, therefore, he is on the edge of a financial cliff. I wonder how often he goes traveling.

"I give you very little distraction," Laurie is telling me. "I'm an artist with a check once a month from a museum trustee, a scholar in Jerusalem. He pays me to reproduce ancient biblical illustrations. I have a brother in San Francisco and parents in New York. I can do a Bronx accent." This portrait she's done of me gives me the same sharp look she has. My mother also gives the people she paints her own expression. It's the true signature. On another wall in this room is a portrait my mother did of me with Jeremy when he was a baby. My eyes, his eyes, are sharp as her eyes.

"Right now, I'm a time traveler," I say. "I'm here from 1946 for a moment, then I stop by out of the fifties or sixties and seventies. I can't tell you a thing about the eighties."

"I think you can," Laurie says. "Come with me."

I go upstairs with Laurie. The children are probably in school, I figure as we climb the steps. There are four rooms on the upper floor.

First she shows me two small rooms like bedrooms. "These are your dressing rooms. They call them 'changing rooms' here," she says, "you can tell which one is Stuart's and which one is yours." That's easy. His is neat.

My changing room looks like a small used clothing store run by someone who doesn't want to sell you anything. The big ficus tree is decorated with ribbons, beads and chains. Hooks on the back of the door are draped with shoulder bags. There's no closet; the clothes just hang from a long chrome rack. A mirror standing on a pile of old *Vogue* magazines leans against the wall. Laurie burrows through a chest of drawers behind a basket piled with heavy sweaters. "Here," she digs out a big cosmetic bag, "from Clinique's 1987 free offer at Harvey Nicks, and these," she pulls shoulder pads from the cosmetic bag, "are all you need to know about the eighties. You loaned them to me every time I went out."

"Did I?" I'm distracted by a trio of chiffon gowns with hand-painted designs and beaded trim, black and red, white with pink and orange, like a fairy queen would wear, and a tawny one like a Navaho princess gown. "Zandra Rhodes." It's not fashion—it's ballet.

"Yes," Laurie says, "and Stuart bought the three of them in one day."

Then I hold up the lemon-yellow linen jacket

"Lagerfeld," she says, "you wore it to Ascot with a coral straw hat with a yellow ribbon." She perches pads on her shoulders.

"The age of the power knee," I say. "I don't remember the rest. Or the year. Don't tell me. I hate knowing how far off I am."

Laurie's slipping on high heels from the boxes under the rack of clothes. "You wear these to try to look like you're taller than I am. But it doesn't work because you can't walk in them. I'm taller."

"You aren't taller than anyone," I laugh.

"You forget. We went through this," she says. "He measured us. I am taller."

"I had a seizure. I grew. It's like a quake." Do all native Californians have this seismic tendency? Pull us too far out of our land for too long and we break up like this, shake into pieces. The swimming was too familiar, too close to home.

We move farther down the hall now. "This is your workroom." The room has dark blue walls, the color of my father's office at MGM, and is covered with posters of my father's plays, framed reviews and letters, a map of L.A. It's like a museum of MGM in the fifties with pictures of my father, the only writer ever to run a studio, with President Roosevelt, Adlai Stevenson, and Sam Goldwyn. And a picture from *The Wizard of Oz*, of Glinda trying to protect Dorothy from the Wicked Witch. The picture Sanford Roth took of Colette.

"My mind stops at 1954—no, here's 1960-something." I turn to Laurie, pleased. "Here's a picture of me with Barbra Streisand."

"You know her," she says.

"We were in a peace march together, I think."

"I think that was before you met," Laurie says. "I think she was in a movie with a peace march, and you saw it."

Maybe I can't tell what's real and what is a movie memory. Will any of my friends move forward in my memory, or are they all fixed here on these walls? Does film stay fixed in memory? Does it record on a different place then reality? Especially with the L.A. brain.

There's a long writing table, pitchers of colored pencils, a silver mug of black pens. Papers and books are piled everywhere. There's a picture on the desk of a little boy in a baseball cap. "That's Justin," Laurie says, "your grandson, Johanna's son."

"Right," I smile.

"You lie," she says, "you don't remember."

Laurie says this cheerful woman here with the tough look behind the smile is Johanna.

"But she just made this paperweight at school," I say, confused. It's a white ceramic globe with bluebirds set in terra cotta hands. What could it be, a year ago? It's as if I've come in at the end of a movie I really wanted to see. I will try to see how it went from what they tell me—I'll have to take it their way. Sometimes I won't be sure. But "not sure" is not the same as "I remember," not the same as "I was there." Their memories may not be my memories. But then I won't know, will I?

I do remember how I sighed when the phone rang and Johanna said, "It's your mother, Mom." Does Johanna really want to hear it's me?

Over the couch, draped with a gray, red, and blue afghan, there's a picture of dark redwoods and pines, like the forest near Stanford University, where I'd sit in the tall quiet, trying to find the focus to write. When my father couldn't write, he'd go for a drive in the canyons. We'd stop and climb up through the trees, not talk, or park and walk along the ocean on the way home. He'd talk about what he'd been thinking about by then. I learned from him that way; how to pull ideas into words.

I rub the fringe on the afghan between my fingers. "My grandmother made this," I tell Laurie.

I lift a picture in a silver frame from a long red table piled with manuscript pages. The picture's of a young man with a tough, tanned face, but there's a curve to his cheek. "He looks exactly like my father—with blond hair." He's standing next to a young woman and holding a baby.

"That's because he's your son, Jeremy," Laurie says gently.

I put the picture back next to the silver mug of pens. I touch the man's cheek, "I can't bear to say it . . . I don't know him. What do I do?"

"You can call. He'll put you on hold, but he'll know it's you."

I may not know him, but I know I never made his life easy.

"I think I'll wait."

"*I* have to tell you something terrible."

"Nothing could be much worse than that you don't remember me. We've done that. It's okay."

Now we're in the living room where my husband works. The walls are charcoal. It has his strong, unpretentious style. I am sitting in the big beige corduroy chair he hates (covering it with the Scottish plaid blanket hasn't helped).

"No," I say, "I can't remember how we met. How did I marry you?" I put my hand out. "You're handsome, I love you, and you're English. But you're not Jewish. How does my father deal with that?" What kind of person am I? I say "handsome" first.

"Jill—," he leans forward and holds my hands in his. He has to say something difficult.

"Stop," I tell him. "What time is it? I mean, what year?"

"It's 1990."

"You don't have to say it. My father's dead."

I can't remember if my mother has died, or when. I will call my sister. Yes, Joy, in L.A. My brother, much younger (maybe) is where?

"Did you know my father?"

"Yes, I met him a year before he died. When I proposed, he stood up. He was fond of ceremony, so I stood up and saluted. He took the bolo from around his neck and placed it around mine, and I promised to love and protect you as long as I shall live."

That feels heavier than just forever.

And he reminds me—most conversation for now is a reminder— "your last husband wasn't Jewish."

"I have enough to remember for now." I stop. "How many husbands?"

"Two. Your first husband was your children's father."

"I really can't find anything there. Not at all." I'm uneasy. "I'm opening a door to a room I don't want to look in."

"You will." He puts his arms around me close, but not clutching. His arms are perfect. I stroke them.

"I remember watching your forearms as you fixed something for your son to eat. So I thought you would be a good father."

The walls of the Englishman's room have agile pictures—are these Miró? And a stylish cartoon of him.

"That's terrific. Who did it?" I ask.

"My older son, Stuart Jr. He's an artist, a writer, a DJ, and he's part of an ambulance crew in Florida."

"So that's all he does?" I look at the picture of Stuart Jr. I can feel the same urgent presence.

I wait until Stuart is asleep tonight and find my children's phone numbers. It will be easier to talk to Johanna than to Jeremy. Daughters, like women friends, enjoy the phone.

"We already talked this afternoon," she says, then quickly adds, "I'm glad you called again. I'd be foggy too if I'd been out as long as you were."

"Did I call Jeremy this afternoon, too?"

"Yes," she says, "and he's really scared. He says you talked to him as if he's a stranger, and had forgotten Grandfather was dead. I told him you'd be fine in a couple of weeks."

"Thanks," I say. "Do we believe that?"

"Absolutely," Johanna says.

We weren't part of a social group in London the way I was in New York. There, friends would be calling, reassuring, dismayed—maybe disbelieving until they spent time with me. Stuart sometimes refers to himself as a troubleshooter. Now we are like a pair of troubleshooters, tackling this problem alone together.

"I told you we were coming," Barbra said, arriving one night for dinner with Donna Karan. I made spaghetti fast. She was baffled, intrigued. How is it that I have not forgotten how to cook? Maybe it's along the same lines as not forgetting a song.

I forgot we were invited to one couple's house for dinner. "Losing your memory is no excuse," the hostess shouted. (Who was she?) "Everyone forgets things. You must keep better records."

I cried so.

Stuart's extraordinary journals of our life together since we met have helped me sort these years out, which doesn't mean I don't fight over things I don't actually remember but don't much care for. Some things just don't feel like me, and I hate some things he says I said. So I say I didn't. Which changes nothing.

Also, he does not mention what I am wearing in most of his journals. And that makes it very difficult. I spend as much time thinking about what I'm going to wear as I do thinking about what to make if you're coming for dinner. These notes add dimension to memory and sometimes they'll place a season, but we fight over what he's added in later.

"No one," I said, when I was looking over his notes for winter '95, "no one was wearing a red tweed Valentino then—not even me."

"But I gave it to you and you loved it."

"Not after '88 for sure." How can I tell him that? It's a gift. I must have it somewhere. I'll wear it. Sometime soon.

In one of his journals for 1984, he says we had fettuccini, poussin, and bread pudding for dinner. He was probably hungry when he wrote that.

"There was no poussin," I'm guessing this part. The eighties are fairly blank, "and I wouldn't have creamy fettuccini with creamy bread pudding. You just wish we'd had bread pudding. So, how did we meet?"

"You'd heard me talk in Westport."

He was talking to a group of people about how he stopped drinking. We both believe that most great spiritual programs do best, like restaurants and movie stars, when they hold onto their mystique. So I won't reveal things about our program because it works, and always has, along its own lines of protocol. One of the principles is you don't talk about it. There's no problem, though, for us to tell our own stories.

"You told all your friends you'd seen this Englishman. One of them told you everyone in Westport knew you'd seen me—and that my best friends were jazz musicians and that I only went out with models. Your friends Marcia and Dolph knew me. They told you that if you thought you'd had trouble—you didn't know trouble."

"So, I was warned—which only made you more appealing."

"You did very well. You found out everywhere I went, everyone I knew. You sat behind me at a lecture by Anatole Broyard and at one of Gerry Mulligan's concerts. You tapped me on the shoulder and, in a very low whisper, asked for a cigarette, which I handed you. I didn't have to look over my shoulder to see who it was. And I knew you didn't really smoke."

"So you were intrigued . . . "

"I'd heard you were smart, a good writer with a rough story. You seemed harried."

Research journalism is excellent training. I can figure out what I might have been wearing, what I might have been working on. But I can research the thrill I had when I saw his dark green Jeep Wagoneer pull into the parking lot in front of the Sherwood Diner in Westport? Yes. Can I measure it up to the catch I feel when I see him coming down the street or walking into my workroom, and hold the sense of it, edgy as it remains? Does he know me? Will he talk to me this time?

"Did you know that was my red Jeep you were parking next to?"

"No, but it was always next to mine when I'd come out after having coffee with friends. I noticed you sometimes sitting at the window wearing Laura Ashley smocks. You were reading *Middlemarch.*"

I was probably trying to look more English than cowboy. "You should have read that by now," Anatole told me.

"Most of the time you were writing."

"Someone told me you worked with Hugh Hefner on a few projects, and I knew that meant models."

"Probably," he says gently.

Your memory is in trouble if, among other things, you repeat the same stories more than once a day. Or is it more than once a week, or less than once a day? Forgetting these memory scales does not worry me.

What interests me is why I remember some things and not others. I remember the acid-green glass candlesticks are from Joanne Segel, but I'm not sure for which wedding. Gil and Joanne gave me my second wedding, but I couldn't tell you when it was. But I do remember everything we ate at Johanna's house this last fall and every word Jeremy has said to me this year. But then, that's because after I talk to him, I write it all down.

I can tell you exactly how to pitch the look I shot across the diner that night I met the Englishman. He had picked up a coffee to go and had just turned and started toward the door.

I put everything I had in that look—didn't spare a second of energy for "Is this a good idea?" I was saying with this look, "I am designed for you. I am everything you need."

"You came across the diner and stood by the table. I have no idea what I was wearing."

"That shows it doesn't matter after all, doesn't it?"

"Yes, but I remember you were wearing a khaki shirt and khaki pants." His big tortoiseshell glasses were perfect for the heavy blond brows and the silky wave across his forehead.

"I asked you if you would care to come and have tea sometime, and you said 'Right now would be perfect.' We forgot about the coffee I was holding. You followed me to my house. Our cars, as you pointed out, were perfect for each other."

"I may forget your name, but I won't forget your car."

We are sitting across from each other on low, soft chairs. The lights are low, too. We're holding tea cups in our hands, as we carefully place each line we say, setting words and thoughts out in front of each other like offerings. Do my responses show I understand you? Is this interesting enough?

I can remember Stuart's house, the house where I went with him that first night. I think it's the American neurologist Barry Gordon who says it helps to arrange words in categories. Houses lead directly to flowers for me.

"There were white lilies on the piano," I tell him. "You were playing a jazz song I'd knew I'd like from then on—but I don't know what it was."

"The song was called 'It Never Entered My Mind,'" he says. "I talked to you first about writing—wanting to write. You said something Martin Luther King, Jr. said, about believing you're everything fantastic you want to be. Trusting your excellence. You remembered things that well then," he goes on, "and you said you'd always loved the idea of going to England. Your favorite teachers and school friends had been English. But you'd never been out of the United States—you'd been working all the time and raising your kids, always into a deadline or a school term. And—this was closer to it I guessed—you said you hated going anywhere you couldn't drive."

"It's a California thing," I say now. "So, did you ever get me out of the United States?" I smile. I love the line of his jaw. Am I really married to this man?

"Where do you think we are now?" He leans forward.

I close my eyes, shake my head. "Well, I guess . . ." and look around the room. Do logic—this is not Connecticut. "Upper West Side?"

"Jill," he says, "we're in London."

"Well, it's been a long day." We hold hands. "Let's stay where we were in the story—about how we began—how you got me here."

"I did say one day I'd take you to London. 'We'll have a Jaguar waiting for us at the airport,' I said, 'and I'll drive you up north to Yorkshire, through some of the most beautiful land you'll ever see.' You said, when you saw it, that it reminded you of chaparral on the Santa Monica Mountains. We stood on the Scarborough cliffs, watching the northern lights. Then, later, we put the car on a ship to France and drove down to the Côte d'Azur, speeding around the Mediterranean."

"You made it sound wonderful—and what I probably thought was, 'Oh, sure.'"

"I wanted you to believe me, but I knew it would take time. When I put on some music, you said, 'You're a nice man. I don't want to throw you,' and I told you I hadn't read your book, didn't know the details, didn't want to know yet. I knew you had some tough, dark years. No one winds up with our determination to change just for a bit of heavy drinking."

"What if I'm somewhere one day and I forget I don't drink?"

"You won't forget. It's something like being left-handed; you know it. One of the most important things you told me then was you hadn't given up on the idea of loving someone. You don't forget that. We had that in common. A lot of people wind up loners, can't imagine finding someone to be with without drinking. You'd been hurt, so I was careful just to talk easily to you," he's holding my hand, "to let you know me, trust me."

He's doing the same thing now, circling in. I can feel that rise you get at the beginning of the titles in a movie you're really going to like. He reminds me about writers I know and love, about this writer's march we went on. Artists we're friends with, concerts we've gone to, how I hated classical music when we met.

"Do I really like it now, or do I tell you that?"

He's like a professor. He has big, clean, and perfect hands. I'm looking his hands over. I put them up, press them close to me and say so quietly, "It's new to be falling for someone you're already married to." And at the same time I'm thinking, *I'm really going to learn a lot here. It may have been this way the first night we met.* "So what did we do next?"

Is he too sweet to talk about sex?

"I could see you liked your reputation as this raunchy authority. But I didn't think you could easily take off your clothes with the lights on; that without drinks, without something, you were shy. I told you that after the hallucinations I had at the end of my drinking, I was scared of the dark."

"How do we sleep if I can't sleep with the lights on and you can't sleep with them off?"

"I told you we weren't at that part yet," he touches my face, "and we aren't."

"So where did we go from there?"

"And you turned away and told me to ignore what you write about sex. You said you were really bad at it, hated it."

"And then . . . ?"

"I figured out you had this thing about trust. The next night we went to a meeting, then I took you to hear John Mehegan play jazz. We all came back to my house, talked until late about the blacklisting in Hollywood. You didn't feel they understood your father's role. They were older, had a different perspective, but you made it clear you had actually been there in the middle and that you never had a child's perspective, but an observer's. I liked you for standing your ground. You are challenging, interesting."

And I'm thinking he's aware and smart. Like my friends, like Sandy, Lynn, and Josie, I have an interesting husband.

"Where are you?" he asks me.

"I'm thinking of all of us together having dinner at Lynn's in New York. Anatole and Sandy, Lynn and Dick, and Josie and Peter."

"Jill," Stuart says, "Anatole Broyard is dead. Lynn Nesbit and Dick Gilman are divorced. And I never knew Josie Davis. She has been dead since 1973."

Will I remember that she is gone the next time I think of Josie?

Johanna Mankiewicz Davis. Every generation has a few mythic losses, potential snapped off, people who were going to be everything. In L.A., Josie had been ours.

Stuart and I are in the living room on Wimpole Street again. He's telling me about the second night we met. "You came back to my house. My son was there."

"You were working on something together, right?"

"The stereo," he says. "After Philip, my youngest son—he was staying with me—went to bed, we began to talk again. Then around dawn, I put on Billy Joel's 'Just the Way You Are,'" he tells me, "and we began to dance."

"Did we?"

He's put on some music now. He dances easy and firm. He lets you move but he's there with you, isn't going to let you go, but isn't holding you back. "I like the way you dance." He holds me tighter. Now he will remind me how it is in bed.

That's what he means. Can he talk about sex? Can I?

But where's the anxiety, that catch that tells you this is love? He feels too safe. He feels like a protector.

Is that sexy?

We are sitting on the edge of the bed. He kisses me. He kisses like movie stars kissed on screen.

Did I kiss movie stars?

I remember as I kiss Stuart that I knew, as I watched him that second night with Philip, he was exactly what I wanted and what my children needed. Solid paternal values. Strong, tawny forearms. Firm hands guiding Philip's hands. Philip, a fairer, slighter version of Stuart. Then, yes, his oldest son, Stuart, Jr., an artist, I think. His daughter, Susan, went to school with Johanna.

"Do our kids get along?"

He stops where we are. "They don't really know each other and they live far apart, but they understand their differences."

Would it have stopped me falling in love if they hadn't?

I put myself first, while I told myself I was putting the kids first. I look at him in the soft light here. He's putting on another record—no—tape— but that's not it, either. Whatever it is, I like how he moves. But then, my kids would have had no interest in the accent or the blond hair. They might not have wanted another father. They might well have preferred to keep things as they were.

"The next morning we slashed our wrists, mixed blood—this was before AIDS—and swore to be together for the rest of our lives. And because you said you tended not to pay attention or to hear only what you want to hear, you swore to listen. I gave you my oath to love and protect you."

A protector is sexy. Even though I couldn't remember what he said, I felt it in his presence. More an animal instinct, the way you do fall in love before there's anything to remember.

"And what did I swear?"

"To always hear me, to listen to what I'm saying."

"Do I do that?"

"Most of the time. Yes, you do."

"Do you hear me?"

"Yes, I think I do."

About two weeks after we'd taken oaths, we sat across from the minister, Ted Hoskins, in his office on the church's second floor. A tall, robust, silver-haired man with a giant presence, he'd be a minister, a whaler, or a sculptor. The sun always lights up behind him.

"But I'm Jewish," I said, "and Stuart's Christian. Would you marry us?"

"There's only one God, isn't there?" he said. "You'll be fine as long as you keep your priorities clear—as long as you have the same priorities." That sounds very simple.

We agreed we'd be no use if we drank again, so that was our first priority. We were each other's second priority. Everything else must come next.

"Children, parents, work?" For me the work had always come first. "My children have resented me more for that than for anything else. Including, I think, drugs and bad men." You can't put a mother down if she puts you first. "I was just beginning to be able to give them everything, to put them first, to give them a home." Maybe it was too late. But I wanted to keep trying.

"Jill, they're twenty-five and twenty-three years old. Maybe you're giving them an opportunity to explore their own lives," Ted suggested. He was putting it in a nicer way.

"I don't agree," I said, "but I want to be married to Stuart."

A year later, we'd married, flown to England, and were standing on the balcony of the round room in the tower of the Holbeck Hotel in Scarborough looking at the northern lights.

You can fear, when you look back and see where it's all come out, that you didn't do the best thing. But you can also understand how you felt then and know you would do the same thing all over again. This is a remarkable level of pathology. Or acceptance.

I come down at 7:15 the next morning. The Englishman is sitting at the kitchen table having blueberries on corn flakes.

Even with my back to him I can tell he's sad. I'm having a test in an hour at the Churchill Clinic. He's probably scared he'll have to take care of me forever.

I woke up early today, read about him in one of his early journals. He had a younger sister whom he had to carry around during the war. And when Stuart—or his mother?—had TB, he lived with his great-grandmother. She ran the movie theater in her town, so he saw movies free, any time he liked, and practiced love scenes coached by older girls.

This is the test: MRI—Magnetic Resonance Imaging. Dr. Rudolph arranges to have me attached to a kind of a sled, my head in a cage, and slid into a steel rocket through a world of gauges, buzzes, hums, taps and quirks. Far below I hear Stuart singing me back through time with the Lambeth Walk, Glenn Miller, and at least twelve verses of "Green Grow the Rushes." Was that a Yorkshire song, or was it a movie with Richard Burton, who sounds just like my husband? Has the same sort of lower lip.

Josie and I followed Richard Burton around Palm Springs one day. Joe Mankiewicz, her uncle who was directing Burton in a movie, had told Josie that Burton was sleeping with Elizabeth Taylor. He'd tell Josie anything, and the look he gave Josie was the look we wanted from Burton. Older men, especially directors, were sexy. They would make good coaches. They know how to light you, move you, and charm you so your face lights up. They'd know how to touch. We wouldn't have wanted our parents to know. The whole point was to move out a bit to test new territory. The men knew how far to go. Some people's parents looked the other way.

Josie hasn't called in ages. I'm scared for an instant. Hate this. Then I remember I don't remember things. Maybe she has called and I've forgotten. It is better to slip that away to deal with another time. I'm not sure why, and by now I don't know what it was I was thinking.

"You see, I'm not going to die," I smile, "there's no brain tumor."

Dr. Rudolph explains that the epilepsy pattern has been managed by the phenytoin, and the blood test shows I can handle a higher dosage if it becomes critical.

"You know, I used to be given phenobarbitol every night as a kid," I say. I understood the sniffs of powdered ephedrine were for the asthma, which made you crayon brilliantly. But phenobarbitol is not for asthma. "Could that have been for epilepsy?"

"That was a customary way to manage epilepsy then."

I always figured I could get around a condition, get outside of it, and have this "Happy Ending" sort of life, but I'm always dragged back to face an item of inventory I've tried to escape. And now, here's epilepsy.

I remember passing out as a kid and being removed from phys ed, which was blamed on the asthma, a far more acceptable condition. You could stop breathing and die. But you didn't wet your pants, foam at the mouth, or have your eyes roll up into your head. None of which worked as an acceptable attention grabber at Warner LeRoy's birthday parties. You'd practice lines.

Jean and Susan Stein's parties had a classy form, like New Yorkers trying to do English aristocracy. Linda and Warner's mom, Doris Vidor, understood L.A. style: fast dialogue and great art.

"Sleep, rest, lower stress, and normal living," Dr. Rudolph taps the results into order, "and your confidence should return as much as possible."

"Sleep, rest, and shopping," Stuart says as we leave the office quietly. What he means is we should take a walk, which along with tea is the British solution to most disagreeable situations. I have not forgotten that I hate to walk or that he has learned to call it shopping.

We cross Oxford Street, which looks like Wilshire at Fairfax. I'm jarred by the faces, the images. He catches that, takes my arm. "You like it when we get to Bond Street," he reminds me.

It's late morning, and the clouds float by animating the figures in the windows. "I think I'm glad I never knew I had this," I tell him.

"Maybe it's part of your imagination . . ."

I interrupt, "Don't even begin to tell me it's okay."

He pulls me back fast from a crossing. "You have to look the other way!"

"I know!"

"You don't—not now. Listen to what I'm saying. I've known since we met that there are fundamental differences in our ways of thinking."

"Exactly. I'm L.A. Female, Jewish. You are completely British Male, Christian."

"What I mean—just hear what I'm saying."

"Bond Street windows—perfect for my concentration. I'm listening."

"You see, I usually work my way through to a conclusion in a rough sort of rational way," he continues. "You almost always jump to a conclusion."

"Immediately," I say. "That's true." I put my hand on his arm, "Sorry."

"I thought you did this because of your 'feminine intuition' or 'artistic insight,' but that's not the complete answer."

"But it is partly."

"Partly, but I now believe that you 'jump' to conclusions the way a person jumps onto a departing bus. You need a resolution while you can still hold onto the topic under consideration. Most of my thoughts are buses parked, waiting for my selection. Your thoughts are transient and have to be jumped on before they leave you stranded."

"By the time I get to it, it may be gone."

"Something like that," he says.

"Nothing could be a bigger gift," I turn him away from the Ralph Lauren window so that he's facing me, "than to have someone think about how your thinking works."

Sleep, shopping, and sex. I hold his hand.

*O*n the shelves and around pictures on the walls of my workroom there are bronze plaques and medallions, humanitarian, film, and theater awards given to my father. A picture of Roosevelt and posters of my father's plays. A sketch of Ethel Barrymore when she was young. I am halfway in my father's room, halfway in my own. I am sitting in the rocking chair, wrapped in the gray, red, and blue afghan my grandmother crocheted for him. I remember turning the wool into balls as she held the skeins up around her hands.

My father was the only writer who got to run a studio, which some thought was like putting a fox in charge of the hens. It was, in the sense that to write you have to put yourself outside so you can see the whole picture. To run a studio well, you have to believe you *are* the whole picture—you have to be everywhere at once.

I used to listen to my father talking to writers when they'd come to watch rushes on a picture that needed more footage, or when they'd call him late at night troubled over rewrites. I'd like to call him now.

I thought I'd put L.A. behind me when I went East to write books, but I guess I catch my voice from my roots, where the rhythm's as easy as the sound of surf rolling back and forth. I hitch up my memory of surf, to get it right. When was the last time I saw surf? How does the movement go?

I look at the date on an award to my father from the Anti-Defamation League. I remember my father's birthday. I try to write down the numbers on a pad of paper from the table nearby with a pen. It's dried out. I take another.

I hear the Englishman's footsteps. He is stopping by here on his way to bed. I catch the Aramis drifting by and the violet-striped Turnbull & Asser robe. Bond Street and its territory are fixed in memory's hard disc.

"I need new pens," I say. He is standing in the doorway. I look at the dates and up at Shaw. "My father's dead, isn't he?"

"Yes. He's been dead for ten years."

"Our family doesn't live much past seventy, that's how I figured it out. He'd have been eighty-five. And you would have said something about calling him, you know."

"He died ten years ago."

"Did we go through this before?"

"Yes."

"I wonder if I remember less if it's something I don't want to know?"

"Of course. It's called denial."

"Was I there when he died?"

"No, you weren't. We were on a plane flying back from our honeymoon. There was a message at the airport from Jeremy."

Jeremy is my son. Now I see it. Jeb is my brother. He is fixed in my mind at fifteen, when we'd drive around town in my new red and white Mercury. Jeb is my father's son. And now, Justin is Johanna's son. A lot of J's. This may make it easier. I don't have to race around the alphabet to catch names. Stay with J's and I'll run into someone I love.

I look Shaw over. "Were you there when your parents died?"

"It wouldn't have made much difference if I was, would it? We went up to Yorkshire every time my mother had a heart attack and it didn't make a difference. She died because that was her time." This, I seem to remember, is the Yorkshire approach.

"It makes a difference to the one who's sick," I say. "It made a difference to me that you were there, even when I didn't know." Which is my family's approach. Break an ankle, and we'll all rush to you on a plane. With Petak's Russian coffee cake. I can tell you the name of the coffee cake, but at this moment here, I'm using my husband's last name.

"I'll be there in a minute," I tell him. He has an elegance in the soft hallway light.

I cannot remember how sex goes with him. More to the point, I don't remember ever being very easy about it.

I am in my changing room. I'm looking at this stack of slender orange Hermés boxes outlined in chocolate, in each one a scarf he's given me. You'd think they'd date them; Hermés dates its narrow brown cotton ribbons, which I have hanging here on branches of my tree. If I'd kept each ribbon with its box, I'd know if this pale blue Christopher Columbus one came before the one with Navajo chieftains. I don't like wearing them so much as I like having them, feeling them. I wore this first one with the gold keys on our honeymoon, wondering how his family in Yorkshire would feel with me so grand and having all these things. I had this scarf on when we rushed from the airport right to Seventieth Street when my father died. My mother touched the scarf when I kissed her. "At last, someone took her to Europe," she told Stuart. Hermés scarves—deductible, perhaps, as basic mnemonic aids.

This may be my favorite, fields of wheat sparked with poppies, corn-flowers—and here—the rabbit with the scarlet eyes. I wore it with the two-piece St. Laurent cotton dress—mistake to give the top away when shoulder pads came in. My daughter is called Rabbit. She's fast, swim-ming or skating. I only wear the red and royal blue Eiffel Tower or the navy zodiac scarves on really outgoing days. I didn't think the French were into astrology. It is convenient that Stuart has the same sign as my mother and my children; an Aries never lets you forget its sign.

I put on the blue and white Lanz nightie patched with bits from the strawberry print that Josie and I bought for old times' sake when she came back to L.A. in the sixties after her mother's first heart attack.

The Rafelsons had just moved in right below me in Laurel Canyon, near Brooke Hayward and Dennis Hopper's house. Josie and I were at Toby and Bob Rafelson's on the Monday night of the big '66 fire. Bob and Jack Nicholson were playing poker with Roman Polanski, who looked at us all like we'd never been anywhere. And I hadn't then. I remember the sound of sirens lacing through the night around Rafelson's and Nicholson's moody dark laughter. I can feel the tension now. Is this the way memory defines itself? It wasn't just the regular summer heat. We'd all been on the gallery walk-around, drinking and catting our way along La Cienega. I was feeling sleek that night. I had hipbones and I'd been on TV with Mort Sahl twice that month, talking fast enough so everything sounded sharp. We were doing our basic down politics riffs, when Brooke called in shreds, taking turns on the phone with Josie and me. Then Dennis came over in a rage. He'd put these pictures out on the lawn to dry, "and Brooke just went out there, man, and turned on the sprinklers. I'm not fucking kidding," he said. Rafelson was already figuring how he'd use this in a screenplay and Toby got Dennis a bowl of something. Because of speed, I don't remember sixties' food, but it was probably chili. Like sex, we did not talk about food then. We just made a lot of it and shared it all around with anyone who might drop in.

In Daniel Schacter's wonderful book, *Searching for Memory*, he talks about the memory wars. Some memory explorers believe once it's gone that's it. The connectors are burned out. Others go for Proust's idea, that the scenes are in the storage vaults, waiting for a "retrieval cue."

I remember this night with Brooke because I hear a siren. I left the Rafelsons—it went something like this, I think—and I brought Brooke and her kids, Jeff, Willy, and Marin, home with me that night.

The fire engine I hear now in London calls up the image of our children lying together on the shaggy royal blue carpet, on Merimekko cushions, the moon coming in the huge window which reminded me of my mother's art studio.

We were hoping they thought this was just a fun overnight. Or is that what I'd like to believe we were thinking then. Did we see their sensibilities as people so clearly before they grew up to tell us?

The siren wails off beyond Marylebone. I'm in our bedroom. Shaw's pulled down the covers. I slip in beside him in my nightgown and hold on tight, patting his shoulder. He kisses me with this big, long Gable close-up kiss.

"Could we turn the lights off, I wonder?"

"Of course," he says.

"It's still light in here," I say. "Streetlamps?"

"Maybe the moon," he says.

"I know you've seen me without clothes on," I say. "I'm sure."

"That's true," he says, "but you're not easy about it, so that's okay." He's even more charming when he's amused because it doesn't happen easily.

"I can't remember you laughing." I look at him lying back against the dark paisley pillowcase (Ralph Lauren, late eighties.) "I can't remember—do you have a sense of humor?"

"You told me yesterday you didn't think so." He's stroking all along the curve of my body, lightly, carefully. "And you said that was fine with you."

"I guess it's not okay—but it's how it is."

"Hush," he says, and his lips are cool and perfect. *Stay,* I tell my mind. *Stay here. In the present.* It slips, like silk, like a scarf. I then feel it starting, that gathering feeling, the arising, rolling, buzz.

"I can't . . . ," I say, "I'm scared I'm having one of these things." Petits mals. That's what they're called. It's a couture condition. Hermés could do a petit mal scarf. I can give them images. If I could catch them, tie them down so they stay in place. "Your hair looks silver blue in the moonlight." I touch his brows.

"How many people," he says, "can begin again? I think it's interesting."

"But you remember where we were before."

"That," he says, "is what makes it so interesting. Do you remember when we first met you told me you couldn't come unless you were tied up to the bedposts? You had a lover who made gift wrap. He'd tie you up in his newest ribbons. But I didn't have bedposts and wouldn't have tied you up anyway. You talked a great game then, the way you wrote, and I knew the charm of it was I had a newcomer."

"So to speak," I say. I lie quietly as he turns towards me and puts his wide strong arm across my body like an honorary ribbon, a banner, the kind Princess Diana had on with badges when I sat next to her at that concert. I don't remember the concert, but I remember her easy, open attention that broke the ice she assumed you'd feel sitting next to her. "Isn't this great?" she whispered at one point, touching me with her arm, the kind of arm that gives a real embrace, sturdy as Stuart's arm on the other side of me.

"What are you thinking about?" he asks. He's now got his leg across me so my thighs stay this way, open.

The wind is coming up from behind the full moon, whipping round and clearing bits of sky so the moon looks set in it like a rough-cut antique diamond. I used to sit at my window when I was a kid. I looked out over the drive winding down between hills covered in English ivy and I imagined I was in an English castle. Then I'd stand at my three-way mirror, sideways, so I'd look over my shoulder the way movie stars do, lifting my eyebrows, trying out smoky glances as I brushed my hair (make it stay blonde, God, let me be glamorous, please). If my parents were out, I'd go down to my mother's maid Dorothy's room. She gave me bourbon. We'd listen to her Bessie Smith jazz records and she'd call me "Glamour."

One night the Ku Klux Klan, in their white pointed hoods, burned a cross on the ivy-covered hill right by the big stone reindeer. This was because black people were not supposed to live in Brentwood.

When I first met the Englishman, he actually had a six-foot-four-inch woman from Jamaica living with him, towering over him. She kept him warm when he got the shakes getting sober. They were a forceful combination, but she left the day after we met. She left her clothes cut up in shreds all across his lawn.

"I can't remember what I'm thinking about," I said, "what do you think about?"

"You," he says.

I doubt it. But it's a perfect thing to say.

He's like a large, endlessly passionate animal; curvy, dense flesh you can disappear under. I'm a ship and he's the sea. Then we turn, rearrange legs and I'm the sea and he's the ship. Can he keep my attention on him, on the present, instead of this kaleidoscope inside my head dense with tough images.

Stay here. Consider how the tongue of the wave curls back down and sucks up the flat spill lying up there on the sand, and what is the word you have for that; it curves up there, never the way you expect it, always getting the edge of your beach towel.

His hand feels like sun.

Set your mind here, on a stone balcony in the village of Èze in the South of France. I'm lying naked in the sun. Like warm silk. Drape it just so it shows this part, like the Eiffel Tower part on the Parisian scarf—and then, with just a twist of your neck or a touch of the wind or his arm around your shoulder, and the ivory triangle comes out like a glimpse of my mother's nightgown. Cut. Start again.

The power builds; the energy's on. It gets still, focused and silent.

"Stop! Don't!" I'm silent, can't talk through the seizure just as you can't talk when you're coming, not really. I can't tell him it's happening. Is it an orgasm or a seizure? I've got to get out, don't tie me into it or I'll go all the way and never come back. I get out from his hand, his leg, and lie here panting, crying against his body. I don't want it to be just sex with him.

Just Sex, she's saying, and Sex is so insulted, having such an open field day in matters of life and death and politics and out of its closet altogether is Sex in this century—the nerve, Sex says, and it is a matter of nerves, I have to remember to ask the neurologist whether in fact the seizure and the orgasm are related, and if it is a kind of come.

I try to turn to loving him, but he's withholding here. "Not yet," he says. Giving sex, "I want to see yours but I won't show you mine," is the oldest child trick. You want to see a grownup so you don't have to spend quite so much time wondering what they (especially the directors) look like without their clothes on. Do you? Want to know, really? Yes. But that's different. Is that adult abuse? Thinking how all your parents' friends, especially the movie stars, look without their clothes on? And what they do, exactly. Especially the Democrats.

The villains, Robert Ryan and Richard Widmark, would have interesting games. They would tie me up and take off one piece of clothing for every line I got wrong. Do they know this is what I am thinking at deli dinners on Sunday nights? Lana Turner went upstairs to hug my brother good night, and he said he could feel her real breast against his face.

I wonder if I saw more, knew more, and, as I think my father did, only let myself feel what I could handle. This I can't deal with. "No, no, no," I twist away, "I can't go there yet."

Find something lovely, like the peonies on the scarf he bought in the south of France. Folds and curves, edged in crimson, dark as it is here, where he's trying to find our connection, carefully, he's winding his way along; a sure tread he has with his fingertips, like a seasoned hiker here, chivvying me along, the way he did down that French mountainside, or was it Yorkshire, or a trail down from Mulholland where I'd sit and watch Lupita Kohner and Maria Cooper taking turns riding Traveller, the school horse, waiting for the weekend when my father would be home and take us for a hike along the trails through the chaparral off Tigertail Road.

My father was easygoing on the weekends; his walk, his voice, the expression on his face changed. He became Jimmy Stewart. We'd take turns building up a story, scene by scene, as we drove up the canyon.

This is not useful for coming. Go red, sharp, dark. Cut it.

Turn on my side away from him, shaking. He's a wonder, says it's okay, hush, and holds me close, rocking me in his firm, steady arms.

6

*T*oday he takes me down the street to Sagne's, a bakery with a platoon of marzipan animals and cakes like white chocolate bouquets in the window. "Princess Alexandra used to come in here every year with her lady-in-waiting to place her order for Easter eggs," Stuart tells me.

"How nice to have someone whose job it is to go shopping with you," I say.

"You do," he says. "When we first moved here, you thought no one knew you. Then one day, when you'd left a cake you'd bought, someone from the shop came by our house with it on her way home. It had a note on it, 'American lady writer—Paid.'"

We sit down for a quick cappuccino. Clement Freud is sitting across from me, glaring down at his cream puff. A trim, sporty woman with a great smile hugs me, reintroduces herself quickly, "I'm Jacquey Visick."

"Does everyone in town know?" I ask Stuart after she's left.

"She's a journalist," he says, "one of your favorite friends. Calls every day to see how you are."

We pick out croissants, almond and chocolate, and a raisin Danish. I ask for some bagels. "You don't like the bagels," Stuart says.

"Maybe I will now. You'll see."

A young woman is in the downstairs waiting room when we come back. She has a little boy with her, maybe four years old, cheeky and restless, sucking on a candy. "Don't even begin to tell me you don't know me," she says, "don't even start."

"Of course," I laugh, "I know you." I do. But not her name. Or his name.

She has curly, expensively tortoised hair tangled into a barrette. Her eyes are round and glittering dark. "It's a good game," she says, "you may get away with fucking murder with anyone else." She tosses aside the *Vogue* she's picked up. She looks at a woman you know is waiting for Fickling the dentist because she's reading *Country Life*. "Yes, I said 'fucking' in front of a kid in broad daylight."

As we go upstairs, she reminds me, "I'm Judith Marcus. I own a company that makes commercials."

She's watching me, concerned. "I thought it was one of your dramas, but you really don't know me." The memory loss is real. She jokes it away. "If you don't remember anything, I can tell you anything and you'll keep it safe. How convenient."

"Can I get the paints?" Noah, her little boy, asks.

"Sure," I hesitate, "if you know where they are."

"You let kids paint on the walls upstairs," Judith says.

We go into the kitchen.

"And you say I'm best," Noah says.

"You are." I hand him a glass of water and some of the brushes from the mug on the kitchen table. Will I remember anything she tells me, and if I don't will I be able to fake it?

"Cesario, my lover, is charming," she explains, "but his days may be numbered. He lives too far away. With our work, his wife and kid, and Noah, it's very hard to make time to see each other."

"So he's married?" I ask.

"Of course. Why can't they be wonderful and single?" she asks.

"They can, but then they'd be less interesting," I say. I can see she gets bored easily; she runs a studio, has a child and a lover and an ex-husband. She surfs through her days like a man does with TV channels.

"I'd always find something wrong so that I can go back to Cesario," Judith says, her face in the refrigerator. "He is perfect, just available enough for entertainment." She peeks around at me. "Not enough to get in the way of a marriage."

"You could always see this analyst downstairs, you know. That's what he does. Works out marriages. Stuart says he's meant to be very good."

"You're saying 'meant to' like that to sound English," she says. "Stop it. His name's Mendell. He's a sex therapist. That's not the problem." She puts her arm around my shoulder.

"So, do you have any idea what happened to you?" Judith sounds tough, but she's far more sensitive and easily hurt than Laurie, who has the self-absorption and assurance of an artist who knows she's a genius. "Can I put out some cold chicken?" Judith asks.

"You see," I say, as I get a blue glass from the shelf, "we had an assignment to write about Champney's, the health spa."

"I know," Judith says, "I told you to do it, that you'd love it. I didn't tell you to get carried away."

"Literally." I tell her about the anger I had when I was swimming. And suddenly I remember why I was angry. "He took chocolate bars with him. And he napped instead of exercising. I guess I got wild with rage."

"I'm about to do that," Judith is putting pieces of roast chicken on a platter. "Cesario's wife thinks they should move back to Italy. How can she do that to me?"

"You know, the very worst thing can turn out to be the beginning of something amazing. Or did I tell you that already?"

"Probably," Judith says, "at least you don't act like you're tired of hearing all this."

"I'm not tired of listening," I say, "but I'd be interested anyway. Even if I hadn't forgotten."

The Englishman has walked into the kitchen and is pouring another cup of coffee.

"Convenient you should turn up now."

"Memory does not matter to her," he puts his arm around me, "she invents everything anyway. I was in an exercise class when they called me and told me she was having a full-blown seizure."

"Convulsion, everything?" Judith lifts her eyebrows.

"It was so bad, he won't tell me what it was like in the ambulance."

"If I were you, I wouldn't want to know."

Noah comes back in for another piece of chocolate croissant. Judith says no. I hand it to him when she gets him a glass of milk. "He knew you'd do that," she says. "So you were swimming?"

"I'd made a mile—or nineteen laps. I remember the sign that it takes twenty laps to swim a mile. So I dove in. The water was perfect, easy water, turquoise pool water. I worked hard from the twelfth lap. By the time I got to fifteen, I knew I'd get there, do the mile, even though it was hard going. I was counting the laps then, turning at the end of each one, to see how far I'd come. After eighteen, I pushed on into that fever you get when you've wrapped something big. It was only a mile—but for me—"

"For anyone," Judith says. "A mile for any of us is a big deal."

"Well, I did it. And lost the rest of the week—and in a way, everything else. I don't know what I don't know until it comes up, and then I realize I don't remember it."

"When Stuart said I was coming over," Judith tosses back her hair, "did you have an image of me in your head?"

"Of course," I say.

"Not at all." She looks me over carefully. She can case you fast as Walt Winchell, as Lenny Lyons. Judith's shrewd and tough on top, full of longing, generous underneath. I wonder if Jeremy is like this.

We set out the gray plates with the clipper ship pattern at the small round table in the dining room. Judith and Stuart are talking about her studio, but when I join them the subject changes to Cesario. This is not unfamiliar.

"I'm really trying to end it." She takes a piece of chicken from Stuart's plate. "He doesn't like white meat," she reminds me.

"Can you just decide to end something, just like that? Give yourself time—otherwise you'll feel terrible when it doesn't work," I say, "like quitting anything."

"I think you can just end it." Stuart is disagreeing with me. "You end with the action. The feelings go in their own time."

"Like you with Peggy?" I snap. Peggy was the girl he stabbed when she went out on him. This was quite some time before we met.

"You remember that?" He's encouraged. He explains to Judith how it was every day when he went to see me—how I'd see him in a different way—regard him with a different expression.

"I'll send you Oliver Sacks's book about the man who mistook his wife for a hat," Judith says.

"Maybe I thought he was a Jaguar, but I wouldn't remember.

Sometimes I hear him play the piano when he's not even home," I say. I haven't told him I've been looking in his journal, trying to catch up on our story.

I am not entirely certain if this is the same day as the last piece of time. Stuart has put postcards on the kitchen wall from holidays we've had together, dinners with Ted and Vada Stanley, Bruce and Lueza Gelb. This interests him even more than the pictures of his own children and grand-children—which we are also taping on the wall next to the kitchen table so I can start to understand, to hold onto who they are. I have lists of their birthdays and their phone numbers and addresses, which I've matched with the pictures. I also have pictures of my children when they were lit-tle, when I seem to remember them best, and pictures of them at other stages. Judith is here and there are croissants, so it may be the same day. Or this may be a regular thing we do.

Judith and I are looking at pictures of my children taken when they were with us during one of the summers Ted and Vada loaned us their beach house. Here we're sailing with Bruce and Lueza. Lueza's standing on the bow of the ship.

And here I'm standing with Barbra. We're looking at each other in exactly the same way as my father and Sam Goldwyn are looking at each other in this other picture over here.

"My father may be younger than I am in this picture."

"He may be the same age Jeremy is now," Judith points out.

"And I don't know Jeremy as well. Is this typical? That we don't know our children as well as our parents?"

"We probably don't let our parents know us," says Judith.

"Probably. I haven't seen him for ages," I say.

"You saw him last Thanksgiving," Judith says, "you were just getting yourself together. Jeremy brought Phoebe with him."

I don't remember, so I move on to the next picture. "This is Justin." He's got a Yankees baseball cap on. "Here's his mother, Johanna." I get misty.

"Don't get that way," Judith says, "Johanna has no patience with that."

"You mean you don't," I say, but then neither do I. "I look at these riveting adults and I don't quite understand who they are."

"How would you?" Judith says. "They've changed. You see Jeremy and Johanna maybe once every year for a few days. How can you expect to know them?"

Is she saying I don't see my children enough?

"I haven't forgotten guilt," I snap at her. "I really don't need you to tell me that I haven't seen them much." I'm too sharp. Lighten up.

"Look," she says, "this isn't memory. We're all different to our parents. If we lived next door, it wouldn't be any easier—maybe harder. Denial is the traditional way to handle family relations."

"Even if we were in America, you wouldn't remember the last time you saw your children," Stuart says quickly.

"You're trying to show me that it's not all your fault, that it's not only because we are living here in England." I'm snappy. That's because Judith's here and they'll go in his room as soon as she can and talk about her work. "Maybe," I tell him, "you're really wondering how much I remember about our own last trip. Do I remember the cliff overlooking the ocean, the tiny donkeys on the beach, and starfish in tide pools?"

"That's so sweet," Judith says, "you do remember."

"Does it matter if I don't know exactly what we saw? It's like splicing a few frames of film to put the story together." I say this to Judith, to remind her that I know about film. I have the defensive determination you get when you're older to remind newer people that you were around in the business, whatever business, long before they were. You do it when they don't include you, because they're trying to show that they've arrived and they want your total appreciation.

But then my defense is usually light-years behind the time, as I probably am. Do they splice? Call it film anymore?

"She's talking about Scarborough." My husband gives Judith another piece of his croissant.

"She knows," I say, and so he knows he's not off the hook, "of course, if we were at home, my kids could come visit and show me who they are. There would be accidental times when we'd run into each other and have ice cream, and be able to make up for the last fight."

"Spontaneity won't come easily," Judith says, "with Johanna in Connecticut and Jeremy in L.A."

Now Laurie's tapping on the door. She says she's come up to ask if we think the landlord will care if she paints her kitchen.

"Why would you do a picture of a kitchen?" I wonder.

"I don't want to paint a picture of the kitchen," she says. "I want to paint the kitchen walls."

"Since when are you cooking?" Judith looks her over.

"I'm not. But if I liked the color of the kitchen, I might."

"So what color is it?" I come into the middle. This is in case we miss daughters who don't get along.

"You shouldn't see the color until you're better; in fact, it could set you back years," Laurie says.

"Years I can handle. I'm very good on 1958. It's yesterday that's a problem."

As my husband puts more chicken on Judith's plate, he tells Laurie, "Mark's looking at the other flat across from you."

I tear out a bite of bagel. I want a flavor to go with how it looks. This is like seeing a movie without the score. "Bagels don't taste like I remember."

"That's because you don't really remember how they taste," Judith says, "and you invent dissatisfaction to distract us."

"I'm not being dissatisfied . . ."—don't let her hurt you—"I'm just puzzled."

"That's possible," Stuart says. Judith splits the chocolate croissant and hands half to him.

Sound sharp, I tell myself. "So who is Mark?" I turn to Laurie. "And what color is the kitchen?"

"Mark is the writer who pretends he's your driver, something I wouldn't expect you to forget," Laurie answers, "and the kitchen is chartreuse. Doesn't that ignite the memory?"

"It's probably easier to remember things you hate," Judith eats.

Not sure. I toss up a set of flash cards, like mug shots, on my mind's screen—former husbands.

"I've thought of showing her movies she hates," the Englishman says, "but there aren't any."

"That's not true," I say, "I hate most movies with Dan Duryea." I'm delighted. "You can't say my memory's all gone if I remember Dan Duryea."

"That's so useful," Judith says.

"Well, it is," Laurie says. "We could put her on a game show."

"I remember chartreuse," I say, "you'd wear it with cocoa, maybe a turban hat—or with fuschia jersey. On its way out, it ended up on leisure suits, and I remember violet, my grandmother's shawls." I brush the crumbs off my favorite placemat, which I put out this morning—"this and the other one with ranunculas."

"But that's not your grandmother's," Judith says, "you bought those all on sale at Liberty."

"I don't think so." I'm dizzy with the confusion I get when I'm wrong.

"It doesn't matter," Laurie says quickly, "they look the same."

"The important thing," Judith says, "is you haven't forgotten the things that matter." She wants to get down to business now. "I need to talk," she tells Stuart, and leads him into his room.

"I could come down and paint your room with you," I say to Laurie.

"That's a perfect idea," she says. But you don't have to remember to sense how someone is about being alone.

Judith pours a cup of coffee for Stuart, throwing in two sweeteners and some milk. I wouldn't have remembered exactly how he likes his coffee. She pulls off a bit of the almond croissant on his plate as she hands him the coffee. I hope she's in love with someone.

Noah wants me to see what he's painted. I take his hand and he leads me upstairs to the wall by my writing table.

C · H · A · P · T · E · R

7

*T*his is a new morning. I look at a blond male; imagine a Henry Moore sculpture you can sleep with. There's a tree outside the window. The man is no more or less familiar than the tree; we are no more or less connected. I go outside the room. I'd like to have some people around. When I'm on my own like this, I feel like I'm on a windy roof. Nothing to hold onto. I'm in the changing room looking at a rack of clothes. I have a lot of chino clothes. I find some pants, a shirt, a jacket. Arthur Miller was dressed like this when we marched down Fifth Avenue in New York. I can't remember what it was about. Here's a picture of my father with President Kennedy. I guess I'm a Democrat. But I can't remember who's President now. Are my values and political attitudes different now? What if Stuart's not antiwar and thinks nuclear testing is a good idea? He's English. Is he fond of the Queen? Will things I used to like to eat be distasteful? Will I love music I used to hate? How much of choice is influenced by association? Will everything be a brand-new choice? Are these khaki clothes comfortable because they bring back a moment I liked? And they are so worn in, it may be more than one moment. I sit down on a needlepoint cushion to pull on socks. Who did this needlepoint? There's a bag of shoulder pads on the floor—for making clothes?

Something. Shoulder falsies, for affectations of height and power. Did I run a company? God help it. How many of these questions did I ask yesterday, and how many have already been answered?

I go into a long mind skid. *Take a ride,* I tell myself.

I've got a Mustang convertible. It will be in the garage. I'll drive out to Santa Monica Canyon to see Sherman and Joan. Sherman Yellen's out here working on his new play.

I go out the front door. Wrong. You're not home. This is certainly not L.A. I walk up this street. There's bound to be a garage somewhere. You can always tell by the car whose house it is. Judith has a Jeep; shows you can run a family and work at the same time. You feel like a World War II general.

I stand at the corner, confused. But this could be Wilshire, around Hancock Park. On a Sunday. I know I'm wrong, but I can't make the connection.

"Are you lost?" a sturdy woman rumbles up along the curb on a motorcycle. Is she picking me up? She has on a red and turquoise Nike outfit, bright helmet; she's a giant toy. "Jill, it's Prue." She takes off the helmet and blonde hair tumbles out.

"Of course. Hi!" I laugh. "I'm fine." I have no idea who she is.

"It's okay," she says. "I haven't seen you in ages."

She's saying that to make up for my embarrassment at not knowing her. The English can't bear embarrassment. And Americans are a major source of embarrassment. Look what I do to this authoritative corner of substantial Victorian architecture, standing here, looking uneasy, having the queasy appearance of an L.A. cliff after a 6.5. She throws a chain around the front wheel of the cycle and padlocks it to the fence of this house just down the street. I stand under the arc of a eucalyptus tree and pinch a bit of the bush to my right. It smells like home. I knew what it was—but now it's gone. She unlocks the old paneled door. This is my house. Don't be crazy. Don't be that crazy, please. We walk in. I look in my pockets for a key to our flat.

No key.

I'm there five minutes when Prue says, "We've got a patient soon, but you can stay in the waiting room."

A small woman with thick silver and black hair comes by, she does an instant freeze frame with her eyes. "I'll call Sagne's and tell Stuart you're here. He's been looking for you." She has hair like my Aunt Lillian. But her hands and her jawline are fragile, exactly like my mother's.

"I've only just gone out," I say.

"No," she looks at the biker, "no, you haven't." She picks up a phone on the table in the black and white marble hall. "This is Laurie Lipton," she knows her name carries weight, "will you tell Stuart Shaw that his wife is back at home." Then she looks at the biker. Prue. Yes, Prue.

"How are you doing?" the biker says to Laurie, who shrugs.

"It's good I live in the basement because I can jump out the window and it won't kill anyone."

"A friend of mine, an opera singer," Prue says, "would really like you to do his portrait."

"I'm open to proposals," Laurie says.

After the biker—yes, Prue's her name—goes into the dentist's office where she works, Laurie gives me tea in the kitchen, which has only one chartreuse wall left. You've been in England over a year when you start serving tea. After five years it's what you really want to drink.

"I'm thinking about this biker I met," Laurie says.

Prue reminds me. "A travel photographer. We might be fine for each other."

"You're never crazy about the one you'd be fine for," I tell her.

"You are," she says.

"Possibly. But maybe we decided we'd save everyone else from the trouble we are and made up our minds to be crazy about each other. It was best of all for the kids. We're here. Out of their way."

"You don't mean that," she says.

"I don't remember if I do. It feels familiar." I know I don't mean it "I might not have a choice." I can change the subject easily and just say I don't remember what we were talking about. "So, you could bike all over—to America even. And you'd have free transportation all over. Fast."

"That's the part you'd like. You're terrible at matchmaking. Besides, I work in black and white. I need someone who dresses in black and white. I think I've met her. She works in the City—smart, funny. Conservative. Ideal for me."

"But can I trust you—to know?" I ask. "Is she also remote and unavailable?"

"So, your memory returns. She will bring me to a new level of despondency."

"That's important if you want it to work." I look over the walls. "That chartreuse is terrible. Thank God you're changing it."

"I told you. I never lie." The black and white drawings are everywhere, big wide-open expressions. The woman eating an apple, which is actually the head of a child. You look and you hear the large voices; you don't have to know them to know them.

"You draw like I wanted my mother to paint," I tell her. "You catch the edge. I used to watch my mother paint gentle, ravishing images filled with love. Then at night, after we'd had our glasses of sherry, she'd tell me the true stories, the savage stories. Why is negative more real than positive?"

"It isn't," Laurie says, "except when I'm in a depression. You don't hold onto depressions well, but you're very tolerant of other people's depressions." She tells me that when she came back after her mother died and had hidden out, I'd left bowls of chicken soup by her door. "You never tried to cheer me up."

"I wouldn't think of it." I look around the neat rooms.

Sheets of paper lean against every wall; each one covered with real people, their reality raised by her fine pencil lines to a rich new level of grotesque precision by the perfect details of the hands, the eyes, grimaces—surreal characters you know are someone's relatives.

Do I write about my family like this? Do I remember my family? From hello, I miss you, to goodbye, I love you, I know more about a person I met an hour ago.

"So why did you paint this wall chartreuse? Pop art?"

"I didn't do it," she says, "you did it because Stuart's grandsons were visiting."

"Really?"

"You took them to Paris after a couple of weeks here," she says. "Nathan, he's the oldest. He's very smart—extremely handsome. And Kenneth, who's original, funny. Kenneth may be schizophrenic. He was diagnosed before you went away. You were talking to your friend Vada about him."

"I don't want to remember this part," I tell Laurie. I look around at the kitchen. "And I hate this green."

"I told you so."

"You never tell someone 'I told you so.'"

"My family always does," Laurie says. "It expands guilt to a remarkable degree. You can't plead ignorance."

"Yes, but in L.A. we have no guilt. We have earthquakes, fires, and total destruction, and get to start all over again every couple of years. How can I have guilt without memory?" I ask.

By not calling my mother, of course. So I call, but it's been so long, her phone has been disconnected. This could be to show me how hurt she is. Or because she is gone. The loss of memory is refined denial.

I don't want to ask him. He's playing Brubeck on the piano—"Take Five."

He has that dreamy, pleased expression on his face when he plays, an expression men have only when they're playing jazz or driving new cars, pastimes that require little memory, only composure.

My mother will see this loss of memory as a new act of aggression; having lost my memory, I may have lost most of her life. For who has more of her memories than I—from old Hollywood love stories to the first edition of *Lady Chatterley's Lover* she gave me when I said I wanted to learn about sex—"It's all here," she said. But you can't see the loss of memory. It's the kind of thing someone like me, who craves attention, designs as an affectation. I can also design ways to cover it up, masks and games and distractions (if I can remember I've decided this). No one really needs to know about it.

Stuart takes the memory lag more seriously than anyone because he's lost as much in it as I have. He's kept his journals every day since we met. I go over them to catch what I can so the next moment we are talking or lying together, I can say, as a lover would, "This reminds me of that morning in Èze village at The Chevre d'Or."

Now, I have read this last night and cannot remember the name of the place. So even when I read the journals, I can't hang onto what he's written long enough to use it. Then, too, if I read it and say, "That was wonderful"—whatever it was—he knows I am not seeing the memory, not catching the colors again; the sound of those waves breaking on that shore, or smelling the roses on that one hot day in London in Regents Park. *A hot day in London,* I say to myself, *can that be true?*

I remember so little of who he is or what he does. But he also knows better than I do what I let just drop and what I really can't hold onto.

While Stuart's playing music, I am going through old papers in my changing room. Well-named room; it is here that I become who I think I am today. I have found a note in a child's hand from my sister, Joy, when she was ten and I was twelve. She's apologizing for antagonizing me.

I cannot remember if I've called about my mother. Why should it be surprising, that the hard things to deal with are the most difficult to remember?

"It's been ages since I've seen you," I tell my sister, "so what are you doing with yourself?"

"I'm seeing my clients." She's catching me up.

"Clients?"

"I'm not in real estate, if you're wondering. You know that." She reminds me she is a psychotherapist. "How long do you think it's been since we've seen each other?" she asks. Her voice has the analyst's seductive concern.

"About . . ." Silence. Throw a number into the air. "Five years?" There's a question mark there. "You've been alone in L.A. with our mother," I won't say "my mother."

"Yes." She's not going to pull me along here. "It's okay to say," Joy says, "that you think she's dead. She is. You sent her packages in the last weeks that she loved—some drawings. She thought you were very dear." My sister uses "dear" the way my mother and father do. Or, rather, used to do. I have to say "hot" or "cool." Never "sweet."

"She lost her memory, too—for a different reason—but she wouldn't have known you had been here moments after you had spoken to her," she adds, "so it didn't matter that you weren't here."

Joy is telling me I hadn't wanted to come. I can imagine (if not exactly remember) that she got the hard part. There wasn't that much of our mother to have around, and during the years when I was there, I tore off more than my share.

*D*r. Rudolph sent the test results to Christopher Earl, a neurologist who will interpret the brain scan. I have three attacks on the
way to see Dr. Earl. He's large, with white hair; probably belongs to the
Lords' Cricket Club. I must send one of their cream flannel cricket uni-
forms to Justin.

Dr. Earl is looking over Rudolf's report like a bank manager going
over exactly why your checks have bounced. "You have a focal abnormal-
ity in the left anterior temporal region, which indicates temporal lobe
epilepsy," Earl says. "You were mortally ill." He's concerned I might not
be taking this seriously enough. He also points out, "The attacks can be
brought on by thinking about it or talking about it."

Chris Earl has sent a note to our doctor, Peter Wheeler, who has an
office on Sloane Street, which has so many great store windows, it is possible to forget you're going to see a doctor. I think I'm on Fifty-Seventh
Street until I'm jarred by a New York accent going by with her husband.
You don't notice American accents at home, which is how I can tell I'm
here in London. The same way a Londoner would suddenly notice an
English accent on Madison Avenue.

Our doctor is tall, stylish, and handsome and stands up to greet us.

"Hello, Peter," Stuart says, and I wonder why Brooke didn't call to tell me they were in town.

Peter shows me his letter from Chris Earl. They write to each other using their first names. Chris is an excellent Christian name. Definitive, one might say. They probably meet for lunch, have port and one of those plates of everything horrid you cut off a pig. Chris has written Peter, "One could make out a good case for her taking regular anticonvulsants and I'd suggest Phenytoin, which you originally prescribed."

We leave the office and walk up Sloane Street.

Let's say I have now gathered together some things about my husband which I can lay out, as I do my scarves, in my attempt to say I know him, or know what he likes enough not to bother starting wars by suggesting things to do that he hates.

He doesn't ride the Underground because he's claustrophobic, which is also why he does not do elevators. He doesn't water plants or cook. And he does not eat anything that is not chocolate, or ice cream, or has not been slaughtered or hooked. He's easily bored, and does not believe what is new is automatically interesting. After reading this over a lot, I remember what's missing: he doesn't go to Hampstead. So I don't go. I might think I'm in Laurel Canyon and never come back.

"You think if we walk on Bond Street and Sloane Street, we'll catch the fever for making money," I say to him. "The shopkeepers nod at you, like you're trooping your colors." I take his arm. He always keeps one clean credit card to refresh the self-esteem during dark days.

We stop at L'Express and stand on the steps, looking down, waiting for one of the tables along the wall in the front. You don't need a memory to walk into a restaurant and know the hot tables. This is a sixth sense, or maybe what Daniel Schacter calls "priming." Like you learn your own mother's voice before you're born, you learn what's a good table. To play it safe, never take the first table you're given at a restaurant where they don't know you.

We sit down and survey the menus. I tell Stuart I'm confused and angry that none of the doctors want to discuss the issue of my missing memory. "Nowhere in the letter did Chris Earl say that he liked me, that he understood why I don't want to be drugged."

"Uninvolved medical remains inconceivable to you, doesn't it?" Stuart says.

In L.A., doctors always want to be your best friend, which our family always thought was a good sign, because doctors were very smart and wouldn't be friends if you weren't interesting—or going to live successfully enough for some time, so there would be social benefits. Friends made midnight visits, and free script, and I'm using "script" here in the pharmaceutical sense, not talking about movie scenarios, although some doctors didn't mind putting in a word here or there about a hospital scene—and maybe getting a mention on the credit crawl.

"A doctor should be your friend," I tell Stuart, "especially if he can't fix you." There's an irritating couple of women at one of the smoking tables in back, each on her own phone. You hear them over everyone, making dates with someone else.

This is the kind of place Brooke and Josie and I would go to at home. I order a fruit punch. They have paper tablecloths. I look at the menu. "I'll have a Caesar salad."

He's surprised. "You usually have a Niçoise."

"I decided to try the Caesar." I can't remember the Niçoise. I take out the pen from the—what's the word for it?—in my terrorist jacket—we bought them in chino and white at Ralphie's when we first came to London. They have dozens of pockets and these fabric racks that look like bullet slots, where I keep pens. "I think Brooke Hayward and I sat here the last time she was in town. That was the time a woman came over and told me that one of my books changed her life, and Brooke wondered who the hell she thought I was. I was hurt, but I'd love it if Brooke walked in today. I miss people I actually know." I'm drawing a purple coyote on the tablecloth. "I haven't done this in years," I say.

"Why would you think Brooke would be here?" he asks, but he's more interested in a tall Nigerian model who has walked in with a man out of Hemingway wearing a rumpled white linen suit and a cigar.

"Because," I said, "we just saw Peter—"

"Jill," he thinks a moment, "Peter Wheeler is not Peter Duchin, Brooke's husband, although he'd be pleased by the confusion. They have a resemblance, and you were having lunch with Brooke in New York when you saw that woman. It was Esther Ferguson. Aside from that, it's fine."

I'm not asking who Esther Ferguson is. "I fucking hate this," I say.

"Are we talking about mixing people up or drawing on tables?" Stuart asks.

"Mixing people. I like drawing. I make a drawing of Stuart dancing with the Nigerian model. Drawing is easy now, not writing. It used to be the other way around.

People say we have a happy marriage. This is because if you ask each of us how we do that we say we do it "his way" or "her way." This, I am seeing, is true in the sense we have figured out what matters most, and we each give in that territory. Except in these two places. First, Stuart cannot watch any one TV channel at a time. He says people who do watch one channel at a time have one-track minds. And second, I do not comprehend how you can love family effectively from a great distance, as he seems to do.

We are quiet, watching stylish colonials in black outfits have lunch with their phones.

"And another thing I've forgotten," I say over my second fruit punch, "is my concept of God."

"You have several concepts," he says, "you change them like clothes, which may have been what brought the subject up. Your concepts all fit. You should read Freud's *Civilization and Its Discontents*. It would help you understand where your beliefs come from."

"They're all from movies, don't give me such credit."

"Don't give yourself so little," he says. "I haven't got patience for that today."

"I'll give you a break," I say as we leave L'Express, "let's walk, but I want to walk home a different way." I'd kick pebbles if there were any to kick. "Let's go down that street," I point to one, "I don't remember it."

"We've done it ten times," he says, "there's nothing to look at; you'll hate it."

"Like that movie I wanted to see which I can't remember—and you said we'd seen it a week ago and I didn't like it! And I'm sure we never did see it. But not sure enough to be absolutely sure." I'm standing still, hands on hips. "This is not fair! You asked me where I wanted to go, and I said. And you don't want to. So we don't."

"The reason I walk you on the same streets is exactly so you will remember them!"

"Could you once do something not for me?"

"Easily," he says.

And we walk home fast on streets with no shop windows, not talking.

He glances at me, and I glance back at him. He must feel that our lives will be empty now—made even darker with my blank presence.

I'm not sure I can retrain my mind to remember, let alone to write books.

*T*oday he is walking me over to see one more doctor, an expert on epilepsy. It's busy downstairs. The dentist who rents an office on our main floor is just coming in. Fickling is a tidy little man in a pistachio doctor's tunic. "Back from the holidays?" he says as he shuffles through the mail and gives my husband a quick smile. "Nice day?" By saying "Nice day" to me he means "Are you okay." They all know. In England you express concern or convey friendliness through references to weather or holidays.

"Lovely day for a walk," Fickling adds. "Lovely day" is when it's not pouring. I hate walking.

This epilepsy doctor has asthma. "Ventolin's great," I tell him as he takes a hit from the blue inhaler. Maybe it's magic to have a doctor with the same trouble you have. I don't think so.

"I can't tell you what it was like without it," he says.

Maybe it's not magic. You want a doctor who doesn't get sick, to show you that it's possible. "I can tell you," I say. "Not breathing is what it was like." I also want this visit to be about what's wrong with me. "Could what's happened to my brain be damage from not being able to breathe? Or drugs? I used to take speed a lot."

"You took what?" He's embarrassed. He's not had an addict in his office.

"It was a long, long time ago," I say, "and it started with the Ephedrine. Remember when you could only get it in little packets of bitter white powder? You'd sit there unable to breathe, waiting for the packets to be opened. I was sure I was going to die."

"You can remember that?" He's suspicious; am I in here for some kind of fix? Or am I certain everyone's suspicious of me?

"The memories are coming back in patches," I say. "I've got bits of this. But L.A. in 1944 is not particularly helpful if you're living in London in 1980-something," I snap.

"Especially," he says as he writes something down, "when it's 1992. This has no connection with drugs." He looks at one of my reports again. "I'm afraid it's not that simple. You have always had epilepsy."

"I don't think so," I say.

"It may never have been active, or you may not remember."

"Someone would remember," I say. I remember Carol Steinman had epilepsy. No one wanted to be alone with her. She was never allowed to be with us. You were warned when you did see her not to upset her. She was like special crystal, she just might fall off and shatter into terrifying, shaking pieces.

"At least it will stop now," I say. "The pills will control it."

"They will modify it. But," he inhaled his Ventolin again—he shouldn't use it so much, but that's something he doesn't want to hear from me. And besides, this is a hard thing to tell me—"it won't stop anything." He shifts up in his chair and leans over his desk, elbows on it, hands folded. "Your husband told me you were a writer." He slips a few pages of my records out of a folder.

"I could have told you that," I say. "I remember. Could I see your notes?"

"Of course," he says.

There are ten letters. How nice. One calls me a sixty-four-year-old authoress. Like ten years older than I am. Another one says I'm fifty-six. And here I'm fifty-one. Do I hear another offer? I'll go for forty-nine. And my birthdate's on each one; but then with all the work it takes to learn anatomy and drugs, it's understandable you skipped subtraction. I'm no one to talk, and here we have all different visions and scan results.

"Jill." Stuart puts his hand on my shoulder, I shrug it off.

"Mainly, I want to know if I'll be able to write again."

"I'd like to reassure you," he says, "but I'm afraid that kind of effort will be very difficult."

"Are you saying it's impossible?" I ask.

"I wouldn't make it that important in your life."

Snap my fingers. So it goes. "You're saying I won't be a writer again." I want to hear it, like you want to see the enemy.

He's sad. "I wouldn't think so. First of all, most patients find that any mental stress triggers attacks. Even minor attacks are debilitating and affect the memory. So the more you work at writing, the more stress and the more likely the memory's affected. It'll be very difficult to remember what you're writing. You'll be able to do social correspondence, that sort of thing, of course, but I shouldn't plan any larger projects. You're going to have to remain on medication."

"Maybe there'll be a new medication," I say hopefully. "You never know."

I've always put writing first, scattering my life and the lives of everyone I've loved, everyone I've known, and now it's been blasted away.

It wasn't just me who was hit. It's a restless Sunday afternoon. Stuart's driving me around the city. I try to look as if I've seen it before. He tries to look as if this is something he feels like doing. "It's like taking a dog for a walk," I say, "isn't it?"

"I'm trapped behind invisible bars," he says, "honor, duty, loyalty—and nothing I give you helps."

"I can't help you fix me," I'm crying now, "and I can't fix me—so maybe you just go. Put me somewhere, and go." I can't think where he could put me. "I don't want to be like my mother, where you have to visit." Or his mother. But I never want him to know I'm not crazy about visiting his mother. "This isn't what I want for you, or for my children. Maybe this has happened to show me. Touché. So just take me to the ocean, throw me in."

"London doesn't have an ocean."

"Well, how the hell did you get to America!"

"The city is built on the Thames, you know that."

"I never heard of a city without an ocean."

"Chicago. You like Chicago when Studs puts you on his show."

We're at a bridge over the river. "Let's go to the other side."

"It's the Valley," he says, "you really don't want to go."

"I want to do something else, something different!" Which we both understand is crazy, since just about everything feels different and new. He stops the car and we are on the other side of the Thames, looking out at Big Ben. "I wish I were looking at Manhattan and coming home," I say.

He sighs, impatient.

"Your writing will come back," Stuart says firmly. "Never mind what they say—it will come along in steps." I used to listen to my father talk over story outlines with his writers when he was running the B unit at Metro. They'd cobble together pieces of ideas and characters and things to say, while my mother painted on the screened porch and my grandmother set out lunches of borscht and latkes, coleslaw and strudel. And it didn't seem possible to do one of these things without people doing the other things nearby in silence. I waited to hear my father telling the writers to listen for, what to watch out for, when to go back in time and to come forward. "Mainly," he said, "watch people and you'll see your stories."

Now we're in my dressing room. "I love the way I've put all my clothes out on steel racks, like it's backstage."

He says, "It's because the house was built before closets were invented, and," he does this eyebrow lift, "I have more fun buying you clothes than closets."

"You don't have to tell me if you don't want, but do you have money?" I pull out a smoky gray violet outfit with wide-legged slacks and a radical jacket with a bias-cut asymmetric hem.

"That's a new young designer, John Galliano," he says. "And no, no I don't."

This is a subject I feel we don't like to talk about. "But we live like we do." I pull on a red striped skirt that goes with a red tweed jacket.

"It's a Valentino," the Englishman says, "I bought it for you in Venice."

"I loved Venice," I reply. The suit is out now. You don't have to know that to feel it. But telling him that is impossible.

"You don't remember Venice," he's telling me.

"But I can remember I loved it." I look at him. "We can go back."

"Not so easily," he says.

"You'll see," I say, "we're partners. I'm going to work again. My mind just needs some pushups. You'll see."

It's around here I started the Red Valentino System.

Judith and I are eating lunch. She wonders, "How can you write a book when you can't remember what you're writing?"

"I'll remember what I'm writing—I just don't remember I've already written it or where it's going."

"So don't worry about that. Just write it in scenes as they come up" Judith suggests, as if it's a film.

"Some mornings it already feels as if I'm going through a lot full of spare parts, and I'm saying 'make a car out of this.' And I'm no mechanic."

"So, maybe you'll make an interesting car. Or do you want to whine?"

So I write down scenes and as they go, I remember another piece, another part of my life that works here. Maybe I'll put it in the spare parts lot and wander through at the end of a day, seeing if there's something I can patch it onto.

Now Judith's looking over the pages. "You've got a lot here," she says, "but you must have liked that red Valentino suit because it keeps coming up." So I put a red Post-it note at every place I talk about the suit. Then I check which one I like best. With different-colored tags, I do the same system with almost everything.

"Talent," my mother said, "is the only thing you'll ever need."

"Talent is fine. Then you have to show up," my godfather, the screenwriter Lennie Spigelgass, said.

I'd come to him for money. He told me, "Put on the pearls I gave you for your sixteenth birthday, buy a black dress at Macy's, and go and get a job at Saks selling dresses." I did. That taught me fast that writing wasn't so hard. Talent, for Lennie, for Gore Vidal and all the writers he gathered in his house on Sunset Plaza every Sunday afternoon, was the thing that always came first. They'd envy each other, tease and fight, but their lives were also about their work.

I think of my brain like a twisted ankle. It will get stronger. I will exercise it carefully.

CHAPTER

10

I open the invitation to Ian's son's bar mitzvah and begin to worry about what to wear. This is built in; worrying about what to wear comes before writing, before worrying what to make for dinner.

"I haven't been to a bar mitzvah, maybe ever," I tell Stuart, who is Ian's business mentor.

"Jeb would have been bar mitzvahed. Ask Joy what to wear."

"She'll ask me why I'm worried. Then tell me, just be comfortable."

"So. Is that so terrible?"

"We get an invitation to a bar mitzvah and you're sounding Jewish. Don't do that," I warn him.

One of my friends says she cannot have sex with Jewish men. They are both too familiar and too couched in the emotional vernacular of their own superiority—and of our superiority. We are like their mothers, and they are like our fathers.

"I think I'll need a hat. Navy blue. And high heels. Can I walk in high heels?"

"No," he says. "Didn't Jeremy have a bar mitzvah?"

I am very still. I must know this. Of course he would have. "Well, for God's sake," I snap, "you were there. You tell me."

"No," he says, "I wasn't there. Jeremy was twenty-one when you and I met."

Twenty-one.

At nineteen I married, left home, and began to learn about life.

My mother sent me long, unraveling letters from New York when they moved there just after Jeremy was born. I hated that my parents had left. She was telling me how much she missed home, but I couldn't hear her. I was too busy missing home myself.

Jeremy once said, "Mom, a real family stays somewhere."

I think of families, places, and memory.

When I visited Johanna's first apartment in Norwalk, I remembered my mother visiting my first place, a Quonset hut in Coronado on the Navy base. She cried. I fed my parents lasagna, which my mother-in-law taught me to cook. My parents had never seen lasagna. This was gangster food, and not Jewish gangsters.

One of the first things you do when you marry is to irritate your own parents with details of the new family's life to show you have moved out. I do the same thing now, but to my children and I get at once jealous and grateful when Johanna talks about her husband's immense, supportive family.

There is no precedent for dealing with the new lives of parents. No protocol for accepting the ways of the new family.

Jeremy didn't really talk to me the last time I saw him.

Stuart shows me pictures from the visit and I remember moments. I remember Jeremy pulled a piece of steak he'd barbecued off my plate and finished it. He cannot hate me that much if he bites where I have bitten.

I watched Jeremy listening to his phone. He's a careful listener. Talking and listening is what he does for work, so no wonder he doesn't call. That is how I choose to see it.

I go with Judith sometimes to pick Noah up after Hebrew school. This makes no amends for what I have guessed I did, which is spend money on Mustangs, not on my children's religious education. Joanne will know and will have a way to fix how I feel. Or do I have to find my own trail here?

This bar mitzvah is in Stanmore at the end of the Jubilee Underground, the long north train out of London. We're talking here about a subway to Rye. I think that's what we're talking about. I don't remember the exact twin city.

Stuart has an easier time with his concept of God—which isn't saying I want to give up mine. I'm not sure I can. It's rooted in there, maybe like the eucalyptus tree in front of our house here. It's looking fairly dead, but I'm not moving it just in case.

"Your fight with who God is," Stuart says when I start this discussion, "may be more about your father. It all starts there, but I'm too tired to go over this again."

Why are women never too tired "to go over it again"? This is not a chauvinist remark. It is the truth.

For the first months, long before writing became a consideration, I practiced reading with Agatha Christie. One book a week. Then I'd test myself. Finally, it was two a day. I am a detective. I see myself slinking along the walls of each day, holding up the magnifying glass. Catch the details and the day will stay with me longer.

Just when I think my memory is all there, I hit a blank patch— always, always, always around the kids. Don't tell me emotion doesn't short-circuit memory.

At the temple, the men are wrapped in white and blue shawls, some wear derby hats, some yarmulkes. Ian's yarmulke is navy velvet with silver, his son's is garnet. Stuart sits stiff and upright with the white yarmulke he's been given perched on the back of his head. The men fling shawls over their shoulders with flair like women with those cashmere wraps Valerie Wade is crazy about. Some drape them over their heads.

I'm sitting with the women in the balcony. Ian's wife, Mira, has her long dark hair swept up and wreathed in gorgeous silk roses. We are leaning over, watching the men freely praying, chanting, and wandering. It's an individual process; some face the wall to mourn, some turn around, some in and out, wandering. It's free spirit. No wonder we drive everyone crazy.

"*Zahar*"—I am looking through the thick prayer book in the rack in front of us. Is this Hebrew for memory? The book says you don't just remember. You ask yourself, "For what?" Remember to what avail? Remembering creates; remembering has action; you must transform the past into a contemporary imperative. And remembrance, here, involves a response to right a wrong. I remember in order to desist, to stop doing something. I shall hold our remembrance. I must remember the covenant I make.

The Nobel Prize winner Gerald Edelman compares the brain more to a dense rainforest than to a computer. That sounds lively, full of surprises. "An ecological habitat," he said, "that mimics the evolution of life itself."

So my memory may not be so much pulling up an image fixed by a program as rummaging through antique markets with Judith and recreating images, rooms, scenes from long-gone decades. This makes memory more like the act of an artist or storyteller, something to be drawn up. I don't have to remember things or situations so much as to be able to do the act, to find the creative trails.

In my mother's painting "Hall of Mirrors," you see her reflection down through several layers in a three-sided mirror, like in a dressing room, only she's set it just so you can't see her face. Catching most memories is something like that. There's an image just out of sight. Petits mals feel like that, like tumbling down through a mirrored tunnel of reflections of past events.

I saw my parents' marriage like that as I grew. I never saw it face to face. (Do we try not to see our parents' marriages? Is that maybe how it's meant to go?)

I watch Ian's wife looking at her son. "Maybe," the woman next to me whispers to her friend, "the reason we keep out-of-date husbands is so we can let go of our sons."

My first mother-in-law knew right away her son's marriage to me wouldn't work. "Do you know anything about being a wife?" She knew. She was married five times. She was between the third and the fourth when we met.

She draped the layers of pasta for her lasagna like a stripper. "Can you do this as well for him as I can?" She sat across from him at the table, her eyes filled with tears. The two families dueled for us. Would my father's projection room outplay my husband's mother's exotic kitchen? The best and the worst thing that happened for our marriage, so that it lasted long enough for us to have our children, was that he was sent off to Korea with his ship.

I wrote around ninety letters a month to my overseas husband, and he wrote me back. His distance was also his particular appeal. When he came home from the service, he was back with his mom, riveted by her forceful, hearty seduction. She couldn't know it, couldn't see it. I couldn't begin to match up to her commanding attachment, her jokes, or her lasagna.

I don't remember eating anything that my grandmother hadn't taught my parents' cooks how to make. Each cook would teach the recipes to the next before she'd go, watching, waiting, until they were just right. The main thing that had to be just right was continuity. No revisions.

MONDAY
Roasted chicken with paprika and egg noodles (not to be confused with pasta)

TUESDAY
Veal cutlets armored in bread crumbs

WEDNESDAY
Lamb chops, always with canned petit pois, stylish in L.A. because they sounded French

THURSDAY*
Beef stew and salad (a wedge of Iceberg with Thousand Island dressing)

FRIDAY
Salmon croquettes (same bread crumbs as veal) or filet of sole (Fish every Friday in case the guests were Catholic).

SATURDAY
Spaghetti or hamburgers (our parents were often out),
Or pot roast with latkes, which no one but Grandma ever got right. Which is how she wanted it.

SUNDAY
Deli

*If our parents were not having a Saturday party, then it would be pot roast on Thursday. You had to have it once a week, like you had to have deli on Sunday.

"It's your mother or me. Her or me." I remember my mother standing in their bathroom, screaming at my father. "This is my house, my life." She hadn't realized that my grandmother and I had come back upstairs, slowly, after my grandmother had finished helping Ethel make the latkes. I'd climbed into my grandmother's bed and wrapped myself around close to her body in the ways you couldn't with parents. "Careful of my hair," my mother would say. "Don't kiss me like that," my father said when I kissed his smile, trying to make a perfect kiss in one long take, the way Lana could do with Gable. My father pushed me away sharply, and now I'm not sure what I felt then, although I remember my father telling William Wellman that Lana Turner told him Gable had the best staying power of anyone in Hollywood. "And she knows," Wellman said. Staying power. I thought it meant a guy would never leave you no matter what, which didn't make sense with Gable, who kept changing wives with just about every movie after he lost Carole Lombard.

During the sixties, when I remembered everything with the anger of my fierce, alerted sexuality, I remembered that I felt rebuffed, deeply wounded. Now, with more distance and the deeper perception of time and satisfaction, I think my father was startled and aware enough to see my competitive games with my mother and to catch his own reaction. So he was short with me.

Daughters and fathers, sons and mothers; we captivate each other. We are our own other.

I could drive like my father and cook like his mother. These, my mother thought, were not class things to do. Why be seen driving when you could have a chauffeur? Why cook or take care of children? Some women, she'd tell me later in our long night talks, also think sex is not a class thing to do and they lose their men to women who know sex has nothing to do with class. You don't have to know anything else to have a man you love. She taught me early, I think, to keep me from attaching totally to my father.

In 1968 I moved to New York. Work for me was getting the gig so I could tell my father, so he'd notice me more.

I had no money. My second husband had gone there to find better poker games. I'd been fired from my job and had not paid rent for about six months. Writers I knew all said I'd have an easier time getting work in New York.

I had watched my father with his nephews and with my brother. I had learned everything I needed to know about the most important things from my parents: romantic love, how to use my talents, and how to work a room. This is why I probably never set much store by schools; neither did my parents.

I liked the bits of fame I could grab. Life was superficial, extravagant, edgy. Even after I learned to listen to stable women with strong marriages and strong relationships with their children, I used my "adventures" as party entertainment.

I didn't talk to my children about where we were going or why. I held them close until they showed interest in the outside world, and then I brought that world in on them in my version of their terms. They were my right and left arms, sunny companions. I raised them in the sentimental Marxist style of hippies—a platform I fell off every time I got my hands on money and near a Mustang. Then we became the Three Musketeers, triumphant with our cars.

I rationalized that I had no use for the closed-in temples and the dusty attitudes; God was in the trees, the curves of the mountains, and you could get close to God best driving on those mountain roads in your car.

With the loss of memory goes the loss of preconception, the loss of references. Then, just when I think the door is locked to some area of my memory, I find a key and discover another rocky old road to climb. If I'd seen all of it at once, I'm not sure I'd have made it. To reach some memories you just have to stretch harder, practice longer, then try again. A lot like the laps in that pool. (And I remember the pool even as I think this through.)

The rabbi at my confirmation greeted me with his palms around my forehead as I came past for my blessing—telling me, "I would have given you the confirmation cup if you'd been a good student because of everything your father has done for the synagogue, but you haven't deserved it."

I hated this formal, self-righteous leader handing out his blessings like traffic tickets. I'd been charmed in the beginning, but that day I felt trapped, locked into a framework, my idea of God all twisted around with how much you'd give for the new benches or whether I'd be pretty enough to marry a man who could buy a whole table to the dinner for the man who donated the new wing.

At the bar mitzvah lunch, we are sitting at a table with eight men Stuart knows and only one other woman. "It would be a minyan," she says, "if you and I weren't here."

"Do you have any children?" Sam, the man on my right, asks me.

"I have a daughter, Johanna, and a son, Jeremy."

"That must have been some bar mitzvah, out in L.A."

I'm sidestepping this. "Where was yours?"

"I didn't have one. My father died when I was a kid, which made me mad. I didn't go to his grave until I was around twenty. He died at thirty-four. I had trouble finding the grave. It was covered with shrubs, vines, and dirt. I found a service to keep the grave clean, but I never went back. I think of my father around some of his birthdays. As time goes on, he has a different role in my memory, do you know what I mean? When I was thirty-four, I saw him as he was when he died. I felt as if I was losing an older brother. Later, I felt like I lost a younger brother. It's harder to stay angry with him now that I'm forty, really old enough to be the father of the young man my father was when he died, if you see what I mean. How old is your son?"

"He's forty now." I'm trying to figure out how old he was when I was forty. This is not memory. This is not being able to do subtraction in my head. Using my fingers, I've figured out he was eighteen when I was forty; five years earlier he was thirteen. That was 1971. Rough years.

There's a message from Judith when we come home. She's got a late-night shoot. Can Noah come over? She reminds me when they arrive that he has homework to do.

"Sure," I say, "right away."

"I mean it," she says.

After Noah paints a giant charcoal robot on his stretch of the wall along the staircase, I say, "Time for homework." I never remember saying that to my own children.

"It's always time for homework," he says.

"The longer you put it off, the more time there is."

"That doesn't make sense."

"I know, but that's what you're here for."

Noah needs to see where letters go. I need to see where my chapters go. Not to mention the characters and their situations, which become more baroque each week as I forget what they have been doing.

We're lying on the floor of my workroom. "I need some more marshmallows," he says.

"And I need another Porsche," I say.

"What about one marshmallow?"

"That's it. But only after you spell 'economic.'"

"What does it mean?"

"It's about money. An economic issue is whether you have the money to get the Porsche."

He spells Porsche in an instant. But the Porsche has a picture that makes the spelling stick in his mind. Even in mine. We make a sentence out of "economic": Elephants Come Over Now On Mondays In Coaches. "So, if you're in a place where spelling *economic* becomes a big deal, you can pull out that image like a kind of video of elephants waving their trunks, leaning out of a huge coach as it comes up your drive."

"One of them might toss the Monday paper on the doorstep," Noah says. "The way I spell economic is I use a laptop with a spell-check."

I don't have space in my neurological attic, my changing room, for this, but it is there, trying on image outfits. The elephants are Republican. They are wearing narrow ties, fanning themselves with folded-up copies of *The Wall Street Journal*. Where did I find that?

Noah's ahead of me in some areas. He can tell you where he lives without even thinking about it. But I spell better.

"However," I tell Noah, "I'm working out a system for spelling, which isn't my idea I'm sure, but I think you're going to like it."

"Could I have one marshmallow?" He goes into the dining room to play with my father's antique banks, while I try to find where I've hidden the marshmallows.

Noah's taken down the bank that actually looks like a bank, with a teller there to take your change when you open the door. I pull a chair over to the window. "Hand me the tape," I say. I gather the fabric falling down from the valance into my hand and put it back up with lassos of double-sided tape.

It's four in the morning. I'm sitting on the edge of the sofa in my work-room. No, you can't call Jeremy and go into tough subjects. Such as bar mitzvahs.

I can't find any characters around, no one I know. I set up a scene. They wander in and stand there in Dacron suits, hands limp at their sides, people uninvited to a party they don't want to go to.

I ball up pages. Throw them across the room. I can call that man who copies instruments, objects, or is it genes? He's from Fulbright—or Oxford? Look it up. What's a passing connection becomes a research project. Yes, here he is—John Halloran. He inserts real things into a computer and reproduces them.

I call Jeremy.

"It's four in the morning there, Mom. What are you doing up?"

"I can't write. I think the doctors knew it wouldn't work."

"Don't you remember what Grandfather told his writers? I think I've told you." He probably told me and thinks I'm pretending I've forgotten so I get a chance to call him. That's fine. "I know I've told my writers and it works." Like Lynn Nesbit's, Jeremy's voice changes when he talks about writing. The tone mellows and the beat slows way down. "Just write your characters a letter, Mom, and they will answer." Pause. I can tell he's look-ing at something else. "Is that all?"

"Yes, that's great."

And he's gone, and I forgot what I really wanted to say.

11

"You're not sleeping," Shaw points out. He's come into my workroom around four this morning.

"That's true. I've tried Jeremy's advice. I have written to two of my characters. I have heard nothing."

"They did not have airmail," he says, "it will take time."

"Don't be funny," I tell him, "it doesn't work for you. You are sexy, interesting. Not funny. I would never sleep with a funny man."

I am afraid, I explain to him, that I've been away from the characters too long. "When you make someone up, their presence can just go, like smoke."

He reminds me I never really make anyone up. "Your role models this time are L. B. Mayer and the original moviemakers."

"In a way," I tell Stuart, "it's coming clear. My father used to sit around a table like this with his writers, Millard Kaufman, Allen Rivkin or Norman Corwin, talking characters alive. I'd like to write about a female mogul, a Doris Vidor or Frances Goldwyn, who inherits a studio."

Stuart says, "So just imagine Judith on a ranch in L.A. in the early part of this century.

"Listen," he adds, "I came in to tell you that it occurred to me, if I were a writer and I'd lost my memory, one thing I'd do is reread what I'd written."

"Did this occur to you while you were sleeping? I like being part of your unconscious."

"It was simpler. I woke up and you weren't there, so I knew you were worried about the book. Look at the pieces you've written for the *Times* in the last few months."

Silence.

". . . on teas in London . . . on the new-style country house hotels . . . "

This kind of short past time collapses like an old balloon and flits off.

"You know," he says, "your writing is best the closer you stay to reality. Always has been."

He doesn't need to add any more to this. But he knows I would prefer to spend a lot of time discussing what he means and how to go about it, so he sits down in my Aunt Lillian's old rocking chair across the workroom from me. As he leans back in the chair, one of the lights in the wobbly old sconces by the fireplace goes out. "I thought we had that fixed," he says.

"That might have been the other one." The light snaps on again. "It's best not to notice."

"Fine," he says, which it is with him. He's not drawn to fixing things. He has this toolbox in his changing room that serves largely as a mnemonic aid for both of us: me for putting memory test objects into; Stuart for reminding me how distracted he'd be if we did live in the old house in Connecticut, where it is the custom to fix what is broken.

Sitting here now, Stuart crosses his ankles exactly the way he did when he was four. His mother gave me a picture of him then. As we grow older, we look more like ourselves as children, or maybe we just try to recall all the possible ways we can be appealing. Little gestures and expressions that got surefire reactions. He is not conscious of these things; I probably am when I do them.

"I guess I ask you about every page ten times," I say. "You're very gracious about not telling me when I repeat myself. Or maybe to avoid going nuts, you just don't pay attention. Is that true?"

"That's not an argument I can win."

"I think I see what you mean." I've half-forgotten the question.

But I have learned when I repeat myself on subjects he's bored with.

It's not exactly that I remember the repeats. I recognize disinterest, like animals being trained to go through a maze by electric shock. In this case, the door of interest snaps shut, so I turn to another subject.

"But you're always great about my work."

"This is true, even though you're complimenting me now to keep me here with you."

"I could go over and stroke you, but then I'd go back to bed with you, and I want to work—have to work."

"I know that," he says.

"When did you figure that out—right away?"

"No, or I didn't exactly. When I first met you, you took me to your therapist, to Gloria . . ."

"Gloria Friedman." I haven't called her, I remind myself. I can't imagine why I wouldn't have talked to her right away. I'm interested now, too, that I can think about that and listen to Stuart at the same time. Have I even forgotten how thinking normally works, that it does fold over as you talk?

"Gloria was very wise," he's saying, "she said everything would work out fine so long as I understood that the book you are working on always comes first."

"Did I remember right away that I am a writer?"

"I told you right away. I knew it was what Gloria would have said to you."

"Would have?"

"She died a few years ago," he says.

I look around the workroom. Posters of my father's plays, a drawing of Ethel Barrymore, and a picture of an ancient forest. Did I put all this here in case the memory went?

"I remember Gloria. Mostly I remember she was always there." I think about it. She'd be there, shifting in her chair with pleasure when she had an idea that would help. "You're always here, too," I tell him quickly. Am I here for him? Do I register what he does with a day? Does he know how little I remember of our years together? How many, how few those may be?

"You mainly have to remember work never just jumps onto the page. You have to trust it will come," he says. "It takes a long time, but you've known that all your life." He gets up now, comes over and kisses my forehead. "Your characters are answering you now. I'll see you later."

That the work takes time I learned from watching my grandmother with her knitting. Even before the war, she made dozens—more than dozens—of caps, sweaters, booties, and gloves for refugees' children. I knew how much time her work took and it always got done. Her hands were always filled with wool, or food—challah, knaidlech, matzo balls—twisting, smoothing, forming it. When she lived with us during the war before my father got her a flat of her own in Westwood, she taught my mother to crochet and knit. They'd sit listening to war bulletins; my grandmother would hold up her hands and my mother would take a new skein of wool and wind it around into a tight ball.

My mother's hands were also always moving, across piano keys, sketching, dappling, sweeping a brush over a canvas. "I'll be okay if I don't try to keep my hands still, doing nothing," my mother said, "the lunching ladies do that. They can't break their nails." My mother spent all day in wedgie shoes and blue denim aircraft workers' overalls the studio fitted for her. She'd wrap them over with denim skirts later on; my father hated the actors she painted seeing the outline of her body.

I look up at the top shelf across from me. I have written five books: *With a Cast of Thousands; Thanks for the Rubies, Now Please Pass the Moon; Bed/Time/Story; Perdido;* and *Dr. Rocksinger and the Age of Longing.* One by one I take them down. They all have "I" voices. So, in this way, I should be no stranger.

But each "I" voice adjusts, more or less, to the slang of her time.

The first book was a cheeky, naive little memoir about life in fifties Hollywood. How blind I was. And it wasn't that you just didn't write about those things; you didn't know. I see a smothered kid here in *With a Cast of Thousands,* which was written in 1963. It was right before I burst out. I wrote about the budget my father showed me for his first years, which included entries for gum, cigarettes and writing paper, the R. H. Brothers Tropical Furniture, and the giant Capehart radio phonograph that you'd sit and watch, like Ishmael, the gorilla.

I say in that early book, "My mother was repelled by infidelity, homosexuality and rudeness." Where did I get that? Her closest friends were gay, rude, and played around. I wrote the book for my parents the way they'd want it to be.

It says, "I was a pig about attention—even bad attention was more welcome than none." My mother, I'm saying, knew the threat of boys talking about me wouldn't have kept me a virgin—only what my father thought of me would. I've always had to have an icon, someone my actions play to.

I have my grandmother in every book, from the Witch Neva Sheba in my second book, a fictional autobiography of Jacqueline Onassis (edited by her godfather, whom I modeled on Gore Vidal, a friend of my own godfather), to the Rocksinger with the silver hairbrush in my fifth book (can you have a lover and a grandmother all at once?). Grandma was in *Perdido*. And in every book I talk about driving and hating to walk; right here, in *Bed/Time/Story*, the husband of the time tells me I don't have to take the kids five blocks to school in a taxi. We can walk.

Suddenly I remember "pig" from writing for the *L.A. Free Press* in the sixties, calling cops "pigs." Or was it thinking of my grandmother and "trayf"? I should simply write about my grandmother and her life in Hollywood with my father and his young friends.

I start to run to tell Stuart I've got the story, then I hear him downstairs, alone, playing the piano. Do not smother him. There has to be a time where we can each see our own days. I don't want to think of that.

It may be the next evening that we're lying on our bed watching *A Farewell to Arms* on television. It's a period that moves me, maybe because when I try to remember my parents and who they really were, it helps to go back to their time and imagine the impact World War I had on their lives.

"I think I'll keep this book closer to my parents' lives, research and talk to people they knew, and then make it how I see it. I can't go back to them, so I'm not locked in by the need to get it right. It's a closed story. I know the ending."

"It might be a relatively more urgent idea to look at your own life," Stuart says, "to see how the shifts and changes hit you and your children—and changed all of you."

"That's also a closed story," I say too quickly, because I fear it is. "And I wrote that book— about the woman in love with the rock singer not much older than her kids."

"But you'd tell a very different story now. Your own story is changing as your needs of it change. The emphasis is different. You're not lying, not even forgetting; you're accommodating their own changes."

"Are you being tough on me?"

My writing won't fix anything with my children. What they'd want is for me to understand how they feel. And the years that affected them are the years I can't catch.

This scene from *A Farewell to Arms* is set in a wooden mountain house near water. "It's probably the Adirondacks. I lived there once," I remind Stuart, "the kids loved it."

They came back to me there after living with their father. I made some money, which I spent in about an hour and a half; as if money would fix it. Band-Aids on deep knife wounds.

"It wasn't the Adirondacks," Shaw says, "you lived in Connecticut in a place called Stonybrook, near Ring and Frances Lardner, with ferns and green slopes, pine and evergreens. You liked living by another writer and you said it reminded you of a canyon in L.A. We lived there for the first three years we were married."

"So, was it like this?"

"A little bit."

"Did my father visit us in Connecticut?"

"Yes. You bought the house because you thought he'd love it. You were also showing what you could do. Those were not easy times for your father and mother. They came for Thanksgiving the year before we married, the year before he died. But I wasn't living there yet."

"Why?"

"We didn't want to live together until we were married."

"That was smart—to get the children used to the idea."

"Not exactly. It was to get us used to the idea. I was used to complete independence and you were used to having total control."

As we're having this light dialogue, I am walking through the Stonybrook house, placing my father in different chairs. Light from the skylight falls on him as he comes in and sets down the bag he carries with maps and stuff on the round breakfast table. I've put a Western scarf over the table, which he'll like.

I see my father sitting in the screened porch in that Stonybrook house telling the children stories about when he was young, the way he did with us. But there never was enough. There never is when work takes its cut of your parent's day.

This is some kind of triumph. I am here in London talking to Stuart—and I am seeing my father in Connecticut. I could not do that a few weeks ago, could not layer thoughts of the past with conversation or an awareness of the present.

A few weeks ago? Well, whenever it was that I couldn't do that.

12

I meet Judith for lunch at Villandry, a little restaurant full of rough tables, big helpings of Provençal food and the only perfect raisin challah in London. People in film and the rag trade and people from Hampstead have jammed in here since it opened up the street from where we live.

Jean Charles, the owner, tells us they are moving. "You are having our last meal here."

"I've seen the new place," Judith sets her phone on the table, "it will be very good." Then adds, "I'm moving, too."

"That's sudden," I say.

"It will make life simpler," she explains. We split another piece of challah. "It's on Cesario's street."

"Even simpler if it was in his house."

"I already told you. He's married."

"Then his wife will be pleased when she gets the change of address card."

"I thought so," she says. Before I can tell her I don't think this is a brilliant idea, she switches to a subject that will distract me. "So, are you okay?" she asks.

"Imagine riding horses who go all over the track," I say. "That's what it feels like inside my head."

It's easy to describe. I just don't like living with it.

"Hard for either of us to imagine riding horses," she says. "Let's say a guy on speed."

"Right," I say, "but I can make myself come up out of one of the attacks. I say 'stop it,' and it does stop, the way I'd not throw up, or stop coming," I tell her.

"We all know how to do that," she says.

Starting, I don't say, is the usual trouble.

The phone rings. She hopes it will be Cesario. It isn't. She's quick on the phone. "That's my friend Geraldine," Judith says. "She's trying to get her life together and manage a rock group. Actually, she wants to be a writer. Maybe you can give her some advice."

"Take up skiing."

"Exactly what I thought you'd say," Judith says. "Maybe I should call Cesario."

As I listen to Judith, I am beginning to remember how very much of my life I have spent on the subjects of sex and waiting for the phone call I wanted.

In every stage of life, there is always someone who has not called. Call it a growth requirement. In the First Act, it is parents I was waiting to hear from. What do they think of the drawing I slipped under their bedroom door? Do they like the card I made? When are they coming back from their vacation? (A holiday was when I went with them.) Is that Lucy, my father's secretary, to say he's on his way home?

Second Act. The friend I loved the most; the guy I loved the most, longed for the most, will not call. I didn't go out in case he calls, or she calls. There was a time, in the dark ages, when there was only one phone. My sister and brother were designed to be on that phone, to keep the call I wanted from Caroline Veiller or Paul Sperry from coming through.

This was also a time when I couldn't go out because the phone could not go with me. Not that this helps. No matter how many phones I have, I am on all of them when the call I want is trying to get through.

And when it does, the sharp, funny things I mean to say—all offhand, throwaway lines that show I couldn't care less—are gone. Breathless? Never. I used to get asthma when Paul called. I said it was because a cat had just walked by.

In this Third Act, most of us have more or less worked that out. Or given up. Which is a way of working it out. This does not mean I am not waiting for the phone to ring.

It is Sunday. By four o'clock I start waiting for my kids to call.

Ten, fifteen years ago, I hated to pick up the phone on Sunday. "If it's my mother, I'm not here," I'd say.

She'd know by the way the phone rang that I was there. The way Stuart's mother knows when we don't pick up the phone on Sunday mornings.

I look at the picture Stuart tells me is Jeremy. This is a picture of a good-looking young man with a drill sergeant's haircut. "Tell me he is not in the Marines." He has the stark presence of a guy you'd see in an industry ad. "Industry" means Hollywood. This is on the hard disk.

"He doesn't like talking on the phone," Stuart has explained. "For an agent it is not a recreational activity."

I decide Jeremy is a combination of the characters on *Friends*. It takes more time than you'd imagine for me to get clear that my daughter, Johanna, is not like the Phoebe character. Johanna, I learn by doing phone brunch with her, is also witty, but earthy and stable. She outgrew whimsy by age ten. Phoebe is also not like Jeremy's Phoebe, whose mom, Romi, I decide, reminds me of Jennifer Aniston.

Don't try logic on it, I say to myself when Stuart switches the channel. Just let it be and you won't pine for whoever they really are. I tell myself to assume that my kids have found worlds as well that are even more reasonably real—could I dare to hope, these days, even actually interactive? And what do I mean by interactive?

After living with no memory, writing postcards I didn't send, and rereading my parents' papers, I decide I might write again the same way I learned to do something else I didn't think I could ever do—to live without speed and drinking. I'll find other people who are trying to do the same thing—to write.

"They could come every Sunday, maybe for lunch," I tell Stuart.

"Maybe," he says, but he isn't listening now.

I want the writers' gathering to have something like the feel of the Friday afternoons when John Lahr held his teas at his house on Primrose Hill, before he began to review for *The New Yorker.* Here people like Betsy Blair, Karel Reisz, and Al Alvarez all gathered around the kitchen table.

Betsy and I threw our arms around each other when I first saw her. She smelled of smoke, of the forties, of my mother. She was married to Gene Kelly then, and I remembered when she posed for my mother in ballet tights.

I already knew I had met my first writer as I spoke to Angie Montague at one of Laurie's exhibits. Angie said she was a poet, but was interested in writing a novel about a painter. A tall blonde, she was trembling with the particular fear it takes a lot of talent to get. You have to know how hard it is to be good.

And she understood right away about the memory.

"I may not be able to remember what I read," I warned her, "and I won't remember you . . ."

". . . or what I'm here for . . . ," she smiles, bashful and wise all at once, "when you leave the room and come back in."

"It can be that bad, yes." She arranges her words, speaking in short, careful lines.

I came home one Sunday afternoon after lunch to find Angie sitting in the large rose velvet chair in the black and white marble lobby of our house. Laurie had let her in. I had forgotten this was the first Sunday we had agreed to meet. She had her arms around a manuscript she didn't really want anyone to read.

"I don't want to read mine, either," I said, "so maybe we'll just talk and see where it goes."

We decided to listen to each other read and make comments as we went along, catching when it doesn't sound just right. Then Angie suggested that during the week, she could help me organize the notes for the book about my parents, which Stuart tells me I'd started years before. This is why Boston University sent me the cartons of papers, letters, pictures, and manuscript pages that are in my workroom.

Angie manages to be totally supportive and needy at the same time. After about a week, she could figure out where I'd be if I wasn't at home when she arrived. I don't know I have a pattern, but everyone else does and can usually find me when I've forgotten where I'm supposed to be.

She helps me to set up a chart of scenes leading to the Happy Ending I am sure my parents' story will have. I will pick up an Oscar for my screenplay of this book about my parents. My father will take off his glasses and, with his head to one side, wipe his eyes the way he does. This is not true. My father told me to stay out of his territory.

It is only a few weeks before there are three of us here for Sunday lunch, talking about what we are not writing and reading what little we have. I met Geraldine at a screening at the British Film Academy.

"If nothing else," she says in her gentle Scottish brogue, "this will be a distraction from making unsatisfying phone calls." As the road manager of a rock group, the novel she is writing makes clear that the phone calls might be to the rock star who is married to her lover.

Geraldine has strong shoulders and long legs. I can see all too fast why she appeals to everyone.

"The book's not what I want it to be, but I'm just writing and that's how it is on the page," Geraldine says. "There's something wrong, but I don't know what it is yet."

"It's probably an easier story to write than it is to live," Angie says.

"Especially," Geraldine says, with a wry charm the brogue adds to everything, "since I know it's not going to have an ending I'm going to like."

After three or four Sundays (do I remember?), Stuart asks, "Are the girls coming today?"

"It's not girls," I say, "Mark's coming, too. And so is Judith."

"I don't think that's a good idea," he says. Stuart sees himself as Judith's mentor, and he's probably right.

The only really good idea, for Stuart, is to be alone with me on Sunday. Quiet. But he also understands that I have to collect attachments to hold in the wings. God forbid I should be alone and have no one here to say, if not "I love you," at least "This is who you are."

"I'll take a walk and see you later," he says.

A walk. Of course.

Angie and Geraldine both understand that when I forget things they tell me, it isn't because I'm not interested. As I set out lunch, I let them read a study my sister, Joy, has sent me from the *American Journal of Psychology* on "The Effect of Activity upon Learning and Retention in Cockroaches." Joy has attached a note, "Thought this might be helpful."

"Cockroaches don't like walking," I say, bringing in the bread, "it disturbs their memory."

"That's why there are no cockroaches in London; they'd have to walk." Mark glances at the study. "This is from 1947, before anyone heard of fitness!"

While Geraldine is showing Angie more notes she's written for her book, my phone rings. "Don't," I say to myself, "don't pick up until the third ring." I can't let Jeremy know I'm sitting here, waiting for the phone to ring. Maybe I should let him think I'm not home, that I do have things to do. "No. Pick up the phone."

Pause.

It's for Stuart. I go back to the kitchen. I have turned on the wrong burner, so the chicken broth for the risotto is still cold.

An attack starts. I hold it out there to look at it, the way you'd step back from a painting. Tell it it's just fear. Cut. Rewind.

"Do you want a glass of water?" Geraldine has walked in. I'm sitting at the kitchen table.

I can't answer. I see flickering images of Anatole dancing with Bliss, dappled Connecticut trees. I want to say a name. I can't find the name. Trigger. Roy Rogers's horse. His wife's name. Taste melted cheese sandwiches. Dale Evans. That was his wife's name. Now I see old trees bent by heavy Connecticut winters. Heads wrapped in gauze, the smell of Shalimar, black cords, and steel clamps.

"Isn't there something you can take?" Geraldine puts her arm around my shoulder.

"This Dr. Earl suggested I up what I'm on to four hundred. I would be completely unconscious and stoned, a condition I've worked rather hard to avoid."

"I can sympathize there," she says.

"I thought you might," I say. You can't be the manager of a rock group and not have a deep understanding of drugs.

"Then don't do it." Geraldine says. "You have to think about it as one more risk."

"But there are some risks not worth taking, you know." I can't forget my role here.

"Sure," she says, "but if you know the answer, if there is no danger, it hardly qualifies."

"Could we talk about danger and you?" I ask.

"Maybe another time. You can't believe how exciting it is to know I'm really going to learn how to make my book right."

"We're learning together." I'm careful.

I can only guess at what I teach, which is that even if I did remember how to write, it isn't easy. I've found enough of my own notes to tell me that. I explain that, but Geraldine's glowing, her light green eyes looking sideways.

"I'm already thinking about new ways to remember it, to put it down, that make more sense. Maybe," Geraldine takes a bite of salad and carries a bowl to the table, "just the act of being together, saying we're going to write, builds the confidence in all of us. I can feel a kind of spirit here."

"Oh please," Judith has just arrived, "don't do that." She has an armful of spreadsheets for Stuart to look over.

While Geraldine and Judith decide whether they'll tolerate each other, I start the risotto again. Mark, who drives me around with a black cap on when he's blocked and can't write, comes in with Laurie, who sits observing our gestures and expressions. Mark adds some fresh basil to the salad. He's sad, and I can't remember why.

Stuart has returned from his walk. He talks to his mother on the phone and comes in for a bite to eat.

"She's fragile," he says to me. He deals with all these people being here by talking to me as if they aren't, at least until he decides what role he wants to play in this domestic scene. Will it be Hamlet in the corner, or Henry VIII, the burly and vigorous host?

"We're going to have to go visit my mother next week," he continues. "She told me I haven't been back since I left for America. She can't remember the last time she saw me."

"How disconcerting," Mark says, "to have it on all sides."

"You'd wonder if you exist at all," Laurie says, "if every time you turn around, someone has forgotten you."

"Maybe you should be the writer," Geraldine says to Stuart, "it's one way to keep track of what you want to remember."

"He is a writer," Mark says. I wonder if Mark sees Stuart becoming a martyr, dutiful and trapped.

"And a spy," Geraldine adds. "That's how Jill said you came to America."

"Jill told me he came to New York as a poet," Laurie says.

"Thank you, Jill," Stuart says. "Actually, I went to Washington, D.C., as a writer and got involved with the Army-McCarthy trials. When the trials were over, I saw an ad for a job at Procter and Gamble. I thought it was a writing job. In a way, it was. I got the job at headquarters in Cincinnati, Ohio, and with luck, I suppose, and my distinctive accent and journalism experience, I transformed myself into a man in a gray flannel suit. I was rather successful as P and G's first foreign executive in the U.S. business world."

He stops for a moment and says, "If you're writing a memoir, Geraldine, the reader wants to feel the writer reaching for the truth."

I'm stirring the risotto slowly, the rhythm coming back the minute the wooden spoon touches the pan, swirling the rice through the heavy green oil, adding the broth.

"But our perception of experience is so individual," Mark says. "My memory of today is completely different than yours will be."

"That's why you write your memoir and I write mine," Stuart says. "If you're going to be a writer," he says, shifting attention from himself, "it has to come before everything else."

"I have a friend," Geraldine says, "who's an Arabian horse dealer. He loves my stories more than anything—or more than almost anything."

After Judith leaves, offering to drive Angie home to Clapham, Mark leaves and Laurie goes downstairs. Geraldine helps me clean up. She says she thinks Mark's very sad. Stuart says Mark's partner is dying. They told us when they were here last week. I'd forgotten about that—set it aside completely.

Then, after everyone has left, I tell Stuart, "I hate the doctor I saw yesterday. Let's look for another one. How can I be a part of anyone's life if I can't hold onto what they need me to know?"

He's wondering about that, too. "You didn't see Dr. Earl yesterday," he reminds me, "and you're switching doctors like you do hotel rooms."

"And tables at restaurants."

"That," he understands, "is in the genes."

I am looking at the pictures on the kitchen wall. "What if I have a thing in front of my children?" I will not say "fit." "I'll never be able to take them on drives."

He's patient. "The grandchildren, you mean. There are other things to do with kids than drive them around."

"Teach them how to paint on walls, for example," I say.

"You can if you want," he replies.

Jeremy and Johanna will never let me be alone with their children. I can barely keep track of myself. I don't see any way to look at it that I like.

Stuart says he wants to pick up some more milk. We had some delivered this morning—I can see it in the fridge as he's telling me. He needs to get out. I'll leave him alone when he comes back. Maybe he'll write.

I hear him come home. After a couple of hours, I come downstairs. He's listening to Carly Simon and looking at pictures of a woman. "I'll understand if you leave," I say to him.

"Don't be crazy." He puts the pictures back in an envelope.

I reach for them. "Who is she?"

"It's Carla," he says.

I'm blank.

"Carla's dead. I knew her before I met you."

I don't even remember my rivals. "Well, you couldn't have known her after we met, because I'd have killed you."

"Maybe I was rehearsing grief," I hear him say.

"Maybe you were. Welcome to my family—it's catching. I should have told you. This isn't easy for you." I stand behind his chair, my hands on his shoulders.

"I'm afraid of feeling fettered," he says, "of my world closing in."

"That's why you take all these little walks. Every time I turn around, you're gone on another errand."

"Maybe you've forgotten that I always come back," he says.

"But you come back, nervously, like you'll find me on the floor, biting my tongue, pants wet, eyes rolled back in my head. It can't be pretty. But I do remember you saying, like Churchill, not to surrender. I'm not going to," I say to Stuart, "don't be impatient with me, but I'm not upping the pills. I'll take the risk, and the little attacks are okay. It beats asthma."

My life is about my work.

It's four in the morning. I walk into my workroom. The notes Stuart has shown me are lying on the desk. Reading whole sentences is a problem. Pages are almost impossible. I can't hold onto an idea. "Excessive irritability hinders the correct response." I have read that. Somewhere. Or was that something one of the doctors said when I said I'd kill him if he told me I couldn't drive?

I look through my notes for a character to meet. Then I wander through my mind, like a vacant arcade; faces peer around columns, like characters in a hide-and-seek game. I am at Chadwick, at boarding school. Lennie Schreiber is riding. I am on the ladder painting the mural in the dining room. Then I'm going home in Susan Simon's limousine. She's not Susan Simon now. How can I call a friend and ask, "who have you grown up to be?" I'll call Jeremy. I'm clear on him tonight.

But he'll put his hand over the phone, saying to the person in the room, "It's Mom."

I call Jeremy. I hang up. It's four in the morning. "I'd be one of those crazy mothers who call people at weird hours and say I forgot what time it was," I tell Laurie the next morning as she comes up to fax a note to her gallery.

"But that's when you always call Jeremy," she says, "it wouldn't seem crazy to him at all. In any out-of-line way, I mean."

I remember the feel of that night. I know where it goes in my story and where I'm going from here (most of the time). This is a very big deal. I give Dr. Zilkha credit for this.

I liked Dr. Zilkha right away. A tiny, portly, electric man in a suit and bow tie, he comes out to greet his patients. A child has been waiting before us. "I'm just your size, aren't I?" he says to the child to put her at ease.

It's my turn. He tells me, to put this child at ease, that not only skills like typing and drawing will come back, but writing will, too. "The brain likes to exercise." He is refreshing. He says I must sleep more. "Some animals have sharper memories and learn more quickly when they get more sleep."

"That's all I'm doing," I say.

He goes over my records, "Not drugged sleep—you're on the wrong medication. Tegretol will help, and you will write."

"Did you know," I tell Judith, pleased with my memory, "goldfish and dogs like a good night's sleep. Rats and cockroaches work at night."

I am looking out the dining room window, down into the little mews below, empty, silent, big old garage doors and empty hooks and chains for hanging planters. Lilia has shown me where I have hidden the key to the silver chest. "Madame, you put it up here," she pulls out a chair, "so no one, not even I, will know where it is. Up here no one can see it." She pulls a chair up to the bookcase, stands on it on tiptoes, and lifts the key out from behind the dried flowers.

"And it is here," she says, pulling out another drawer, "we have all the bandannas for serviettes." Serviettes? Yes. Napkins.

"Every color." She's probably right. "Most of all red." They're folded neatly, color by color, in a drawer.

"My father keeps his silk handkerchiefs just like this," I tell her, "each color monogrammed and placed in its own stack."

"I show you something," Lilia says, leading me upstairs to the Englishman's changing room. With a magician's flourish, she pulls out the small top drawer in his dresser, "and here, Madame, the very same." And, true, here are silk squares, each one in its place in the spectrum.

I confuse my life with the lives of my parents. This way, they are not dead.

A woman stands with her back to me, looking in a three-way mirror. She is painting a portrait of a child standing on a tall chair, like a bar stool.

My mother was a painter. Equally crucial was her facial paralysis. Half her face was glowing, expressive; half her face was frozen and grim, the eye exposed, unable to close. I knew she was always watching with that eye, even when she slept, and certainly when I slept. So my mother saw everything. She never missed a mirror or a reflection. She always checked to see if, maybe, it had gone away.

I am on a stage in the halfway land between reality and petit mal.

"Are you all right?" Stuart says it again.

I have had a couple of these things already today, but this one is hard to get out of. I hold on tight to his shoulder.

I can't answer. I'm in this glass bell, a film's stuck. Now the voiceover commentator's at the track: "They're off! The ribbon man's tying her down. The hat's too tight. L. B. Mayer's white house is coming into line. Here's his new wife. There's a runaway horse. Sharon Disney's passing a plate to Nora Ephron and, on the right, we're sliding down the wet ivy, spinning down."

Now I'm back.

"Sit down," he says.

"No, I'm fine." I'm clinging to him. "It's just one of these things—like time flips—well, more like . . ." I try to imagine how to say it as it happens again, to catch it and hold it, looking at it like one of my father's crystal paperweights, from every angle. "Imagine," and as I say this, I think I have said it before, which does not stop me. "Imagine your mind about to throw up, on the verge, and again, on the verge, and once more, whoa, a swoop, and it's one of those loop-em turn car rides I'd never go on and I can see why not now." I've had these things for years. I thought they were leftovers from speed, brain damage you learn to live with. Suddenly, defined, they're scary. Suddenly, I understand they can go further.

"I was reading somewhere—today, I think," I say, "that you don't forget skills, like typing. I wonder if cooking's a skill?"

He's being courtly and careful. "I think it's great that you remember what the doctor said. And you don't have to wonder about the cooking—this you have not forgotten."

The slow swirl of the olive oil into the cream face of the cobalt blue Le Creuset pan takes my mind off the rent. The rental agent, Mr. Barclay, has a crush on Laurie, and I know that because she's the only one fastidious enough for Barclay and it keeps him coming back, giving us hints on ways to keep the house. Are we losing the house? Where does that come from? Don't ask. You never mix money with cooking.

I first thought I'd learned to cook from watching my grandmother Belle make lunches of gefilte fish, borscht, latkes, applesauce, and chicken for the young comics home on furlough, like Red Skelton and Jack Benny, who came on Sundays to pick over her Yiddish stories and jokes, the way the kids picked over the cloaks and hats. They longed to be sexy and handsome, and were stuck being funny. My grandmother directed them like a master chef with a brigade of sous-chefs, showing the moves, the eyebrow angles, how to do comedy with top-of-the-chart grace.

Though my grandmother was a storyteller, my mother was a listener. Stars would come to her studio to pose and tell her their troubles. The wide, high window slanted light across the huge room of warm, unfinished wood, where big canvasses hung and slid into racks and two huge easels, like the gallows in *Tale of Two Cities*, rolled across the floor. They'd choose something from her baskets of costumes and props, comfortable, wearing what they wanted, and feeling like intellectuals—with the smell of paint, with classical music playing in the background, the stars would tell her everything.

My mother started out to be a concert pianist, but when her paralysis hit (was it a fall or an illness?—it was never clear), she refused to go onstage.

"Remember," Joy says, "the night we were watching rushes for *High Society*. Dad looked at the close-ups of Grace Kelly and kept saying, 'That face. Look at that perfect face,' and I looked back at mother and she was devastated."

My mother had studied at the Art Students League and worked their formal technique with ease, like a seasoned chef, slipping in the right proportion of linseed oil to turpentine while she was talking, the way I do when I make a salad. I did learn the flip confidence I have with cooking from my mother, even though she never went in the kitchen, claimed she didn't know where it was. But now she's here, perched on my shoulder, with the golden art nouveau roach holder Gloria Swanson gave her slipped on her forefinger. Ashes always fell into the mix she made up of her paints, she'd eye whomever she had lying on this lounge and squeeze out fresh dabs of fresh oil paint round in a rainbow on the marble slab table.

She'd underpaint in sienna and cadmium white. Then do a sketch in terra cotta, to place the image, then she'd pour another bit of sherry in her glass. "If you only drink Bristol Cream," my mother said, "you're not an alcoholic." And, using burnt umber for the darker outlines, building the underpainting, with shadings of viridian green, molding and warming with venetian red, she'd comfort her models. When I said our governess was crying a lot, my mother painted her picture.

It's late-night lighting: I push the model's chair off stage right.

My mother wheels the easel off stage left.

She returns in a long satin negligee, pushing a door on a frame. She stands inside the frame, holding the door. I am sitting in a pink chair.

My mother explains Milly is "frustrated, so she's seeing Dr. Greenson for a while." I ask what "frustrated" means. My mother bites her forefinger. I pick at the silver roses painted on the pink brocade chair.

My mother is lying back and looking up at the face she hates splintered into rainbow fragments in the crystal chandelier above her bed.

Her bedroom defined *boudoir*. Like their generation of Hollywood couples, my parents had separate rooms. But they didn't do it, they said, for independence, but to be like the East Coast American aristocracy, the presidential families, who did it to be like the European aristocracy.

Frustration was the major issue of the fifties. Unless you'd read *Lady Chatterley's Lover* or Havelock Ellis, my mother said, you most likely had no idea about sex. It's a sad, new kind of frustration to read about women suing men for coming on to them. How captivated we were when Helen Gurley Brown first wrote about our sexual independence. We just couldn't wait to exercise our new freedom to relieve our frustration.

"Frustration," my mother explains, "means she isn't having sexual intercourse." That makes it sound so formal. You'd do whatever it was with your robe on over your stockings. Stockings were important. Men were crazy about stockings, but you had to keep the seams straight or they'd leave you. Chipped nails, messy hair, broken-out skin, all, absolutely all smells, especially there, would scare men off like skittish horses when they see snakes.

But my mother did say that sex was beautiful. I imagined it would be as fragrant and silky as her Juel Park chiffon nightgowns, and might carry with it the thrill I'd get when I'd hear her play thundering moves from some of the great Russian piano pieces.

I remember someone telling me my mother knew nothing about mothering. "She wasn't designed as a mother," I said, "she was designed as an artist."

On those long nights, she'd lean against her pillows, sipping her sherry. She'd drink a few glasses every afternoon at tea time when she'd come in from painting to go over the day's messages with Betty, her secretary. They'd both have Harvey's Bristol Cream with ice cubes. Later, my mother would switch decanters, kept filled all around the rooms she might be in. She'd tell me how great my wedding night would be. I'd get that shiver I got when I'd look at some men's loins during chariot movies.

Grooming was just the beginning, along with thank you notes. You couldn't hold on to anything without writing perfect and fast thank you notes. My father corrected mine. Even the good notes could be better if I said it like this. He could write, even with the gloves he wore because of this terrible rash on his hands. He'd slather them with mason cream every morning, then wrap them awkwardly in gauze, and pull on the large white cotton gloves. I got the rash, too, and wore gloves. It was after that my brother and I had to stop picking our nails. Joy didn't pick her nails. Jeb and I were told we'd get fungus. The Marines coming home from the tropics had fungus. We'd hear the big-bellied planes roaring in late at night. And then the ambulances in the distance, bringing the soldiers to the veterans' hospital off Sawtelle. Every month there were more white-crossed graves.

I'm in London. The writers have left, we're cleaning up. "You did that very well," Stuart says. "No one would have dreamed you had, once more, no idea who the hell they were when they arrived. But I could tell you had another seizure when I was there having dessert with you."

"Don't be gentle just because you hate having them here," I snap. "And these are not—those aren't . . ." My words stumble. It's late. I'm tired, the words are like marbles rolling around. I'm trying to catch them with thongs—no, that's not it—prawns, but shrimp don't fish. Images are off. Tongs. Maybe.

"Don't call them seizures," I'm angry, "they're petits mals." Like petits fours. Charming little things you have for tea. "I don't know why they happen—there's no pattern—what really happened was that I really can't deal with reality. You always say, 'What's the point?' This is the point, to keep adding to the group so I won't wind up reading to myself."

"No," he says, "so you won't wind up in a room by yourself where you'd have to write—not just talk about how you can't."

Stuart goes into his room with the charcoal walls and puts on a new CD Gerry Mulligan just sent him.

When there's trouble with us, it's safe to say I am probably reacting to my parents. That first act of my life is the hard disk. Whatever my memory has dropped, the walls of photographs, shelves of books and portfolios of letters at my fingertips bring it right back.

This may be the next Sunday. Debbie arrives with a bunch of pink roses. Debbie is small. Her skin is pale, her hair and eyes are dark, shadowed, damp, like a child's. She catches a look at the antique toys around the shelves and on the floor and she's okay.

I have reread the note her father sent me before she arrives. He wrote that it might have slipped my mind, but we met at the first gathering of the new Fulbright Commission. He told me his daughter, a writer, was going to study at Oxford the following year and, in the meantime, he knows she would love to talk to another writer about her novel.

"It's nice of you to see me," she says, braiding the fringe on her woolen muffler, "but I'm not sure I can do this."

"I'm not sure what this is," I say, "but you wouldn't be here if you didn't think so."

I remember when I gave my father the book I wrote about my second marriage and addiction. As a father he was horrified, but as a writer, he said, "Welcome."

I liked that. You have to shock your parents to make some kind of leap. But there's the other leap into becoming the parent, the audience—the teacher.

"I have my story here with me," Debbie says. She has this shy persistence I understand. "It's a difficult story," she adds, and looks away.

"About an older man?"

You can't write without sex coming into it (even by an obtrusive absence), and if you're young and female, it could well be an older man. How easier in our world to see it as his intrusion; how much more naturally that moves from the page to the reader than that forceful longing you might have had for a colorful older man in your life.

"An idle guess," I say, "so come in." I put my arm around her and explain that I do confuse things.

"My dad told me," she said, "and you told me yourself when I called you last week."

After everyone else leaves, Judith comes by with Noah for dinner.

"Did you talk to Jeremy today?" Judith looks me over.

"You know I didn't," I snap.

"So why don't you call?"

"Because I don't want to be like that, you know, where the phone rings and you know it's your mother."

"When was the last time I could have talked to our mother," I never called her mom, "do you know?"

And when, I could also say to my brother, Jeb, who has just answered his phone, was the last time I talked to you? But I'll leave that.

"You were there when Mom died," my brother says. He has an "I'm going to tell you a story" pace to his voice. He says hello, and you wait for it to begin.

Dad had that, but with him it was hello and the cut of the story was likely to be, "This is what you should be doing."

The hateful parental role.

"You were there for a week right up to the end with Mom in the hospital every day. Then you had to go back to London, two or three days before she died, which was two days before my birthday," my brother says, "and I was bugged with you, leaving. It was those years after Dad died that I got close to her. Do you remember the scene about his Oscar?"

It's like a set of one of my father's plays: the family scenes he wrote over and over, missing his own, catching the powerful mother, the renegade showy brother, the witty sister, and the earnest kid brother with the big dreams.

This was their apartment in New York on East 70th. Jeremy was organizing plans for the memorial service. My mother made it clear she wasn't speaking.

My father had not made a will. He knew he was dying. As he looked around their rooms in their new apartment, there was both too much to sort out and not enough. That was the hard part.

In the family tradition, he'd spread his money around, helping all of us when he was making a lot. Now, what was left were masses of books, even after the fire, china, crystal, and silver. Lots of bronze and silver engraved awards, prizes, and cups.

My brother tells me how it was.

Mother was sitting off to the side, her neck arched, jaw jutting up, her skin frosted crystal. She was aloof, almost contemptuous. My mother's emotions—her pain and her love—were unique.

My brother stood by the fireplace, watching as we cased the scene. The only thing we didn't want to deal with was Mother. Did my father ever think she'd outlast him? Did she think she would? Or, the question I ask, thinking of her last lonely years, hands crippled with arthritis, not painting, not near any of her children, did she outlast him? These years of my mother's life I don't want to remember. But I do now. They began that day, watching us eyeing the pieces of their lives as we talked about the memorial.

Joy was organizing speakers.

First I asked my mother, "When would you like to speak?"

"I don't want to," she said.

"But you have to."

"No," she said, "I'm not speaking."

Joy was tearful. I detest that Joy can cry. I envied her tears. I hated that I was in such control, sitting next to my mother, who shrugged me aside, keeping me from touching her.

Jeb said nothing at first, looking off out the window. After a long western pause, he said, "I'm not talking."

"But you're his son," Joy said. We knew how much that mattered. My mother used to say, after nearly dying giving birth to Jeb, "I'd rather have died than not give your father a son."

"But you have the name," I told my brother.

"I said I'm not. I don't want to parade around what I'm feeling."

"I felt," my brother tells me now, "I was out of line, but I said, 'it's not going to happen.'"

Mother looked at him. "I understand exactly."

"She saw I didn't want to share it," Jeb says. "'It's none of their business. You do what you want.' And suddenly," my brother says, "I thought, there's something here for me with this woman. And I'm going to give her my time. She didn't want to speak, didn't want to look at it. I should pay attention to this woman. There's more here than I know."

We talked over the Oscar. Joy thought she should have it for her son, Saul, who loved films. I said, "Jeremy should have it; he's in the business." And Jeb said, "The name Schary is on the Oscar. My name's Schary. It's my fucking Oscar."

"So," Stuart says when he reads this, "do you remember what you said at your father's memorial?"

"I didn't speak."

"You did. You talked about your mother. You stood at the mike and you talked right to her, about their attachment, about the support she gave your father, about how much you learned from her about love."

I cringe as he tells me. "I have a hard time remembering good things I've done."

But I see her sitting there, in black, her face like chalk, her expression stark. No matter what I said, the only thing that ever really mattered to my mother was gone.

14

"If you made a list you wouldn't have to go back and get things," Judith points out. She has picked me up on Marylebone High Street after my second trip to the market this Sunday.

"But if I made a list," I explain, "I wouldn't be working my memory." This is one of my favorite strategies. It is not popular with people who have to get things done.

Dr. Barry Gordon has straightforward strategies, advice, and memory aids. He suggests notebooks. I tend to lose them or fill them with drawings and give them away.

I repeat, write down what I want to remember.

I put Post-it notes on things I have to remember so I'll notice them. Stuart's son Philip has told us a brilliant new thing is coming: a watch that has, he says, a global positioning system, so when I'm lost, a map comes up and tells me where I am. This will work if I've written down where I think I'm going.

Be consistent. I always do things in little routines so they become familiar. I brush my teeth with the red toothbrush in the morning and the lilac one at night. Hello. And good night.

I connect everyone to someone else. I try to remember people I really want to remember by setting up a ready-made memory theater: starring them in a favorite movie, putting them in a scene I'm wild about. But then I think of the part and not the person. Nothing works every time.

Barry also says, "The less you worry about memory lapses, the less likely you are to have them."

It's the connections of reflections, of ideas, of concerns that make the point. People I love who really remember me aren't thrown—it's one more quirk.

"The memory you really need can come naturally." Don't, as James Billington, the Librarian of Congress, says, confuse information with memory. The real memories are the emotional connections, like the wonderful song from *Gigi* that I can't remember when the two people once in love, long ago, talk of their times together. They each get the where and the when wrong, but they agree it was wonderful.

I tell stories, incidents and scenes I want to remember, over and over, fast. They will become part of my repertoire.

Learn in small bites.

Have a memory partner. I'm well covered. Susan Granger in Westport, Sandy's in Boston, Holly in New York, Joanne in L.A. Stuart is my memory partner in London.

Gordon also points out, most helpfully, that there may be things I don't have to remember.

I've been holding onto old plots, old addresses, and, really useless, old hostilities. Characters killed off in old novels. I write them all down. Tear them up and throw them away. Put them into scenes I cut. I think they'll disappear.

So I don't, before going on a trip, say, fill my head with packing. I draw all the things I need to pack, put the pictures on the changing room door, and when I think of packing, I can scratch them off. So I don't worry about leaving something behind, I put the list of pictures in the suitcase.

Paying attention: If I don't remember someone, it's often because I wasn't interested. The artist Andrea Tana introduced me to a lawyer years ago named Simonetta. She smokes a pipe. That made me pay attention.

Then I watched and listened to her. I have never forgotten her. (To catch attention, do something no one else does. They'll see you're memorable.)

Where that's all far too simple, consider what the poet Simonides accomplished 500 B.C.E. He'd gone to a party to do the toast celebrating an Olympic victory by a very popular wrestler in town. He left right after giving his poem, only moments before a landslide collapsed the hall. The dead guests were unrecognizable. Simonides had taught himself to fix faces in their setting, as parts of an entire image. So he remembered where everyone had been sitting and in that way identified the bodies. Cicero formalized this approach around the first century, and it was picked up again by the Russian Shereshevski.

For example, I am going shopping. Before I go out, I imagine the things I need really clearly in my mind placed on some particular spot in my dining room: fettuccini on the chandelier, Stilton cheese on the board on the table, foil on the silver tea caddy L. B. Mayer gave me for my first wedding—and so on.

This system works for me when I absolutely have to remember a few things, so much so that I do not throw in such distracting details as how I got the tea caddy and of how many ways Judith reminds me of L. B. Mayer and other moguls. Even on a simple day, like a Wednesday, I can only place and remember seven or eight things at a time.

Sunday is never a simple day for us.

And then, no day is simple since I have been trying to write again. The main thing that happens is angry nightmares about not writing that turn into petits mals. And the writing lies dead. I ask Stuart to listen as I read. My voice does not charm him into lying about the work.

"It's a nice idea," he says.

"This isn't where it will really go," I explain.

"I'm sure," he replies, "it's good—it's different." He smiles.

He tries. I miss my women friends, the network. I look over my friends' books from long ago. Josie had just published her book when she brought me up to her agent, Lynn Nesbit's, office. I think I was wearing the fifteen-dollar midi skirt I bought at Macy's. I take the books down from the work-room shelves, dusting them off, rereading. I remember sitting with Lois Gould in a restaurant, switching chapters we'd pull out of our bags, and I see a big room overlooking Central Park West. Was it Betty Friedan's or Alix Kate Shulman's? The entrance halls were full of roller skates.

We were with each other in the sixties. Or was it the seventies?

Life Signs—Josie had the perfect title. The world seemed ahead of us, we were stepping out into it, out of the isolated kitchens and away from the dreary corner desks into what felt like careers, jobs. Real writers.

Now writing feels like a conceit, I tell myself as I sit in front of a yellow legal pad in my London workroom, Victorian rooftops framing the gray sky. I don't have the smart pacing you get from having an editor down the line, like when I was writing for Helen Gurley Brown. She was a tough copy director, writing advertising copy for Foote, Cone and Belding in downtown L.A. Helen taught me how I could write ninety commercial radio shows for women stuck at home, thinking long and hard about laundry and what to feed the kids for supper; neither of which subjects came to our minds in a given day.

"Do you think I can pretend I am Helen teaching me?" I ask Stuart.

He is sitting at his gray birch tree desk, working. I have this knack for knowing when it is a particularly bad time to start talking about my writing. Always on a Sunday evening, after the writers are gone, when he's got a conference here on Monday morning and he's putting his notes together.

"You act as if you are Helen when you are working with someone else, sharp and organized." He wants me to be sharp and organized and let him get back to his own work.

I like making it easy for people who meet me by talking about the memory problem. That was what I loved about my mother; right away, if a friend of mine came over, she'd tell a fresh story of how she'd fallen or how it happened, an inspiration to me, particularly now. Not-remembering is like situps for the imagination.

This Sunday, Judith is here with Stuart, and Geraldine and Debbie are here with me.

Debbie always brings flowers. She has added this suspense to the group: can she keep her shy distance while turning out these dark, original pages? She writes I fear out of her own memory. She tells me today, when I am missing what I still call home, "Rilke suggested trouble may be guarding the gate to Paradise. Maybe what we miss is what we shouldn't have."

I pull the chicken, roasted golden with sweet paprika, out of the oven, and reach up and take down one of the colanders for draining the fettuccini. "If I learned cooking by watching my grandmother, why didn't I pick up piano by watching my other grandmother teach my cousin, Julius Katchen, to play the piano?" Different part of the memory.

I hand some red bandannas to Geraldine. I see that by piling them carefully according to pattern and shades, I can now remember how many I have, which restores my confidence on days when I forget what I did last night.

"Today I have remembered you don't eat mushrooms," I tell Debbie. I put her flowers in a pitcher and bring them into the dining room. But maybe it's Angie who doesn't.

I sit in the chair at the head of the table in our red dining room. Geraldine always sits on my left, facing the fireplace painted like a merry-go-round by my granddaughter Phoebe and me, looking out on stacks of books on the windowsills, hanging paper masks, mechanical toys, antique banks, carousels, and Shaker boxes. Angie usually sits on my right, opposite the picture of Justin in his Yankees cap and the pine buffet with its parade of tureens and the movie star plates Stuart found, balanced on both sides by Laurie's picture of us looking at each other and her portrait of me seated, writing, with a giant theater backdrop.

Mark sits next to Angie farther down the long oval table, which I've covered in large swatches of dark red Liberty prints to go along with the ones swagged up above the lace curtains on the front bay of windows overlooking the street. Mark is late. And one of the swags needs tacking up. Angie is not coming. "I have met someone." She is very private, but she says "someone" as you say it when it's really someone.

Low early-winter light dances off the crystal chandeliers and filters in from the window overlooking the mews I see from my father's old Early American desk, where his brass student lamp with the emerald green shade lights up my family photographs.

Stuart's life-size plaster ram looks down from one of the big book-cases, all topped with deep thickets of dried leaves, branches of dark red, sienna, garnet, and plum; bunches of heather; and giant bright crepe paper poppies.

The knife, fork, and spoon from Schary Manor, my grandmother's catering place, are framed to my right. This week is more like my grand-mother's Sundays, like my parents'—it's not just Geraldine, Mark, Debbie, and I passing around food and reading out what we've written this week, and then, all so carefully, telling each other what we think, the goal being more about staying with it than cutting it up, although I never exactly said it like that, but you look at any one of us and know that's the deal.

The writing group has lasted longer today because they all have something going in their lives besides writing. Mark's uneasy because Archer has flown off to Mexico City because there's supposed to be a great new treatment for him there.

"Archer's fine," he says. "Did you really like my pages or were they too long?"

"No, really, the pages are fine . . ."

"Archer is not fine," Geraldine says in a low, sympathetic voice.

"He's comfortable," Mark doesn't miss anything, "of course he's not fine. You're right." He turns back to me. "Are the pages only fine?"

"No, no, Mark, they're wonderful."

"But do you really remember them, or is that to make me feel better?"

"I take notes as I read, you know that—you can see."

Before Geraldine leaves, Stuart comes into the kitchen for coffee and Geraldine hugs him. "Sometimes you are both like parents to me."

But "like parents" is not parents. "Like children" is not children.

Have we made up surrogate families who see us as we wish to be—this ideal romantic couple? How do we look to the families we've left behind in America?

Johanna knows the best way to keep me in touch is not to remind me how much farther apart the distance puts us every year. We deal with it by our phone talks, creating a radio series relationship, all neat and chatty, with only a few teary scenes now and then.

Stuart reminds me that Jeremy sent me a ticket to visit him and to begin to know Phoebe. "He made it clear that means a lot to him—for you to be there." I was there, staying with Jeremy in L.A., but I don't remember that trip.

I have come into Stuart's room. It is the twin to the dining room, except it is dark gray, beige and neat. Judith wants to stay to talk to Stuart about her studio and the new ways in which she hates it this week. And Laurie has come upstairs to show him the contract her new gallery has sent over.

This is the kind of Sunday I love—and exactly the kind he hates.

Now the phone rings. It's Archer from Mexico City. "He wishes he could just be here," Mark says.

"Why not," Stuart says, "everyone else is here." Stuart takes the phone.

"He has this infuriating way of talking to people in front of you without letting you know what they're saying," Judith says.

"No wonder. He was a spy," I say

"When did you know that," Laurie says, "or did you just make it up?"

"He was," I say, "in Hungary."

"She doesn't forget what interests her," Judith says. "That panel over the fireplace is really terrible," she points out to me. "You'd have great stones under there if you took it off and put some tiles above . . ."

"Not this year." This year rent is the issue. He'll kill me if I told anyone, but by tomorrow he'll have me convinced we're fine.

"It's not stones," Laurie says, "I have the same fireplace. It's brick-work—hideous . . ."

"Oh, one of your valances in the dining room is falling down," Judith tells me.

"I know," I reply, "and my lace curtains need washing." Suddenly I remember myself telling my mother her silver wasn't being polished enough.

"I hate nets," Judith says. "That's what we call these lacy curtains over here, or did that slip your mind?"

"You're cranky today," I say, "or is this how you are every day and I've forgotten?"

"No," Judith says, "this is unique."

"Yeah."

"The nerve."

"The Cat's in the Cradle" thing is true. In this latter season of life, you do wind up paying for every bitchy, ratty, thoughtless moment. Tough if you can't remember them. The payback itself is usually enough to open the code. I snap my fingers and say, "Oh, this is for that."

15

*M*emory is a series of chips. You draw a card and you can jump a whole stack of chips, or throw the dice, never knowing where you'll wind up or in what piece of time. One great thing about being older than you thought you'd want to be is there's so much more to remember, to mix up and to put back together.

It does not surprise me to be in England. It's a cold pink-and-blue dawn. The rain hasn't come around yet.

When I was a child, one of Hollywood's main concerns as it became alert to the Nazi intent, before the rest of America, was to keep America interested in the war. The government and the military were aware of Hollywood's importance and our lives were filled with people from these worlds; the way the war caught our hearts was in the stories of England, the faces and voices of the English actors who came over as refugees. A lot of their children went to our school, and my favorite teachers were English. England was small, valiant, and had a courtly class system, just like home. London looks like several sets of itself and works like light comedy.

I'm sitting at my father's old desk, looking at pictures of him with Cary Grant. Here's one of them out driving. I call my brother in Texas. "Where were they driving together, Cary and Dad?"

"That was a scene from *The Bachelor and the Bobbysoxer*. Funny movie. Dad played Cary's friend in that scene."

I stay up all night, going over this last talk I had with Cary Grant about my dad, all wound around in notes, the way I do, half drawing, half writing.

I met with Cary Grant on a Bel Air patio, surrounded by camellia and hibiscus bushes.

I arrived five minutes early, so that I must wait—a procedural memory of protocol picked up watching costume movies about medieval courts that screenwriters copied from Hollywood's social scene. Cary, Spencer Tracy, Robert Ryan, Humphrey Bogart and Gene Kelly were probably the actors my father knew best and the ones who were closest to him, from his earliest days in Hollywood. Spencer Tracy starred in *Boys' Town*. My father won his Oscar for the screenplay.

My father went on to be a producer for L. B. Mayer's son-in-law, David Selznick, who was married to L. B.'s daughter, Irene. After my father left Selznick, he ran production at RKO so successfully L. B. asked him to come back to head up MGM's production. There, in a coup by Archer Schenck and the East Coast stockholders, my father was put in to replace L. B. Mayer, even though Selznick warned my father that running a studio which is not your own never makes anyone happy. The stockholders at the Board thought my father would be more manageable, and more economical.

Cary and I talk first about England, where Cary came from "with an acrobatic troupe in 1920. There was a modernity, an excitement to New York," he said. "I met your father first in New York at the St. Regis Hotel. He did a scene with me just before I left for the Coast. We met again in L.A. when Dore was writing for Metro. L. B. Mayer was a moralist and he hated writers, but I always insisted on writers being on the set. Directors never could get the timing right unless the writers were there. You could look great riding the boom with the pipe, but looking like you're directing and directing are two different things."

"Mayer pulled stunts," Cary remembers. "He'd get Dore on the intercom and give orders in a tone and a manner that indicated he had someone in his office, that Mayer wanted to show he was calling the shots. He'd never talk like that if he were alone. Your father told me, 'The son of a bitch has a roomful of people in there.'"

There is no bad light for Cary Grant. With the sun on his weathered tan skin, shadows shape even deeper charm into each expression, if such is possible.

"Dore was sexy," Cary says, "I should say, a sexual man. But, first of all, your father was crazy about your mother; she was the guardian demon. Miriam was the only person I ever had a relationship with exactly on her terms."

"I'm not sure I want to see my father with anything approaching what people call reality," I say. "I don't want to detach from him, to view him with dispassion, or to put him in perspective. I'm not interested in taking him apart. So I'm not current—I won't excavate my parents' lives to answer my own questions."

"I don't think you mean excavate," Cary says.

"No, but you know what I mean. Look, I'm sure there's no more grief in my father's story than in any story of any creative, disarming man's rise to that kind of unmanageable power, but people expect you to come up with dark stories."

"Exactly," he says. "A lot of people in this town resented his goodness. He intimidated some people. He had an almost religious respect for academics. He'd fill the house with academics to demonstrate he was of a studious turn of mind, but they'd be bored to find each other there— 'Where was Lana Turner?'"

Or, which he doesn't say, "Where was Cary Grant?"

My father had the star's way of walking into the room and being the center of it. This makes a lot of people in L.A. hate you automatically, but they know they have to handle it, not fight it or ignore it, or they'll lose out.

It's a particularly difficult thing in a large family. Some other people aren't going to like you for this, but each gathering you do show up for lights up more for your being there. Our family had its share of "A list" types. Their most disastrous impact is on brothers-in-law, or actually any people who marry into the family without taking the status game seriously.

The outsiders, the philosophers, rabbis, and psychoanalysts who came for deli dinners, watched my father as closely as the movies he'd show, as curious about his idiosyncrasy in Hollywood as he was about them. He'd watch them talk, and I wonder if he was saying somewhere to his own father's critical spirit, "See where I am? See, they even listen to me."

"He wanted to be considered the innately educated man. His lack of education irritated him," Cary continued. "He enjoyed giving the academics he had over what they didn't have—and then their education might rub off.

"Dore never saw himself as an employee. But then, L. B. treated Dore like his idea of a son."

His idea, maybe—but then, I doubt if my father knew what a son was supposed to be. His own father left his mother and went somewhere when his business failed—I have the impression it was England. I stop to wonder if my kids see me like that.

My grandfather never sent anything back home except an occasional wild piece of Victorian china. I remember (and suddenly I really do) a giant punch bowl supported by six naked cherubs with garlands of flowers. Three feet across. I loved the punch bowl. The cherubs were naked and "uncircumcised," my mother said with a sexy look.

My father walked sharp through the MGM back lot, maintaining his gait the way he taught us to walk on our hikes along Tigertail. He surveyed his sets like L. B., with assistants keeping up around him and the studio photographer sprinting on ahead, backwards, snapping every exchange. This authority and fast delegation didn't come easily for my father. He liked the reflective pace and shifting concerns of a writer. This is why other writers didn't run studios, and why my father spent a lot of this time in bed on his back.

He had leadership he liked to use; ideal for becoming a producer, as Gene Kelly said, "He was a born executive, not a born writer. Eyes gravitated to him."

Cary says, "I think Dore preferred the idea of being a writer more than actually writing."

"But that," I say, "may be the first symptom of the writing problem." I don't remember how, but I do remember I don't like it and must do it.

"Do you think, as someone said, my father was the ultimate naif?" I ask Cary.

"No," Cary holds his hands up together, fingers touching the way my father used to do when he was thinking something over carefully, "I think Dore found himself in situations he didn't understand because he was either unequal to them, or incapable of impugning any wickedness to other people's motives. Your father was the audience, no less dazzled. He didn't do it for acknowledgment; he believed it. He wanted recognition—we all do. Perhaps, more than anything, Dore wanted congratulations."

We talked about the Sunday nights and the other nights when MGM's head editor, Margaret Booth, came over. Cary was one of the few actors who was close enough so he could just drop over to watch his own scenes.

"Your father started running films at home, and a darn good idea, too. Dore was modern, but he may have had too much imagination to be a mogul. Moguls deal in economics; not that writers or actors can't. Why divorce the actor from the businessman? If you enjoy acting, you'll do well with it. Dore had more of that same knowledge, that streetwise sense you get from actors.

"You know as an actor when someone's real with you. Of the best actresses I had the good fortune to ask for, the best was Grace Kelly. Hitchcock thought the same thing—there was a contact, Grace could listen. Most actresses aren't fully listening; they're wondering how they look. But Irene Dunne had great comic timing, and Betsy [Cary's third wife, Betsy Drake] wrote dialogue very well."

You become so much more conscious of World War II when you live in England, and you're more grateful and slightly protective about being Jewish. We go to Corinne Laurie's for a Sabbath dinner every Friday in London.

I met Corinne at Andrea Tana's, the American painter who has created a Mediterranean garden in Kensington. Andrea knows everyone interesting in London.

I was grabbed right away by Corinne's dry humor and flair. She whizzes around London and the whole world with such snappy style, you'd never guess the grave losses she's had.

Stuart says we have been picking up Corinne's father, Max, for a couple years to go to Sabbath dinner. People our age may be considerate to people who are really old because we're just beginning to see we won't be able to escape it. What I really feel in these months of Fridays is that I'm an expatriate—like Max. Except my family is not dead. I sometimes say being here is the best thing I can do for them. Do they want to deal with my anxieties, fears, and demands, my needy ways and yawning frustrations, which I cover by cooking, drawing, and changing clothes? If I feel this distance from my land, what must Max feel?

When I was young, I never wanted to be near old people. I might pick up mannerisms, fading attention, less snazzy language. Words like "snazzy."

We were stuck in traffic this one Friday and it occurred to me to ask Max if he left Germany before the war. "No," he tells me, just like this, "I was in the German army during the war. It was a terrible time, and to be part of a nation that is doing something you hate. My family went to the camps. They died in Buchenwald." I am wrestling to hold onto moments so I'll have a past—while his whole life is really gone. His gears seem stuck at times. He repeats and repeats a sentence. I stop. Do I do that? Max is living in a recurring cyclorama, old films going around in the head day and night, the suction getting stronger. He shakes his head sometimes, over and over, as if he's stuck in a thick, terrible place. The wheels spin, and I hate myself for getting impatient.

It's too close for comfort. Closer for comfort is when I'm watching Corinne with her grandchildren. As they bring out the family albums, talking together, passing 'round the newest baby, laughing over the pictures, I catch what I've ripped from my children. I am their memory, and as my own memory is gone, so I've taken theirs.

My father's own father told him he'd ruined his business after some of my dad's friends showed up and sabotaged the first catering event my grandfather ever let him host for him. In reading and talking with my cousins, I realize the catering place fell apart in the Depression.

How much of what we accomplish stirs our parents' ghosts? Maybe their disappointment in us isn't the real issue, and what we're remembering are their own big dreams that blew up in their faces.

I spent my school years studying my parents and their world more than anything else. But now, when I consider my father's fastidiousness, which I used to lay on his being a Virgo, I'm sure it had far more to do with the influenza epidemic around the time of World War I. The way he described how it was, in just his house alone, makes me snappish when people call me now and say they've got the flu, when all they've got is a cold.

People were sick on all five floors, my father told us. His mother, weak and drenched with fever, was clutching her new baby, running down the stairs from her room. My father was twelve; he knew that the baby was already dead. Plumbing had frozen. He was surrounded by the stinks and sights and sounds of sickness.

He told us the story when we were kids. And I colored it up for story time at school. I said that all of my father's brothers and sisters died during the flu epidemic and he became a writer after he wrote about them for his mother so she wouldn't forget. Perhaps, I thought, reflecting on my father as he was during the years when Jeb was always desperately ill with asthma, my father wanted to be sure that in her grief, his mother didn't forget she still had him.

The principal of our school, Mrs. Dye, who had lost her own son during the war, called my father to tell him how well I'd done and to talk about what a shattering thing that must have been for his mother to lose so many children at once. My father gently explained to me how important it is to separate what really happens from the story you write and to be careful with other people's real lives; to keep memory and storytelling on separate shelves in your mind, like reference books and novels.

I remember, as I read this, asking Cary if it was true what Ralph Greenson said about my father, that "he was defeated by his own goodness."

"There wasn't anything devious about him. People were accustomed to evasion—it almost embarrassed them. Dore recognized integrity, but he often failed to recognize its absence. That," Cary said carefully, "is how I would say it."

16

"*Do* we fight every Sunday?"

"Just about," he says. "I like to be alone and quiet. You like to have as many kids over as possible."

Last Sunday night I had Tim and Lucy Mellors and their three children for dinner. The kids painted on the walls. I made my grandmother's pot roast for supper, mashed juniper berries for the jelly, latkes, but I did not avoid thinking of Jeremy and Johanna—not for a second.

They liked the dessert of crème fraîche mixed with strawberries, chopped almonds fried up into a kind of toffee with butter and brown sugar, and croutons of pound cake. This used to be severely good—but now it's kind of like eating Sara Lee shoulder pads. Did I cook all of this for the Mellors or for Joanne and Gil Segel? In Santa Monica Canyon? It's best not to talk about it. He knows I invite kids because I miss mine.

He puts down *The Financial Times*. "This isn't a fight. This is how we are. We knew right away there would be times when we'd want to be on our own. I'd want to go hear jazz. You'd want to spend evenings with your kids."

"Did I want to spend evenings in the city and you want to be with the kids? Your kids?"

When Stuart's daughter first came to visit after we told her we were getting married, Susan was as anxious and uneasy as Johanna, but she hadn't the sharp cover Johanna had invented. One day we went to the City together. When families join, it's a kind of ballet; everyone has to do a *pas de deux* with everyone else before being able to join up for the *corps de ballet* finale. Susan was a kid I could never have raised. She has the gentle assurance of a child raised with order and discipline. She follows me around Bloomingdale's peering at me, not the merchandise.

"So why did you decide to be a writer?" Susan asks me. We are having coffee in a cafe on Lexington. The shopping didn't interest her much after all. This made me regard her with a new and intense curiosity. It could be because she was born in Ohio—some women born in the Midwest become serious and live meaningful lives because they do not actually like to shop. A friend of mine said that staying out of stores was a shortcut to excellent sobriety, one she did not expect me to master.

Has Stuart spent time with my kids?

Don't get into this. It is prime fight software. I can feel myself storing it away, saving it for another day.

This Sunday we will go to the movies.

We have been wanting to see a movie called *The Ice Storm* by Ang Lee. We say we want to see it because it's set in Connecticut and because Ang Lee is a great director. As much as I say I want to see this picture, I also avoid it.

So, it's Sunday afternoon. "We can catch the six o'clock in Leicester Square," he says. He looks at his watch. "We'll have to leave by five-thirty."

Our other fight is the being on time fight, a variation that assumes real significance when it involves catching a plane. I've explained this to him. And, as a compromise he doesn't really appreciate, I always let him have an easy win on the plane timing. I am ready at the time he tells me we need to leave, "and this is cutting it close," he'll add. This means we have two hours to kill at the airport, during which we do not speak to each other because the English don't fight in public.

I try, however, to win such other leaving-the-house games, like going to movies in time to see the commercials. They're a fast way to catch up on the best and worst new ideas. Leave too early and there's no suspense about getting there.

I like to go out to see movies, to catch the crowd reaction; as if it's my responsibility to pick up where they get restless, whether the laugh scenes go over. Some of the times, when I was a kid, we had to stay home and watch movies in each other's projection rooms because of kidnap threats from whatever radical political group our fathers' pictures had most recently offended. (This is why they made a lot of musicals.) Some parents would not have noticed if the kids were gone. The governesses and chauffeurs also liked us to gather in projection rooms so they didn't have to hang around with the actual public. I loved to feel the public's reaction to a movie. It was completely different from a projection room or preview reaction, and you could tell if your work really came off. When I was around eight and writing my first short stories, I'd go downstairs to Dottie's room where Ethel and Mabel used to hang out at night and read aloud. They'd tell me what they really thought. Sometimes they'd sit there. They'd rather be listening to the radio and the characters they knew better than the families they'd left behind in the East or the South.

"I hate seeing commercials. They shouldn't have them in movies. Do I need a raincoat?" Of course I need a raincoat.

The phone rings.

"You haven't got time for that." He looks at his watch.

"I'll just answer. Not talk."

He sits down and crosses his ankles.

"Hi, it's Steve. Steve Lewin. We said we'd call when we got here." He has a New York accent. "So we're calling." West Side. Steve Lewin. This could be the name of Erica Jong's new husband. Erica and Steve. A possible combination. "You told us about that little French restaurant you love—we'd like to take you for lunch."

"Sure." I've been in London a lot of years and I love seeing anyone from home. L.A. is really home, but New York's a close second. I lived in New York for a long time before I came to London. It's been three acts: L.A., New York, and London. Actually four. There was also Connecticut. The only difference between really living in New York and Connecticut is when you live in Connecticut, you still say you live in New York—you just have this house in Connecticut.

This man who I've decided is Erica's husband and I agree to meet at Villandry at 1:00 on Thursday. I hang up the phone. Put on the answer thing.

"I'll just call Danielle and make a reservation."

"Do you want to go?" Stuart asks, patience thin. "You don't have to worry about the commercials now."

I was working at Saks when I met Erica. She was small, round and uneasy, with long blonde curls like a girl in a Kate Greenaway illustration. "I'm doing a poetry reading at the Y," she said, "and I need a dress."

"This is not where you need to be." I pulled her aside and sent her over to Norma Kamali, a new young designer I was crazy about.

Erica invited me to her reading and I said I'd written a couple of books. She sent me an application for a grant from the National Endowment for the Arts, which made it possible for me to leave my job and begin writing again.

I'll read some of Erica's last book again before we have lunch—where did I put it? Remembering a line brings the writer, the friend, to life again—for a moment. Erica once told me, "You do not die from love, you only wish you did." She wrote a poem from that remark. Most writers never exactly talk to you. We test lines. You are material, you become a character. Your stories are our rough drafts. I loved living around writers in New York. I worked to keep my dialogue sharp. There was a better chance I could be someone else's character and not have to worry about getting hold of a story or an image long enough to make it live on my own pages.

"Maybe," I'm saying in the taxi to Leicester Square, "I am putting it off because it will remind me of Connecticut." I'm looking out the window of the taxi. "This is a great section of town."

"This is Soho. You were here last week visiting Judith at her office. Maybe," he adds, "you don't want to see *Ice Storm* because you're afraid it will remind you of nothing."

This is true. I don't have to say it. I grip his hand. So much of that last time living with my children has great silent, empty gaps. For my kids, the gaps are filled with people barely out of adolescence, left in charge while I was writing, taking better care of the books than I was of them. If you were old enough to drive, you were old enough to take care of yourself, was my idea—kind of a medieval concept of minimalist child care.

As I watched shots of the dry winter forest of birches, as fractured as the images glittering later through the ice-crusted branches, I saw pieces of those years, images of my children's faces, sunny, laughing, in their cars, at their parties, with their friends, reading, sleeping, angry. How many of those images are from snapshots? How much is gone because of my memory problem, and how much because I can't bear to see how it really was? I catch their anger and disappointment, but in my own voice. I can't always catch their voices.

In *The Ice Storm* there was a seventies key party (which I never heard about in Connecticut), where the women would throw their car keys onto the coffee table and take home whichever man picked them up. This was not a practical idea in Connecticut, because most of the cars would have to be jump-started from the cold. What you wanted was an auto mechanic.

I thought Connecticut marriages would be difficult and resigned, like John Cheever stories. "We don't play Westport," Susan Lardner said, "we're too depressed." Susan and Fred Hellerman, like most of the couples we knew, exchanged dialogue like they were practicing for *New Yorker* cartoons. These were the conversations to master; like duels, you slashed each other with lines about other people, movies, manners, and, above all, how they'd dress, move, and speak. Style was the thing to master.

But in how you decorated your house, not in your clothes. "What are you wearing?" was not a question. "Have you heard from the kids?" was interesting, especially when the kids were six and seven. And always, "What are you making for dinner?" "Can you use an orange quilt as a tablecloth with hydrangeas?" These were the questions we were asking Martha, Andy Stewart's wife, who was not having an easy time, even though she was working and running her house perfectly. You knew she'd rather just stay home and make it wonderful. Martha lived in Greens Farms, open, easy to find, with lots of land.

Erica's house was not so easy to find, Stuart pointed out the first time we went over there together. You're never fond of each other's friends' houses at first. How, you wonder, do I fit into this picture? Not easily.

Erica and her then-husband, Jonathan Fast, were living in Weston then in Erica's big, modern, perfect Connecticut house set on a hillside in a net of trees.

I try to get pointers on confidence by listening to Erica. When she asked Stuart what he was doing, she was the novelist, observing her dialogue and moves. "Now I am leaning over, asking him what he thinks. I toss back my thick blonde hair and laugh. I have a deep-throated laugh and he's enticed."

Sometimes Erica talks like her own biographer—some sentences have footnotes. "I'm doing a speech in the city next week; very much like the one I did in '79 at the New School. It was reprinted in the author's bulletin as well as my graduate newsletter. They published it with a great photograph."

Jonathan's father, Howard Fast, was there. (Howard was blacklisted in the fifties, which makes him something of a hero.) Stuart, interested, asked Howard if he felt frustrated as a former Communist watching America become increasingly polarized.

"I don't think that's true," Howard said. He picked at his food. "The working man has more advantages than he's ever had. I was over at Fleetwood Cadillac last week—any man can go in there and pick up a Cadillac at a very reasonable price. I haven't noticed it's gone up much beyond what it was five years ago."

"Jonathan's very cold and remote," Stuart said, "and Erica can't cook. But she's warm, I like her. Perhaps she can't cook because she really likes to write and she actually does it all the time."

This is something I can't understand. Erica lies awake at night and thinks about her writing—making it work for her. I lie awake at night and think about whether you could make a good jam out of juniper berries. I know I can make a jam, even an interesting jam.

Do most people think like this? Is having an actual memory like being saddled and bridled, or running on a track?

When I drove (am I more upset about not being able to drive than not being able to write?), I liked to drive on Mulholland or way up in Topanga finding dirt road connectors to Mandeville. I used to do rides like that with the kids in Connecticut. We'd just take off, winding way up in New York State, and come back down 59 over near Weston, near Erica's.

Her first husband, Alan, seemed cold and remote to me. Because he was Chinese? Culture is always a good excuse for difficult distinctions. Stuart is more private, more formal; "I don't believe in telling everyone everything." That's English. The land has a lot to do with it. No wonder Americans are open—we've got all this land, and some of it's warm and easy to live in.

I don't suppose, if you asked him, Alan would say that he was just being a stereotype. It wasn't the same with Jonathan. You looked at him and expected Woody Allen.

"He needs to be Woody Allen," Stuart said.

I'm in my changing room, dressing for lunch with the Lewins. I've changed clothes three times. I like American friends to think I am different now. So I won't wear the American frontier-look suede cowboy jacket everyone around here is used to. I put on my Sonia Rykiel pants and sweater.

I'm walking along Weymouth now, which still has the look of Regency England. I'm trying to remember which of Erica's husbands this is. There was Chip Wheat (a fine name for a hero of a story about a cracker). Chip was sweet, but rather in over his head.

Steve Lewin. He could be a doctor, or a dentist, like Fickling.

It is pouring by the time I cross Wimpole Street. It will stop when I arrive at the restaurant. England is not an island, but a small planet around which clouds circle like a flock of slow planes, dropping rain wherever I happen to be walking.

As a Californian, it never occurred to me to walk anywhere until I moved to New York. Then I recognized you could avoid the walking problem by moving to Connecticut. The English do walk everywhere, but London suits me; I can sit on park benches or in coffee places, framing people into incidents. Quick studies with a beginning, middle, and end. Nothing to connect. No continuity, no yesterday, and no tomorrow. There's only today. And most days there's only right now.

My house has a Wimpole Street address, but it sits on Weymouth Street, which goes into Marylebone High Street just below Villandry, which opened a couple of years ago. A tiny food shop/restaurant, crammed with nests of herbs, of mache lettuce, fresh breads in warm linen towels, challah, shelves of jams, cheeses, and sausages packed as tight as the people waiting for tables. It's a triumph. Now the owners, Jean

Charles and his wife, Roz, want to expand. They're bidding for the huge abandoned stable across the road where the Queen's guard used to keep her spare horses.

A small, dark couple out of a Truffaut movie, with wide nervous smiles, Jean Charles is from Paris, Roz is English. They were designers and decided it would be more secure to have a restaurant. We share the same sense of logic. I decided I'd rather be a writer than an artist because I didn't want to be working alone all day. My mother says you never call yourself an artist. Someone else will decide if it's art. My mother doesn't think much of it was. I think I've told her I see Clement Freud at Sagne's every morning where I have coffee. My mother likes his work. I must tell her he looks very much like the cream puff he has.

I had lunch at Villandry a week or so ago with Laurie just after she came up to say her mother died. She was sobbing and I held her in my arms. "It will be okay," I said, "and you forget, you didn't get along."

"It's you who forgets," she reminds me. "You didn't get along with your mother. I did."

The night before Laurie left for her mother's funeral, I was trying to remember if my own mother was dead and if I made up with her before she died.

I am thinking about this as I stand at the stop light.

Erica's mother is a painter, too, and probably alive. Mothers who thrive on conflict live longer. The ones who can say right out "You'll be sorry when I'm dead" don't need to die. My way to deal with this: don't write about it, just write Johanna a letter. Can I learn to be with her on terms not entirely my own? It might help if I was there.

Even though I live in London, I'm probably closer now to my mother in some ways than I've ever been. If I were going to be able to support my kids, I'd need power and a kind of shrewd, speedy toughness I don't see in my mother. My father had it. I tried to stay close to him so I could learn to be like him, not disturbed and fragile, the way I see my mother. But then I was too immature, too crazy, to realize that she had the guts to let me know her as an artist, real, varied, and conflicted, in a way parents don't usually show themselves. I hated her for doing that. I wanted her to just be my mom—consistent and not too close.

My mother is in me in all her ages and images. I miss her terribly. As I wander down the street and pass the windows of estate agents, stationers, and beauty parlors, I see my mother's paintings in an invisible gallery: portraits of the trees in our Brentwood garden, of movie stars in their costumes, of screenwriters, and of the Cape Cod seashore during the last happy summers when my father was writing his plays and they were alone together.

I couldn't have remembered those summers for my mother in exactly that way until now. At first I cast those summers in the fury I felt that they'd sold the house I grew up in. Now I see they had come back to the territory of coaching in summer camps, of theater—the territory of their new romance. The old memories are fixed from the stories they'd tell at dinner during visits from Moss and Kitty Hart.

I arrive at the restaurant and it's not Villandry at all. It's dark olive green enamel; and, like a nightmare room, it's almost empty.

I've done this before, I think. I walk up the street slowly to Daunt Books, a store of travel books built like a giant galleon, each deck devoted to books about a different continent. London is a perfect place to be if you don't remember people. I say, in my quiet London voice, "I seem rather confused." This doesn't seem to surprise them. "Could you tell me if Villandry has closed?"

"Oh, it moved—a few months ago now—over on Great Portland." He checks with someone else in the shop, perhaps to mellow any embarrassment I might feel. "You just walk along Weymouth and you'll run into it. Shall we ring Villandry and say you'll be along shortly?"

"Lovely," I say.

I go back to Weymouth Street, then across Portland Place, which comes down from the Regent's Park Gate, down past the Architectural College, which has its own Pâtisserie Valerie, which is where I will take my mother for lunch if she comes to London. I am planning all of this to make a deal with God: if I'm terrific with my mother, Jeremy will be great with me when I come to L.A.

As I cross the broad road into the new Villandry, I pick up my pace so it appears I'm pressed for time—as if I've just dashed over. I walk into the new restaurant through an enclosed forecourt like a French street market set in a huge art gallery. Baskets of miniature potatoes, morels, pink eggplant, baker's racks of warm olive and European sourdoughs, of challahs crusty with sesame seeds and marble counters spread out with platters of food to take home. You'd come here, I think, mainly to walk through this market. Then I do sort of a Kramer screech-to-a-halt entrance and scan the scene. But Erica is not here. I am late, of course, because I got lost, but they would have waited. And Daunt's did ring— but it only just occurred to me that they didn't have to ask me for my name.

There's no one here I remember I know. Then I spot a couple looking up and waving. Americans who have been here a while like to think we can pass as English, but we can't. We talk bigger, use larger gestures, are more animated. The English do not look up when you come in. The smallish man is standing. He is a potential Steve Lewin. Erica's husbands have been slight. The woman here, although possibly an Erica, is not that Erica Jong. But the tweeds guarantee they are Americans, dressing the way we do when we visit England. Unless we're of the later West Coast school, which wears fitness black everywhere.

"Hi," the husband says, "I'm so glad you could meet us. Great place." He looks around the restaurant.

"They only put the lamps up last week," I say. Since this couple knows me, I can pretend that I know who they are until we hit an impasse and it becomes clear to them I've lost my mind. "The architect is married to a friend of ours," I say.

"You told us last summer," Steve says. "His wife was just moving back to Yale to complete a paper."

"Oh, really?" I say. Would they go on, would they fill me in?

"Were you able to keep your house?" he asks.

"We're wrestling with that right now," I say. When you tell everyone everything, it helps you stay in touch with yourself at all times.

"And how's Laurie?" they ask. So they know Laurie. They must have bought one of her pictures. Yes. That's certainly it.

"Did you call Laurie, too?" I ask the Lewins.

"Yes, we thought we'd look at her new pictures, but she wasn't in. We left a message."

Jean Charles comes by the table. I still don't know Mrs. Lewin's name. I'll introduce them in fast French. Americans assume if you live in London you pick up French just like that. They don't know that the French believe the English have no grasp of any spoken language. The French use sign language in London, as the English do in L.A. Jean Charles tells us three of the lunch dishes aren't available today; he shrugs and smiles. Chaos is one of Villandry's distinctions. "We have ninety-three reservations and, as you see, we serve only fifty-two, so," he shrugs, "you can see how this is for the chef just now. Roz walked out," he shrugs, flings out his hands and laughs. Roz, the chef, is his wife.

"Should I come to the kitchen and help?" I laugh. This is a perfect way out. "I am so sorry," I will say. "I must cook." That way, the Lewins will think I am a little crazy, but have a talent for cooking known all over London. Not simply that I have no memory.

"No, no," Jean Charles puts his hand on my shoulder, "it is not necessary."

"Why would you take ninety reservations?" Lewin's wife asks, putting her glasses on to consider the menu.

"These things, they happen," Jean Charles explains.

This is excellent. We have a subject to discuss for the five minutes after he has disappeared into the kitchen—a subject that doesn't need any precedent. "It's difficult to figure how many cancellations you'll have, and at lunchtime people usually eat faster. But, here, they stay longer. There's more time spent on puddings."

"Puddings?"

"That's what we call all desserts here." I love saying "we" to Easterners. I'd never say it to a Londoner, and probably not to a Californian.

By the time we have finished the little onion tart appetizers, I look at them. "Listen, this is crazy," I tell them, "I don't know who you are."

"Jill," she laughs, "We met last summer in the Hamptons," They will dine out on this lunch.

But then, so will I. Except I may not remember it by the time I get home. "You see, I have a memory problem."

"Oh, we all have trouble with that," he says, maybe worse than forgetting is fearing you are not memorable.

"I feel really awkward here," I say as I look from one to the other. I case her crisp red hair, freckles, rosy cheeks. Up front authority in the fast smile; the eyes work the room with the wily routing of a London Courier bike. "But I don't know who you are—and," I add quickly, "that's not your fault. You'll have to tell me how we know each other." I look from her to him, quickly dipping ciabata into olive oil. "You see, this thing happened—when was it—a few years ago perhaps—and I really have lost my memory."

"So, how's Erica?" he asks when I come home. He's got a meeting on, so I simply say, "Fine. She sends love."

"Sometimes I'm tired of making it funny," I tell him later. "I remembered our first bad fight in Connecticut."

"Really?"

"It was about Sunday. I wanted to have everyone over. You wanted quiet."

"Yes, I did."

And now, too.

In Connecticut, I stormed out of the main little ranch house where he was working, out into the snow, across the yard to the studio house with the bed where we slept. I stamped up the steps to my desk in the loft.

He had called his friend Townie, who listened for a minute, then just said, "You want to stay married?"

"Sure."

"Then do the opposite of what you feel like."

So he took off all his clothes, crunched through the snow in his boots, pulled open my door, and stood there and shouted, "Let's make love!"

And I shouted back, "Fine!"

"Good idea," he says now.

C • H • A • P • T • E • R

17

*T*his is now. We are watching a television show called "Why Men Don't Iron," which explains the radical difference between the way men and women think. Women think verbally. Men learn in action in images, which is why, for example, men are generally better at physics. Women tell you what they think. Men don't. This explains to me, once again and rather better than I've seen it done before, why it is that Stuart doesn't talk about his family and rarely sees them, but really cares about them and thinks about them as much as he says he does. Stuart rarely misses a day ringing his mom, even if they are on the phone no more than a minute—Stuart listens while Hylda tries to find a ramble intriguing enough to keep him on the line, to keep the sound of his breathing there a bit longer. Mothers of sons will get what I am saying here.

Yorkshire life is about work. This is why I understand Yorkshire, where Stuart grew up, better than London.

They once made licorice candy in Pontefract, his hometown, but it's mostly about coal mining. It's much easier to be in a one-craft, one-industry town. Even if you meet someone new, you have a hook for conversation. You fairly well know they'll talk about what happened at work today, and there's always going to be something disastrous in Pontefract.

The community is about work, like Hollywood and New York. In London, society seems to operate outside work. We don't go out with people we work with, and you don't ask people you socialize with what they do until you've known each other quite a while. Work and "society" are separate, exclusive.

Stuart is his mother's star—he's everything she waits for, the point of living this month, this year. His voice on the phone is the light of her day. He calls on Thursday to tell her he'll be there, Sunday, for lunch.

Sunday's her birthday. Mine is the day before. I read in his journals that we were in Pontefract for her birthday last year, too. Last year, he wrote, he gave me the Zodiac scarf. We gave his mother Elizabeth Taylor perfume in a purple satin bag, and a rhinestone heart locket with a matching pin. Stuart had written, "She's eighty-four years old and still has all her silver hair, so I'll have mine, too!" He wrote about talking with his brother and sisters about what to do when their mother got older. "I won't have her sitting in a home, surrounded by people who have forgotten their lives, staring at each other, not having a clue who they are or who they might have been." He couldn't imagine anything worse.

Hylda, his mother, calls on Friday evening to say we never came. So he reminds her we won't be there until Sunday. And this is only Friday.

Then Hylda calls on Saturday morning to see when we are leaving, and doesn't exactly remember who I am.

"I'm not certain myself," I say.

"Can I speak with my Stu's wife then?"

I know she means Margaret. The mother of the children remains the real wife.

Stuart's driving the Jaguar himself to Yorkshire. Mark brought it around from the garage up the street and washed it for Stuart before he took off to the hospital to visit his partner, Archer. Lilia has made a plate of brownies for Archer and a ginger cake for Stuart's mother before she left for her French lesson last night. She also gives me a birthday present, "not to open until the day," it says on the card where she's drawn her own coyotes. I ask Lilia when was the last time she went home to see her mother. "A year and a half. Maybe two years. My sister is the one who wants to be there. So she stays there. I want to be independent." She stops for a moment, then says, "You will be back on Tuesday and we will fix the plants. This is for real?"

"Absolutely," I say, "don't worry."

She stands, watching, waving as we leave.

There is no speed limit on English freeways. Stuart starts at eighty and moves up from there.

Last night I read his journals again to get his family's names right. He writes that he has secretly bought my birthday presents. By the time we leave, I have forgotten what they are.

Hylda will be calling again to see why he isn't there yet. So he asks me to call from the car to say we're on the way.

"On the way where?" she asks.

"To see you," I answer, "I'm calling for your Stu"—get the jargon right so I don't sound so foreign to her, although they don't mind the western American accent in Yorkshire so much. They remember it from cowboy movies. So do I. And I use it.

"Is Stuart coming today?" she asks. She'd have been up at dawn this morning, worried sick he might not be coming, wondering to Marlene, Stuart's sister, how he'd be out so late and gone so early.

He reminds me we always drive up to Scarborough on the coast the day before we visit his family inland, across the moors. Scarborough's like old Santa Monica. We walk along the boardwalk in the moonlight on Saturday evening, eating fish and chips. You need to eat them wrapped in a newspaper to catch the point.

So I understand Yorkshire. But I didn't understand Stuart and his relationship to his family.

Stuart's mother lives like a salty little queen in her cottage on a hillside nest of a village outside Pontefract, whipped by the mixed air of heather, coal, and coming rain. Perhaps when you're old, memory's loss is a blessing. I'm not certain. Hylda's working at being cheerful, but as Sunday wears on she's increasingly lost and sits fingering her handkerchief, watching her family seated around her. The family doesn't visit a lot and they finish what they have to say in a minute or two.

I always start talking and keep at it until I find what I mean to say. But a Yorkshire person decides the one thing he needs to say before he sees you, saves it for the best moment, and says it as fast as possible. Once when we stopped to buy his mother Pomfret cakes and Allsorts on a visit, the sign on the shop's door just said SHUT. When Holbeck Hall, the hotel we loved to stay in fell into the sea, a notice on what remained of the cliff said "GONE."

On these holiday visits, some of us stare at the heater as if it's the fireplace that used to be there, while the men stare at the TV sports until after lunch, when his brother, Philip, comes up from the mines to go with his brothers-in-law and nephews to watch the TV sport at the pub. It has taken a while for me to catch on that Philip the brother is not Philip, Stuart's son, who is blond, lives in Portland, Oregon, and has a baby, Tucker, who lives somewhere else.

Stuart's sister, Lynn, pitched a bucket of water on Philip once and Hylda winked at Stuart and threw him a switch of her sturdy hip. I saw how she must have seemed to him growing up—do you really want a sexy mom?—I saw how it was during the war with his father away for years, and lonely boy soldiers protecting the town. "But I'd lie on my bed at night," he said, "my mother was around twenty-eight by then, and I'd hear her with soldiers. That's when I discovered what to do with the feelings I had."

Philip has dark curly hair; he looks like Heathcliff and stares mournfully at you, so you invent sad stories to feed him of all the young English refugees in L.A. during the Second World War, so many kids on their own. Then I sit with the nieces telling them watered-down stories of L.A. in the sixties, until Philip whispers, "How are you doing now?" We shake our heads at each other. Like his wife who they call Lambsy, I'm from another town and no one knows my family. Sometimes I help with the washing up, but I never want to show my cooking because it's too off the road and you want to play things down when you're a newcomer.

Hylda asks me how the children are—and I know she means her own grandchildren, Young Stu, Philip and Susan. I give her glowing reports based upon my memory of Stuart's talks with them and my impressions of who they might be. Like complex square dance partners, we start in one family, two figures break away, link arms, spin off, form another set, make two more, which break away, and you have all these whirling groups doing the same dance, but related in no other way.

When a driver applies for a license to drive a black London taxicab, he has to have passed "The Knowledge," the rigorous course of learning London's streets and alleys, squares and mews, which one is a dead end, which one changes names midway, and so forth.

It's no less complicated to come into a family.

We are adaptable creatures, the way we can, if uprooted, slide into a new family. After a time, we pick up the ways, the games, and customs, and even catch bits of stories to toss back and forth. A quick memory helps you mime the ways; helps you catch the Knowledge.

All the men go to the pub, except Stuart. He walks with them a while, then comes back. "So," he says to his mom, "where's your bank book?" He sends her money every month. "I want to see how you're doing."

She's sitting in her chair, by the radiator set into the empty fireplace. You think Mrs. Tiggywinkle, but the expression is Margaret Thatcher, which is how Hylda got through the death of one child and raising five others while she was working in a factory, surviving TB.

"Not on your life." She pulls herself up straight and clasps her purse to her breast. The purse all English women carry over the forearm—from the Queen Mother, who will wear it in the grave, to the Queen herself. (How do you tell the American woman? She has a shoulder strap.) Even the Prada backpack you carry on the forearm. Hylda clutches the bag tightly, "You can't look at my bank book." She looks up at him, "Only my son, Stuart, can see my bank book."

"But I am Stuart."

"I know our Stuart," she insists, "and there he is," and she points a finger at the photo of Stuart on the mantelpiece; the young man in his RAF uniform. "There's my Stuart," she says proudly, and looks her son over, "and that's not you."

"That's true," he says, "and neither is this. I asked my wife the other day and she didn't know who I was either."

"You see," his mother looks me over, "I'm right. Stuart isn't married. And certainly not to you." Just to make that really clear.

When we get back to Scarborough, Stuart and I walk on the trail down to the sea, where I sit by the starfish pool with a couple of kids my grandchildren Justin's and Phoebe's ages—I think. I look at their hands and their cheeks and remember the song lyric, "If you're not with the one you love, you love the one you're with."

But it's not true. Family is family, and you feel the difference. I don't know how. It may not be what you'd call memory. It goes back further than anything so conscious.

"Strange family, isn't mine?" he says, by way of comforting me for missing my own family, which he understands and can't do much about right now. "Or is that a redundancy?" We pick up toffee apples and he sits with me for a moment on a rock, looking out over the fishing boats coming in. "My family only reconfirms my gut feeling that families are artificial constructions—they are what you make them. I suppose I've chosen to make very little of mine, so I have very few discernible feelings."

"I see your feelings very clearly. You just don't want to go on about family like I do. To you it's a built-in responsibility. The feelings don't need exploration any more than how you feel about me. You commit yourself to each attachment in a clear, decisive way. And that's forever. It's a balanced, honest judgment of a role." I'm crying now. "I'm not like that at all." I stand facing him on the edge of the cliff, the wind sweeping my hair back off my forehead. I can't hide a lie. "Stuart, I can't give enough, say enough, be there enough. All I do falls short of what I want to give—but 'whither thou goest' I've done."

I grip his hands. "How hard it is for you with me forgetting you on one side and your mom on the other. She forgets chests of the chocolates you've sent, the great hams, the Yorkshire puddings, the strawberry cream cakes, the poems and pearls and all the letters and the love—and even you. I'm sorry, sorry for what's happened, but I'm sorry for my own as well."

We walk along the beach to Alan Ayckbourn's townhouse and then back past his theater to the hotel rose garden which is built on a cliff no firmer than the ones along the Pacific Palisades, a cliff, Stuart tells me as he holds me, "may not be here next year."

And, I think, neither may I.

18

$\mathcal{L}$ ike any limb you've broken, you work it carefully, bring it back slowly, moving as if you're made of glass. Like exercise, I'll do more each day. It sounds simple.

I start by writing one postcard each day to a friend in America. It takes forever to decide which postcard is perfect for which person. And then what I say isn't perfect. "Hello, how are you?" isn't witty. But it's what I see written on the card. "Just thought I'd write . . ."

A helpful friend I don't remember calls to tell me about a girl who had epilepsy and was operated on and now has the two sides of her brain each making its own decision. "And they rarely agree, isn't that interesting?" she says. "I know that isn't what happened to you, but I thought you'd want to know about it."

"Wouldn't have missed it," I answer.

"I thought you'd find that helpful," she says.

"Ever so." If I knew who she was, I would send her the old postcard from Savannah that says, "I've been meaning to write . . ."

Each time I write a sentence, the other side of my mind, the aspect of myself that says, "You never write well in that shirt," says it has a better idea. "Go change again," it says.

I go to my writing table. I fall asleep after every paragraph. Stuart says maybe I should go to write in a place where it is not advisable to sleep.

The British Museum's Reading Room is like an opera house, filled with carved galleries and rows of bookshelves. It's centered with row after row of long tables where you sit up and read the books.

"This," he says, "is where you'll write."

"Don't think of anything else," he says that night as he wraps himself around me, "just write for yourself. Read and write."

I turn back to the L.A. of long ago. This seems easy in England, which shares the same strong class system. The accents remind me of governesses; the galleries of noblemen are like stars' houses with their favorite portraits; the parks are like great Bel Air gardens with an invisible gardener always in attendance. I can't find the finishing fever without deadline tension.

Then one day a woman I've been watching at the library comes over and sits across from me. She comes in every morning, sits in the same place; she isn't so much reading as studying, writing, crossing out, going over words, rewriting. In America after a week we would have had lunch together. Here, after a month, we are nodding. I know by looking at her books that she is Russian. She can see, because we reveal ourselves in a hundred ways, that I am an American. I want her to know that my ancestors were also Russian, so we have something in common. But my families were Jews and chased out of Russia by pogroms of her family's making.

There's an interesting difference between a refugee and an expatriate. A refugee makes me think of desperation and a brave attachment to a world that may not want you, certainly not on any terms you understand. An expatriate's an escape artist, something of a hustler, running from something. If it had been going so well, why would you have left? I think of battered linen suits and endless talks, and tables cluttered with bottles and glasses—even if the bottles are only Diet Coke and San Pellegrino fizzy water.

It has been six months.

Her name is Svetlana. "So," she says one day, "I know you are a writer." She has astonishing long fingers, like bony serpents; she needs to be a star.

"No, I was," I say, "I'm just practicing now."

"I don't think so. And I want you to show me. I want to tell my mother's story. This is important."

"I can't, really." I don't want to tell her we can barely talk, and I can't remember writing—can't hold onto a visual image—writing's even harder. "You should do this with someone who knows you both best. Your best friend."

She touches her chest, and with a sweep of her hand spreads her fingers across my breastbone, "But this is you—you are my best friend."

My mother's maiden name was Svet, so Svetlana is unforgettable. Svetlana writes in English with a strong Russian accent, which is hard to pull off. She has a harder time finding words when she speaks. She smacks her lips, furrows the brow. I'm with her when she loses the word, but I never dare to come up with it; a taboo thing, throwing in someone's missing word. "It's good to let me try, the hard way is how to remember," she says. "Invitation!" she exclaims, "come to our house. I will tell you where it is and you will write it down."

The Englishman is appalled. "You know she's Russian? This is her address, her husband's name is Sergei, and you met her at the Reading Room? These are all excellent reasons for going over to a stranger's house for dinner in a neighborhood I don't go to." The English accent was made for dismissal.

"She's in the theater, works with top artists, and I met her at the Reading Room."

"It's not a café, you met her *in* the Reading Room, and just because someone reads and speaks two languages, you assume she is smart and would make a perfect friend for us. Not for me."

I explain Laurie is also invited. "She will meet people."

"Good," he says.

But he goes, and on the way, Laurie asks what we think about Jennifer, whom she'd brought over for tea. "It's easy to see you're in love," I say.

"But she's clear," Laurie sighs, "she'll never bring me home to meet her parents. I'm Jewish, American, and gay."

"And an artist," Stuart says. He prefers to stay out of these talks when he knows nothing he says will change anything. But he adds, "You'll never keep her in the style she's used to."

"But she's a banker. She could keep me!"

"She won't. She's already putting up limits," Stuart says. "I'd say just have a good time and don't expect her to change, but that's not how it goes with you."

"You're projecting," Laurie says.

"On experience," he says. "That's different."

"Not seeing her anymore is hardly an appealing idea," I say. "Something will work out. What is happening with the new gallery?"

"Not that you're changing the subject," Laurie says. "He's coming back next week with his partner."

"This could be exciting," I say, "falling in love with a banker, and a show, all at once."

"You have lost all sense of reality," she says. "You have to keep her inside," she tells Stuart, "she can only do damage."

Stuart is sitting on a white garden chair next to Svetlana's ninety-year-old mother, shadowed by one of the dark lilac trees in Sergei and Svetlana's garden in Clapham. There are soft potato pancakes, borscht, fish cakes with dill, dumplings, and cucumbers for dinner. Svetlana's mother has my mother's long slender jawline that grows ever more arched to compensate for the posture she can no longer adjust. She is alone during the party, looking grim and desolate until Stuart sits down beside her.

He's talking in the international language of gestures. He doesn't put on acts to the extent I do (hard to do), but this—Poet Revealed—is one of his best. Just the way he was when he kissed Ninette de Valois. He introduced me to her after the ballet one night. He adores elegant older women. "I had a book of hers, the *Penguin Book of Ballet,* and I fell in love with the book." Suddenly, he's reciting Verlaine and quoting *"Dans le vieux parc . . ."* in one sentence, and having things to say about it, too. They patch together a conversation in French. Svetlana's mother is now sitting up straight, looking him up and down. I remember this expression of his. I remember him meeting my mother and the same thing happened. He is good at courting mothers.

But I don't remember how he courted me. I don't remember how we met. The deeply blotted-out patches don't seem to have a form. It's as if

a bottle of ink was spilled from far above; and very occasionally, a bottle
of remover is spilled, bringing something else clear again.

After supper, friends of Svetlana's play Russian songs under the willow
tree with the enthralled expression real musicians get when they play. I
have never seen a writer smiling at work. I am watching Svetlana's friends
and, like the Cheshire Cat in the tree, I remember Michael Tilson
Thomas playing the piano with this same look at Corinne's on a Friday
night. Stephen Sondheim also looked like this the summer he visited with
his mother. Stephen smiled when he played. Not when we took him to
the beach club, a new club, the first one Jews could go to. He went for
manners, a big thing then. And then my cousin Julius Katchen used to get
this glow on his face when he'd come out from Newark to be with us for
his holidays. He'd practice, smiling, on my mother's Steinway. He was a
prodigy and Mr. Chenoweth, our piano teacher, was breathless with
admiration, and Julius would go across the street to visit Artur Rubinstein
for tea and recitals. Artur's daughter Eva would greet Julius at the door,
towering over him and looking at me on my bike like I was the chauffeur.
You'd think Julius could not possibly eat more, but they'd give him cakes
there, which he'd tell us about after he came back home with this same
smile.

"I have a cousin who's a concert pianist," I told Michael when we met,
"you'd like each other, I think." They would hate each other, of course.
How pleased I would definitely not be if someone came up to me and
said, "My cousin is a writer and you really ought to meet."

Michael tried to be pleasant. "A wonderful pianist," he said, "Brahms
especially."

"So then you know him?"

"Yes," I said, "and Julius has a son who is, I guess, really troubled."

"I can think of a reason right why he might be troubled," Michael
said. "Julius is dead."

Stuart slipped in here and gently reminded me about our trip to Paris
to visit Julius's widow, a tough Parisian who had been living with an
Algerian man.

That night I remembered only the widow's legs, bare, tanned ankles in old high-heeled shoes. Tonight I remember all of this as we sit in Svetlana's garden, clouds the shade of creamy tea drifting by behind the poplar trees, black silhouettes against the sky still larkspur blue at midnight.

"You are so low and quiet," Svetlana says to Stuart. Svetlana's one of those women men who don't usually talk will talk to. European women see men's humanity more than I do. If a man caricatured me in the way I tend to do to the men I've claimed to love, I'd dismiss him as a chauvinist.

"Odd days, that's all it is," Stuart says. "I'm waiting for something to break. And Jill's wrestling exhausts me," he adds, and looks at me. "I know it's hard for you, but sometimes it's even harder for me to watch. I wonder, can you handle this? Should you? Maybe this suspense is the feeling you have before dying. Waiting for Godot. Or maybe it's all the deadlines."

"You are both doing this same thing," Svetlana says.

"No, he's been cheering me and everyone else," I say, "his mother, his children. He's planning our next trip and living for next year, the next paycheck."

"Maybe," Svetlana says, "you need to both stop." She looks at us closely. "You are adjusting all the time. No wonder he's exhausted."

I don't wait for him to answer. "So maybe I have to be more independent, whether he wants me to or not." I turn to him. "If I just go ahead, you'll see it's all right."

19

I'm on my knees in this garden in England's long twilight, a choir
singing inside the church, and I'm praying to believe this makes any
sense. A happy voice filled with American confidence has invited me to
come to High Table at Oxford.

This probably began when I got an invitation from Ron Clifton, the
cultural attaché at the American Embassy, asking me to serve on the
Fulbright Commission and to be in charge of selecting the writer for the
Raymond Chandler Award.

To receive a Fulbright was very impressive when I was a teenager.
The grant funded you so you could stay in Europe and work on a particular project. Senator Fulbright set up the scholarships because he'd
been in Europe during the war. He'd realized that few Americans had a
sense of how it feels to live in the rest of the world. We like to torture
ourselves with this, to add it to the list of things we hate about being
Americans so we don't get too grandiose, but not a lot of Slovenians,
Finnish, Chinese or French like anywhere else either. If you can live
somewhere else, it gives you a perspective, an edge, and a new tolerance
for irritation, which is useful.

To be a Fulbright Commissioner was even more of a very big deal.

For four years you'd help choose the awards and go to events at the embassy.

"Do they know I didn't finish Stanford?" I asked Stuart.

"You've written five books and hundreds of . . ." He doesn't need this discussion. He's reading.

". . . of articles. I don't want to hear the litany of stuff I've done again. That's not the point."

"That's exactly the point," he says. "You're bored by that, which means you remember it. Boredom is an excellent sign." He looks at me over his glasses, the right brow gathered up in circumflexes. Where have I seen this expression? Yes. Victoria. Am I always irritating when I'm writing? Even when I'm actually not?

And another problem here. How do I choose the best manuscript for Fullbright when by the time I read one sentence, I have forgotten the one I read last? That's the short-term memory problem. When it's this bad, you don't have what they call a working memory, one that can keep more than one bit of information on hand.

Mine is unemployed.

So give it a job, and it will figure out how to do it.

Handing out a grant for the best detective novel proposal couldn't be better.

I'm looking for the memory. The writers are looking for a university where they can work in exchange for giving a few lectures.

All of us are detectives. However, the mind has its own shorthand. When you're reworking a memory, it needs coaching. This is a perfect project. As I go through proposals of plots, I draw images of characters. Which one comes easier? Who is faster to cast? What dialogue grips me? The project isn't so automatic for me. I bring no preconception to meeting these characters.

The wonderful thing is that certain events are fresh each time. Oxford High Table is one of those. Larry Beinhart, the second writer I chose for the Raymond Chandler Fulbright Award, invited me the first time. He came to lunch at my house last Sunday with his kids, so his wife, Gillian, could work on her writing in Oxford. Noah showed his kids the walls to paint on.

Everyone at my Sunday lunch watched Larry carefully, the way we'd watch new visitors to John Lahr's teas on Primrose Hill. Every gathering you go to has an element of suspense. Will this person show up with that person we all hate? Will he really bring him when he is there? Will she tell that story again, and in front of her? The more of us who were there and the more restless we were to get on with our own riffs, the longer everyone else's chat would go on and the more difficult questions about increasingly obscure political issues would come up.

The elements of suspense at our Sunday gatherings are all about our writing. The routine now is to bring three pages of the same project consecutive to what we were writing the week before. We read aloud to catch if the rhythm of our writing feels true to the pace and tone of our voices. My writing feels like cold cream labels. Does the first page of what I am writing have any connection to the next? Will Geraldine have a rock concert drug scene, a sex scene, or both, and will Mark have a new subplot set in a different Asian embassy this week? Will the sharp new writer Bramley be writing a screenplay or a novel? And will I remember what anyone read last week?

I can't remember who has invited me to High Table this time, but unlike the situation with the person who was also Erica, I can guess it has something to do with Fulbright.

Since I'm wearing my old Ralph Lauren commander's jacket, several Americans at the Paddington train station asked me what time the train was leaving and where is the track for Liverpool. I might just as well have told them, because people I ask say the time has changed or they're not familiar with that route. Americans like to go to Paddington. They think it will be a wise little bear of a station. It's a huge, up-to-date station, complete with a flashy overhead timetable crawl and a cappuccino bar—which in no way affects its authentic eighteenth-century operation.

After maybe forty minutes on the train to Oxford, looking out over the rolling hills and green trees, I think I am in northern California, arriving at Stanford University with my parents in one car and my suitcases in another. I'd been accepted solely on the grace of several short stories. I had no real school background. I'd been tutored at home during the war. I thought it was because of the war. I remember staying overnight with my friend Judy Lewis, Loretta Young's daughter. We went to a Catholic

Church for Mass the next morning. The priest rang a bell and I thought it was an alarm that there was a Jew in church. The next thing I knew, I was in a hospital.

The same thing had happened at Chadwick boarding school. I went out horseback riding and woke up in a hospital. I was told I'd fallen off the horse and had a mild concussion. I remembered riding, moving from a trot into the rocking force of confident canter. I didn't remember much after that, except leaving school (which I didn't mind) and being set up with a program of tutors from my old school who had organized a plan of classes that would, exams permitting, be acceptable to Stanford.

Once there, I couldn't memorize by rote, which made science and math classes difficult. I see now I memorized history by visualizing characters that would disappear as soon as the exam or the paper was finished, but my writing grew in assurance. One day I was out driving, faded out, drove into a truck, and once again found myself in a hospital, once again on phenobarbital, which made me drowsy. I could not stay with the stories my teacher, Hannah Greene, told me were so full of promise. This was a reason I was given amphetamines during the day.

All of these instances of passing out were rationalized, excused and no connection among them was ever made. This was only natural in the time I grew up, when epilepsy was seen as an unmanageable and unmentionable disease, like alcoholism.

So even a visit to Oxford feels like a very big deal, in case I have not reminded you for a moment that I am here, walking up to the gatehouse entry at Corpus Christi College. I'm forty-five minutes early. The gatekeeper says I can walk in the garden. On the way I walk by a chapel and hear singing. I slip inside, and listen to students rehearsing hymns. During a break, I walk along an arcade winding on. I wound my way through lavender, forget-me-nots, sweet alyssum; drifts of mint and thyme softened walls of stone, along with pansies, pinks, and deep velvet sage. Safe here, with the privacy I need to pray, I kneel down and ask whatever force is listening to help me come up with words fast, to be buoyant and fresh, not to sound like an idiot tonight. Prayer works for setting me firm on a course of concentration and helps make me less self-absorbed.

There's a tap on my shoulder and I see a tall, gaunt man, his long black cloak drifting behind him, falling open over a white shirt, a tie, and over that, like a bright weskit, an Andy Warhol t-shirt. "Your friends are waiting for you," he whispers. I follow him carefully to the gatehouse and, with the bravado it takes to be an American in Oxford, I switch on a big smile and meet the Hallorans. I launch into my memory riff, the fast version.

Susan reassures me, "You explained about your memory to us. It's okay. John's here on a Fulbright and we met at the embassy last year."

It was too appealing to be a Fulbright Commissioner, granting the Raymond Chandler award, to point out that I wouldn't be able to remember an applicant's book from one page to the next. I would have to figure out a way to do it.

By making notes, as I read, on what I thought was fresh and interesting—even surprising—and adding up how many times during the reading of a book I stopped to mark that down, I was able to choose the winner. The one who gripped me the most times won.

John Halloran wasn't a writer. As we walk to the dining hall, he explains in what is probably his short riff that he's a scientist. "I'm working on a project where we'll be able to take an object, say this glass"—we've come into the huge, medieval dining hall—"describe it to a computer, which then speaks to a computer, say in L.A., which then creates an actual replica of the glass there in L.A."

"John's particularly happy," Susan says, "because he's been working with sculptors, and the latest thing," they beamed at each other, "is you can take a bone that's been crushed, a jawbone for example, and create a new one to replace it."

I turn to the man on my other side, James Griffin, and ask what he does. "I'm a philosopher," he says with sort of a challenge in his voice. I looked him over. He's said it maybe five thousand times in his long life and has seen this blank look, likely followed by "Oh," and a quick switch to the weather.

"What's your philosophy? Or do you teach all of them?" I ask.

"I'm a philosopher of values."

"That's difficult right now, to find any to think about," I say. "Is it likely that since my values have changed since I was in my thirties, I will shift my memories to suit my values?"

"Possibly," he says, "and you may not be aware you're making that shift, since you may not remember what your values were."

I stop eating the comforting roast lamb, served this way since the beginning of time, and look at James. "You're an American."

"Yes," he says, "they're fond of us here, if we keep a low profile. I've written forty books and the university's published all of them. I've been here a very long time."

I've been watching the new writer, Anatole's daughter, Bliss Broyard, all evening. I can't believe she doesn't know me, but perhaps Sandy, her mother, has told her about the memory and she may not want to embarrass me.

We move to another room for dessert, where James says, "If you like, I'll introduce you to the young woman you have been watching all evening."

It's not Bliss. It's Andrea Ashworth, whose stark violent memoir, *Once in the House on Fire,* has just been published. A friend of mine, Laura Roman, a junior fellow at Oxford, said, "You have to. Yes."

Andrea's complex story about her parents, her battle to get away to Oxford grabs me. "My memory holds when it sees what it wants," I tell Andrea, "and what I want is to read more, to catch that force you have."

I don't want to leave Oxford. "I think if someone gave me a course to teach and a room with a bed and a desk, I'd stay," I say as we move for the dinner's third act to the sitting room for coffee.

"What would you teach?" James Griffin asks.

"Hollywood myths and legends—the fictional history of America as seen through its filmmakers' eyes. Something like that," I answer.

That's not what I'd teach at all, I think, standing now in the Oxford station just before midnight surrounded by loud, crazy students bashing each other around. This isn't the Oxford you have in mind, I tell myself as I duck to miss a flying bottle. I'd teach the art of memory. That's what I'd teach.

I think of John Halloran's great new magic trick. I can do that. I can take this evening, put it in my particular mind and it will disappear. Voilà! Or come out in such a way that no one who was there will recognize it at all.

20

*J*ames Griffin, the philosopher I sat next to at the Oxford High Table dinner, wrote me a note, suggesting that I visit Dr. Martin Davies, a philosopher with an office in one of the psychology departments at Oxford.

When the train stops in Oxford, I don't look at the note I'd made myself because I know I remember where I'm going. So I take a taxi to the wrong college, where a girl from Texas who went to Yale tells me where I should be—not Christ Church this time, but Corpus Christi College, one of the smallest colleges in Oxford.

I follow Dr. Davies through a warren of crannies and up several flights of steps to an office with a small table for six and a few hard chairs and one easy velvet chair.

"James Griffin has the impression I work in memory," Dr. Davies begins, "because I have an interest in acquired language." I wonder if acquired language is one you buy when you forget your own. I keep this confusion to myself. He continues, "A philosopher such as James has an interest in perception, which is how we learn about the world now. Memory, of course, is how we learn about the past."

Martin Davies has a lot of thick, dark curly hair that he keeps lacquered down, a mustache, sharp eyes, and the eagerness of the ten-year-old just discovering his genius, the ten-year-old who keeps his delight at it.

He presents each comment like an unsettled idea he's heard something vague about. Then, as you listen, you pick up that it's a major new theory he's learned everything about. "To begin with," he explains, "there are two kinds of memory. The first is semantic, or factual, where you know the meaning of things without any memory of how you learned it; as in 'a rose should smell like this.' The second is episodic, as in, 'I became uneasy with dogs when my mother's dog bit me when I was four years old.' You learn because of a specific event."

"For example," I say, "I love this garden because I was in my new bare sundress, sitting up in this olive tree, looking out over the pool, when Clark Gable came through the gate to see my father? Is that what you'd call episodic?"

"Colorful episodic, a perfect example," he says. "It's also called a memory of particulars."

"So, I may be learning something here. A semantic memory might be that I love sitting in olive trees. Or am I confused?"

"No, your memory of association may be gone, but your aesthetic–or neurological–memory is there," he says. "You'll remember, say, that olive trees have a sultry charm to them, a protective, romantic glamour, and I like sitting here."

"So we're both fond of sitting in olive trees," I smile. And, now, as I write this, I remember it wasn't me seeing Clark Gable, but my friend Judy Lewis. This was the story she told me. The story I wrote about in *Perdido*.

"If someone has no memory of dates or events, such a person would have difficulty having any concept of a past." He looks me over.

"I may be almost such a person," I say. "Would it help to restore my memory if I were smarter, or are there exercises, things I can learn?"

"I wouldn't confuse memory with intelligence," he says, "although I suppose if you have a high IQ, you'll devise new skills to hold and retrieve information—if, that is, your skills are okay. You can refer to skills, or routine tasks, as hard-disk memory, although I prefer the term 'procedures' instead of 'skill.' Sometimes we don't even know we keep them. You might be asked, 'Can you type?' and you'll say 'No,' but put a typewriter here and you'll be able to do just fine. Sometimes short-term memories are important enough to put into the stacks."

"Like in the Bodleian Library?"

"Exactly. Some people remember everything so firmly that there isn't room for a new idea. There are people," he likes this idea, "who speculate that because autistics don't always see how things work together, they're able to break out of their mindsets more freely."

"You know, I couldn't recognize my husband at first. Now, sometimes when I see him after a couple of hours away—like when I come home from Oxford this evening—I'll be startled by him. Is that odd?"

"No," he flutters his hand, dismissing the seriousness of the condition, "you at least see the problem. One patient was so bad, I'd have her take the tests, she'd fail miserably," he's laughing now, "forget how badly she'd done, and talk about how good her memory was!

"Here," he says, "try this. Take three letters of the alphabet and hold them in your mind."

"Okay, S, Q, and R."

"Now, count backward from thirty."

It works. I'm pleased. I've remembered the letters.

"Like any exercise," he says, "it doesn't seem to have a point until you need it." He's quiet for a minute, going through files of ideas in his mind, like the piles of books and papers scattered around the room. Then he continues.

"There's a book about face recognition by Vicky Bruce and Andy Young, published by Oxford University Press, that's tied in with an exhibit of faces at the Scottish Gallery. You'll find memory's information there, like in the Bodleian.

"There are two systems of recognition, the first of which is 'who is it.' Face recognition may have a separate neurological system. Even though sometimes faces go and stay gone, they may also come back."

What he's said means, of course, it goes both ways, but he didn't want me to be discouraged. "That's one system of recognition, 'who is it.'"

"Then," he says, "there's the second system of recognition, 'how do I feel about it.' You might not know it is your husband, but you know how it feels. And there's another thing," and this interests him. "It looks like your husband, but you don't feel what you expect to feel. Someone's taken your husband away and they've put this ringer here. I remember a case like that. This woman believed a robot had been put in the place of the person she loved. It became pathological. To prove it, she decapitated the person!" He's fascinated by that.

"Then there's another story: Here everyone else—the daughter, the son—knows this is not the woman's husband." Like a wizard from Yiddish folklore, he sees science as a story. But, it's fine with the woman—"We get along," she's told him. "She'll deal with it."

"John Marshall at the University of Psychology talks of situations where you remember episodes, but no longer get the buzz. For example, you know this is who you are married to, where you fell in love, and how it was, but," he shrugs, "that may be less to do with memory and more to do with electricity."

"Or you may just fall out of love," I say.

"And it has nothing to do with memory. But," he looks out the small windows overlooking the towers and trees of the campus, "the skin conduction has changed. There's something called galvanic skin response. If someone loses face recognition, you can test the skin and the electrodes will show if this is your mate."

I remember playing with the children on the beach at Scarborough. Their hands touched mine as we built sand castles, and I closed my eyes, imagining they were my own children as they dusted sand off my cheeks. But they weren't my own.

"Maybe that's almost a genetic characteristic," I say, "the 'touch' of your own genes."

I'm so interested in talking to him that my own memory's disappearance seems beside the point. So when I went over these notes, the meeting with Dr. Davies comes back quite clearly. Maybe the less stress distracts it, the more memory holds on.

Before I leave, I ask him, "Would you have any idea why I'd rather draw now than write?"

He thinks about that, listens to some of my background, and says that if memory's gone, whatever inhibited me from art would also have gone, and the art may be showing through. This leads us around to the earlier theory about autistics and originality.

About short-term memory, it's hard to find the logic. By the time I had left the room where we talked, I couldn't tell you what tie Dr. Davies was wearing, but that was a "fact," and only on the soft disk. I could, however, draw a picture of the chair he said I should sit in. I probably made a character, an image out of it, thereby putting it away in the stacks.

And I have not forgotten that Dr. Davies says, "Your memory of fear can also be gone." This explains why I'm not afraid to travel alone now—or was the fear a learned response, and never basically there?

"Not only," I say to him, "did I make this trip to Oxford, but I did it wrong and was still able to get to the right place after all." I write that down to remind myself that there's no disaster if I go to the wrong place. Go early enough. Leave room for mistakes.

*T*he basic way we deal with a serious war—I don't remember this, but fall into it by reflex—is to move into silent retreat. I am lying firmly on the far side of the bed the way you do when you haven't made up.

Do the opposite of what you feel like. I turn to Stuart, stroke his shoulder, and look across him out our window to the full moon shining through the tree outside, the light outlining his jaw and his arm. I could frame this window, heavy lace at the edges, furled like sails with rough ropes wound into strong curving knots.

I'm back draping one of the small mannequins I dressed with fabrics my aunt, Hope Skillman, sent me from her company in New York. Her catalogues on the floor become storyboards I've put up with lists of costumes we made for Warner Leroy's Ram's Head Productions at Stanford. I dyed the white ballet tights by filling the bathtubs and lying down in them in the dye to make sure the color came out even. But I couldn't master the sewing machine in freshman-year costume design. You can't be a great designer without sewing perfectly. You can't cut offbeat if you can't cut a straight suit, can't do a riff if you can't write a declarative sentence. I turn over to him and touch his shoulder. Even in his sleep, Stuart always turns and puts his arm around me.

He must miss his jazz friends. So many are gone. Gerry—was it just last year? We must visit Franca in Milan. Stuart fits around me as easily as an Armani. Can you play jazz if you don't know your scales?

Aunt Hope wanted me to be a designer, my mother wanted me to be an artist, and then I watched Barbara Bel Geddes in my father's picture *I Remember Mama.* The camera froze in closeup—showing memory at work as Barbara told how she was writing up the memories of her childhood and her mother—then went off focus, dissolving into the next shot to show you the past. A perfect flashback.

Try this. Go to a mirror. Stare into your own eyes. Focus on what you can catch of the scene you want, even a corner. What you are wearing. Move in even closer. Layer today over yesterday, slide today away, so slowly, again.

Cut to black. Try again. Like striking matches on jeans, the moment you want doesn't light up at first. You have to believe the whole scene is back there on file.

Barbara Bel Geddes was older than I was, but not so much that it was one of those adult ages I didn't ever expect to be. I wanted to be East Coast elegance, like Kitty Hart in black velvet. Or to be a tough woman from a Mitchum movie with a straight whiskey voice, like Jan Sterling. I'm leaning forward over him. Was she married to Paul Douglas? Edie Wasserman had powder-white matte breasts, smooth above the draped bodice of the black crepe cocktail dresses she wore with diamond Tiffany clips, like quotation marks, on either side of the bodice.

Some had breasts shining with suntan oil, like Sidney Sheldon's wife. Sidney had a stud look. You could see him doing real estate deals. He was one of my father's protégés, but he wouldn't speak to me when I was trying to write a biography of my father for Michael Korda, the ideal editor for that one. He said my books had only been an embarrassment to my family.

Killer cuts have mnemonic overdrive.

God talked to me in this dream and made me fly and said writing's not a lot different from breathing. Neither is this. But how does God feel if you're thinking about Him while you're doing this? God invented the idea. Loving—writing—all—like breathing—works as long as you don't for a second believe you can't do it. Hang on like it's a glider. Do you think you can't go here or there? Slower now. It'll go as long as I stay in close to the heat—to the power source. Keep going, long, slow, and steady. Am I thinking of loving or writing? You can do it, are doing it, it is a song, and another one. I go and go, up over everything, never stop. Flying out, out over the coast.

I do actually love this person on automatic, like I love my father, and my room, and my children. I stop. Chill out. Like they used to say on juvenile delinquent warning signs, DO YOU KNOW WHERE YOUR CHILDREN ARE NOW? DO YOU KNOW WHO THEY ARE?

I pull away. "Are you okay?" He touches my hair. "Fine."

You can't be there and be here. Don't do that. Don't think of home; this never works when you have any of the kids on your mind, mainly yours. But deep as a sword's slash comes the longing to see Phoebe's face. I want to catch every darker new angle to my grandson Justin's voice. Did he get the cricket uniform I sent?

Where do you think the big romantic stories, happy endings, come from—you fall for your parent, you come so close you singe the feathers. I love you so, I'm thinking, but I hate the feeling. He'll never get off unless I think of models with endless legs, how do they say it; limitless, legs through the roof, over the top, did he say Picasso lived so long because he did this every day, or did Picasso say it? It doesn't matter. Picasso isn't here to say that he never said it and Paloma wasn't there to say yes or no; and it doesn't matter yes, because he's believing it and that's the wonder, when I think of it. He's here.

Look to this moment. It's getting light outside.

Look to this day. When I was in school, we used to stand on the lawn with our arms raised to the sun and say, "Look to this day, for it is life, the very life of life," and the day I'm having will give me the way to find the memories I need. I can write as long as I like, like the songs in a big show, the words will keep coming and coming. I'll have everything to say, everywhere to go. Don't ask how you get here or if there's something beyond beyond—because it's there. He has it.

Does personality remember who to be, how to be, if you've lost everything else? Or does it watch what it sees and find new riffs, a new voice? *Listen,* I remind myself, *the best way to find what you need is to construct a strong new present.*

I don't want Lynn, my agent, to know how bad it is. Angie works with me, walking me through chapters she maps out the way you'd take a blind dog through a park.

I haven't told Lynn Nesbit that French *Vogue's* editor, Joan Juliet Buck, called from Paris last Thursday and asked me to do a story on Liz Hurley.

"She was really friendly," I told Valerie Wade, one of my best friends here, by which I mean she does not expect me to remember what she tells me or that I have been over to her house. "That," Valerie says, "is because Joan and you have known each other for years. I think you met her in Leo Lerman's office in New York."

"Great," I said to Joan. Presence of mind here. I did not ask who Liz Hurley was. Or if I did, I do not remember what she said.

Lynn knows. She called Friday. "You're throwing away your work on little magazine stories." This is exactly what I need to hear. More, more. She has a closet of tough lines tailored to each of us, like an S & M couturier in Soho. I bet I have a tough line from her, like a caption, under every piece of my work. She's the teacher you really learn from. Others threw me out of class, but she's sticking with me.

The writers and Judith are here this Sunday. I am spending more time on lunch than writing. Today it's chicken paprika and poppy seed noodles.

"You're cooking, not writing," Geraldine says.

"I try to tell her that, too," Stuart says. He has come by for a plateful.

"This is not stopping you eating," I point out.

"Give him a break," Judith snaps. She is his person. If we are surrogate parents, I am the eldest daughter's annoying mom.

Judith has brought Stilton cheese and grapes, which Stuart loves. She goes in the refrigerator, takes out the terra cotta dish with foil. "Polenta? Do I like that?"

"You could try it. I'll heat it up."

"And some of the, what is that?"

"A peach crumble."

"Yes, with a little ice cream. I've got to stop eating."

"I think I'm leaving," Stuart says. He returns to his dark gray room where he'll spend the rest of the afternoon.

"The thing about him that is so remarkable," Angie says, "is he's here even when he isn't. His personality stays in the room after he's left."

"It's true," Geraldine says, "he's the center of the room even when he doesn't talk. His is a stalwart presence."

I must discuss presence with this Professor Steven Rose—if he answers my letter. But then, presence is not the part of the brain he studies. He is the biochemist who has written *The Making of Memory*. Memory and presence. Is presence a brain thing or a body thing? Or is it spirit? I think of Stuart when I should be thinking of the work. Does he matter more than my work? That might be new. If I don't remember my old character traits, can I figure they're dusted? And I put you first. I really do love.

Stuart's particularly grim today because Geraldine has her kid, Sam, here and Noah is upstairs painting.

"What does Liz Hurley do?" I ask after we're settled around the table.

"She's a model, gown held together by safety pins, and she's having an affair with an actor," Geraldine says.

"By the time you get the story done," Judith points out, "the rest of the world won't remember who she is either."

"You just say that because you can't wear the clothes she does," Mark says.

"Or doesn't," Geraldine says.

"That's not your kind of thing to say," Mark tells her.

"I'm testing a new character," Geraldine says.

I can't remember whether Geraldine's new character, Deodora, is the star or the manager in love with the star. Is that the writer's problem or mine?

"If French *Vogue* is doing a piece," I say, "then she must be someone. But I will be doing it for the wrong reason. I want to be translated into French."

"You are already affecting a French accent," says Judith, "and it's bad."

"But, of course."

"You could ask her how she'll feel being remembered for one dress."

I won't. I show them the picture of Liz Hurley they've sent over. She does not want to be remembered for the curve of safety pins coursing down her body in Versace's dress. I feel the tracks of those pins, the quiver of tension in the taut pull of the dress. The curve is like the snake draped around Eve, outlining to Adam what he's not likely to get (unless he really toes the line). '

"I'm not giving Versace, any Klimt or Erté title so fast, but this dress on this woman is about now."

"But will you remember 'now'?" Debbie wonders.

"This has taken you away from your book," Geraldine says. Geraldine is worried about the book in the way I forget to be.

"The book's going through a personality change."

"We know that," Svetlana says. "How do you say, 'in retreat'?"

"True." It is, but I don't want her telling me. It's okay if Judith said that. I should try to remember that when Svetlana's sharp it means she's needy.

As if to prove what I mean, Judith remarks, "You have a new habit— I'd watch it. You look in the mirror all the time. You have a lot of them around and now you don't miss a glance."

"Thanks," I said, "that's reassuring." I look at Noah's new drawing of another rocket diving into the painted nasturtiums on the top landing.

Martha has had highlights put in her heavy, dark curly hair. The highlights give her eyes glances of gold I can't figure, as if the light hit the expression center inside. It's very sharp. Just when I decide I'm intimidated, I always glance at her delicate lower lip, trembling slightly—will she be in control no matter what comes up? What you say may hurt. Worse, what she says, before she realizes it, may hurt you, and she hates that.

Someone has given me an architect's book, *Chambers for a Memory Palace*. Maybe with memory coming all around me, with learning about it, I will lure it back. Like an act, if I understand how it works, what some ideas are, how it looks, I will at least give the impression I have it. If I can remember, that is, what I am learning.

Memory palaces are a variation of the memory theaters I first read about in Steven Rose's book. The ancient thinkers hated writing and worked out many ways to have their ideas and stories remembered forever without writing things down (for themselves, they had scribes).

Plato said Socrates thought writing was inhuman and established outside the mind what could only be in the mind. And Cicero thought writing weakened the mind. "You put it down, you lose it."

By the way, the mind, Steven Rose makes clear, is not to be confused with the brain and its properties, structures, processes. The mind has sensations, thoughts, emotions. "The mind is the dramatist, the poet. The brain does the homework, edits and remembers structures."

Yes, Gavin, the architect who lives downstairs, brought me the book, *Chambers for a Memory Place*. Donlyn Lyndon (with Charles Moore, who died before the book was finished) writes that two thousand years ago, before Cicero would make one of his two-hour speeches to the Senate without notes, he'd construct a theater in his mind filled with balconies, rooms and arcades. He'd go through it in his imagination, setting around furnishings and statues to remind him of each specific idea he was going to talk about.

Ideas and events, allied with particular images and their distance, their placement and proportion, became memorable in spaces that had clear, recognizable, permanent order.

When I read about this ancient understanding of memory, I was reminded of *Fahrenheit 451,* Ray Bradbury's story about the loss of literature. I saw his characters in togas and sandals wandering through arcades, making sure the stories, poems, and novels are remembered. The arcades are draped with ivy and wisteria; images representing the characters, the ideas, and the values are set into sun-dappled niches, or up on shadowed balconies like those around the Bel Air Hotel.

I want to do that with my years; give a year to a friend and be able to call up and, "Okay, February 1967—so where was I?" I'd like to have it clear what we thought that year.

The ultimate book Steven Rose recommends, *The Art of Memory* by Frances Yates, is the exquisite, detailed history of all the ancient techniques of using your imagination to place ideas and images in order, all the medieval and·Renaissance approaches, the masters' names and techniques. I am inspired.

I will put good lines into niches, characters into balconies, scenes on stages, and garland chapters along arcades, so I can simply walk through my place and pick up what I want to recall.

While everyone's quietly eating, looking at the memory book, and going over pages, waiting to see who decides to read first, I look around my rosy red room here on Wimpole Street with red and magenta candles lit, the fragrances of dark pink lilies, sage, the onions, the paprika, oranges. I don't know where it's all from or how exactly it was put together, but what I'm not sure of yet is, will this remain even when I'm away? And will I remember it when I am not here? Will I be able, like Rose explains, to store what I want here on this shelf, or in this silver tea caddy? Little by little, will I put more things and people I need to remember around my house? As I can handle it or as it becomes necessary, I will, I suppose, put up shelves, bring in extra galleries and invent an attic with chests and old statues representing scenes and moments.

To begin, I pasted up family pictures around the walls in the kitchen and my workroom. This has become my memory theater, and as the days go on, I can tell you before I come into a room whose picture is where. I am not certain where each picture was taken, but in no picture is it raining.

Stuart is the lead player. Most of what I do remember about him is what I need to know, which is that he is always here. I have no fear that if he goes out he won't come back. But if this is true, why does my breath catch each time I see him? The parts of my life that are almost completely blank are these recent years with him. Then the years with my children when they were on their own with me are faded, shadowed out. Negatives held up to a hot sun. I have them in my theater on the stage, to the right and to the left, giving them independent entrances and exits. I must stop referring to them as "the children." This gives each child his own spotlight, an accessory, an image. Johanna's smile, her rosy cheeks. Her husband, Rob, the fireman, brave, silent. Justin, my grandson who loves baseball and hates talking on the phone, but no more so, Johanna tells me, than Jeremy, who is here with his daughter, Phoebe.

"Memory theaters," I tell him, "refresh and organize intimate family relationships."

"Intimacy and family," Stuart says, "are not to be confused."

"Especially if you don't live anywhere near your families," I remind him, "and, therefore, cannot make them intimate."

This was still the serious weekend issue. I miss home, especially childhood Sundays, filled with people playing tennis, swimming, eating deli from Nate 'n' Al's, eyeing each other and going for tops in charades—fast lines, low cuts (dresses), long looks and salty digs. (Doris Vidor, Linda and Warner Leroy's mom, always won at those.) I can't exactly place myself there. But that may have been the point. I stayed outside—watching.

Stuart says I tried to imitate those L.A. Sundays when we lived in Connecticut, and now again by having my writers' group here on Sundays.

"Possibly," I say, "so now we can fight about me missing my kids all day on Saturday."

After the writers leave, Judith goes into Stuart's room and sinks into the leather couch, holding the needlepoint cushion she made him.

"Cesario can't leave his wife or his work around my birthday so that we can go away. He is simply not going to be here for me."

Maybe Judith needs the anger. Fear's paralyzing.

"Maybe, Judith, let him go." I hedge when I'm firm. Is this my style?

I do remember, in *Bed/Time/Story*, not of course in my real life, someone telling me to dust the guy. And it was hard for me. Now I see it was hard for my friend to say that, too. We don't like to tell anyone to cut the losses when the loss is love.

I've gone too far.

Tears.

"I can't."

"So why ask me for advice?"

"Because I do. Then you tell me it will never work and that won't help."

"Sometimes all I want on a Sunday is for Stuart to say I've got a ticket to go home. You aren't the only one who feels like hell."

"Maybe," she says, "someday you'll get your book together, you'll get your own ticket for the States—now, there's a concept—and you're going to say, 'I'm going home.'"

But is that what I really want? Or just this weekend?

What Judith is actually here to talk about, until Stuart's finished going over this latest contract from Laurie's new gallery, is Cesario.

"Like all intriguing men, he wants you to be his enchanted mirror. He'll polish the mirror, give it things to reflect upon. Do you want to be a mirror?" I look at her hard. Turn it around: this way she has complete independence.

That night Stuart and I are in our separate workrooms. I am not working on the book. I am playing old movie scores and working on my memory theater: my father is on the aisle in the front (this isn't exactly how they'd organize these theaters then, but it's working for me). This is where he'd watch runthroughs of his plays, with his assistant next to him with a clipboard making notes. He loved himself best at this time in his life, felt closest to himself. He was back in the theater, where he'd seen himself when he was a kid. He loved the intimacy of theatrical control. He grew up in the small family catering business, with the show business urgency and flair where, like the theater, each scene is on and over in an instant.

My mother is at the piano, in the orchestra. This part is easy. The part I work on every day involves placing and shifting other characters as the day's play changes.

In a classic memory theater, the values you need to recall are placed in arched alcoves around the courtyard, virtues being more important players in your life than human characters. And they would last longer.

You store the thing to be memorized at the base, like in a little drawer the statue is standing on. Or you can put it on a platform, a slope or stairs that climb and pause. I could start with the loft above my mother's studio where I had a place to paint and write. Steep stairs, not so easy to slip up to and invade. The other stairs were the spiral staircase from the projection room to my father's bedroom—so he could work in bed when his back was bad and studio people could visit without disturbing my mother. There were back stairs so we could get from our children's wing to the kitchen and the breakfast room. I had a class problem about being a kid. I liked taking the broad front stairs and going through the dining room, then through the swinging door to the kitchen with some clear authority.

After Judith leaves, I go down to see Laurie. On the way, I glance in the mirror on the stairs.

Laurie opens her door. I hug her, admire her new picture, then say, "Judith says I've been looking in the mirror a lot. Is this true?"

"You probably don't have a strong sense of yourself right now, so you're looking to see who you are—here—to see what you look like." Laurie gets a camera from the bookshelf to the right of her easel. "Just look at the camera."

"Don't take a picture. I have nothing on. You know what I mean. Makeup."

"Be quiet."

The picture is taken.

Does Elizabeth Hurley have a place in my memory theater? After I have tea with her tomorrow, will I remember where I'm coming back to? A whole new fear. Maybe that's why my rooms are so busy, so bright—if they pale out in memory while I'm away, there'll still be something here.

Liz Hurley doesn't meet me at The Ivy, nor in the satiny boudoir dressing rooms old stars liked. She decides to meet in her office, a film company set in a couple of floors of an old Victorian house, large whitewashed rooms with giant posters of Hugh Grant propped up against the walls, the way you place paintings you may not keep.

She clomps across the bare floor in wooden high-heeled clogs with brass studs, suede vamps in Jil Sander palomino pink. She folds herself down into a deep yellow and white sofa.

"Until this year, I only had running shoes, everyday boots, black high heels. Now I have masses of high heels, beautiful high heels," she says. "I always wear monster heels. These are low for me, slippers."

"Do you know," I point out, "Rita Lydig, who wore a tricorn hat and was sculpted by Rodin and painted by Sargent and Boldini, had three hundred pairs of shoes?"

Something she's been just waiting to hear.

"That's almost as many shoes," I continue, "as the tartes tatins Bill Hayward made last year. Bill made one every day. (Have I told you this?) He's Brooke Hayward's brother—their sister and mother died when they were young—Brooke wrote the story in her fine book *Haywire*. Now I realize Hurley does not know Bill Hayward's dark legacy, and doesn't want to. This is like coming to London and not wanting to know all about the places with the blue plaques. You can't really be in the movies without knowing all our family scenarios. But what beginner wants that. What all she wants is that we should know her.

"I had an hour's sleep last night," she continues, "I look absolutely awful. Really dreadful." She's wearing dirty white jeans with button studs up the front. Her high breasts shimmer under the iridescent silver threads knitted into the bare midriff sweater.

Cecil B. De Mille told Paulette Goddard when she went out looking ratty, "You're a star. You never even cross the alley unless you're dressed to the teeth." Stars, my father said, always need to be told they look terrific, that they're doing a great job. So I won't agree that she looks dreadful.

"I would like to look this dreadful," I say, then, "How did you come across the Versace dress?"

"A friend told me someone had a rack with PR stuff, to 'go have a look,' so I went and I said, 'Um, yeah.' There is a problem of having no hips, completely flat from here to here. But last summer Versace cut a lot of little suits to give me a little wiggly bottom and hips, which I wore with Estee Lauder spray-on tanner—nicer than nude tights. This fall everything I've chosen from Versace's couture line is winter white. Dare I wear it?" Suddenly she's Pamela Harriman, statesmanlike responsibility to Fashion.

"So I asked Liz Hurley, 'What sign are you?'" I report the following Sunday after I finish reading the story I've written to the group.

"It would be difficult to be from L.A. and not ask this question," Angie agrees.

"So what was she?" Geraldine asks.

"Gemini. We were thrilled with each other for an instant."

"Then, only because it's next to 'what sign are you' in that kind of question, I asked, 'Where will you be on New Year's Eve, the night this century changes?' and she said she'd probably be sitting very sadly, 'by myself, on a foreign film set.'"

I am looking again at Laurie Lipton's picture of the slight woman with a steely glance and a vague resemblance to Alan Rickman. The woman has a pen in her left hand, a writing pad on her lap and is sitting in front of an intricate theatrical vision, an imaginary movie studio set, with swags and floodlights, stars and crew—and there, in the front, a left-handed little girl making notes.

Laurie has given me the perfect memory theater. Everything I love is here. And the woman here is okay.

But these aren't the sharp, tough, critical people I've heard I once knew. So who did I know? I remember my brother and sister and I dressed up to meet Easterners, senators, moguls, stockholders, theater owners. I always told them I was going to be a writer. So I was a kid, three feet high—you never know. I damn well might do that. We wouldn't want you growing up remembering us in a way we wouldn't like.

Maybe this was a way I got you to pay attention to me when I was a kid.

The next morning I mail off the piece on Hurley. When I come home, I have a message from Professor Rose, who has agreed to see me when he returns from a lecture tour in America.

It's as if the characters are writing me back. It's not much, but it's a beginning. This is the book I am writing. The dimension I am in is the present.

23

Steven Rose began studying at Cambridge in the late fifties, when he discovered what he calls "the exciting hinterland between chemistry and physiology" and named the science of neurochemistry, the biochemistry of the brain. Rose is now a professor at the Open University an hour north of London.

In the car, whizzing past the industrial plains bordering any freeway, my body's clock forgets where it is. It careens in and out of time zones: New York, Los Angeles, or here. Where is here? I take a quick look at my datebook.

My day is a charade—signs are held up, expressions, gestures tossed at me: Who is this? Where is it from? What does this have to do with that? Get a grip.

The university spreads flat and starkly threatening, like giant blocks, across acres of flat land. I won't remember one corner, one path beyond the huge white reception building.

Don't have to. Someone is meeting me. A positive approach is not to worry about remembering what you don't have to.

The professor's assistant leads me down a bright hall to his office. Steven's standing, instantly engaging, with wide, enthusiastic light eyes.

He's good at capturing eager attention, but at the same time, you sense that he'd rather be immersed in his work.

"So, baby chicks everywhere," I say, "I'd know it was you."

There's a toy windup baby chick and a kind of wooden paddle toy with several chicks. "The Ukrainians bought that for me," he says.

One of the things I liked best about his book is the sense you get of the man writing the book, of his own experience with memory: being in an air raid shelter; the childhood artifacts, like a silver mug, that trigger his own memories. I stretched harder to understand what he was talking about.

I'm looking him over so I can remember how to describe him. People are not used to someone casing them so carefully.

"I'm sorry I'm dressed like this," he says. He's wearing dark slacks and a dark tie, and the soft deep ultramarine shirt fits his torso well. You expect him to be heavier because of the warmth of his writing. But given how much he does, he doesn't have time to eat. You also expect him to be in baggy khakis and the mindless patterned sport shirt that thinking men live in.

"I have to go to one of those dinners tonight," he explains, "so that's why I'm dressed like this."

"It's okay," I say, "I won't think you're intimidating."

There is a desk, a computer and a round table with royal blue chairs where we sit and talk. In the center is a large square fish bowl filled with light gold water; inside is a human brain, which looks smaller, trimmer than I'd expected. In his book, Steven talks about doing his early research on kosher cows' brains so that when the work was finished, he could use them for his dinner. I will not ask if this one is marinating.

"I have some questions, but the embarrassing thing is they haven't stayed arranged in my memory theater. You've talked about Hyden and how cells change their properties as a result of experience; that large cells deep in the brain concerned with balance don't change . . ."

"That was back in the sixties." How fast he reaches back and connects. But, to me, with time unfixed slipping like Mercury, the sixties are yesterday, and I only know the eighties by that red Valentino suit.

"Now, this is the question I've underlined here—I've got four stars next to it."

"I see that," he says.

"I was wondering if under a large shock, say a grand mal fit, would the structures react and reset so radically that the whole character of the memory changes. One of the things that has surprised me the most, particularly when I go back and reread things I wrote before, my attitude and angle have changed, and my appreciation of the memory and understanding—now, this may be age or maturity—but it seems that some things are just radically different."

"It's a difficult question, isn't it? I have the experience of reading things I wrote fifteen or twenty years ago—firstly, I have no recollection of writing them at all. Secondly, I look at this thing and don't recognize it as mine, so I don't think that's as it were unique to a post-fit situation. In fact, my partner, a sociologist, says exactly the same thing." He speaks of her often and with affection, and I'm thinking how much more I'd like to have them over to dinner than to learn how my brain works. Or, to be precise, if it still does.

He smiles. His eyes light up when he's onto his subject; it's a physical sign of enthusiasm. Does it show in the neurons and so on, or only in the eyes, to be caught by untrained eyes like mine? Ed Doctorow's eyes lit up like this when he'd talk about a character he liked. You'd see this electricity in the eyes of some movie stars in the first dailies on a new picture. And always with Fred Astaire, always Gene Kelly.

It's his fresh involvement that makes me reach to catch what he means. One of the things that happens after an epileptic seizure, electric shock treatment, and so on is you get random bits of nerve cell death. "On the whole," Steven says, "they don't get replaced in adults, so, in a sense, there're going to be spots that are disconnected. We know a great deal more about the mechanisms involved in learning than we do when we try to remember something, as it were, inside your brain. The mechanisms for scanning and refinding that memory are almost entirely unknown and uninvestigated. We still don't know what changes in the brain to create memory storage. We know a change is required in the biochemistry and structure of cells, but we don't know where this happens, either."

"But you said there are medications now that can improve memory." I don't forget this idea.

"Yes, but the complete change and adjustment of memory is not likely to happen with a pill." He's careful. "That would be like trying to fine-tune a radio by jamming a screwdriver into it."

I see it as fixing antique lace: as tying and threading small connections, picking up beads, examining them in the light to get each shape and shade in place. Once it's here, it looks together and may even (if you don't go too close) look like it used to, but you mustn't confuse it with the original. Make the same demands and it will shred apart into pieces, as airy and dead as cinders.

"There's a whole literature about so-called 'smart' drugs," he continues. "Most of them don't work. Some of them are designed for people with Alzheimer's disease and I think they're pretty tough to take, and I wouldn't advise taking those at the moment. There is one substance that is used in Europe—it's not licensed here—that is completely innocuous, it does no harm at all. It might well be worth trying in your situation. It's called Piracitan—I know the company that manufactures it, and we've used it in the lab. I don't think it would do any harm to try it. You can order it off the Web."

Before we go on talking, we go to the commissary for lunch. I am reminded of school cafeterias—and the commissary at the studio where an actress would have a dish of cottage cheese, and you'd see her watching the director eat a big plateful of goulash and noodles. I have chicken and tomato sauce with pasta, and he has a herring and onion salad with a baked potato, which looks like a far better idea.

I love institutional lunches. I have the big white visitor's badge clipped to my sweater and I feel I am involved. I do belong. Instantly I look around to see which rank I'm in. Wherever I go, I'm figuring out a way I can muscle in, get a gig. Is this because I don't relate in any gripping way, once I am not there, to any place?

We're going back to his office now through a labyrinth of walks and hallways.

"I'm glad I'm with you or I'd never get back," I say.

"Not being able to find your way around is one of the things I would expect to happen," he says, "a fairly logical step if you've had some sort of disconnection.

"The part of the brain called the hippocampus is associated both with short-term memory and the transfer of short-term to long-term memory, and with spatial representation, that is, making maps of where you are."

It's as if here I'm reassured. I know exactly what he means. "I not only don't know, but I don't know I've been there."

"But I bet you're unimpaired at riding a bike," he says. "That's procedural memory. People with Alzheimer's disease, a progressive loss of memory, can remember how to ride a bike, long after they may have forgotten a bike is called a bike. The first thing to go is autobiographical episodic memory—'Did you see that film last night?' To know that a film is a film—to remember the days of the week (semantic memory) is easier—but to know what did I do last Tuesday is harder."

I think about that. I don't.

"What interests me is that my writing is off. I have trouble remembering sentences or who a character is, but my drawing is better than ever."

I'm not clear again on what Steven Rose means when he says, "It is always declarative rather than procedural memory that suffers."

But I woke up late one night, went into my workroom, and decided not to try to write, but to send something to Phoebe. I picked a tiny notebook and I sat there with the colored pencils, filling pages until the book for Phoebe was finished. I remembered how to shadow, to feel where the line's going before the pencil touches the paper. I remembered the strokes and curves to take to bring coyotes, bears, and starker characters to some sort of life. I remember learning from my mother. But I don't remember where she died or when.

"In order to write now," I tell him, "I start by sometimes drawing my way in. It's almost like I'm fooling the brain, relaxing my brain so it won't think about it."

"If I were a clinician listening to that, I would begin to suspect there was damage to the left hemisphere rather than the right hemisphere."

"That reminds me," I say quickly, "I wanted to talk about the left-handed rats and the right-handed rats."

"Those were very early experiments," he says. "The man who invented them influenced me and shaped the direction of my research back in the sixties. He trained rats to reach for food down a glass tube and noted whether the rats reached with their right or left paw. Then he made it necessary for them to reach with the opposite paw. It enabled him to study these particular cells and that particular region—so he designed his task to be related to the certain cells he was studying at the time. Of course, methods are much more sensitive now and those techniques are completely unused. Humans are the only organisms that are not lateralized; there's only a small proportion who are left-handed. If you look at other animals, about half prefer their right paw and half prefer their left paw. However, that's not true for birds. They have a very sharp lateralized brain."

"And a good sense of color." I read this in a book by Barry Gordon, an American. Gordon is a psychologist who works directly with people.

"Is memory DNA?" is my next question. A man named McConnell wrote about this issue in the *Worm Runners Digest,* which was not a journal for fit worms, but a study of worms who had been trained by light, then cannibalized by other worms to see if they'd remember the game the food worms had been taught. It seemed that the worms who ate the light-trained worms did change their behavior as if they remembered "the conditioned response their food had learned." This created quite a stir for a few years, until, as worms do, they turned and refused to duplicate the experiments for other scientists.

Steven gave me a book for children called *Brainbox,* which he wrote with a twelve-year-old friend of his. He'd asked his young friend what he wanted to know about the brain, and being a very democratic young man, the twelve-year-old polled his class and came back with a list of fifteen questions, of which the last two were, "How does your brain make you happy or sad?" and "Are you the same as your brain or different?" Steven was deeply impressed.

"I think I'll think about that last question for a long time."

"I think many people have," Steven says.

"I'm wondering, is recollection shadowed by emotion?"

"Oh, yes. Why do we remember things? Not in order to have cognitive skills, to be able to remember the letters of the alphabet—but to be able to survive in the world. To survive in the world is entirely about emotional rather than cognitive things."

"What I fear I've done," I say, "is reinvent rather than recollect."

"One always does," Steven says. "Every act of memory is a reinvention, isn't it? When you tell a story or have an experience, the memory shifts as the tale is a little different next time it's told. Its character also changes depending upon who you tell it to."

"And how you're feeling as you tell it this time."

"I know that when I tell a story out loud, it changes as I adjust my own memories to my listener's response. I never tell my father's stories or my own exactly the same way to everyone. Times and attitudes change, subtle language changes restyle a memory.

"That's why this whole debate is going on—the psychotherapists' memory-false memory debate in the States. People are supposed to be able to remember sexual abuse or whatever when they were kids. So if I asked you to remember something now—which is your favorite childhood memory—you'd be remembering it as you changed it the last time you remembered it. Once a psychotherapist has persuaded you that you were abused as a child, that memory's real to you—it's in the brain. It's as real to you as if in fact it had actually happened. We all tell ourselves our stories. Memory isn't intended, as it were, as an absolute record. It's an active process going on inside the brain."

I am lying in our bed in the soft gray morning light. I am not going back into old time. Stay in a place you know here. Here is London. I am in Regent's Park. I'm walking along the path to Venice. Is that what it's called? And I'm in a gondola. (This may be on a trip to the real Venice, not London's Little Venice. Not L.A.'s Venice.) Did we go to Venice with Judith and Cesario? Yes, and they fought. She flew home, Prada bags on her back, slung over forearms, and swinging from her shoulders.

Never mind. Now I'm carefully guiding this gondola around rivers of nerves through my body, bumping along by the joints, hearing the vibration of the veins like the shimmering of leaves. This once led me to see that I could stay in touch without drugs; that, in fact, they muzzled the connections. Since then, I can connect but I can't see the memory. I've never been able to find it.

I will respond and connect my spirit and my mind to my body. And it will work. I think of Professor Rose's floating brain. Do I remember the part of my brain that writes? Can I image the connections to fix them?

Possibly. Steven did say that when neurons, cells, die, it gives more space for connections with other cells to grow—so it's not necessarily a bad thing. In the first ten to twelve years of life—our development is really rooted in these first years—there's a huge overproduction of neurons. The brain is a very redundant structure—there are many pathways to get from one place to another—there's more than one way to skin a cat, so to speak. "So if some neurons died in your seizure," he shrugs, "you'll just find another way to do the same thing." I thought about Kohler's chimpanzees, who got the idea to put short sticks together to reach their bananas. When animals learn a goal in a maze, even if you turn it around, change it, they'll find the way to their goal.

Maybe scientists who do not work with people may take a more positive view of things. Working with five hundred rats and baby chicks that don't make it, it's the one that does that counts.

I'm going to be the one. I'm going to find another way to do hours and days—and scenes and chapters.

Steven Rose has a memory test in his little book, *Brainbox*, which I've adapted, changing some of the color images so the drawings will be clearer in black and white. Look at these things for one minute. Then see how many you remember.

This is what I remembered the first time I took the test: lemon, orange, feather, safety pin, pencil.

"Theater is memory," John Lahr says, "that's its function. Theater is an historical memory; a way of taking an audience and making it imagine the past, a way of working through the past, a way of reviving memories to reflect on their own lives. All of Shakespeare's history plays help an audience recall in themselves parallel universes, see if they can find those feelings in their own stories."

John eats with the busy vigor of a historical character, smiling, eyebrows as alert to flavors as to his own brisk delivery. John loves to eat. Loves to think. Loves to talk about what he's thinking.

I'd called John a few weeks after I saw Steven Rose. I had John's number in my book, and I knew we'd met. Or maybe I'd been given his number because John and I have something of a similar background. I think. He's the theater critic for *The New Yorker* and his father was Bert Lahr, the Cowardly Lion in *The Wizard of Oz*.

"John . . . Hi, we met years ago in L.A. I can't remember if we went to school together, but . . ."

"Jill . . . ," he was amused, patient. I loved his voice right away. Now, is this because I remember its character, or because from the sound of his voice I know it's one of those which easily tumbles over into laughter. "You were here in Primrose Hill a few months ago."

"Not the Upper West Side?"

"No. You got lost, but not that lost," John says. "Why don't I come over—let's talk about memory."

"I'll feed you," I say.

"That's what I hoped," he says.

"The first time we met," John explains when he arrives, "was when our books came out—*Notes on a Cowardly Lion* and *Bed/Time/Story*—and we were on this show as the children of famous people. But we really met when you and Stuart came over to England, your friends and mine, Leslie and Arthur Kopit, gave you our address in Hampstead. You'd arrive for tea with muffins, always tied in red bandannas, and jalapeño jelly."

"No—not muffins—chili corn bread—yes. Or Tex Mex scones!"

"So you remember food?"

"Far better than anything."

"You struck up a relationship with my son, Chris. You were very nice to him," John says. "You always brought either strawberries or a strawberry tart just for him. You'd just come and schmooze with everybody, and then you'd call for your car, which I thought was rather magnificent—that you had a car. Then the guy who made *Four Weddings and a Funeral* was giving a party and you and Stuart were there.

"Do you remember where our teas were in the house?" John asks. "They were at the top of the house. Once you got to our house, you had to go up another set of stairs."

I lay out lunch and John sits down. "Of course," he says, "theater is memory."

"When you lose your memory, you don't think you're very smart anymore. Being without memory in a territory of writers and artists is like being in L.A. and not driving."

So my idea that memory is theater and John saying theater is memory restores my self-confidence, which is why I'm sure, when I go over what we talk about, I see that I've remembered more than usual.

Like me, John started out knowing he was a writer, because "I could do that better than anything else. I got a lot of pleasure out of it." Like me, he began with political journalism.

John was at Yale when they integrated Ole Miss and they sent him down there to cover the story. "They were rioting on the campus, it was all aflame, and they had banned all reporters because someone from *Paris*

Match had been murdered. But I put my secret society pin on (it just happened to have a chapter at Ole Miss) and I was able to walk on campus as a student. I scooped the nation for one day and won that year's Yale Writing Prize."

How quickly memory shifts from our own lives to our parents'. "My early desire to be famous came," John says, "from my parents. That was all they respected, all they knew, and it was the world I lived in. I didn't know anyone who wasn't famous."

We've dined out and well on the material they are. But memory is what all writers use. It's the fabric; the trick is how you cut it.

John slices another piece of challah, and I wonder if I know a writer who does not eat much.

"It's a very strange and unsettling feeling thinking of your parents not knowing—intellectually," he continues. "I was always interested in words and in being able to use words, and I think that has something to do with what my parents didn't have."

"I think it can go two ways. My father loved words. He made them so real you could almost see them, like characters and, like you, John, at the teas, he was a generous presence. He made sure you got to do your own riffs, unless you went on too long. He liked quieter writers and actors like Robert Ryan or Richard Widmark and doctors and political friends who could write their parents in Detroit, Cleveland and Philadelphia and say they'd arrived. Doctors picked up the style of the storytellers and each week was like an *ER* episode. They'd battle not only over who had the most famous patients, but which one was in bigger trouble.

But my father's favorite friends were academics. They were famous in their own universities so, I think, he felt they gave him a certain exclusive credibility. "When he had Abraham Kaplan to dinner, this almost made up for not going to school. This is not unlike me liking to write about going up to Oxford, as if I can catch some of that, it's as if I can say my brain has arrived. The way people go to Hollywood to catch stardust."

John says, "I wrote a novel called *The Autograph Hound,* about a guy who pursues famous people, and I was trying to explore those feelings.

"I'm embarrassed I don't remember it."

"I wouldn't expect you to," he laughs. "Even after I've written a book, I'm getting on with the next thing, so I've completely forgotten that information because more information has come in. I don't know anybody who rereads their books. The book represents a little time capsule of who you were in that period, what your concerns were, even stylistically.

"So we do change. Maybe it's true that you can't really write for too long from who you really are. You start out as a basic, clear and wonderful creature. Then the memories pile up and the pressures of who you ought to be now, the pressures of the time, your physical condition and the pressure of how much money you have—all these start pushing and shoving this talent's morality; and as you work through life's struggles, it affects how you express yourself. You change your 'look,' as it were, because you are thinking about what you want to project. You can't do that in writing—you do see people do it, but they're very bad writers who want to project an image. They want to be Henry James or Roger Burbank. What it communicates is their emptiness or their confusion. It doesn't let the reader in—you're trying to let the reader see you in as honest a way as possible."

"Do you take notes at the theater, or do you remember a play and moments or lines?"

"I do take a few notes, but I like to applaud. Most critics won't applaud at the end of a play—they're not part of the experience. I go out and rediscover the play over the next couple of days when I'm analyzing it. Very recently, I went to see *Electra*. I went with a friend and afterwards we were talking about the play and she said, didn't you love the moment when the servant picked her up in his arms, and for that one brief moment she fell asleep suddenly, the only moment she was able to relax? And I said, what are you talking about? I didn't see that, what do you mean she relaxes? What happened, I think I was writing in my note pad—I missed that moment, it just didn't exist for me. So I went back to see it again—it was a very good play. Having seen the play once and having gotten to know the parameters of the play, I felt very comfortable with it. I could listen to it in a different way. So the second time through, I not only saw the moment my friend had mentioned, which was a very important moment, my opinion of the play was clearer for me—I was completely in the play.

"That's one of the ways I know if it's a really good play or not. I've had some wonderful times at the theater when I was never 'at the play.' If it's not fully dramatized or if it's boring, I'll sort of go off and follow something in my own head. I'll make something up or I'll be thinking about something before I came to the theater and I'll just time travel and dream away. That's another reason I don't like to take notes. The fun of going to the theater is you enter that world and stay in that world."

"I'm not sure I enter my life," I say. "I live as though I'm saying, how am I going to write about this? how can I use this character, where? So much of my life is . . ."

"Scavenging," he says.

He's right.

"Yes!"

"You are, to a certain extent, using your memory predicament to scavenge yourself. There are a lot of people you can go back and say, what happened? What do you remember? Of course, the sad thing is that what one person selects may not be the thing that you may have selected from a particular occasion."

We start to talk about John's teas, which are part of what little I remember from my first years in London. "They reminded me very much of Friday afternoons in New York, when the *Vogue* editor, Leo Lerman, had us gather in his office. He reminded me of Monty Woolley in sharp thirties roles. I think I mean the thirties—but, yes, that's where I met Joan Buck. She was also a young writer and I could feel her excitement. You'd come with your lines sharpened like pencils. Leo was like a professor. If you were fast, he'd cue you in like this week's star."

There was a little of that feeling at John's teas. Breathless before you'd talk—is this a smart angle? I don't say that now, because in memory's favored soft light I felt at home. The teas were more like our Sunday dinners.

"Remember, there was only one rule," John says, "which was that nobody was to write about those times."

"Because I will write about it . . . or, as you say, scavenge." Which I have already done.

"No, it's okay," he says. "For me, too, it was a non-self-conscious time—it was a way to be with people—'cause we were solitary a lot of the time. We did the teas for a decade—we never knew who was coming, we never invited anybody, they knew it was there, they knew it was happening. The teas were unvarying. Never, in ten years, did we have a Friday when no one came. We provided the tea and everybody brought something. One summer, when we left to go on holiday back to America, they didn't want the teas to stop, so we left the teas with Francesca and they had tea at our house even when we were away! We had the brown tiles on the floor, sort of Provençal tiles, and a pine table. It had a very American feeling to it."

I remember it had, to me, a very English feeling, like what Josie and all of us wanted to feel we had in the Village, as if we'd just come over from Oxford and started our first novel. But I am probably remembering what I want to.

"The teas would start at four-thirty and they'd end when they ended—Steven Spielberg could be there, Richard Avedon, anyone who was passing through. It was like a novel—everything happened over that table over a period of ten years. Lives changed, people separated—in fact, in the end, Anthea and I separated. I carried the teas on for a while until I got *The New Yorker* job and it got to be too much—plus, it had been part of our old life, not my new life. It was a lovely memory. When Anthea left, I put a lot of money into the flat—redecorated it, completely redid the bedroom—went upscale. We had been married twenty-three years. I wanted to lose the memory—instead of regain a memory. It's odd in that sense. In those twenty-three years, I was only away from the house for five nights. If you ask me now what I remember—I do remember things to do with Chris—I don't remember a lot of it. It's surprising how you can will that stuff away. There are some scenes I'll never forget, especially at the very end of our marriage—like Bergman scenes. Sometimes when I'm waiting for Connie at the end of the day to pick me up, I'll stand at the window—and just when I'm doing that, I remember Anthea waiting by the window, waiting for her soon-to-be-husband to pick her up, and I find that very painful."

"You talk of standing by a window. My parents put a window seat in this window where I'd look out over the driveway, and I'd sit there, watching my father leave, waiting for him to come home. He was the center in the house. The captain. When he was gone, I felt we'd go aground.

"I think I was sitting in that window watching my father drive off at three-thirty one morning. I'd been up reading. The medicine they gave you for asthma then, ephedrine, was like speed, so I heard the phone first when it rang in the hall off the children's wing. It was Monty Clift calling and he sounded terrible. My father sped off too fast, down the drive, to see him, but by the time he got there, Montgomery was dead."

"Didn't your dad make a picture with Clift—Nathaniel West's *Miss Lonelyhearts*—much later?"

I think that over. "Of course. Then I've seen that wrong, that was *Raintree County*. And Monty did survive." I remember the call from a different time.

What I remember is the call, the voice, the fragility, and fear. And my father's concern as he rushed off. But Monty didn't die that night. And all these years I've remembered it that way. What I probably saw from the window is my father rushing off the night my grandmother died.

How important it is to logic memories through whenever you can. The sadness I felt that night, the worry about my father, was mixed up with my grandmother's death.

"You know," John says, "Bergman makes no distinction between the past and the present. The past isn't a shadowy ghost, and the people in the present time are in constant conversation with people in the past. I think what writers do when they close the door and start to imagine a world is to be able to call out of themselves these ghosts and they become very real and alive. I've had one dream where my father appeared to me—I could smell his cologne, I could feel his cashmere coat—it felt incredibly, deeply real. No writer would not admit to talking to themselves when they write—with these figures of their past who haunt them—in my case, it's my mother and father, and Anthea—although both my parents are dead. Writing is one way, one socially acceptable way, of communicating with the dead. My mother wanted to kill certain memories, so she just wouldn't tell us. We are left with very little about her early life. Memory gives a sense of coherence to a largely incomprehensible world, just to make a pattern so you can feel at home in the world—and if you don't have that, it's a frustration."

I tell John the story about Stuart's mother. No matter how ill she was, as we'd turn the corner up to her house set so alone with the bleak indigo moors stretching out on all sides, she'd be there, dress shuddering in the wind and her sweater shawl round her shoulders, waiting outside for him. My memory of the story changes now as I tell it to John. And my memory of the moors—sometimes they're lavender and embracing. I tart up the story as some writers do when they're together.

John tells me now that a few weeks ago, he came across a conversation he'd had with his mother when she was losing her memory. "Although there was a certain essential 'momness' to her, actually, without memory, you lose a sense of who you are, a sense of self, because really the self is only a collection of associations and memories of things done and done to you and where you've been—and without that, it's very hard to get any definition on who you are. In the end, she could only speak about one or two sentences that she could remember. I used to go visit her in the end—and it's hard to visit, knowing that when you close the door to leave, she won't remember that you've come. She was in a constant state of feeling that no one visited her—of waiting for visits she couldn't remember. Memory allows you to have relationships with the outside world. You have to remember who's talking to you and something about them in order to engage them. Mom's last spoken words to me were—'You think I'm stupid. This house is closing, now and forever.' It was extraordinary language—not at all like the rhythm of the few sentences she regularly spoke at the end of her life—she had left. But the experience of being with her when she lost her memory—there was nothing to share—she'd lost her identity."

We're picking at tarts, a bit of cherry, a touch of apple. We keep eating to keep talking—I'll have another bite if you'll hear me.

Before he goes, John says, "When you write about memory you'll be saying, 'I lost my memory, and you're seeing me trying to retrieve, and here are some of the things I've found out.' That's very powerful—it's like a mystery—it's really clues to yourself. It will be powerful for a reader because you're so vulnerable, it's upsetting, embarrassing, shameful, distressing, the trap that memory has for people. That's why we forget certain memories, because they're too horrible to remember. We doctor them."

"I could say it's all fiction. Lay it on a character."

"That's a disclaimer. You can probably get Frances Yates's book on the Internet," John says, "it's very simple." He sits at the computer . . . and there it is.

Then he takes another cookie. "These are excellent," he says, and he is gone before I can say I didn't bake them.

The day after John has been here, I can't remember what we had for lunch. "You had a good rice dish," Stuart tells me, "roast chicken, and a raisin challah from Villandry, which you ate three quarters of."

"That's all right. Like the chili corn bread, I'll remember it in another eight years or so when it's turned into long-term memory."

I keep finding myself doing things that I remember I don't do. "Here I am at a symphony," I say to Shaw during the intermission at this stark concert hall on the wrong side of the Thames. It feels like the Valley.

"We've been going to London Philharmonic concerts," he reminds me, "for around fifteen years. We have the same seats every season, center aisle, fifth row."

"That may be why all of the players in the orchestra are as familiar as the faces on my kitchen wall," I say.

The fourth bass player who looks like Errol Flynn. The Brazilian cellist, the only one who talks to the young fat cellist. The tall blond is lead violinist, wild for Kent Nagano, the conductor with the long black hair.

Stuart comes to hear the music. I come to continue the soap I've made up about all the musicians.

"That," he says, "was my plan. Patterns build security. You liked your childhood because there was a routine."

"I hate habits."

"No, you don't. You like the meetings you know. And when the writing is hard, you wear your Sundance sweatshirt every day."

"I do?"

He's right, which I do not tell him.

I don't like classical music. My mother once said, and I remember this, "It's vengeance against me for making you take piano lessons."

Did I also tell you (and how many times) that I hate walking? And now I am walking with Luise Rainer after a visit to our friend Corinne's today.

"I saw this viola player from Russia last night," I tell Luise. Perhaps it was the night before. But I remember his expression. This is progress. "I can't remember if it was the dark pull of the viola or the fling of his long black hair that has caught me so."

"It must be the music," she says. "My first memory is of listening to my mother play Beethoven. I remember every note. I was two and I sat under the piano. Much later, of course, Gershwin played at our house when he stayed there, and Marian Anderson, too. I loved Rubenstein, but he blew so with his nostrils when he played."

Luise's voice is deep, Austrian. Under her fur coat she wears gold lame knit sweaters, tights and caps. Does she dress like a miniature Oscar to remind us she won two in a row, back-to-back for *The Good Earth* and *The Great Ziegfeld*.

I also sat under the piano listening to my mother play. I remember her red toenails, not the music. The polish was Arden's Victory Red. She pressed her foot down and down, again, harder on the pedals in her blue maribou mules. I wanted to slide my fingers in between her soft toes.

Luise is so tiny, so slender she's translucent, as I remember my mother was at the end of her life. I must not confuse them. Luise is electric and demanding. Asking for what you want may be longevity's real secret. And running. Luise was the fastest runner at her school in Hamburg.

"Centuries ago," Dr. Rose wrote, when he explained the memory theaters, "special people, the elderly, the bards, became the keepers of the common culture, capable of retelling the epic tales which enshrined each society's origins." The survivors, like Kitty Hart and the photographer Eve Arnold, whom I watch as a trip guide into the 'third act,' seem to operate on curiosity, on a dogged, exasperated intrigue about life right now. Nostalgia does not play a huge role here. It keeps its place. But Luise is different.

My mother told me after I asked Ethel Barrymore if she'd met Queen Victoria, "You don't ask someone really famous to talk about the past because it's like saying you aren't famous right now, and the only thing that makes life bearable is being famous."

What matters now to Luise seems to be walking and reading eccentric new books. But I still want Luise to tell me the stories. I'm counting on her to bring back that time, but she's living now.

She lifts her sharp jaw in what I see as a period expression. My mother did this. It comes out of the scenes when the star (Luise) would look up into the man's eyes. "Memory and the soul are one," she says. "I am the soul. The body is borrowed. I have been lucky this time—it is a wonderful one."

If the soul is a matter of faith and if the memory and soul are connected, one might have more faith in memory turning up when you really need it.

As we cross the park, Luise turns up the collar of her coat and becomes, with strides, the officer she's telling me she was in the Middle East during the Second World War. "I was married then, too. I miss him some days—more often." She stares across the park as if it's a stretch of time. "Of course, I do not want to be alone. You say you will come and have lunch again. You say you love me and yet I never see you."

How can I say I forget I know you? You cannot forget a legend.

"So, I saw your picture with your friend in *The Evening Standard*," Fran Curtis, a friend of Stuart's who had us over for dinner, says. "Jill *knows* Streisand." She says to this other couple she and Roger have over.

I can pretend I have forgotten what Fran's talking about. When you are friends with a star, what you have to offer is discretion and privacy.

"Oh, yes," I say, "this is great smoked salmon. Is it Selfridges's?"

"No," Fran says, "I went to Villandry. You told me they have the best. Don't you remember?"

We always say smoked salmon now. It was lox in L.A. and only my mother and Mildred Jaffe called it smoked salmon. It's the easiest and most expensive starter here. I would rather eat the plate.

Or anything to avoid the discussion Fran is determined to have. I can see now why I have been invited.

The other couple, Abigail and Ben, are London establishment. I knew when I opened the dashed-off little white card inviting us to dinner, handwriting thin as Fran's stiletto heels, that we were being asked for a purpose. "Do you see Barbra every time she comes to London?"

"Sometimes. Is that a Jil Sander top? I like it."

"Yes," Fran lifts her shoulders, "it's sweet, isn't it. I bought it in L.A." There has to be a reason to say one bought something in L.A. "Our house in Malibu isn't far from your *friend's* house, you know," she says.

I know exactly. She'd like to meet Barbra.

"So where do you live?" I cut right across and ask Abigail. In London, that's a little fresh, asking 'where do you live' before you know someone really well. But since the husband, Ben, owns real estate, I feel it's okay.

"We live upstairs," Ben says.

"That's how we met," Fran says.

"And after the smoked salmon, I'm going upstairs to work," Ben says.

"He means," Abigail says, "that he's going upstairs to drink."

Fran winks at Stuart quickly. Maybe she thinks he'll talk to Ben about drinking. Second on Fran's agenda.

"He walks everywhere," Abigail says, "you could go together."

"There's an idea," Roger says. He and Stuart nod at each other. We all know this will not happen.

Fran says, "I wonder what a movie star does when she wants to go window shopping. Personally, I like just walking with friends so much."

"Me, too," I say.

"That's absolutely *not* true," Stuart says. He picks up the last chocolate from the plate.

"I'd love to come to your writers' group," Fran says before we leave. "I'm writing a wonderful screenplay. So what do you all wear?"

A movie star does not go window shopping. This star has enough trouble shopping.

Fran was referring to a photograph in the *Evening Standard* of me behind Barbra, leaving a London Store. This happened a while ago. Barbra had seen something at the restaurant Le Manoir aux Quat' Saisons, which the maître 'd, Alain, had told us we could find at John Lewis.

"But it's like Macy's," I say, "you'll be mobbed."

"This will be different," Barbra says. "It's England, and we'll slip in and out." Her tone of voice makes it clear we're going. She sends her limo to pick me up. Fame moves through a crowd like one of those dog whistles you can't hear, like the sonic control or whatever it is that sends messages without wires. Stars have it. They are satellite personalities to a major degree, like the one in your family everyone gravitates around, only more so.

But Barbra is right—it *seems* different in England. As we shop, everyone notices. The difference here is no one says a single word, no one comes up to her with a card to sign, a song or movie idea. Just enough excitement flurries the staff into action.

One very cool aspect of shopping with a star—everything is possible. Immediately. If I wanted to do star for a day, it would probably be to get things fixed and delivered fast.

Although the English shopping public may be more reserved than we are, the press is just the reverse. A manager suggests that the car be brought around to a service exit. But by the time we get there, the press has found the same door. We burrow through the reporters and the snapping lights until we slip into the dark silence of the limo's back seat.

"I've been famous since I was a kid," she says, with exhaustion. She says it like fame is a kind of affliction.

And suddenly I remember how it had always seemed that way to me. It always seemed like an emergency—watching stars being rushed around, scared into time panics by studio and guards, crumpled breathless into limousines, watched over and pampered like little kids, never just free to come and go with no one watching, no one knowing where you were every minute, no one inviting you 'just because.' But then, if they don't invite you, you wonder if something's gone wrong. I'd wonder about my father's last picture, whether the box office was okay. But then every kid worries if the parent's scene changes: will the mood change?

My mood changes when Barbra calls. Another time: I am in my changing room taking things off. I'm down to sheer black pantyhose and black satin shirt, which is good for going into Stuart's changing room. Then the phone rings and it's Barbra's assistant, "She's got extra tickets for the theater tonight. Can you be ready in an hour?"

I put down the phone, dash into Stuart's changing room, already dressing; will he change plans? Agree to go out?

I don't want to tell him how being with her somehow pulls up a longing, for home, makes it feels so strong. But he knows. And, he'll go. Says he won't, but he's getting dressed. Now, that is.

"The friendship is about memory," Stuart says. "Barbra likes to hear your memories about Hollywood. And sometimes when you're with her, you remember how it was to be with your father. It's like coming home to a time you don't quite remember.

"She is also interested in the way you and I get along. We are real for her because she wants to see the truth—what really matters. A lot of her best friends have strong marriages."

"Not easy to find," I say.

He shows me pictures of times I've forgotten, of couples gathered around Barbra's sedar table. Are we like bookends, holding up our stories to keep them straight, easier to dust?

Line up her pictures in order and I'd guess the roles she's picked have tracked the evolution of my options as a woman.

"Barbra expects you to write again, trusts that you will do it, always asks how your work is going—and listens to the answer. Her curiosity's intense, like a journalist or a researcher. 'What do you mean by that?' 'What do you do with this?' You like that she's curious about you."

And then, I like to see how stardom has evolved.

Stars like Grace Kelly and Ingrid Bergman, Judy Garland and Elizabeth Taylor were frustrated by not having the power to do what they wanted. They would have had to be crazy to say 'No,' or 'This is what I want. Do it again. Do it my way.' Write their own books, like Shirley, invent their own personas, produce and direct their own movies like Barbra? Choose their co-stars? It would never have occurred to them.

Barbra's success allows her to do that. She's never pretentious. Perhaps because there's nothing Barbra has to pretend to that she isn't already.

I remember watching Barbra in her cream suit, heels, and fedora, looking at herself in the mirror at Le Manoir aux Quat' Saisons, an English country house hotel. All independent authority, she considers, adjusts. She's the director and the star.

Quite another matter when I watched Grace Kelly looking in a mirror in Helen Rose's costume design studio at MGM in 1955. This star stood with the preferred deference of the time, almost a condition of the contract, manners. I sat sketching quietly, waiting for the fitting of my first wedding gown. Whether Grace Kelly's gown was for the real wedding to Prince Rainier or for the wedding in *High Society*, any appearance was a part, a job. Every move had to be fresh but not unsettling, endearing but never sexual, stylish but not original. Expressions must be sincere, authentic, but not extraordinary. A flick of the eye this way, a slide of the smile there, and it's off—you've disconcerted the camera. The exchange is cut, the photographer loses faith. The expression, the voice—once they're gone, you can't find where you are. Even in a real day you were on. You didn't have a real day.

So here I am, one more time, walking.

Stuart's taking me out because I'm depressed about the one thing he can't fix: family. He never even tries. Distraction, as he knows, works best.

Before we go out, Johanna calls to tell me that Justin really doesn't want to fly alone to visit us this summer. "You don't know how it is to fly alone when you're a kid. You never went anywhere alone," Johanna says.

"Neither did you. I was with you. I'm sure I was. Or Nannie was."

Nannie was the Scotswoman who stayed even when there wasn't any money, fended off the landlord, and drank with me all night listening to my latest pages. Great for me.

"No," she said, "that's not true. We flew across the country alone all the time when we were eight and ten."

"I can't believe that!" I hate this.

"Mom, you don't remember."

"It's true." That's the darkest area, so dense with shame.

So before the phone can ring again, we leave the house. We are just about to cross Oxford Street, which in no way bears the élan of its name. Think Thirty-Fourth Street. Or Wilshire at Fairfax.

"I'm cold," I say.

"That's a warm coat," he says.

"I have to change."

"You don't like the coat."

That's true. I'd seen it reflected in some dark windows as we'd walked along. It looks awkward, but I say, "I'm just really cold." We go back and I change into the khaki leather coat from Loewe's. Excellent.

So we're coming down Bond Street. He's going past the windows as fast as the TV flicker, and here's Donna's store, all lit up, ready to open. And here's Donna—tall, wrapped in black wool up to her ears.

"See," I say, after we've hugged and looked around the store and gone on our way, "see, you never know who you'll run into. It's a good thing I changed."

"Donna's really going to remember that," he says, "as if you'd care what Debbie wears for Sunday lunch."

I think about all of us—Angie, Geraldine, Debbie, Svetlana, Judith and Laurie. I don't know what we wear. Only Mark dresses, when he can be there. But that's because he can't ever tell when Stuart will need him to drive somewhere.

We go to the café at the Intercontinental, where we will listen to an American jazz musician and drink Aqua Libra. They have a buffet where I can have sushi, which he won't eat, and he can have roast pork and everything else I won't eat.

I have worked out the longing to call Johanna back, to talk it over when it's too fresh will only make it harder. The thing to do is finish the book, and then go home to see my kids. Is home always where you started from?

Stuart's walking in his sturdy, rolling gait. I keep up with him easily, which is probably how he's worked out this walk. This street is more a mews: dark, winding, hidden, with doors open to narrow stairways lit by bare red lightbulbs. On the walls are pictures of women and terse job descriptions.

I look at Stuart in the dark lamplight. He once wrote, "Single men are designed around wall units, each woman another module."

Most men of his time spoke of women as numbers, car models, or graded them in numbers. Men did this especially when they were around other men, who assumed the more dismissive grief they said they gave women the more potent they appeared. Smart women (who believed this was a profitable approach) let men maintain that impression.

I hold his hand and listen to our footsteps along the cobblestone road.

26

*Y*ou don't have to watch me now, I want to say to Stuart as he leaves early this morning to meet with some business friends up north. I am okay. I know you'll come back. But then every time I hear your key in the door, or see you on the street coming to track me down, my heart skips a beat.

Just before he comes home, my friend and one of my favorite writers, Kennedy Frazier, calls me about a story for *Vanity Fair* that she doesn't want to do, a story she thought would be ideal for me. "It's sexy, Hollywood—not my kind of story, but perfect for you. So may they call you, is that all right?"

"Is that all right?" I say. "That's divine." Mainly what I hear is the chance to go to L.A., to see my kids. (As usual, I place them both conveniently in one spot.)

Five minutes after I hang up the phone I'm terrified. Where do I stay? Oxford is one thing. How will I manage L.A. on my own?

And then, to go home and not drive. But it will not happen. I won't get the job. That is the real dark fear.

I hear the key in the door. I'm not going to tell him about Kennedy's call.

"I had a bite after the meeting with Carl. Then Jeff joined us, all optimism of course."

"I figured."

He puts down his leather envelope on the hall table, flings his black raincoat over the banister, hurls the umbrella into the copper stand.

Stuart likes to do his own coffee. Then he goes into his gray room, tosses the evening paper onto the table by his blue-green leather chair. Then he sits at his desk and looks at messages and starts to open mail with his paper knife.

"Will Carl be all right?"

Stuart sips his coffee, slashes open another envelope, "It's a weakening proposition, scientifically and legally."

"How do you tell him?"

"You help him come up with a positive new proposal before you tell him how much trouble he's in."

"The sixteenth degree of denial."

"Of course," he says, "here I am trying to bolster his confidence about himself and his company when my own position is so vulnerable."

"You'll see." Our friend Mike has described us as "defying the laws of financial gravity." This is a particularly defiant time. "Something may come along." I could raise his hopes so fast, but this is no more than the kind of positive new proposal he invents for Carl. I stand behind him and rub his shoulders. "Don't do the mail now . . ."

I was going to say "like all men," but it's like all of us. He leaves so upbeat—crisp bow tie, fluffy hair. Then he comes back from a meeting with a company—any meeting, any company—telling me it went fine in a particularly deliberate way, which tells me nothing interesting happened and any expectations he might have invented didn't come off. This kind of reentry takes about twenty minutes.

I am glad I have not told him. No one has called. Would I really want to do the story? Maybe it's time I cleaned up my act. What act? Disappointment moves into heavy denial.

I can't leave him right now anyway. Next week Stuart is having angioplasty, a kind of surgery where they slip a slender wire into the heart to see how it feels, sometimes by that very act shocking it into action. Or that's how I see it. The doctor has tried to make it clear this is a routine procedure. We have made it serious, if not critical.

I am no more an accessory of his life than he is of mine; no more, no less, an accessory than the heart to the body.

I sleep in his arms the night before he goes to the hospital. Do I imagine his heartbeat is off? My grandmother lived outside the arena of the sexual century. I loved curling around her body, wrapped close in her arms. I'd press my head close to her breast, hearing her heart working hard to beat, praying these beats were okay. I used to try to count the beats.

I listen to Stuart's heart beating now. Does it flutter, like a moth trying to lift up when its wings are wet? Is this a long, drowsy beat, and has there been too long between this one and the one before?

We have talked about what happens if he dies. Before one of his operations, my father said to my godfather, "If I die, don't tell Miriam."

Stuart said, "When I die, our wills are upstairs in my dresser."

"Under the silk pocket handkerchiefs."

"Yes."

"With your latent supply of Cadbury's."

"Exactly. So you'll out my chocolates."

"You bet."

Judith comes with us to the hospital. I fill in the application blank, which has a place for "title." I put "Sir." They look at him and believe it.

Class behavior still works in a few corners of England; it works because the upper class is a security class. Upper-class people will provide things: work, a place to live, chocolates. It's a godparent class, handing down tidbits of reassurance.

Laurie is here waiting with me during the operation. "Don't clutch this hand," she tells me, "I'll never draw again. Sit on my other side. Here's my right hand."

The operation goes fine. This does not mean I don't need to watch him all this next night in the hospital, sleeping. The move of the triple circumflexes above his brows, now the right, now the left. They give sexy emphasis, a touch of surprise, where someone else might smile. His eyelids are shadowed in lavender and taupe, two of the better colors of the silk hankies in the drawer; heather like the Yorkshire moors, like the small veins in his big, smooth hands.

Over each brow there's a pearly knob underscored by the curvaceous frown line. The ram's horns were hacked off here at birth so no one would pick up that he is unreal.

After three hours, Laurie convinces me he will live even if I am not watching. She is clever. "Maybe *Vanity Fair* has called. You could, you know, tell me what the story is and you won't b'shri it."

"Maybe," I say.

I kiss his forehead, and we walk home together. I make some chicken soup, then bring some down to Laurie's flat.

Laurie's room is square with two arches. She is making color reproductions of medieval Biblical illustrations for a Dutch collector, and you almost expect to see some of those medieval figures standing in the arches. On the blue skirt of a woman doing laundry, "a symbolic washing away," Laurie explains, there's also the glow of firelight on her skirt. "See, I'm a middle-class artist with her feather duster," she says, as the gray and copper feathers whisk away microscopic pencil ash from the picture.

"Is the soup for us or really for Stuart?" Laurie asks.

"For him, but he's not eating. Making it is for me."

She has the chicken soup. I am lying on Laurie's couch while she listens to classical music with the particular silence of an artist working. This is like being with my mother in her studio—the gift of meditation. With her left hand lightly moving like a harpist, you can't tell whether it's music or drawing—the arts all mix together.

She sits in a sturdy black artist's chair, a kind of working chair that does everything; it adjusts for your feet, your back. On either side of her easel she has white carts on rollers with pencils, a really good straight-edge ruler, small dolls from a flea market—Ernest Borgnine, Bionic Woman, Cindy, Action Man, "much better than anatomical models," she's told me—music tapes divided by classical, pop and jazz ("my brother had his in alphabetical order, which frightened me, so I pulled them all out and had to put them all back") and racks of books.

"So tell me the story," she says.

"They want someone to find the girl everyone said Polanski raped. I could go to L.A."

"So what if she's not in L.A.?"

I had not considered this.

"She could be in Battersea, or Detroit," Laurie suggests.

"Where I have no family," I say.

"So," Laurie says, "what's to b'shri?"

Halfway through reading my pages that Sunday, a riff about my father and Adlai Stevenson, I stop and I tell the writers about the *Vanity Fair* proposition.

"You're packing now," Mark says. They're ecstatic, encouraging.

"Stuart will never trust me to go by myself," I say.

Oxford was miles. This is time travel. I could go and never come back to the present.

"Do you trust yourself?" Geraldine asks. "That's the point."

"So . . . ," I'm careful as I tell Stuart about the story that night, "I haven't been to L.A. for years. But Jeremy does want me to be with Phoebe. I haven't asked, but I'm sure I could stay with him."

"We were there last year, Jill. You wrote about L.A. for a travel magazine. I played the piano, Phoebe danced, and you had a family reunion."

"Don't say it like an accusation. You have reunions, too. And family."

"Family," he says, looking at mail, "nostalgia . . . melodrama . . . and severe editing."

Thinking about my family leads to considerations of denial. Losing memory is sometimes yesterday's denial—and I do that. Denial is not acknowledging what I see right now. Then, when I do find it in the memory store later, it will have been redone, will look the way I want it to look.

I see it in the way I can handle it, although I am trying, here, not only to remember, but to remember that time as it was. But doesn't that mean as I saw it? Aren't I accused, if lovingly, of seeing things in the sentimental spectrum of old Technicolor?

It's just that I don't think reality is always the harsh side; you don't always have to look with the cold, clear eye. It's an irony that the sexual era coexists with this looking at everything real. Sex does so well with romance, which needs to wear a little denial behind the ears, to flick it on the lashes and spray it on the throat before you say a word.

"I've almost finished reading your journals," I say to Stuart this morning. "I stayed up all night."

As the journals progress, they're filled with more scenes of his own memory, tough writing about the years at Procter & Gamble, the part of his life I don't want to see, when he seemed to be the contained forceful male, like my father was when he ran MGM. In his journals, Stuart writes about the fear, the restlessness, the conflicts, and how they're brought into focus by dealing with me, caring for me. Once again, he is the contained male. The story he wants to write about his own life is jetting out of these journals.

"Were the journals helpful?" he asks quietly. He's reading the *Herald Tribune* and I'm distracting both of us from the issue at hand—L.A. on my own.

I'm kneeling by his blue-green armchair, stroking his pink flannel robe, the one with pictures of ice cream cones on it. "I never saw the pain and difficulty you went through, not just because of how little I registered during these years, but because of my fragility—you've been so trapped. You must have felt like a keeper stopping me from being lost, confused, or frightened into blowing a fuse forever. You also dealt with such tempers!"

"Those were not new," he says wryly, "but you did throw yourself into the street in front of cars more often. Your temper was just exaggerated by the early medications." There were scenes he had to just mellow down for fear I'd work myself up into a seizure. And there was always the question, was I aware he wouldn't retaliate because he was scared I'd crack?

"Stuart, listen, through every year," I continue, "as you write in your journals, you talk about not writing your book. Yet you're writing it. It's here, in the journals. You never told me how much you were missing it, how hard it must have been doing work you hated so that I could lie around trying to connect fragments of sentences."

"I will write my book when the time is revealed." He already looks tired of the conflict he'd have to have with himself to write it.

"In 1990," I remind him, "you wrote, 'I won't be writing in 1990,' and you also wrote, 'That is unacceptable.'

"You also said that some consultants concentrated on making money—others, you, as you said, 'tried to perpetuate a dream of management.' You even try to make business creative, like a figurehead of a character in an old skyscraper movie. Stuart, you believe so in whatever you do. You didn't think you could support your family by writing, so you thought of business like writing or directing, having an image, working with people, shaping their stories, like a director. It's also like teaching, like counseling, which I've watched you do brilliantly. Maybe that is what you want."

He hates when I do this. "I can't talk about this now. I need to get dressed, take a walk to pick up some coffee."

"Of course, the minute I start to talk about you—your writing—or not writing—you have something you need to go and pick up."

"Jill," he stops, "I watch you. I've seen how it was. I'm the only one who knows." He switches glasses, puts down the newspaper. "I can't pretend it would be easy to see you go."

He sits forward in the chair. "I can't ignore what I see, even when I don't tell you."

"What you think you see is your mom."

"I can't help that. I see how hopeful it was when the new doctor changed her medication. Our phone calls were lively, encouraging. She kept up the snappy exchanges that lure me into calling. She reacted with excitement, not fear, to the notion of visiting London, the way, on good days, you have no trouble thinking about going anywhere. But a day later and she's gone again. She's forgotten all the joking, the teasing, the poems, the organ playing, the old songs, histories retold, days, nights, and old times recast, reshaped to fit the present; the Christmas hams, the Stilton cheeses, the chocolate Yule logs."

"You think I'll go up and down like your mother, and wind up out there down and alone. But I'm not her. I don't have what she has. And I'm not alone. My kids do care."

"But,"—it's heating up—"right here—look at right now—you've forgotten that your children and I do get along. I'm the one who reminds you. You forgot Jeremy's Thanksgiving visit when Phoebe was still in their arms. You forgot how he strolled with me and we talked of buying land together."

"But when you remind me of things—you remind me of your mother."

"Stuart, I have my weird days—but hardly as many. I know you're afraid of me going somewhere. Maybe that's what's happening. But it will never happen," I tell Stuart, "because they'll find out I can't write anymore."

"Look, they know you've written several books. Has that slipped your mind?"

"That was before. And the last one got reviewed in New Jersey."

"The condition was to write, to be published—and you've done that."

"You're cranky," I say, "because you don't want me to go."

"No," he says, "you're cranky because you're scared to go, and you think if I get mad, I'll stop you. I don't want that. This is a great chance for you."

*S*ex was the opening move in L.A. conversation in the sixties. Now it's "What's your favorite meeting?" or "Where does your kid go to school?"

It's very likely, with the sensibility I have now, that I choose to see those days as evil. Most of the books and articles I read, most of the people I talk to, speak from today's sober approach. In the sixties, we spent more energy looking back in anger at our parents than we put into our own kids. Our children have become the parents we now wish we had been.

First of all, I want to talk to Polanski. I find someone who will give him my number. I call people who will be interesting about that time; people who might have clues to the girl; people who knew Polanski; people who were there.

For most of us, far more important was the murder of Polanski's wife, a bloody enough event to throw any man. So what, I think when I read the two stories again with today's attitude. We threw him out of America for this?

I call Rafelson and his ex-wife, Toby. I call Brooke Hayward and Dennis Hopper. Brooke says, "Polanski is a bitter man." She last saw Polanski in Paris in 1981. "He hadn't felt he'd made a great film in years." That was long ago the way lives go these days.

And then you can talk to any artist on any given day, or night, and hear that all the work they've done sucks rats. "Don't trust any artist who doesn't doubt his work," my mother said.

I decide to call someone else. Someone who was, as I saw it, outside the sixties scene, I think.

I'm not sure Bob Redford will remember, but we were in class together at school. I like the pictures he chooses to make. And he keeps a balanced perspective. He's involved and maintains a cool, objective eye at the same time.

His assistant was careful. She'd get back to me, she said.

Gillian Farrell, the mystery writer and Larry Beinhart's wife, reminds me, "Polanski's name came up a year ago when we were here for dinner. It was just after you did that travel story on L.A."

"I did?"

Andrea Tana, the painter with the auburn hair, was here that night. They all come over again to refresh my memory. "We agreed that from the Hollywood perspective, the sixties ended when Manson killed Sharon Tate in 1969," Andrea says. "I heard the people who bought that house have tours through it—like a monument to murder."

The candles on the table tonight flicker. In even the worst movie of this scene, they would not do that.

"Is Polanski still in Paris?" Larry asks. Larry's rugged John Garfield face is directed by challenge.

"Sure," Gillian says, "in exile. Remember we wondered what happened to her?"

"I still think it was just a story—someone set him up. If it was real she'd have been on TV, written a best-seller by now. No one even knew who it was."

By "no one" we mean us, privileged insiders. If we don't know, it isn't true—never happened.

"But it was this young actress," Andrea mentions her name, "I know that."

"I've never heard of her," Larry says.

"Young actress," Gillian says, "not a big star."

"Clearly," I say, "since no one has her name right."

"But why wouldn't she talk about it?"

"Someone she loves doesn't want her to. She's in her thirties now. Would you want to talk about it if you had kids?"

"Do we know if she has kids?"

"TV actress in L.A. doing nothing. Why hasn't she come out with it?" Sure. Why wouldn't she want the bestseller, the movie deal? Suppositions work the room. Gillian says she'll talk to her friend Leuci, a great detective in Rhode Island.

She calls the next evening. "He'll talk to you."

Leuci has the voice. You'd cast him right from "Hello."

"Where do you begin?"

He says he has an idea, and he'll call me back. Each phone call has that waiting time, like waiting for a date.

"The public never forgave Roman because someone murdered his wife and shocked them," Toby Rafelson says. She has a salty, wise Eastern voice, Sara Mankiewicz. The Rafelsons' house was a place to talk, to eat. L.A.'s Central Park West.

"He was supposed to be chaste forever. Perhaps Roman's exile is an anxious xenophobic reaction to his dark work, a confusion of what happened to Sharon. Somehow the public believed if he had never been there this would never have happened."

I want to hear from my agent and from the detective, who are both doing the same job, looking for something I don't believe I'll get. Who will call back first?

Waiting. Writers do this very well.

The trick is to get out of the house before you think the phone might ring. Then you do not watch the phone. And when it is a call from New York you are waiting for, it will not come until you sit down to eat dinner. The phone is far more likely to ring, however, if you are out.

But the call will not come on Monday. People are then dealing with stuff they didn't do on Friday, and they've come in late because of the weekend traffic.

Tuesday they are dealing with urgent things. Writers are not urgent.

Wednesday is their best day to do lunch. After a long lunch, there's barely time to go back to the office before you have to meet someone over drinks. (Meeting over drinks is work talk. Meeting for drinks is another thing.)

After drinks, it will be too late to call London.

Thursday could be a day for calls. But then they're cleaning up for Friday, when it's just as well to work at home and miss the weekend traffic.

I contemplate the story. I reread Cheryl Crane's tough book about her shattering childhood and triumphant recovery. Raped and battered by two of her mother's guys, accused of murder when she was trying to save her mother's life, Cheryl was raped from the time she was ten. This might give me a clue to this girl's angle now.

Cheryl's mom, Lana Turner, was the perfect silver screen star in black and white, all creamy, pearly luster; complete glamour, and marrying, marrying, marrying. Cheryl used to watch movies in an empty screening room. Bob Topping told Cheryl her real father, Stephen Crane, a night-club owner, had died, so Cheryl would call Bob "Dad." Loretta Young won't admit, even now, that Judy is her own child. Judy thought she was adopted until her wedding night, when Jack Haley Jr., son of the Tin Man in *The Wizard of Oz*, told her she really looked a lot like her father, Clark Gable. My mother told me during one of the long night talks just after she'd finished Judy's portrait.

"She looks more like her father there," I said.

"I think so," my mother said.

I asked Judy if she ever saw her father, and this was long ago, when she said only once, when she was sixteen and getting out of the pool in her new red bathing suit. And there was Gable at the garden gate, looking.

"Perfect," I said and knew I'd steal it for a story.

Big tanned Tarzan Lex Barker took Cheryl Crane into the sauna, where she'd never been. Where the only light came from the dark gold bulb on the ceiling; quizzing her, touching her, "did he ever do anything like this?" He took it out, rubbed it, said it was his rabbit. "Remember, from now on this is going to be our secret, ya got that?"

You see a spirit ennobled by a lousy childhood; a girl put into reform school for saving her mother's life by stabbing her lover. Naive, scared, she slashed him sharp side up. Cheryl was her mom's protector. The giant child-like ego needs all the attention it can get. The wise child attempts to get anything from its parent, so it becomes the listener, the home audience, the comforter, the parent.

Jeremy and Johanna could dine out well with Cheryl.

Gillian calls me a week later, after midnight. She's excited. "Leuci's trying to reach you, and he has someone for you to talk to."

Leuci's daughter, Santina, produces the show called *Hard Copy*. Larry Silver, this lawyer for the girl who was raped, has called her. He wants $100,000 for the story.

When I actually get Silver on the phone, I tell him, "I want to do something serious, to show how kids can reinvent their lives." I talk about how the fame plague rips right down through families, about the marketing of kids from the beginning of time.

I talk fast, tell Silver I've been there, written about it, "every woman who's been drugged or drunk knows about rape. It's not something you want to explore again if you get through it."

He's listening. He's got hearings, he'll make some space if I call him next week.

"I know I shouldn't have trusted Santina," Silver says. He's had a "week from hell." He's going to try to turn it into an epic. Some people who do that make it worse. But then, some come through better than the ones who say, "Sure, right away!"

"It's *Vanity Fair*," Stuart says.

That's early. I dash to the phone. It's all over, probably. There's no hello, and I never heard of this person. But then, if I had, I wouldn't remember.

"We had a call from Robert Redford's office." This is not my editor's voice, not George. This voice has attitude. It's in the job description. "We don't like our press to call stars unless you've been given clearance."

"I am not press!" I say, shaking. Anger, embarrassment, or fear. Who cares. Let it sound imperious. Think Hepburn. "Look, I know movie stars you haven't even heard of. Redford and I went to school together long ago when Sepulveda was just a pass and there were trolleys downtown. Don't tell me anything about L.A., its people, or who I can talk to," and hang up the phone.

"Terrific!" Stuart says. "You did that well."

"And killed the job. And I just vaguely remember Redford. He won't remember me."

I spread the Liberty cloths with the big scarlet poppies across the dining room table. One cloth has an ivory background, the other black. The poppies remind me of the acres of poinsettia fields stretching from back of the Sawtelle Veterans Administration Hospital, all the way along the Sepulveda Pass, back when that was the main way to the Valley.

I do know L.A. That is, and was, my town. This kid assistant wouldn't know what I mean if I talk about the poinsettia fields that carried on about as far as the tunnel.

Debbie, as always, is the first of the writers to arrive. She dresses like a very small, impoverished French model, with tiny tops and skirts that no one else could figure out how to wear. Her black curls mix into the shaggy black scarf. She hands me tulips and begins untangling herself from her coat, shoulder bags, and sweaters.

"I was thinking of you and all the men you must have slept with," Geraldine says, "if I can say that."

"Well, you just did," says Debbie.

"But I mean," Geraldine says, "how hard it must be to have forgotten all that. You can study us for women characters, but who can you turn to when you want to write a man's character who isn't Stuart?"

"No one says she can't look," Judith says.

Do I even bother to remember? Or are they all Stuart, which is why it's not working?

"Can I read," Judith says, "because I have to leave early."

So she reads, "Sylvia wrote a list of what men do. She rode the tube. She watched them for a whole day: jeans hitchers, belt hikers, watch checkers, wallet tappers, ear scratchers, brow twirlers, neck stretchers, shruggers, hand wranglers, chin rubbers with their invisible beard, or no beard at all, but pulling jaw skin up, nose rubbers and pickers, hand washers and crackers, ball shifters, bald guys rubbing like that would bring the hair back. And then guys with glasses got a whole world: pulling them down to rub their noses, looking up over them, taking them off, twirling, spinning, clicking.

"It's hard to find one," she reads, twirling her pencil between her right forefinger and thumb, jiggling her right knee and twitching her left ankle, "hard to find one who sits still, and harder than that to find one you'd want to sleep with."

"Well," Debbie says, "you do look." Debbie is still slight, translucent with postadolescence, which makes her sharp sentences startling.

Judith glares, "But it's good, isn't it?"

"Great," Angie says, "you can just hear Sylvia!"

"I like that. You're so good when you keep her close to you. You watch them like you're making a movie."

"Because that's what Sylvia's character wants to do," Judith snaps.

After Judith leaves, we have some tea and honey and eat the muffins.

"So," I say, "I was reading about the Acropolis in the memory palace book. It was the most important image of the ancient Athenian world, its crowning image—and I was wondering if each story or book has a crowning image, a moment we're going for that a particular character never loses sight of. Finding the girl is as far as I can imagine now."

Can I imagine that far? Does memory's break amputate the ability to project, to imagine ahead? My Acropolis today is really seeing L.A.—getting home.

Debbie is also almost always the last to leave. I'm in the kitchen when the phone rings. Debbie's bringing in the ice cream dishes, which now only hold cut-up fruit. Have our writing styles changed as much as our eating habits?

"Would you pick that up, luv?" You learn to say "love," not "darling," and after five years, you say it with some slight shift, which means it's got a "u" in the middle. (Don't try. You have to be here.)

"Jill," Debbie comes whispering in, her cheeks scarlet, "he said, 'Hi, this is Robert Redford.' And it is!"

"Okay, okay." I fluff my hair in the mirror over the kitchen sink and dash to the phone.

"Hi," I say, "I'm sorry. I didn't mean to bother you, but I think you know me . . ."

"Jill, you think I'll know you?!? We've known each other since school and I was in one of your dad's plays, don't you remember? It was my first try on Broadway."

I explain to him about the memory thing, leaving out the epilepsy bit. I also hate to say it was a stroke, which sounds old, so I probably said what I do, which is "this thing happened and I was in a coma and lost my memory." No one asks "what thing?" if you say it all fast enough.

"I'd love to see you and talk to you. Just call when you get to L.A."

28

"So, you believe in keeping everything you have ever worn?" Valerie Wade has come to help me pack for L.A. I have not let too many friends into my changing room. It is here that I become who I will be today.

"Now I understand how you do it," she says, "you make up outfits the way I make up rooms." Valerie has the definitive interior design shop on King's Road. "You take old pieces and invent another look for them. But what could this have been?"

She holds up the patio circle skirt Loretta Young made for my mother the Christmas "everyone was doing one." It has royal blue and emerald green hydrangeas and is scattered with sequins.

"It's wonderful with a chartreuse ascot shirt and a delphinium cummerbund."

"I don't see it for slipping in and out of rooms trying to find the girl."

"I may have found her." I put the skirt aside. And Ralphie's ancient knitted golden cardigan.

"You're kidding! Not really?!"

"One of the Fulbright award winners, you know, for detective novels, knows this lawyer in Boston whom I called. The lawyer sounds exactly like the guy in *NYPD Blue*—Slovensky or something." The man you marry after the one you knew you shouldn't have married gets away. Cranky. Smart. Heavy. Maybe Slivowitz, protective and loyal. "Anyway, he says he thinks he may have an idea but he'll have to make a call. It may be nothing."

I toss the gold sweater into the bag. "There is nothing better than this and a white shirt."

"Except the tan Donna Karan one you've already packed. But I mustn't discourage you. So, have you heard back from Polanski?"

"Nothing. He told me to leave him alone. I don't want to find her before I get there anyway."

"This is something you tell us all the time."

"So, it's no news?"

"None."

"I'm not sure Jeremy remembers me."

"Are you sure you remember Jeremy?"

"Fair question." Tough question.

We wanted to raise our children in a way different from the way our own parents did. I remember bedtime was of no interest, and why go to school if a peace march was coming together. This was political consciousness, just a new take on my father's approach.

The night before I go, Polanski does call me back from Paris. He's charming. I don't want to lie to him, but I try to talk to him about the changes in Hollywood. He was taken in, he tells me, by the "ingenuous time of the sixties in Hollywood"—the notion that everything was all right, that you could do anything.

He says, "The sixties ended when Kennedy was killed. Sharon's murder and the landing on the moon changed everything—when man walked on the moon some romantic idea of the moon was over. I believed in romance when I was with her—but then the magic illusion was gone."

We talk about the fear, the bitterness running through his dark, complex love stories. Could innocence still turn him on?

He's careful. "The artist catches violence. If it's there in the culture, he'll reflect it."

I am thinking of questions, such as, "Did your own longing freeze at that time? Did you need someone new to begin again? Would you have bolted if you did it again now?" These are questions I might better ask myself.

"But," Polanski says, "we all did things we might regret. Sex and power and celebrity are all the same in America—which has taken the mystery out of sex." He spoke dismissively. "Now when you speak to an ingenue, you hear a baby crying in the background." Like many great directors, he's swift and icy, until you're into the scene he wants and then he's totally there with you, until he wants to move on.

"If you read my autobiography you will see all you need to know about that day."

He says he hasn't time to see me. And there's no point in telling him his autobiography is out of print and not in London libraries.

I saw my brain in a dream last night, spread out around me like this oatmeal cashmere blanket Jeremy sent me. I was stroking it to appreciate the things it was doing, showing it off in fact, when I saw under a puff of the blanket there was a fire. I put it out quickly only to see another, and on and on, as if all over neurons were exploding into tiny bonfires.

Do I trust you, brain, from one day to the next? Can I go along to this corner, certain you're not sabotaging another place I've forgotten to lay my attention? Can I catch it all?

29

I am flying home, jetting back to a world I know.

Last night I reread bits of *The Cause,* the novel I wrote about the sixties for Ed Doctorow when he was a young editor. I would chronicle the world I felt bursting around me. This was my destiny. I was full of naive drive—and speed. I couldn't make the last draft.

This story is different. I know about rape. I know the sixties. I am this girl.

Stuart's son Philip calls it "The Golden Age of Sex." "So, what was it like?" he said when he visited. He's blond, with loose, long-limbed, an-idea-a-minute vitality. If there are period faces, Philip has the tough, tender thirties man face. Maybe it was last week—or Thanksgiving. The point is what he meant was the time after the Pill and before AIDS.

I was just as fast then, except I'd take stuff so I could listen more intently to my mentors and coaches. I must be something to be in their awesome presence. I never saw their desperation. They needed my young wonder as much as I needed their wisdom.

At thirty I almost killed myself because Sylvia Plath was a famous poet and I wasn't. What chance would life have if you weren't a legend by thirty?

It isn't the custom now to speak of sex in our old easy way, in the style of the "Golden Age," as Philip put it. Sex was a craft then, as readily picked up and discussed as basket weaving. To keep its mystique alive, we had to come up with new ideas, new taboos to spring free of. Initiative and imagination mattered.

When you're young you think you can get away with anything—now that I'm grown, I see what a hustler I was. I no longer wanted to be seen as this kid who had everything. To be a real writer I needed to know what real trouble was like. If I'd held on, life would have come to me. But I went looking. I wanted to walk the high wire.

My first marriage, to my children's father, was crumbling. I was hardly trying. My book came first, neck and neck with sex. This was 1962 and the art of sex was in the pretense, in the invention of new ways to lie together. "We did it standing!" I whispered to one of my girlfriends who had been married longer. "So," she shrugged, "we did it with the lights on."

"And your eyes open?"

"Really," she nodded.

No one talks now about how it felt then to suspect there was something more to sex, something more than even these gymnastic positions we thought we'd discovered.

My first husband looked like Raymond Burr, who played a detective in a TV series; every description was in reference to a TV or movie star, or a car. He also looked like a mid-fifties Buick. This was a heavy car with large swashes of chrome. Escada clothes look like Buicks, so in a way my first husband reminded me of a line of clothes that hadn't been invented then. His mother, on her fifth marriage at the time, would have been comfortable in Escada.

On this night he had fallen asleep again in front of the TV. This made the room the color of a black-and-white movie. He had his cigarettes in the pocket of his pajama shirt. He was snoring softly, but looked entirely attractive in the slate-gray light.

I felt damp and raw and breathless with longing, and I'd taken off my clothes and poured myself over him the way you do, kissing, licking, reaching. He was heavy on me; I was a treadmill, a trampoline, and the thrill of just the idea of doing sex had gone. "Doesn't anything satisfy you?" he said. There had to be a catch to it, and I didn't know what it was.

I wanted it to feel at least as surreal as the sensations I'd have a few times during the day. I thought they were from speed.

They felt like falling and flying all at once—like dreams I'd had of how sex would be. So I went to see a serious Freudian analyst who had experienced enough, we all believed, to tell us hard things. He had known all our parents. He'd look at you at family gatherings and you'd dig in for your worst ideas and figure, if you were feeling lust, envy, or fear, you were onto an authentic track. He liked to use Latin sex words around kids. Our parents snapped to attention. We'd blush; he'd wink. I'd read it all in Latin, the only foreign language I learned carefully because the very good parts of Havelock Ellis's *The Psychology of Sex* were all in Latin. I didn't know exactly what they meant, but I'd whisper "fellatio" and "cunnilingus" to myself when I thought of Gable's leer or Brando's loins.

"Many men don't understand women's sexual response," the analyst said. The words were unbearably hot. Did he want to show me?

I explained to my husband that there must be another way to make it work. But every time I'd get close, I'd feel the way I did as a child, when naked, raw images crackled in my head with a warm hum, the world would go black, and I'd wake up somewhere else. If this was coming, I couldn't risk getting to the other side.

We were trying once again. Hating the surreal images creeping into my brain, I wanted it to be all his fault. I wanted to stop, but you couldn't be the quitter. It would be a long time before imaginative coaches got me to take the leap, convincing me, even, that the suspense was seductive.

The phone rang just in time. "What?" I shouted into the receiver.

"Bobbie's in trouble," I snapped at my husband. "I have to go."

"That's one more excuse to go hang around with all your friends." This was, of course, true.

Bobbie, my friend Roberta Neiman, was not in trouble, but she could hear I was. Bobbie said she'd pick me up on her way to the Ferus gallery.

Every Monday night the art galleries on La Cienega were open late. The artists Ed Ruscha, Ed Moss, and Andy Warhol and dealers like the Easterner Richard Feigen, who visited every summer since he was a teenager, and Molly Barnes, who had always been part of our world, were here to see the scene. Artists cruised, checking out the space, the crowds, and the prices the dealer put on their buddies' work. Later, after the dinners at El Coyote, much later at the Beanery, they'd talk about the work, their dreams of glory.

On most Mondays the time we spent hanging out after the galleries closed began to last longer than the time looking at the pictures. We'd start at one gallery and wander on. Unless there was an opening, like tonight. And the pictures, like Ed Kienholz's assemblages, were sometimes not pictures. Art, like our lives, sprawled and leapt outside its frames. The art spilled out first, then we followed. The things Kienholz assembled for us to stroll around were pictures from the darker images of *True Confessions*.

Larry Bell and James Rosenquist (and, when they were around, Roy Lichtenstein and David Hockney) used to come over to Lynn and Don Factors' on Sundays. Theirs might have been the first severely modern house on a Beverly Hills street, stark and white in a procession of Venetian, Moroccan, Federal, and Tudor mansions. Hockney wore tennis flannels and so did Irving Blum. Feigen wore ivy league shirts. Don Factor had a court, so maybe he used to play. When my father broke his back and couldn't play anymore, he tore down the tennis court.

"You know," Lynn Factor said, standing there in her smooth new JAX dress, "these are like the tableaux we used to have around Christmastime along Little Santa Monica, little stables full of straw. It's like you've done dark tableaux."

"I've been waiting for you to tell me what I've done," Kienholz says, sucking at his cigar and looking her over. Bald and burly like a Harley rider, his chin's a match for his beer belly. Tiny, piercing eyes. I thought of Sylvia Plath's poem about the Nazi. How dark can I go, how down? Can I file away the elegant cover of my family image? Can I show someone who I really am, and then see, somehow, if I can be loved even so? Can I be someone even so? Can you touch me now? What about this? And after this and look at this—not now, you'll never look back now—testing, testing, how far can I go down and still get back?

I'd learned that the way to pass for hip was to say nothing.

He looked me up and down and asked if I'd like a joint. I didn't like pot so I sidestepped, asked him to be on my radio show.

"You don't want me on your show," Kienholz said.

He looked like a construction worker with his jeans down low, backside cleavage and burly shoulders. But he did do his constructions after learning the academic way. Like my mother said, you didn't take off into new abstract worlds until you knew what you were taking off from, until your own line was steady and clear enough to give your work a presence.

We were standing in front of his royal blue car assemblage with the couple doing heavy petting in the backseat. "I'm not about talking 'look at what I do,'" he said.

"Maybe you'll see what you really want to think about," I swung around to the door. "I have a deadline I have to make."

"Make me," he said so quietly.

"Later," I said and fled.

I had an office by then in the Writers' Building in Beverly Hills. The building, long and not too high, was built to last through a good quake. My office was on the third floor. I found a bright yellow Mexican rag rug and paper flowers on Olvera Street one Sunday when I took my kids downtown for tacos. The office was twenty-five dollars a month and my payments were usually late.

I said I took the office so I would discipline my writing. I'd go for several hours every day. I couldn't work at home surrounded by reverence in every antique bank, every painting and silver candelabra; chaos reflected in every unanswered letter, crumpled manuscript, and smashed glass, leftovers from last night's fight, which I'd triggered to distract from the terror of writing.

I had a typewriter in my office, packages of typing paper, and yellow pencils. I knew not to have a phone. The screenwriter downstairs, married to my son's godmother, let me give the number to Nannie.

Here I'd try to finish the novel about the woman looking for a cause to give her life to, as her liberal father and his friends seemed to do during the war and the years of blacklisting. I had no such gift of focus, no real fervor in spite of the snappy jargon I tossed around on TV with Mort Sahl. The only thing that drove me forward, screaming along empty beaches, was sex.

But you couldn't write about that.

I had my father's old writing desk in my office and a canvas director's chair. "I need something to lie down on," I told Brooke and Dennis. "You have to sleep yourself into some scenes and stories."

"Kienholz has an old psychiatrist's couch that would be ideal," Dennis said.

"Just think," Brooke said, "of the ghosts of old Freudian dreams you can pick up."

I met up with Kienholz at Barney's and followed him up to his house in my car. You could make it with any artist (even if you weren't so sure it was art, after all), but you couldn't drive in a car with any man if you had kids you had to support.

Some of this was the beginning of feminism. For art, it was the last decade of the presumed male.

His pickup truck sputtered and chugged up the canyon, and I staggered behind him on the trails to his house, where he climbed over his harem of embracing, lunging, hovering mannequins; bodies and limbs like car parts (some were car parts).

"She can't collect art," Lynn Factor once told a photographer from New York she introduced me to, "so she's collecting artists." She laughed.

"In what way?" Her friend leered down over me, his big square jaw shadowing his ascot printed with peacock plumes.

"I eat them for breakfast."

"No wonder art in L.A. is so prolific. Heady meals. I knew it," He said.

Kienholz's territory was like a hillbilly hideout ambling round in the far back of Laurel Canyon. There were lizards drowsing on the old car parts, a large one with blue flecked paint on its stubbly tail, and I knew he'd look like that, stubby, when he slipped his jeans down even farther. The nakedest part of a man anyway is the back of his neck, where you'd pick him up with your jaw and carry him off to your cave. You own him when you bite him there.

The lump on his neck rose above his undershirt. There was more than one lump, a varied musculature of severe power. I thought it best to back off. But I did him. You try to think of it as conferring a kind of artistic grant.

You could look down at night and see La Cienega, which he said was as close as he wanted to be to the art scene. No artist says he wants to be part of the scene, but in the beginning they have to play it to survive. Hang out in a corner, look angry, depressed, or chilly. Come late. Leave early. Do not dress in any hip way, or like an average artist in jeans and a shirt.

My art teacher, Howard Warshaw, gave an impact to the wombat in his pictures that you wouldn't have suspected, and laid more truth on the rule that the worst-dressed guy at the gallery was the best artist—until art got hot and artists wore Ralph Lauren. I am not talking about women artists, for this was the edge of the sixties and there were no women artists to speak of in L.A.

If there were, I didn't want to hear about them because my mother was as good as any of them—and I didn't want to know how she was feeling. You don't know some things until it's too late.

I didn't kiss Kienholz that day. It wouldn't exactly be adultery (still a major concept of some deep concern back then) if you didn't do certain things.

You would not kiss lips.

You would not stroke hair. No problem with Kienholz, he had none to think about.

You would not say love words such as "darling."

You would not smile up at them (or down at them, depending upon where you happened to be in the arrangement).

You would keep it tough.

"Snakes are aphrodisiacs to German shepherds," Kienholz pointed out as we finished this turn through his chaparral trailer park territory, winding through tossed-off ideas, sawed-off mannequins, loops of cloth, heaps of limbs, tins, paints, stone, marble, board, canvas, and twine.

Artists like to tell you scientific facts so you don't think they have their heads up there all day in the clouds.

I could see that his German shepherd was taking his time over a rattlesnake he was just finishing up. I turned toward Ed. "This is like the kind of question I'll ask you." (I was throwing "like" and "sort of" into sentences to give the impression I had been an early beat person from the North.) "What makes you think you're a real artist? When do you know?"

"You don't ask the question if you are," he said, rubbing his forefinger along my backbone. I had my clothes off by now. This was no longer a strange phenomenon for me: neither having them off with a stranger, nor suddenly discovering they were off when only a second before they had seemed to be on. These discoveries were one of the amusements of the new chemistry of the time.

The dog had come along into the room where I was sitting on the black leather chaise longue. "And you don't talk all the fucking time about art in our time and all that bullshit, and you don't say no to anything. Schultz wants you." Schultz is the German shepherd.

I could do a lot of dangerous things in one go. "Schultz is German, uncircumcised, and has rattlesnake stuff in his mouth," I pointed out. "I am allergic to dogs and he's turned on by snake venom. So don't try to tell me the dog thinks I'm someone."

I am someone, but my definition and Schultz's definition of "someone" are far removed.

I started writing a screenplay. It would not be about marriage. You could not have a good marriage and be a real writer. Choose one. I chose. It seemed natural to make it a movie. I could see the picture. It would be the story of a woman who was a stylish wife and mother by day, and a man, an artist, at night.

I watched Brooke and Dennis. Brooke was everything the woman should be, elegant and clinically aware. Dennis was everything the man must be, romantically sullen, difficult, radical.

One actress would play both parts. But when she played Jordan, the man, an actor's voice would be dubbed in. The sets would be designed by the new artists. The crazier I got, the darker the book's ending became. At first the woman killed the male artist. She burned his pictures and freed herself to take care of her children.

I heated up my drive to write by talking around pools and in living rooms with friends. Jeremy and Johanna were friends with Peter and Julie Rafelson. Their parents, Bob and Toby, landed in the center of our lives with East Coast authority. I watched Toby host the mixture of artists, filmmakers, and Easterners who would come out to observe Hollywood's transition, and I wondered what happened to us. There was no question when I'd sit on the high backseats in our projection room watching friends that Warner LeRoy would be running the town. If I could have chosen the son to be, it would have been Warner.

I'd assumed, growing up, that we'd slip into our parents' or even grandparents' roles with easy aristocratic grace. Assumption doesn't do the work. Charm doesn't help. It only makes you feel even more entitled. While you're lounging back telling entrancing stories, the ones you aren't inviting are at home, working out how to make the goals you say you have happen.

Us. Who were we? Usually whomever Josie Mankiewicz had sitting nearest to her at the Sand and Sea Club. Even Sharon Disney came down from her club to be near Josie. Nora Ephron was different. Her mother was a working writer, which may have been one of the most useful things that could happen to determination and wit. You don't know how different the attitude toward working women was then.

It was another thing to have a mother who was a star. This was an automatic tragedy, but in those days that didn't mean a book deal. It meant denial.

I thought I wrote the scene about the woman in the book burning the man's (her own) pictures the night after Brooke called me, sobbing, to say that Dennis was going to kill her, could she come with the kids and stay with us. For $135 a month, I rented a wonderful small house overlooking the sea in Santa Monica Canyon, with a living room like an artist's studio and more than enough space.

"He put his paintings out on the lawn to dry—and I turned on the sprinklers. We'd just planted a new lawn after the fire and I'm very careful about it. It's been so dry."

Lawns are a source of accomplishment and trouble in L.A. When I was around eleven or so, I was furious with Angelo, our gardener, for telling my father that these boys I had over, Bob Redford and Billy Keane, were kicking holes in our lawn playing football. My father was working at home. He came out, yelled at them, and sent them home. I was embarrassed. Devastated.

I'd actually invited only Bob because he was good at drawing and I thought he'd be interested in my mother's studio. I'd been disappointed when he brought Bill, but boys did that then. You never did get to see one on his own. If you really got along, then what could you do about it? You couldn't just be friends; someone for sure would point out that this was strange. What kind of guy has a girl as a friend?

I was friends with Dennis. He'd been on my radio show. We talked, the way I talked with the other artists, about the work and the impact the change in art was having on Hollywood, on behavior and attitude. Was it, I wondered, the other way around? You could talk that over for a long time.

Dennis would show up at least once or twice a week, and I'd read scenes. I wanted Jordan, the artist in my screenplay, to sound like Dennis, the artist wrestling with fame and his talent's hundred or so hot drives.

Dennis listened. "You're way off." I'd try again. "I feel so different and scared. Like I don't know what I'm doing here and I don't want to fuck it up," he'd flash this grin, "but I am, aren't I?"

"Absolutely."

Looking back, I know I was in love with the idea that I could share this drive, this art, with a man. We could be wild, creative, on the same wavelength, all new. It was a revolution.

I was never this girl I am looking for now.

S unset. I see it from the air as we turn in for the landing. That's all I need to see to know I'm here. Phoebe is here to meet me, with Jeremy, who has his grandfather's smile; the rest is Bruce Willis. He has what my father used to call "the motor." I know where he is standing before I am off the plane.

I am at Jeremy's house only five minutes before Judith calls from London. "My mother knows a young guy who would be interested in driving you around."

"Terrific," I say. "So, how are you doing?" I ask. I pull her face into focus. Yes. It's here.

"You've hardly left," she says. "I'm fine."

I'm watching Jeremy on his other phone—foot jiggling, clicking channels, and reading. It occurs to me how much Jeremy and Judith may be alike. Above all, they are desperate not to let anyone know how much they do for people they care about. Judith's seen to it that I have a driver. There's a dinner party tonight and my luggage is on the wrong plane. "Go to Armani, charge it to me," Jeremy says.

The next morning Jeremy's gone to work. Phoebe's at school. And the Girl's lawyer "is in court all day."

I take the dog and walk the half-mile from Jeremy's house to where the house I grew up in used to be. I am looking for more here than the girl Polanski raped.

The night my parents' house burned, I had awakened from a nightmare that my parents were enveloped in a sheet of flames. As I sat up, shaking, I realized the phone was ringing. My father was on the phone, sobbing, telling me the house had burned.

Now, as I walk, I can't remember why I didn't go right to him.

I cross Sunset, turn down Burlingame, and as I come near Marlboro I see the hill where we'd roll down the ivy. I don't want to go further, but I see the chimney, the thick rustic shingles of the high Tudor roof. I go left up Marlboro, hard hill to climb on my first bike, on up to the even steeper curve of the drive.

There are gates here now. And this is our house—it didn't burn down.

"That fire was in New York," my brother tells me.

He's here from Dallas on a shoot, and we meet for dinner in Santa Monica, not far from where we were taken to the merry-go-round so Tucky, our governess, could meet up with Mickey, the Marine who came over for naps.

Jeb looks like a giant cowboy: tall, stocky, bald, with sharp green eyes. "You know what was strange about that fire," he says, "was that the autographed pictures of presidents, the pictures that burned, were the ones that could be replaced. The ones of Kennedy, Roosevelt, and Truman were untouched."

The driver, Charlie, found me exactly where Judith said he would. As he opens the door to his 1983 dark blue Chevy wagon, he tells me he's a writer.

"So, tell me what you're working on," I say. He's driving me to see Howard Koch.

"I'm writing a screenplay about the Mayan sacrifices. They'd kill their own thirteen-year-old daughters, sacrifice them to the snake god. Quetzalcoatl."

Maybe that's what happened with the girl who got mixed up with Polanski. Did her mother sell Little Red Riding Hood to the wolf?

Charlie pulls a black curl through his silver earring, winds it out and round his forefinger. He is wearing an old purple velvet frock coat with his Mozart t-shirt, his jeans, and Timberland boots.

He tosses questions around when we're at STOP signs.

"Do you see big changes since you lived here?" He looks me up and down, eyebrows raised.

"I'm not sure." Is today's answer the same as yesterday's? "I think it's more like a big city, but I only really see what I remember," I say. "I block out what I don't want to see. I remember the roads the way they were when I was driving with my father, but he's gone."

"How long?"

"Almost twenty years."

"Does twenty years feel like a long time to you?"

"Not as long as it does to you."

"Do people know when they're old?"

"Maybe they know," I say, "when they're asked that question."

He's quiet. We've hit a long stretch of Sunset where you can still use some driving style and wind up ahead of the traffic. Not a tree, not a patch of green has changed. I can't remember the name of these dark bushes with the slender pale blue flowers. I sat sucking the honey out of them, watching, the day Billy Keane and Bobby Redford came over and played football on the new grass.

We're at a stoplight. He pops a handful of salted almonds into his mouth, tossing his head back.

"Thirteen," Charlie says, "is the end of sexual wonder, which is why sacrifice never really bothered anyone. Magic ends. Life gets practical. Why go on?" His voice is flat.

The Girl is thirty-something now. Can I ask her about sexual wonder? Time speeds. The question seems archaic today.

"You have this story here every week. Charlie Chaplin, Fatty Arbuckle, Errol Flynn—those are just the ones you know," says Howard Koch.

Howard used to race around in a wood-paneled convertible. Now he makes movies from a wood-paneled office that looks like a library. He knows more than a lot of guys who don't talk so readily. He's at ease with himself, which puts big directors and big stars at ease around him. "The great ones all have temperaments," he says. "You can't expect them to change."

"She really was just a kid. The mother was the real trouble maker. She made the judge angry, too. If it had been someone else, the studio would have got some top lawyers for him. The judge was thrown off the case, you know. That's a big story."

That evening I go to the opening of Judy Chicago's amazing "Dinner Party" at the L.A. Museum of Contemporary Art, the spectacular production that Harry Hopkins first brought to the San Francisco Museum of Modern Art in 1979. I gaze at this symbolic history of women spread out here in iconic glory, each place setting a different artist, and I'm pitched back to the Banner Party on the beach where we each brought banners we made. We tried to be the art. We became the assemblage, spending a dark, hallucinogenic night burrowing under one giant banner, slithering out at dawn.

The following day, I drive to La Jolla with Dennis Hopper to see a retrospective exhibit of his photographs, which have the originality of his crafty eye. Like old cowboy buddies, we eat at a western restaurant. It could have been old rustlers, old roundups we go over, careful, distant. He talks of his son, Henry. I talk about my grandson Justin's batting average.

We talk carefully of the sixties and of the art scene in L.A. thirty years ago. "The sixties started at the Pasadena Art Museum," he says, "with Walter Hopp's show with Hockney and Oldenberg in 1963."

The whole town was changing then; as one part of L.A. became more conscious and sophisticated as an artistic center, its core enterprise, the studios that put the town on the international map, was turned over to corporate investors.

"The big change in Hollywood started even earlier," Dennis reminds me, "it started with Jules Stein. He hired people like Wasserman who would run it like a business. The old guys knew how to deal with artists."

Did they really? Some of them understood the temperament, the nervy bravado one day, the steely need for isolation the next. Some of them sheltered all that, but also used their artists, seducing, coercing, possessing them, running them like racehorses. Today Barbra directs her own pictures, and Dennis can choose the parts he wants to play.

His hands are worn and rugged, but so are mine. "There aren't even any theaters left where you can show an art film, an independent picture. When I go to Europe, I'm blamed for being part of the American industry."

We all have our own way of seeing it. Dennis is idealized in Europe for being one of the first actors to bring the wild American cowboy into the twentieth century.

I see him more as the shy, pale young theater actor Brooke was walking with one evening (maybe it was in New York), just after he'd done *Giant* and hadn't invented the camouflage you need to survive fame. His eyes were wide and gentle. The two of them were holding hands and, I thought, defining love.

And then we talk about what I'm doing here. "One of the editors told me it's the story of the century," I tell Dennis.

"If this is the story of the century," Dennis says, "then the century has a problem."

"I'll get in touch with you Monday or Tuesday, possibly sooner, but I'd hate for you to be terribly disappointed if she's deciding not to tell her story. The only reason that she's willing to is she's in dire straits." I can hear the shrug over the phone.

"Is she fragile?" I ask. I imagine her still this little kid.

"She was tiny then," he says, "but she's a big woman. Very attractive."

"If she's uneasy, what about if I go to see her?" I could tell Silver I may not even remember her name. "If I meet her, she'll realize she'll be giving her story to someone she could trust. I could tell the story of her survival."

The next day Charlie is busy writing. Jeb's son, my nephew Zachary Schary, a guitarist with my father's eyes and my brother's cowboy way, speeds me out to the Valley in his maroon onyx '66 Mustang convertible. The high school the girl would have gone to is gone. The boy on the phone who works in the junior high store says he's not sure where the high school is, or how late the shop is open. He just works there, you know. He says they might have some old yearbooks from '77, but he doesn't think so.

Larry Silver calls to say, "My client might be interested in The Big

Idea. You can't tell anyone you've gotten this far. You have to give me your oath and I have to trust you."

The oath I give is not to use her name or tell where she lives.

"So I'm going to patch you through now." Thirty seconds of silence goes like a month until he says, "Jill, this is —— ——."

"Hi!" We laugh.

"Hi." She does sound like a kid. "I've never known what to say about it." She has the light just-south-of-L.A. drawl, not quite a twang. "What if it becomes a movie? I don't know how I feel about that."

"What I think I want," Larry adds, "is to be in on all your conversations." He feels like a man who wants to "watch."

"Sure," I say, "if that's okay with ——. I find it harder talking in front of a guy, but that's up to her." I may learn something from her.

"I don't mind," she says. "So what do we do now?" she asks. "I just don't want to do anything that will be hard for my kids."

She asks what I'm really writing about. I say I'm writing about how some of us reinvented our lives in the sixties. I've written about being raped and dealing with mixed feelings.

Then when I point out some of the other people I'm talking to about the sixties, she's concerned. She says, "I thought this story was all about me."

I've been told by another detective, a guy in Hollywood named Warren, that I'd be smart to drop the Polanski story, stay out of it.

"I'm not that smart."

"She's living in a place out on the fringe of Santa Monica around Federal," the detective says, "but I'm not sure what name she's using."

"That's where nurses at the old veteran's hospital shared houses during World War II," I tell Charlie as we drive in to Hollywood to meet Warren.

The word you use to describe where you're going is very important here. You go "in" to Hollywood; "over to" means the Valley; "up" is one of the canyons; "down" is Sunset to the Coast Highway; and "out" is to Malibu.

"Maybe you took speed to bring back that war panic." Charlie likes to think of me doing drugs. It shows a hip fallibility. Or maybe it shows you can do drugs longer than he did and live forever.

Warren says this actress named Lisa is absolutely the right girl. "It got me a lot of good parts," she says when I call her at her apartment off Mulholland (on the Valley side). "Actually two," she said, "they weren't big ones. But I didn't discourage the idea. To be linked up any way at all to a famous name in this town is useful. You can always do something with it. I haven't figured out what."

Not yet.

Lisa mainly needed to talk, which I understand. She had been alone in her house for a week. She wasn't certain if her husband was in jail or had forgotten where they lived. He had a two-hour memory range that he hadn't found a new chemical to enhance; and if he did, he'd forget where he'd written down the source's phone number. And it would be unlisted. She reminded me that all good L.A. phone numbers are unlisted.

"Do you know any good agents?" she asked me after we talked the third time. "Maybe we could work it into a screenplay together."

"I don't think Lisa is the girl," I tell Charlie, "she doesn't have that permanent edge in her voice."

"What do you mean, permanent edge?"

He'd have to listen to the girl to know what I mean.

All weekend a Santa Ana rages round the city. The coyotes sound closer, wilder, as more of the chaparral, their homeland, burns. Down in the shoplands the air's smoky and you can see the burning patches on the mountains.

I meet Army Archerd and his wife, Selma, at Drei's on Bedford. Just opened that week. The owner, Victor, tall and French, spins down the aisles ecstatic over the rush. Drei was a friend of Polanski.

Army saw Roman six months ago. "Roman feels abandoned. Jack's dropped him. Bob Evans. All of them. Sure Roman's arrogant. That has nothing to do with his work. So he's tough to work with," Army shrugs. "Some of the best talents in the town are tough to work with."

None tougher than the lawyers.

On Wednesday, I'm up early making a birthday cake for Jeremy with Phoebe. Lots of fresh coconut and lemon juice fixes the frosting flavor. The red crystals, the rose in the center, the almond toffee, the raspberries and the strawberries. "It's brilliant," she says.

When we come back from a walk with George, the golden retriever, there's a message from Silver. I call back at 11:55. His office says he's on a conference call, "he'll be a minute. Do you want to wait?" "I'll wait." He's still on the other line.

We do the jockeying, the game, the "what are we going to do here?"

"Why do I think I trust you?" he says.

I don't tell Larry I've heard the thing to see is the testimony.

"So, I have a friend who says you're a great lawyer."

"Do I know him?"

"He's a lawyer. He's heard of you."

How long will we play?

He patches in the Girl. This time I talk to her for maybe ninety seconds. She has a hesitant, shy kid's voice. She speaks L.A., which clarifies only when you get out of town long enough to miss it. I talk to her long enough to believe she's real.

"So," she asks, "what are you going to do?"

"I thought I'd come to see you."

"Maybe you could send me something of yours to read. And we could talk about questions so I think about them. I'm doing this so he can come back and just let it all be finished."

I sent her a couple of pieces I'd done for the *New York Times* and a few ideas I felt we could talk about.

Then when I call on Monday Larry can't talk to me. On Tuesday, "It's a week from hell."

"You've had that week. Listen, I can't just sit around out here." It's not going to happen.

"Come in tomorrow," Larry says, "I'll have things for you to read no one's ever seen."

I am waiting at Nate 'n' Al's. Delicatessen is one of the things Polanski has told me he misses about L.A. I taste the rye bread, the new pickle. I tear into a bagel.

I am waiting for my father. He's got on his cardigan and the hat he wears coming on Sundays to pick up everything for our deli dinner. My father must be having trouble parking the wagon. He always brings the wagon on Sundays . . . I freeze.

Images skid by. Jeremy's red room, cactus garden, Josie's car. Sit very still. The Wilshire Palms, Cary Grant on the balcony, tanning, reading a script. Pale blue cover. Arrowhead.

No wonder they're called "mals." This one is not petit.

Slowly, too slowly to feel safe, it's going out of sharp focus, fading like a shuddering, uneasy come, and I'm unclear. Time and place are off.

I look for my father. Tears. Don't. Look for his tennis sweater. Lennie's friend's shop. Go there, they'll call. Smarter move—go nowhere.

Yes!

I see Lew Wasserman. His hair is platinum today. He always looks like a classy piano player at a good club.

Wasserman is my father's agent. Even when he makes house calls, he wears a black suit, white shirt and a black tie. He's like a tough editor, the art dealer, the teacher. Every artist needs one around. He and Edie stay pale so you'll never take them for westerners. He smiles at me, kisses me, say he hears great things about my son. The confusion may be his, but Wasserman has never been confused. "Wasserman was the first one to get an actor a piece of the action. He got James Stewart ten percent," Alan Ladd Jr. told me. "That was probably the end of the studio system." A subject that alternates in consideration with Sharon Tate's murder as the end of the sixties.

This information comes on like a slide even as I am lost here in midimal time.

I am shivering, numb, but I know to look in my Week-At-A-Glance. Yes, I am to see a lawyer named Larry Silver at 3:00. This may be about our divorce. I thought Bert Fields would do it, but he was at our wedding.

Finding my way is no problem. I'm blank right now, but I can still tell you every street in Beverly Hills.

There are different memory road plans. For example, there's the grid system, where characters interlock. You have to make clear choices here, and now here again.

I'll take the axis, a direct route, but I'll have enough shapes and distraction to make me think I'm on a wandering path. Wandering paths are a favorite in England and Japan; you can feel you're lost or go directly. A good museum is planned like a wandering path so you can feel you're strolling along with idyllic stopping places. You know where you are, the way you do on a fine axis street like 57th, but you can also be lost at any moment exploring Regent's Park or Fifth Avenue or Sunset Boulevard.

On the way down Beverly Drive, I pass a Hasidic rabbi in pedal pushers. Cannot be a bad sign.

I go into the lawyer's office. The walls are gray, carpet a sea gray. No, it's not the divorce. It's something to do with Slipkovitz. Yes, that's it. Am I doing a story for *NYPD Blue?*

Don't, above all, appear confused. Do not ask revealing questions. Try to gather clues.

Silver may dye his hair. Under his glasses one eye wanders. Maybe that's what makes me feel he's disinterested, not paying attention. There are piles of cardboard boxes and cartons, one turquoise office chair, five brown ones. Like the new cars, the chairs are all shaped like eggs. It's sort of high-tech in midlife crisis here. There are crumbs and ashes on the glass-topped wood table and a small cobalt blue Indian wall hanging.

It's not an MGM set. Doug Shearer did not do this.

I leave the office. I have taken notes from pieces of testimony Slipkovitz had me read in front of him.

"Listen," I'm still smart, just addled, "if I'm taking notes, why can't I just have a copy? It's only one page."

"Because if you use it, I can always say you made it up."

A chance here for a clue. "Use it for what?"

"Don't play games with me. We both know what's going on."

"Sure," I say, tough. I'm copying the dialogue here.

Silver says he'll call me tonight. I tell him I've got other fish frying. That's always safe in any scene.

Feeling daunted, I'm sitting on a stone bench outside this skyscraper on what I know is Wilshire. Worse than being seen walking is being seen not driving. It does something to the tone of your walk in Beverly Hills when there aren't keys to a good car in your pocket. Not to drive in L.A. is to lose virility. I consider hitching. Would anyone know what that is?

A young man comes to the curb. I know the car. "I think I'm doing a TV series, yes? And you are?"

"I think you're tired," he looks at me, puzzled. He has a Mexican accent. "I'm taking you home."

Phoebe cartwheels down the hall to meet me when Charles drops me off at UTA, Jeremy's agency. Phoebe and I work on some drawings in Jeremy's office as he twists the phone cord, taking calls, checking papers slipped in front of him. He's exactly like I'd like to be.

"I haven't been here in a while," I say.

I can't tell him how it feels to be sitting here, watching him so cool and alluring. He is distinctive in his distant style, achieving, then moving beyond the most elite Hollywood manner. That's how I see it.

Not that, like any self-absorbed mom, I drive him crazy, and that the way to deal with me is distance. After all, isn't that how I have dealt with him?

Later, there's a message from Silver. As I wait for him to answer, I wonder if I'll make this first draft of the story before I short-circuit. I thought the needy panic, the hysteria I saw in my mother when she was getting work done before an exhibit, or in some stars before a movie would wrap, was a creative prerogative, maybe the only way to set yourself up for the last burst of energy. But I can't dare that. Chill out.

"I don't think we want to do it," Silver says, "we've got a TV offer now." Pause. "If you agree to publish after the TV show, maybe we'll see what we can do."

"Larry, don't play games with me." This is aloof. "I'm going ahead."

With what, I ask myself.

What's startling is when someone not only remembers you, but comes up with a quick image that gives you a new take on who you thought you were. Even as a kid, Bob Redford drew new compositions and took unusual angles on each group of figures he'd draw.

Bob is sitting in the back of a restaurant I've never heard of, at a table you'd never see, in an angle of glass high in the trees looking out over a stretch of the city I never knew. "I do know you very well!" I say, surprised.

And he's always taller than I remember. He was a tough, kind of edgy kid, an outsider like me when I first knew him at Brentwood Grade School.

I'd been sent to public school for the first time. I was here because my father took stands. "That's your American responsibility," he said.

I thought we had to leave our private school because at the parents' meeting they decided to expel the kids of blacklisted writers. We couldn't go to other private schools in L.A., because they either had quotas of no more than 20 percent Jews or show business students at any time, or none at all.

This is how my memory works today. I write this down. I know it is wrong after I see it on the page. This is only part of the story. We left that private school because the head of the parents' group thought Robert Mitchum's sons ought to be expelled because Mitchum had been busted for smoking pot.

Ed Lasker, a lawyer and one of my father's best friends, was going to the meeting. My father said Eddie was too hot-headed, so he'd go. He could keep his temper. My father "slugged the SOB" and we were, of course, in public school the next day.

This is how my father told the story. He liked to say "slug" and "SOB" Looking at it even another time, I figure he took a firm stand, then, once defeated, stalked out.

Since there had been letters threatening kidnapping, we couldn't just go to school in a station wagon driven by our governess, who could at least pass as a mom. We had to go in the limousine. Other Hollywood kids have talked about having the limo drop them off a block or two away. Donovan, our driver, wouldn't do that. He'd just gotten out of the Army and needed the job.

The spaces on the playground were huge and circled with high wire fences. At school they tried to teach you to be good at everything. If I'd been running schools, I would have let you do what you were really good at and left it at that. No phys ed. No math for me.

I'd sit on this bench, picking off flakes of gray paint. They couldn't repaint because of rationing. I looked up at the wire fence. I couldn't imagine how you'd get out. There were no trees, sparse palms around the outside. I noticed Bob first when he was playing ball. He'd gone after a ball no one else could have caught.

Even in the middle of team sports, he was detached, the way I was. He'd rub his bristling reddish hair and size them up.

I envied the childhood I thought Bob would have. It would be like the childhoods you saw in textbooks. Most arithmetic problems included pies. We'd remember numbers given familiar images. We did not have homemade pies. Perhaps if the books had pictures of kreplach.

"If Jane's Mom bakes six apple pies, and Dad lets Dick mow the lawn seven times, and Uncle Fred says they each take twenty minutes to finish, who is ready to take Jane and Dick to the beach first, Mom or Dad?" I couldn't figure out the answer. I was picturing the simple intimacy of such a life.

Inside the classroom, Bob sat away from others and looked out the window a lot. He was fixing his attention out of here and into his head, which I understood.

I watched him without talking and managed to sit near him without catching the attention of teasing kids or teachers, which was a trick and entirely due to his subtlety with moves and placement. He could be in the center of the room here answering a question, disappearing the next. "One day I just couldn't bear it, so I went to the boys' room, opened the window and left. They put a monitor on me after that."

Here with Bob tonight, he is an artist. He listens with the intensity of the artists I've known—with my mother's early sharp perception. And like men who are artists, once you are alone with them, they can match you even in talk.

"I was telling Stuart how I'd watch you draw action—and how still my drawings looked next to yours. He said it all comes down to the masculine and the feminine."

The arrow and the womb, waiting, is what Stuart actually said. And I am remembering, as I write this now, a story by John Updike. And I've found it, here. "These pairings," Updike said, "are like the Royal Albert Hall, round, capacious and rosy, and the phallic spike of the Albert Memorial."

I could place them, I was pleased to see, as I read. They are on the other side of Hyde Park . . . how long it took me to remember Hyde Park in London is not F.D.R.'s house.

When the teacher was occupied in another direction, without talking about it, Bob and I drew. It went like this. I'd draw one picture, usually knights or early Americans in an important scene. You had to put men in drawings, or at least buildings, to convince boys you were good at art. I never did figure out a way to be interested in drawing men sitting in plain business suits. Bobby Redford's pictures moved. Legs were really running. You could see the arms reaching back. My pictures were pretty, but they stood still.

At private school, Sue Sally Jones and Jane Fonda had had the patent on horses. No one else could draw horses or try. "I'll draw dresses," I'd agreed when we were laying out the territories. "Fine," Sue Sally had said. This was like someone saying "I'll take Catalina Island." Who cared about dresses?

To know an actor, look at his hands. He's learned to stage his face. Bob's hads are young and wiry and worn all at once. Tense, lithe and bow-legged fingers from riding a range of pencils, brushes, gestures. I'd guess he gets bored faster than the characters he's drawn up there for us, but then, he talks like an artist. You can see him roaming around in his head over the lay of a sentence or the shape of a scene, the speed with which he'll want to get to a story's point. He listens and watches you like an artist. In which way will you apply to a character? As John Lahr says, we all scavenge each other; we are each other's best material.

"You live with the dark and the light, so you use the dark. Put it in the work. All my best work is personal, like *The Milagro Beanfield War.* The great villain now is real estate."

"Yes," I say quickly. I can talk about the land wars that are going on now in Malibu, but I don't remember this movie of Bob's, and how can I say that so I told him about the memory thing, windup with this bit.

"Sometimes I'll say I want to see a movie, and Stuart will tell me we saw it last night. I won't know."

"Then you may not remember," Bob says, "that the first time you invited me over to play, and we tore up the grass? Well, when I was sched-uled for a tryout for a play on Broadway—I was terrified your father would remember me and I'd never get the part."

"But that's not what my father remembered about you," I say, "he remembered you were shy and had talent." If you know someone as well as I knew my father, you can play a safe hunch on what he'd remember. Memory goes more on hunches than you think.

"He was a nice man. He understood actors."

"I think he understood actors because he understood artists," I say. "I couldn't bear how much of himself he gave to my mother, and now I watch my own husband do that with me."

We speak of our children and political influences. "When I was thir-teen, Richard Nixon gave me an award," he says. "I remember feeling he was cold and wooden."

Then we talk of kids we both remember from then, of the first girl he kissed when she was ten, of the juvenile delinquents, "kids who could get you into bad scenes."

"They looked like John Derek," I say, "so you didn't care."

"They were fine until they'd go near your kid sister. You could deal with them. Then, too, most juvenile delinquents were more interested in your mom than your kid sister. The idea of kids and sex was gross," he says.

And we move on to the sixties, because that's when the story I'm here to write really began.

"It wasn't so much when the sixties began as when the fifties fell apart. But the Beats weren't embraced like the hippies were," Bob says. "I think it really goes back to the quiz shows. Remember how we felt? How Van Doren shook our belief system when he crashed and burned? It's hard to imagine an America where a guy who cheated on a quiz program shook us as badly as a violent act, but this was moral violence. Decibels so low we'd shrug it off today."

Bob didn't want to be kept in, but he had ranged far enough in those early years to be able to work with a disciplined vision later. "The big changeover has been in the feel of fame and creativity. The sense of being an artist is different from fame. Responsible fame requires playing a political role, but you still have to have a broad enough base of privacy to ramble around in."

"Polanski had never had it. He was like a kid in a big candy store.

"It was sad to watch people get sucked in. When Manson hit, some bubble burst. But Kennedy—that was the shock. People walked around numb."

We order finally. I'm not paying attention to the food. I think Bob keeps his privacy by talking mostly about you, but when he tells stories in scenes; setting them up, then standing back like a director. He talks of his friendship with Carol Rosson, whose dad was blacklisted. How he put himself through hell earlier in Utah. "When I was sixteen, I was going out with a woman who was twenty. I thought I'd be a lawyer, went into pre-law.

"But my sixties began in the late fifties with a trip that expressed the whole time—wide open and raw. I took off in a car with a woman who understood I was freewheeling—an artist. I came back, alienation a shell around me. I loved the art, but couldn't connect with the movement. I loved—almost survived—the spirit.

"The sixties came to be about support; if we band together there will be power. What I was doing was about the opposite. I was giving up that freedom to be with someone. I also loved what I was feeling. I didn't like classrooms, the group behavior of sports."

"I'm just surprised," I say, "that you remembered me."

"I'd see you come to school in the limousine like a princess and stand there so aloof and unapproachable. I'd want to talk to you because we both liked to draw."

I never saw myself like that. It was so excruciating to be seen being dropped off, and watched. I knew I was despised for this distinction, so I didn't try to show off or push my way in. "You were observing," I say. I have forgotten this cringing, despised pale kid I was.

"Aloof has some strength," he says.

"I like that," I tell Bob.

This is going to be my new style. Unapproachable. How much work you can do when you are unapproachable, and how useful it will be to be aloof with Silver and the Girl.

Stephen Kabak is who you call when you need to know something on record. He has the lead to the right city offices. He would be played by Ben Kingsley.

I am going down to the Hill Street courthouse to get the transcripts of the testimony no one ever saw. Gittes went there to get the papers in *Chinatown*. I'm standing outside the car down here at the library when suddenly I am the person I was then, the person I was in the sixties and seventies. When I was a kid, I wanted to be Helen Gahagan Douglas. I wanted to be serious, to be political. That was another kind of importance, not like being a movie star.

I scramble with Charlie down three basement levels into the archives of the courthouse. Movie posters are taped on walls: *Disclosure, Night of the Running Man, Imaginary Crimes.*

"Did you see the man who works here?"

"It's the Sequestered Department," we're told.

"I know, that's why I'm here. Is Cameron the guy I'm looking for?"

The man who doesn't work here asks another man walking by, *"La señora quiere ver viejos archivos del tribunal. ¿Necessita hablar con Cameron?"* Even though I can't speak Spanish, I get the drift: This woman wants to see the archives. Does she have to talk to Cameron?

"No, necessita hablar con Walsh."

No, she'll have to talk to Walsh.

Walsh is the name of Gittes's guy in *Chinatown*. This is perfect.

"So, can I see him?"

To Charlie he says, *"No, no puede."*

"No, he's not here."

Charlie tells me, "He's just stepped out."

"¿Puede ver el archivo?"

"So when is he likely to be around?"

"Es muy raro." I sit down, discouraged. *"No sé si vayamos a encontrarlo."*

"Hardly ever."

Charlie talks to someone else. *"Ella es buena onda."* "She's a kind of good guy," Charlie says (or something like that). They look back at me. The court guy leaves for about fifteen minutes and returns with the document, which resembles a screenplay. He hands me the testimony. Even when it's a terrible story, there is this excitement about seeing something no one else has seen. This is probably called prurient curiosity. I start to read it, to take notes.

At approximately 2:30 on Thursday, March 24, 1977, she is called as a witness before the Los Angeles County Grand Jury. She raises her right hand and solemnly swears that the evidence she'll give in this matter now pending before the grand jury of the County of Los Angeles will be the truth, the whole truth, and nothing but the truth. So help her God.

She is thirteen. The man asks all these questions in a cool, matter-of-fact tone. When asked if she lives with her mother and her twenty-year-old sister in Woodland Hills, she says, "Yeah."

She's advised that she should answer "yes" or "no."

So she says "yes," and she tells her story:

This is what I want. "Charlie, I have to have it."

He talks to the guy who looks me over, shrugs, *"No puede llevarlo."*

More talk. Then there's a conference with someone else. *"Dile que regrese mañana. Quizás tendremos alguna noticia."*

Charlie can come back. They'll have a copy tomorrow.

I stay up tonight reading the court transcript. I imagined myself at thirteen saying some of this out loud to a group of people. They are mostly strangers, which is at once better and worse.

When your first sexual experience is bad, you can be destroyed by it, because every time the sensations of sex come up you have that image. If you're lucky and work it out, it fades away. Secrecy maintains the sexual force of the iconic images. I would guess there's this girl out there who sees Polanski for an instant every time she gets off. The worst thing with this is you feel bad about yourself, certain everyone else sees the face of her lover in her arms.

A legal advisor I talked to said, "At thirteen a girl is not emotionally ready to handle this. She won't be just fine."

Maybe she's fine enough to know it won't be right for her to risk more by what we call this sharing. Maybe she's a fine enough person not to do a public tell off of her own mother. Maybe she's one of the sixties children who has grown up. Will I have the grace to let her be?

I call Silver back. I am very clear now who he is. "Another thing we have in common besides rape is asthma." I need my inhaler.

"But my client doesn't have asthma, don't you get it? She said she was having an asthma attack so he'd stop. Polanski didn't pick up on it, because she thought it would frighten him that she was having an attack. One of the things about rape is that you try to resist. Let me put it this way," he slips into the legal voice, "in order to demonstrate that it was rape, you have to prove that you tried to do something to stop it, and because she did pretend that she had asthma, that was proof enough that it was rape."

How did she know to do that? Maybe it's built in. A girl I know told her stepfather she had AIDS. "My mom's nephew died of it," she told him, "so he'd believe it was in the family."

"So where are we?" I ask Silver.

"You're a nice lady. I don't want to disappoint you."

"Then don't. How often have you seen Polanski?"

"Only a couple of times. I hate his attitude about women." He stops. "Look, I'll talk to my client."

I'm sitting here on Jeremy's patio looking out at Phoebe directing the golden retriever, and I'm listening to the girl's voice. It's Saturday. The girl is easy, open—that's the surfer cover. "I'm just worried about my children, their privacy. And do I have to go over what happened then?" We go over all the fears and restrictions. "What if it becomes a movie?"

"We'll think about that when it happens," I tell her.

Larry calls. "She wants to do the interview." Then he has to take another call. I hold and hold and hold. "The music is Aaron Copeland," Larry says, "could be worse. She'll do it, but I want to protect her rights."

Three days later it looks like arrangements have been made to meet the girl. The day before I take off to meet her where she lives, Larry calls again. "This happens to be a coincidence," he says, "she's coming to LA."

I talk to the girl again. "Larry says you want to do the interview. What a great coincidence that you're coming here."

"I really don't want my family mentioned or my name or where I live."

"Of course not," I say quickly.

On Tuesday, Larry calls again. The girl wants to change the place to the Disneyland Hotel. She's bringing the children there. They'll go off with their dad. The first priority is the kids. Her husband probably hates the idea.

I call the Disneyland Hotel and talk to a guy named Joe for directions.

The next day Silver's changed his mind. There are new demands. This time I say, "We'll have to pass."

"All my clients promise me I'm going to be famous," he says, "and nothing ever happens."

It happened. I wrote the story, and George Plimpton included it in his anthology *The Best American Movie Writing 1998*. I never used the Girl's name or said where she lived. If you ask me, I say I've forgotten.

But a month after *Vanity Fair* published my article, she came out and told the world. You can't get this close to fame and not bite.

35

*W*e are going to New York. Then I am going on to Connecticut to see Johanna and Stuart is going to Boston to see his daughter Susan and her mother, Margaret, Stuart's first wife. Margaret and Stuart have lost one of their grandsons, Kenneth, who was found at the bottom of a cliff in Montana. Stuart Jr., Kenneth's father who is an artist, an original, and Kenneth's brother, Nathan, will also be in Boston.

Stuart and I are fighting. "Maybe we always fight before we're going to be apart? Is that true?" I say.

"I didn't notice we were fighting," he says. He's in his tweeds, back from the Regent's Park walk.

"Maybe we do need the space," I say.

"I don't," he says, "you're just working up to a fight because you have just about finished your book."

Each chapter is laid out on the dining room table. Angie, Geraldine and I met last Sunday and they helped me lay it out. Angie read the new beginning of her book, the first real work she's done since her daughter Delilah was born. Geraldine's *Tempo* is ready to send out. Svetlana is posing for artists again. "I hate to write," she said. "That," Geraldine says, "doesn't stop me. I hate to write."

The night before we go, Laurie comes up for supper. "News!" she says.

She has been asked to go to Russia by a man who is the benefactor of an entire village, the last place where they do those paintings on black enamel. "They asked me how I make my pencils," Laurie tells me, "so I thought I ought to ask how they make their brushes. 'First,' I was told, 'we catch a squirrel.'"

Again Stuart and I are looking over chapters.

"What matters is I can remember exactly where each scene is."

I was triumphant, until it occurred to me to change several scenes around. Which is how it would go if I switched images in Steven Rose's memory test.

Arguing generates adrenaline. I also am missing my children. "They're hardly in the book," I tell Stuart. "There's just this one last bit."

I call Johanna. "I really haven't been there. I'm reading over the book and I haven't written about your life—your kids, your husband."

"Maybe you haven't written about it because it's my life," she says. "So, are you at the fighting-with-him stage?"

"How do you know?"

"Put Stuart on the phone and I'll remind him you must be finished if you're being awful and sending out for pizza."

"I just made brisket and applesauce."

"So it's another week," she says.

"Your children might hate being in the book much more than they mind being left out," Stuart says. "They're more private people."

"Everyone's more private." I turn on him. "What about you? Do you remember how I just rip pieces out of your own writing when I can't think of how you'd say something?"

"Yes, but you don't want to remember right now that I gave my journals to you."

"But why? And what about that, how you've just tossed your whole life down the pit of my neediness with this illness, with my writing, always my writing. Do I write about that?"

"It isn't my whole life. And whatever you talk about, you will write about. I knew that the minute I fell in love with you. This is our reality. You'd never have stayed with a man who put money and power first."

"Do you have to put it first to have it?"

"You know the answer to that better than anyone," he says.

"Do you question that choice?"

"Jill, why talk about it? Could we go back and change that? Would we?"

I'm digging deeper into an area I don't know how to write about. "Think of the women, the writers I knew in New York in the seventies." I can only see, now, looking back with my adaptive memory, how close we were. "I can't think of any of us who write about our adult children."

The look I get now over the plate of brisket is, "Would you know? Do you talk? Look out for each other?"

"Don't," I tell myself, "think you'll be going back to that New York, any more than the L.A. you saw while researching the Polanski story was any of the L.A.'s you'd known."

But I wonder where my children are in this consideration of these last few years. It's not because I don't care, not because I've forgotten. It is because this is the last taboo. Am I stepping across that line? We go after our parents, our mates, particularly former ones, but what of our children? What of this deep, complex time in this most perplexing relationship?

Do they all hate what we do, and that we're doing it for more years than ever before? Did they tolerate the writing as a single mom's job, something that would sometimes pay the rent?

I understand my own mother only now. I may have my talent, but I caught the obsessive drive from my mother.

Before I leave London, Phoebe calls me from L.A. Like her father, she's fast on the phone. I communicate with her best by making small books. "Grandma, there's a Britannia Bear Beanie Baby," she tells me, "I really need to have it."

The Brittania Beanie Baby is symbolic of everything I need to be. Scratch the book.

Fenwick's doesn't have it. Selfridge's has no idea where to find it. We call Harrod's, who gives up a number to call back. "You can try Hamley's," Corinne suggests. Hamley's has a waiting list. We get the Harrod's number when it isn't busy. A message says, "If you're American, don't call because we're not selling to American distributors." Or grandmothers with American accents. I fly off without the Beanie Baby.

When I call Johanna to say I have arrived in New York and that I am staying at Bruce and Lueza's, she reminds me Jeremy might be coming to New York. He might be bringing Phoebe. Or might not. And we might all be going trick-or-treating together. Or might not. "And," she says, "he might drive you to Connecticut."

"Jeremy drive me?"

"Yes, Mom," she says, "he drives."

They've been talking. I like that. Look how long it took for me to really talk to my brother, Johanna reminds me.

There might also be a confrontation, or might not. The images of their past must be so powerful. How else can they get over the anger?

The night before Stuart goes to Boston, we go with Ted and Vada to an event. I see faces I know and can't place. Do they know I don't mean to not remember them? And how do you go up to someone and say, "I'm crazy about you, who are you?"

Then suddenly, here's Brooke. Her face is glad to see me. During these last years, I thought we'd met sometime in the sixties. Is it the music playing—and I don't remember what it was—which creates the connection; or, as Schacter might say, electrifies the engram. But I suddenly see Brooke and myself and we are six years old. And I know the image I saw in London of our children lying on the floor in my house in Santa Monica, has stayed with me because it reminded me of all the times Brooke and her brother and sister, and me with mine, played in the barn Brooke's parents built for the children next to their Brentwood house. After we'd worn ourselves out, we'd flop down on the floor together, drawing and making up stories.

"I've known you forever!" I say and we hold each other tight.

The next morning the phone rings at the Gelbs' at six in the morning. "Who's this," I say into the phone.

"It's Jeremy."

"Really—you?" I want him to call so much that by the time he does, I've worked so hard to drop it, I can't place the voice. It's like when my father would call when he'd gone to New York. I'd always dash to pick up the phone, to be there first, to catch it before my mother, and surely before my brother or sister. It's the way it is when, at last, you meet the hero, and stand there dumbstruck.

There are no games here; he presents the agenda. I've won the lottery. We'll have dinner tomorrow, take Phoebe to FAO Schwartz Friday morning and to the theater Friday night. "I'll drive you to Connecticut Saturday and we'll go trick-or-treating, and Phoebe might stay over."

Actually, this is a game, and the game is minimalism. Can I keep the conversation more direct, more simple than you can? "I can't do theater. Sorry. But I'll see you tonight." I stop. Is this too much? The main thing is not to be boring. They talk faster. I'd shape words into sentences before I'd present them to Anatole or Leo Lerman; sentences that might lure them when I wanted to catch their attention. Don't fool yourself. They were just as fast. Anatole picked up the phone and said, "Yes." Leo would say, "Four-thirty. That's fine."

By the time you said "Fine" back, he was off the phone. "Phone" is not the same as conversation. "Phone" is not to be confused with talk. "Phone" is like Morse code. We used to talk about people who gave great phone. You'd talk and never have to see them. Giving phone is not the same as phone. You don't give it, talk it, or do it. "Hello" is over. "Goodbye" is gone.

With e-mail, you don't even have to talk. The typewriter meant you no longer had to show your handwriting, and now e-mail means you don't have to reveal the style of your letter paper. Tiffany's on Bond Street no longer sells stationery. Cicero would be so relieved. Writing's over.

I had wanted to be at Jeremy's hotel, to meet him there, but Stuart would have told me that might seem overeager. I should wait until Jeremy calls. You can be the perfect mate, but the exchange between parent and child is different. The complexity passes down through the genes. Maybe I'll just go over there.

I throw off my jeans skirt. It's New York. Black will be the thing.

"Does this look too odd?" I ask Lueza, taking off the wired black necklace with the spacemen. "Trying too hard?"

Jeremy called the day Phoebe was born and talked about how everyone was driving him crazy. And Stuart said to me, "Isn't it great you're not there?" But I'm different. Maybe too different, so it's best I wasn't there, coming up with distinctive ways to be helpful.

This is exactly like waiting for a date to call. No, it's not. It's more, and I remember what it's like. It's like waiting for your parents to come home from a trip. Or wondering if they'll come to see you read a story at school. At night I'd wait to see what my father thought of a poem I'd leave on his pillow. Would there be one of his notes on the yellow-lined paper folded on the breakfast table in the morning?

How many times in the self-absorbed years of the sixties and seventies did I miss the cue? Maybe I won't miss the cues with the grandchildren.

I can remember loving my father because he understood how writing went, for knowing the movies I would love and talking them over with me on the same level. He gave me Ralph Lauren pajamas the year he knew he was dying—a gift he couldn't afford. Did I let him know how much that meant? Did I know how much it meant to him to give me something I'd like, to know he was still in touch?

Do I know what Jeremy would like? Or Johanna? Is that another reason I keep close to these writers and to Laurie, so I can grasp their generation? This isn't so much memory as keeping the spirit supple.

The phone rings. "He's here!" I grab it.

"Where are you?" Phoebe says.

"I'm here."

"You were going to be here by now." Grandchildren are the reward for all the cool years. You cannot be too much there. You also cannot say I forgot.

"I will be right there." I pick up my black scarf and throw my coat over my arm, and I'm off.

No lights have been so long, no traffic so heavy. I hear the Englishman's voice. "You could walk this faster."

You can't walk that fast in New York because you'll see people you know; between Sixty-Seventh and Fifty-third on Madison, I'll hurt twelve people's feelings. "I didn't know you were in town." "I'm not, actually, but I'll call when I am." I dash by, "I can't ever remember to call."

"It's so smart of you to wear black," Phoebe says, "that's what I always wear in New York."

Phoebe is seven, an early preteen. You're not just a child now, you're categorized by your economic power. A mid-preteen doesn't have enough allowance to get an older brother or sister to pick up a video she isn't supposed to watch. In a top executive partnership where both parents work, the post-preteen films her own video.

I can't take my eyes off Phoebe, who is sprawled across a sofa in the living room of their suite. Her black fur coat and hat, which have the look of a turn-of-the-last-century sealskin, are draped around a purple Teletubby. Jeremy is on the phone. Blair, Jeremy's fiancée, is warm, friendly, and easy, with short dark hair and the organizational momentum of someone who does well in L.A. She can get a few people who have very different agendas to appear to pull it together for a while, to move in the same direction, without inciting rebellion. Jeremy has the crisp, tough attitude that gets Phoebe to consider tossing her coat on the floor and saying "no," and makes me want to have a talk about where we're going and what we're doing later.

Blair sizes up the characters, gets our coats on, gets us out the door and down the elevator in minutes.

What I do best with Jeremy is attend to Phoebe. He has a twenty-second-century mind. This is a Hollywood technique he's mastered: from the beginning of time in Hollywood, the idea is to be ahead of you. New Yorkers, you'd guess, would be better at it, but they're not.

The day in New York is bright blue. The streets are filled with women I understand.

"I'll meet you at Schwartz at a quarter to nine," Jeremy says.

Do I tell him I don't think it opens until ten? How do I remember that? I tell him.

"How do you remember that?" he says, then adds, "I've got a buyer meeting us there early so I can shop for Johanna's kids."

Phoebe will have FAO Schwartz to herself for an hour. I remember Miss Frenault meeting us at Saks and having three dressing rooms filled with clothes to try on. It wasn't a big deal.

Phoebe's first question is, "Do you have the Furbies?"

"We're sold out, but they should be in tomorrow."

Phoebe has been given a budget for the day. She keeps to it, knows she can't have everything. I never knew that. And then I told my kids they could have everything, and I never made rent.

Jeremy and Blair discuss which latest computer space radar game Justin and Ethan would like. Phoebe wanders about, trails the coat, dances. "I should have my hair done," she says after a look in a mirror. "I saw a place on the way to dinner. We can go after we're through here. It was cool."

"Do you know where the place was?"

"No, but I'll know when I see it. We'll just taxi up Madison." She's dropped "Avenue." She moves from L.A. to New York with perfect cool.

For Halloween, she's wearing a Ginger Spice English flag chemise dress Jeremy bought at auction. She takes a magnanimous preteen view of Alice's pink butterfly outfit. "She might like a wand," Phoebe says. She wants it clear that she's not into that kind of thing.

"Do you think I should wear a wig?" Phoebe asks as we start up Madison. I want to show her the new Chinese shop, Shanghai Tang. "My mom got a red silk shirt from there," she says. "I don't think they have a kids' department."

It's important for me to be right with Phoebe. If she likes me, it will get around to Jeremy that I'm not brain-dead. You want your kid to think you're smart and, most importantly, you want him to trust you with his kid.

"I'm sure they do," I say. Michael Chow takes us downstairs, where Phoebe picks out a red satin jacket.

Life is a circle. I see myself smiling in the red satin Chinese jacket my children's father brought home from Hong Kong when he was a naval officer.

"Perfect." Phoebe regards herself with a calm, distant appraisal, exactly the way she does after a ride up Madison to the hair salon, where she sits quietly. We both meditate upon her face and José's choreography of the dryer, brush, and Phoebe's long dark-blond hair.

"Now I don't want to go to Connecticut," I tell Lueza the next morning, "there's going to be one of those confrontations. They have them on the *Jerry Springer Show*. Like the public circus in Rome. I don't know if I want to ride up to Connecticut just to be shouted at."

The worst capper of all the things I did to my children was leaving them in the bloom of their lives, in the pride of their time; when, above all, you want to show your parents who you have become and to share with them the glory of your own children—even, perhaps, to show them "this, you see, is how I would have raised me."

I am part of the first generation who expect to see our children into the beginning of what once would have been called their old age. We are showing them how to live on into realms of life where we'd once have been content to hang around watching our grandchildren once a week. I say this as if this is not one of life's most exquisite goals.

Jeremy picks me up at the Gelbs with Phoebe and with Blair, whom he is going to marry. I want to show them to Bruce and Lueza. The more I connect all the wings, all the branches of my life into one network, the less likely it is to go totally blank. "You'll see Jeremy and Phoebe and meet Blair," I tell Lueza. "Then if I say I haven't seen them yet this trip, someone will say, 'But you did, Jill, I was there.'"

Jeremy is driving Johanna's Jeep. I want to buy things for the kids.

"You already gave me my TV," Justin says.

"That's progress," Johanna says. "Mom took an ax to our TV, wouldn't let us have one."

I thought of it as political action.

We all go to a market the size of England. Who is the painter who did giant food? Here are giant hamburgers, iceberg lettuce big as globes, giant ivory bread loaves, slices soft as cold cream, big cordovan apples, carrots long and orange, string beans, bricks of cheese, barges of scarlet meat and Caucasian fleshy chicken, tubs of butter, tanks of ice cream.

Johanna's son Justin is thirteen. I was thirteen when I hated my cousin Julius and being indoors. I wanted to have a ranch and to be the first Congresswoman in frontier pants.

Justin's eyebrows are thick and calm. He is silent on the ride home.

"So, how do you write your stories for school?"

"I write on a computer," he says. He's watching the highway. "You know, Mom, the only billboards are for cars, cigarettes, and alcohol."

"Maybe," I say, "we'll go to New York together one day."

"I don't like New York. It's like a big mall to me," he says, "and I hate museums."

"You just want to ride and think about stuff?"

"I guess."

As we drive along, Justin watches out the window and broods, inventing attitudes and approaches, considering pitches and catches, and keeping himself steady through the distracting chaos of his younger brother and sister. He watches out the window and broods, but doesn't miss what's happening in the family around him—like a pitcher who knows when the guy on second is planning to steal third. Justin knows when the kids are using him, using some of his energy.

Ethan, who isn't shy, invents distractions, shouting, goading, until Justin turns on him. Then he's quiet, tugs at my sweater and says, "Do you know they have a class at my school and they call it art and we can just draw?"

Alice, like Ethan, is crazy about new words. "What's sex?" she says.

I say, "It's a game adults play."

"No," Johanna says firmly, "it's something two adults do as a way of showing they love each other."

Riding with Alice's head against my arm, I see pieces of Connecticut life, of Anatole and Sandy, Bliss and Todd, of Lynn and Dick with Priscilla and Claire, of Marcia and Dolph, Holly and Roger.

When we come home, we walk together—the colors of Connecticut are shifting, fading. We slip down piles of leaves, toss them into the air, the children's faces shift as quickly as the leaves, which crackle like old hands reaching as we tumble through the woods up along the hillside. My memory slips between now and then, cuts between the cold air, the ash smell, the snap of twigs. Shots from old scrapbooks.

I expect the confrontation will come now. Ideal, while the kids are getting their costumes together. We've eaten. Johanna's sitting here in one chair. I'm at one end of the couch. Jeremy turns on the TV, lies on the couch, puts his head in my lap and goes to sleep. This, of course, is the point of the confrontation.

It's Halloween Night. The moonlight shines down as we wander across lawns and driveways, all open (no security gates), with the doorways marked by lighted pumpkins and banners. Bags are filled with Hersheys and Milky Ways.

Jeremy tells me before he leaves Phoebe with us for the night, "I can imagine how it felt when I said I didn't need you. Today I told Phoebe I'd always take care of her and she said, 'I'll be a big girl and take care of myself.'"

Phoebe is already ahead of me.

Now the kids are watching *Men in Black* in Johanna's living room—Mr. Smith and Mr. Jones protecting the Earth from the scum of the Universe. Johanna and I are in the kitchen. I take cups off hooks to wash them. "This one's white with chubby crossed legs."

"Gloria Cole gave me that," Johanna says, "careful, it's put together with glue."

Johanna has drawers of linens and on every surface, baskets, books, tiny china houses, and like her mother, masses of artificial flowers in the dining room, on the round table like the ones my mother's models held in their arms while they posed.

It's night. I am with all my grandchildren in Justin's room with the sapphire plastic bubble chair—as space age as Vada's blue diamond. Darth Vadar made from a kit glares at me from a small chest. Yankee posters on the walls—*Star Trek: The Next Generation,* covers of *Baseball Weekly,* Bernie Williams, Derek Jeter, Andy Pettitt.

I sleep on a Marimekko pillow and Johanna carries a Marimekko bag I found in London just like the ones I'd buy from Flax—or, no, Design Research, in the very late fifties, when Mondrian was the look you needed.

We watch Justin's TV games. The one I can understand is where we invent characters—vests and wristlets, gauntlets, helmets and belts, flicking through colors and sizes, heights and faces, flipping through names and races, character traits, like accessible, easygoing, fast, angry, slow and secretive, highly charged.

Then I teach them charades the way my brother and sister and I played it. The Director invents a scene and tells the Actor how to play it. Then the person playing the Producer guesses what it is. There is no Writer.

"You're not like a regular grandma," Justin says.

Most memories I'd apply to rapture were about falling in love.

I thought, too, that hard drive was full. I'd done all the roads to rapture. Memory charges up, like a good old battery, and here's an entirely new road to go. Showing them how to draw coyotes and telling them stories of how it was, and learning from them how to send cartoon roses on e-mail and listening to their stories of how it is.

Now Ethan and Alice are wrapped around each other on the floor in thick duvets, and I'm in the lower bunk with Phoebe wrapped around me and vice versa, Justin thrashing in the bed above us. The breathing around me settles, hushes into sleep. They are my memory's link to eternity.

36

*T*hink about this: exercising memory as heavy aerobics.
A complex mnemonic goal was to envision all the planets, all the constellations, including astrological passages, all surrounded by wheels holding an encyclopedic array of arts and science knowledge. All of these concentric circles, an atrium of memory rooms you are looking down upon, observing the details of how the planets, the tides, the seasons, all the forces impact upon each other.
—Adapted from *The Art of Memory,* Frances A. Yates, 1966

I have just about finished my memory book. Then Stuart suggests I go back to talk with Zilkha, the doctor who said I would write again. "He'd be interested in hearing how you've done."

"You could tell him," I say. My attitude about doctors is a little like shopping. If you don't go into the store, you don't buy something.

We are in Zilkha's office. As I said, you say hello to a doctor and right away he wants to see you. "There's a new twenty-four-hour telemetry test, which will tell you something interesting," he says.

"I'm finishing my book," I say, "I really don't have time."

I hate being in hospitals. Hate tests. Tests also always lead to something else.

"I have an interesting book you should read, *Women and Epilepsy*," Zilkha says. "Let me see if we can set up the test next Tuesday." Zilkha asks his assistant to find the book. "You can look it over while I make the arrangements."

The assistant hands me the book. Everyone who works with Zilkha is crazy about him. It's like being a runner for Cicero.

"I can't loan you the book," Zilkha says, "but if you see anything you'd like to think about, we can copy those pages for you."

Stuart and I sit in the waiting room. He picks up *Vogue*. I flip through *Women and Epilepsy*.

"Is it interesting?" Stuart is watching me.

"Too much," I say. I note the pages I want to read again.

"It's the temporal lobe I want to see," Zilkha says when we've gathered again in his office.

I fear I know what he means. It's suddenly all too simple, all too elementary, my dear Zilkha.

We are driving to the Cromwell Hospital, through Hyde Park past children gathered for pony lessons. The black taxi is driven by a young woman. That's how long I've been in London. Black taxis remind me of our old black lunchboxes. My mother told the governesses they were classic. The bright colors on the lunchboxes Nona and Binnie had were painted with enamel: (a) to which we were allergic, (b) were made by a right-wing company, or (c) by a company that didn't hire Jews or blacks.

The park is sunny and I can see how appealing it would be to walk here today. That's also how long I've been in London.

Dr. Zilkha has the wizard's gift of sudden appearance. I've just hung up my jacket in my hospital room, put this blanket Jeremy sent me on the bed, and Zilkha is here.

"Did you go over the *Women and Epilepsy* pages?" he asks.

"Not yet." I have them with me, "but when I feel this taken care of, I don't think the brain's going to leap up for attention."

"But I do expect we'll see some abnormalities," he says.

I'm here to have an MRI test, followed by the new telemetry test, where, as I write, draw, or sleep, my brain will be on camera for twenty-four hours. Will this brain offer up another clue?

Stuart has left. He has written "Stuart loves Jill" on the white noteboard on the wall opposite the bed.

The MRI test is simple. I lie down on a surgical table with my arms across my chest. A glass mask is clamped over my face. I'm slid into a giant cannon, so that Con Ed can test the sound impact of new drills for forty-five minutes.

Now I am back upstairs, alone in a beige room with beige built-ins and a pale, sea-blue cover on the bed. I see a jet crossing a rare sunny March sky above rows of large West Kensington Victorian houses. Around the corner Andrea Tana is painting. She is using exactly this shade of blue. If you painted on Wimpole Street, you wouldn't get this color as a reference point. This is why over in Wimpole Street territory one tends to draw in black and white, like Laurie.

Tracy is a neurological technician from Australia. She is gluing electrodes onto my head and asking me questions about what she calls "events." How many? Does it feel like sexual release? Any kind of release? How long do they last? Grand mal?

The electrodes are thirty-six-inch-long thin cords in sky blue, grass green, dark pink, lavender, yellow, and pearly gray. They are stuck to my scalp with glue dabbed onto their silver tops. I have become my own telecommunication system.

I could wear this, plug it in to e-mail, and you'll know what I'm thinking. Never mind the writing coming through my hand, sharing, showing you or letting you catch the sound of it with my voice. We will wave it across to each other. I am preparing for when you live on Mars and we'll exchange signals.

Are my brain waves unique?

The box by my side is sending signals to the screen in the nurses' watch room. The box is set into exactly the kind of white shoulder bag I'd like for a trip we're going on. It holds the key to this brain.

I am being watched as I study and write for twenty-four hours. There was no test like this ten years ago. This may not fix anything, but knowing how deep my space-outs go will help me know how safe I am, how safe my memory is, and most of all, how safe I am for a kid to be alone with.

I am to keep a diary of what happens. Three columns: the time, what I'm doing, and the Event.

I think of prizefights, charity dinners, and premiers as Events, but these have one similarity, a singularity in one's day. They are notable. Has my brain elected to have these events in order to grab attention fast? The heart-wrenching subject of the charity (far more appealing than the woman going to lunch); the powerful victim/hero of the prizefight, triumphant through pain; the panicked, fenced-in star.

Can the brain will trouble on itself, as it can pitch the body down the stairs? Can it make an Event without a committee?

My guess is, if Freud hadn't been left behind some time ago, that it all started when I saw my father leave his typewriter and come dashing to me when I was sick. Just as he dashed to his mother. Do heart attacks come from a warmer emotion than attacks of the brain?

After Stuart leaves, I decide I'm not going to use the phone tonight. I'm not running from what I've got here or from what I can learn, even though I can no longer trust convenience amnesia.

I read about a twenty-year-old woman who "from the age of four had had seizures due to a right temporal lobe astrocytoma. The attacks were essentially paroxysmal sexual manifestations, which could be triggered by fantasies in which the parental image appeared" (adapted from M. R. Trimble, ed. *Women and Epilepsy,* 1991, ch. 13).

So I wasn't evil when I'd have this indecent dizziness and imagine my parents making love, or late at night, after leaving my mother's room, I'd swoon, ostensibly turned on by the vision of her in her chiffon gown. These were seizures, which I thought were some kind of punishment for undressing everyone in my mind. It was the other way around. The mixed-up electric charges in my brain generated the erotic imagery and responses.

I am really looking. I feel anger, like when I realized I am an alcoholic. I am furious. "Why didn't anyone tell me?"

Images from the past tumble over. I hold them here. Freeze frame: the time I found myself thrown by the horse, certain I'd seen it buck, startled by an image of a naked man who suddenly appeared in front of me. I knew he wanted to rape me.

Sexual seizures associated with temporal lobe foci assume various forms. An eroticized aura may consist only of a diffuse sense of heightened arousal.

—Women and Epilepsy

I was quickly taken out of the school. Another time: I was driving down from Palo Alto on the Coast Highway. I had this wave of longing. Then I saw a naked man driving in the car next to me, handsome shoulders and neck. I woke up in a hospital. I was told I'd driven head on into a truck.

I could spend a lot of time listing incidents and reciting denials, which have nothing to do with my life today. "Denial," the book says, "is common and may be constructive, leading to planning for the future.

"It may also be destructive," says the next sentence. I thought of all the years I drove with my children in the car.

I look over Table 5.

Table 5. Adolescent epilepsy coping mechanism
Insight/acceptance—ideal, but unlikely
Denial—common
Constructive—allows development, planning
Destructive—increases non-compliance
Intellectualization—permits mastery
Rationalization—uncommon, fatalistic
Regression—common in early adolescent
Reaction formation—mastery
Projection—anger, frustration, alienation
Withdrawal—poor, promotes non-compliance
Panic—outbursts, diffuse hysteria
Acting out
Temper outbursts, aggression
Manipulation, non-compliance
Running away, verbal abuse
Flirting, suicide gestures
Drug abuse

—Women and Epilepsy

These mechanisms are not a lot different than addict and alcoholic coping mechanisms. But then, does anyone go through adolescence easily?

So my brain has a bad paste-up, like "what's wrong with this picture." I am not, then, essentially mythically evil.

I'm far more interested in the subject of memory. I flip the electrodes, hanging from my scalp like pastel dredlocks, over my shoulder, lie down, and read along in Frances Yates.

My mind eats up the stories, characters parading around the stage of this vibrant study of the time when memory's art was a discipline. Just as in my childhood, learning by rote was a discipline. We repeated multiplication tables until we remembered them—one of the vestiges of the art of memory. Today our children and grandchildren have calculators; their memories develop in new, audiovisual ways.

To excel at the art in earlier times, you'd devise systems filled with planets and zodiac signs, galaxies and mythic characters. Memory images could be comic—Furbies would fit ideally into memory images designed by a man named Publicious. One of his was a character called Unhappy Envy. (Is there a Happy Envy? Useful Envy?)

Guilio Camillo, famous in the sixteenth century, built a wooden memory theater with a working secret only the King of France, who paid for it, ever knew. Camillo dictated his theater's plan, with its seven concentric rows and seven aisles standing for the seven planets' attitudes, in seven days.

I far prefer imagining these complex plans using mythological figures as memory objects than looking at the stark, simple truths about my memory fault and its impact on my life.

In 1600, the Renaissance philosopher Giordano Bruno was burned at the stake because the church feared people would remember his buoyant, illustrated memory system.

Did I have to travel as far as I did? Could I have summoned up the images of my own past simply through the occult system of movies, pictures and old legends I have in books and notes around me? By flying miles back in time, I spun my mind back years. And now, is this wired-up twenty-four hours an allegorical event for my memory? No more nor less than reaching High Table at Oxford, when only a few months before that I couldn't make it home from the corner. Only five years ago, I couldn't have spent twenty-four hours alone with my memory. It would not have found enough to do.

The sun is down, the traffic's muffled and soft, like a dark cloth has settled round it.

From the Middle Ages there was "a change in attitude to the imagination," and classical memory systems were being regarded as "artificial memory." Memory was no longer part of Rhetoric. Man, the Renaissance said, could grasp a sense of a Highest Power behind his own image, beyond appearances. Maybe the Highest Power was the Scientific Age, when ideas no longer wore outfits; were no longer set around in galleries of niches, long and shadowed deep plum, like the windows on the dark sand Victorian brick houses I can see from the hospital window across from me. I could turn the windows into niches and put one of the stories I want to remember into each one. But I've got them here in this brain with me.

Just as the neurological department isn't certain exactly where memory rests in our brain, Frances Yates isn't sure where memory belongs as a study.

Is it a philosophy, psychology, or is it, in fact, an art? Or, as she seems to prefer, is memory a part of the soul and, therefore, is it part of theology?

Maybe memory is everywhere.

The sky is softening down to the color of pale gray Armani suede sneakers. A friend of mine says, "Why do you put brand names in your books? It dates them."

Exactly. Brands become mnemonic devices. Tell me Lanz and I see Josie, and I remember I forgot to mention the barbecue Jeremy had when I was in L.A. "Mom," he said, introducing me to a tall, blond young man, "this is Tim Davis." Tim is Josie's son. I'd know those eyes anywhere. Tim is a writer; Jeremy is his agent. Do we need to say a word about life's circles?

But I was thinking of suede. That's what the brain in the glass case in Professor Steven Rose's office looks like, butterscotch suede. I walk to the window. I can hear, by the sound of the cars, the last people leaving work. At once more determined and more diffuse, the traffic is background music to the point and tuck of my brain's moves across the screen, telling its long and curious family love story. But the road has always been a part of the story. The only thing I don't get is why there are miles of empty space.

Barry Gordon prefers the "contextual" organization of memory, that memories are linked by constellations formed around landmark events.

That's how it is when I hear a piece of an old movie score, and I am on the set watching Gene Kelly and Cyd Charisse whirl across the sound-stage. Then I'm at Emerson Junior High, watching Carol Rosson and Bob Redford dance in moonlight shining through the windows of the gym. What was it, "Mr. Sandman"? And I see Sandy Burns and Warner LeRoy dancing at Chadwick. I remember some of the words of the songs, and even more about what we were all doing and what our lives and our parents' lives were like at that time.

Would I ever fall in love? I remember my father, dancing stiff in his back brace, and my mother, her cigarette on her forefinger; how much love can go through and still look like that after all.

When I started writing again about old L.A., I'd play tapes of MGM movie musicals, and classical albums like the ones my mother played in her studio. Like a switch flicked, the time comes on. When I want to remember these last twenty years, I play Stuart's jazz albums and the music we danced to.

Long-running love is a rare thing, and as time goes by and you realize there's inevitably less time ahead than behind you, all the "memory" songs tear your heart out. But they always did; from the moment there's life, you've got loss: "Try to Remember," "Memory." I hear Barbra's voice and I can see her dancing under the menacing helicopters, at her wedding to Jim Brolin, in her garden when the lavendar roses reminded me of the wisteria shading my sister as she glided through the arbor on my father's arm at maybe the last event in our house. The images spin into a montage of the weddings of all my children.

I see the edge of light, like a last thought, above the rooftops, scalloped behind the chimney pots, fading up into a steadily dimming sky. Does my mind dim down with the light? I used to be a night writer. I want to keep awake with my brain tonight.

Remember my version of Steven Rose's memory test? This is how many I remember today (I looked at the test twelve hours ago!): lemon, orange, feather, leaf, cherries, safety pin, key, button, scissors, pushpin, paintbrush, paint, screw, nail, pencil (blue), scissors, shell, thread, acorn, pen, and book.

This is nineteen out of twenty. Fifteen is considered good. Fifteen is what I scored last night. But nineteen is what stayed with me. I remembered because I put the things in particular rooms in my mind. The paintbrush and paint, the pencil and the feather are in my mother's studio. The cherries, leaf, orange, lemon, acorn are in the kitchen. The safety pin, shell, button and thread are in my bathroom. And the push-pin, screw, nail and scissors are in the toolbox in Stuart's changing room. The book and pen are on my desk. I forgot the key. I always forget my key.

I have not remembered them in order exactly. I have to go up and down the stairs in my mind to find what I want, but at least I can remember most of it.

I have worked my art. Giving and receiving.

We now remember truths (and things that aren't so true, things that shouldn't be true) through our cinemythology. We remember war from war movies. We worry that some may make it funny, too readily heroic or too clean, because the sharp images we see repeated become the mythic images.

So should I say how quickly I remember people when I ask their signs? It's been a favorite mnemonic device again for the past thirty years, really, something like the magician's mnemonic games with cards, which suggest numbers. The signs suggest personalities we already know how to remember.

The sky's royal blue. Morning is here, and I exercise hard, jogging in place. My brain paces along steadily.

I am worried. What if a seizure doesn't come? What if they're watching and it doesn't happen? What's wonderful is I am not alone when my mind is with me. So maybe the MRI will show something in the temporal lobe. The issue over why I have lost some periods of memory and not others is not going to be so clear.

One theory is that memory is split into files by a psychological event, stored separately. This would explain why the events right before and after the swimming pool scene at Champney's don't register, but not why I've also lost so much about the eight to ten years before the swim.

But then, this theory also considers that the memories you acquire in one personality state are stored one place, and those picked up in another condition are stored elsewhere.

Of course. This is why I have almost surreal clarity of my memories of my childhood and of the sixties, when I was given the white powder called ephedrine, presumably for asthma, but, now I think, as much to counter the effects of the phenobarbital I was given every night. This, I read tonight, was the standard treatment for epilepsy when I was a child. The thing they didn't understand was addiction, and the catch that the very thing that stopped the seizures also triggered abuse.

The clarity changes, like a focus being adjusted, after a space-out, while the memories of the last years in Connecticut and in England are softer in the tones of monotone, an early russet and aqua color film.

The split personality idea is obvious and I think it's a condition any performer would understand. It just may be more extreme. When I'm quiet, writing and drawing, I go back to my best childhood times easily.

But when I'm in a group being funny, being "on," I lose all memory, go into routines. If I stop the "routine," the "riff," to really remember, to reflect on the people around me, to hear them so I can remember them, so I can write about them, I lose the riff. I can't go back into it. This would explain why, if you meet a performer "out of sync," she'll seem cold, distant. It's as if you put on outfits. I have trouble taking off the coat. Or is it a mask?

Kids see it. They're used to dressing up. That's why I'm far more at ease with them.

I can remember last night. I can remember what I have read.

The doctor and Tracy come to see me again. "How's your diary?" she asks.

"Nothing happening," I say. It is empty under 'Event.'

Zilkha says, "We haven't read the chart yet."

I have a feeling he already knows the answer.

Then at 10:05 in the morning, the Event comes, the gathering in, the looming fear. I look in on spinning men lying on their backs, legs open like Ziegfeld dancers, centrifugal force, a fugue, big color sheets blown out, scarlet, marigold and cobalt blue, clipper ships make a getaway, and I'm shuddering down, in, clattering down like the last tiger-eye marble rolling home across the glass.

Unlike some other people who smell and taste things, my space-outs are filled with color. Rats have no color sense, but they remember taste and smell. Birds remember color, but not smell or taste.

I turn to the book, to the page I've marked with a red tab. Here's the description, what Zilkha wanted me to see.

> A sudden libidinous feeling, sometimes associated with a sense of familiarity . . . as if she had suddenly been cut off from a sexual experience. There is no resolution.
>
> —*Women and Epilepsy*

So they have something to see, and it no longer terrifies me. We are sprung from our own land after all, and it is only fitting my brain should be built round a fault.

This twenty-four hours alone with my memory here has been an allegorical trip, as I've looked at all the ways I've trained it, pushed it, encouraged it and set it off, never sure it was there for the trip. It took me to the corner, to Oxford and to L.A., where what I really found, looking for the Polanski girl, was recognition of my own losses, which had little to do with sixties' melodramas and much more to do with the recognition of emotional responsibilities, of academic and political ambitions I tossed aside.

In these last years, for each image of physiological intrigue in Steven Rose, for every dense line of historic passion in *The Art of Memory,* I have faced another connection, which might well be a paragraph of *Women and Epilepsy.* And another sentence from an article by Peter Wolson, who talks about "Adaptive Grandiosity" (*Psychoanalytic Review,* 82[4]:).

Woolson, unlike a lot of analysts, says artists do need a powerful belief in their creative power to learn. It isn't easy for a young prodigy, for example, to focus when she, or he, is surrounded by maestros who know they'll never achieve what she will, or to function with that peculiar outsider's sensitivity in a world of curiosity, envy, a world waiting for the "hitch." If you don't have enough of this particular confidence that keeps you certain you're the best, no matter that you still have to practice or revise, you might be afraid to give yourself enough alone time for the talent to flourish, the ideas to evolve. Without this steely assurance, you might get into a room with a piano, a paintbrush, or a pen, and say, "Why bother?" Adaptive Grandiosity is the gut instinct that the world needs what you're doing.

I've always wanted to be unique. I hate when I don't get the table I want at the restaurant. (And it is never the first table.) At the same time, I want to be really liked; I ask a dozen times, "Do you think this works?" or "Should I wear this?"

Love is a man who will take you back so you can change your outfit. Stuart has Adaptive Grandiosity. He says, "This is what I'm wearing."

Most importantly, I've faced my own family, seen my parents and my children, and their children. What I lost, and what is there to find, to hold onto.

In the seventeenth century they worried that the Art of Memory was over. As, step by step, I've picked up my past, I wondered if there was anywhere to go. Could I remember more, and what would there be? What they did in the seventeenth century was apply aspects of *The Art of Memory* to these new explorations in the scientific method. So, here in this hospital, seeing the action in the temporal lobe of my brain, is the answer to these seizures, these gripping auras. But what I do with any answers I have found, how I apply them to my life, to time with my family, to working with my writers, is what matters.

I have applied this new memory muscle to the consideration of memory in all its guises and to aspects of my life I've never wanted to see. And I have learned that the only old idea about looking at the past is that there's nothing new to see.

The Englishman is sitting at the ash desk in his tan shirt. "What movie do you want to see tomorrow?" he asks.

I tell him.

"We saw that a month ago," he says.

Sometimes I'm not sure if that's true, or if he just doesn't want to see it. I do not want you to think I have a perfect memory for all things at all times.

"I told Judith we would have dinner with her Friday night," he says.

"Can't," I say, "we're going to Corinne's. It's Sabbath."

"I guess," he says, putting his hand on the arm I've wrapped around him, "I guess I forgot."